MOTIVATION IN EDUCATION
Theory, Research, and Applications

SECOND EDITION

Paul R. Pintrich
The University of Michigan

Dale H. Schunk
*The University of North Carolina
at Greensboro*

Merrill
Prentice Hall

Upper Saddle River, New Jersey
Columbus, Ohio

Library of Congress Cataloging-in-Publication Data

Pintrich, Paul R.
    Motivation in education : theory, research, and applications / Paul R. Pintrich, Dale H.
Schunk.—2nd ed.
      p. cm.
    Includes bibliographical references (p.) and index.
    ISBN 0-13-016009-1 (pbk.)
    1. Motivation in education. 2.Motivation (Psychology) I. Schunk, Dale H. II. Title.
LB1065 .P52 2002
370.15'4—dc21

2001045034

Vice President and Publisher: Jeffery W. Johnston
Executive Editor: Kevin M. Davis
Editorial Assistant: Autumn Crisp
Production Editor: Mary Harlan
Production Coordinator: Marilee Aschenbrenner, Carlisle Publishers Services
Design Coordinator: Diane C. Lorenzo
Cover Design: Jason Moore
Cover Photo: International Stock
Production Manager: Laura Messerly
Director of Marketing: Kevin Flanagan
Marketing Manager: Amy June
Marketing Coordinator: Barbara Koontz

This book was set in Berkeley by Carlisle Communications, Ltd. It was printed and bound by Maple-Vail Book
Manufacturing Group. The cover was printed by Phoenix Color Corp.

Pearson Education Ltd., *London*
Pearson Education Australia Pty. Limited, *Sydney*
Pearson Education Singapore Pte. Ltd.
Pearson Education North Asia Ltd., *Hong Kong*
Pearson Education Canada, Ltd., *Toronto*
Pearson Educación de Mexico, S.A. de C.V., *Mexico*
Pearson Education—Japan, *Tokyo*
Pearson Education Malaysia Pte. Ltd.
Pearson Education, *Upper Saddle River, New Jersey*

10 9 8 7 6 5 4 3
ISBN: 0-13-016009-1

To our families,
for their motivation, love, and support

Liz and Bill
Caryl and Laura

Preface

The field of motivation has undergone many changes in recent years as psychological theories have increasingly incorporated cognitive concepts and variables. Explanations of behavior have moved away from stimuli and reinforcement contingencies and instead emphasize learners' constructive interpretations of events and the role that their beliefs, cognitions, affects, and values play in achievement situations. Even more recently, within the field of educational research, there has been an interest in social and cultural models of learning that stress the situated nature of learners' beliefs and cognitions. This situated perspective has led to an increasing emphasis on how the local classroom context and other contextual factors shape and influence student learning and motivation. These two developments that stress student cognitions and beliefs and the influence of the classroom context have led to much more important and relevant research on motivation in education.

Motivation involves processes that occur as individuals instigate and sustain goal-directed actions. Although many professionals feel comfortable with this cognitive perspective, considerable disagreement exists about what processes are involved in motivation, how these processes operate, how motivation relates to learning and achievement, and how motivation can be enhanced and sustained at an optimal level. Moreover, it is important to understand how these processes operate in classroom and school contexts if we are to improve education.

We believe that motivation is an important quality that pervades all aspects of teaching and learning. Motivated students display interest in activities, feel self-efficacious, expend effort to succeed, persist at tasks, and typically use effective task, cognitive, and self-regulatory strategies to learn. Motivated teachers feel that they can help students learn, put extra time into instructional planning, and work with students to help ensure their learning and mastery of knowledge and skills. When motivation declines, other educational outcomes also suffer. Teachers must not only impart knowledge and teach skills, but also establish a motivating environment for learning.

The first edition of this text grew from a conversation the authors had at the 1991 American Educational Research Association (AERA) convention in Chicago. At that time, each of us had been active in the field of motivation for several years as researchers and specifically in the Motivation in Education Special Interest Group of AERA. In addition, both of us had been teaching graduate level courses on motivation in education and felt the need for a textbook that would be appropriate for our courses. We wanted to write a book that would provide students with a solid theoretical and empirical grounding in motivational research as well as illustrate how the principles and research findings might be applied to education. The first edition of this book was well received by our own students as well as other students and faculty members nationally and internationally. We have been quite gratified by the positive comments from colleagues and students about the first edition. Nevertheless, the field of motivation is developing, and it seemed to be an appropriate time to prepare a second edition that would update the text and reflect current theory and research in motivation.

Objectives

The primary objectives of this new edition are the same as those of the first edition: (a) to present the major motivational theories, principles, and research findings in enough detail to help students understand the complexity of motivational processes, and (b) to provide examples of motivational concepts and principles applied to educational settings in order to suggest ways to facilitate motivation in these settings. Although different perspectives on motivation are presented, the text places primary emphasis on the role of personal cognitions and beliefs during teaching and learning. This focus is consistent with cognitive accounts of human behavior that view learners as active, constructive learners, not passive recipients. At the same time, the text focuses on motivation in education with an emphasis on how motivation is situated, facilitated, and constrained by various classroom and contextual factors.

Organization

The text comprises 10 chapters. After the first introductory chapter, the next six chapters focus on the six main theoretical and conceptual perspectives that stress the role of personal cognitions, beliefs, affects, and values in motivation. Accordingly, there are chapters on expectancy-value theory, attribution theory, self-efficacy and self-regulation theory, goal theory, intrinsic motivation theory, and interest and affect theories. These chapters reflect the general cognitive perspective of the text. The final three chapters of the book highlight the importance of various contextual factors in promoting motivation and focus on the teacher and the classroom, the school, and then other sociocultural factors such as peers, families, and communities. These three chapters represent the emphasis on the contextual factors that can facilitate or constrain motivation.

All of the chapters are organized in a similar fashion to ensure some consistency throughout the book. Each chapter begins with a scenario that illustrates some of the processes discussed in the chapter. The chapter then discusses key theoretical principles and constructs and important research findings. We summarize basic studies, testing hypothesized influences on and effects of motivation, as well as applied research investigating the operation of motivational processes in classrooms and other learning settings. Where appropriate, we also address the moderating role of developmental factors in motivation, along with important individual difference variables such as gender and ethnicity. Our intention is not to highlight differences, but rather to show how personal cognitions and motivational constructs may help to explain the relation between these age and individual difference variables and student outcomes.

Throughout each chapter, we discuss the implications of the theory and research findings for educational practice. In addition to numerous informal examples in the text, each chapter includes detailed and specific applications with suggestions for incorporating motivational principles into instructional contexts. We have geared most examples to K–12 education, but many of the suggestions are readily applicable to other learners (e.g., postsecondary) as well as other contexts (e.g., out-of-school settings such as homes, museums, and even the workplace).

New to This Edition

The second edition of this text is similar in many ways to the first edition, in particular in its emphasis on the psychological and educational theories and empirical research on motivation. At the same time, there are a number of important changes that we hope are improvements over the first edition. First, the chapters are now organized differently. In the first edition, there were two introductory chapters: a general chapter and a historical chapter. The historical chapter has been removed and that material has been deleted or moved into the appropriate theoretical chapters.

More important, the first edition had the six main "theory" chapters organized around general constructs, not theories. In the first edition, for example, one chapter on the construct of self-perceptions of competence had material from the expectancy side of expectancy-value theory as well as self-efficacy from self-efficacy theory. Another chapter on values and affect had material on values from expectancy-value theory and the attribution-affect link from attribution theory. Although many people liked this emphasis on general constructs and our attempt at synthesis across theories, we also found this original organization somewhat awkward in writing and in teaching with the text.

Accordingly, in this second edition, the six main "theory" chapters are organized around six main theories that represent current cognitive perspectives on motivation. All of these chapters are updated, but there are other significant organizational changes in the new edition. There is just one chapter on expectancy-value theory that includes the research on both the expectancy and value components of motivation, which were discussed in two different chapters in the first edition. There is just one chapter on attribution theory that includes the role of attributions and affect instead of having these two aspects of the theory in two different chapters, as in the first edition. There is one chapter on self-efficacy theory that now includes a new and expanded discussion of different perspectives on self-regulation. There is one chapter on goals and goal orientations that presents several different models of the role of goals in motivation. The chapter on intrinsic motivation theory is similar to the first edition, except the research on flow theory is moved to the chapter on interest and affect. Finally, the chapter on interest and affect includes an expanded discussion of the role of emotions in motivation as well as other key constructs such as self-worth and test anxiety.

The remaining three chapters on contextual factors include two chapters that are similar to the first edition. The two chapters on teacher and school influences are updated, but organized in the same way as the first edition. The last chapter, on sociocultural influences, is completely new to this edition and discusses the role of peers, families, and communities in motivation. This last chapter reflects the increased interest in factors other than teacher and school effects in the study of motivation.

In addition to these changes, we have added a glossary of terms to this edition to help the reader in understanding motivational terminology, which can be quite daunting for the novice. Terms that appear in bold in the text are listed in the glossary. We have also updated the text considerably. The first edition included more than 600 references; the second edition now includes more than 800 references, representing a more comprehensive and current perspective on motivation theory and research in education.

The book is designed for use by psychological and educational researchers interested in questions of motivation. It is also for educational practitioners, graduate students, and advanced undergraduates who have some prior knowledge in education and psychology and want to learn more about motivation in education. The book will be appropriate in courses in which motivation is covered in some depth; for example, in introductory courses in learning, development, motivation, and educational psychology, as well as graduate courses or specialty courses in these areas. While we assume that students will have some familiarity with psychological concepts and research methods, the text contains minimal discussion of the statistical aspects of research results.

Acknowledgments

We want to thank many people for their assistance during the various phases of production of both editions of this book. We owe a sincere debt of gratitude to our many professional colleagues who have provided us with valuable insights into motivational processes. In particular, we have found our activities and interactions with colleagues in the Motivation in Education Special Interest Group of the American Educational Research Association (AERA) personally rewarding and fruitful. This group is a model for how a scholarly community should conduct itself, pushing its members to research important issues and to think hard and critically, but always in a respectful and motivating manner. We always enjoy coming "home" to the Motivation in Education group at the annual AERA convention.

Dale has benefited from many conversations with colleagues across the country, including Albert Bandura, Curt Bonk, James Chapman, Peggy Ertmer, Carolyn Jagacinski, Judith Meece, the late John Nicholls, Frank Pajares, Don Rice, Claire Ellen Weinstein, and Barry Zimmerman. At Michigan, the faculty and students in the Combined Program in Education and Psychology have provided Paul with a consistently stimulating and collegial environment for research on motivation. His faculty colleagues—Phyllis Blumenfeld, Jacque Eccles, Stuart Karabenick, Marty Maehr, Ron Marx, Bill McKeachie, Carol Midgley, Scott Paris, and Kai Schnabel—have provided critical feedback and constructive support that have benefited him both personally and professionally. Allan Wigfield, while at Michigan and since he has been at the University of Maryland, has been a source of many great ideas, cogent advice, and stimulating conversations as a colleague and best friend for Paul. Finally, and most important, Paul has had an excellent group of graduate students involved in his research program over the years, including Eric Anderman, Lynley Hicks Anderman, Juliane Blazevski, Stasia Danos Elder, Teresa Garcia, Barbara Hofer, Lidi Hruda, Toni Kempler, Lisa Linnenbrink, AnneMarie McEvoy, Helen Patrick, Rob Roeser, Allison Ryan, Karen Strobel, Tim Urdan, Scott VanderStoep, Chris Wolters, Allison Young, Shirley Yu, and Akane Zusho. These students from the Competence and Commitment Project, the College Research Group, and the Motivation Research Group have worked collaboratively with Paul on problems of motivation and learning in classrooms and have been an indispensable source of motivation and inspiration for him over the years. In addition, most of them have been students in his doctoral seminar on motivation and were the original audience for many of the ideas in this book.

We also acknowledge the agencies who have funded our research over the years, including the Office of Educational Research and Improvement in the Department of Education, the National Science Foundation, the Spencer Foundation, the Kellogg Foundation, the National Institute of Mental Health, the University of North Carolina, the University of Michigan, Purdue University, and the University of Houston. In addition to our funding sources, we thank the administrators, teachers, and students from a large number of school districts who have collaborated with us on our research.

With respect to the book's production, we thank Kevin Davis, our editor at Merrill/Prentice Hall, for his support, patience, and guidance over the years of working on both editions. In the high-turnover world of publishing, he has been a beacon of stability and good sense. The book would not be the same without his help. We look forward to many more years of productive collaboration with Kevin. This edition has been ably guided through the production process by Mary Harlan, Sue Dillon, and Marilee Aschenbrenner. Several colleagues provided excellent critiques of earlier portions of the first edition. In particular, we thank Carol Midgley from the University of Michigan and Allan Wigfield from the University of Maryland for their cogent and helpful feedback on several chapters. We also gained valuable feedback from graduate students at Michigan and Purdue who previewed the book in draft form. At the University of Michigan, Carol Birmingham and Loralyn Rudy assisted with word processing, indexing, and other administrative details on the first edition. For the second edition, Fran Maszatics and Marie Bien at Michigan did a wonderful job on the references, all with good humor and in a timely fashion. Their careful and hard work made the writing and production tasks much easier.

We would also like to express our appreciation to the reviewers of this text: Martha Carr, University of Georgia; Margaret W. Cohen, University of Missouri–St. Louis; Lyn Corno, Teachers College, Columbia University; Julianne C. Turner, University of Notre Dame; and Allan Wigfield, University of Maryland.

Finally, we express our heartfelt thanks to our parents, Teresa and Paul Pintrich, and the late Mil and Al Schunk, for their love and encouragement. We owe the deepest gratitude to our wives, Elisabeth De Groot and Caryl Schunk, and to our children, Bill De Groot and Laura Schunk, for their patience, understanding, and support throughout this project. Although we know they became quite tired of our divided attention and a few lost weekends as we worked on "the book," they were always supportive. We also thank Liz and Caryl for several of the ideas for the applications in the book as they drew on their years of experience as teachers and principals in the public schools. We also are very happy and grateful that this book project gave us many hours of stimulating conversation with each other and created a friendship that will endure over our careers.

Paul R. Pintrich
Dale H. Schunk

About the Authors

Paul R. Pintrich is Professor of Education and Psychology and Chair of the Combined Program in Education and Psychology at the University of Michigan, Ann Arbor. He also has served as the Associate Dean for Research for the School of Education at Michigan. He has a B.A. in psychology from Clark University in Worcester, Massachusetts, and an M.A. in developmental psychology, and a Ph.D. in education and psychology from the University of Michigan, Ann Arbor. His research focuses on the development of motivation and self-regulated learning in adolescence and how the classroom context shapes the trajectory of motivation and self-regulation development.

Paul has published over 100 articles and chapters and is co-author or co-editor of eight books, including the *Advances in Motivation and Achievement* series. He also has served as editor of *Educational Psychologist,* the American Psychological Association journal for Division 15-Educational Psychology. His research has been funded by the National Science Foundation, the Office of Educational Research and Improvement in the Department of Education, the Spencer Foundation, and the Kellogg Foundation.

Paul has served as President of Division 15-Educational Psychology for the American Psychological Association and is currently President-Elect of Division 5-Educational and Instructional Psychology for the International Association of Applied Psychology. He is a Fellow of the American Psychological Association and has been a National Academy of Education Spencer Fellow. He won the 1999 Best Research Review Article Award from the American Educational Research Association. He also has won the Class of 1923 Award from the College of Literature, Science, and Arts and the School of Education at the University of Michigan for excellence in undergraduate teaching.

Dale H. Schunk is Dean of the School of Education and Professor of Curriculum and Instruction at the University of North Carolina at Greensboro. He holds a Ph.D. in Educational Psychology from Stanford University, an M.Ed. from Boston University, and a B.S. from the University of Illinois at Urbana. He has held faculty positions at Purdue University (where he served as Head of the Department of Educational Studies), the University of North Carolina at Chapel Hill (where he also was Chair of the Academic Affairs Institutional Review Board), and the University of Houston.

Dale has edited six books, is author of *Learning Theories: An Educational Perspective* (Prentice Hall, 2000) and over 80 articles and book chapters. He has served as President of Division 15-Educational Psychology for the American Psychological Association and as Secretary of Division C-Learning and Instruction for the American Educational Research Association. He is presently a member of the editorial boards of three professional journals.

Dale's teaching and research interests include learning, motivation, and self-regulation. He has received the Early Career Contributions Award in Educational Psychology from the American Psychological Association, the Albert J. Harris Research Award from the International Reading Association, and the Outstanding Service Award from the Purdue University School of Education.

Brief Contents

Contents

Motivation: Introduction and Historical Foundations

K eith Mitchell teaches seventh-grade social studies at a middle school. His fourth-period class is quite typical of the students he teaches. The 12 male and 13 female students have varied socioeconomic backgrounds, but most are middle class. Although they represent a range in achievement, students generally perform well in class.

The students are engaged in small-group work. As Keith takes a break from walking around and checking on the groups' progress, he scans the room. As his eyes settle on the following students, he thinks about each in terms of motivation.

1. *Matt.* Matt is intelligent but has little motivation for social studies. He would rather be playing his electric guitar or hanging out with friends. He is motivated to be a great guitar player. Keith wishes he could increase Matt's academic motivation.

2. *Sharon.* Sharon is an intelligent student who enjoys learning for its own sake. She is motivated to learn new things and enjoys the challenge. She sets goals for herself and checks on her goal progress. Keith wants to ensure that Sharon's academic motivation remains at a high level.

3. *Eric.* The main thing that seems to motivate Eric is doing better than everyone else. Eric is not content to be second best. Whenever he works on a task, he compares his work with that of others to determine how well he is performing. Keith's goal is to try to replace Eric's emphasis on beating everyone with a desire to cooperate and to find satisfaction in learning for its own sake.

4. *Deanna.* Deanna is motivated to avoid being the slowest student in the class. Whenever the students work on a task, Deanna compares her work with that of others to make sure she is doing better than at least one other student. She wants Keith to think that she is not the dumbest student in the class. Keith wants her to stop thinking of herself in this negative fashion.

5. *Tamika.* Tamika is interested in schoolwork but has very low self-confidence for performing well. A few years ago, her older brother was an honor student in high school and attended a prestigious university. Tamika has never considered herself to be as competent as her brother. Her low self-confidence adversely affects her motivation. She works lackadaisically on difficult tasks and gives up easily when she does not understand.

6. *José.* Unlike Tamika, José does not know what it means to give up. He is a tireless worker who believes that hard work will conquer almost any problem and lead to success. Keith appreciates his persistence, but occasionally it leads to problems, such as when José works endlessly on a task he does not understand rather than asking Keith for assistance. Through his diligent efforts, José completes most of his work and earns decent grades.

7. *Kris.* Kris is a good student who works hard and makes good grades but takes little credit for her success. When she performs well, she feels that she was lucky or that the task was easy. She never says that she is good in the subject area, nor does she believe that success derives from her effort. Keith is concerned because Kris takes little personal responsibility for her successes and failures.

So different, thought Keith, and yet in many ways so much the same. After school that day, Keith went to the faculty lounge, where he and some other teachers talked about their students. The conversation shifted to a discussion of why students act as they do.

"It seems to me," said Keith, "that students act the way they do because of how we treat them and what we expose them to. People react to their surroundings. If we treat people well, they will treat us well in return. If we don't treat them well, we can't expect much nice from them."

"I agree with you, Keith," said Sara Wylie. "I think sometimes we create problems for ourselves. Look at competition. No wonder kids are so competitive. They're exposed to competition at home, on the playground, in school. We just make them more competitive by emphasizing grades and doing well so they can make the honor roll and get into college. That's why I think we need to stress cooperation more in school. Having kids work together should help make them more cooperative and less competitive."

A. K. Buerso was shaking her head. "You two think students are puppets. We pull the strings and they react. Since when does that happen so automatically? Aren't you forgetting about something? These kids are their own personalities. They're so different and I'm not sure we have much to do with it. I think their personalities are so heavily determined from birth. They come into the world and they're going to act certain ways. Look at so many things babies and preschoolers do. They couldn't learn them. They must be genetically determined."

"Oh sure, A. K.," said Keith. "I suppose you're going to tell me that most of what my kids do was present at birth. Did Tamika lack self-confidence at birth? Was Eric competitive? Did Deanna not want others to think she was the slowest baby in the nursery? How do you explain these?"

"No, not everything is present at birth," A. K. continued. "Traits come out over time, unfold so to speak. But I think many of the predispositions are present at birth. Students change, sure, but it represents more of an unfolding or maturing. My point is that I don't think we have much influence on how students behave."

"Well, there is another way to look at it," responded Sara. "How students act isn't due just to what they bring with them into the world or to how we treat them, but rather a combination of the two. The characteristics that are there interact with the setting and behavior results. Put an aggressive child in an environment that does not reward aggression and the child will act less aggressively. Put the same child in an environment where aggression is encouraged and aggression will become worse. I think as teachers we can affect our students' behaviors but we always must contend with some pretty strong tendencies or dispositions that they bring with them. We succeed when what we do complements those dispositions. We have problems when what we do goes against their grain."

This discussion on the causes of behavior highlights some different views of motivation. Keith espouses the behavioral and environmental view, A. K. stresses the role of inner causes, and Sara provides a compromise by stating that both are important. These students, representative of a typical class, illustrate the various motivational patterns that present challenges for teachers to understand. The discussion also shows that teachers do have implicit or intuitive theories about how and why students are motivated for academic learning and these theories can and do guide teacher behavior in the classroom (Patrick & Pintrich, 2001).

Keith's students also highlight the point that motivation is an important quality that pervades all student activities. Motivated students display interest in activities, work diligently, feel self-confident, stick with tasks, and perform well. When students perform poorly, teachers may say they were not motivated to learn but that they would do better if they tried harder. Given that motivation affects all aspects of schooling and contributes to students' school success, improving students' academic motivation is a worthwhile goal of schooling. Each year, many school workshops and in-service programs are devoted to motivational topics. Teachers often list motivating students as one of their chief concerns.

Despite its intuitive importance, there is much we do not know about motivation. Professionals disagree over what motivation is, what affects motivation, how motivational processes operate, the effects that motivation has on learning and performance, and how motivation can be improved. Our knowledge is further limited because many earlier research studies used people engaged in artificial tasks (e.g., ringtoss games) or laboratory animals in boxes or mazes. Such research does not capture the complexity of motivation as students think, learn, and solve problems. Fortunately, much recent research is school based and involves students engaged in academic tasks.

This chapter discusses some basic issues in the field of motivation. We begin by defining motivation, after which we discuss the relation of motivation to learning and performance and examine the role of theory in the study of motivation. We follow with sections on types of motivation research and on methods of assessing motivation to include indexes of motivation and research strategies. Actual research studies are discussed to illustrate differences in research methods and tools of assessment.

We then present a brief historical walk through the field of motivation, beginning with the early part of the twentieth century and continuing to the emergence of cognitive perspectives around 1970. We make no attempt to discuss these theories in depth or review all relevant historical work because this is beyond the scope of this text. Readers who are familiar with this material may wish to omit it; those who desire further information should consult other sources (Heckhausen, 1991; Heidbreder, 1933; Hunt, 1993; Mook, 1987; Weiner, 1985b, 1992). Following the historical material we discuss **metatheoretical models**, or models (paradigms) of research that offer a way to organize theories and understand their basic assumptions.

After studying this chapter, you should be able to:

1. Define motivation and explain how it can affect learning and performance.
2. Describe the critical features of the following research paradigms: correlational, experimental, qualitative, laboratory, and field.
3. Discuss advantages and disadvantages of direct observations, ratings by others, and self-reports as assessment methods.
4. Summarize the key assumptions of the following historical perspectives on motivation and critique these views for their adequacy as an explanation for human motivation: volition/will, instincts, Freud's theory, conditioning theories, drive theories, purposive behaviorism, arousal theories, cognitive consistency, functional autonomy of motives, and humanistic theories.

MOTIVATION DEFINED

The term **motivation** is derived from the Latin verb *movere* (to move). The idea of movement is reflected in such commonsense ideas about motivation as something that gets us going, keeps us moving, and helps us complete tasks. Despite these commonly held ideas, there are many definitions of motivation and much disagreement over its precise nature. These differences in the nature and operation of motivation are apparent in the various theories we cover in this text. For now, we will say that motivation has been conceptualized in varied ways including inner forces, enduring traits, behavioral responses to stimuli, and sets of beliefs and affects.

As we discuss later in this chapter, many early views linked motivation with inner forces: instincts, traits, volition, and will. Behavioral (conditioning) theories view motivation as an increased or continual level of responding to stimuli brought about by reinforcement (reward). Contemporary cognitive views postulate that individuals' thoughts, beliefs, and emotions influence motivation.

Although there is disagreement about the precise nature of motivation, we offer a general definition of motivation that is consistent with the cognitive focus of this book on learners' thoughts and beliefs and that captures the elements considered by most researchers and practitioners to be central to motivation:

> **Motivation** is the process whereby goal-directed activity is instigated and sustained.

Let us examine this definition in depth. Motivation is a *process* rather than a product. As a process, we do not observe motivation directly, but rather we infer it from such behaviors as choice of tasks, effort, persistence, and verbalizations (e.g., "I really want to work on this").

Motivation involves **goals** that provide impetus for and direction to action. Cognitive views of motivation are united in their emphasis on the importance of goals. Goals may not be well formulated and may change with experience, but the point is that individuals have something in mind that they are trying to attain or avoid.

Motivation requires *activity*—physical or mental. Physical activity entails effort, persistence, and other overt actions. Mental activity includes such cognitive actions as planning, rehearsing, organizing, monitoring, making decisions, solving problems, and assessing progress. Most activities that students engage in are geared toward attaining their goals.

Finally, motivated activity is *instigated* and *sustained*. Starting toward a goal is important and often difficult because it involves making a commitment to change and taking the first step. But motivational processes are critically important to sustain action. Many major goals are long-term, such as earning a college degree, obtaining a good job, and saving money for retirement. Much of what we know about motivation comes from determining how people respond to the difficulties, problems, failures, and setbacks they encounter as they pursue long-term goals. Such motivational processes as expectations, attributions, and affects help people surmount difficulties and sustain motivation.

We now turn to a topic of critical importance to schooling—the relation of motivation to learning and performance.

RELATION OF MOTIVATION TO LEARNING AND PERFORMANCE

Keith Mitchell's perceptions of his students exemplify our intuitive understanding of the role of motivation in classroom learning and performance. Motivation can affect both new learning and the performance of previously learned skills, strategies, and behaviors. Activities such as drills and review sessions involve performance of previously learned skills, but most class time is spent learning facts, beliefs, rules, concepts, skills, strategies, algorithms, and behaviors.

As an example of the effect of motivation on performance, suppose that Keith tells his class to complete some review material. The students, being less than enthusiastic about this assignment, work lackadaisically. To boost students' motivation, Keith announces that they will have free time as soon as they complete the assignment. Assuming that the students value free time, we would expect them to finish their work quickly.

Such performance effects often are dramatic, but the role of motivation during learning is equally important. Motivation can influence what, when, and how we learn (Schunk, 1991b). Students who are motivated to learn about a topic are apt to engage in activities they believe will help them learn, such as attending carefully to the instruction, mentally organizing and rehearsing the material to be learned, taking notes to facilitate subsequent studying, checking their level of understanding, and asking for help when they do not understand the material (Zimmerman & Martinez-Pons, 1992). Collectively, these activities improve learning.

In contrast, students unmotivated to learn are not apt to be as systematic in their learning efforts. They may be inattentive during the lesson and not organize or rehearse material. Note taking may be done haphazardly or not at all. They may not monitor their level of understanding or ask for help when they do not understand what is being taught. It is little wonder that learning suffers.

A key point is that motivation bears a reciprocal relation to learning and performance; that is, motivation influences learning and performance and what students do and learn influences their motivation (Schunk, 1991b). When students attain learning goals, goal attainment conveys to them that they possess the requisite capabilities for learning. These beliefs motivate them to set new, challenging goals. Students who are motivated to learn often find that once they do, they are intrinsically motivated to continue their learning (Meece, 1991).

MOTIVATION THEORY AND RESEARCH

This section examines the role of theory in the study of motivation. Throughout this text we integrate theoretical principles and show how they relate to research and practice. We believe that a good theoretical understanding of motivation and knowledge of different types of research paradigms are necessary to appreciate the role of motivation in settings involving teaching and learning.

Theory and the Study of Motivation

Like most teachers, Keith, Sara, and A. K. have theories about what motivates students. Their theories reflect their intuitive understandings of their students and help guide their actions. Such intuitive understanding is beneficial in many ways. In this section, however, we discuss theory from a scientific perspective and its role in systematic empirical research. We define a **theory** as a scientifically acceptable set of principles advanced to explain a phenomenon. A theory provides a framework for interpreting environmental observations and helps link research and education (Suppes, 1974). Without a theory, research findings would be disorganized and have no common referent.

Consider the following example. Much research shows that students' beliefs about their capabilities relate to motivation. Students who feel self-confident about learning and performing well in school seek challenges, expend effort to learn new material, and persist at difficult tasks (Schunk, 1991b). Although interesting, these findings are unrelated to other knowledge about motivation and do not inform teachers about ways to raise student motivation. If we link these findings to any of the several motivation theories that stress the role of perceived capabilities in motivation, we see how such beliefs fit into a broad motivational framework. We then have a better idea about what affects beliefs and how they influence motivation.

Theories reflect environmental phenomena and generate new research through the formation of **hypotheses**, or assumptions that can be tested empirically. Hypotheses state what conditions ought to accompany or follow other variables. We could, for example, test the following hypothesis in a research study: If students' perceived capabilities improve, then they will display greater academic motivation (choice of tasks, effort, persistence). When research data support hypotheses, the theories are strengthened. Hypotheses not supported by data may necessitate revision of the theories. Scientists strive to make sense out of research results and relate them to their prior theoretical beliefs (Pintrich, Marx, & Boyle, 1993).

How this process might work in teaching can be illustrated with an example from Keith's class. From his interactions with Eric and his parents, Keith has come to an intuitive (naive theoretical) understanding that Eric's desire to outperform everyone stems from a basic insecurity. Eric is the youngest child in a family in which his older brothers and sisters have performed very well in school. Keith believes that Eric does not want to appear any less competent than his siblings. Thus, his behavior of trying to do better than everyone else represents a means of performing well.

Based on this understanding, Keith formulates the following hypothesis. If Eric can see himself as a worthwhile and competent person, then he will become less competitive. Keith employs methods in his class that he believes will convey this impression to Eric. Keith provides Eric with ample feedback showing how his work is exemplary and how he is improving his skills. He tries to assuage Eric's fears about not performing well by encouraging Eric to work diligently. Keith structures tasks and presents material that he believes Eric can master. Keith also makes frequent use of small student groups that work cooperatively to accomplish a task. Keith hopes that by decreasing Eric's opportunities for competition, Eric may develop greater motivation for learning. Keith will evaluate his hypothesis by observing Eric's behavior, talking with him, and gauging the reactions of his classmates. This example demonstrates the role of a teacher's intuitive or implicit theory and how he or she might test it as well as act upon it in the classroom.

From a scientific perspective, theories are much more formal and complex than Keith's ideas, but they are still subject to testing and revision based on empirical data. A good example of research data that did not support a hypothesis and required revision of the underlying theory comes from Hull's (1943) systematic behavior theory. Hull postulated that amount of reward was a critical variable for learning such that behavior was strengthened when a large reward was given immediately after goal attainment and that as reward size decreased, behavioral strength declined.

Although intuitively appealing, this idea was not supported by research. Studies by Tolman and Honzik (1930) on latent learning showed that rats learned to run mazes without being rewarded. Other research demonstrated that shifts in performance (e.g., speed of maze running) occurred after the behavior had been learned and depended on changes in reward size (Crespi, 1942). The latter finding could not be due to altered strength of behavior because learning was hypothesized to increase slowly with repeated reward.

Eventually, Hull (1952) modified his theory to include an **incentive motivation** factor. Spence (1960) explored this factor in depth and concluded that reward did not affect learning but rather performance, and that incentive motivation was a performance variable. Although many researchers today believe that motivation affects both learning and performance, this example illustrates how theories undergo revision as a result of hypothesis testing.

Sometimes we conduct research with little theory to guide us. When that happens, we may formulate objectives or questions to be answered rather than hypotheses. Regardless of whether we are testing hypotheses, addressing objectives, or answering questions, we need to state the research conditions as precisely as possible. In examining research, it is important to understand the procedure that was followed, the measures used to assess motivation and other variables, and the characteristics of the participants, in order to adequately evaluate the research.

Motivation Research Paradigms

This section discusses the paradigms (models) that are commonly employed in motivation research. We describe, compare, and contrast the correlational, experimental, and qualitative paradigms and then discuss the attributes, advantages, and disadvantages of laboratory and field studies. Readers who are knowledgeable about research methods may wish to skip this section. We present this material for the benefit of individuals with little research background and those new to the field of motivation.

Correlational and Experimental Research

Researchers employ different research paradigms to investigate motivational processes (Table 1.1). One distinction is between correlational and experimental studies. **Correlational research** deals with relations that exist between variables. A researcher may hypothesize that student motivation is positively correlated with (related to) perceived capabilities, such that the more confidence students have in their learning abilities, the higher is their motivation. To test this relation, the researcher might measure students' perceived capabilities and their motivation as demonstrated on a task. The researcher could statistically correlate the perceived capability and motivation scores to determine the nature and strength of their relation.

Pintrich and De Groot (1990a) conducted a correlational study that explored the relations among motivational, cognitive, and academic performance variables. Seventh-grade students completed the Motivated Strategies for Learning Questionnaire (MSLQ).

Table 1.1   Research Paradigms

Type	Qualities
Correlational	Examines relations that exist between variables
Experimental	One or more variables are altered and their effects on other variables are assessed
Qualitative	Concerned with intensive description and interpretation of meanings
Laboratory	Project conducted in controlled setting
Field	Project conducted where participants typically go to school, learn, or work

This self-report instrument measured students' motivational beliefs and learning strategies. The motivational beliefs component assessed 3 factors: self-efficacy (perceptions of capabilities), intrinsic value (importance), and test anxiety. The learning strategies component comprised 2 factors: cognitive strategy use and self-regulation.

Correlations among intrinsic value, self-efficacy, strategy use, and self-regulation were positive and significant. Test anxiety showed a significant, negative correlation with self-efficacy; correlations of test anxiety with all other variables were nonsignificant. The researchers also computed correlations among these five variables and measures of academic performance: in-class seatwork and homework, quizzes and tests, essays and reports, and grades. Intrinsic value, self-efficacy, and self-regulation correlated positively with all academic measures; strategy use correlated positively with academic measures except for seatwork (nonsignificant); test anxiety was negatively correlated with grades and quiz/test scores. This study was correlational because Pintrich and De Groot looked at the existing relations among variables and did not attempt to alter them. The results show that motivational variables relate in important ways to cognitive factors contributing to classroom success (strategy use, self-regulation) and to measures of academic performance.

In an **experimental research** study, the researcher changes one or more variables and determines the effects on other variables. A researcher interested in the effects of perceived capabilities could conduct an experimental study by systematically altering these beliefs and gauging the effect on student motivation. For example, the researcher might have a teacher systematically praise low-achieving students to raise their self-efficacy and determine if this increase enhances motivation.

Schunk (1982) conducted an experimental study that investigated how forms of effort attributional feedback (see chapter 3) influenced students' achievement outcomes during learning. Elementary-school children who lacked subtraction skills received instruction and practice opportunities over several sessions. While children solved problems individually, an adult monitored the seatwork and periodically asked each child on what page in the instructional packet he or she was working. For some children (the prior attribution group), after they replied with the page number, the adult linked their progress with effort by remarking, "You've been working hard." For others (the future attribution group), the adult stressed the value of future effort by stating, "You need to work hard." Those in a third condition (the monitoring group) were queried, but the adult departed without comment after the child replied. Children in a fourth (control) condition were not monitored.

This study was an experiment because Schunk altered the type of feedback children received and looked to see whether differential effects on achievement outcomes resulted. Schunk hypothesized that prior attribution would be the most effective because it supports children's perceptions of their progress in acquiring skills and conveys that they can continue to improve through effort. This prediction was supported. Prior-attribution students outperformed children in the other conditions on measures of self-efficacy and subtraction skill. Prior-attribution group students also displayed higher motivation than did future-attribution group and control group students as assessed by the amount of problem solving during the independent practice portions of the sessions. The results of this study suggest that it is better to link students' past successes to effort than to stress the future benefits of hard work.

Each type of research has advantages and disadvantages. Correlational research helps clarify relations among variables. Correlational findings often suggest directions for experimental research. The positive correlation obtained by Pintrich and De Groot (1990a) between intrinsic value and academic performance suggests further research exploring whether increasing intrinsic value leads to higher achievement. A disadvantage of correlational research is that it cannot identify cause and effect. The positive correlation between intrinsic value and academic performance could mean that (a) intrinsic value affects academic performance, (b) academic performance influences intrinsic value, (c) intrinsic value and academic performance affect each other, or (d) intrinsic value and academic performance are each influenced by other, unmeasured variables (e.g., home factors).

Experimental research can clarify cause-effect relations. By systematically varying type of feedback and eliminating other variables as potential causes, Schunk (1982) could specify how changes in attributional feedback affect achievement outcomes. Clarifying causal relations helps us understand the nature of motivation. At the same time, experimental research is often narrow in scope. Researchers typically vary only a few variables and try to hold all others constant, which is difficult to do and somewhat unrealistic. Schunk altered only one variable—attributional feedback. Classrooms are complex places where many factors operate simultaneously. To say that one or two variables cause outcomes is probably overstating their importance. It usually is necessary to replicate experiments and examine other variables to better understand effects.

Qualitative/Interpretative Research

In recent years, another type of paradigm has gained currency among researchers. The theories and methods used are referred to by various labels, including qualitative, ethnographic, participant observation, phenomenological, constructivist, and interpretive (Erickson, 1986). These approaches differ from one another but are generally characterized by intensive study, descriptions of events, and interpretation of meanings. Such a research model is not new in the social sciences, but its application to education is of recent vintage.

Qualitative research is especially useful when researchers are interested in the structure of events rather than their overall distributions, when the meanings and perspectives of individuals are important, when actual experiments are impractical or unethical, and when there is a desire to search for new, potential causal linkages that have not been unearthed by experimental methods (Erickson, 1986). Such research is well designed to answer the following types of questions:

1. What is happening, specifically, in social action that takes place in this particular setting?

2. What do these actions mean to the actors involved in them, at the moment the actions took place?

3. How are the happenings organized in patterns of social organization and learned cultural principles for the conduct of everyday life—how, in other words, are people in the immediate setting consistently present to each other as environments for one another's meaningful actions?

4. How is what is happening in this setting as a whole (i.e., the classroom) related to happenings at other system levels outside and inside the setting (e.g., the school building, a child's family, the school system, federal government mandates regarding mainstreaming)?

5. How do the ways everyday life in this setting is organized compare with other ways of organizing social life in a wide range of settings in other places and at other times? (Erickson, 1986, p. 121)

Research within this tradition is quite varied and can range from microanalyses of verbal and nonverbal interactions within single lessons to in-depth observations and interviews over much longer periods. Methods may include classroom observations, use of existing records, interviews, and think-aloud protocols (i.e., participants talk aloud while performing tasks). It is not the particular methods used that characterize this tradition; all of the preceding procedures are frequently employed in correlational and experimental studies. Rather, the hallmark of qualitative research is the depth and quality of analysis and interpretation of data.

Using ethnographic methods, Meece (1991) examined classroom characteristics that help to explain teacher differences in students' goal patterns. During a school year, science lessons were observed repeatedly in elementary and middle-school classes; each class was observed for an average of 600 minutes. Observers collected detailed observational records, including field notes and audiotapes. They transcribed the lessons and analyzed such activities as instructional presentations, teacher and student questioning patterns, forms of feedback, grouping practices, evaluation methods, and motivational strategies. The results are lengthy and will not be summarized here. Meece obtained evidence of important differences among teachers in the preceding activities, which, in turn, related to differences in students' goals.

Qualitative/interpretive research yields rich sources of data that are much more intensive and thorough than those typically obtained in correlational or experimental research. This research paradigm also has the potential of raising new questions and new slants on old questions that often are missed by traditional methods. Because this approach is not concerned with the aggregation of usable knowledge for teaching practice, it is not a means for providing practical answers to teaching problems (Shulman, 1986). Studies are usually conducted with few participants, which raises the issue of whether findings are reliable and representative of the population being studied (e.g., teachers, students). Another concern is that if researchers do not attempt to interpret data in light of a theoretical framework, findings may not be linked and interpretation will prove difficult. Nonetheless, as a research model, this tradition has provided much valuable data in the study of motivation, and its influence will continue to grow.

Laboratory and Field Research

In addition to the differences among experimental, correlational, and qualitative research, another distinction exists between **laboratory research** studies conducted in controlled settings and **field research** studies conducted where the participants go to school, live, and work. Much early motivation research was conducted in laboratories using such infrahuman species as cats, dogs, and rats. Such research was appropriate, given the influence of conditioning theories (discussed later in this chapter), which contended that common processes occurred in animals and humans and that controlled experiments could isolate these processes and eliminate extraneous influences. Motivation research also has employed humans in controlled laboratory environments. With the increasing emphasis on motivation in schools and other applied settings, much current research is conducted in the field.

The Meece (1991), Pintrich and De Groot (1990a), and Schunk (1982) studies are examples of field studies because they were conducted in students' schools. In contrast, a study by Jagacinski and Nicholls (1990) is a laboratory study. College students reported in small groups to the room where the study was conducted. They were given written scenarios and asked to imagine that they were taking an intelligence test in a class and at a certain point got stuck. Their task was to evaluate possible responses to the question, "What will you do to avoid appearing to lack intelligence?"

An advantage of the experimental laboratory is that it offers a high degree of control over extraneous factors: telephones, people talking, windows to look out, and other persons in the room (unless the experiment involves group behavior). The light, temperature, and sound can be controlled. The laboratory also allows researchers to have their materials and equipment at their immediate disposal.

Such control is not possible in the field. Schools are noisy and it often is difficult to find space to work. There also are continual distractions. Students and teachers walk by, bells ring, announcements are made over the public address system, fire drills are held. Rooms may be too bright or too dark, too hot or too cold. Because rooms may be used for other purposes, researchers must bring and set up their materials and equipment each time they work. These extraneous influences can affect an experiment's results.

An advantage of field research is that results can be generalized to similar settings because studies are conducted where students are. Generalization of laboratory findings to the field, however, is typically done with less confidence. Laboratory research has yielded many important findings on motivational processes, and researchers often attempt to replicate laboratory findings in the field.

Whether we choose the laboratory or the field depends on such factors as the purpose of the research, availability of participants, costs, and the use we will make of the results. If we choose the laboratory, we gain control but lose generalizability, and vice versa for the field. With the latter, we need to minimize extraneous influences so that we can be more confident that our results are due to the experimental factors we are studying.

ASSESSING MOTIVATION

The topic of assessing motivation is important for researchers and practitioners who are concerned with understanding the operation of motivational processes and with ways to optimize student motivation. We begin by discussing some commonly employed indexes of motivation: choice of tasks, effort, persistence, and achievement. We then discuss the measurement of motivation by direct observations, ratings by others, and self-reports. As with the preceding section, readers with research backgrounds and those familiar with motivation research may wish to omit this material.

Indexes of Motivation

We noted earlier that there is disagreement about the nature of motivation and the operation of motivational processes. At the same time, most professionals agree that we infer the presence of motivation from the behavioral indicators shown in Table 1.2. One indicator is *choice of tasks,* or interests. When students have a choice, what they choose to do indicates where their motivation lies. This is an important indicator for Keith. What students do (or say that they do) in and out of school when they have free time and can choose among activities indicates their interests.

Lepper, Greene, and Nisbett (1973) is a good example of a research study that employed choice of tasks as a motivational index. Preschoolers were observed during free play. Those who spent much time drawing were assigned to one of three conditions. In the expected-award group, children were offered a good player certificate if they drew a picture. Unexpected-award children were not offered the certificate, but unexpectedly received it after they drew a picture. No-award children were not offered the award and did not receive it. Two weeks later, children were again observed during free play when they could choose tasks to work on. Expected-award children chose to spend less time drawing following the study compared with children in the other two conditions. The expectation of an award decreased children's motivation as assessed by their choosing to draw during free time.

Despite the intuitive appeal of choice of tasks, choice often is not a useful index of motivation in school because in many classrooms, students typically have few, if any, choices (Brophy, 1983). *Effort* is a second index. Learning often is not easy. Students motivated to learn are apt to expend effort to succeed. For motor tasks, effort is physical. When skill learning is involved, cognitive effort is an appropriate index of motivation

Table 1.2 Indexes of Motivation

Index	Relation to Motivation
Choice of tasks	Selection of a task under free-choice conditions indicates motivation to perform the task
Effort	High effort—especially on difficult material—is indicative of motivation
Persistence	Working for a longer time—especially when one encounters obstacles—is associated with higher motivation
Achievement	Choice, effort, and persistence raise task achievement

(Corno & Mandinach, 1983). Students motivated to learn are likely to expend greater mental effort during instruction and employ cognitive strategies they believe will promote learning: organizing and rehearsing information, monitoring level of understanding, and relating new material to prior knowledge (Peterson, Swing, Braverman, & Buss, 1982; Pintrich & De Groot, 1990a). The usefulness of effort as an index of motivation is limited by skill because, as skill increases, one can perform better with less effort. Many students expend high effort to learn in Keith's class—Kris, Sharon, Eric, Deanna, José—although their goals differ considerably.

Salomon (1984) assessed students' mental effort and found that it related to self-efficacy. Children judged self-efficacy for learning from television or from written text, watched a televised film or read the comparable text, judged the amount of mental effort necessary to learn, and were tested on the content. Students judged mental effort greater for text and demonstrated higher achievement scores from text. For text, self-efficacy correlated positively with mental effort and achievement; for TV, it correlated negatively. Students who observed TV felt more efficacious about learning but expended less effort and achieved at a lower level. Schunk (1983a) assessed children's perceptions of how hard they worked during mathematics learning. Schunk found that providing children with feedback linking their performance to effort expenditure raised their perceptions.

Persistence, or time spent on a task, is a third index. Students who are motivated to learn ought to persist at the task, especially when they encounter obstacles. Persistence is important because much learning takes time and success may not be readily forthcoming. Persistence relates directly to the sustaining component in the definition of motivation given earlier, and greater persistence leads to higher accomplishments. In Keith's class, many students persist at tasks, but José's persistence is very high.

Persistence is commonly used by researchers as a measure of motivation. Zimmerman and Ringle (1981) had children observe a model unsuccessfully attempt to solve a puzzle for either a long or short time while verbalizing statements of confidence or pessimism, after which children attempted to solve the puzzle themselves. Children who observed the high-persistent model worked longer on the task than children exposed to the low-persistent model. Children who observed the confident model persisted longer than those who observed the pessimistic model. As with effort, the usefulness of persistence as a motivational measure is limited by skill. As students' skills improve, they should be able to perform well in less time. Persistence is most meaningful during learning and when students encounter obstacles.

Finally, student *achievement* may be viewed as an indirect index of motivation. Students who choose to engage in a task, expend effort, and persist are likely to achieve at a higher level (Pintrich & Schrauben, 1992; Schunk, 1991b). Many research studies obtain positive relations between achievement and motivational indexes of choice, effort, and persistence. Schunk (1983a) found that the more arithmetic problems children completed during training (which reflected effort and persistence), the more problems they solved correctly on a posttest (a measure of achievement). Teachers are convinced that such effects occur in their classes.

Methods of Assessment

Motivation can be assessed in various ways, for example, by direct observations, ratings by others, and self-reports (Table 1.3).

Table 1.3 Methods for Assessing Motivation

Category	Definition
Direct observations	Behavioral instances of choice of tasks, effort, persistence
Ratings by others	Judgments by observers of students on characteristics indicative of motivation
Self-reports	People's judgments of themselves
Questionnaires	Written ratings of items or answers to questions
Interviews	Oral responses to questions
Stimulated recalls	Recall of thoughts accompanying one's performances at various times
Think-alouds	Verbalizing aloud one's thoughts, actions, and emotions while performing a task
Dialogues	Conversations between two or more persons

Direct Observations

Direct observations refer to behavioral instances of choice of tasks, effort expended, and persistence. These behaviors are valid indicators of motivation to the extent that they are straightforward and involve little inference on the part of observers. By focusing only on overt actions, however, direct observations may be superficial and not fully capture the essence of motivation. Earlier, we said that motivation was inferential: We infer its presence from behaviors. Direct observations ignore the cognitive and affective processes underlying motivated behaviors. For example, Sharon, Eric, and Deanna all show relatively high levels of effort, but their reasons for trying hard differ greatly. These reasons represent important cognitive and affective processes that motivation researchers try to understand in their research.

Despite the latter concern, direct observations are commonly used to gauge motivation. Most of what Keith knows about the motivation of his students he has learned by observing them. When Keith says students are motivated to learn, he bases this on his observations of their persistence at tasks, the effort they expend to perform well, and how willingly they engage in tasks.

Bandura and Schunk (1981) used direct observation to assess students' intrinsic motivation in arithmetic. Students received subtraction instruction and practice over seven sessions using seven sets of material. Some children pursued a short-term goal of completing one set each session; a second group received a distant goal of completing all sets by the end of the last session; a third group was given a general goal of working productively. To assess intrinsic motivation, the researchers gave children subtraction problems and digit-symbol problems. Children could work on one or both tasks and worked alone for 25 minutes. Observers recorded which tasks they chose, whether they changed activities, and how much work they completed. In the Lepper et al. (1973) study discussed earlier, observers recorded the length of time students engaged in the target activity as the measure of motivation.

Ratings by Others

Another way to assess motivation is to have observers (e.g., teachers, parents, researchers) rate students on various characteristics indicative of motivation (e.g., Would Tiffany rather read a book or work at the computer? How much effort does Larry expend to solve difficult problems?). An example of a rating instrument is found in a study by Skinner, Wellborn, and Connell (1990) that focused on students' perceptions of control and engagement in academic tasks. Students' perceived control was assessed with a 50-item, self-report instrument comprising three dimensions (strategy beliefs, capacity beliefs, control beliefs). Student engagement in activities was measured with a 10-item scale in which teachers rated children on class participation (e.g., When in class, this student participates in class discussions) and emotional tone (e.g., When in class, this student seems happy). The results showed that teacher reports of engagement correlated with all aspects of perceived control.

One advantage of ratings by others is that observers may be more objective about students than students are about themselves (i.e., self-reports). Ratings by others often attempt to capture motivational processes that underlie behaviors, and thereby provide data not attainable through direct observations. At the same time, ratings by others require more inference than do direct observations. It may be difficult to judge students' levels of cognitive engagement, interest in learning, and so forth. Ratings by others also require observers to remember what students do. Because memory is selective and constructive, ratings may not be valid indicators of student characteristics. Nonetheless, ratings by others are commonly used in motivation research and add a dimension beyond that attainable through direct observations.

Self-Reports

Self-reports capture people's judgments and statements about themselves. Questionnaires, interviews, stimulated recalls, think-alouds, and dialogues—roughly ordered from least to most natural—are types of self-report instruments.

Questionnaires present respondents with items or questions that ask about their actions and beliefs. Respondents may be asked about the types of activities they engage in and how often or how long they engage in them (e.g., "What do you like to do in your free time?" "How many minutes did you study last night?"). They typically make ratings on numerical scales corresponding to their feelings and beliefs ("On a 5-point scale ranging from 1 (low) to 5, mark how certain you are that you can learn how to add fractions with unlike denominators") or answer open-ended questions ("How do you usually feel when you are in school?"). The Skinner et al. (1990) perceived control instrument is an example of a self-report questionnaire, as is Pintrich and De Groot's (1990a) MSLQ. For the latter, students rate each item on a 7-point scale ranging from *not at all true of me* (1) to *very true of me* (7).

The **projective test**, which involves presenting individuals with ambiguous pictures and having them respond to questions, is a special type of questionnaire (or interview). Projective assessments are based on the assumption that people possess personality characteristics and underlying motives and fantasies. Presenting them with ambiguous material may lessen their objective tendencies and allow them to subconsciously project their motives and fantasies onto the situation. Responses are recorded and scored to determine the type and strength of the underlying motives. The Rorschach test is a well-known projective measure whereby participants tell what is suggested to them by a series of inkblot designs (Lilienfeld, Wood, & Garb, 2000).

The Thematic Apperception Test (*TAT*), which was developed by Murray (1938) to study personality, is a well-known projective measure of achievement motivation. McClelland and his colleagues adapted it to assess the achievement motive (McClelland, Atkinson, Clark, & Lowell, 1953). Respondents view a series of pictures of individuals in unclear situations and respond to four questions: "What is happening?" "What led up to this situation?" "What is wanted?" "What will happen?" They are given 4 minutes to write each story. Responses are scored using various criteria. Scores from individual stories are summed to give a total score for strength of achievement motive. The TAT has been employed in many research studies and often relates positively to achievement outcomes (Spangler, 1992). At the same time, it has been shown to have low reliability and its correlations with other achievement measures are not always strong (Weiner, 1985b). More recent research suggests that the TAT measures implicit motives (those not accessible to consciousness) in contrast to more cognitive or conscious motives, what McClelland, Koestner, and Weinberger (1989) have called self-attributed motives, which are best measured by self-report questionnaires. McClelland et al. (1989) suggest that implicit motives and self-attributed motives are separate constructs and should not necessarily be correlated with each other. Lilienfeld et al. (2000), in their analysis of the construct validity of projective techniques, suggest that the scoring of the TAT for need for achievement (an implicit motive) has validity. It seems clear that as the interest in unconscious processing and implicit motives is revived after the dominance of cognitive and social cognitive models of motivation, there will be more use of projective techniques in research on motivation.

An **interview** is a type of questionnaire in which the questions or points to discuss are presented by an interviewer and the respondent answers orally. Zimmerman and Martinez-Pons (1990) developed a self-regulated learning interview to assess self-regulated learning strategies (e.g., self-evaluating, organizing and transforming information, goal-setting and planning, seeking information, keeping records). During the interview, different learning contexts are described (e.g., "When taking a test in school, do you have a particular method for obtaining as many correct answers as possible?" "What if it is a difficult test question?"). For each context, students specify the methods they would employ. Zimmerman and Martinez-Pons scored students' answers, assigned answers to categories, and tallied responses within categories. They found that use of self-regulatory strategies was positively and significantly correlated with students' mathematical and verbal self-efficacy.

For **stimulated recalls**, individuals work on a task and their performances are videotaped. Subsequently, they watch their tapes and attempt to recall their thoughts at various points. Investigators typically stop the tapes at different times and ask questions to help respondents recall their thoughts. By linking thoughts to specific behaviors, stimulated recalls avoid the problem of forcing people to make judgments about their typical behaviors. At the same time, stimulated recalls rely upon respondents' memories. If the recall procedure is delayed for too long after the videotaping, people may have difficulty recalling what they were thinking about at that time.

A stimulated recall procedure was used by Peterson, Swing, Braverman, and Buss (1982) with fifth- and sixth-grade students during instruction. Students were videotaped during the lesson. Afterward, they were shown segments of the tape that portrayed critical incidents. Students were interviewed individually and asked such questions as "Try to remember what you were thinking about. What were you thinking about?" "Were you paying attention?" "Were you understanding the part of the math lesson that you just saw?" Interviews were coded and scored for the presence of various cognitive processes. Students reported a high degree of effort to understand the teacher and the problems. Students who reported that they understood the material also performed well on the seatwork problems and the achievement test.

Think-alouds refer to students' verbalizing aloud their thoughts, actions, and emotions while working on a task (Ericsson & Simon, 1993). Verbalizations may be recorded by observers and scored for the presence of statements relevant to motivation. Think-alouds require students to verbalize, but students in school are not accustomed to verbalizing aloud while working. It may seem awkward to some students and they may feel self-conscious or otherwise have difficulty verbalizing their thoughts. Investigators must prompt students if they do not verbalize.

Diener and Dweck (1978) explored motivational processes during failure. Children were identified as mastery oriented or as learned helpless, based on their attributions of failure to lack of effort or to factors beyond their control. (In Keith's class, Sharon seems mastery oriented whereas Tamika may be learned helpless.) They were presented with stimulus cards containing two figures that varied in color, form, and symbol in the center. Children had to form a hypothesis about the correct solution and choose one of the two figures for each card. They received feedback indicating their choices were wrong regardless of their answers.

Children thought aloud while working. To dispel inhibitions about verbalizing, the experimenters pointed out that they might think aloud about many types of things besides the task, including what they will do after school and what they will have for lunch. The experimenters were interested in how children's cognitive strategies changed as a result of continual failure feedback. Verbalizations were recorded and categorized. Helpless children showed a progressive decline in the use of good problem-solving strategies and an increase in ineffective strategies. Mastery-oriented children did not show such a decline and some actually became more sophisticated in strategy use.

Dialogues are conversations between two or more persons. A researcher might record a classroom conversation as students work on a task or as teacher and students discuss an issue. The conversation is subsequently analyzed for the presence of motivational statements. Dialogues have the advantage of using actual interactions; however, they require interpretation and may be subject to problems in that regard.

Thorkildsen and Nicholls (1991) collected dialogues in a second-grade class. The following excerpt from their work shows that the youngsters were discussing motivational concerns:

> "You want a challenge," argues Jacob . . . "You could challenge yourself to get more than someone else."
>> "But maybe a person is trying all they can and can't get up higher," counters Joan.
>> "Everyone learns things," answers Jacob.
>> "But," Joan insists, "they might have done best as they can and can't get up more . . ."
>> "You can just keep on trying," counters Jacob. "If they just say they can't do it and quit, in a few years they'll say I don't have any money and they'll sit around saying, 'What'll I do?' "

"They can just do their best," suggests Alan.

"Their best is all they can do," adds Matt.

Alan wants to claim more. "If you believe you can do a thing, you can." (pp. 361–362)

Thorkildsen and Nicholls related this and the remaining dialogue to the topic under discussion and provided interpretation of children's thinking and its relation to issues of schooling.

There is no one, best type of self-report measurement. The choice of instrument must match the purpose for the assessment and the research problem. Questionnaires are useful for covering a lot of material in a fairly efficient manner. Interviews are better if researchers or practitioners are interested in exploring feelings and beliefs in depth. Projective methods allow individuals to subconsciously project their motives and fantasies onto the testing situation. Stimulated recalls ask respondents to recall their thoughts when the actions took place, whereas think-alouds examine present thoughts. Dialogues offer unique opportunities to investigate interaction patterns.

Self-report instruments typically are easy to administer, complete, and score, although problems often arise when inferences must be drawn about students' responses. Under these conditions, it is essential that the scoring system is reliable. Other concerns about self-reports include whether students are giving socially acceptable answers that do not match their beliefs, whether self-reported information corresponds to actual behavior, and whether young children are capable of self-reporting accurately. Guaranteeing confidentiality of data can help promote thoughtful responding. A good means of validating self-reports is to use multiple forms of assessment (e.g., self-reports, direct observations). There is evidence that beginning around the third grade, self-reports are valid and reliable indicators of the beliefs and actions they are designed to assess (Assor & Connell, 1992). However, researchers need to use self-reports judiciously and design studies to minimize potential problems.

HISTORICAL THEORIES OF MOTIVATION

This section examines some early views of motivation that have played a key role in motivation research. Although many of these theories are no longer viable, several contemporary ideas about motivation can be traced to historical theories.

Before we turn to our historical presentation, we will discuss differences between behavioral and cognitive theories of motivation. Understanding general assumptions about these theories provides a better grasp of the concepts underlying human motivation and of how theoretical principles are derived.

Behavioral and Cognitive Theories

The process whereby motivation occurs is a basic issue. **Behavioral theories** view motivation as a change in the rate, frequency of occurrence, or form of behavior (response) as a function of environmental events and stimuli. A response to a stimulus becomes more likely to occur in the future as a function of how often it has been paired with the stimulus or what has happened following it. Reinforcing consequences make behavior more likely to occur in the future, whereas punishing consequences make the behavior less likely (Skinner, 1953). From a behavioristic standpoint, motivation is defined by the rate or likelihood of behavior. Compared with students low in academic motivation, those who are motivated to learn are more likely to engage in tasks, persist at them, and expend effort, all of which are behaviors.

The rise of behaviorism in psychology occurred against the backdrop of introspection (discussed later in this chapter). Behaviorism's most strident early supporter was John B. Watson (1924), who contended that if psychology was to become an objective and experimental science, it had to concern itself with observable and scientific phenomena, as the physical sciences did. To psychologists, behavior was observable, whereas introspection, which dealt with subjective states that may have no basis in reality, was not observable and therefore not scientific. Watson (1914) argued that if consciousness could only be studied through introspection, then it should not be studied at all because introspection is too unreliable.

Many historical views of motivation are behavioral because they explain motivation in terms of observable phenomena. Behavioral theorists contend that explanations for motivation do not need to include thoughts and feelings; rather, people are motivated by environmental events. In the preceding scenario, Keith seems to be espousing a behavioral view.

In contrast, **cognitive theories** stress the causal role of mental structures and the processing of information and beliefs. Motivation is internal; we do not observe it directly, but rather its products (behaviors). Although cognitive theorists are united in the importance of mental processes, they disagree about which processes are important. Different cognitive theories of motivation stress such processes as attributions, perceptions of competence, values, affects, goals, and social comparisons. A. K.'s comments place greater emphasis on internal processes.

These conceptualizations of motivation have important educational implications. Behavioral theories imply that teachers should arrange the environment so that students can respond properly to stimuli. Cognitive theories emphasize learners' thoughts, beliefs, and emotions. Teachers need to consider how such mental processes may manifest themselves in the classroom and how instructional and social variables affect not only what students do, but also their thoughts.

We now begin a largely chronological look at important historical perspectives on motivation. Readers who are familiar with historical theories and want to focus on current views may wish to omit this section. At the beginning of the twentieth century, motivation was not a separate topic of study as it is today, but rather was ill-defined and fell under the purview of the newly emerging discipline of psychology. Views of motivation, and psychology in general, were rooted heavily in philosophy. Two prominent conceptualizations of motivation were in terms of (a) volition/will, and (b) instincts.

Volition/Will

Many early psychologists drew on the views of such philosophers as Plato and Aristotle and conceived of the mind as comprising-knowing (cognition), feeling (emotion), and willing (motivation). The **will** reflected an individual's desire, want, or purpose; **volition** was the act of using the will.

Wilhelm Wundt, who studied volition and helped establish psychology as a science with the first psychological laboratory in Germany in 1879 (Hunt, 1993), introduced the method of **introspection**, which required individuals to verbally report their immediate experiences following exposure to objects or events. If they were shown a picture of a tree, they might report their perceptions of its shape, size, color, and texture. They were to avoid labeling the stimulus ("tree") and reporting their knowledge of it and the meanings of their perceptions because labels and meanings masked the organization of consciousness. Introspection helped demarcate psychology from other sciences but was problematic and unreliable. When viewing a tree, people naturally think of its verbal label and their knowledge about the tree. Forcing people to ignore these attributes is unnatural and does not allow researchers to study higher mental processes (e.g., thinking, problem solving).

Philosophers and psychologists disagreed over whether volition was an independent process or rather a by-product of other mental processes (sensations, perceptions). Wundt felt that volition was a central, independent factor in human behavior. It presumably accompanied such processes as sensation, perception, attention, and formation of mental associations, and helps translate our thoughts and feelings into action.

Wundt's ideas about volition were quite general and difficult to validate. William James, another psychology pioneer, studied volitional acts in depth (Hunt, 1993; James, 1890, 1892). James believed that consciousness helped people and animals adapt to their environments. Will was a state of mind in which we desire a particular action and believe that its manifestation is within our power. Volition was the process of translating intentions into actions. At times, a mental representation of the act was sufficient to motivate action, but at other times, an additional conscious element "in the shape of a fiat, mandate, or express consent, has to intervene and precede the movement" (James, 1890, p. 522).

James (1890) cited an incident of getting out of bed on a cold morning as an example of how volition was minimal because a mental representation of an act can motivate action:

> Now how do we *ever* get up under such circumstances? . . . We more often than not get up without any struggle or decision at all. We suddenly find that we *have* got up. A fortunate lapse of consciousness occurs; we forget both the warmth and the cold; we fall into some revery connected with the day's life, in the course of which the idea flashes across us, 'Hollo! I must lie here no longer'—an idea which at that lucky instant awakens no contradictory or paralyzing suggestions, and consequently produces immediately its appropriate motor effects. (p. 524)

It may seem that many actions occur automatically, but volition often plays a role because it helps execute the intended action by activating a mental representation. Volition has its greatest effect when various intentions compete for action. This is the reason why so many ideas we have do not result in action. We need the type of volitional "fiat, mandate, or express consent" to translate intentions into actions and will ourselves into action.

Ach (1910) pioneered the experimental study of volition, which he viewed as the process of dealing with the implementation of actions designed to attain goals. This is a narrow view of motivation because it does not address the process whereby people formulate goals and commit themselves to attaining them (Heckhausen, 1991). Ach referred to processes that allowed goals to be translated into action as **determining tendencies**. In a series of studies that employed introspection, Ach found that determining tendencies compete with association (previously learned) tendencies to produce action even when the action conflicts with prior associations. Thus, instructions to perform a task (attain a goal) in response to a cue that conflicts with the type of task performed previously can trigger determining tendencies that allow accomplishment of the goal. Action is determined by the tendencies to attain the goal.

Many ideas in the psychologies of Wundt, James, and Ach were vague and difficult to test empirically. The use of introspection was often problematic. Although conscious willing of action seems plausible, the will may actually reflect our interpretation that our thoughts cause action rather than the cause itself (Wegner & Wheatley, 1999). Volition offered an incomplete perspective on motivation because volition was limited to implementing actions designed to attain goals. How people formulated goals was ignored or downplayed. Nonetheless, we will see in chapter 4 that in modified form, volition is reflected in contemporary motivation and self-regulation theory.

Instincts

Another early perspective on motivation stressed **instincts**, or innate propensities that manifest themselves in behavior (e.g., imitation, emulation, anger, resentment, sympathy). James (1890) believed that instincts could not explain all behavior but provided a base upon which experience builds by developing habits. He thought that instinctive behavior overlapped reflexes and learning.

McDougall (1926) believed that all behavior was instinctive. Instincts were not dispositions to act in particular ways, but rather included cognitive, affective, and conative components. The *cognitive* component refers to awareness of ways to satisfy the instinct, the *affective* component denotes the emotions aroused by the instinct, and the *conative* component is the striving to attain the object (goal) of the instinct. Thus, students with the curiosity instinct know how to satisfy their curiosity, will feel emotionally aroused when curious, and will attempt to attain the objects of their curiosity.

McDougall believed that objects triggering instincts can be changed. By linking school activities to objects or events that elicit children's curiosity, the activities themselves may eventually trigger the curiosity instinct. Instinctive behaviors can also be changed. Infants' curiosity is satisfied by grabbing and crawling, but with experience curiosity is satisfied in other ways (e.g., reading, solving puzzles). Instincts can be altered when many are triggered at once, such that the resulting instinct represents a combination. Curiosity at school is sometimes coupled with anxiety about learning; the resulting behavior may reflect ambivalence. Instincts can become attached to objects or situations; for example, students whose curiosity is not rewarded at school may display it only at home.

The instinct position is compatible with the points made by A. K. Buerso, who believes that students have (innate) dispositions and that many behaviors—especially those of young children—do not reflect learning. The instinct position remains current; for example, the "nature-nurture" controversy over which human abilities are learned and which are inherited.

Instinct theories are compelling, but have problems when viewed from a scientific perspective. Classifying all behavior as instinctive downplays the role of learning. A theory of motivation needs to specify where instinct ends and learning begins. It also is true that instincts are impacted by learning. Thus, the capacity of people to learn language is innate, but language is learned through social interactions. Finally, labeling a behavior as instinctive does not explain it. A complete theory of motivation must be able to explain what causes an action, what factors interact with it, and how it can be modified.

Freud's Theory

Another early psychological theory with relevance to motivation is Sigmund Freud's. Freud is well known for his theory of personality and for the psychoanalytic method of psychotherapy. We do not provide a detailed explanation of Freud's theory; readers are referred to other sources (Freud, 1966; Heidbreder, 1933; Hunt, 1993; Weiner, 1985b). A summary of motivational principles from Freud's theory follows.

Freud conceived of motivation as **psychical energy.** He believed that forces within the individual were responsible for behavior. Freud's concept of *trieb,* the German word for *moving force,* bears a close resemblance to motivation. Trieb was translated as *instinct,* although in meaning it seems closer to **drive.**

Freud believed that people represent closed energy systems. Each person has a constant amount of energy, although its form may change. The psychical energy builds up in the **id,** a personality structure devoted to attainment of basic needs. Energy develops when needs exist; needs are satisfied by channeling energy into behaviors that reduce needs. Need reduction is pleasurable because a build-up of energy is unpleasant. The aim of energy is its goal (satisfaction); its object refers to the means whereby the force is satisfied; and the source denotes bodily processes activating the energy. For example, a child neglected at home has a need for attention. The aim of the force is to satisfy the need, so gaining attention from an object (teacher) is pleasurable and reduces the source and the energy. Eventually other objects (friends) may satisfy the need for attention, or the energy may become *fixated* on a particular object (teacher) to whom the child always turns for attention.

Energy also can be **repressed,** which means that individuals resist the force to the point where it is not recognized. We resist forces when activity related to them causes more pain than pleasure. Repression does not eliminate energy; rather, repressed energy manifests itself in distorted ways (e.g., neurotic behavior). Repression may be largely unconscious; we may not be fully aware of the forces at work or why we are acting the way we are. A behavior may not represent the motive it appears to represent. For example, repressed sexual energy can disguise itself as overeating.

Freud's theory is so extensive that it makes little sense to ask whether it is correct. Some aspects have been shown to be valid; others have not received support (Weiner, 1985b). Westen (1998) has suggested that there are aspects of Freud's legacy that remain useful today. In particular, the notion that there can be unconscious aspects of thoughts and behavior that individuals do not have access to is in line with current theories about implicit motives (McClelland, Koestner, & Weinberger, 1989) as well as general research in social and personality psychology (Bargh, 1997; Bargh & Ferguson, 2000; Kihlstrom, 1990). On the other hand, by assuming that most of an individual's motivation stems from inner forces that often are unconscious, the theory downgrades the importance of personal cognitions and environmental factors. To improve students' motivation, teachers need to know their goals, interests, and values; how students are affected by teachers and other students; and how to design instruction that teaches and motivates. Freud's theory offers no guidance on these points.

Conditioning Theories

Conditioning theories became preeminent in the United States early in the twentieth century and maintained their dominance in American psychology until the last 30 to 40 years. In contrast to Freudian ideas about unconscious, or even conscious, internal processes, these theories concentrated on the analysis of observable behavior. Three important conditioning theories are those of Thorndike (connectionism), Pavlov (classical conditioning), and Skinner (operant conditioning). Although these theories differ, all are behavioral theories that emphasize the association of stimuli with responses as the mechanism for learning. These theories are relevant to motivation because at the behavioral level, motivation involves the probability or rate of responding.

Conditioning theories posit an additive view of behavior. Complex behaviors can be reduced to a series of simple behaviors; behavior change is continuous and occurs by combining behaviors into larger sequences. No new principles are needed to explain complex behaviors; rather, these theories involve principles that can be applied to all behaviors.

Connectionism

Thorndike's (1913) **connectionist** theory contended that learning involves the formation of associations (connections) between sensory experiences (perceptions of stimuli or events) and neural impulses that manifest themselves behaviorally. Learning often occurs by trial and error (selecting and connecting). Organisms (people, animals) find themselves in problem situations where they attempt to reach a goal. From the various responses they could perform, they select one, perform it, and experience the consequences. Learning occurs gradually; successful responses become established and unsuccessful ones are abandoned. Connections are "stamped in" or "stamped out" by being repeatedly performed or not performed.

> The **Law of Effect** is a central principle:
> When a modifiable connection between a situation and a response is made and is accompanied or followed by a satisfying state of affairs, that connection's strength is increased: When made and accompanied or followed by an annoying state of affairs, its strength is decreased. (Thorndike, 1913, p. 4)

The Law of Effect states that the consequences of behavior are motivating and produce learning. Responses that result in rewarding consequences are learned and those that produce punishing consequences are not learned. Thorndike (1932) subsequently revised the Law of Effect because research showed that rewarding consequences strengthen connections, but punishing consequences do not necessarily weaken them. Connections are weakened when alternative connections are strengthened.

Another principle relevant to motivation is the **Law of Readiness**, which states that when one is prepared to act, to do so is satisfying and not to do so is annoying. Applying this motivational idea to learning, we might say that when students are ready to learn, engaging in activities to foster that learning is satisfying and produces better learning than when they are not ready to learn. Alternatively, when students are forced to learn and they are not ready, learning is annoying.

An important implication is that students are motivated when they are ready to work at an activity and when the consequences of engagement are pleasurable. Students should possess the prerequisites to learn and experience desirable outcomes of learning: performing new skills, recognizing the value of learning, and receiving positive feedback. Despite the intuitive plausibility of Thorndike's principles, his theory has limited applicability to the complexities of motivation in education because it ignores cognitive processes.

Classical Conditioning

Pavlov's (1927, 1928) classical conditioning theory is important in the field of learning and can be applied to motivation. Conditioning involves presenting an **unconditioned stimulus** (UCS) to elicit an **unconditioned response** (UCR). In a prototypical experiment, a hungry dog is placed in a harness. The dog salivates (UCR) when presented with meat powder (UCS). Conditioning involves briefly presenting a neutral stimulus (e.g., a ticking metronome) before presenting the UCS. In the early trials, the ticking of the metronome produces no salivation. Eventually, the dog salivates in response to the ticking metronome. The metronome has become a **conditioned stimulus** (CS) that elicits a **conditioned response** (CR) similar to the original UCR (Figure 1.1). Repeated presentations of the CS alone cause extinction—the CR diminishes in intensity and disappears.

Receipt of reinforcement (the UCS) strengthens the CS–UCS connection. Through repeated pairings with the UCS, the CS acquires the motivational potential of the UCS to generate a response (CR). Thus, neutral stimuli can acquire motivational properties by being paired with stimuli possessing those properties. Although Pavlov believed that conditioning occurs with repeated CS–UCS pairings, research shows that conditioning is not automatic, but depends on cognitive processes (Fuhrer & Baer, 1965). For

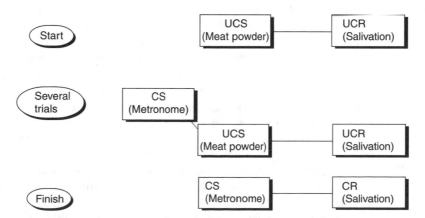

Figure 1.1 Pavlov's classical conditioning (UCS = unconditioned stimulus, UCR = unconditioned response, CS = conditioned stimulus, CR = conditioned response)

conditioning to occur, the CS must inform individuals that the UCS is likely (Rescorla, 1972, 1987). The CS helps people form expectations about the time, place, quantity, quality, and so forth of the UCS. If people do not realize there is a CS–UCS link, conditioning will not occur. Even when a CS is predictive, it will not become conditioned if another CS is a better predictor. Expectations formed through conditioning apparently motivate individuals to anticipate reinforcement.

In like fashion, emotional reactions can be conditioned to neutral stimuli by pairing them with UCSs. In school, students may develop anxious reactions to teachers, classrooms, or buildings when they are paired with aversive events (e.g., test failure). Alleviating symptoms requires counterconditioning the anxiety-producing cues by pairing them with stimuli that elicit pleasant feelings. If the classroom becomes an anxiety-producing cue, the teacher needs to associate the classroom with pleasant events (e.g., praise, positive feedback).

Pavlov's theory has many ideas of interest to education. The notion that learning should be accompanied by pleasurable consequences is important, and teachers generally try to make their classrooms pleasant. Conditioned emotional reactions are apparent in school phobia and test anxiety. Because the theory ignores cognitive processes, however, it offers an incomplete account of behavior. It also represents a passive view of learning and motivation; if conditions are right, conditioning will occur regardless of what people do. In fact, research shows that conditioning is never automatic (Rescorla, 1987). Further, we show throughout this text that learners are mentally active and they exert much control over their learning and motivation.

Operant Conditioning

B. F. Skinner's (1953) operant conditioning theory is an influential theory for motivation, especially in the field of education. This theory examines the external variables of which behavior is a function. The basic conditioning model is:

Antecedent ⟶ Behavior ⟶ Consequence

In this ABC model, an antecedent stimulus sets the occasion for a behavioral response to be performed, which is followed by a consequence. The consequence is any stimulus or event that affects the future rate of responding or the probability that the response will be performed when the stimulus is present. **Reinforcement** increases the rate or likelihood of responding. A **positive reinforcer** is a stimulus that, when presented following a response, increases the future rate or likelihood of the response occurring in that situation. **Positive reinforcement** involves presenting a positive reinforcer following a response. Students who work productively in class may be praised by the teacher. If students then are more likely to work productively or sustain their efforts at a high level, we conclude that praise is a positive reinforcer.

A **negative reinforcer** is a stimulus that, when removed following a response, increases the future rate or likelihood of the response occurring in that situation. **Negative reinforcement** involves removing a negative reinforcer contingent on a response. In the preceding example, students who work productively may be told by the teacher that they do not have to do any homework. If students then continue their productive work, we say that homework is a negative reinforcer and that its removal is negative reinforcement.

Punishment decreases the rate or likelihood of responding. Punishment may involve either removing a positive reinforcer or presenting a negative reinforcer following a response. In the preceding example, suppose that the students are wasting time. The teacher may take away their free time or assign homework. If they then become less likely to waste time (i.e., more likely to work productively), we say that they were punished for wasting time by having a positive reinforcer (free time) removed or a negative reinforcer (homework) presented. Reinforcement and punishment are exemplified in Table 1.4.

Once a response becomes established, it can extinguish. **Extinction** refers to a lack of responding produced by nonreinforcement of the response. Students who raise their hands in class but are never called on may stop raising their hands. Extinction depends on reinforcement history. Extinction occurs quickly if few preceding responses have been reinforced. Responding without reinforcement is more durable with a longer reinforcement history.

Operant conditioning requires that we determine the effects of behavioral consequences. What functions as reinforcement and punishment may vary from person to person and moment to moment. Although most students are reinforced by praise much of the time, praise sometimes does not reinforce and may actually punish (e.g., when a student does not desire teacher attention). Even valued reinforcers can change. A reinforcer applied too often can produce satiation and lead to decreased responding.

The **Premack Principle**, which states that the opportunity to engage in a more valued activity reinforces engaging in a less valued activity, offers a systematic means for ordering reinforcers and predicting how consequences will function (Premack, 1962, 1971). Determining in advance which reinforcers are likely to be effective is critical in planning a program of behavior change (Timberlake & Farmer-Dougan, 1991). Value is defined as the amount of responding or time spent on the activity in the absence of explicit reinforcers. The Premack Principle predicts that (a) if the value of the second (contingent) event is higher than the value of the first (instrumental) event, the likelihood of occurrence of the first event will increase (the reward assumption), and (b) if the value of the second (contingent) event is lower than that of the first (instrumental)

Table 1.4   Reinforcement and Punishment

Event	Stimulus	Response	Consequence
Positive reinforcement (present positive reinforcer)	Teacher gives student work to complete	Student studies	Teacher praises student for good work
Negative reinforcement (remove negative reinforcer)	Teacher gives student work to complete	Student studies	Teacher says student does not have to finish work
Punishment (remove positive reinforcer)	Teacher gives student work to complete	Student wastes time	Teacher takes away student's free time
Punishment (present negative reinforcer)	Teacher gives student work to complete	Student wastes time	Teacher assigns homework

event, the likelihood of occurrence of the first event will decrease (the punishment assumption). For example, if during free time Emily often works at the computer rather than on math, then the opportunity to work at the computer (the contingent event) will be an effective reinforcer for working on math (the instrumental event).

Operant conditioning requires no new principles to account for motivation. Motivated behavior is increased or continued responding is produced by effective contingencies of reinforcement (Skinner, 1968). Internal processes that accompany responding (e.g., needs, drives, cognitions, emotions) are not necessary to explain behavior. The causes of Kara's behavior reside within her reinforcement history (what she has been reinforced for in the past) and the present environment (Skinner, 1953). Students display motivated behavior because they have been reinforced for it previously and because effective reinforcers for it are available in their environments.

Operant conditioning includes many educational principles. The motivational importance of reinforcement and punishment for schooling is apparent in such practices as praise, criticism, time out, free time, rules, privileges, grades, and token/point systems. Some examples of principles of operant conditioning and other conditioning theories applied to teaching and learning are given in Application 1.1.

It is important to note that all of the applications in this book are suggested as general strategies for teachers to use in their classrooms. Teachers must be aware that there are different motivational strategies that are best used in different situations, depending on their goals, the classroom context, the students, and the academic tasks. The application suggestions must be applied in a thoughtful and reflective manner by teachers. In this strategic sense, the applications are "tools" that may be used to accomplish or "build" certain things. Continuing this tool metaphor, different tools have different uses and can be used effectively in different ways (a hammer can be used for many tasks, but it is better for some tasks than are other tools). In the same way, there is a need for builders to use their tools appropriately and thoughtfully and use the right tool for the right job. It is the same for these applications. They are offered as tools for teachers to help motivate their students, but the judicious use of the applications must be based on the teacher's own professional knowledge and judgment.

APPLICATION 1.1

Applying Conditioning Theories in the Classroom

1. *Ensure that students have the readiness to learn.* Ms. Walker, a fourth-grade teacher, will teach addition of fractions. Before she begins this, however, she checks whether her students can add whole numbers. Two students are still having problems adding whole numbers, so she spends extra time with them until they can add correctly.

   Mr. Tamborina tells his fifth graders that after they learn how to divide, they will be able to compute baseball players' batting averages. Midway through the school year, he feels that they can divide well enough, so he teaches them how to figure batting averages (total number of hits divided by total number of times at bat).

2. *Help students form associations between stimuli and responses.* A third-grade teacher is teaching her students to put headings on papers. She has them write headings on papers in all subject areas—math, writing, spelling, and social studies. She wants them to learn that when they start working on a paper (stimulus), they are to put on a heading (response).

    An elementary teacher works with his students on multiplication facts by giving them brief review exercises each day. His goal is for them to associate the stimulus "$9 \times 7 =$" with the correct response "63."

3. *Associate learning and classroom activities with pleasing outcomes.* A fourth-grade teacher decides to start cooking in the classroom each Friday to help her students with measurement. After the students have prepared the recipes with accurate measurements, they get to cook and eat what they have made.

    Ms. Kincaid, a middle school art teacher, has been working with her students on various sculpture and glazing techniques. After they have completed several small projects, the students are able to create a large piece for their homes.

4. *Reinforce desired behaviors and extinguish undesired ones.* Mrs. Wazulski moves around the classroom and monitors students' seatwork. She comments on desirable aspects of their work (e.g., "That's good, Jim, you're working very well.") and shows students how to perform better ("That page is a bit sloppy, Mara. Look at the example here. Try to work it this way.").

    Jason pushes Sam out of line. Mr. Christo spots this and immediately says, "Jason, we do not push people. You know that the penalty for pushing is no free time, so you lose your free time today." The next day, Jason does not misbehave in line. Mr. Christo says, "Jason, you can be line leader on the way back from lunch since you are doing such a great job of walking and not pushing."

5. *Reinforce progress in learning and behavior.* Mr. Green has his high school English students keep a portfolio of their writing. Periodically, he sits down with students individually to review their work and point out the areas of improvement. They feel better knowing that they are making progress in writing.

    Mr. Leland, an elementary music teacher, has a second-grade class that has been having difficulty learning six songs for the spring program. Mr. Leland makes a chart with the six songs listed. He tells his students that each time they learn a song, he will put a star on the chart. After they have earned six stars, they will have a popcorn party in class.

6. *Make participation at valued activities contingent on working on less-valued ones.* Alfonso, a fifth-grade student, does not like to finish his reading assignments, but he loves to write stories on the computer. Mr. Willet, his teacher, tells Alfonso that he may have extra time at the computer if he completes his reading work.

    Ms. Sherrill, a high school drama teacher, tells her students that to perform in the senior play they must be present at 15 of the 20 play practices.

Conditioning principles have practical usefulness, but the theory offers an incomplete account of motivation. Operant conditioning does not distinguish motivation from learning, but rather uses the same principles to explain all behavior. We stress in this text that although motivation and learning are related, they are not synonymous (Brophy, 1983; Schunk, 1991a). Another issue is that reinforcement and punishment motivate students, but their effects are not automatic; rather, they depend upon students' beliefs. Students engage in activities that they believe will be reinforced and avoid activities that they believe will be punished (Bandura, 1986). When reinforcement history conflicts with present beliefs, people are more likely to act based on their beliefs (Brewer, 1974). Research has identified many cognitive processes that motivate students (e.g., goals, social comparisons, attributions, expectancies for success). By ignoring these processes, operant conditioning cannot fully account for the complexity of human motivation.

Drive Theories

Conditioning was not the only influential perspective on learning and motivation during the first half of the twentieth century. Drive theories emphasized the contribution of internal factors to behavior. *Drives* are internal forces that seek to maintain **homeostasis,** or the optimal states of bodily mechanisms. When an organism experiences a need because of deprivation of an essential element (e.g., food, air, water), a drive is activated, causing the organism to respond. Drive is reduced and the need is satisfied when the element is obtained.

Drives possess intensity, direction, and persistence (Woodworth, 1918). *Intensity* refers to the extent that a drive activates behavior. Intensity varies from too low to activate behavior to extremely high. *Direction* denotes the object or goal of the drive. When a drive is triggered, it activates behavior explicitly oriented toward satisfying the need; for example, a hunger drive leads persons to seek food rather than water. *Persistence* refers to the continuation of behavior until the goal is obtained and the need is reduced.

Much research in the drive theory tradition was conducted using laboratory animals engaged in simple behaviors. A typical experiment might vary conditions and measure the time it took for hungry or thirsty animals to run mazes to obtain reinforcement. The concept of drive may explain simple behaviors by animals and humans, but it has been found wanting as an explanation for the complex behavior that characterizes much human motivation (Weiner, 1985b).

Systematic Behavior Theory

In addition to drive, Hull (1943) postulated that habit strength and inhibition were important for behavior. **Habit strength,** or the strength of the stimulus-response association, increases with the number of reinforced stimulus-response pairings. **Inhibition** refers to fatigue due to responding and to the reinforcement derived from not responding when one is fatigued. Whereas drive and habit strength led organisms to make responses, inhibition caused them to not respond. **Effective reaction potential,** or the likelihood of behavior, is a function of drive, habit strength, and inhibition.

Motivation is "the initiation of learned, or habitual, patterns of movement or behavior" (Hull, 1943, p. 226). Innate behaviors usually satisfy needs and learning occurs only when innate behaviors prove ineffective. Learning represents the organism's adaptation to the environment to ensure survival. Much behavior was not oriented toward satisfying primary needs. Secondary reinforcers (e.g., money) acquire reinforcing power by being paired with primary reinforcement (money buys food).

One problem with Hull's theory is that needs do not always trigger drives aimed at drive reduction. Needs for food or water can be outweighed by nonphysiological needs (e.g., desire to finish important tasks). Drives can exist in the absence of biological needs. A strong sex drive can lead to promiscuity even though sex is not immediately needed for survival.

Another concern is that much human behavior is aimed at obtaining long-term goals: getting a job, obtaining a college degree, or winning a championship. People are not continuously in a high-drive state while striving for these goals. High drive is not conducive to performance over lengthy periods or on complex tasks (Broadhurst, 1957; Yerkes & Dodson, 1908). Over time, people typically experience alternating periods of high and low motivation. The key to long-term success is to not remain for long in a slump!

Incentive Motivation

Hull's theory subsequently was refined to better address motivation. The theory originally specified that reinforcement increased habit strength and effective reaction potential. Hull (1943) postulated that large rewards led to better learning (i.e., greater habit strength) than did small rewards and that strong habits were developed when large rewards were delivered immediately after goal attainment.

These ideas were not substantiated by Tolman's research on latent learning (discussed later in this chapter), which showed that rats learned to run mazes without being rewarded. Other research demonstrated that shifts in motivation (e.g., speed of maze running) were due to changes in reward size (Crespi, 1942). This shift cannot be caused by altered habit strength because habit strength presumably increased with repeated reinforcements.

Hull (1951, 1952) modified his position to include incentive motivation, which refers to motivation for goal attainment and is a performance rather than a learning variable. Spence (1960) postulated that incentive motivation combines additively with drive to produce a complex motivational variable. The idea that reward influences behavior, but not necessarily learning, has been substantiated in the ensuing years (Bandura, 1986), and is addressed by many cognitive theories of motivation.

Mowrer's Theory

Mowrer (1960) developed a drive theory that stressed the role of **emotions**, which are intervening variables that mediate (bridge) the relation between stimuli and responses. Cues associated with the onset of emotion become capable of eliciting the emotion before the emotion-producing stimulus does. Such anticipatory emotion produces instrumental behavior to approach or avoid the stimulus.

Mowrer's theory postulated four primary emotions: fear, relief, hope, and disappointment. *Fear* instigates behavior designed to avoid perceived danger and represents the anticipation or expectation of pain. Fear occurs from increased drive brought about by such situations as food deprivation and being shocked. *Relief* occurs when fear is reduced by a response that removes the organism from the feared situation. Relief becomes linked with stimuli that are present when fear cues are removed. If a light comes on in an experimental apparatus immediately before an animal may be shocked, and pressing a lever turns the light off, the sight of the lever can become conditioned to produce relief in the animal.

A decrease in drive can be accompanied by *hope*. If a hungry animal is taught to press a lever to obtain food, then obtaining food reduces drive and produces hope. Cues associated with lever pressing (e.g., a light by the lever is on when food arrives) become conditioned to elicit hope because they signal that a decrease in drive and an increase in hope are imminent. *Disappointment* occurs when hope is diminished by the consequences of a response, as when hope cues predicting a decrease in drive do not lead to drive reduction (e.g., suddenly the light goes off and lever pressing does not produce food). Disappointment, like fear, is negative and motivates organisms to remove the cues signaling disappointment. Thus, an animal may cease pressing the lever and begin making other responses to see if they produce food.

Mowrer's theory represents a plausible account of how some motivational responses are learned. Behaviors are motivated by emotions that become conditioned to cues. Fear, hope, relief, and disappointment are common emotions among students in response to school situations (e.g., tests).

Mowrer's theory can account for the performance of established behaviors but not the instigation of new behaviors (Miller, 1963). Once a laboratory animal learns that cues in a maze are associated with hope because food is at the end, the animal's behaviors will continue, but the theory does not explain why the animal explores the maze the first time. Also, emphasizing a small number of emotions limits the role of personal cognitions and the explanatory potential for achievement motivation.

Acquired Drives

Hull viewed drives as innate mechanisms for survival, but drives can be learned. Miller (1948) explored these **acquired drives** using a box in which two compartments were separated by a door. Rats were shocked while in the first compartment, after which the experimenter opened the door so they could escape to the second compartment. Subsequently, rats were put into the first compartment but not shocked and could escape through the door to the second compartment. They then had to learn to turn a wheel and press a lever in the first compartment to open the door leading to the second compartment. About half of the rats learned the two responses and showed improved performance across trials. Rats that did not learn the responses developed habits (e.g., crouching in place) that interfered with learning.

Miller's study showed that neutral cues associated with the first compartment became associated with shock and motivated the rats to learn new, arbitrary responses (wheel turning, lever pressing) that were reinforced by the rats escaping to the second compartment. Motivation to avoid the first compartment was acquired through pairing it with shock. This motivation helped the rats learn behaviors to avoid shock. As with other drive theories, the explanatory potential of this view is limited because it downplays cognition and assumes that all human motivation is ultimately linked with primary drives.

Purposive Behaviorism

Tolman's (1932) theory of purposive behaviorism, which stresses goals, stands in contrast to the mechanistic conditioning and drive theories. Environmental stimuli offer means to goal attainment and must be studied in the context of actions. High school students who want to attend leading universities study hard. A focus only on the studying neglects its goal. Students study not only because they have been reinforced for studying, but also because they believe studying promotes learning and high grades and enhances the likelihood of college acceptance.

Although Tolman went beyond stimulus-response associations, he qualified his use of cognitive terms by noting they were defined objectively. People and animals act "as if" they are pursuing goals and "as if" they choose means for goal attainment. Despite its behavioral focus, Tolman's theory alludes to cognitive mechanisms.

Expectancy Learning

Tolman (1932) defined expectancies as involving relationships between stimuli (S_1—S_2) or among a stimulus, response, and stimulus (S_1–R–S_2). Relations between stimuli concern what stimulus is apt to follow what other stimulus; for example, if I see lightning (S_1), thunder will follow (S_2). In a three-term relation, people develop the belief that a certain response to a given stimulus will produce a result; for example, if I study (R) this book (S_1), I should make a good grade on the test (S_2). Simple stimulus-response contiguity is often sufficient to produce an expectancy. Expectancies help one attain goals. People form **cognitive maps**, or internal plans, comprising expectancies of which actions are needed to attain one's goals. Individuals follow signs to goals, learn meanings rather than discrete responses, and use cognitive maps to attain goals (Tolman, 1949).

Tolman tested his ideas in clever ways. In one study (Tolman, Ritchie, & Kalish, 1946), rats were trained to run an apparatus, after which it was replaced with one in which the original pathway was blocked. Conditioning theories predict that animals will choose a pathway close to the original one because its cues are associated with reinforcement. Instead, the most frequently chosen path was aimed toward the original location of food, which supports the idea that animals respond to a cognitive map of the food's location.

Latent Learning

Additional evidence to support cognitive map learning came from experiments on **latent learning**, or learning in the absence of a goal or reinforcement. Such learning contradicts the operant conditioning principle that behavior change requires reinforced practice.

Tolman and Honzik (1930) allowed two groups of rats to wander through a maze for several trials. One group was always fed in the maze; the other group was never fed there. Rats that were fed reduced their time to run the maze and the number of errors; time and errors for the other group remained high. When some rats from the nonreinforced group were given food for running the maze, their times and number of errors quickly dropped to the levels of the group that always had been fed. Running times and error rates for rats who continued to be nonreinforced did not change. This showed that rats in the nonreinforced group learned features of the maze by wandering through it.

Tolman demonstrated that learning can occur without reward or drive reduction and that incentives affect performance rather than learning (Weiner, 1990). Teachers sometimes try to motivate students to perform what they know (e.g., review sessions), but much time is spent motivating students to learn. The educational message that learning can occur without reward is an important one. Despite providing this insight, Tolman's theory does not fully capture the complexity of influences on motivation.

Arousal Theories

A different historical perspective on motivation is found in theories that construe motivation as a level of emotional arousal. These theories are not behavioral in nature, but neither are they entirely cognitive. Arousal theories postulate that motivation depends strongly on affective processes. Researchers are increasingly showing that affects play an important role in school learning and motivation (see chapter 7).

In this section, we discuss the James-Lange theory, ideas about optimal levels of arousal, and Schachter's theory of emotion. Readers interested in further information on arousal theories are referred to other sources (Arnold, 1968; Mook, 1987; Russell, 1970).

James-Lange Theory

Toward the end of the nineteenth century, a popular view held that emotional arousal mediates the relation between perception of a stimulus and behavior. For example, if we encounter a threatening snake, the perception of the snake gives rise to fear, which leads to escape. This may be depicted as:

$$\text{Perception} \longrightarrow \text{Emotion} \longrightarrow \text{Behavior}$$

James (1884, 1890) and Lange (1885) independently challenged this view. The **James-Lange theory of emotion** (as it became known) stipulated that emotion is a consequence of behavior rather than an antecedent (cause) and involves perceptions of responses to arousing situations. Responses include actual behaviors as well as reactions of the autonomic nervous system—rapid heart rate, sweating, bodily pains. Emotion is the conscious experience of overt behaviors and internal responses. According to this view, we see the snake and then escape. While escaping, we realize what we are doing and we experience internal symptoms that produce the emotion or the conscious experience of fear. This causal sequence is:

$$\text{Perception} \longrightarrow \text{Behavior + Internal response} \longrightarrow \text{Emotion}$$

The James-Lange theory downgrades the importance of emotion because it is an effect of behavior rather than a cause (Cofer & Appley, 1964). The motivation to run arises from factors other than emotions (e.g., learning that snakes are dangerous).

Cannon (1927) disputed the validity of this theory. Cannon showed that emotions can be experienced even when bodily changes that provide feedback to the brain are eliminated. He removed nerves from cats to eliminate bodily changes, but the cats still showed rage in response to barking dogs. He also demonstrated that the same bodily changes accompany the different emotions that we experience. During rage and fear, for example, blood sugar increases, pupils dilate, and heart rate accelerates. These internal responses cannot determine emotion as predicted by the James-Lange theory.

Cannon's alternative postulated that internal responses and emotion are coeffects of perception:

Perception ⟶ Internal response + Emotion ⟶ Behavior

Emotion-provoking stimuli activate circuits in the *thalamus* (a brain structure). These circuits send messages down the spinal cord to evoke autonomic bodily arousal and up to the *cortex* (a higher brain system) to evoke emotional experience. We see the snake and simultaneously experience autonomic symptoms and emotional awareness. This view stresses the role of emotion in motivation because emotion helps determine ensuing behavior.

Optimal Level of Arousal

Different theories postulate that an optimal level of arousal is motivating. Hebb's (1949) neurophysiological theory of learning stipulates that motivation results from **cell assemblies** that represent knowledge that are gradually developed through repeated stimulation. Cell assemblies become linked into phase sequences that are the physiological equivalents of cognitive processes' guiding behavior. Moderate levels of arousal are needed to keep cell assemblies and phase sequences active. When arousal is too low, sequences do not function properly; when it is too high, sequences are disrupted.

In Berlyne's (1960, 1963) theory, arousal is roughly equivalent to drive. Berlyne postulated that exploratory activity is often accompanied by increased arousal and that collative properties of stimuli (e.g., novelty, ambiguity, incongruity, surprise) affect arousal. Arousal is adaptive and we attempt to maintain an optimal level. If it goes too low, boredom sets in and we are motivated to increase it; if it becomes too high, we are motivated to lower it. Novel or incongruous stimuli motivate behavior directed toward exploring them because they produce a desirable shift in arousal.

Hebb (1966) postulated that moderate changes in arousal are reinforcing because the brain requires activity. Hebb linked arousal to play, which occurs when other needs are not active. Play can be physical or mental because many games require memory of past events and rules. Play occurs as a result of boredom and provides an optimal level of arousal.

Berlyne and Hebb stress that deviations above and below an optimal level of arousal trigger motivation to return arousal to this optimal level. This view contrasts with that of Hull, who believed that motivation represents a drive to reduce arousal and return the organism to homeostasis (calm state). Berlyne and Hebb thus expanded the motivational functions of arousal. Application 1.2 provides examples of these ideas.

APPLICATION 1.2

Applying Arousal Theories in the Classroom

Teachers know the value of using novelty, uncertainty, and incongruity in the classroom to raise student alertness, interest, and motivation. Teachers routinely use brightly colored displays, demonstrate surprising results, and present contradictory information (e.g., "If space is black, then why is sky blue?"). At the same time, too much novelty and uncertainty can disrupt classrooms and create in students uncertainties and doubts about learning. Arousal is important for motivation and we should strive to maintain an optimal (moderate) level of student arousal. Some suggestions for doing this are as follows:

1. *Maintain student motivation at an optimal level; avoid periods of boredom and high anxiety.* A new seventh-grade science teacher had many students finish their work quickly and then play around in class. Realizing that his students were bored, he developed several hands-on, center activities for the students to do when they completed their written work. Within 2 days, student behavior had improved.

   Mrs. Hall, a kindergarten teacher, was concerned because several children were crying each day. After conferring with the other kindergarten teachers, she realized that the cause of the crying might be that she was expecting the students to complete too many activities. After she adapted her plans to include fewer activities, the children calmed down and participated with more confidence.

2. *Incorporate novelty and incongruity into teaching and student activities.* A high school science teacher developed a unit to teach students how various substances react to certain chemicals. To make the unit more interesting, she gave pairs of students an unknown liquid and asked them to determine what the substance contained, based on its reaction to the chemicals.

   A third-grade teacher took his students on a field trip to a wooded area to collect leaves and tree bark. The students used the items they had collected in a classification lesson.

3. *Develop in students positive emotions about learning rather than uncertainty.* Susan was having difficulty with long division. Her teacher, Mrs. Kush, told her, "Susan, I'll be glad to help you after school. I know you can learn how to do long division if we work together."

   "Thanks, Mrs. Kush. My teacher last year told me I never was going to be able to learn anything about math," replied Susan.

   Mrs. Anderson was frustrated with her resource students because they were having trouble getting their science projects finished. She suspected that they felt they were not smart enough to keep up with the students in the regular classroom. She met with children individually and helped them develop a schedule to ensure they would finish their projects on time.

Schachter's Theory of Emotion

Schachter (1964; Schachter & Singer, 1962) proposed that emotion involves physiological arousal and a cognitive label or attribution (perceived cause). If either is absent, the emotion experienced will be incomplete.

In most situations, we can label physiological arousal because it is accompanied by cues. If someone walks up and deliberately pushes you, you experience emotional arousal and a clear cue for labeling the emotion as anger (i.e., someone deliberately pushed me). Schachter felt that cognitions determine the emotion experienced (e.g., anger, fear, rage). Cognitions arise from the present situation and are interpreted in light of our prior experiences. There are times, however, when we experience arousal but the cues for labeling the emotion are not clear. When this happens, we search the environment for an explanation.

Schachter and Singer (1962) tested these ideas with adults who were led to believe they were participating in a study on the effects of vitamin supplements on vision but actually received either epinephrine or a placebo. Epinephrine causes increased blood pressure, heart rate, and respiration rate, and flushing. People who received epinephrine were correctly informed about what to expect (informed condition), were misinformed about the effects by being told it might cause numbness of the feet and itching (misinformed condition), or were told that it would have no side effects (ignorant condition). Participants were paired with an experimental confederate, informed that the confederate also had received the vitamin supplement, and told to wait for a few minutes, during which time the confederate acted angry or euphoric. They were observed unobtrusively and later completed a self-report mood measure.

The ignorant and misinformed participants reported greater euphoria compared with informed individuals. The unobtrusive observations showed that misinformed people behaved more euphorically than did ignorant ones, who behaved more euphorically than informed participants. Results for anger were similar although not statistically significant. Schachter and Singer proposed that informed individuals had an attribution for the bodily changes they were experiencing because they were told of the drug's effects. Both ignorant and misinformed people had to search for cues to explain their symptoms. The presence of an angry or euphoric companion apparently led participants to label their experienced emotions as anger or euphoria.

This view is similar to the James-Lange theory except that Schachter added cognitive attribution as a cause of emotion. Like Cannon, Schachter emphasized the cognitive aspects of emotion. Schachter's formulation presents a strong case for bodily arousal and cognition being required to experience emotion.

There are some methodological problems in the Schachter and Singer (1962) procedure, and not all attempts at replication have been successful (Cotton, 1981). Debate continues in professional circles over the nature of emotion and its role in motivation. We discuss attribution theory in chapter 3, which also highlights the role of cognition in emotion. An important implication is that the ways that students interpret events affect emotion and motivation. Chapter 7 also discusses other theories and constructs that are related to the role of emotion in motivational processes.

Cognitive Consistency

Cognitive consistency theories were developed around the middle of the twentieth century. These theories broke with behavioral theories by addressing people's cognitions and how these affect behavior.

Cognitive consistency theories assume that motivation results from relations between cognitions and behaviors. They are homeostatic because, when tension occurs, there is a need to make cognitions and behaviors consistent and thereby restore internal balance. Two important views were propounded by Heider and Festinger.

Balance Theory

Heider (1946) postulated a tendency for relations among persons, situations, and events to be cognitively balanced. The basic situation involves three elements, with relations as positive or negative. Balance exists when all elements are positively related or when there are one positive and two negative relations. Thus, if I like Dave and Jamal, and if Dave likes me and Jamal, and if Jamal likes me and Dave, the triad of me-Dave-Jamal is balanced. Imbalance exists with one negative and two positive relations and when all elements are related negatively. An example of the former would be if I like Dave and Jamal and if Dave and Jamal each like me, but Dave and Jamal do not like one another. The theory predicts no change when the triad is balanced, but people will try to resolve conflicts when imbalance exists.

That people seek to restore cognitive balance is intuitively plausible, but balance theory contains problems. It predicts when people will attempt to restore balance but not how they will do it. The theory also does not adequately take into account the importance of unbalanced relationships. We care very much when imbalance exists among people we value, but make no effort to restore balance when we care little about the elements. As a theory of motivation, balance theory is incomplete.

Cognitive Dissonance Theory

Festinger (1957) postulated that people strive to maintain consistent relations among their beliefs, attitudes, opinions, and behaviors. Relations can be consonant, irrelevant, or dissonant. Two cognitions are consonant if one follows from or fits with the other (e.g., I don't like Joe and I avoid Joe). Irrelevant cognitions bear no relation to each other (e.g., I like blue and my dog's name is Fido). Dissonance is tension with drive-like properties leading to reduction. Dissonant cognitions exist when one follows from the opposite of the other (e.g., I don't like Joe and I see Joe all the time). Dissonance increases as the discrepancy between cognitions increases. The importance of the cognitions also is taken into account. Large discrepancies between trivial cognitions do not cause much dissonance, whereas even a small discrepancy between important cognitions may cause dissonance.

One way to reduce dissonance is to change a discrepant cognition. If I change my belief to "I actually like Joe," dissonance will be reduced. Another way is to qualify cognitions (e.g., I see Joe all the time because I work with him). A third way is to downgrade the importance of the cognitions: It's not important that I don't like Joe because there are a lot of people I don't like. Finally, I can alter my behavior by avoiding Joe.

Dissonance theory calls attention to how cognitive conflicts can be resolved (Aronson, 1966). The idea that dissonance motivates us is appealing. By dealing with discrepant cognitions, the theory is not confined to triadic relations as is balance theory. But dissonance theory has many of the same problems. The dissonance notion is vague and difficult to verify experimentally. To predict whether cognitions will conflict in a given situation is problematic because they must be salient and important. The theory does not predict how dissonance will be reduced. Additional factors are needed to explain motivation. Shultz and Lepper (1996) formulated a model that may reconcile discrepant findings from dissonance research and integrate dissonance better with other motivational variables.

Functional Autonomy of Motives

Trait psychology was an active area of theorizing and research during roughly the period 1930 to 1950. **Traits** are unique realities within individuals that help to account for the relative consistency of behavior across situations (Hunt, 1993). Trait psychology played a critical role in the evolution of motivation theories from behavioral to cognitively based.

Gordon Allport was an influential trait theorist. Henry Murray, whose work on needs is discussed in chapter 5, was another key individual during this era. Interested readers should consult Winter, John, Stewart, Klohnen, and Duncan (1998) for a comparison of their theories.

Allport (1937) believed that people were best viewed as unique systems constantly evolving and striving toward goals. Traits are part of this system but are idiosyncratic and can be studied only with reference to particular individuals. Allport rejected the ideas of Freud, McDougall, and Murray that motives derive from forces in early childhood or from particular classes of needs or instincts. Rather, he proposed a functional autonomy of motives:

> The dynamic psychology proposed here regards adult motives as infinitely varied, and as self-sustaining, *contemporary* systems, growing out of antecedent systems, but functionally independent of them. Just as a child gradually repudiates his dependence on his parents, develops a will of his own, becomes self-active and self-determining, and outlives his parents, so it is with motives. Each motive has a definite point of origin which may lie in the hypothetical instincts, or, more likely, in the organic tensions and diffuse irritability . . . Theoretically all adult purposes can be traced back to these seed-forms in infancy. But as the individual matures the bond is broken. The tie is historical, not functional. (Allport, 1937, p. 194)

Traits can lead people to view different situations as similar or functionally equivalent, which accounts for consistency in human behavior across situations. Cross-situational behavioral consistency has been hotly debated in motivational circles. For example, it means that persons who possess the trait of honesty will believe they should be honest and behave honestly in such diverse situations as receiving change back from purchases in stores, finding valuables belonging to others, and asking friends to perform favors. There is conflicting evidence about the extent that human behavior is consistent across situations (Mischel, 1968).

Allport's ideas were adopted by the humanistic movement in psychology with such advocates as Maslow and Rogers. His ideas are general and do not lend themselves readily to empirical testing or practical application. His major contribution to human motivation is that he called attention to the force of traits as they manifest themselves in different situations.

Humanistic Theories

Like trait theories, humanistic theories challenged behaviorism's tenets. Two well-known humanistic theorists were Abraham Maslow and Carl Rogers. Maslow's theory, which emphasizes motivation to develop one's full potential, is discussed in chapter 5. In the following, we summarize assumptions of humanistic theories and Rogers's theory.

Assumptions of Humanistic Theories

Humanistic psychology emphasizes people's capabilities and potentialities. As the third force in psychology (after psychoanalysis and behaviorism), humanistic psychology stresses that individuals have choices and seek control over their lives. This is an important assumption in intrinsic motivation, as we will see in chapter 6. Humanistic psychology does not explain behavior in terms of unconscious, powerful inner forces and does not focus on environmental stimuli and responses as determinants of behavior.

Humanistic theories have many common assumptions (Weiner, 1985b). One is that the study of humans is holistic. In order to understand people, we must study their behaviors, thoughts, and feelings. Humanistic theories do not follow the behavioristic approach of studying individual responses to discrete stimuli; rather, they emphasize individuals' subjective awareness of themselves and their situations.

A second assumption is that human choices, creativity, and self-actualization are important areas to study (Weiner, 1985b). In order to understand people, researchers should not study lower organisms. The uniquely human aspect of motivation asserts itself in the study of people who are attempting to be creative and maximize their capabilities and potential. Although motivation is necessary for the attainment of basic needs, humans have fewer choices of ways to obtain food, clothing, and shelter as compared with ways to maximize their potential.

A third assumption concerns methodology. A goal of psychological research is to perform well-controlled studies. The literature is replete with instances of a complex methodology applied to a trivial research problem. Importance of problems must be the primary criterion used to select topics to study. From the humanistic perspective, it is better to study an important problem with a less-refined methodology than a trivial problem with a complex methodology.

Client-Centered Therapy

Carl Rogers was a famous psychotherapist whose approach to counseling became known as client-centered therapy. According to Rogers (1963), life represents an ongoing process of personal growth or achieving wholeness. Rogers labeled this process the **actualizing tendency** and believed it was innate. The actualizing tendency is the fundamental motivational construct in Rogers's theory (Rogers, 1963); all other motives (e.g., hunger, thirst, shelter) derive from it. The actualizing tendency is oriented toward personal growth, autonomy, and freedom from control by external forces.

> We are, in short, dealing with an organism which is always motivated, is always "up to something," always seeking. So I would reaffirm . . . my belief that there is one central source of energy in the human organism; that it is a function of the whole organism rather than some portion of it; and that it is perhaps best conceptualized as a tendency toward fulfillment, toward actualization, toward the maintenance and enhancement of the organism. (Rogers, 1963, p. 6)

Need for Positive Regard

Although the actualizing tendency is presumably innate, it is influenced by the environment. Our experiences and interpretations of them foster or hinder our growth. With development, people become more aware of their own being and functioning, or what he termed self-experience. This awareness becomes elaborated into a concept of self as a result of interactions with the environment and significant others (Rogers, 1959).

The development of self-awareness produces a need for positive regard. **Positive regard** refers to such feelings as respect, liking, warmth, sympathy, and acceptance. We experience positive regard for others when we have these feelings about them; we perceive ourselves as receiving positive regard when we believe that others feel that way about us. These effects are reciprocal. When people perceive themselves as satisfying another's need for positive regard, they experience satisfaction of their need for positive regard.

People also have a need for **positive self-regard**, or positive regard that derives from self-experiences (Rogers, 1959). Positive self-regard develops when people experience positive regard from others, which creates a positive attitude toward themselves. That attitude is then strengthened as a result of one's experiences.

A critical element in the development of positive regard and self-regard is receiving **unconditional positive regard,** or attitudes of worthiness and acceptance with no strings attached. Unconditional positive regard is what most parents feel for their children. Parents value or accept ("prize") their children all the time even though they do not value or accept all of the children's behaviors. People who experience unconditional positive regard believe they are valued regardless of their actions. The actualizing tendency can then strive toward growth because individuals accept their own experiences, and their perceptions of themselves are consistent with the feedback they receive.

Problems occur when people experience **conditional regard,** or regard contingent upon certain actions. People act in accordance with these conditions of worth when they seek or avoid experiences that they believe are more or less worthy of regard. Conditional regard can create tension (because people feel accepted and valued by others only when they behave appropriately) and thwart the actualizing tendency and growth. Anxiety triggers defenses that people use to protect themselves. These defenses selectively perceive or distort experiences or deny their awareness.

Unfortunately, people typically experience conditional regard because society does not distinguish people from their actions, and rewards acceptable behaviors and punishes unacceptable ones. People can function with a certain amount of conditional regard, but become defensive and cannot grow when it is excessive.

Rogers and Education

Rogers applied his theory to education in the book *Freedom to Learn* (1969). Meaningful, experiential learning has relevance to the whole person, has personal involvement (involves learners' cognitions and feelings), is self-initiated (impetus for learning comes from within), is pervasive (affects learners' behavior, attitudes, and personality), and is evaluated by the learner (according to whether it is meeting needs or leading to goals). Meaningful learning contrasts with meaningless learning that does not lead to learners being invested in their learning, is initiated by others, does not affect diverse aspects of learners, and is not evaluated by learners according to whether it is satisfying their needs.

Rogers (1969) believed that people have a natural potential for learning, are curious about their world, and are eager to learn.

> I become very irritated with the notion that students must be "motivated." The young human being is intrinsically motivated to a high degree. Many elements of his environment constitute challenges for him. He is curious, eager to discover, eager to know, eager to solve problems. A sad part of most education is that by the time the child has spent a number of years in school this intrinsic motivation is pretty well dampened. Yet it is there and it is our task as facilitators of learning to tap that motivation, to discover what challenges are real for the young person, and to provide the opportunity for him to meet those challenges. (Rogers, 1969, p. 131)

Meaningful learning is perceived as relevant by students. They believe it will maintain or enhance their selves. The best learning occurs through active participation. Learning requires self-criticism and self-evaluation by learners and the belief that learning is important.

Learning that can be taught to others is inconsequential and has little effect on behavior. Teachers do not impart learning but rather act as **facilitators** who establish a classroom climate oriented toward significant learning and help students clarify their purposes in learning. Facilitators also arrange resources for learning to occur. Facilitators are resources and make themselves available to students by sharing their feelings and thoughts.

Providing students with the freedom to learn requires modifications. Instead of spending a lot of time writing lesson plans, facilitators should provide resources for students to use experientially to meet their needs. Individual contracts should be used rather than lockstep sequences in which all students work on the same materials for the same amount of time. Although contracts impose structure on the learning process, they also allow students considerable freedom in setting up the contract and in deciding on the goals and time lines. Freedom itself should not be imposed; students who want more teacher direction should receive it. Rogers advocated greater use of methods of inquiry, simulations, programmed instruction, and self-evaluation as ways to provide freedom.

Rogers's theory has seen wide psychotherapeutic application. The focus on helping people strive for challenges and maximize their potential is relevant to teaching and learning. At the same time, the theory is developed only in general terms and is replete with technical constructs that are difficult to define and measure. Greater specification is needed on how one's self-regard affects behavior and can be improved. Another problem is that the actualizing tendency is not firmly linked with goals. Rogers emphasized striving toward growth, but this process is vague. Much research shows that specific goals motivate individuals better than general ones (Locke & Latham, 1990). A third concern is that it is unclear how positive regard for others may influence them or how social factors (e.g., rewards, social comparisons, feedback) can affect regard and self-regard. Fortunately, research continues in the humanistic tradition that will help to clarify these concerns. Examples of humanistic principles in the classroom are given in Application 1.3.

APPLICATION 1.3

Applying Humanistic Theories in the Classroom

The following are some suggestions on how to use humanistic theories in the classroom:

1. *Show positive regard for students.* Mrs. Sarver, a second-grade teacher, was working with her students on a cooking project in the school's kitchen. Bryan was afraid of the very large oven they were going to use to bake cookies. Mrs. Sarver hugged Bryan and let him stand far back from the oven whenever she used it.

    Mr. Shah, a high school civics teacher, asked his class a question. Steven raised his hand and said, "Mr. Shah, I don't get it. This is probably a dumb question, but could you go over that first part again?"

    Mr. Shah replied, "Steven, there are no dumb questions in this class. What you and the others have to say is important. Yes, I will review that again."

2. *Separate students from their actions; accept them for who they are rather than for how they act.* Ms. Barret had in her English class C. J., who was known to be one of the neighborhood gang leaders. Other teachers in the building kept telling Ms. Barret negative things about C. J. Undaunted, Ms. Barret worked with and praised C. J. to develop his outstanding writing ability.

    Jenny, a first-grade student, frequently hit other children on the playground. Mrs. Moore told Jenny, "I really like you and I'm glad you are in our class, but I don't like your behavior. You are not to hit other students."

3. *Encourage personal growth by providing students with choices and opportunities to initiate learning activities and establish goals.* Lisa, a mildly handicapped fifth-grade student, was excited about moving into Mrs. Myers's class for language arts. Mrs. Myers used literature books for reading and had her students do a lot of writing. Lisa loved to read and write. Mrs. Myers met privately with Lisa before the class and explained the activity centers and the reading and writing assignments. She told Lisa to select those activities she felt most comfortable with at first. Then each week she could increase the number of activities to do.

    A high school civics teacher gave his students a choice of participating in five different community projects. The students were to select a project and establish their own participation and completion schedule, according to what would work best with their daily personal and family commitments.

4. *Use contracts and allow students to evaluate their learning.* Mrs. Adams met with each student to develop contracts for completing a social studies unit. The contract included readings from the text, in-class activities, and assignments in the media center. When students completed the contract, they took a test and wrote a report. They then graded their own test and met with Mrs. Adams to discuss it, go over the report, and assign a grade to the overall unit.

    A reading resource specialist worked with his students by developing contracts to complete writing assignments. After completing each writing activity, students met with him to evaluate their work and to make a list of improvements to be incorporated into the next assignment.

5. *Facilitate learning by providing students with resources and encouragement.* A fifth-grade art teacher let his students select their own projects to complete during the last 6 weeks of school. He provided them with ample resources (e.g., clay, paint, chalk, paper, scissors) and encouraged them to work with the media they had liked best during the year. Then he moved about the room throughout the 6 weeks assisting and providing positive input.

Mrs. Hagaman, a second-grade teacher, developed a unit on homes for animals. She divided her children into groups of three and let them select materials (e.g., blocks, sticks, yarn, glue) to create a make-believe animal and its home. While the students worked, she circulated in the classroom to check on progress and provide encouragement.

METATHEORETICAL MODELS AND METAPHORS

We have concluded our discussion of historical theories that have relevance to motivation. Being confronted with all of these theories can seem overwhelming and create confusion about how they differ, or which aspects are most useful in the study of motivation.

One way to distinguish theories is in terms of the larger metatheoretical models, or **paradigms**, of research that they reflect. Metatheoretical models provide a way to organize theories and understand their basic assumptions. For example, in specifying causes of motivation, theories may focus on environmental factors or on underlying characteristics, cognitions, or affects.

Metatheoretical models also contain metaphors that can help us understand theoretical assumptions, concepts, and principles. A metaphor is a figure of speech with an implied comparison. A word or expression typically used in one fashion is applied in a different way. A metaphor relates in a relatively surprising and occasionally dramatic fashion two items that are not usually conceptualized as similar (McReynolds, 1990). Because they relate new material to what we already know, metaphors help us understand phenomena (Leary, 1990). Metaphors are common in everyday language (e.g., He had butterflies in his stomach. Love makes the world go 'round. She really blew her stack.), and they often are used in science to explain unfamiliar phenomena (Leary, 1990).

Unfortunately, metaphors are not always precise, so we may not be able to apply them literally (Weiner, 1991). It also is true that the principles and assumptions of many theories reflect more than one metaphor. A one-to-one correspondence between theory and metaphor is not always found. In the scenario at the beginning of the chapter, A. K.'s statement that Keith and Sara must think that students are puppets is an example of a metaphor.

In this section, we discuss three metatheoretical models, along with their associated metaphors, that reflect the central assumptions of theoretical approaches to motivation. We will refer to these models as *mechanistic, organismic,* and *contextual* (Lerner, 1986; Overton, 1984). Table 1.5 highlights their central assumptions. We have categorized each of the theories discussed in this chapter as reflecting one of these three models; however, keep in mind that many motivation theories do not fit neatly under one

Table 1.5 Metatheoretical Models in the Study of Motivation

Model	Scientific Perspective	Relation of Complex to Simple Behavior	Continuity between Levels of Behavior and Stages of Development	Metaphor Used to Explain Behavior	Applicable Theories
Mechanistic	Natural science: Laws of natural science are basic laws of the world	Reductionistic (complex behaviors can be broken into simpler ones), additive (behaviors sum to form more complex ones)	Behavior change and development proceed in continuous fashion, levels differ quantitatively	Machine	Freudian, conditioning, drive, purposive behaviorism
Organismic	Human development: Progressive changes in organisms	Nonreductionistic (complex events cannot be broken into simpler ones), multiplicative (behaviors combine to form behaviors more complex than the sum of the parts)	Behavior change and development proceed in discontinuous fashion, levels differ qualitatively	Living, growing organism (plant)	Volition/will, instincts, trait
Contextual	Interactionist: Relation of person to environment	Nonreductionistic and multiplicative	Mostly discontinuous	Historical event	Arousal, field, cognitive consistency, humanistic

45

metatheoretical model, but rather share assumptions of two or more models. Freud's theory, for example, is mechanistic in that it treats bodily energy in a machinelike fashion, but it also is organismic because it discusses the development of personality processes.

Mechanistic Model

A fundamental assumption of the mechanistic metatheoretical model is that the laws of natural science are the basic laws in the world and that, ultimately, everything is reducible to them. The mechanistic model is **reductionistic**; that is, complex events can be reduced to simple phenomena. Reductionism implies *continuity*. No new laws are needed to explain psychological phenomena because they can be reduced to simple events. Basic and advanced behaviors differ *quantitatively*. To move from a basic to an advanced behavior, one simply adds more elements. The mechanistic model is *additive* because complex phenomena represent the summation of many basic phenomena.

A metaphor often applied to the mechanistic model is that of a machine (Overton, 1984; Weiner, 1991). This seems appropriate because the natural sciences involve physical laws at fundamental levels of analysis. Machines are reductionistic in that complex functions can be reduced to simpler operations. There is continuity because no new principles are needed to explain more complex operations. Machines also differ quantitatively. Functions can be added to provide greater complexity.

To apply the machine metaphor to people, we would say that they display many of the qualities of machines in terms of input, operation, and output. Important components of machines are that they have parts and a structure, there is a desired function and the parts operate to achieve this function, actions are involuntary and performed without conscious awareness, reactions to stimuli are necessary and predetermined, and there is an interchange of force and energy such that the system stays in equilibrium (Overton, 1984; Weiner, 1991).

In the opening scenario, Keith used a machine metaphor because he implied that people respond to forces from the environment much like machines respond to the forces that act on them (e.g., temperature, pressure, electrical current). Neither A. K. nor Sara agreed with Keith and suggested different perspectives for viewing students.

Among the theories we review in this chapter that reflect the mechanistic model are Freudian theory, conditioning theories, drive theories, and purposive behaviorism. Freud's theory is mechanistic because it deals with the distribution of energy in a machinelike fashion (i.e., it is dissipated or transformed via repression). We noted earlier that there is an overlap of theories among categories, and Freud's theory is an example. It is also organismic because it emphasizes inner processes that seem to unfold and over which individuals may have little control. We group it here as mechanistic because that theme captures its predominant characteristics.

Conditioning theories are mechanistic because they postulate a reductionistic, continuous, and additive view of behavior. Complex behavior can be reduced to many simple behaviors. Behavior change is continuous and takes place when behaviors are combined in additive fashion. Drive theories reflect a mechanistic orientation because they view the body as a machine and drives as the machinelike processes that keep the body in proper condition (homeostasis). Although Tolman's purposive behaviorism mentions cognitive processes and is contextual because it emphasizes interpreting behavior in light of goals, it remains mechanistic because it postulates behavioral responses to stimuli largely in machinelike fashion. Although not formally discussed in this chapter, many cognitive models of information processing (including parallel distributed processing models) are mechanistic; they rely explicitly on a computer-machine metaphor for understanding cogniton and learning.

Organismic Model

Proponents of the organismic metatheoretical model assume that changes in organisms are often qualitative and cannot be reduced to previous behavior (Overton, 1984). This is especially true in the area of human development, where new cognitive, physical, and social capabilities appear suddenly and bear little resemblance to previous capabilities. Lerner (1986) points out, for example, that 1-year-old children display many behaviors that can be explained by stimulus-response associations. By the time children turn 2, however, they have begun to develop a language capability that allows them to engage in actions they could not have performed earlier (e.g., imitate actions long after observing them). The capability for symbolic representation helps to explain many actions. Trying to reduce complex behaviors to a summation of simpler behaviors is inappropriate.

The organismic view is a *discontinuous* position because it assumes that changes can emerge suddenly and do not emanate smoothly from earlier behaviors. Some theorists within this tradition posit stages or phases that individuals pass through that are qualitatively distinct from one another. This perspective also stresses the quality of actions and not simply the quantity (e.g., rate, frequency, likelihood). The organismic model is *multiplicative.* The impetus for change is overt and subjective activity. People interact with their environments and help to construct meanings of events.

An appropriate metaphor for this model is that of a living, growing organism like a plant (Overton, 1984). Plants grow and develop, but the course of growth is uneven. Sudden growth spurts occur, followed by slower growth. Some changes are quantitative (e.g., leaves become larger), but many are qualitative (buds appear, followed by flowers and then seeds). A fully-grown plant is not simply a larger version of a tiny seedling. With regard to people, similar changes occur in the areas of cognitive, linguistic, social, and emotional development.

In the opening scenario, A. K. espouses an organismic position because of her emphasis on students' predispositions and how characteristics emerge over time. Theories covered in this chapter that reflect organismic assumptions include volition/will, instincts, and trait theories. The volition/will theories of Wundt, James, and Ach are organismic because they assume an unfolding of inner processes that proceeds without conscious awareness or direct human control. With their emphasis on inner propensities and dispositions, instinct theories are organismic. Trait theories stress the energizing role of inner motives, which, although not necessarily instinctual, are internal mechanisms that develop and change in ways not entirely predictable from environmental events. In terms of cognitive theories that were not discussed in this chapter, Piagetian and neo-Piagetian models of cognitive development are very good exemplars of organismic models that focus on the unfolding or development of children's cognitive capabilities.

Contextual Model

The contextual metatheoretical model represents a compromise between the mechanistic and organismic positions (Lerner, 1986). This view accepts underlying organismic patterns of change but contends that environmental conditions play a greater role in such change than is allowed in an organismic model. Students may become developmentally ready to display new competencies, but unless the environment is conducive, the behaviors will not be displayed. Whereas the mechanistic model stresses the environment and the organismic model emphasizes the individual, the contextual model places importance on the individual in relation to, or in dynamic interaction with, the environment (Overton, 1984). This view shares many of the assumptions of the organismic model: *nonreductionistic*, *nonadditive*, and *discontinuous*.

An appropriate metaphor for this model is that of a historical event. Historical events do not operate in isolation; to understand events, one must know something about the dispositions of the principal individuals involved and the conditions prevailing at the time. Wars, for example, are complex events. To understand the causes of a war, one must have knowledge about the leaders of countries that become involved in the war and the prevailing historical, political, economic, and social conditions. Further, an event in one domain (e.g., economics) will affect other areas (politics, daily living). Change is constant and each change produces others. Thus, developmental changes affect the situations in which people find themselves; in turn, environmental events can stimulate developmental growth.

In the opening scenario, Sara presents a contextualistic perspective because she states that although students may have predisposing attributes, their emergence depends largely on environmental factors. Theoretical positions reflecting contextualistic assumptions are arousal, cognitive consistency, and humanistic theories.

Arousal theories are contextual because they highlight the interpretation of arousal in light of environmental cues or cognitive processes. There is some organismic emphasis (e.g., optimal level of arousal), but the context is essential for understanding motivation. Cognitive consistency theories are contextual because efforts to restore balance or reduce dissonance depend on a person's level of cognitive development, prior experiences, and cues in the present situation; balance is not achieved automatically but is context specific. Humanistic theories are contextual because they view behavior in holistic fashion and contend that to understand people, we must interpret behavior in light of personal attributes (e.g., feelings, values, thoughts) and present circumstances. Finally, in terms of general cognitive models, Vygotskian, neo-Vygotskian models of development and learning are based on contextualist perspectives and metaphors.

This metatheoretical perspective is highly relevant to education. Today's educators emphasize providing developmentally appropriate experiences for students. Cognitive growth will not occur if experiences are too advanced, and motivation suffers if material is too basic. With appropriate experiences, teachers can help facilitate cognitive, physical, and social growth in students.

In subsequent chapters, we refer to these models and metaphors to help organize contemporary theories and approaches to motivation. We believe this approach will give readers a more unified understanding of the field of motivation than if we simply summarized theories without attempting to relate them to broader perspectives or to one another.

SUMMARY

Motivation refers to the process whereby goal-directed activity is instigated and sustained. Motivation affects all classroom activities because it can influence learning of new behaviors and performance of previously learned behaviors. Learning and performance are related in a reciprocal fashion to motivation because what one does and learns influences one's subsequent task motivation.

Although individuals use intuitive ideas to understand motivation in themselves and others, the scientific study of motivation requires guiding theoretical principles. Motivation research proceeds by testing hypotheses, addressing objectives, or answering questions. Researchers conduct correlational studies that deal with relations existing between variables, experimental studies in which some variables are altered and their effects on other variables are determined, and qualitative studies characterized by intensive description of events and interpretation of meanings. Research studies may be conducted in experimental laboratories or in field sites (e.g., classrooms). Each type of research paradigm has advantages and disadvantages. The choice of instrument depends on the purpose of the study.

There are various indexes of motivation: choice of tasks, effort, persistence, and achievement. Motivation can be assessed through direct observations, ratings by others, and self-reports. Direct observations refer to instances of behavior. Ratings by others are judgments by observers of students on various characteristics indicative of motivation. Self-reports, which refer to people's judgments and statements about themselves, include questionnaires, interviews, stimulated recalls, think-alouds, and dialogues. Each method has advantages and disadvantages; the method of choice must reflect the researchers' aims. The use of multiple forms of assessment is likely to provide richer data than does a single measure.

Many early theories of motivation were behavioral, defining motivation in terms of overt actions and looking for causes in the environment. Contemporary cognitive views examine the underlying mental processes involved in motivation and how these are affected by personal and environmental factors.

Early views of motivation defined it in terms of will (desire, want, purpose) and volition (act of using the will). Another early perspective stressed the role of instincts or innate properties that manifested themselves in behavior. In the field of psychotherapy, Freud conceived of motivation in terms of psychical energy.

Conditioning theories emphasize the association of stimuli with responses. Prominent conditioning theories are Thorndike's connectionism, Pavlov's classical conditioning, and Skinner's operant conditioning. Drive theories stress internal forces that seek to maintain homeostasis, or optimal states of bodily mechanisms. Drive theories were formulated by Woodworth, Hull, Spence, Mowrer, and Miller. Tolman broke from the behaviorist tradition and stressed purposive behaviorism, or the goal directedness of behavior. His views on expectancies and latent learning were important precursors of cognitive theories.

Some theories link motivation with level of emotional arousal. The James-Lange theory contends that emotion is a consequence of behavior and involves perceptions of responses to arousing situations. Theories by Hebb and Berlyne postulate the importance of an optimal level of arousal for bodily functioning. Schachter proposed that emotion involves physiological arousal and a cognitive attribution.

Cognitive consistency theories are homeostatic and assume that motivation results from relations between behaviors and cognitions. Heider's balance theory and Festinger's cognitive dissonance theory are cognitive consistency theories.

Psychological trait and humanistic theories focus on innate, qualitative differences in psychological processes that emerge with experience and development. Allport proposed a functional autonomy of motives in which motives grow out of antecedent systems, but with development become independent of them. Allport's ideas are reflected in many humanistic theories. The humanistic psychologist Carl Rogers developed client-centered therapy. Rogers believed that the central motivating force in people's lives is the actualizing tendency, or the ongoing process of personal growth and achieving wholeness. People have a need for positive regard and self-regard, and a critical element in developing both is receiving unconditional positive regard. In education, the teacher's job is to facilitate learning by arranging resources, helping students clarify goals, and establishing a climate of positive regard. Rogers's theory suggests the use of contracts, inquiry methods, and opportunities for self-evaluation.

Theories of motivation can be organized into larger metatheoretical frameworks or paradigms that have defining characteristics and metaphors used to explain behavior. The mechanistic model reflects the laws of science, is reductionistic and additive, posits continuous changes in behavior, and is exemplified by a machine metaphor. The organismic model derives from principles of human development, is nonreductionistic and multiplicative, assumes that changes are discontinuous, and is exemplified by a growing organism metaphor. The contextual model is based on an interaction between person and environment, is nonreductionistic and nonadditive, posits that most changes are discontinuous, and is characterized by a historical event metaphor. Contextualism is becoming increasingly influential in the field of motivation.

Expectancy-Value Models of Motivation

*S*everal junior high students are talking during lunch.

Kevin: *How are you doing in social studies? Did you think the test we just did was too easy?*

Rachel: *Well, not really. It's more just boring. I mean, who cares about what happened 200 years ago? That has nothing to do with my life.*

Kevin: *Really? I like it. It's interesting. I think what happened before does matter today, plus I'm really good at it. I think I did well on the test today. I always think that I'll do well in social studies because I always get a good grade on the tests and the reports we have to do. I've been getting good grades in social studies ever since elementary school. I might even major in social studies when I go to college.*

Jacob: *Yuck, are you kidding? What a nerd! I hate it! I never seem to do well on those tests. I'm sure I flunked this one. All those true/false questions, they just confuse me. I think the teachers just make those up to trick us. Plus, do you know how hard it is to write a report? I can never think of what to say. It's too hard. I just end up copying out of the book. I'd rather play soccer. I'm really good at that and I love it. I'm not good at social studies and I hate it.*

Rachel: *I hate sports, too. I'm not good at social studies or sports.*

Kevin: *Well, I'm not too good at soccer. I never do well at that, but I'm pretty good in baseball. I really like to play baseball. I would love to play in college and then in the pros. You can get a scholarship to play sports in college and then make a lot of money in the pros.*

These students are discussing their beliefs about their capabilities to succeed, including their expectancies for future success as well as their interest and value for schoolwork and athletics. They are concerned with their ability to succeed at a task, whether they have the skills or knowledge to do well, and what they expect will happen if they do attempt to do the task. They also make comments about whether they like or hate something or whether they think it is important or relevant to them. All of these students are discussing, in one way or another, two central constructs in many motivation theories—the role of expectancy and value beliefs.

The concept of expectancy represents the key idea that most individuals will not choose to do a task or continue to engage in a task when they expect to fail. They may be interested in and value a task, but if they try a task and experience repeated failure, and expect that failure to continue in the future, then eventually they will not engage in the task. Kevin notes that he does well in social studies and speculates that he may choose it as a college major. Jacob does not expect to do well in social studies and thinks it is too hard for him. Rachel thinks she is not very good at either social studies or athletic endeavors. As shown in the vignette, the **expectancy construct** reflects individual's beliefs and judgments about his or her capabilities to do the task and to succeed at it. In more colloquial terms, the expectancy construct concerns the answer to the question: "Can I do this task?" If the answer is yes, most people will choose to engage in the task. If the answer is no or there are doubts about one's capabilities to succeed, individuals are less likely to engage in the task. This is a basic idea in most motivational theories, but it is represented most explicitly in expectancy-value models.

The other half of the equation involves the **value components** of motivation. Values refer to the different beliefs students have about the reasons they might engage in a task. In colloquial terms, it concerns the answer to the question, "Do I want to do this task and why?" Students might have a variety of reasons for why they want to do a task, such as it is interesting to them, they like doing the task, they think it is important or useful to them in some way, they will get a reward (e.g., grades, points, candy) for doing it, they want to please their teachers or parents, and they want to avoid being punished or avoid getting into trouble. In the vignette, all of the students make comments about how much they like or dislike doing schoolwork. Rachel notes how she finds social studies boring (the opposite of interesting) and Jacob says he hates (the opposite of liking) social studies, although he likes soccer and would rather play soccer. In contrast, Kevin thinks social studies is interesting to him and he may even choose to major in it. For all three students, however, these beliefs about liking and interest do seem to be related to whether they want to engage in the academic or athletic task in the future.

In expectancy-value models of motivation, both the expectancy and value components are seen as important for predicting students' future choice behavior, engagement, persistence, and actual achievement. Students may be confident that they can do well and expect to succeed, but if they don't value the task, they will be less likely to choose to engage in the task. In the same way, students may believe that a task or activity is interesting or important to them, but if they don't think they can do the task, eventually they will not engage in the task. In expectancy-value models, it is important to understand both expectancies and values to be able to predict student behavior in the future.

After studying this chapter, you should be able to:

1. Define and explain the differences between various expectancy and value constructs.
2. Describe and understand how expectancy and value constructs are linked to different motivated behaviors and outcomes.
3. Compare and contrast how expectancy and value constructs and their relations to outcomes may vary by age, gender, and ethnicity.
4. Analyze how findings from expectancy-value theories and research can be used to improve classroom teaching.

HISTORICAL PERSPECTIVES ON EXPECTANCY-VALUE MODELS

Expectancy-value models spring from a general cognitive perspective on motivation and reflect the cognitive metaphor of the individual as an active and rational decision maker in contrast to earlier behavioral models of motivation. However, even early on in experimental psychology, there were behavioral psychologists who stressed the cognitive nature of learning and utilized expectancy and value constructs in their models. For example, as noted in chapter 1, Tolman (1932) proposed that rewards did not just "stamp in" associations between stimuli and behavior, but that even animals learn expectancies about what will happen to them if they perform a certain behavior. They then come to expect the reward (or punishment) when they engage in the behavior in the situation. For Tolman, this cognitive notion of expectancy replaced the mechanistic concept of habit from Hullian drive models (Weiner, 1992). In achievement terms, students who expect to succeed or do well on a task will tend to do that task again in the future.

In terms of value, in Lewin's (1935) theory, the term **valence** was used to signify the value a person attached to an object in the environment. An object acquired valence because it satisfied a need of the person given the range of other objects in the environment. For example, if a person is hungry, food objects will have more positive valence than other objects in the environment (TV, work, books, other people) because food will satisfy the current need. In this case of a hungry person, the person will tend to approach the food objects, rather than watch TV or do work or other activities. In addition, objects may become more attractive the longer the need is unsatisfied. That is, the amount of valence that accrues to an object is a function of the intensity of the need. A person who has not eaten all day will find food objects in the environment more attractive, or more positively valenced, than someone who ate just a few hours ago. In addition, some objects might have more valence due to intrinsic properties. Some food objects may be more intrinsically appealing (i.e., a lobster and steak dinner versus bread and water) and people will tend to approach these objects over less appealing ones (Weiner, 1992). In achievement terms, if students are curious and active learners (a need to learn), some objects may be more appealing or positively valenced for students, such as computer activities or other intrinsically interesting tasks.

As part of the general shift from mechanistic, behavioral models that stressed rewards and habits to more organismic, cognitive models that stressed expectancies and values, there was less of a conceptual need for postulating some instigator or energizer of behavior (i.e., an instinct, a drive, a need, a habit). When concerned with a rat in a maze, there is a place for thinking about what motivates the rat to run the maze (e.g., hunger). However, once a general cognitive model is proposed that assumes that humans are innately active learners, constantly seeking to learn and adapt to their environment (White, 1959), the problem of what motivates behavior is not a salient theoretical issue. There is less of a requirement to postulate needs or drives, but the issue of directionality becomes paramount. Accordingly, cognitive motivational theories became concerned with how individuals make decisions about which goals or paths they will choose to pursue, and about the direction in which they will focus their innate energy, curiosity, and activity.

Lewin (Lewin, Dembo, Festinger, & Sears, 1944) proposed that the construct of **level of aspiration** could capture this more cognitive decision-making process by incorporating both expectancy and value components. Level of aspiration was defined as the goal or standard that individuals set for themselves in a task, based on past experience and familiarity with the task. The traditional research paradigm that was used to assess level of aspiration was the ringtoss game, in which individuals were asked to toss rings over a peg while standing at different distances from the peg. Distances farther away from the peg were given more value because they obviously made the task more difficult. The subjects were given some experience with the game (usually 10 trials) and then asked to state their goal for the next 10 trials (How many are you going to try to get over the peg in the next 10 trials?). The combination of different distances and values allowed the experimenter and subject to estimate both expectancy (probability of success for a toss) and value (distance from peg).

A great deal of empirical research was done using this level-of-aspiration paradigm and several important findings emerged (Weiner, 1992). First, subjects were most likely to feel successful when they met the goals they set for themselves (subjective goal or level), not the actual objective level of attainment (e.g., five successful tosses). This type of situation occurs in the classroom when two different students get the same good grade of 85 out of 100 points on a test (same objective level of attainment), but one student is quite unhappy with the grade because of expectations of a higher grade, whereas the other student, who had a lower level of aspiration, is quite content with the grade. A second general finding was that level of aspiration was related to prior experience with the task and that prior success generally led to increases in level of aspiration, but failure usually decreased level of aspiration. Finally, the research found that there were individual and group differences in level of aspiration. Subjects high in ability tended to set higher aspirations than those low in ability. In addition, subjects were influenced by group goals and performance and adjusted their level of aspiration to the group norms (Weiner, 1992).

Building on these general constructs of expectancy, value, and level of aspiration from Tolman and Lewin, Atkinson's (1957, 1964) model of achievement motivation attempted to combine the constructs of needs, expectancy, and value into a comprehensive theory. His model proposed that behavior was a multiplicative function of these three components, which he labeled **motives**, **probability for success**, and **incentive value**. Motives represented learned, but stable and enduring, individual differences or dispositions and included two basic achievement motives: to seek success (**motive to approach success**) and to fear failure (**motive to avoid failure**). These motives were affective in nature but included an aspect of expectancy in terms of emotional anticipation (Covington, 1992). The motive for success was assumed to represent individuals' hope for or anticipation of success and reflected their "capacity to experience pride in accomplishment" (Atkinson, 1964, p. 214). If the motive for success was high, individuals would likely approach and engage in achievement tasks. In contrast, the motive to avoid failure represented individuals' capacity to experience shame and humiliation when they fail. When this motive was high, individuals avoided engaging in achievement tasks.

In the voluminous research on this model, the motive for success was usually measured using the Thematic Apperception Test (TAT) (Atkinson, 1958; McClelland, Atkinson, Clark, & Lowell, 1953), a projective test in which individuals were asked to tell stories about a set of pictures. The pictures displayed people at everyday tasks (e.g., two men in a machine shop) and the stories were scored for achievement imagery (e.g., The two men are working on a new invention that will change the industry). In contrast, the motive to avoid failure was usually measured using the Test Anxiety Questionnaire (TAQ) (Mandler & Sarason, 1952), which was a more objective self-report measurement that asked people to rate their anxiety and worry about testing situations (e.g., "While taking an intelligence test, to what extent do you worry?"). The TAT has been criticized for problems of reliability and validity, although a meta-analysis of research on the TAT and questionnaire measures of need for achievement suggested that both types of measures show approximately the same relation to actual behavior (Lilienfeld et al., 2000; Spangler, 1992). There continues to be development and research on the use of the TAT and other more objective measures of the need for achievement (Smith, 1992). In fact, Lilienfeld et al., (2000) conclude that as a measure of the implicit motive of need for achievement, the TAT scoring system developed by McClelland et al., (1953) does have reasonable construct validity and scientific utility.

In Atkinson's original model, these two motives were assumed to be orthogonal to one another, although most subsequent research usually examined the motive for success and operated as if there was a single continuum anchored by high motive for success on one end and high motive to avoid failure on the other end. More recently, Covington (1992) has suggested that the original model based on the independence of these two motives provides a more comprehensive picture of different approaches to achievement. If the two motives are conceptualized as orthogonal, a two-by-two matrix is created with four cells generated to describe four different approaches to achievement (Covington, 1992; Covington & Omelich, 1991; Covington & Roberts, 1994). This quadripolar model suggests that there are four general types of students and ways of approaching achievement tasks: success oriented, failure avoiders, overstrivers, and failure accepters (see Figure 2.1).

The *success-oriented* student who is high in motive for success and low in fear of failure would be highly engaged in achievement activities and not be anxious or worried by performance. In chapter 1, Sharon represents this type of student because she achieves at a high level and does not worry or become anxious about doing well. A student who is a *failure avoider,* high in fear of failure and low in motive for success, would be very anxious and attempt to avoid failure by procrastinating and using other self-handicapping strategies (Covington, 1992; Garcia & Pintrich, 1994). This type of student would be very reluctant to even engage in academic achievement work. These two types are the most often researched and described by a simple continuum between the two motives.

Figure 2.1 A quadripolar model of need for achievement

From "Self-worth and College Achievement" by M. V. Covington and B. Roberts in *Student Motivation, Cognition, and Learning* (p. 160) edited by P. R. Pintrich, D. R. Brown, and C. E. Weinstein, 1994, Hillsdale, NJ: Erlbaum. Copyright © 1994 by Lawrence Erlbaum Associates. Adapted by permission.

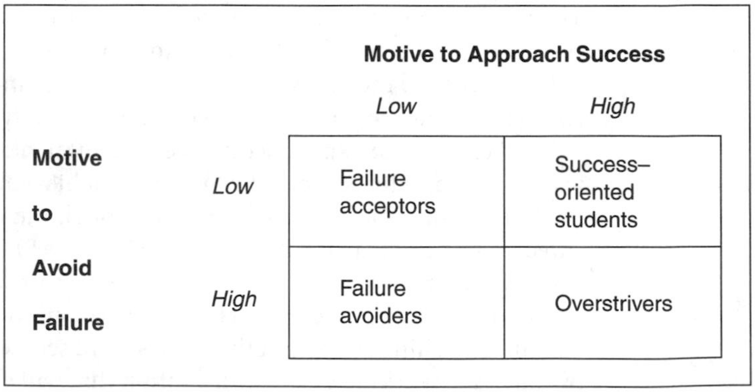

The off-diagonal cells in the quadripolar model, however, suggest that there are two other types of students (Covington, 1992). *Overstrivers* are students who are high in both motives; they try to approach success but simultaneously fear failure greatly. These students work very hard at achievement tasks but also feel very anxious and stressed because of their fear of failure. In more social cognitive terms, these students are similar to defensive pessimists (Garcia & Pintrich, 1994; Norem & Cantor, 1986). Overstrivers are students who almost always do well in class, but are constantly asking the teacher about their grade and show signs of anxiety and worry about doing well. Finally, Covington labels the students who are low in both motives as *failure accepters*. These students are basically indifferent to achievement, although this indifference may be due either to lack of concern and caring or active anger and resistance to achievement values, as some have suggested is the case for minority students (Covington, 1992).

These two motives (to approach success and to avoid failure) represented the internal and personal contribution to motivation in Atkinson's model. Atkinson also included expectancy and value constructs in his model that represented the environmental side of the equation because they were assumed to be more closely tied to the situation or task. In Atkinson's model, his expectancy construct was very similar to Tolman's idea about the formation of expectancies regarding the associations between responses and rewards. Atkinson's model and research used human subjects, not rats, so the construct was more cognitive in nature and reflected a person's subjective belief about the probability of success. **Expectancy** (or probability) **for success** was often measured using the same ringtoss method as developed by Lewin (e.g., How many rings will you be able to get on the peg?) or by giving subjects a set of puzzles and asking them to estimate how many they would be able to solve (Weiner, 1992). These subjective beliefs about expectancy for success, although certainly reflecting an individual's own beliefs, were also assumed to represent one of the environmental influences on motivation because they could reflect task difficulty (e.g., how far away from the peg the person stood, normative information about how many puzzles others solved). In this sense, the model tried to take into consideration external factors, although it is still basically an organismic model focused on the individual.

The third component of motivation in Atkinson's model was the incentive value of success. Incentive value of success was defined as an affect, specifically, pride in accomplishment. Tasks that are too easy usually do not generate much pride in accomplishment or seem very attractive, whereas difficult but manageable tasks do seem attractive and generate more pride and self-worth when individuals are successful (Weiner, 1992; Wigfield & Eccles, 1992). Thus, incentive value covaries inversely with task difficulty. For example, the incentive value of receiving an *A* in a difficult course would be higher (more pride experienced) than the same grade in an easy course (Weiner, 1992).

In addition, probability of success covaries inversely with task difficulty, obviously with easy tasks having higher probability of success than harder tasks. The incentive value of success was assumed to be inversely related to the probability of success. For example, as the expectation for success went up, as in an easy task, the incentive value went down because it was assumed that the person would not value succeeding at an easy task. In the same way, for a difficult task in which probability of success is low, the incentive value would be high. Given these relations, Atkinson was able to logically define incentive value as 1.0 minus the probability for success. This relation means that incentive value will be higher for tasks in which probability of success is lower; that is, people will tend to value more difficult tasks in comparison to easier tasks. For example, people may value certain careers or professions (e.g., medical doctors) more highly and assign them more prestige and salary because of the perceived difficulty of attaining them (Weiner, 1992).

Although this inverse relation between incentive value and probability of success is logical and also makes intuitive sense, by defining incentive value as 1.0 minus the probability of success, Atkinson made probability of success the component that had to be determined in his mathematical model (along with motive for success, of course). In effect, as Wigfield and Eccles (1992) point out, this equation "removed" incentive value from the model. Researchers did not have to measure incentive value as long as they could determine the probability of success. Incentive value would simply be 1.0 minus whatever the probability of success was determined to be. This convention led to the long-standing focus on probability and expectation for success in most research on achievement motivation. Incentive value was ignored in empirical research for the most part until relatively recently (Eccles, Wigfield, & Schiefele, 1998; Parsons & Goff, 1978; Wigfield & Eccles, 1992).

Given the inverse relation between incentive value and the probability of success, Atkinson's mathematical model predicts that motivation will be highest when tasks are of an intermediate level of difficulty. When the probability of success is .5 (the person will succeed at the task about half the time), the incentive value of success also will be .5 (incentive value = 1.0−.5, which is the value for probability of success). The product of multiplying the probability of success by the incentive value (as in all expectancy-value models) is greatest at this intermediate level (e.g., .5 × .5 = .25) in comparison to other conditions. For example, suppose that the probability of success is .1 (the student will succeed only 1 time out of 10), then incentive value will be high for such a difficult task (1.0 −.1 = .9) and the multiplicative product of these two numbers (.1 × .9 = .09) is lower than the number generated at the intermediate level of difficulty (.25). This is true for all values of probability of success and incentive value given the assumed inverse relation between probability of success and incentive value.

This generalization that motivation is highest at levels of intermediate task difficulty is one of the most often-cited findings from achievement motivation research. However, it is interesting to note that variations on this generalization are represented in other theories as well. Behavioral theories, such as Gagné's, suggested that instruction should be designed to be within several steps of a student's prior level of competence (Gagné, 1985). Of course, in applications of Piagetian cognitive developmental theory, it was suggested that students should only be taught concepts that were representative of the next immediate stage (+1 modeling/instruction), not concepts that were more than one stage above the students' current level. More recently, we have seen a great deal of interest in applying Vygotsky's socio-cultural theory and his concept of the zone of proximal development, which also represents the notion that instruction should be designed to be just beyond the students' current level of development. The task or instruction should not be too difficult to be far outside the students' range of capabilities or too easy to be repetitive for the students (Vygotsky, 1978). Although these theories are not conceptualized as motivational theories and tend to downplay or ignore the role of motivational constructs, the general principle that learning will be fostered when students are working at a task that is somewhat beyond their range of current capability fits with these behavioral, cognitive, and socio-cultural theories as well as with most motivational theories. The real challenge is determining the students' current capabilities and the most propaedeutic difficulty level of the academic task.

Weiner (1992) summarized the motivational research on this generalization regarding an intermediate level of difficulty and concluded that the laboratory research on task choice and persistence is supportive. However, he did note that in Atkinson's model, the third determinant of motivation, the motives for success and fear of failure, played an important role beyond the expectancy and value components. Atkinson's model predicted that individuals high in the motive for success and low in fear of failure (what he called "high need for achievement") would be most likely to choose tasks of intermediate difficulty, whereas individuals high in fear of failure and low in the hope for success (what he called "low need for achievement") would choose very easy or very difficult tasks. In the latter case, for individuals high in fear of failure, a choice of a very easy task ensured success, thereby minimizing fear of failure. The choice of very difficult tasks by individuals high in fear of failure did not maximize the fear of failure because there was the expectation that very few people could succeed at the most difficult tasks. Atkinson's model and reasoning here were based on the general hedonic principle of maximizing positive affect and minimizing negative affect (Weiner, 1992). However, the actual empirical findings did support the differential predictions for individuals high in fear of failure. It appears that most people, regardless of their motives for success and failure, choose tasks of intermediate difficulty, although there was a tendency for individuals high in the motive for success to choose intermediate tasks more often than those high in fear of failure (Weiner, 1992).

Weiner and others (e.g., Trope, 1975) suggested that this choice of intermediate tasks could be explained in terms of an informational principle rather than the hedonic principle. They suggested that choosing tasks of intermediate difficulty provided the most information to individuals about their own effort and capabilities (too easy and too difficult tasks provide more information about the task than the individual). This information about personal capabilities is useful for self-evaluation and, in the long run, accurate self-information is functional and adaptive (Weiner, 1992). In any event, the finding of very little differential choice of tasks by motives and of a larger role for expectancy for success and incentive value suggests that these more cognitive and environmental constructs might be more important than the stable personality dispositions of motives.

In sum, the early research on expectancy and value constructs was important because of the focus on cognition and beliefs in contrast to overt behavior and the related constructs of drives, needs, and habits. These theories and models moved motivational psychology away from a dependence on a simplistic Stimulus-Response (S–R) psychology to a more rational and cognitive paradigm that is still dominant today. Moreover, these early cognitive models of motivation stressed the importance of the individual's perceptions and beliefs as mediators of behavior, thereby focusing motivational research on the subjective and phenomenological psychology of the individual. In particular, these early models developed the distinction between beliefs about being able to do the task (probability and expectancy for success) and beliefs about the importance, value, and desire to do the task (motives, incentive value) and posited that it is the multiplicative combination of the two that results in motivated behavior. Accordingly, we may feel capable of doing a task, but if we do not value it, then we will be less likely to engage in it. In the same way, we may value a task, but if we do not feel able to do it and expect to fail, we will be less likely to engage in the task. Current research on expectancy and value constructs continues in this tradition of focusing on these two general beliefs of the individual, although researchers do attempt to include contextual influences in their models. In the remainder of this chapter, we will discuss a current expectancy-value model of motivation.

A CURRENT EXPECTANCY-VALUE MODEL OF ACHIEVEMENT MOTIVATION

Although there are many motivational theories that include some type of expectancy and value constructs, we will focus on one model that has generated the most theory and research on academic achievement in classroom settings. The model comes from the work of Eccles and Wigfield and their colleagues (e.g., Eccles, 1983, 1987, 1993; Eccles et al., 1989; Wigfield, 1994; Wigfield & Eccles, 1992, 2000) and is derived from and bears the closest resemblance to the early expectancy-value models of Lewin and Atkinson (for other current expectancy-value models, see Heckhausen, 1977; Pekrun, 1993; Rheinberg, Vollmeyer, & Rollett, 2000). This social cognitive model focuses on the role of students' expectancies for academic success and their perceived value for academic tasks and springs from a general organismic perspective based in personality, social, and developmental psychology.

A simplified version of this elaborate model is displayed in Figure 2.2. The two most important predictors of achievement behavior are *expectancy* and *task value*. It is important to note that these are basically two of the three components specified in Atkinson's model. In Atkinson's model, the expectancy construct was called *probability for success* and the task value construct was labeled *incentive value*. Reflecting a social cognitive and more situational perspective, the Eccles-Wigfield model does not highlight motives such as need for success or fear of failure, but these implicit motives could be part of the affective memories component, which can give rise to the more cognitive task value beliefs. For example, fear of failure might be related to the anticipated psychological costs, while need for success would be related to attainment value or interest. Most importantly, in the Eccles and Wigfield version, task value has a much more important and differentiated role to play than just being the inverse of probability for success, as in Atkinson's original model.

As shown in Figure 2.2, achievement behavior is predicted by two general components: expectancy and value. These constructs are within the dashed lines in the figure to represent the fact that they are internal, cognitive beliefs of the individual in contrast to the achievement behaviors, which can be overt and observable. In colloquial terms, the value construct refers to a student's response to the question, "Why should I do this task?" (Eccles, 1983; Eccles, Wigfield & Schiefele, 1998). Responses would include interest (I'm interested in this topic), importance or utility beliefs (This topic is important or useful to me for my future career) and costs (If I take this difficult course, I will not be able to play sports). Rachel's expressions of boredom and lack of care about social studies and "hate" for soccer are expressions of value beliefs.

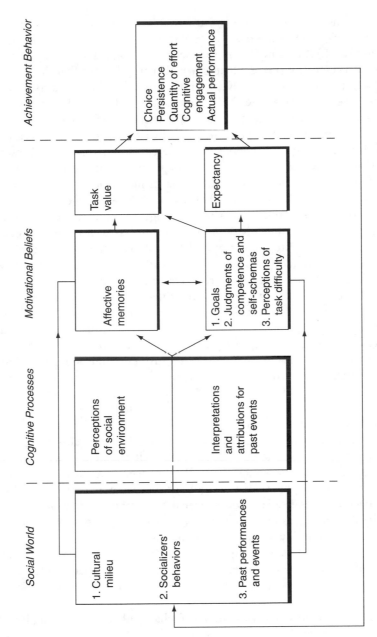

Figure 2.2 A social cognitive expectancy-value model of achievement motivation

Social World · Cognitive Processes · Motivational Beliefs · Achievement Behavior

Social World

1. Cultural milieu

2. Socializers' behaviors

3. Past performances and events

Cognitive Processes

Perceptions of social environment

Interpretations and attributions for past events

Motivational Beliefs

Affective memories

1. Goals
2. Judgments of competence and self-schemas
3. Perceptions of task difficulty

Task value

Expectancy

Achievement Behavior

Choice
Persistence
Quantity of effort
Cognitive engagement
Actual performance

In contrast, the expectancy construct refers to the question, "Am I able to do this task?" (Eccles, 1983; Eccles et al., 1998; Pintrich, 1988a, 1988b; Wigfield, 1994; Wigfield & Eccles, 1992). In Figure 2.2, expectancy refers to actual beliefs of students about their future expectancy for success; that is, whether they believe that they will do well on an upcoming test or some future event. In our example, Kevin expects to do well in social studies, whereas Jacob and Rachel do not expect to do as well. This construct is usually measured by asking students to predict how well they will do in the future on some task or in some domain (see Table 2.1). Accordingly, expectancy for success is more future oriented than simple self-perceptions of competence. In a great deal of research by Eccles and Wigfield (as well as many others), higher expectancies for success are positively related to all types of achievement behavior, including achievement, choice, and persistence (Eccles, 1983; Eccles et al., 1998; Wigfield, 1994; Wigfield & Eccles, 1992).

Referring again to the model shown in Figure 2.2, the next two motivational components include students' goals and self-schemas as well as their affective memories. **Affective memories** are a less empirically explored aspect of the Eccles and Wigfield model, but refer to individuals' previous affective experiences with the type of activity or task. These memories can be activated by anticipation of engagement in the task and can lead to different positive or negative values for the activity through classical conditioning mechanisms or direct association. For example, if an individual had a bad or embarrassing early experience in trying to play baseball, this affective memory might be classically conditioned such that the next time the opportunity to play baseball arose, the individual would activate the same negative emotions along with less positive values for baseball. This could lead to avoidance of baseball and could even generalize to other athletic activities. In the same manner, students might have negative experiences with school subjects such as math that could lead to less value and interest in math and subsequent avoidance behaviors.

The other motivational component refers to **goals** and **self-schemas** which includes individuals' short- and long-term goals as well as their general self-schemas. Self-schemas reflect individuals' beliefs and **self-concepts** about themselves. For example, people have beliefs about what kind of person they are and what kind of person they could become (possible selves, ideal selves), including beliefs about their personality and identity, as well as more domain-specific self-concepts about their physical attractiveness, athletic ability, academic ability, and social competence (e.g., Eccles, 1983; Harter, 1983, 1985a; Markus & Nurius, 1986; Marsh, 1989, 1990b). The domain-specific judgments of competence or ability are similar to self-efficacy judgments in Bandura's (1997) theory; they are not just outcome expectations (Eccles et al., 1998). Self-efficacy beliefs are discussed in chapter 4.

Goals are cognitive representations of what students are striving for or trying to attain. Short-term goals might include "getting an *A* in this chemistry course," while a long-term goal might be "to become a doctor." These goals can be shaped by self-schemas and self-concepts. For example, an individual who has as part of her self-schema or identity the idea that she is "someone who helps others," may set a long-term goal of becoming a doctor, teacher, or social worker. Short- and long-term goals are discussed in chapter 4, but it is important to note that these goals in the Eccles and Wigfield model are not the same construct as goal orientation (mastery or performance goals), which is discussed in chapter 5.

Table 2.1 Different Self-Report Items Used to Measure Various Expectancy and Value Constructs

Expectancy Constructs from Expectancy-Value Theory	Perceptions of Competence (Harter)	Task Value Beliefs from Expectancy-Value Theory
Rated on a 5- or 7-point Likert scale.	Harter uses a 1–4-point, forced choice scale. Children choose one side (positive statement) or the other side (negative statement) and then within that side choose a number (1,2) or (3,4).	Subjects are asked to respond to items using a Likert scale that ranges from 1 to 7 (or 1 to 5) with anchors at the endpoints such as *not very important* (interesting, useful) to *very important* (interesting, useful) or *not at all true of me* to *very true of me*.

Expectancy for success
How well do you think you will do on your next math test?
Compared to other students, how well do you expect to do in math this year?
How well do you think you'll do in your math course next year?
How well do you think you will do in an advanced math course like calculus?

Task-specific self-concept
How good at math are you?
If you were to rank all the students in your math class from worst to best, where would you put yourself?
Compared to most of your other subjects, how good are you at math?
How have you been doing in math this year?

Perceptions of task difficulty
Compared to most of your other subjects, how difficult is math for you?

(Harter column items:)
I remember things easily.
I'm good at schoolwork.
I finish my schoolwork quickly.
I'm just as smart as other children.
I understand what I read.
I can figure out the answers to schoolwork.

(Task Value column items:)
Attainment value or importance
How important is it to you to get good grades in math?
I feel that being good at solving problems that involve math or reasoning mathematically is
It is important to me to learn the course material in this class
Understanding the subject matter in this course is very important to me

Interest
In general, I find working on math assignments
How much do you like doing math?
I am very interested in the content area of this course
I like the subject matter of this course

Utility value
How useful is high school math for what you want to do after you graduate and go to work?
How useful is what you learn in high school math for your daily life outside school?
I think I will be able to use what I learn in this course in other courses
I think the course material in this course is useful for me to learn

Perceived costs
Is the amount of effort it will take to do well in your math course this year worthwhile to you?
How much does the amount of time you spend on math keep you from doing other things you would like to do?

63

The last aspect in the goals and self-schema component includes perceptions of task demands. Task perceptions concern students' judgments of the difficulty of the task (not unlike Lewin's and Atkinson's models) as well as other features of the task (such as how interesting the task appears). Again, Eccles and Wigfield assume that these task difficulty perceptions are relatively domain specific. In their own empirical work, they have used general school subject areas (e.g., English, math, science) as their operationalization of the domain, not unlike other self-concept researchers such as Harter and Marsh. Of course, they would allow that there may be even more domain specificity in these beliefs that could influence achievement (e.g., differential self-concept and task difficulty beliefs for algebra versus geometry versus calculus), but more research is needed on the level of specificity for conceptualizing domains. Specificity of domains is one of the biggest issues that needs to be resolved for any cognitive or motivational theory that proposes domain specificity of constructs. What are the boundaries of a domain and at what level—the individual task level; the project, unit, or topic level; the course level; the discipline level—do we need to specify them?

These beliefs are influenced by two other general constructs in the model (see Figure 2.2). One includes other cognitive and internal processes concerning how students perceive and interpret different events that happen to them. In particular, this interpretative process is driven by the types of attributions a student makes for past events and actual performance. Attributions are crucial to the formation of self-perceptions of competence and expectancies and are the focus of chapter 3, so they are not discussed here. The other aspect of cognitive processing includes how students perceive their social and cultural environment. This includes their perceptions of various socializers' beliefs (parents, teachers, peers) as well as how they perceive and interpret social roles such as gender roles and stereotypes about different activities. It is important to note that in keeping with a general cognitive and constructivist approach, this model assumes that students' beliefs about themselves, their expectancies, and values are influenced by how students perceive their social environment and what happens to them as they move through it. Accordingly, it is not just that parents' or teachers' beliefs and behaviors have a direct influence on students, but rather that these aspects of the social environment are mediated by the students' perceptions of the social environment. For example, a female may not perceive a bias by the teacher against her in a mathematics classroom. So, even if there is a bias, but it is not perceived by the individual student, there will be less of an influence on that individual's subsequent motivational beliefs.

The other general construct that influences students' beliefs is the actual culture and social environment, including the general cultural and societal milieu; the nature of the students' interactions with parents, peers, and other adults (e.g., teachers); and their past performance and achievements as well as their actual capabilities. These final influences are represented on the far left of Figure 2.2 outside the dashed lines because they are assumed to be external to the student. Nevertheless, these external factors can have a large influence on students' motivational beliefs as they set the context for the students as they move through different situations in academic and nonacademic activities. These contexts provide opportunities for and constraints on the individuals' beliefs and behaviors. Accordingly, although the general model places a great deal of emphasis on how students construct their motivational beliefs through social cognitive processing, it is assumed that these beliefs are grounded in the larger social and cultural contexts that make up the students' worlds.

The Role of Expectancy and Self-Perceptions of Ability Constructs

There are a number of different outcomes that might be related to expectancy and **self-perceptions of ability or competence** constructs. We have organized our discussion of the role of these constructs around three general outcomes: actual achievement or performance, involvement in the task including cognitive engagement as well as effort and persistence, and choice behavior. Achievement outcomes include student's performance on standardized achievement tests, grades from different courses, and other learning outcomes such as performance on classroom tests or tasks. **Cognitive engagement** refers to how cognitively engaged the students are in the tasks, including their use of different types of cognitive or metacognitive and self-regulatory strategies. Finally, choice behavior concerns the types of choices students make when given some autonomy in their decision making. For example, do they choose to take more math or science courses in the future when they are not required by the school curriculum? Do they choose to do one type of task or activity over another? Do they intend to major in one discipline versus another discipline? These outcomes should be positively related to individuals' expectancy beliefs and their self-perceptions of their ability. There has been research on these questions from both an expectancy-value motivational perspective as well as research from a self-perception of ability or self-concept perspective.

In a series of large-scale correlational field studies, Eccles and Wigfield and their colleagues (Eccles, 1983; Eccles et al., 1989; Wigfield, 1994; Wigfield & Eccles, 1992) investigated the role of expectancy and ability perception constructs in achievement. These studies used both cross-sectional and longitudinal designs. Upper elementary and junior high students were given self-report measures of their self-perceptions of ability and expectancy for success, as well as task value beliefs, in math (see Table 2.1) and English at the beginning of one school year and at the end of that same year. In some of their studies, these same students were then followed for a number of years and given the same self-report measures, again at the beginning and at the end of subsequent school years. At the same time, the researchers also collected data on the students' actual achievement on standardized tests and course grades. They then used path analytic and structural equation modeling techniques that allowed them to examine the relative effects of expectancy and ability perceptions versus grades on subsequent perceptions and grades. These studies have consistently shown that students' self-perceptions of ability and their expectancies for success are the strongest predictors of subsequent grades in math and English, even better predictors of later grades than were previous grades. These studies also found the same relation for self-reported outcome measures of effort and persistence in these domains. These general findings emerged across a number of studies highlighting the importance of students' expectancies and self-perceptions of competence as mediators between the environmental or cultural context and actual achievement behavior and involvement as proposed in Figure 2.2, again demonstrating the importance of student beliefs and the constructivist nature of motivation. In addition, these studies were conducted in actual classrooms and followed students over a number of years, resulting in high ecological validity and increasing the generalizability of the results.

Besides actual achievement on tests, teacher-assigned grades, and reports of effort and persistence, other researchers have linked students' expectancies and self-perceptions of ability to students' cognitive engagement. For example, Pintrich and his colleagues

(Pintrich, 1989, 1999; Pintrich & De Groot, 1990a; Pintrich & Garcia, 1991, 1993; Pintrich & Schrauben, 1992; Wolters, Yu, & Pintrich, 1996) investigated the relations between self-competence beliefs and students' use of various **cognitive strategies**, such as elaboration (paraphrasing, summarizing), and metacognitive or self-regulatory strategies (planning, checking, monitoring work) in a series of correlational field studies. These cognitive and metacognitive strategies result in "deeper processing" of the material to be learned, not just more effort at the task, and should be related to higher levels of deep understanding and learning. Although they used self-report measures of both motivation and strategy use, Pintrich and his colleagues consistently found that higher levels of perceptions of competence were correlated with more reported use of cognitive and metacognitive strategies in both junior high and college student samples. Other researchers have found similar relations (Paris & Oka, 1986; Shell, Murphy, & Bruning, 1989) between self-perceptions of competence and cognitive engagement.

In contrast to these relations between competence perceptions and cognitive engagement and actual achievement, the findings for choice are not as clear-cut. Although earlier research by Atkinson and others showed that expectancy beliefs related to students' choice of distances in the ringtoss experiments, more recent research on student academic choices does not show as strong a role for expectancy beliefs. Eccles and Wigfield and their colleagues find in their field studies that the value concerning the students' perceptions of the importance, utility, and interest in the task was a better predictor of their intentions to continue to take math and of their actual enrollment decision (Wigfield, 1994; Wigfield & Eccles, 1992; also see Feather, 1982, 1988). Accordingly, from an expectancy-value perspective, it appears that expectancy beliefs are more closely tied to actual achievement and cognitive engagement but that value beliefs are more closely tied to choice behaviors that would provide the student with the opportunity to achieve in the future.

The Role of Self-Concept Beliefs

The research on students' perceptions of their own competence and self-concept (Harter, 1982, 1985a, 1990, 1998) is very similar in some ways to the research on expectancy-value models. Specifically, the definition of self-perceptions of competence is isomorphic with the definition of task-specific self-concept in Eccles and Wigfield's research. Self-perceptions of competence are students' self-evaluative judgments about their ability to accomplish certain tasks (Harter, 1985a). Self-perception of competence is the more cognitive evaluation of ability in a domain (I can do math), *not* a general measure of self-esteem or self-worth that concerns how individuals might feel about themselves (I am happy with the way I am) (Harter, 1998; Wigfield & Karpathian, 1991). At the same time, this research on perceptions of competence springs from a more developmental perspective on the development of the self and personal identity in contrast to the focus on motivation in expectancy-value models. Given this different heritage, there are some differences in the research and theoretical underpinnings.

First, some of the research on students' perceptions of competence is closely related to the more general research on children's conceptions of their personal identity (e.g., Damon & Hart, 1988) and research on self-concept (Harter, 1998; Markus & Nurius, 1986; Marsh, 1984a, 1984b, 1990b). An important issue in the research on self-concept is the domain specificity of individuals' perceptions of themselves. Much of the early research on self-concept was not very theoretically based, good definitions of the construct were not developed, and many researchers assumed that self-concept was a rather global construct (Wylie, 1974, 1979, 1989). Research now focuses on how children distinguish their perceptions of competence by domain (Byrne, 1984). Although self-perceptions of competence become more differentiated with age, most researchers now accept the idea that even fairly young children (first and second graders) have self-perceptions of competence that are domain specific (Eccles et al., 1998). In addition, whereas there is disagreement about the levels of specificity of the domains, most researchers at least distinguish among academic, social, and physical domains of competence (Harter, 1982, 1998; Wigfield & Karpathian, 1991).

The academic domains concern students' perceptions of competence at school tasks. The perceptions of competence shown in Table 2.1 are from Harter's perceived competence scale (1982) and reflect a general sense of competence for schoolwork. Another self-concept measure, Marsh's Self-Descriptive Questionnaire (SDQI for preadolescents, SDQII for adolescents, and SDQIII for late adolescents and adults), has domains for reading, math, and all school subjects. See Byrne (1996) for a review of measures. The social domain reflects individuals' perceptions of their competence in interactions with others. Harter's revised perceived competence scale, now called the Self-Perceptions Profile (Harter, 1985b), and Marsh's SDQ both have separate scales for relationships with parents and relationships with peers/close friends. In addition, both Harter and Marsh have scales regarding competence for romantic relations with others for their adolescent and adult measures. The physical domain on Harter's and Marsh's measures includes perceptions of competence at physical activities like sports as well as general perceptions of physical attractiveness/appearance. Students' scores on these different domain scales show moderately positive intercorrelations, but the research suggests that these are empirically separate domains. Accordingly, students may have differential perceptions in different domains (high in math, low in reading, high in physical ability, low in peer relations, etc.). Researchers and teachers need to be sensitive to these domain differences in perceptions of competence and not assume that students have a single, global self-concept that is related to their performance in all domains.

Although the simplistic idea of a global self-concept relating to performance across many domains is not accepted, the assumption that there are domain-specific self-perceptions of competence still begs the question regarding the hierarchical nature of these self-perceptions. The issue revolves around the problem created by multiple domains and the specificity of those domains. For example, if a student has different self-perceptions of competence for different academic domains such as English, math, science, and social studies, the question becomes: Are these self-perceptions ever integrated into a general academic self-concept? This academic self-concept then might be at the same level in a hierarchy of selves as a physical self-concept (an integration of self-perceptions for different physical activities such as running, tennis, gymnastics, soccer, baseball, etc.) and a social self-concept (an integration of self-perceptions for relations with close friends, other classmates, parents, and other adults).

The research on this issue is somewhat mixed. Harter (1983, 1985a) suggests that the results of her studies with factor analysis of the domains from her student perceptions profile support a nonhierarchical model, reflecting support for the taxonomic position (Byrne, 1984). In contrast, the work of Marsh and Shavelson and their colleagues (Marsh, 1990b, 1993; Marsh, Byrne, & Shavelson, 1992; Marsh & Hattie, 1996; Marsh & Shavelson, 1985; Shavelson & Bolus, 1982) suggests that the self-concept is hierarchically structured, with separate domains of academic competence fitting into a global academic self-concept, although they find that the strength of the hierarchical structure differs with age (less hierarchy in older adolescents and adults). Wigfield and Karpathian (1991) suggest that these different findings may be due to developmental differences in the students and reflect a general developmental movement from non-hierarchical to hierarchical back to nonhierarchical self-concepts over time. Most of Harter's research has focused on younger students who may be less able or less motivated to integrate the different domains of their self-concept. In contrast, Marsh's early adolescents may show hierarchically organized structures because they are now able to integrate diverse information cognitively and, given the adolescent "life task" of achieving identity, be more motivated to attempt to fit together the different self-domains. Finally, Marsh and Shavelson's older adolescents and adults again may show less hierarchy because they are not actively involved in all domains (most adults are not involved in academic learning of math, science, social studies, etc.) and are less concerned with differences in domains and less upset with having multiple identities or self-concepts. Of course, as Wigfield and Karpathian (1991) point out, most of this research has been cross-sectional. There is a need for longitudinal research to examine the developmental trends and the suggested explanation of the findings. Harter (1998) also suggests that there may be individual and cultural differences, not just developmental differences, regarding the hierarchical nature of the self-concept. She notes that there is a proliferation of theoretical models of the self (possible selves, multiple selves) that do not rely on hierarchical assumptions regarding some unified, hierarchical model of the self.

A third important issue related to the domain specificity and hierarchical nature of perceptions of competence is the relation between perceptions of competence and global self-esteem. As already noted, after some confusion in the early research on self-concept, there is now widespread agreement that self-perceptions of competence and self-esteem are two theoretically and empirically distinct constructs (Harter, 1998; Wigfield & Karpathian, 1991). To reiterate, perceptions of competence are more *cognitive* judgments of personal skills and abilities, such as the belief that you are able to learn social studies, or that you can play soccer (recall Kevin, Rachel, and Jacob), or that you can make friends. In contrast, self-esteem is a more global, *affective* reaction or evaluation of yourself (e.g., you feel bad about yourself because you don't do well in social studies, or good about yourself because you play soccer well, or bad because you don't have many friends). Empirical research by both Harter (1985a, 1986) and Marsh (Marsh & O'Neill, 1984; Marsh & Shavelson, 1985) has shown that global self-esteem is an empirically separate dimension from self-perceptions of competence, although the two show positive moderate correlations. Obviously, perceptions of competence should be related to self-esteem, but the exact nature of this relation is unclear.

One of the early leading American psychologists, William James (1890), speculated that self-esteem was a ratio between one's "successes" and one's "pretensions" and that self-esteem would be higher to the extent that individuals were able to succeed in meeting all of their goals. More recently, Harter (1985a, 1986, 1990, 1998) made a similar argument and suggested that global self-esteem is related to both self-perceptions of competence in different domains and the importance the individual assigns to those domains (paralleling expectancy-value theory predictions). Accordingly, if students have low perceptions of competence in several academic domains, they may not necessarily have low self-esteem if they do not think those domains are that important or central to them in comparison with other domains (e.g., social relations with peers, personal physical abilities). Harter (1986) found evidence for this type of "discounting" in a sample of fifth through seventh graders. Students with high self-esteem had much less discrepancy between their importance and competence ratings in comparison with those with low self-esteem. Wigfield, Eccles, Mac Iver, Reuman, and Midgley (1991) also found similar results with junior high students. Steele (1988, 1997) has suggested that many minority students, particularly African Americans, use this type of discounting strategy by lowering their value for academic domains in which they have lower perceptions of academic competence in order to affirm their self-worth and self-esteem. In contrast, in a study of high school and college students, Marsh (1986) did not find that self-esteem was related to perceptions of competence and importance, but rather self-esteem was best predicted by only perceptions of competence. Developmental differences may be responsible for the different results, but clearly more research is needed on the relations between self-perceptions of competence and global self-esteem (Wigfield & Karpathian, 1991).

Finally, self-concept researchers have been concerned about the nature of the relation between perceptions of competence and self-concept and achievement. As noted previously, children's perceptions of their ability have been linked to most achievement behaviors in expectancy-value research, including cognitive engagement and actual achievement. However, within the tradition of research on self-concept, researchers have been concerned about the direction of the causal relation between self-concept and achievement. Some researchers have argued that self-concept is causally predominant over achievement, while others have taken the opposite position that achievement determines self-concept (see Byrne, 1984; Caslyn & Kenny, 1977; Hansford & Hattie, 1982; Scheirer & Kraut, 1979 for conflicting views). These different views obviously have implications for instruction. The self-concept enhancement version suggests that teachers should ensure that students believe they are capable, and students' subsequent achievement will improve. The achievement-first model suggests that teachers should ensure that children have the academic skills to succeed and their perceptions of competence will follow from their successes. The most sensible view of this controversy is that "it is relatively fruitless to continue to pursue the general question of which causes which" (Wigfield & Karpathian, 1991, p. 256). Clearly, the relation is reciprocal; self-concept influences future achievement and actual achievement shapes and constrains self-perceptions of competence. Moreover, there may be individual, developmental, and contextual differences in the nature of the relations between self-concept and achievement (cf. Marsh, 1990a; Skaalvik & Hagtvet, 1990). In terms of future research and educational practice, it seems wise to realize that the relation is complex and that simple, linear models do not map onto the reality of classrooms. Future research should concentrate on understanding how self-perceptions and actual achievement work together to predict future behavior at different ages, for different students, and in different contexts. Teachers should focus on teaching their students the appropriate cognitive skills to master academic tasks and, at the same time, ensure that students have the motivational resources, including appropriate self-perceptions of competence, to engage in these tasks.

In sum, the research on expectancy and self-perceptions of competence constructs has investigated the role of children's self-evaluative judgments and their links to motivational and achievement outcomes. In general, the research consistently shows that students who believe they can do the task and expect to do well are more likely to achieve at higher levels, be more cognitive engaged, and try harder and persist longer at the task. Moreover, current research suggests that self-perceptions of ability are domain specific, not global, although there is not agreement about the specificity of the domain. Nevertheless, it seems important for future research as well as educational practice to recognize that in the academic domain, self-perceptions of competence need to be specified at least at the level of general subject areas (i.e., English, math, science, social studies, foreign language, art, music, etc.). It probably will not be that helpful, moreover it is potentially misleading, for teachers to label children as having low self-concept as a global trait that applies across all academic, social, and physical domains. Teachers need to differentiate more carefully and recognize that children can and do differ within those domains in terms of their self-perceptions of competence and that these intraindividual differences can result in differences in motivated behavior. Application 2.1, later in the chapter, provides some suggestions for facilitating students' expectancy beliefs.

The Role of Task Value Beliefs

Although research in the Atkinson tradition did not really examine incentive value as a separate component due to the fact that it was the inverse of probability for success, there were other researchers who did attempt to investigate values. For example, Battle (1965, 1966) developed the term attainment value and defined it as "the importance to the individual of achievement in a given task . . . [that] should determine the length of his persistence in working at it" (Battle, 1965, p. 209). Battle also distinguished between absolute attainment value, which referred to the importance of the task overall, and relative attainment value, which referred to the importance of the task relative to other tasks (Wigfield & Eccles, 1992). Battle (1965) found that both expectancies and attainment value were positively related to persistence on a math task in a sample of junior high school students. Crandall, Katkovsky, and Preston (1962) found that attainment value predicted early elementary students' choice of intellectual activities, especially for girls. In a second study that examined junior high students' actual performance in math and English, Battle (1966) showed that expectancies were more strongly related to performance than to relative attainment value or overall attainment value. This pattern of expectancies relating to actual performance and attainment value being more closely linked to choice or persistence has also been found in research by Wigfield and Eccles and their colleagues (Wigfield & Eccles, 1992). However, Battle (1966) did show, contrary to Atkinson's model, that expectancy and attainment value were positively correlated with each other, not inversely related as suggested by the formula of incentive value being equal to 1.0 minus the probability of success. Accordingly, it seems that students tend to value tasks they expect to do well on and expect to do well on those tasks that they think are important (Wigfield & Eccles, 1992).

Feather (1982, 1988) has also been one of the main researchers in the expectancy-value tradition concerned with the value side of the model. His model of values integrates Rokeach's (1979) general values with the more traditional achievement motivation expectancy-value constructs. Rokeach (1979) proposed a general model of values that defined values as "core conceptions of the desirable within every individual and society" (p. 2). These values guide cognition, motivation, and behavior by serving as general beliefs and standards against which to make judgments about which behaviors are desirable and should be approached and, by implication, which opposing values and behavior are undesirable and should be avoided. Rokeach (1979) discussed 18 terminal values, such as sense of accomplishment, wisdom, freedom, self-respect, comfortable life, mature love, world peace, inner harmony, and national security, that he believed represent life's ultimate goals. These terminal values are similar in many ways to the general goals found in Ford (1992). Rokeach also proposed that there were 18 instrumental values, such as being ambitious, honest, intelligent, independent, courageous, loving, helpful, polite, obedient, clean, and self-controlled, that are modes of conduct for achieving the terminal values. It is interesting to note that interest in teaching virtues in education (see Bennett, 1993) proposes some of the same values as Rokeach's instrumental values.

In Feather's (1982, 1988) expectancy-value model, personal values are the larger, more general values based on Rokeach's instrumental values. These personal values are assumed to determine the values individuals have for specific tasks, called **task value** in Feather's model. Task value is similar in function to incentive value in Atkinson's model and, along with expectation for success, should determine achievement behaviors like choice, persistence, and actual performance. Feather (1988) found that college students' enrollment in either a humanities, social sciences, or science course of study was related to both expectations and task value for math and English. Students who had higher task value for math and higher perceptions of their ability in math were more likely to enroll in science. Similarly, students who had higher task value and perceptions of their ability in English were less likely to enroll in a science course of study and more likely to enroll in humanities. Moreover, Feather found that task value for math and English was related to different types of personal values based on Rokeach's instrumental values. Students who were high in restrictive control personal values (high importance ratings of clean, obedient, polite, responsible, and self-controlled personal values) were more likely to have higher task value for math. In contrast, students who were high in prosocial concern (high importance ratings of forgiving, helpful, and loving personal values) were more likely to have higher task value for English. These personal values of restrictive control and prosocial concern did not have a direct relation to course enrollment; their effect was through math and English task values. It seems that these more general personal values do influence specific task values, but the specific task values relate more closely to achievement behavior, at least in terms of choice of a course of study. Feather (1988) also found that expectations were positively correlated with task value, similar to Battle (1966) and counter to the theoretical assumptions of Atkinson about the inverse relation between expectancy for success and incentive value.

Current Conceptions of the Components of Task Value

The most current model and research on task value components is the work of Eccles and Wigfield. They define achievement task value in terms of four components. Each component can influence achievement behaviors such as choice, persistence, and actual achievement. These values should also be related to implicit motives such as need for achievement or fear of failure in terms of attainment value or costs, respectively. They use the term *subjective task value* to signify that these beliefs are individuals' perceptions of their own values and interests for the task or activity. Of course, there can be a sense of an "objective" value for certain tasks, at least as defined at a societal level (e.g., school tasks might generally be valued in a society). However, given that this is a constructivist and psychological model of individual motivation, the most important aspect is the individuals' perceptions and beliefs about value. The four components and sample items that are often used to measure them (see Eccles & Wigfield, 1995) are displayed in Table 2.1. Three of these four (attainment value, intrinsic interest, and extrinsic utility value) have been shown to be empirically separable constructs in confirmatory factor analyses (see Eccles & Wigfield, 1995).

In this model, **attainment value** (or, more simply, **importance**) is defined as the importance of doing well on a task, similar to Battle's (1965, 1966) definition. In addition, attainment value is defined as the extent to which a task allows individuals to confirm or disconfirm salient or central aspects of their self-schema (Wigfield & Eccles, 1992), hence the arrow between goals and self-schemas and values in Figure 2.2. For example, doing well at an athletic event may be very important for a student because an important aspect of her self-identity is her concept of herself as a good athlete. In this case, her attainment value for most athletic events would be very high. For another student, her academic self-concept may be more central to her identity and, hence, academic tasks would be likely to have higher attainment value. As Wigfield & Eccles (1992) point out, other values, such as the importance of masculinity and femininity values, may be more or less salient in an individual's self-schema. To the extent that tasks allow these more general values to be expressed, attainment value would be higher for these tasks. For example, if mathematics is stereotyped as a "masculine" activity and at odds with "feminine" values, girls who have these feminine values would have a low attainment value for mathematics and would be less likely to engage in it. By linking these more global personal values such as masculinity and femininity to attainment values, Wigfield and Eccles (1992) attempt to incorporate the more general values of Rokeach (1979) and Feather (1982, 1988) into their model.

In addition, as shown by the link between affective memories and values in Figure 2.2, an implicit motive such as the need for achievement might be linked to attainment value with individuals high in need for achievement having higher attainment value for achievement-type tasks (doing well in school, excelling in sports). In contrast, an individual high in need for affiliation or belongingness might have higher attainment value for tasks or activities that do not stress achievement as much as they stress working or being together in some manner.

The second component of task value is **intrinsic interest**, or **intrinsic value**, defined as the enjoyment people experience when doing a task, or their subjective interest in the content of a task (Wigfield & Eccles, 1992). It is conceptually similar to intrinsic interest in the intrinsic motivation theory of Deci & Ryan (1985), which is discussed in chapter 6, as well as the work on personal interest and flow discussed in chapter 7 (Csikszentmihalyi, 1975; Renninger, Hidi, & Krapp, 1992; Schiefele, 1991; Tobias, 1994). In some ways, it is more related to the means of doing a task and the pleasure of doing a task, not the ends in a means-ends analysis. When intrinsic interest value is high, individuals will be more engaged in the task, persist longer, and be intrinsically motivated for the task (Wigfield & Eccles, 1992).

The third component of task value is **utility value**. Utility value is defined as the usefulness of the task for individuals in terms of their future goals, including career goals. It is related more to the ends in a means-ends analysis of a task. For example, a college student may not have much intrinsic interest in organic chemistry, but because she wishes to become a medical doctor, this course has a high utility value for her. In this sense, utility value is similar to some of the extrinsic reasons for doing a task in Deci and Ryan's (1985) model.

The fourth and final component of the model is the **cost belief** attached to engaging in the task. This component has not been researched as much by Eccles and Wigfield in their empirical work, but it is defined as the perceived negative aspects of engaging in the task (Wigfield & Eccles, 1992). When individuals engage in one task, it usually means they cannot engage in other tasks at the same time. Accordingly, along with any choice of one specific task, there are some costs associated with it. Eccles and Wigfield assume that costs include the perceived amount of effort required for the task as well as anticipated emotional states (e.g., performance anxiety, fear of failure). For example, a college student might not choose to continue in science or math because he perceives that the costs in terms of the effort required are too much for him to bear at this time. If these courses require too much effort and study time, they take time away from other activities such as dating, sports, and social events. In terms of the anticipated emotional costs influencing behavior, a researcher may not participate often in conference presentations because of his performance anxiety about speaking in front of large groups and his fear of failure. These costs and negative affects might be generated from the affective memories of earlier experiences with similar activities, as suggested by arrow from affective memories and values in Figure 2.2.

These four components of task value are assumed to operate together to determine the achievement value a task might have for an individual. Accordingly, individuals will generally have perceptions of the attainment value, interest, and utility value of a task as well as the costs associated with a task. In this sense, this model is a rational decision-making model of motivation, not unlike other expectancy-value models and goal theory models (Locke & Latham, 1990) and does fit under the godlike metaphor suggested by Weiner (1992). However, in their empirical work, Eccles and Wigfield and their colleagues have focused on how these value components combine with expectancy beliefs to influence student achievement behavior in actual school settings. Given this high level of ecological validity, their research is very relevant to understanding student motivation in K–12 schools in comparison to laboratory studies of college students or field studies done in business settings.

Most of Eccles and Wigfield's empirical research on values has focused on late elementary through secondary school students' values and expectancies for math and English. The studies were correlational and longitudinal in design and used survey methodology with large samples of students. The general pattern has been to survey students about their values and expectancies at one point in time and then examine the predictive power of these motivational beliefs for subsequent achievement in terms of grades and performance on standardized tests at a later point in time. Because they have been interested in choice behavior—in particular, student decisions about whether to continue taking math courses—these researchers have asked junior high students about their intentions to keep on taking math in high school and college. In addition, in longitudinal studies, they have actually followed the students over time and collected data on actual math enrollment decisions as well as the values and expectancies of the students.

The main effects of these studies are fairly easy to summarize. As noted in the previous section, expectancy beliefs, including self-concepts, ability perceptions, and expectancy for success, seem to predict actual achievement in terms of grades and performance on standardized tests. Values are positively correlated with actual achievement, but when both expectancy beliefs and values are used to predict achievement, expectancy beliefs are significant predictors, and values are not significant predictors. In contrast, in terms of intentions to take future courses and actual enrollment in those courses (choice behavior), value beliefs, including attainment value, intrinsic interest, and extrinsic utility value, are better predictors than are expectancy beliefs (see Eccles, 1983; Meece, Wigfield, & Eccles, 1990; Wigfield & Eccles, 1992).

It appears that achievement values may be more important for choice behaviors and are responsible for students enrolling in courses. Once in the course, however, students' values are not as important for actual performance as are expectancy beliefs. This implies that it may be more important for teachers to encourage appropriate expectancy and self-competence beliefs in order to improve students' classroom achievement than to worry about increasing students' value and interest in the course material. Of course, increasing the value and interest levels may result in students electing to continue on in the subject area at a later point and, given the positive correlation of values with achievement, will not have detrimental effects on actual classroom achievement.

There are several other consistent findings in this program of research that bear on the theoretical and conceptual relations among the constructs in expectancy-value models. First, in their construct validity studies using confirmatory factor analyses, Eccles and Wigfield found that the different expectancy constructs such as self-concept, self-perceptions of ability, and expectancy for success are not differentiated into separable factors empirically (Eccles & Wigfield, 1995). Accordingly, although self-concept of ability may be distinguished theoretically from expectancy for success in terms of the former being considered somewhat more stable and general and the latter being more task and situation specific, it appears that students do not make these distinctions, at least in their responses to a self-report questionnaire. Second, their research has shown that the three value components of attainment value, intrinsic interest, and extrinsic utility value are empirically distinct from one another and from the expectancy component. It appears that students do make differential judgments about importance, interest, and utility and that there can be intraindividual variability on these dimensions for the same task. For example, students may be intrinsically interested in English but report low levels of importance or utility value for it. Moreover, Eccles and Wigfield's research shows that these value components are positively correlated with an expectancy component, such that students tend to value those activities in which they think they do well and vice versa (Eccles & Wigfield, 1995). This positive association gets stronger with age (Eccles et al., 1998).

These results, taken together with Battle's (1966) and Feather's (1988) findings, offer strong empirical support for the idea that expectancy and value components are positively related to one another, not inversely related as originally proposed by Atkinson (1964). Although expectancy and value beliefs have been shown to be positively related to one another, Eccles and Wigfield do note that at this point in their research, there is still an open question as to which is causally predominant (Eccles et al., 1998). That is, it is still not clear whether children develop competence at a task and then begin to value it or whether value leads to more time spent doing the task and, hence, competence develops out of this increased engagement. Their future work will examine this issue, but it does bring up questions of development. Application 2.1, later in the chapter, provides suggestions for facilitating students' value beliefs.

DEVELOPMENTAL AND GROUP DIFFERENCES IN EXPECTANCY-VALUE CONSTRUCTS

Current research on expectancy-value models demonstrates the importance of these constructs for student choice, engagement, learning, and performance. As noted previously, two important generalizations emerge from this work. First, students with positive self-perceptions of their competence and positive expectancies will be more likely to perform better and learn more as well as engage in an adaptive manner on academic tasks, including exerting more effort, showing more persistence, and demonstrating more cognitive engagement. Second, students who value and are interested in the academic tasks are more likely to chose similar tasks in the future as well as perform better, learn more, and be more adaptively engaged in the tasks. Given the importance of these two generalizations for education, it is crucial to determine if there are any exceptions to these generalizations. That is, do these generalizations apply to all types of children? To all ages of children? Do they apply equally to males and females or to different ethnic groups? We first explore developmental differences in these constructs and then consider how gender and ethnic status might moderate these generalizations about expectancies and values.

The Nature of Developmental Differences in Expectancy and Value Constructs

Given the importance of self-perceptions of competence in achievement, there has been a great deal of developmental research on the age-related changes in children's self-perceptions of competence. There is an important distinction in this developmental literature between the level and accuracy of children's self-perceptions of competence and their definitions of ability and effort (Blumenfeld, Pintrich, Meece, & Wessels, 1982). The latter have to do with the psychological meaning of ability and effort and will be discussed in chapter 3 on attribution theory. In this chapter, we are concerned with the level and accuracy of children's self-perceptions of competence.

The research that has examined developmental differences in children's self-perceptions of competence has consistently shown a decrease in the mean level of self-perceptions of ability as children move into adolescence (Eccles & Midgley, 1989; Eccles, Midgley, & Adler, 1984; Eccles et al., 1998; Harter, 1990, 1998; Stipek & Mac Iver, 1989; Wigfield, Eccles, & Pintrich, 1996). In particular, the average level decrease seems to be the greatest when students move into junior high schools or middle schools in seventh or sixth grade, respectively (e.g., Eccles, 1993; Eccles et al., 1998), although Marsh has found the lowest point to be in eighth or ninth grade (Marsh, 1989). Most of this research has been cross-sectional in nature, but the few longitudinal studies also show a decrease over time with age (Eccles et al., 1998; Wigfield et al., 1991). There are three general explanations for this age-related drop in mean level of self-perceptions of competence: methodological, cognitive developmental, and contextual.

First, there is a simple methodological explanation. Most measures of students' self-perceptions of competence use some version of a Likert-type scale whereby students rate themselves on one of several numerical scales from the lowest level of self-perceived ability (a *1* on the scale) to the highest level of self-perceived ability (a *4, 5, 7,* or *11,* depending on the scale). It may be that young children (early to middle elementary grades) are more likely to use only the endpoints of the Likert scale, especially the higher end of the scale. As they get older, children may be less likely to use the endpoints and distribute their responses across the continuum of the scale, resulting in a general mean level decrease. Although this may be the case, it is not clear that this tendency to use the endpoints on a Likert-type scale reflects a methodological artifact of Likert scales per se. Assor and Connell (1992) argue that Likert scale items are acceptable and valid measures of children's self-perceptions of competence as long as some precautions are taken in their design and administration. They do note, however, that a 4-point scale may provide all the needed precision with younger children and there may not be a need for scales with a larger range.

This brings us to the second general type of explanation for the developmental differences in perceptions of ability, which is more substantive and has to do with internal cognitive psychological mechanisms that might show developmental differences. Two issues are related to a cognitive explanation of the overall drop; one concerns the accuracy of self-perceptions and the other concerns the overall optimistic self-perceptions of younger children.

The first issue regarding accuracy assumes that there is some objective indicator of children's competence that can be used as a criterion against which to assess the congruence of their perceptions of their competence. In most studies, the objective indicators in the academic domain have been standardized tests, teacher grades, or teacher ratings. In general, the research suggests that in the middle elementary grades (third, fourth grade), there is less congruence between children's self-perceptions and more objective assessments, whereas the congruence becomes much better in the later elementary grades and later junior high school (eighth and ninth grades) (Eccles et al., 1998; Harter, 1985a). Moreover, most of the incongruence in the early grades occurs because the younger students have fairly high self-perceptions of competence. Their self-perceptions then become more modest as they move into the later grades (Frey & Ruble, 1987; Harter, 1985a; Stipek, 1981, 1984; Weisz, 1983), thereby making them more veridical with other more objective assessments of competence (Phillips & Zimmerman, 1990). Nevertheless, this high level of competence ratings in the early grades for most children means that correlations between perceptions of competence and actual achievement will be attenuated. In many studies, the correlations are quite low in the early grades and then become much stronger in later elementary and junior high school grades (Eccles et al., 1998). Of course, this result means that age does moderate the generalization that perceptions of competence are positively linked to actual achievement. It appears that this generalization is more true of older students than students in the early elementary grades.

In any event, it is probably best for individuals to have somewhat optimistic perceptions of their competence and efficacy (Assor & Connell, 1992), although not to be too overly optimistic and certainly not too pessimistic (Phillips, 1984, 1987). Nevertheless, given the general social cognitive and constructivist perspective of current motivational theories, the accuracy of these perceptions in terms of their correspondence to objective measures of achievement is not as important as the fact that these perceptions do have motivational and achievement consequences. Assor and Connell (1992) review a number of studies of both the illusion of competence (children who overrate their competence, given their actual achievement) and the illusion of incompetence (children who underrate their competence, given their actual achievement) and conclude that, in both cases, these perceptions have important consequences. Students who overrated their competence were more likely to be engaged and achieve at higher levels, whereas those who underrated their competence were more likely to avoid tasks, report more anxiety, and not achieve that well. Assor and Connell conclude that these inaccurate perceptions are "real" because they have real consequences in motivational and behavioral terms. Accordingly, the accuracy of perceptions in terms of a match to external criteria like teacher ratings or achievement tests is not as important a validity consideration as whether measures of children's self-perceptions actually reflect the children's own perceptions of their abilities. As Assor and Connell (1992) state,

> Surveys of relevant research findings clearly demonstrate that, beginning in the third and fourth grade and extending through high school, in populations ranging from upper middle-class Caucasian American youth, to lower and middle class Israeli children, to primarily poor African American adolescents, there is no empirical justification for viewing self-reported appraisals of academic competence and efficacy as invalid measures of performance affecting self-appraisals. (pp. 41–42)

Moving beyond the accuracy issue, the second issue regarding the cognitive explanation concerns the optimistic beliefs of young children. Assor and Connell (1992) note that there may be some positive advantages for having "inaccurate" self-perceptions of competence when they are higher than should be expected given actual performance. They report that these "inflated" self-reports actually are related to positive performance outcomes 2 years later in a longitudinal study of high school students. They also note that students who have inaccurate self-perceptions that are lower than they should be (deflated self-assessments) perform at much lower levels, which coincides with other studies as well (Phillips & Zimmerman, 1990). Accordingly, in line with a motivational and constructivist perspective, individuals' personal and subjective self-perceptions are important for future achievement behavior, regardless of the "accuracy" of the perceptions in terms of their match to grades, standardized tests, or ratings by adults. Researchers must still be careful, however, to get accurate and valid perceptions that really represent children's own beliefs about themselves, not modesty or social desirability effects.

Besides the general developmental differences in accuracy of self-perceptions, there also seem to be some individual differences in the inaccuracy of self-perceptions of competence. Inaccuracy in self-perceptions of competence can result from overestimation of competence (believing you are more competent than suggested by objective measures) and underestimation of competence (believing you are less competent than expected by objective measures). Phillips (1984, 1987; Phillips & Zimmerman, 1990) examined three types of students in terms of their accuracy of competence perceptions. In her studies, she used samples of only high-achieving third-, fifth-, and ninth-grade students (defined in terms of a combination of standardized test scores and teacher ratings), but still found that there were overestimators (higher perceptions of competence than warranted by actual achievement), accurate perceivers (congruence between perceptions and achievement), and underestimators (lower perceptions than warranted by actual achievement). This latter group, all of whom had the "illusion of incompetence," was of particular concern to her because all of her sample students were actually achieving in the top 25% on nationally standardized tests. These underestimators were most likely to hold very low expectations for future success, to believe that their parents and teachers had low perceptions of them, to be more anxious, and to be less willing to try hard and persist on academic tasks (Phillips & Zimmerman, 1990). Accordingly, whereas most students do become more accurate in their self-perceptions of competence as they progress through school, there are still some very able children who have the illusion of incompetence and show negative motivational outcomes.

Given the argument that children's perceptions are real and younger children are more likely to have higher perceptions, we still need to account for this phenomenon, not just attribute it to inaccurate or invalid measures. The cognitive explanation offers a cognitive developmental rationale for the generally optimistic perceptions of younger children. This explanation is based on a developmental argument that these children may not have the information-processing skills available to integrate the information and make the types of social comparisons necessary (Blumenfeld et al., 1982). For example, Parsons and Ruble (1977) have shown that young children have difficulty utilizing all of the cues presented to them to make accurate predictions about future performance. Other researchers have shown that children do not interpret feedback about task difficulty in the same manner as adults. For example, Meyer and colleagues (Meyer et al., 1979) found that ninth graders and adults were more likely to believe that praise after success at an easy task implied low ability and criticism for failure at a hard task indicated high ability, but that third and fifth graders used praise as an indicator of higher ability regardless of the task difficulty level.

Besides these differences in information processing, a number of studies suggest that younger children use less comparative standards or criteria to judge ability in contrast to the more relative standards of older children and adults. For example, Blumenfeld, Pintrich, and Hamilton (1987) have shown that younger children (second graders) are more likely to use an absolute standard to judge their competence and focus on completion of the task (I can read, I can do my math). Older students (sixth graders) were more likely to invoke comparison information (I can do my math faster than other kids) when asked to judge their competence. Ruble and her colleagues (Ruble, 1983; Ruble & Frey, 1991) have shown that younger children do not always seek out social comparison information, let alone use it to make a judgment of their ability. The lack of interest in and failure to use social comparison information by younger children suggest that they will maintain higher perceptions of ability. If younger children do not make comparisons of their performance to others, then they will be less likely to adjust their self-perceptions downward as they see some other children do better than they do on different academic tasks.

The third general explanation for the drop in ability perceptions as children grow older is contextually based and focuses not on the changing cognitive and information-processing skills of children, but on the changing developmental environments through which they move. Obviously, one of the environmental factors that changes is the nature of classrooms and schools. As a number of researchers (Blumenfeld et al., 1982; Eccles, Midgley, Wigfield, Reuman et al., 1993; Marshall & Weinstein, 1984; Rosenholtz & Simpson, 1984) have pointed out, elementary and junior high schools differ in a number of organizational and structural ways that can influence students' ability perceptions. First, the nature of the class structure changes in junior high, with children moving among several different classes and teachers for subject areas instead of one teacher for most academic subject areas as in most elementary schools. Second, the nature of evaluation changes. Most elementary classroom teachers use a simple criterion-mastery system of grading. Children are graded on their performance on worksheets, projects, tests, and so on without reference to how others perform. In contrast, in junior and senior high classrooms, teachers often use some type of relative grading system whereby students' grades are partially determined in reference to how other children perform. In these cases, children are given information about their ability relative to other children. For those who do not do as well, it is not surprising that they begin to lower their self-perceptions of ability. In addition, tracking by ability level begins to emerge in the upper grades. This can have a detrimental effect on lower-ability children's perceptions of their ability (Mac Iver, 1988; Rosenholtz & Simpson, 1984).

In effect, many aspects of the classroom change as children move to junior high and most of these changes serve to increase the information available to students upon which to make relative ability judgments. Not all students lower their ability judgments (Mac Iver, 1988; Reuman, 1989), but both the cognitive developmental and classroom/school changes seem to increase the variance in students' ratings, so that all children's ratings are not clustered around a higher mean. This situation results in more dispersion of ability self-perceptions and also a lower overall mean as children get older. It seems likely that some aspects of both the cognitive developmental and contextual explanations are operating to foster a decrease in children's ability perceptions. Future research should examine how these two explanations can be integrated to help us understand the developmental differences in children's competence perceptions.

In terms of developmental differences in values, one of the hallmarks of Eccles and Wigfield's research on task values has been the focus on how these values develop over time in school settings. In fact, the original study that spawned their program of research was concerned with the more pragmatic question of why elementary and junior high female students do not continue on in upper level math courses in senior high or college when their actual math achievement in the early grades is remarkably similar to that of males. As developmental and motivational psychologists, Eccles and Wigfield approached this problem in terms of examining how expectancy and value beliefs developed over time, become situated in home and school contexts, and how these motivational beliefs then influence future achievement behaviors.

In terms of developmental differences, Eccles and Wigfield and their colleagues have addressed several issues in their research. First, they examined the differentiation of the different value constructs over the course of development. In general, they find that fifth through twelfth graders do distinguish among the three components of importance, interest, and utility (Eccles & Wigfield, 1995). However, Wigfield and Eccles (1992) report that children in the early elementary grades do not reliably distinguish the three components of task value. In confirmatory factor analytic studies, they find only two value components—interest and utility/importance. Interest seems to be differentiated early on in development and the distinction between utility and importance appears only in later elementary school (Eccles et al., 1998). It appears that the development of task value beliefs follows the general orthogenetic principle of Werner (1957), with task value beliefs becoming more differentiated with age and experience. As children have more experience with a variety of tasks and activities that engage their interest and ideas of importance differently, they will begin to differentiate these components of task value beliefs. Although task value beliefs may not be differentiated into the three principal components in early elementary school, Eccles and Wigfield have consistently found that expectancy and task value beliefs are distinguished from one another in the early elementary grades (Eccles, Wigfield, Harold, & Blumenfeld, 1993; Eccles et al., 1998; Wigfield & Eccles, 1992). Moreover, these same studies found that young children did distinguish between expectancy and value beliefs for different domains such as math, reading, computers, music, social activities, and sports. Accordingly, even very young children in the early elementary grades can make distinctions about what they like or think is important to them versus their perceptions of competence in different domains (Eccles et al., 1998; Wigfield, 1994; Wigfield & Eccles, 1992).

The second issue that is of developmental importance concerns the change in the level of children's achievement task values. The general finding for academic task value beliefs is fairly easy to summarize: Older children's ratings of interest, importance, and utility for school subjects decline in comparison to the mean levels of younger children's ratings (Eccles & Midgley, 1989; Eccles et al., 1998; Wigfield, 1994; Wigfield & Eccles, 1992). There are some domain differences with students in upper elementary grades rating mathematics as more important, interesting, and useful in comparison to students in junior and senior high schools. In addition, this same research showed that students' task value beliefs for English increased across the elementary to high school samples (Wigfield & Eccles, 1992). Other research in this tradition has shown that the transition from elementary school to junior high school is marked by a significant decrease in students' interest and importance ratings of math and English (Eccles et al., 1989; Wigfield et al., 1991). In contrast, research on developmental changes within elementary schools using a sample of first, second, and fourth graders has found that math task value ratings did not decline across grade, although math was not rated very highly in comparison to other subjects or activities (Eccles, Wigfield et al., 1993). The ratings for reading, music, and computer activities were lower in older children, and these children rated sports as more interesting and important to them. In a follow-up longitudinal study of these same children, Wigfield, Eccles, and their colleagues found that within subjects, only reading and music task value ratings declined, whereas interest in math and sports did not decline within individuals over time. As Wigfield (1994) points out, these findings highlight the importance of examining task value beliefs by domain and activity as well as by age of the child. Accordingly, although children's general task value beliefs decline with age, there are important domain and developmental differences in this generalization.

There are two general explanations for the decline in children's task value beliefs. The cognitive developmental explanation focuses more on internal changes in children's strategies and beliefs, paralleling the explanation for the drop in self-competence perceptions (Blumenfeld et al., 1982; Wigfield & Eccles, 1992). For example, as children get older, their beliefs about the nature of ability change (see chapter 3) from a more incremental view of ability as malleable, to a more entity-like view of ability as stable and unchanging (Dweck, 1999; Dweck & Leggett, 1988). If students do poorly in certain school areas, such as math, and attribute this poor performance to low ability that will remain stable, they may lower their perceptions of the value of math to protect their overall self-worth (Steele, 1988; Wigfield & Eccles, 1992). In addition, as students get older, they become more interested in social comparison with others as well as more able to integrate social comparison information with their own beliefs (Blumenfeld et al., 1982; Ruble & Frey, 1991). These developmental changes in ability to use social comparison also can lead to lower perceptions of ability, as noted earlier. In any event, given the generally positive relations between ability perceptions and task value beliefs, if ability perceptions decline with age, value perceptions should as well.

The second explanation for the decline in task value beliefs reflects a more experiential and contextual argument about the power of the classroom context to shape students' beliefs. Eccles and her colleagues have proposed that in most junior high schools, there is a developmental mismatch between beliefs and developmental needs of the students entering the school and the structure and organization of the school. They suggest that students entering junior high school are likely to have high needs for autonomy and control and also the cognitive skills to exercise self-control and regulation. The researchers go on to note, however, that in most junior high and senior high schools, there is actually little opportunity for student autonomy and control. Rather, the students encounter lower cognitive level tasks, more emphasis on normative and comparative grading practices, and less criterion-referenced grading. This mismatch between the students and the school results in a significant decrease in young adolescents' motivation for school (see Eccles & Midgley, 1989; Eccles et al., 1984; Eccles, Midgley et al., 1993; Eccles, Wigfield et al., 1993; Wigfield & Eccles, 1992). This argument is similar to the proposal made by Rosenholtz & Simpson (1984) regarding the decline in children's ability perceptions

An integration of these two positions regarding cognitive and contextual changes represents the most viable explanation for the drop in values and expectancies. There are both internal cognitive developmental and motivational changes as well as environmental changes that reciprocally interact with each other that are responsible for the decline in students' motivation for school. Accordingly, we need to develop models that incorporate both types of changes in order to explain student motivation.

The Nature of Gender and Ethnic Differences in Expectancy and Value Constructs

Besides the developmental differences that are found in ability self-perceptions and value beliefs, studies have also found gender and ethnic differences in these constructs. However, there are a number of problems with making broad generalizations about gender and ethnic differences in motivation. First, by concentrating on overall group differences, many of the studies ignore the more significant within-group differences among females or among minority children. Second, it is often difficult to evaluate the relative contributions of gender and ethnicity to these group differences because the influence of socioeconomic status (SES) is not considered simultaneously (Graham, 1994; Pollard, 1993). Many of these studies confound SES with ethnicity by comparing middle or upper-middle income Caucasian students with lower-income African American students. Moreover, as Pollard (1993) points out, there may be important interactions among gender, ethnicity, and SES on children's motivation or achievement. Studies that do not take into account the multiple statuses and roles that students can play as a function of membership in different groups can be misleading and result in simplistic conclusions being drawn about one characteristic (e.g., ethnicity) when the reality is much more complex. Third, much of the research on ethnic differences has been atheoretical in terms of conceptualizing motivation and has often relied on deficit models and compared different ethnic groups on constructs that allow for simple dichotomies between those low and high in certain characteristics (Betancourt & Lopez, 1993; Graham, 1994; Pollard, 1993). Accordingly, any generalizations about gender or ethnic differences are problematic, albeit there are some trends that should be noted.

In most cases, when a gender difference is found for perceptions of competence, the difference is that females have lower self-perceptions of ability than males (Wigfield et al., 1996). This is particularly surprising because many studies that have examined actual achievement or performance (see Linn & Hyde, 1989) show that there are few gender differences and that in many cases, females actually outperform males; yet other studies still show females as having lower self-perceptions. Although this discrepancy between actual achievement and self-perceptions of ability may be due to a response bias, with boys being more self-congratulatory and girls being more modest (Eccles, Adler, & Meece, 1984; Wigfield et al., 1996), the difference appears often enough to be taken seriously. Again, it appears that gender may moderate the general finding that self-perceptions of competence are tightly linked to engagement and actual achievement.

Eccles and Wigfield and their colleagues have consistently found gender differences in self-perceptions of ability, but these gender differences are moderated by the cultural gender-role stereotyping of the activity as well as how much the individual student endorses the cultural stereotype (Eccles et al., 1998). For example, they find that males have higher self-perceptions in math and sports, two activities that are stereotyped as being more masculine, whereas females have higher self-perceptions of their ability in domains that are usually stereotyped as being feminine, such as reading, English, and social activities (Eccles, 1983; Eccles & Harold, 1991; Eccles et al., 1989; Eccles, Wigfield, Harold, & Blumenfeld, 1993; Eccles et al., 1998; Wigfield et al., 1991). Marsh (1989) also reports gender differences in his data on self-concept. Although he finds that the gender differences account for only 1% of the variance in self-concept, he finds that males have higher self-concept scores for their self-ratings of physical appearance, physical ability, and math, whereas females have higher self-ratings for verbal and reading tasks and general school self-concept (Wigfield et al., 1996). Phillips and Zimmerman (1990) also found that females had lower perceptions of their competence than did males, although the gender difference did not emerge with third and fifth graders, only with ninth graders. Other studies, however, have found that gender differences in ability perceptions do emerge at earlier grades. For example, studies by Entwisle and Baker (1983) and Frey and Ruble (1987) both found that even in early elementary age children, females were more likely to have lower self-perceptions of ability than males. Clearly, there is a need for more research into the nature of these differences as well as more programs to change school and classroom practices that can give rise to these gender differences (Bailey, 1993; Kahle, Parker, Rennie, & Riley, 1993; Meece & Eccles, 1993).

Much less research has been done in terms of ethnic and racial differences, and the research often confounds race and ethnicity with social class differences by comparing middle-class white children with lower-class minority children (Graham, 1992, 1994; Wigfield et al., 1996). Two general issues are often addressed in research that examines ethnic differences. First, are there ethnic group differences in the mean level of self-perceptions of ability and values or other motivational constructs? Second, do the motivational constructs operate in the same fashion for minority group students as they do for other groups, or do we need different models of motivation for different ethnic groups?

In terms of the first question, Graham (1994), in a narrative review of published studies of African American students and their achievement motivation, found little support for the general hypothesis that African American students should have lower expectancies for success or lower self-concepts of ability because of their poor school achievement or general economic disadvantage. In terms of expectancy for success, Graham (1994) reviewed 14 experimental studies that used a common format of presenting a task to African American and Caucasian children and then asked them to predict their expectancy for success. In addition, some of the studies asked the students to make judgments of their expectancy for success after they had received either manipulated or actual success and failure. In 12 out of the 14 studies, African American students had higher expectations for success than did Caucasian children. Graham (1994) also reviewed 18 studies that examined self-concepts of ability. Again, she found very little evidence for the idea that African American students have lower self-concepts of ability. Only 2 of the 18 studies reported group differences in favor of Caucasian children, 7 favored African American children, and the remaining 9 had mixed or no significant differences between the two groups. In a meta-analytic follow-up to Graham (1994), Cooper and Dorr (1995) found that there were generally reliable differences in self-concept, with African Americans having higher levels than whites.

This finding is counter-intuitive to the general idea that African Americans should have lower perceptions of competence, given their often low levels of actual achievement on standardized tests and GPA. In addition, it suggests that the generalization that competence perceptions and actual achievement are closely linked may not be true for African Americans. For example, Stevenson, Chen, and Uttal (1990) found that white children's perceptions of competence were related to performance, but this was not the case for African Americans. From a motivational perspective, as Graham (1994) suggests, this discrepancy may be adaptive—having generally high perceptions of competence would be motivating and help students maintain their engagement, even if they do not eventually achieve at high levels. It also may be a self-protective mechanism, as African American children say they are doing well in order to protect their self-esteem (Graham, 1994). However, on the other hand, from a self-regulatory perspective, the discrepancy between their judgments of competence and actual performance suggests that African American students may not be very accurate, or "calibrated," in terms of the match between their judgments of competence and performance. If this is the case, the miscalibration may lead them to think they are doing fine and may not motivate them to change or regulate their cognition or behavior to do better in the future (Pintrich, 2000d). For example, if a student is reading a text and thinks he comprehends it, when in fact he does not, he will be less likely to go back and reread it or to use other cognitive strategies to repair his comprehension. In any event, this issue of calibration between judgments of competence and performance in different ethnic groups needs to be examined in more detail in future research.

In terms of the second issue, some studies find that self-perceptions of ability or efficacy are linked to academic achievement in the same fashion (e.g., moderate positive correlations) for minorities and other groups (Pollard, 1993; Taylor, Casten, Flickinger, & Roberts, 1994). However, Graham (1994) notes that in many of the studies she reviewed, the actual performance measures, such as grades or standardized achievement tests, showed that African Americans had lower levels of performance, yet had higher self-perceptions of ability. This would suggest that the relation between self-perceptions of ability and actual achievement is not as strong in African American students as it is in Caucasian students (see Stevenson et al., 1990). There have been many reasons proposed to explain this weaker relation. For example, some researchers (e.g., Fordham & Ogbu, 1986; Steele, 1988, 1997) have suggested that the motivational dynamics are different for African American children and that they may devalue academic achievement (a task value belief) because of their repeated school failures. In this case, they may have relatively high self-perceptions of competence (or relatively low perceptions), but their perceptions of competence are not linked as closely to actual achievement as they are in Caucasian children. Other reasons include the use of different social comparison groups; for example, African Americans compare themselves to other African Americans rather than the more advantaged Caucasian group, thereby maintaining high self-perceptions (Rosenberg & Simmons, 1971). They also attribute their lower performance to external factors such as prejudice, thereby maintaining high self-perceptions (Crocker & Major, 1989).

Graham (1994), however, notes that these explanations are not supported in the general motivational literature. She suggests that motivational principles that are used in current theoretical work on motivation should also apply to minority students. In this sense, it may be more important to examine within-group individual differences rather than between-group differences. For example, why do some minorities or females seem to maintain their achievement even in the face of many different obstacles? Graham suggests that there is less need for a different psychology of minority student achievement, although more minority students must be included in future research on motivation, and samples must include a range of socioeconomic levels and different groups of minorities. In any event, there is a need for more research on these issues, both to evaluate the nature of the differences in perceptions of ability between minority and other children and to evaluate the claims that different theoretical models of motivation and development are necessary to explain the linkage between minority students' motivational beliefs about competence and their actual academic achievement.

There has been little research on ethnic differences in task values, but Eccles and Wigfield have examined gender differences. Their empirical research shows some gender differences, but the findings vary across studies and age groups (Wigfield & Eccles, 1992). They found that male and female adolescents do differ in the relative value they attach to various subjects such as math (males value more) and English (females value more), although these gender differences did not always emerge with younger children. In fact, Wigfield and Eccles found no differential valuing of math or computer activities by gender in a study of elementary school students, although boys reported more value for sports activities and girls valued reading and music more (Wigfield & Eccles, 1992). There is a need for more research on how these gender differences emerge in the context of classrooms and how these gender differences may then moderate the relation between value beliefs and other motivational outcomes such as choice, persistence, and actual achievement.

Although Eccles and Wigfield and their colleagues have assessed the task values of a large number of students, in most of their samples there was not much variation in ethnicity, precluding an examination of ethnic differences in values. In two recent studies, Graham, Taylor, and Hudley (1998) examined the achievement values of African American, Latino, and European American sixth through eighth graders. They used a different methodology than self-reports of values, due to their concerns about the social desirability of endorsing typical value statements about the importance and utility of education. They asked students to nominate peers who they admired, respected, and wanted to be like as an indicator of achievement values. They found both gender and ethnicity effects, with girls (across African American, Latina, and European American girls) more likely to nominate high-achieving girls as those they admired and respected. Most importantly, both African American and Latino boys were more likely to nominate low-achieving boys as those students they admired and respected most. In contrast, European American boys nominated high achievers as students they admired and respected, a pattern similar to that of girls. The results of these two studies do suggest that African American and Latino boys do not value achievement behaviors in the same manner as do girls and European American boys. Of course, the measure used is an indirect measure of task values as defined in expectancy-value theory, but the results from these two studies are rather sobering.

Of course, there have been similar arguments made about the dynamics of African Americans' motivation and value for education and schooling. For example, Mickelson (1990) has suggested that African Americans come to devalue education because they see no contingency between their efforts and success, due to persistent racial inequality. Ogbu (1987; Fordam and Ogbu, 1986) has suggested that African American students perceive their peers who work hard to do well in school as "acting white" and that there can be a general devaluing of school or achievement behaviors. However, the empirical evidence for this specific argument is mixed with some studies showing little support for the devaluing of achievement by African Americans (e.g., see Ford & Harris, 1996; O'Connor, 1997; Taylor, Casten, Flickinger, & Roberts, 1994). Research on **stereotype threat** (e.g., Steele, 1997) seems to have much more empirical support. This work shows that when a negative stereotype about performance is activated (girls can't do math, minority students don't do well academically), there is a decrease in performance. Steele (1997) has suggested that this stereotype threat can lead to disidentification with schooling with concomitant problems in performance and achievement.

Although much of the research has focused on African American students, similar arguments have been made for Asian Americans, albeit in the opposite direction. In this case, given their generally high levels of achievement and labels such as the "model" minority group, there have been suggestions that these positive effects are due to Asian Americans' high value for education and beliefs about the importance of effort in school (e.g., Chen & Stevenson, 1995; Holloway, 1988; Slaughter-Defoe, Nakagawa, Takanishi, & Johnson, 1990). At the same time, it is not clear how these values are transmitted or if there are variations by immigrant status and length of enculturation and socialization into American society (e.g., Fuligni, 1997; Hess, Chang, & McDevitt, 1987; Sue & Okazaki, 1990). This area of research on ethnic differences in motivation, particularly values, is a very active area of current research and new findings are emerging continually. Nevertheless, there is a clear need for more theoretically based research on how different ethnic groups are motivated and the links between their motivational beliefs and their actual achievement and educational attainment.

APPLICATION 2.1

Applying Expectancy-Value Models of Motivation in the Classroom

The research on expectancy and value beliefs provides a number of implications for teachers. These general principles reflect the research results, but given that psychology is a probabilistic, not a deterministic, science, the principles may not apply in all contexts and situations. That is, psychology is not like chemistry, in which one can predict with great precision what will happen in a new situation based on previous research. Rather, findings from psychological research can be used to appraise the probability of different events occurring in the future. In this sense, research in psychology can be used as a guide for educational practice, not as the determiner of practice. In some cases, we can say that following certain principles will most likely result in positive motivational outcomes, but there are always exceptions and problematic situations in which educators must use their best professional judgment.

There is disagreement in the teacher education literature about whether teachers actually can use principled knowledge in their teaching or whether their pedagogical knowledge is all case-based and develops from experience. Our position is that teachers can use and benefit from principled knowledge, albeit their use of it and their representation of it may be in the form of cases. Hence, we offer the follow suggestions as a guide for teacher practice. These principles will need to be adapted to the specific classroom context, but we trust that truly professional educators will be able to apply them in a thoughtful and pedagogically sound manner.

1. *Help students maintain relatively accurate but high expectations and perceptions of competence and help students avoid the illusion of incompetence.* Mr. Dearborn tries to provide positive but accurate feedback to all students on their written work. He writes on their papers about their demonstrated level of understanding of the content as well as their level of effort (at least as perceived by him). Some students do a very hasty paper and he makes sure to note this in his written comments. He often speaks with the students individually to ask them why they did not try very hard or did not do very well. Given this information, he tries to help the students see how they can increase their effort or performance. Sometimes, he shows them other students' papers (with the names removed to protect confidentiality and limit social comparison) so they can see a model of a good paper. He talks to the students about how they might go about doing a paper at the level of the model. At the same time, Mr. Dearborn is very careful to make sure that all students know what they did incorrectly; he does not give insincere feedback to boost self-esteem.

   As the research has shown, students are motivated to engage in tasks and achieve when they believe they can accomplish the task. Teachers need to provide accurate feedback to students to help them develop reasonable perceptions of their competence but, at the same time, communicate that their actual competence and skills will continue to develop.

2. *Students' perceptions of competence develop not just from accurate feedback from the teacher, but through actual success on challenging academic tasks. Keep tasks and assignments at a relatively challenging but reasonable level of difficulty.* Ms. Rivera has available many different levels of classroom assignments for her junior high school science students. Over the years, she has collected a number of different projects, experiments, labs, and workbook assignments that provide her with a diversity of tasks with differing levels of challenge. All of the students in her class do a common set of seventh-grade science tasks, but she also has extra-credit assignments available for those who can go beyond the basic seventh-grade material. In addition, she has other extra-credit assignments that are below grade level that she uses with stu-

dents who are struggling with the content. This mixture of common and individualized tasks allows most children the opportunity to be successful and at the same time be challenged.

Although practice on easy tasks is very helpful for building automaticity of skills, children also need to be challenged by tasks in order to be motivated and to actually learn new skills. Tasks should be set at a level of difficulty where most children in the classroom can master the assignment with some effort. They should not be too easy and especially not too difficult that most children fail at the task.

3. *Foster the belief that competence or ability is a changeable, controllable aspect of development.* At the beginning of this chapter, three students were talking about their self-perceptions of competence for social studies. Kevin had high competence beliefs, whereas both Rachel and Jacob had lower beliefs about their capability to do social studies. In this case, if there are many students in the classroom who have the same level of beliefs as Rachel and Jacob, the social studies teacher might want to have a class discussion about how different students study for social studies tests. During the discussion, different types of learning strategies might be mentioned that some children don't know about. Most likely, different levels of effort and amount of time studying would be mentioned as factors that influence test performance. The social studies teacher could then use the ideas generated in the discussion to help all of the students in the class see that performing well on social studies tests is something that they all can learn to do. He could do this by reemphasizing the importance of effort, the amount of time spent studying, and the use of different learning strategies. In addition, he could express his belief that all students can learn to do well in social studies. This type of teacher talk about social studies would communicate to students that the teacher has high expectations for all of them and that learning in social studies is not a stable ability or trait that some students have or do not have.

The vast majority of the knowledge and skills that are taught in K–12 schools can be learned by all children who do not have serious disabilities. Of course, some children may take longer to master the knowledge or skills than others, but there are very few inherent limitations that are stable traits of students. If students come to understand that they can master the material with some effort, they will be more likely to engage in the material. The teacher needs to communicate this type of positive high expectation for all students, younger and older, high and low ability, females and males, and minority and others.

4. *Decrease the amount of relative ability information that is publicly available to students.* Ms. Morgan, a math teacher, has one bulletin board in her room that lists all of the assignments for her class and all of the students' grades for each assignment. She likes having the information posted so that everyone can see it. It helps her keep track of what students have done and it helps the students see what assignments they have finished and which ones they still need to complete. In particular, she finds that it is a very effective management tool because when students are done with their assignment for the day, they can check the board and see what else they have to do without bothering her. Since she started using this system, she is not constantly being asked by students what they should do next. This freedom allows her to work closely with small groups or individuals on their math work without too many interruptions.

Ms. Morgan also has found as the semester goes along, however, that there are always a few students who fall behind in their work, get poor grades, and seem to give up. When she asks them what is going on, they often point to the board and say things like, "Look what I have to do. There's too much. I'm too far behind. What's the use?" or "I'm too stupid to do math. Every day I come in here, some of the nerds make fun of me. They point to the low grades I got on the board and laugh. I really hate math and anyone who is good at it is just a nerd anyway." These comments are upsetting to Ms. Morgan because she wants her students to do well and also to like and enjoy math.

Some teachers facilitate social comparison by posting all students' scores and grades on wall posters in the room or by having students call out their test scores in class while writing them down in the grade book. These types of practices can increase the amount of social comparison information available to children and help to lower some children's (those doing less well) self-perceptions of competence. In Ms. Morgan's case, her management practice with the bulletin board seems to be undermining some students' perceptions of their competence to do math. The students who are not doing so well are having negative interactions with some other students and making negative social comparisons about their ability to do math. The board presents to all students in the class, in a highly public manner, everyone's tests and assignment scores. Ms. Morgan should try to avoid these types of public practices that heighten the differences between students. She could keep the grading information private and use it in assigning final class grades, but it may not be that helpful for all students to have public access to it. If she still wants to use the public bulletin board for management purposes, simple check marks for completion may serve just as well as the public posting of grades. On the other hand, there may be more individualized and more private ways (e.g., individual student folders or portfolios) to keep track of her students' completed work.

5. *Students' perceptions of competence are domain specific and are not equivalent to global self-esteem. It is more productive for academic learning to help students develop their self-perceptions of competence rather than their global self-esteem.* At the beginning of this chapter, Rachel, Kevin, and Jacob all showed the domain specificity of their beliefs about school tasks and athletic tasks. Their teachers provide them with accurate feedback about their performance in their subject area. The teachers avoid global and nonspecific feedback ("You are a good person" "You are all special in some way" or "You should feel good about yourself") in favor of specific feedback about their actual performance.

Although global self-esteem can be important for general mental health, in the academic domains, it is more important for students' learning that they have accurate feedback about their performance and begin to develop accurate and positive perceptions of their competence. General self-esteem improvement may not be that helpful, particularly when students can see that they can't do a certain type of math or science problem. In this case, older children from later elementary school onward will quickly surmise the insincerity of the praise and discount it in terms of their perception of ability to perform the specific task.

6. *Teachers should offer rationales for schoolwork that include discussion of the importance and utility value of the work.* Brophy (1983) has noted how seldom teachers

actually convey this type of message in the course of instruction. Brophy (1998, 1999) also provides some suggestions for how to increase the value and utility perceptions of students.

Ms. Brennan, a seventh-grade science teacher, discusses with her class how important science is, not just for understanding life outside school, but for keeping certain career options open. She points out how engineers and medical doctors need to take a great many science courses in both high school and college. This links the science course and content to utility for certain types of careers.

7. *Model value and interest in the content of the lesson or unit.* Brophy (1999) notes how teachers can model and scaffold not just cognitive aspects of a task, but also motivational aspects of both value and interest.

Mrs. Green is teaching a high school English course and the unit she is focusing on includes Shakespeare's Macbeth. Throughout the unit, she talks about her own interest in the play and how it makes her feel and think about different issues. She also tries to relate how the themes of the play make her think about issues in present-day life in terms of relations with others, such as parent and child relations, ambitious people, etc., and how the play can help her think about different ways of handling these issues.

8. *Activate personal interest through opportunities for choice and control.* Although it can be very difficult, impractical, and probably unnecessary to develop a wholly child-centered curriculum based on students' individual interests, teachers can provide opportunities for students to exercise some choice and control over their learning.

Ms. Wong has collected a very large number of reading books and stories for her fourth-grade classroom. These books and stories range from first grade to junior high reading level (range of difficulty levels) and cover a great many different topics. She allows her students to choose their own reading books based on their interest in the topics and their own perception of the difficulty level of the books. She finds that most students are fairly good at picking out books that match their level of reading competence. Moreover, she scaffolds her instruction by helping those who pick books that are too hard and encourages students to try harder books if they seem to perseverate on choosing books that are too easy.

SUMMARY

Expectancy-value theories have a long-standing tradition in achievement motivation research and current expectancy-value models have some of the strongest empirical support in educational settings. The expectancy construct, in various guises, is one of the most important mediators of achievement behavior. Early research on expectancy constructs moved motivational psychology away from a dependence on a simplistic behavioral psychology to a more rational and cognitive paradigm that is still dominant today. Moreover, these early cognitive models of motivation stressed the importance of the individual's perceptions and beliefs as mediators of behavior, thereby focusing motivational research on the subjective and phenomenological psychology of the individual. These early theories focused on people's expectations for success and their value for the task. Current research on expectancy and value constructs continues in this tradition of focusing on these two general beliefs of the individual, although researchers do attempt to include contextual influences in their models.

Eccles and Wigfield and their colleagues have revised Atkinson's expectancy-value model by making it more social cognitive in nature to reflect the current cognitive paradigm of motivation. They have focused on students' expectancy for success and perceptions of ability as well as values for academic tasks in a number of large-scale correlational and longitudinal studies in schools. This research reflects some of the best ecologically valid studies of student motivation, given the focus on school and classroom tasks and the fact that they have followed the same students over time to actually investigate how motivational beliefs predict future behavior. They consistently find that students' expectancy beliefs about their capabilities to do a task and succeed at it are closely related to actual achievement on standardized tests as well as course grades. Their work also suggests that value beliefs, such as attainment value, utility, and interest, are closely tied to choice behaviors such as future course enrollment decisions.

The research on self-perceptions of ability and values has had a developmental focus and has investigated constructs in young children, adolescents, and adults. Current research suggests that self-perceptions of competence and value beliefs are domain specific, not global, although there is not agreement about the specificity of the domain. Self-perceptions of competence are also theoretically and empirically distinct from self-esteem. Perceptions of competence concern students' judgments of their capability in a domain and, hence, are more cognitive evaluations, whereas self-esteem is a more affective and global reaction to the self. Most students, even relatively young elementary school children, have relatively accurate self-perceptions of their own competence in specific domains. Moreover, when they are inaccurate, most children overestimate their competence, not underestimate it, although there are negative consequences for those who do underestimate their competence. Current research suggests that perceptions of competence are related in a reciprocal manner to actual achievement and performance.

There are developmental, gender, and ethnic differences to consider in children's expectancy and value beliefs. In terms of developmental differences, research suggests that younger children are more likely to have relatively high perceptions of their competence and that the overall mean level of these perceptions declines with age. Values show a similar decline with age. In particular, the research suggests that the decline is greatest when students make the transition to junior high school. There are both psychological and more sociological explanations for this drop. The psychological explanations focus on the changes in children's cognitive skills and beliefs as mediators of this age difference, whereas the more sociological explanations stress the changes in the nature of the school environment as the children move into secondary schools. The trends for gender and ethnic differences are much harder to summarize given the vagaries and confounding of gender, SES, and ethnicity in the samples or analyses in the research. Nevertheless, there appear to be some important gender and ethnic differences that moderate the basic generalizations about the role of expectancy and value constructs in motivational dynamics. There is a need for much more theoretically oriented research on these group differences.

C H A P T E R

3

Attribution Theory

Roy and Akane are ninth graders in a high school algebra class. Roy is an average stu- dent, not the best student in algebra, but he is passing the class. He usually gets B's and an occasional C^+ on the big end-of-chapter tests. On his daily homework, he might miss one or two problems, but normally he gets most of the problems correct. Akane is one of the best math students in the class. She usually gets A's and only occasionally gets a B^+. Her homework is almost always perfect.

The class is now studying quadratic equations and how to graph them. The whole class is having a little more difficulty than usual with this part of the course. The teacher, Mr. Kiley, spends a lot of time working through one or two examples of how to graph the problems, but doesn't stop for student questions very often. Both Roy and Akane listen hard and pay atten- tion in class, but Akane asks questions often; Roy never asks questions.

Roy seems to be missing most of the problems on his homework on quadratic equations, but he is not sure why. When he looks at his corrected homework, he wonders to himself, "What did I do wrong here? I just don't get this material. It seems so abstract and it's hard to see how this relates to anything. I just can't do this. It's too hard for me. I think I'm just not cut out to be a math person." Roy does not work as hard on this material as usual.

Akane also has been having a little more trouble, missing more problems than usual on her homework. However, when she gets back her homework, she looks it over and says to her- self, "I don't understand this, so I'll have to ask Mr. Kiley about this problem. Maybe I'm just not studying hard enough. I'll have to go back to the book and my notes and see what I'm do- ing wrong." She increases the amount of time she works on algebra.

The algebra class as a whole does not do very well on the end-of-chapter test; the overall class average is lower than usual. Roy gets a D^- and Akane gets a C^+ on the test. Roy is very embarrassed and ashamed by the D. He wonders why he did so poorly on this test compared to other end-of-chapter tests: "I know I have been having trouble on the homework and didn't work that hard, but I didn't think I was this dumb. Maybe I just have no ability for higher level math. I think maybe I've gone as far as I can go in math given my ability for it." Roy is so ashamed of his grade, he doesn't talk to anyone about it. For the remainder of the course, Roy puts forth even less effort in algebra and spends more time on his other classes. His math grades show a drop over the course of the year, and he ends up getting a C for his overall math course grade.

Akane's affective reaction to the C^+ is one of shock and displeasure. She has never gotten a C before in her life on any test in any subject. She thinks to herself, "Oh my god, my par- ents are going to kill me. I'll be grounded for sure. I studied pretty hard for this test, and it is so embarrassing to get a C^+. I know Mr. Kiley will think I blew it off. I wonder if everyone *else did poorly. I'll have to see what my friends got on the test. Maybe it was just a very hard test and that's why I didn't do so well." She talks to other kids in the class and finds out the highest grade was a B by the reigning math star. She feels better and keeps on trying hard in math. She gets an A for her final course grade.*

This little case study illustrates a number of important aspects about attribution theory. We will refer back to Roy and Akane as we discuss the model in this chapter, but what is your prediction about the level of their expectancies for success and self-efficacy beliefs for math at the end of the year? What are your predictions about them in terms of their choosing to go on to take more math courses?

The preceding chapter discussed the motivational constructs of expectancies and values and their links to achievement behaviors. Given that these expectancy and value constructs are very central to motivational dynamics, it is important to understand how individuals construct these beliefs and what influences the development of these beliefs. In this chapter, we discuss the various psychological and social cognitive processes that help to shape the construction of individuals' expectancy beliefs and their affective reactions to different experiences. We focus on attribution theory and research on the attributional processes that have a direct link to individuals' expectancy beliefs and their emotions. Although there has been a great deal of research on attribution theory, the one person who has made the greatest contribution to attribution theory in achievement contexts is Bernard Weiner. Our explication of this theory and approach relies heavily on his research and writings (e.g., Weiner, 1979, 1985a, 1986, 1992, 1995).

After studying this chapter, you should be able to:

1. Understand the factors that influence the attributions that individuals make in different situations.

2. Categorize different attributions into the three main dimensions of locus, stability, and controllability and describe the functions of these dimensions in attributional theory.

3. Analyze the expectancy beliefs, emotional reactions, and subsequent behaviors that will result when individuals make different types of attributions for academic success and failure.

4. Understand the role of responsibility judgments in generating emotions and behaviors in attributional theory.

5. Apply the concepts from attributional theory to classroom situations and educational practices.

OVERVIEW OF THE ATTRIBUTIONAL MODEL

Attribution theory is a cognitive theory of motivation and is based on a general "god-like" metaphor of the individual (Weiner, 1992) that suggests that individuals are conscious and rational decision makers. This metaphor is in contrast to the machine metaphor that equates human behavior with a nonconscious automaton that can produce "output," or behaviors, in reaction to stimuli in the environment or as a function of certain types of internal drives. Two general assumptions are derived from the god-like metaphor in attribution theory.

The first assumption of attribution theory is that individuals are motivated by a goal of understanding and mastering the environment and themselves (see White, 1959). This goal is the main instigator of behavior, and the theory does not propose any other goals, needs, motives, or drives (e.g., motive for success, fear of failure, need for affiliation, need for power, intrinsic motivation). The metaphor of person as scientist is often used and just as scientists are motivated to understand the natural world in order to predict and control future events, individuals are motivated to understand and master their own world in order to make it more predictable and controllable. As Kelley (1971) notes, "The attributor is not simply an attributor, a seeker after knowledge; his latent goal in attaining knowledge is that of effective management of himself and his environment" (p. 22). This striving for mastery and understanding has a functional value for individuals that allows them to learn and adapt to their environment.

The second assumption of attribution theory states that people are naive scientists, trying to understand their environment and, in particular, trying to understand the *causal determinants* of their own behavior as well as the behavior of others. Although this scientific perspective may not be popular in a postmodern world, it still has utility for understanding how individuals might perceive themselves and others. Accordingly, as a function of their search for mastery, individuals seek to understand *why* things happen and why people say and do the things that they do. For example, in the schooling context, students may seek to understand why they failed or passed an exam, as did Roy and Akane. A teacher may attempt to understand the reasons why one student in the class can learn to read so easily and another one has difficulty. In our example, Mr. Kiley, the math teacher, probably did wonder why Akane, who usually does so well in math, got a lower grade than usual on that test. In fact, he should try to determine why all the students did so poorly on this material and if his teaching is part of the reason. In the same way, attribution theory can be applied to other aspects of everyday life, such as affiliation behaviors, in which individuals may try to understand why someone will not go out on a date with them. Besides the achievement and affiliation domains, the search for causes is commonplace in many other domains, such as sports ("Why did your favorite team win or lose?"), politics ("Why did this person win the presidential election?"), economics ("Why did your friend lose his or her job?"), and even in criminal justice ("Why did this person commit this crime?"), with implications for behavior and affect in these domains as well.

This search for cognitive mastery complements the general pleasure-pain principle that is the cornerstone of Freudian and drive theory models of motivation. Attribution theorists do not disavow the empirically documented fact that individuals often strive to increase pleasure and avoid pain, but rather they suggest that there are occasions when individuals will not act in accordance with this general principle. For example, rewards do not always result in increased activity, as shown in the research on intrinsic motivation and the overjustification effect (Lepper, Greene, & Nisbett, 1973). In addition, as Weiner (1986) points out, there are occasions when seeking information (i.e., how other students did on a test, what kinds of material goods your neighbors have) can result in painful negative affect (loss of self-esteem, jealousy, envy). Nevertheless, individuals often do seek out social comparison information in order to evaluate their own capabilities and performances. Akane actively asked other students about their grade on the test in order to help her figure out why she did poorly. Accordingly, we do not always operate under the pleasure-pain principle. The addition of a general goal of cognitive mastery provides another principle that is more in line with the general cognitive perspective of individuals as active and adaptive learners rather than merely passive responders.

The general attributional model is displayed in Figure 3.1, although the model can be much more complex (see Weiner, 1986, 1995). The remainder of this chapter will provide a detailed explanation of this figure, but a quick sketch of the most important points may be helpful as an advance organizer. As shown in the second and third columns of Figure 3.1, perceived causes and the causal dimensions that underlie them are the heart of the model. The perceived causes of an event will be influenced by two general types of antecedent conditions: environmental factors and personal factors (shown in column 1). The influence of these two factors on the generation of attributions is termed the **attribution process** (Kelley & Michela, 1980). Environmental factors include specific information (e.g., if the teacher told Roy and Akane that they did poorly on a test because they did not study hard enough) as well as social norms and information (e.g., how others did on the test, how math is generally perceived in the culture). Personal factors include a variety of schemas and prior beliefs that individuals might hold about the test and about themselves (e.g., both Akane and Roy have perceptions of their math ability based on past experience prior to the quadratic equation test). These two general factors influence the actual attribution individuals will make in terms of whether they attribute their failure to low aptitude, bad luck, a hard test, lack of effort, a bad mood, fatigue, or just about any other reason that could be generated for failure at a test.

It is important to note that these attributions are the causes *perceived* by the individual. They may or may not be the *actual* causes. When Roy concludes that he did not do well on the test because he lacks math aptitude, this perceived attribution is the one that produced a psychological consequence (shame) and behavioral consequence (less future effort in math), regardless of the actual causes of the event (he may not have tried very hard and the test was very difficult). In this way, attribution theory is a phenomenological theory of motivation that gives precedence to the individual's construction of reality, not reality per se, in line with other constructive accounts of cognition and learning (e.g., Bruner, Piaget, Vygotsky). Accordingly, although there may be concerns about the accuracy of individuals' attributions (Nisbett & Wilson, 1977), from a motivational perspective, the accuracy of an attribution is not important in order for an attribution to have psychological and behavioral consequences.

The consequences of attributions for an individual's motivation, affect, and behavior are described as the **attributional process** (Kelley & Michela, 1980). As shown in Figure 3.1, attributions can be categorized along three dimensions (stability, locus, and control), according to Weiner's (1986) model. It is these causal dimensions that have the psychological force to influence expectancy for success and self-efficacy beliefs as well as influence affect and actual behavior (columns 4 and 5 in Figure 3.1). These dimensions are described in more detail later in the chapter, but attributional theory assumes that even though there are an infinite number of actual attributions, they can be categorized along these three dimensions. The stability dimension refers

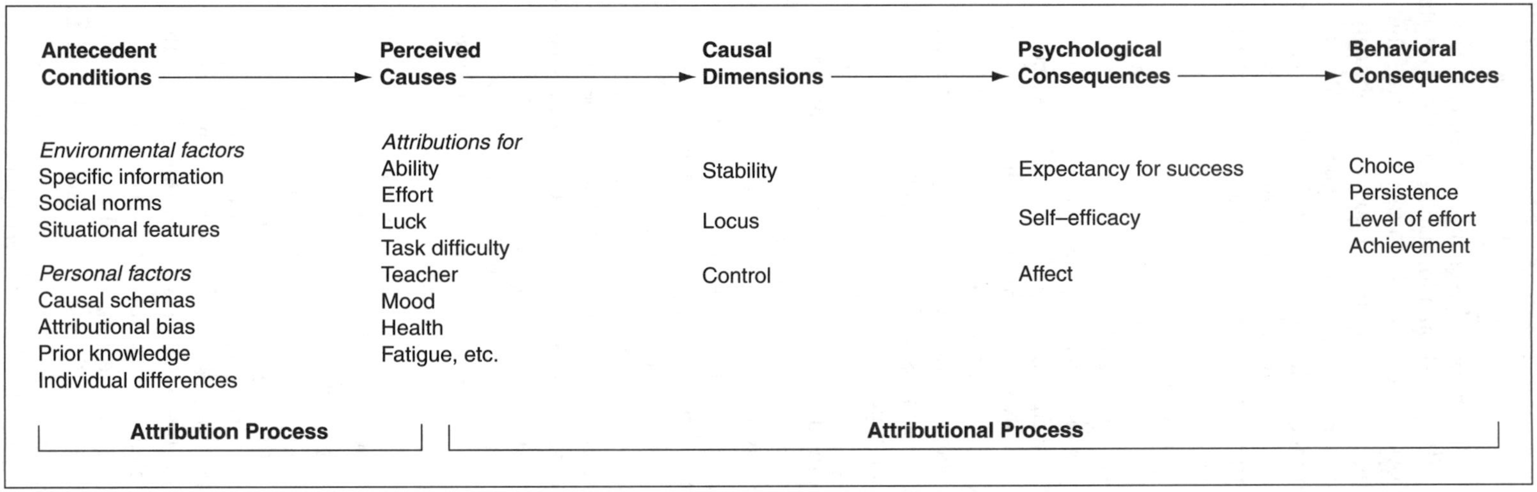

Antecedent Conditions	Perceived Causes	Causal Dimensions	Psychological Consequences	Behavioral Consequences
	Attributions for			
Environmental factors	Ability	Stability	Expectancy for success	Choice
Specific information	Effort			Persistence
Social norms	Luck	Locus	Self–efficacy	Level of effort
Situational features	Task difficulty			Achievement
	Teacher	Control	Affect	
Personal factors	Mood			
Causal schemas	Health			
Attributional bias	Fatigue, etc.			
Prior knowledge				
Individual differences				

Attribution Process

Attributional Process

Figure 3.1 Overview of the general attributional model
Material drawn from Weiner (1986, 1992).

to how stable the attribution is over time and ranges from stable to unstable. Causes can be classified as being internal or external (locus) and as controllable or uncontrollable (control).

Accordingly, in the case of Roy, the normative categorization of low aptitude would be that it is stable (his low aptitude will remain the same over time), that it is internal to Roy, and that it is not controllable by Roy (there is not much he can do to change his math aptitude). Attributional theory and research have shown that it is the stability dimension that is most closely related to expectancy for success (Weiner, 1986). In our example, Roy did poorly on a math test and attributed it to a stable cause (low math aptitude); thus, he should not have a very high expectancy for success for future math tests. Conversely, if Roy had succeeded and attributed his success to high math aptitude—again, a stable cause—then he should expect to do well on the next math test. In contrast, Akane also did not do as well as in the past, but she attributed her performance to a difficult task (external) and she expects to try harder in the future, so her attribution does not seem to have the same debilitating effects. The links between the dimensions of attributions and affect in attributional theory (Weiner, 1986, 1992) suggests that esteem-related affects are related to the locus dimension (e.g., we generally feel pride when we think that something internal to us was responsible for a successful outcome) and that social-related affects such as guilt and shame are related to the controllability dimension (e.g., we often feel guilt if we fail due to something under our control or shame when it is not under our control, as in Roy's case).

These expectancy beliefs and affects are then linked to actual behavioral consequences as the final step in the model. As noted in chapter 2, students with high expectancies and values will tend to choose to pursue a task as well as try harder and persist longer at that task. This engagement should result in higher levels of actual achievement. In the same fashion, positive emotions should result in more motivated behavior such as choice, effort, and persistence, whereas negative emotions should lead the individual to avoid the task in the future. In our example, Roy begins to decrease his effort in the math class after the low grade and his attribution to low math ability. In contrast, Akane attributes her failure to task difficulty and increases her effort and persistence in math. In this way, attributional theory incorporates the pleasure-pain principle as a governor of the linkages between affect and behavior. Given this brief overview of the model, we now turn to a more detailed description of how attributions are formed and their psychological and behavioral consequences.

THE ANTECEDENTS OF ATTRIBUTIONS

As a cognitive model of motivation based on a metaphor of the naive scientist, attribution theory assumes that the individual will use a variety of information sources as data in order to make inferences (attributions) about the causal determinants of behavior. As noted in Figure 3.1, this information can come from two general sources: external cues and information in the environment as well as knowledge and schemas internal to the person. As the individual attempts to assign causality for an event, traditional attribution theory defines the central task of the perceiver as one of detecting covariation between causes and effects (Heider, 1958).

The Role of Environmental Factors

Specific Information and Social Norms

There are a great number of cues and sources of information presented to individuals that help them detect covariation and causality. First, individuals have access to specific information that provides them with direct knowledge of the causes of their behavior. For example, in the case of Roy and Akane doing poorly on the math test, both of them know how hard they studied for the test. If they did not study or prepare for the test at all, this lack of effort may be sufficient to cause the failure. Both of them studied, so they cannot attribute poor performance to a complete lack of effort. Interestingly, Roy and Akane have access to this information about their actual level of effort, but their teacher may not have such ready access. Accordingly, Mr. Kiley may make a different attribution for their performance, lacking the specific information about their level of effort. In fact, Akane wonders if Mr. Kiley thinks that she blew the test off; she worries that Mr. Kiley will think she didn't study for the test. This example highlights an important distinction in attribution theory between the actor (Roy/Akane) and an observer (Mr. Kiley) that we will discuss in more detail later. However, it is important to note that actors generally have more specific information about their behavior and what led up to the outcome than do people who only observe the behavior and the outcome (e.g., Mr. Kiley really doesn't know how much they studied at home, but he may infer little effort for Akane, particularly given her past record of success). At the same time, this example also points out how an actor's own behavior can be external information that the actor can "read off of" to make inferences about causes. In this sense, attribution theory parallels Bem's (1972) self-perception theory and Bandura's (1986) social cognitive model, in which individuals make inferences about the self from observing their own behavior.

Other types of specific information that can influence an individual's attributions include specific feedback from the task or from others. One of the most direct types of information that students receive is teacher feedback. Teacher classroom feedback can influence students' perceptions of their ability and effort in a fairly straightforward manner (Pintrich & Blumenfeld, 1985). Teacher feedback usually stresses effort ("I know you can do better if you try harder"), however, and few ability attributions seem to be made by teachers (see Blumenfeld et al., 1982; Blumenfeld, Hamilton, Bossert, Wessels, & Meece, 1983). If Mr. Kiley were to tell Roy specifically that he did poorly on the math exam because he lacks the aptitude for math, then Roy (in the absence of other information) may accept this attributional statement by the teacher as the major cause of his failure. This attributional feedback about lack of ability may be particularly salient given the infrequency with which teachers seem to make ability attributions. More research is needed on how students integrate the usual and frequently occurring classroom feedback with other more infrequent, yet potentially very salient, feedback (see Blumenfeld et al., 1982).

Information about the task, in particular, task difficulty, can influence the types of attributions that are generated as explanations for the outcome. Weiner and Kukla (1970) provided subjects with information about the relative success or failure of others on a task (ranging from 99% of others were successful to 1% successful). Subjects then rated whether a target person was responsible for success or failure. The results showed that subjects were likely to attribute the outcome to the task when there was consistency between the target's and others' outcome. If most everyone succeeded or failed, then the target's outcome was attributed to an easy or hard task, respectively. In contrast, if the target succeeded when most people failed or failed when most people succeeded, the attribution was made to the person (Weiner, 1992). Continuing with our example, if almost all the students in Roy's math class fail the exam, then he is not likely to attribute his failure to something about himself; rather, he will probably infer that the exam was a very difficult task. If he is the only one to fail the test and everyone else in his class does well, however, then he might see it as an easy task and attribute his failure to some personal characteristic (e.g., lack of aptitude, low skill, low effort, bad mood, etc.). This type of information about the relative difficulty of the task given other students' performance demonstrates how individuals can use social norm information to make attributions (Weiner, 1992).

Consensus, Consistency, and Distinctiveness

Although specific information and social norms do provide cues to the perceiver about what type of attributions to make, Kelley (1967) proposed that all information can be categorized according to several factors that will influence the attribution process. Kelley, working from the intuitive scientist metaphor, believed that the basic question confronting the perceiver was how to assign causality to the person or the environment, reflecting the general Lewinian principle that behavior is a function of both: $B = f(P, E)$. To answer this question, the perceiver uses a process that parallels the analysis of variance (ANOVA) model that researchers use to determine the covariation among independent and dependent variables. In the case of making attributions for an outcome (the dependent measure), there are three factors (the independent variables) that can influence the attribution process: the *distinctiveness* of the entities, the *consensus* across persons, and the *consistency* over time and situations.

The classic example from Kelley (1967) that illustrates the operation of these factors and their influence on the attribution process concerns a movie. If Anne recommends a movie to Roger, and Roger must decide whether to go see the movie, he must determine whether the movie (the entity) is good or if Anne's recommendation should be attributed to something about her (the person). If Roger knows that Anne responds differentially to some movies and not others (high distinctiveness), then Roger will probably infer that it is something about the movie (the entity) that is good. At the same time, if Roger hears from other people besides Anne that the movie is good (high consensus), this consensus across people increases the probability that an entity attribution will be made (the entity—the movie—is good). In the same way, if Anne has gone to see the movie several times and still likes it (high consistency across time) and also has seen it in several different situations (with friends at a theater, watching a video at home alone—high consistency across situations), Roger will tend to make an entity attribution (the movie is good). In this case of high distinctiveness, high consensus, and high consistency, an attribution to the entity—the movie—is most likely to be made. In contrast, if there is low distinctiveness (Anne likes all movies) and low consensus (other people don't like the movie), a person attribution is most likely to be made (e.g., it is something about Anne that makes her like the movie).

These three dimensions of distinctiveness, consensus, and consistency can be applied very readily to the attribution process in classrooms. For example, Ms. Early is a seventh-grade science teacher who is trying to determine why Carla, a student in her first-period class, is misbehaving. Of course, in many situations like this, the effect (misbehavior) may be a function of the interaction between the classroom (entity) and student (person), but depending on the distinctiveness, consensus, and consistency dimensions of the information, different types of attributions may be made. If Carla only misbehaves in Ms. Early's classroom and not other classrooms (high distinctiveness) and always misbehaves in her classroom (high consistency), it increases the probability that something about Ms. Early's classroom may be responsible. If Ms. Early finds that many other students in her first-period class are beginning to misbehave (high consensus across persons), then it seems likely that it is something about her class that is the causal factor. In contrast, if Carla misbehaves often in all classroom situations (low distinctiveness) and no other children misbehave in Ms. Early's class (low consensus), then an attribution might be made to Carla.

Kelley's covariation-ANOVA model is a very rational model of the attribution process and there is evidence that individuals do not always use all three types of information equally (Fiske & Taylor, 1991). In the social psychological literature, it generally appears that consistency information is the most often utilized and consensus the least utilized (Kruglanski, 1977; Major, 1980; Olson, Ellis, & Zanna, 1983). In reviewing research on classroom teachers, expectancies, and attributions, Peterson and Barger (1984) suggest that consistency information is the most salient to teachers. They concluded that teachers are most likely to make attributions for a student's behavior that are consistent with prior beliefs about that individual student. For example, when a normally high-achieving student does well, the teacher is likely to attribute that performance to the student's ability, thereby maintaining prior beliefs. In contrast, if a normally low-achieving student does well on a task, this is inconsistent with prior beliefs and will be attributed to some unstable factor like luck (Clark & Peterson, 1986).

The Role of Personal Factors

The information presented to individuals obviously influences their attributions. However, given the cognitive assumptions built into attribution theory, a number of personal factors also influence the attribution process. We have divided them into four general categories: (a) causal rules and schemas, (b) attributional biases (a certain type of causal schema), (c) prior knowledge, and (d) individual differences (see Figure 3.1).

Causal Rules and Schemas

Causal rules and schemas include the various principles and beliefs that individuals have about causality that they use to make attributions. These rules and schemas are assumed to be learned, stored, and represented cognitively by the individual and can be differentially activated by different situational cues in the environment. First, there are some basic principles that individuals seem to use to establish causality, and these principles seem to be established at a fairly young age, by about age 3 (Kassin & Pryor, 1985; White, 1988). Fiske and Taylor (1991) suggest that there are six general principles that individuals have learned to use to judge causality:

1. *Causes must precede effects.* Even children as young as 3 know that events that occur after the target event cannot be causal factors for the target event. In our example of Roy failing the math exam, the fact that he had a fight with his girlfriend 2 weeks after he took the math test cannot be a cause of his failure on the exam.

2. *Events that share temporal contiguity with the target event are more likely to be seen as causal factors.* If Roy had a fight with his girlfriend the night before the math exam, he might readily attribute his failure to this emotional event.

3. *Events that are spatially contiguous are more likely to be linked in cause-and-effect relations.* If the school band is playing outside the classroom window the day of the math exam, Roy might attribute his failure to that distraction, in contrast to the case in which the band is playing on the football field, quite a distance from the classroom.

4. *Perceptually salient stimuli are more likely to be seen as causal than stimuli that are in the visual background.* Salient events like a fight with a girlfriend the night before an exam might be seen as more causal than mundane events like not keeping up with the daily math homework.

5. *Causes resemble effects. Individuals tend to attribute "big" effects to "big" causes and "little" effects to "little" causes* (Fiske & Taylor, 1991). In Roy's case, a big event like failing a final exam and failing the course might be attributed to a more traumatic event like a romantic breakup or his parent's divorce than "smaller" events like not keeping up with the work.

6. *Representative causes are attributed to effects.* Individuals often compare a current outcome to similar outcomes and then infer that the same cause of the related events are determinants of the current event (Fiske & Taylor, 1991). For example, Roy may have failed math exams in a previous course that was taught by a poor teacher. This leads him to infer that his present teacher is also poor and that is why he failed the math test.

Besides these general causal principles that individuals might use to make attributions, several general causal schemas can be used to make causal inferences. These schemas may be used when there is not complete information available in terms of the three general sources of distinctiveness, consistency, and consensus. These schemas are general beliefs held by individuals that help guide their information processing in terms of attributional search and inference. In particular, they are often used when there have not been multiple occasions of the event, such as surprising events (e.g., failure at a task when success is the norm) or novel situations (Weiner, 1992). First, as Heider (1958) proposed, there is a general *compensatory* schema whereby individuals believe that one cause can compensate for the absence or weakness of another cause. In the achievement context, it is generally assumed that effort can compensate for ability and vice versa (Weiner, 1992). So, in Roy's case, most people will believe that if he has low math aptitude, higher levels of effort should compensate for his low ability and lead to a better outcome than low effort coupled with low aptitude.

Kelley (1972) proposed two specific causal schemas that help individuals make causal inferences when there is not complete information available. The **multiple sufficient** and **multiple necessary schemas** can be used to determine causality and also predict effects given the existence of different causes (Weiner, 1992). Both schemas refer to the case where there is an effect (E) that is related to two causes (A and B). The multiple sufficient schema describes the *disjunctive* relation among A, B, and E; that is, for E to occur, only A *or* B have to be present. In contrast, in the multiple necessary schema, both A *and* B have to be present for E to occur—the *conjunctive* relation. In the achievement context, aptitude and effort are often seen as two causes that can lead to success or failure.

For example, Kun and Weiner (1973) provided adult subjects with information about a target's success or failure, the ease or difficulty of the task, and the target's ability or effort level. The subjects were then asked to rate how certain they were that the "other" cause, which they did not have information about (either ability or effort level), was present or not. In success situations in which the task was difficult, students who were told that the target had high ability (or high effort) also rated that the target had high effort (or high ability). In this case, the multiple necessary schema was used by the subjects; both effort and ability were seen as necessary for success on a difficult task. However, in the case of success at an easy task, subjects were unlikely to judge that the compensatory cause (effort or ability) was present. In this case, the multiple sufficient schema was invoked and the subjects assumed that just high effort (or high ability) was sufficient for success at an easy task (Weiner, 1992). For the failure outcome, the results were somewhat the reverse. If the target failed at a difficult task with low ability (or low effort), then the subjects were not likely to rate that low effort (or low ability) was present as well (multiple sufficient schema). In contrast, for failure at an easy task with low ability (or low effort), subjects were likely to rate that low effort (or low ability) also was a cause (multiple necessary schema). As Weiner (1992) points out,

> One is reminded of the saying that a chain is only as strong as its weakest link; that is, all components must be strong for "success," and the absence of strength in any of the sub-parts is sufficient for "failure." It therefore appears that the attributions for success and failure might be governed by somewhat different psychological rules. (p. 242)

Attributional Biases

Research on the attribution process suggests that there are a number of schemas or inference rules that people may use to make attributions that are often incorrect or can lead to biases on the part of the perceiver (Fiske & Taylor, 1991; Nisbett & Ross, 1980). Table 3.1 lists some of the common strategies and how they might be used by both students and teachers in different situations.

1. *The fundamental attribution error.* This common inference error involves the attribution of others' behavior to dispositional or personal factors, ignoring situational factors that might be partially or even more causally related to the outcome (Heider, 1958; Nisbett & Ross, 1980; Ross, 1977). This bias has been documented in a large number of experimental studies in which the situation clearly determines the behavior, but observers will still make an attribution to the target's personality or attitudes. For example, in the classic study by Jones and Harris (1967), subjects were asked to read essays or listen to speeches on controversial issues (defending Castro's Cuba, legalizing marijuana). The subjects were told that the writers or speakers were assigned to present one side or the other. Nevertheless, the subjects still attributed the opinions expressed in the essay or speech to the disposition of the writer or speaker, not to the fact that they had been assigned to write from that point of view (Ross & Nisbett, 1991). As shown in the examples in Table 3.1, this could happen easily in the classroom context, where teachers might be likely to attribute a student's behavior to something about the student instead of the classroom.

Table 3.1 Common Attributional Biases from the Student and the Teacher Perspectives

Attribution	Student Perspective	Teacher Perspective
Fundamental attribution error Attribute others' behavior to a disposition or trait	Student perceives all teacher behavior as function of a disposition "Ms. Baker is always mean." "Mr. Smith is prejudiced against minorities and women."	Teacher perceives all student behavior as a function of disposition "Sam is just a very lazy person. He never tries hard." "Sally has no aptitude for science."
Actor-observer perspective Attribute others' behavior to disposition, but own behavior to situation	Student perceives his behavior as a function of situation, but attributes teacher's behavior to a disposition "I hit him because he was bugging me, but now you are punishing me because you don't like me and always pick on me."	Teacher perceives his behavior as a function of classroom, but attributes students' behavior to disposition "You are a very aggressive boy and I'm just trying to keep control of my class."
Self-serving bias Accept personal responsibility for success, deny responsibility for failure	Student perceives her successes are due to her behavior, but attributes failures to other factors "I did well in math because I'm smart at that, but poorly in English because the teacher is terrible when she teaches English."	Teacher perceives her success as due to her behavior, but attributes failures to other factors "I did a great unit in math, but the students aren't motivated to study English literature."
Self-centered bias Regardless of success or failure, accept more personal responsibility for a jointly determined outcome	Student will perceive that he is more responsible for an outcome, even when it is due to his and others' behavior "I did more of the work on this project than all the other students in my small group."	Teacher will perceive that he is more responsible for an outcome even when it is due to his and other's behavior "Third-period class discussion was excellent. I'm a really good facilitator of discussions."
False consensus effect Assume that your beliefs and behavior are typical of most people	Student perceives that her beliefs or behavior are representative of most other students "I hate math and most girls hate it just like me." "All the other kids are cheating, so I can too."	Teacher assumes that her beliefs or behaviors are representative of most other teachers "Like all the other teachers in this building, I think the biggest problem is that the kids are just not motivated."

103

2. *Actor-observer perspective.* This bias refers to the propensity for individuals to make differential attributions depending on their perspective as an actor in the situation or as an observer and is related to the fundamental attribution error. Attribution research has shown that actors often attribute their own behavior to situational features, whereas observers will attribute actors' behavior to some personal or dispositional characteristic of the actor (Jones & Nisbett, 1972; Weiner, 1992). In a classroom situation, this bias would lead students to make dispositional attributions about the teacher and teachers to make dispositional attributions about the students (see examples in Table 3.1).

There is some empirical support for both a perceptual and an informational explanation for this bias (Fiske & Taylor, 1991). The perceptual explanation suggests that when an observer sees another person doing something, the most salient stimulus is the person acting, not the situation, which becomes background to the observer. In contrast, from the actor's perspective of the situation, the features of the situation are most salient, not her or his own behavior. Given these differences in perception and attention, actor-observer differences will arise (Storms, 1973). The informational explanation suggests that actors have access to a great deal of information about themselves, including their thoughts, feelings, and intentions in the situation, as well as information about how they have acted in similar situations in the past. This information allows actors to note how differences in the current situation might produce differences in their behavior. In contrast, an observer does not have access to this information and often does not see an actor across different situations and so may make a dispositional attribution (Eisen, 1979; Fiske & Taylor, 1991).

3. *Self-serving or hedonic bias.* This inference error is also called the ego or self-enhancement bias, the ego-defensiveness or self-protective bias, and the beneffectance bias (Weiner, 1992). It refers to the propensity for individuals to take personal responsibility for successful outcomes (a self-enhancing bias) and deny responsibility for failure outcomes (a self-protective bias). For example, when you win at tennis, it is because you are much better than your opponent, but if you lose, it is because of bad luck or poor court conditions. This self-serving bias has been empirically demonstrated in a number of different contexts including athletics, politics, gambling, and classrooms (Mullen & Riordan, 1988; Weiner, 1992) as well as cross-culturally (Fletcher & Ward, 1988).

There may be several reasons why people make these types of self-serving attributions. First, it seems likely that most individuals want to look good, and these attributions can be used to manage others' impressions of them. Second, as suggested in the hedonic bias label, these self-serving attributions can act to protect individuals' egos and sense of self-worth in keeping with the pleasure-pain principle. Finally, besides these motivational mechanisms, there are cognitive or rational explanations that suggest that most people expect to succeed (particularly the oft-tested college student who has a history of success). They also strive to succeed, and when they do succeed, are more likely to recall other instances of success when they had control and, therefore, attribute the current success to their own behavior (Fiske & Taylor, 1991; Weiner, 1992).

In the classroom context, the research is mixed regarding the propensity of teachers to make self-serving attributions (e.g., it is my superior teaching when students do well, but it is their lack of motivation when they do poorly) for their students' performance (Clark & Peterson, 1986; Peterson & Barger, 1984). A number of studies (Beckman, 1970; Brandt, Hayden, & Brophy, 1975; Johnson, Feigenbaum, & Weiby, 1964; Wiley &

Eskilson, 1978) have shown that teachers do make ego-enhancing attributions. However, as Peterson & Barger (1984) have pointed out, three of these studies were experimental studies (all except Wiley & Eskilson) with preservice teachers or psychology
students assigned to teach a "fictitious" student who was then either successful or unsuccessful. In contrast, studies by Ames (1975) and Ross, Bierbrauer, and Polly (1974),
in which college students were assigned to be teachers or students and actually interacted with each other, showed that the "teachers" were more likely to attribute success
to the student and failure to their teaching, a counterdefensive attribution (see Clark &
Peterson, 1986). It seems that the different results can be explained by the presence or
absence of a "real" student and face-to-face interactions between teacher and student. In
the presence of real students and actual interactions between teachers and students (as
would be the case in classrooms), the studies show that teachers will be more likely to
make a counterdefensive attribution.

There is evidence that people are more likely to make a self-enhancing attribution
and accept credit for success than they are to make a self-protective attribution and deny
responsibility for failure (Fiske & Taylor, 1991; Miller & Ross, 1975). In fact, attributing failure to some internal characteristic that an individual has control over can be
adaptive. If the individual fails and attributes it to poor effort or lack of a learnable skill,
then it is possible to actually change effort levels or attempt to learn the skill and increase the probability of success for the future. In contrast, if individuals continually
protect their self-worth by making attributions for failure to external and uncontrollable
events and even engage in some self-defeating behaviors (e.g., staying up late and partying before an exam), in the long run this type of attributional pattern and behavior is
not adaptive. Accordingly, whereas the self-serving bias can help to maintain self-worth,
it also has costs associated with it (see Covington, 1992).

4. Self-centered bias. In many situations, an outcome is determined jointly by the individual and the situation, including other people. The self-centered bias occurs when individuals take more responsibility for an outcome, regardless of the actual success or failure.
For example, the self-centered bias would be operating when both husband and wife think
that they do more than half of the housework or two co-authors both think they were more
responsible for the research and therefore deserve to be first author on the resulting empirical article. As shown in Table 3.1, in the classroom context where most behavior is
probably a function of both teacher and student, this bias would lead the teacher to believe
that he was more responsible for a good discussion, rather than the fact that the students
were also prepared and willing to discuss the class material. The other example in Table 3.1
may arise more frequently, given the current popularity of small-group instruction,
whereby students, operating under the self-centered bias, may claim more responsibility
for a group project for themselves rather than recognizing the contributions of others.

5. False consensus effect. As noted previously, one of the sources of information that
individuals use in making attributions is consensus concerning others' performance or
behavior. The false consensus effect occurs when individuals come to see their behavior
or attitude as typical, as representing how most other people would respond in the same
situation. There are a number of viable explanations of this effect, including a tendency
for individuals to seek out and affiliate with others who share similar views; a propensity
to focus on their own opinions and ignore or discount other, divergent views; a tendency
to interpret new situations in light of previous beliefs and predetermined courses of

action; and a need to see their own beliefs as good, right, and typical, and so they maintain these beliefs to preserve their self-esteem (Fiske & Taylor, 1991). In the classroom or school context, this type of bias could result in teachers who share similar views on instruction to seek each other out and reinforce for each other the "correctness" of their beliefs in contrast to those of other teachers or administrators. This particular situation could result in rather rigid beliefs about students or instructional practices that could impede school change and improvement.

Prior Knowledge and Individual Differences

Along with these biases, prior knowledge and individual differences can also influence the attribution process. Both prior knowledge and individual differences represent, to some extent, exceptions to the general "laws" or principles of attribution theory. Most social psychologists concerned with attribution theory have focused on the general principles just discussed in the previous section, whereas personality psychologists have been more concerned with the individual differences in the attribution process.

Prior Knowledge and Beliefs.   First, in terms of prior knowledge, the original models of the attribution process (e.g., Heider, 1958; Kelley, 1972) proposed that the various attribution processes such as use of distinctiveness, consistency, and consensus information and causal schemas were "content-free" processes that would operate in any domain. However, more recent research suggests that individuals have prior knowledge about specific domains that they use to guide the attribution process (Fiske & Taylor, 1991). Hilton and Slugoski (1986) have proposed an abnormal conditions attribution model that suggests that people only look to explain events when the outcome is unexpected. In these situations, individuals will search for the conditions that gave rise to this "abnormal" event and attribute the event to these abnormal conditions. In addition, this model assumes that people have a great deal of prior knowledge about "scripted" events—those situations in which there is a fairly high degree of consensus about normal behavior in that situation (e.g., a script for eating at a restaurant in terms of the order of events). If something out of the ordinary happens that results in a deviation from the script, observers will search for the conditions that gave rise to this unexpected deviation and attribute the outcome to these conditions.

For example, in a school context, teachers and most students, except for very young children perhaps, have a wealth of general knowledge about classrooms, instruction, and learning that they can activate to explain classroom events. This prior knowledge makes for more automatic processing and reduces the load on information processing by limiting the attributional search to the causes that are most likely to be operative, even though there are an infinite number of causes for any classroom event. In addition, many of the activities in a classroom are scripted and both teachers and students know what is expected. Deviations from the norms of the script can lead to an attributional search on the part of the teacher or students for the causes that give rise to an abnormal event, such as a normally easy-going and pleasant teacher "losing her cool" and shouting at the students. In this abnormal case, the students may be likely to attribute the shouting to a personal problem (bad mood, bad day) of the teacher, or, perhaps, to something they actually did to deserve such behavior because the teacher does not normally shout at them. This would be in contrast to a teacher who shouts and screams at the students all the time. In this case, the students would be less likely to attribute this teacher's behavior to something they did, and most likely would attribute it to the teacher and his personality or usual instructional behavior.

These scripts are for general knowledge about schools, classrooms, teachers, and students. However, in a similar fashion, individuals can have personal knowledge or scripts or self-schemas about themselves that represent consistent, individual differences in the way they perceive and respond to events. For example, most individuals have perceptions of their competence to do different tasks and have self-concepts about different domains, as discussed in chapter 2. This type of prior self-knowledge can influence the types of attributions that individuals will make in different situations (Ames & Felker, 1979). For example, if a student has a relatively high self-perception of competence in math, yet encounters a failure situation occasionally, this student may be more likely to attribute the failure to a hard task or lack of effort, not to lack of ability, in contrast to a student with a generally low perception of competence. In addition, individual differences can extend beyond personal knowledge and conscious self-schemas to particular ways individuals have of interpreting events that can lead to differences in the attribution process.

Individual Differences.   One of the most consistent individual differences that is related to the types of attributions individuals might make is **locus of control** (Rotter, 1966). This construct from social learning theory refers to the tendency of some people, labeled *internals,* to perceive a contingency between their behavior and reinforcement, and others, labeled *externals,* to perceive that there is not a strong link between their behavior and reinforcement. In terms of how this individual difference might influence the attribution process, internals would be most likely to make internal types of attributions given an outcome, whereas externals would be more likely to make external types of attributions. Although there has been a great deal of research on the locus-of-control construct in general and in motivation and education specifically (e.g., Crandall, Katkovsky, & Crandall, 1965), the general locus-of-control construct has been superseded by other constructs that represent a more fine-grained analysis of the role of control beliefs (e.g., Connell, 1985; Peterson et al., 1993; Skinner, Chapman, & Baltes, 1988b). In addition, Weiner (1986) has shown in both logical and empirical analyses that the locus-of-control construct systematically confounds two dimensions that need to be separated theoretically and practically: one regarding the internality–externality and the other concerning the controllability–uncontrollability of an event. Given this more current research, there is little utility in continuing to use the general locus-of-control construct in motivational research.

Learned helplessness theory and research (Peterson et al., 1993) is a more recent formulation of the importance of controllability. Attribution theory, as formulated by Heider, Kelley, and Weiner, is concerned with the development of general principles of social psychology and social cognition. As such, it has not been concerned with individual differences. In contrast, the work on learned helplessness theory grows out of the interest of personality and clinical psychologists in individual differences that reliably predict adaptive behavior. The learned helplessness model assumes that individuals search for causal explanations of events (especially "bad" events like school failure, interpersonal problems with friends or lovers, poor health, loss in sports) and that these causal explanations and the dimensions that underlie them influence expectations about future events. In turn, these future expectations determine behavioral reactions such as passivity, affect, anxiety, and depression (Peterson et al., 1993). The learned helplessness model is basically the same as that displayed in the attributional model of Figure 3.1.

The main difference between the two models is that learned helplessness theory proposes that there is an individual difference construct, called **explanatory style**, formerly called attributional style (see Peterson & Seligman, 1984), that influences the types of causal explanations that individuals will make in different situations. Explanatory style refers to a habitual way of explaining events that is a cognitive characteristic of the individual (Peterson et al., 1993). This construct is often assessed with the Attributional Style Questionnaire (ASQ) (see Peterson, Semmel et al., 1982) whereby individuals are asked to explain why 12 common events (6 with good and 6 with bad outcomes) might happen to them and then rate the causes in terms of internality–externality, stability–instability, and globality–specificity. The research on the ASQ suggests that there are consistent individual differences that emerge from this questionnaire, with some individuals much more likely to attribute common events to internal, stable, and global causes.

Other research has shown that these stable, individual differences can then predict the types of attributions that people might make in a new situation (Peterson et al., 1993). In a learning theory sense, the individual difference of explanatory style is "generalized" to a new situation and the person interprets the new situation in terms of her explanatory style. In a cognitive, schema theoretic view, explanatory style is a particular type of prior knowledge or belief that is activated in the new situation and then guides information processing and the attribution process. In the classroom situation, if a student has an explanatory style that explains his school failures to internal, stable, and global causes (e.g., "I'm just generally stupid and I can't change it"), then when he goes to a new school (transition to middle school, high school, or college) and has a failure experience, he will likely make the same attribution, even when there may be very strong situational determinants (e.g., the new school is much harder).

In sum, both environmental and personal factors influence the attribution process. Attribution theory, based in social psychology, stresses the situational nature of attributions and considers both the features of the situation and the general cognitive rules and schemas that individuals use as possible influences on the actual attributions that will be made in a specific situation. In addition, research from more of a personality and individual difference perspective has suggested that there may be stable, individual differences in terms of self-beliefs and explanatory style that can influence the attribution process. Application 3.1, later in the chapter, highlights some of the strategies based on the attribution process that teachers can use in their classrooms.

We now move on to a discussion of the attributional process (see Figure 3.1) and an examination of the motivational consequences of making certain types of attributions.

THE CONSEQUENCES OF ATTRIBUTIONS

As shown in Figure 3.1, the outcome of the attribution process is an attribution about the perceived cause of the event. The model assumes that given a particular outcome for an event (success or failure on a test, winning or losing in sports, positive or negative interpersonal interaction), an individual will search for the perceived causes of the outcome. This is a crucial step in the model, because without an attribution being made regarding the perceived causes, the remaining steps in the model (see Figure 3.1) would not be followed. The attribution process we have described thus far concerns the *content* of the attribution that might be made given the various environmental and personal factors operating in a specific situation.

Conditions That Foster Spontaneous Attributional Search

The attribution process does not actually specify *if* and *when* an attribution might be made at all. There is some controversy over this issue of spontaneous attributional thinking in the attribution literature (cf. Smith & Miller, 1983; Weiner, 1985a, 1986). In general, critics note that many of the studies were experimental studies that specifically asked for subjects to make attributions about an actual lab-induced event or to make attributions for an imagined or hypothetical event. The experiments used both open-ended questionnaires, whereby subjects generated their own attributions, and rating scales, whereby specific attributions were listed by the experimenter and rated by the subjects. Critics note that all of these studies were reactive and claim that the attributions were elicited by the experimental procedures but did not reflect individuals' actual causal thinking about the event (Weiner, 1986). In fact, some researchers claim that people did very little spontaneous attributional thinking in real life and that attributions were of little importance (Smith & Miller, 1983).

Weiner (1985a, 1986) has summarized the research on the spontaneous use of attributions and concludes that there is good empirical evidence that individuals do make attributions in real-life situations. He bases his conclusions on the results of studies that used methodologies quite different from the classic experimental studies in which subjects were asked to rate a list of attributions. These methodologies included the analysis of written material such as newspaper articles, reports, letters, diaries, and journals for attributional statements. On any daily newspaper sports pages, it is likely that there will be at least several attributional statements about why a team won or lost or why an individual player did well or poorly. In fact, Peterson and colleagues (Peterson et al., 1993) suggest that professional athletes' attributional statements about their past successes and failures are related to their future performance, with those attributing their success to skill doing much better than those who attribute it to luck. Two other procedures are more experimental in nature and involve the coding of verbal statements from think-aloud protocols (subjects are asked to talk out loud about what they are thinking or feeling as they do a task) and indirect measures whereby students are asked to do a free recall task or a sentence completion task under the guise of a nonattributional experiment. In all three cases, there is a great deal of evidence that individuals do engage in spontaneous attributional search and make attributional statements (Weiner, 1986).

There are, however, certain conditions when individuals are more likely to engage in attributional search. As Weiner (1986) notes, if an event is unexpected, an attributional search will often occur. In keeping with the general cognitive perspective, individuals have prior knowledge, beliefs, and expectations about what will happen in a situation in general (scripts) and what might happen to them (personal expectations). For example, after a few years in school, most students have self-perceptions of their competence about doing schoolwork and expectations about future success and failure. If these personal expectations are violated, as in the case of a usually high-achieving student failing an exam (e.g., Akane not doing well on the math exam), then it is more likely that this student will consciously search for the causes of this failure. In contrast, if the student gets a high grade as expected based on past experience, that student is not likely to engage in attributional search. For example, a college freshman who has had an excellent high school record enrolls at an elite university and in the first semester suddenly is getting grades of C and lower in all classes. In this situation, it is likely that this student will engage in a great deal of attributional search about personal ability to succeed at this university.

In a sports context, the expectancy disconfirmation principle also holds and there is more likely to be an attributional search when a favored team loses or an underdog wins (Weiner, 1986). In a social context, if someone violates the norms of a well-accepted script (e.g., talking out loud during a lecture), there is a higher probability of an attributional search for why the individual did not conform than for why everyone else did follow the script and kept quiet. In the same way, in the context of interpersonal attraction, consider two people who have been dating regularly every weekend for a semester. If one partner suddenly claims to not be available this coming weekend, this will probably lead to an attributional search by the other partner for the perceived causes of the rejection. In contrast, the rejected partner probably did not engage in attributional search the previous weekends when the couple did go out as usual.

Weiner (1986) also notes that the studies of spontaneous attributional search suggest that a negative outcome to an event, regardless of prior expectations, will likely lead to an attributional search. Accordingly, students are more likely to search for the perceived causes of failure than they are for the causes of success. In the same fashion, teachers are probably more likely to make an attributional search for a lesson that did not go well rather than for a lesson that went smoothly. This reaction to failure is adaptive; if individuals understand the causes for failure, they can attempt to do something about them. Students can change their effort or learning strategies, and teachers can change their lesson plans and attempt something different next time.

Besides these two general conditions for the activation of attributional search, Weiner (1986) suggests that there may be other conditions that increase the likelihood of an attributional search. There is a need for more research in general, and experimental research, in particular, to support these conditions. One condition put forth is whether an event or outcome has great interest or importance to the individual. For example, a poor grade on one of the many weekly worksheets in a math class might not generate an attributional search because it does not carry the same importance as a poor grade on the final exam for the class.

Another occasion when attributions might be more likely is in a relatively new situation in which the individual does not have a great deal of prior knowledge or fully formed expectations. In this case, attribution theory would assume that a general cognitive mastery goal would be operative and the individual would be searching to understand why things are happening and searching for the causes of these events. For example, when students move to a new school or make a transition to a new school level (e.g., middle school to high school, high school to college), they might be more likely to make more attributions given their unfamiliarity with certain aspects of the new environment. One of the authors of this book has noted an increase in his own attributional searches when he travels outside the United States. He often analyzes everyday interactions with shopkeepers, waiters, and others to understand the way he was treated ("Are they treating me this way because I'm an American or because of something I've done that has violated the local norms, or is this the way they treat everyone here in this culture?"), In contrast, in the United States, he doesn't give these common interactions a second thought and certainly doesn't do an attributional search to understand the interaction.

In conclusion, there is ample evidence from a number of studies employing a range of methodologies for the existence of spontaneous attributional search. Individuals do engage in a cognitive search to understand the causes of the outcomes of different events. Moreover, this attributional search is most likely to occur when the event is unexpected, negative, or important to the individual. We now move on to discuss the content of attributions.

The Content of Attributional Thinking

As Weiner (1986) points out, there is a large body of work on the types of attributions people make for any number of outcomes, including success and failure in achievement contexts (e.g., tests, sporting events, games, occupational performance) and more general situations such as interpersonal attraction (acceptance or rejection of an invitation to go to a movie), political elections, health issues, affluence and poverty, and criminal justice problems. Table 3.2 displays some of the common attributions for several different domains. These listings are not meant to cover all of the possible causes of any event offered by any individual. In fact, there are probably an infinite number of possible causes for the outcome of an event. In addition, it is important to note that the causes for one domain might vary significantly from another domain (e.g., government policies as the cause of poverty is a reasonable attribution, but it is unlikely that policy would be invoked as a cause of an individual's failure on an achievement test). At the same time, there is some overlap across domains, so that poor health might be used to explain failure in an achievement situation as well as to explain interpersonal attraction or wealth/poverty (Weiner, 1986).

Table 3.2 Summary of Perceived Causes in Different Domains

Achievement	Interpersonal Attraction	Wealth/Poverty	Health/Illness
Aptitude	Physical attractiveness	Family background	Heredity
Skill	Personal style	Intelligence	Personality
Stable effort	Physical hygiene	Effort	Family history
Unstable effort	Personality	Schooling	Life stress
Task difficulty	Status	Government policies	Fatigue
Luck	Timing and availability	Prejudice and discrimination	Good/poor habits
Interest	Health	Luck	Weather
Mood	Mood	Health	Exposure to germs
Fatigue	Wealth		Luck
Health			
Help from others			

From *An Attributional Theory of Motivation and Emotion* by B. Weiner, 1986, New York: Springer-Verlag. Copyright © 1986 by Springer-Verlag New York, Inc. Adapted by permission.

In terms of achievement motivation, early research on attributions often had exper-imental subjects rate only four causes—ability, effort, task difficulty, and luck—as rea-sons for success and failure. As more research on the role of attributions was done, experimenters began to use more inclusive lists with up to 8 or 10 attributions to be rated, or used a free-response format whereby the subjects were asked to generate their own attributions. The studies that used these open-ended and more inclusive method-ologies generated more potential causes of achievement success or failure, but all of them included the original four (ability, effort, task characteristics, and luck) as well as intrinsic motivation, teacher competence, and mood (Weiner, 1986). Cross-cultural studies have also found that ability and effort are perceived as common causes of suc-cess and failure in most countries. For example, Triandis (1972) found this to be the case in American, Japanese, and Greek cultures; India being the only exception of the four he examined. Miller (1984) found that Hindus in India were less likely than Americans to give dispositional or trait attributions for why people engaged in prosocial or deviant behavior. Fletcher and Ward (1988), however, in their review of cross-cultural research on attributions, suggest that the content of most attributions is somewhat similar across Western and non-Western cultures such as Japan and India. Beyond the content of at-tributions, what may differ in Western and non-Western cultures is how these different attributions are classified in terms of the dimensions. From an attributional perspective, these dimensions are the most important for motivation.

The Motivational Dimensions of Attributions

The list of causes for success and failure provides a description of the content of attribu-tions, but these attributions, in and of themselves, are not particularly motivational in na-ture. In other words, it is not clear what attributions contribute to the motivational dynamics of behavior; that is, how do attributions "motivate" behavior? In attributional theory, the motivational "push" of attributions derives from their classification into di-mensions based on an analysis of the causal structure of attributions. These dimensions provide the psychological significance and meaning to the simple attributions. The prop-erties of a dimension in terms of its stability, internality, and controllability have implica-tions for students' expectancy beliefs and emotions, and expectancy beliefs and emotions are implicated in almost all types of motivated behavior.

In addition, the dimensional analysis of attributions has several advantages for the-ory building. First, if there are a small number of dimensions that capture the important aspects of attributions, there is parsimony, particularly given the infinite number of at-tributions. Moreover, although there are a number of different and unique attributions that can be made in different domains (i.e., achievement versus affiliation), the dimen-sional analysis allows for the comparison of these "phenotypically" different attributions along "genotypically" similar lines. This increases the power of the theory as it can be shown that the dimensions work in the same ways across very different domains and given very different actual attributions (Weiner, 1986, 1995).

The analysis of the causal structure of attributions has proceeded in two general ways: logical analysis and empirical analysis (Weiner, 1986). Logical analysis appeared first and was a part of the early conceptual work in this area (Weiner et al., 1971). Logical analysis was based on attributional researchers' examination of different attributions and subsequent placement of them in different categories or along dimensions (e.g., an internal versus external cause) based on theoretical considerations. Empirical analysis appeared later in research on attributional theory and involved the use of factor analysis and multidimensional scaling to determine how individuals' ratings of attributions actually clustered together (Weiner, 1986). In both the rational and empirical analyses, a fair amount of consensus has emerged about the importance of three general dimensions of causal structure: (a) a **locus dimension** concerning how internal versus external a cause is perceived as, (b) a **stability dimension** concerning how stable versus unstable a cause is perceived as, and (c) a **controllability dimension** concerning how controllable versus uncontrollable a cause is perceived as (Weiner, 1986). Although there is some disagreement about the exact nature of these three dimensions, there is agreement that each of the dimensions has implications for individuals' motivation and affect.

The Locus Dimension

The locus-of-causality dimension concerns whether a cause is perceived as being internal or external to the individual. For example, ability and effort are both classified as internal causes, whereas task difficulty and luck are classified as external causes. This basic distinction between causes that are internal versus external corresponds to the central question in attribution theory regarding the relative influence of personal and environmental factors on an individual's behavior (Heider, 1958).

Historically, the most common application of this dimension as a psychological construct was the work of Rotter (1966) on what he called locus of control. Rotter was a social learning theorist who was interested in individuals' perceptions of the contingency of reinforcement on their own behavior. People were classified as internals if they believed that the rewards or reinforcement they received was due to something they did (e.g., their own effort) or something about them (e.g., their ability); that is, reinforcement was contingent on their own behavior. In contrast, externals were individuals who perceived reinforcement as somehow outside their control and due to factors such as luck, fate, or other people. In the classroom setting, internal control students would believe that their grades depended on their own ability, skill, or effort, whereas external control students would believe that their grades were just a function of luck, or the teacher, or some other external factor. Teachers can be internal or external as well. Internal teachers would believe that their students' learning is under their control to some extent and that their skill and effort can make a difference for students. In contrast, external teachers would believe that there is little they can do to influence students' learning, that luck, or chance, or other external factors (e.g., parental and home environment) are the major determinants of student learning.

Research on this construct of locus of control was incredibly popular in psychology in the 1960s through the 1970s, with probably thousands of studies done on both the antecedents and consequences of locus of control, not just in educational settings, but also physical and mental health, sports, business organizations, and so on. A similar construct to locus of control was proposed by de Charms (1968), who suggested that people were **origins** (internal locus of control) or **pawns** (external locus of control). More recently, in social cognitive theory, Bandura (1986) proposed a construct he labeled **outcome expectation** that is very similar to control. Connell and Skinner and their colleagues (Connell, 1985; Skinner, 1996; Skinner et al., 1988a, 1988b) have revived interest in the nature of control beliefs and have specified a number of important distinctions about different kinds of control beliefs (see chapter 6).

The Stability Dimension

The locus-of-control construct has a very intuitive appeal and can be readily applied to our own lives. However, early on in research on attribution theory, Weiner and colleagues (Weiner et al., 1971) proposed that the locus-of-control construct really confounds two different dimensions of causality, namely, internality and stability. Weiner and his colleagues reasoned that there were some important differences regarding the stability of different internal causes. For example, ability may be seen as relatively stable, whereas effort can vary across situations. Although both ability and effort are internal causes and should have similar consequences under Rotter's theory, attribution research has shown that they do not have the same consequences (Weiner, 1986). For example, if an individual fails at a task, it is better for future expectancies to attribute it to lack of effort than to lack of ability. Both logical analysis and empirical data supported the need for a second dimension of stability beyond the locus dimension.

The stability dimension refers to whether the cause is fixed and stable or whether it is variable and unstable across situations and over time. In a personality psychology tradition, stability refers to whether the attribution would be considered a trait of the person or a more statelike or situational aspect of the person. Figure 3.2 displays how attributions could be classified according to both locus and stability. The first and original scheme (top part of Figure 3.2) was a simple classification of the four main causes investigated by attribution researchers. Ability and effort were both classified as internal, as would be expected under Rotter's locus-of-control theory, but these two attributions differ in terms of stability, with effort usually seen as unstable and ability as stable. In contrast, task difficulty and luck were categorized as external (as in Rotter's theory), but luck is usually perceived as unstable and task difficulty as stable. This was the original classification scheme used by Weiner and his colleagues in their early experimental work.

It soon became clear, however, that these four general attributions, or at least their original labels, could be somewhat misleading in terms of the locus-by-stability classification scheme. More recent work suggests that the terms shown in the bottom half of Figure 3.2 are a more accurate reflection of the naive phenomenology of people (Weiner, 1986). Accordingly, *aptitude,* signifying a stable, unchangeable, internal characteristic of an individual, is a better term than *ability*. In contrast, *skills,* which connotes abilities that can be learned over time, is a better term to represent internal but unstable abilities. For example, some individuals might have a great aptitude or talent for music or art or athletics that makes them outstanding in their field, but at the same time, there are skills that most people can learn over time that can influence their performance in different domains. In the same manner, individuals can put forth effort for a specific task (e.g., trying very hard on a final test for a math course) as well as be continually hard working and industrious in general for many different tasks. Of course, the opposite situation would be not trying very hard on a final math exam just this one time due to mitigating circumstances, instead of continually not putting forth effort (being lazy) for many tasks

Figure 3.2 Original and revised locus-by-stability classification scheme for attributions

From *An Attributional Theory of Motivation and Emotion* by B. Weiner, 1986, New York: Springer-Verlag. Copyright© 1986 by Springer-Verlag New York, Inc. Adapted by permission.

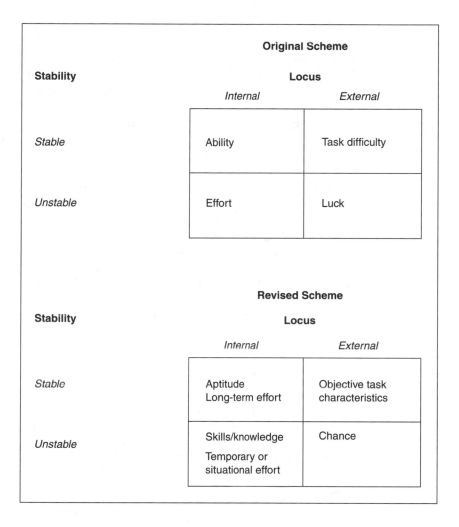

over time. Effort, depending on the type of effort involved, therefore, can be both stable and unstable, although it is always classified as internal.

The same type of clarification was done with task difficulty and luck. Most people perceive task difficulty as being relative to an individual's ability and effort levels and changeable over time. However, in the original classification scheme (see Figure 3.2), task difficulty was categorized as external and stable. Weiner (1986) now suggests that instead of task difficulty, the appropriate term for one cause that is external and stable is *objective task characteristics,* which stresses the nature of the task, independent of the individual who is attempting the task. Finally, luck is often perceived as a stable trait of some people (e.g., "He is always lucky, he wins all the games he plays"), so Weiner suggests that a better term is *chance,* which reflects a focus on the opportunities presented by the environment rather than a trait of an individual.

Related to this stability dimension, is the dimension of **globality** as defined by researchers working with the construct of learned helplessness (e.g., Peterson et al.,

1993). The dimension of stability generally refers to the attribution's changeability over time. However, implicit in our previous examples regarding short-term effort versus long-term industriousness for a variety of tasks was the notion that effort may cut across domains or situations, being more or less global in nature. Peterson and his colleagues have proposed that individuals' attributions can be classified along a global-specific dimension, paralleling the distinction between traits and situational specificity of behavior in personality theory. For example, individuals may make an attribution that they have no aptitude for all academic subjects (global), or they could make an attribution that they have no aptitude for math (fairly specific) or no aptitude for geometry (even more specific). In learned helplessness theory and research, the globality–specificity of an attribution is an important dimension, with more global causes seen as generalizing to a number of situations that can lead to learned helplessness (Peterson et al., 1993). Weiner (1986), on the other hand, notes that in almost all of the factor analytic and multidimensional scaling studies, globality–specificity has not emerged as a separate factor. Peterson and colleagues (Peterson et al., 1993) acknowledge that in their empirical work, they have only found two factors instead of the three they predicted, with locus being a separate dimension and stability and globality being highly correlated. Accordingly, pending further research, it seems that there is an important dimension concerning both the stability and the globality of an attribution, which we will subsume under the label stability, in line with Weiner (1986).

The Controllability Dimension

Logical and empirical analyses also have suggested that there is a third dimension of causality—controllability—which refers to how much control a person has over a cause. As noted in the label for Rotter's construct of locus of control, the dimension of controllability was included as part of his original conceptualization of internals versus externals. However, as Weiner (1985a, 1986) has pointed out, the construct of locus of control really confounds two separate dimensions of causality: locus *and* control. For example, both aptitude and effort would be classified as representing an internal locus of control in Rotter's model, but most people see effort as something they have volitional control over, whereas aptitude (i.e., artistic ability, physical coordination, musical talent) is usually perceived as something they have little control over (Weiner, 1986). Accordingly, it is important to have two separate dimensions—locus and controllability—not one construct that conflates the two dimensions.

Although the locus and stability dimensions can be crossed quite easily in a two-by-two matrix and have an entry in all the cells (see Figure 3.2), there may not be eight full cells in a locus-by-stability-by-controllability matrix. In particular, there are disagreements about whether there can be causes that are external to the individual that are still controllable. Some researchers (e.g., Stipek, 1998) suggest that these cells are empty because, by definition, a cause that is external to the individual is not under that person's control. Weiner (1986), however, argues that there may be causes that are external to the individual that are not controllable by that individual but are controllable by others. For example, a student who fails a math test and believes that his failure is due to the teacher being biased against him would still hold the teacher accountable because the bias could be controlled by the teacher. The other example Weiner offers is a student failing an exam because her friends did not help her. Again, he suggests that the help of friends is controllable by the friends, although it is not controllable by the student. Figure 3.3 displays the full matrix with eight cells and common attributions classified by the three dimensions of locus, stability, and controllability. In this figure, we have included entries for external and controllable causes.

As in the discussion of the stability dimension, there is often another dimension mentioned when there is a discussion of the controllability dimension. This other dimension, intentionality, occasionally appears in the empirical factor analytic and multidimensional scaling studies. In addition, as Weiner (1986) notes, there may be good logical reasons to distinguish intentionality from controllability, although they usually covary considerably. In an achievement context, he uses the example that individuals may intentionally not exert effort, but that rarely do people intentionally use a "bad" or poor strategy to solve a problem. That is, individuals may use a bad strategy in terms of some objective criterion for solving a problem or from the perspective of an expert in contrast to a novice problem solver, but from the individuals' point of view and knowledge, they do not think it is a bad strategy. Both strategy and effort are controllable (see Figure 3.3), but the intentionality of effort versus bad strategy use does add to our understanding. In fact, in the literature on the teaching of learning strategies (e.g., Weinstein & Mayer, 1986), this distinction is crucial. Most programs to teach learning strategies assume that students are not using good or effective learning strategies because they do not know about them or do not know how to use them properly, not because they intentionally decide to use poor or bad learning strategies. Besides this achievement example, Weiner (1986, p. 70) notes that intentionality is at the heart of the distinction between manslaughter and murder. A driver may not have intentionally tried to kill a pedestrian, but the driver should have been able to control the speed of the car before it hit the pedestrian.

Locus

Stability	Internal		External	
	Controllable	*Uncontrollable*	*Controllable*	*Uncontrollable*
Stable	Long–term effort	Aptitude	Instructor bias/ favoritism	Ease/difficulty of school or course requirements
Unstable	Skills/knowledge Temporary or situational effort for exam	Health on day of exam Mood	Help from friends/teacher	Chance

Figure 3.3 Achievement attributions classified by locus, stability, and controllability dimensions

From *An Attributional Theory of Motivation and Emotion* by B. Weiner, 1986, New York: Springer-Verlag. Copyright© 1986 by Springer-Verlag New York, Inc. Adapted by permission.

Weiner then goes on to note that although this distinction may be useful, intentionality usually does not refer to a cause per se. For example, it is difficult to say that aptitude or effort or any other attribution is "intentional." People are intentional, or acts are intentional, but a cause is usually not considered intentional. Accordingly, if the dimensions are to describe the nature of causes and attributions, intentionality is difficult to use. Weiner (1986) suggests that intentionality be subsumed under the controllability dimension, much as the globality dimension is subsumed under the stability dimension. Future research may be able to untangle these dimensions, but for our current purposes, the three dimensions of locus, stability, and controllability are sufficient.

Linkage of Dimensions of Attributions to Expectancy Beliefs

The three dimensions of attributions can be shown to have important consequences for individuals' expectancy-for-success beliefs. Using a logical and intuitive analysis, it seems clear that if an attribution for success is made that is internal and stable (e.g., "I did well on the test because I have the aptitude for it"), the individual will expect to succeed in the future. By the same token, if an attribution for success is made that is unstable (e.g., test-specific effort or luck), the individual will not expect to do as well in the future. For failure situations, the logic works a little differently—the more adaptive attributions to make would be unstable and controllable. For example, if a student failed an exam, it would be better to attribute it to not studying (lack of effort) for this specific test. The lack of studying can be changed and is controllable by the student; as long as the student puts forth the effort in studying for the next exam, he or she might expect to do better. Following this logic, a stable, internal, and uncontrollable attribution for failure (e.g., "I failed because I have no aptitude for math") would have the most detrimental consequences for future expectancies for success.

Besides the logical analysis of the relations between the dimensions and expectancies for success, there are a great many empirical studies that have linked attributions and the dimensions to expectancies for success. Weiner (1986) summarizes the many correlational and experimental laboratory studies of these relations by concluding that the stability dimension is the most closely linked to future expectancies for success, not locus, as would be expected by Rotter's social learning theory. These studies show for both success and failure outcomes that the stability of an attribution is linked to expectancy change. When an outcome occurs and the attribution made is classified as stable, the individual will expect the same outcome in the future. In contrast, if the attribution made is perceived as unstable, the expectation for the future is that the subsequent outcome may change. Weiner (1986) summarizes this research by proposing a general principle for behavior along with three corollaries:

Expectancy principle: Changes in expectancy of success following an outcome are influenced by the perceived stability of the cause of the event.

Corollary 1: If the outcome of an event is ascribed to a stable cause, then that outcome will be anticipated with increased certainty, or with an increased expectancy, in the future.

Corollary 2: If the outcome of an event is ascribed to an unstable cause, then the certainty or expectancy of that outcome may be unchanged, or the future will be anticipated to be different from the past.

Corollary 3: Outcomes ascribed to stable causes will be anticipated to be repeated in the future with a greater degree of certainty than outcomes ascribed to unstable causes. (pp. 114–115)

For example, if students attribute their success on a test or in a course to their own aptitude for the course content (a stable cause), they will expect to do well in the future in exams or courses on that course content (higher certainty of expectancy for future success). Teachers who attribute their success in teaching to their own aptitude for teaching similarly will expect that they will be able to teach future students and classes with success. In the same way, students or teachers who fail and attribute their failure to a lack of aptitude will expect to fail in future situations (corollaries 1 and 3). In contrast, if students ascribe their success to an unstable cause, such as believing they did well on the test or in a course because of luck, they may not expect to do well in the future, and their expectancy for success will be lower than that of someone who attributed success to a stable cause. The same would be true for beginning teachers who attribute their success in teaching to beginner's luck or to the idea that they just happened to have a really good group of students their first year. They would not necessarily expect to be as successful in their second year of teaching (corollaries 2 and 3). It is important to note that in deriving the implications of these corollaries, there are three "variables" that are being coordinated: the outcome (success–failure), the attributional dimension (stability-instability), and the certainty of future expectancies. All three have to be considered simultaneously.

It also is important to note that in these principles and the studies on which they are based, it is the perceiver's classification of the attribution in terms of stability that has the psychological impact on future expectancies. Accordingly, although the empirical findings and normative attributional theory predict that aptitude is usually classified as stable and effort is perceived as unstable, what is most important for future expectancies is how the individual perceives the dimension of the attribution. This idiographic position is in keeping with the general phenomenological perspective of attribution theory, giving precedence to the individual perceiver and his or her construction of reality. For example, if students make an attribution to math aptitude for failure on an exam but perceive math aptitude as something that is unstable and that they can change through learning, this attribution will not have as detrimental an influence on their expectancy for math in the future, in contrast to the normative position in which math aptitude is perceived as a stable and unchanging aptitude.

In much the same fashion, cross-cultural research suggests that different cultures may classify specific attributions along different dimensions. For example, Holloway (1988) suggests that the internal–external dimension that defines causes as internal or external to the individual may operate somewhat differently in Japan, where the primary social unit may be the family or household unit, in contrast to the individual as the primary social unit in the United States. In the case of Japanese culture or other collectivist or interdependent cultures, individuals may give what are normatively considered external attributions (i.e., "I tried hard in order not to embarrass my family or disappoint my teacher"), but these attributions are not perceived as being external to the individual because the individual identifies with the social group. Similarly, Weisz, Rothbaum, and Blackburn (1984) suggest that the dimension of controllability may not operate in Japan in the same manner as in Western cultures, where the emphasis is on an individual's

primary control of others and events as opposed to what they term **secondary control**, which involves adjusting to others and to events and being satisfied with this type of accommodation (Holloway, 1988). At the same time, Fletcher and Ward (1988) suggest that much of the empirical cross-cultural research in social psychology finds support for the classification scheme inherent in the three-dimensional model. Accordingly, although any single attribution may be classified in a different cell from the normative classification displayed in the eight-cell matrix shown in Figure 3.3, the three dimensions seem to be fairly generalizable.

Clearly, there is a need for more detailed and careful research on these issues by psychologists and anthropologists from both Western and non-Western cultures. There is a great deal of interest in cross-cultural or cultural psychological perspectives in social psychology currently (e.g., Fiske, Kitayama, Markus, & Nisbett, 1998; Hong, Morris, Chiu, & Benet-Martinez, 2000). There is a diversity of perspectives and models in this emerging area, but one general assumption is that individuals in different cultures might hold different implicit (or explicit) theories about a host of domains. These theories then guide their perception, reasoning, thinking, motivation, and behavior. In addition, this constructivist perspective allows for the possibility of different theories among individuals in the same culture as well as for "theory" switching or differential activation of theories by the same individual depending on the local situation or context within cultures. In terms of attributional theory, the beliefs that individuals have about effort and ability and other attributions in terms of their stability, locus, and controllability should be sensitive to these cultural differences. In this way, a general constructivist position on attribution theory recognizes that individuals in both Western and non-Western cultures may classify attributions along the three dimensions in an idiographic manner. Given this constructivist assumption, it is most important to understand the individual's classification scheme for attributions. By combining that knowledge with the general links between expectancies and dimensions, one can understand the individual's motivation. Application 3.1, later in the chapter, provides some strategies for teachers related to this issue.

Linkage of Dimensions of Attributions to Emotions

Attributional theory is in the family of general expectancy-value models, but it does not really include value constructs such as attainment value or utility value as in the Eccles and Wigfield model discussed in chapter 2. In Weiner's attributional theory (1986), value is defined by the emotions, such as pride, shame, guilt, and pity, that are generated by the attributional process. These emotions, combined with expectancy beliefs as in any expectancy-value theory, are then predictive of choice, persistence, and achievement behavior.

Attribution theory as developed by Weiner (1986) is one of the few social cognitive theories of motivation that explicitly incorporates emotions into the motivation–achievement behavior process. As in most social cognitive models of motivation, cognitions (attributions in this case) are one of the most important determiners of affect. That is, in this model, emotions are basically outcomes of the cognitive process of making attributions, or, to put it more colloquially, how we *think* influences how we feel (Weiner, 1986). This view of emotions as being dependent on a cognitive appraisal process is consistent with other cognitive models of emotions (e.g., Lazarus, 1991; Ortony, Clore, & Collins, 1988; Schachter & Singer, 1962). It is quite different, however, from psychodynamic models in which emotions arise from unconscious processes, and from behavioral models in which emotions are represented as drives or outcomes of reinforcement contingencies. Of course, as Weiner (1986) points out, this cognitive approach to emotions does not deny that there can be emotions without cognitive appraisal, such as in the case of classically conditioned emotions (e.g., a child's ongoing fear of dogs due to an earlier dog bite) or emotions linked to physiological changes (e.g., hormonally induced depression). Weiner also recognizes that emotions can influence cognitions, as when a depressed person consistently uses a particularly explanatory or attributional style (Peterson et al., 1993). Nevertheless, Weiner assumes that one of the main influences on emotions is how we perceive and think about what happened to us (Weiner, 1986).

Of course, attribution theory recognizes that some emotions are not a function of cognitive appraisal processes. These emotions are labeled *outcome-dependent emotions* and are a function of the outcome—success or failure—of a task. In general, these outcome-dependent emotions are relatively simple, or primitive, positive or negative emotions that are linked to the outcome. For example, individuals feel generally happy when they do well on a test, are successful on the job, or perform well in an athletic situation, and they feel sad or frustrated when they perform poorly in those situations. Accordingly, these simple emotions can be generated by the actual outcome without any cognitive appraisal on the individual's part. In attribution theory, however, the more complicated emotions are not really experienced until the individual engages in an attributional analysis.

Figure 3.4 shows the basic attributional model for the linkages among the causal dimensions, affects, and behavior outcomes. Following the logic of attributional theory, it is not the simple attributions in and of themselves that generate emotions, but rather the three dimensions of locus, stability, and controllability that are the prime determiners of subsequent emotions. In a number of experimental studies, Weiner and his colleagues have shown that these dimensions are linked to the various types of affect individuals will report. Many of these studies were laboratory studies in which individuals were asked to read vignettes or stories about a situation and then report how they would feel or how

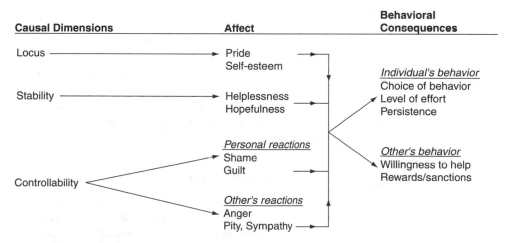

Figure 3.4   Relations among causal dimensions, affect, and behavior
Adapted from Weinter, 1994.

they think others would feel if in that situation. In some of the studies, individuals were asked to think of a time when they felt anger, pity, guilt, or pride and then asked to rate these self-generated events in terms of how the causal dimensions apply to the events (Weiner, 1986). It should be noted that these studies are more cognitive in nature; they may not evoke the actual emotions but simply the memory of the emotions and the accompanying cognitions. In contrast to the research on the accuracy of attributions and their link to future expectancies, questions regarding the validity of the emotions in these laboratory studies are appropriate. It is not clear that the people in these studies actually experienced any emotions, but rather reported on their cognitions or implicit theories about emotions. Accordingly, the links between attributions and affect may not be as straightforward as those between attributions and future expectancy beliefs. There is a clear need for more research in general and for more ecologically valid research specifically on the relations between attributions and emotions. Nevertheless, the findings are very consistent across a number of different studies with different groups of individuals, making it likely that attributions do play a role in the generation of emotions.

The Locus Dimension and Affect

The research does demonstrate empirical linkages between attributions and affect that are logical and intuitive as well as in line with psychological and, perhaps, evolutionary, theory (Weiner, 1986, 1994). As suggested in Figure 3.4, the studies have shown that the locus dimension is generally related to feelings of pride and self-esteem or self-worth. If individuals experience a success and attribute it to an internal cause, they are likely to take some pride in the success and experience an increase in self-worth. A failure that is attributed to internal causes, however, usually results in a lowering of self-esteem. Weiner (1986) notes that even Kant was aware of the link between locus and pride by suggesting that everyone at a meal could enjoy it, but only the cook could experience pride. Teachers may help to manage a student's self-esteem by suggesting that the student's failure on a task was not due to something about the student, but that the task was too hard. Failure in athletic events often generates a similar type of external attribution by the participants or others, such as coaches or parents (e.g., "It was really windy. That's why you misjudged and dropped that fly ball to right field"), that helps the individual maintain self-esteem. In the same way, Weiner (1986) summarizes attributional studies of affiliative situations (e.g., asking a person for a date) by noting that most individuals are well aware of the potential damage to another person's self-esteem if rejection for a date is predicated on an internal attribution (e.g., "I won't go out with you because you are very unattractive physically"). In fact, Weiner notes that many people will not tell the "truth" in this situation but rather provide some other excuse for affiliative rejection in order to protect the rebuffed individual's self-esteem.

The Stability Dimension and Affect

The stability dimension has been linked to feelings of hopefulness or hopelessness, paralleling the findings for the link between stability and future expectancy for success. As noted previously, Weiner (1986) proposed the expectancy principle such that attributing an outcome to a stable cause will result in an expectation that the outcome will occur again in the future and that attributing an outcome to an unstable cause will lead to an expectation that future outcomes will be different than earlier outcomes. Following this logic and applying it to emotion, Weiner suggests that attributions to stable causes for failure should result in feelings of hopelessness. For example, if a student fails an exam and attributes it to a traitlike lack of ability, he may experience a feeling of hopelessness about being able to perform better in the future because he believes his ability cannot change. In contrast, an athlete who fails in a competition but attributes her failure to poor training and preparation can still feel hopeful about the future competitions because training and preparation can be changed. Weiner, Russell, and Lerman (1978) found some support for this linkage between feelings of helplessness, depression, and hopelessness and causal attributions to both internal and stable causes for failure. However, Weiner (1986) notes that not as much research has been conducted on the links between the stability dimensions and emotions in comparison to the links between controllability and emotions.

The Controllability Dimension and Affect

The research on the controllability dimension and emotions has focused on both personal reactions experienced by individuals as they react to their own performance and the affect experienced by others as they evaluate or react to an individual. In terms of the personal reactions of individuals to their own performance, the research suggests that personal controllability is associated with shame-related emotions and guilt (Weiner, 1986). Weiner (1994) argues that controllability is related to personal responsibility. If a cause is seen as controllable, the individual is deemed responsible, whereas uncontrollable causes generate a perception of less personal responsibility for the outcome. The attribution–emotion sequence for a failure situation when an attribution is made to ability (which is normatively classified as uncontrollable) is that the individual will feel shame, embarrassment, or humiliation (Brown & Weiner, 1984; Covington & Omelich, 1979). Moreover, these negative, shame-related emotions will probably lead to disengagement in the task and performance decrements (see Figure 3.4).

For example, a student who fails an exam in science and thinks it is due to his lack of ability, which he believes is not controllable, will likely be embarrassed by his failure. These feelings of embarrassment could lead to the student not choosing to take science courses in the future and could also have an adverse effect on his performance in his current science course. In contrast, if a person fails and attributes it to lack of effort, which is controllable and under her personal responsibility, she is likely to feel guilty (or experience guilt-related affects such as regret or remorse) about her lack of effort and poor performance (Weiner, 1994). This guilt can be harnessed to increase effort for the next exam and the increased effort should lead to better performance for the student. Of course, students may not feel guilty even if the cause of their performance is seen as personally controllable, but Weiner (1986) suggests that if guilt is experienced, some element of personal responsibility is usually present as well. For example, students may feel guilty that they are letting their parents down when they do poorly on an exam, or feel guilty when they are caught cheating on an exam, or feel remorse when they are caught in a lie, but these situations are usually perceived as personally controllable (Graham, Doubleday, & Guarino, 1984; Weiner, Graham, & Chandler, 1982).

The reactions of others as they evaluate an individual's performance are also shown in Figure 3.4, but are represented by the paths from controllability to the emotions of anger and pity and then on to the behavioral consequences. The attributional analysis of how evaluators might feel and react as they judge a target person's performance corresponds directly to the teacher-student interaction when the teacher evaluates and reacts to the student's performance. In fact, many of the attributional laboratory studies have asked the participants to imagine that they are teachers. The participants are presented with vignettes about hypothetical students who demonstrate different levels of performance and are then asked to make judgments about these hypothetical students, report on their affect toward these students, and report their behavioral reactions to the students.

These laboratory studies have shown that the emotional and behavioral reactions of the evaluators are linked to the controllability dimension (Weiner, 1986). For example, if a teacher believes that a student's failure is due to lack of ability (an uncontrollable cause), that teacher is likely to feel pity or sympathy for that student. The reasoning is that the student is perceived as not being responsible for the poor performance due to lack of ability. This link between uncontrollable causes and the emotions of sympathy and pity aroused in others is complementary to the personal reactions of shame when failure is due to an uncontrollable cause (Weiner, 1994). In addition, lab studies have shown that teachers are also likely to report that they will not punish a student who, as perceived by them, is not at fault for not doing well (Weiner, 1986). Moreover, Brophy and Rohrkemper (1981), in a study with actual teachers reacting to vignettes about different types of problem students (e.g., defiant students, hyperactive students), showed that the teachers were much more likely to offer more help, instruction, and support when the cause of the problem was seen as uncontrollable for the student. When the problem behavior was seen as controllable by the student (e.g., defiance), however, the teachers were less likely to report that they would offer help and more likely to react with threats or punishment. Other studies of helping behavior (e.g., Barnes, Ickes, & Kidd, 1979; Weiner, 1980a, 1980b) have shown the same pattern with peer help. College students are more likely to offer their class notes to a student who missed class due to illness (uncontrollable cause) than to a student who missed class to go to the beach (controllable cause).

In contrast to the positive emotions generated (sympathy) and the positive behavioral reactions (no punishment, more help) when another's failure is perceived as uncontrollable, if the failure is seen as controllable, the evaluator usually reacts with negative emotions and behavior. For example, if a student fails and the teacher or parent attributes the failure to a lack of effort, the emotion most often expressed in the vignette studies is anger (Weiner, 1986). The teacher or parent perceives the student's lack of effort as under the student's control and as the personal responsibility of the student and feels angry that the student did not try harder on the task. This link between a controllable cause and an evaluator's emotional reaction of anger complements the personal reaction of guilt felt by an individual who did not try hard. The research on behavioral reactions of evaluators to a failure due to controllable causes also shows that evaluators will be more likely to punish the student for lack of effort (Weiner, 1986; Weiner & Kukla, 1970). As already noted, students will be less likely to get help from others when they are perceived as not having tried hard or having control over the problem.

These linkages among the dimensions of an attribution, the emotions experienced, and the subsequent behavioral reactions can help us understand both student and teacher affect and behavior in the classroom. Although there is a need for more research on attributions and affect in actual classroom settings, the linkages are supported by empirical research and also make sense theoretically, logically, and intuitively. Many teachers have experienced anger when a student is able to do a task but does not try hard and then performs poorly. Even more so than teachers, many parents, especially those with adolescents, may experience anger when their sons and daughters clearly have the ability to do well in school yet do not put forth any effort for academic work. Many of us, as either teachers or students, have probably felt guilty when we have performed poorly due to low effort. By using attribution theory, we can help students and teachers understand their emotional reactions. As they become more aware of how these attributional–emotional dynamics may work, they will be better prepared to cope with their emotions and regulate their behavior. This is especially important for teachers because their behavioral reactions to students in terms of help, instruction, and support are crucial for student learning and development. Application 3.1, later in the chapter, highlights the importance of these issues in the classroom context.

The Role of Responsibility Judgments

Weiner (1995) has proposed that responsibility judgments provide a theoretical linkage between attributional theories of personal achievement motivation and attributional theories of social behavior. This chapter has focused on personal achievement motivation, but it is important to note that the linkages among attributions, dimensions of control and personal responsibility, emotions, and behavioral consequences apply to many domains of everyday life, not just to teachers, students, and classrooms. Weiner (1986, 1992, 1995) has pointed out that judgments of personal responsibility and the behavioral consequences that are generated from these judgments underlie many domains. For example, discussion of the provision of welfare or unemployment benefits often turns on the perception of controllability and personal responsibility. More liberal individuals in the United States are inclined to favor the wide provision of government benefits because they are likely to attribute an individual's need for benefits to factors that are not controllable by that person, such as macroeconomic structural factors, poor educational institutions, persistent race and class discrimination, and so on. In contrast, conservatives are more likely to attribute the problem to controllable factors, such as lack of personal effort, habitual laziness, or unwillingness to learn. By branding welfare mothers or the chronically unemployed as lazy and not motivated to get a job, control and responsibility are shifted to the individual, which leads to the conclusion that it is really up to the individual to remedy the problem, not the government through welfare benefit programs.

Weiner (1986, 1992, 1995) has also shown that these dynamics regarding controllability and personal responsibility can play a role in parole decisions, medical decisions, reactions to AIDS patients, reactions to obesity or alcoholism, aggression, and marital distress. For example, in laboratory studies, individuals' reactions to AIDS patients, obese individuals, or alcoholics were more positive when the cause of the condition was perceived as uncontrollable (e.g., AIDS due to blood transfusion, obesity due to a thyroid problem, a genetic predisposition to alcoholism) than when the cause was perceived as controllable (unsafe sex, overeating and lack of exercise, personal choice of excessive drinking). Following this logic, Weiner (1992) notes that medical doctors often treat patients when their condition is perceived as personally uncontrollable, whereas mental health professionals often treat

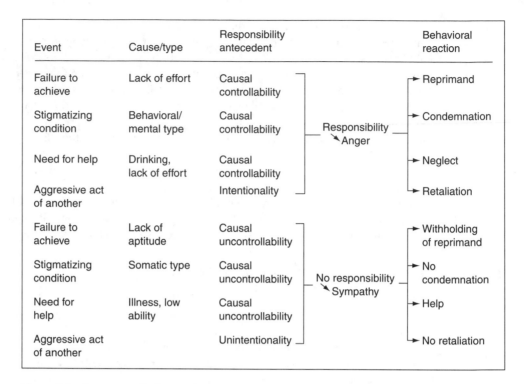

Event	Cause/type	Responsibility antecedent		Behavioral reaction
Failure to achieve	Lack of effort	Causal controllability		Reprimand
Stigmatizing condition	Behavioral/ mental type	Causal controllability	Responsibility ↘ Anger	Condemnation
Need for help	Drinking, lack of effort	Causal controllability		Neglect
Aggressive act of another		Intentionality		Retaliation
Failure to achieve	Lack of aptitude	Causal uncontrollability		Withholding of reprimand
Stigmatizing condition	Somatic type	Causal uncontrollability	No responsibility ↘ Sympathy	No condemnation
Need for help	Illness, low ability	Causal uncontrollability		Help
Aggressive act of another		Unintentionality		No retaliation

Figure 3.5   Summary of relations between events, attributions, responsibility judgments and outcomes

From *Judgements of Responsibility: A Foundation for a Theory of Social Conduct* by B. Weiner, 1995, New York, Guilford Press. Copyright 1995 by Guilford Press. Reprinted by permission.

those patients who are seen as personally responsible for their condition. In a marriage, negative events (being late for dinner, missing an important family engagement) can generate discord if the cause is seen as controllable (choosing to work late) rather than uncontrollable (being stuck in rush-hour traffic). In the same manner, an aggressive act, such as bumping another person accidentally on a crowded street versus intentionally bumping into someone, is judged differently and generates different emotions and behaviors in these empirical studies. The accidental act will not generate anger or retaliation, while the intentionally aggressive act usually generates anger and some kind of retaliation.

Figure 3.5 displays a summary of the role of responsibility judgments in achievement and social behavior dynamics. The events are listed in the first column and reflect various outcomes that people react to and can give attributions for why the event occurred. For example, the failure to achieve, a stigmatizing condition such as AIDS or obesity, or the need for help with a drinking problem or academic help, all can generate certain types of attributions, as shown in Figure 3.5. In the top part of the figure, the attributions are all classified as being controllable by the individual. The person fails to achieve because of a personal lack of effort, the person has AIDS because of his or her own unsafe sexual activity, or is obese because of overeating and lack of exercise, or chooses to drink, all of which are seen as controllable. These acts and an intentionally aggressive act are deemed to be the responsibility of the individual and generate anger (see Figure 3.5).

In terms of behavioral outcomes, the teacher or parent judges the student as responsible for failure due to lack of effort and usually feels anger and will reprimand the student. Individuals with AIDs or obesity problems who are stigmatized when they are deemed responsible for these problems, are usually sanctioned in some way, including condemnation. Individuals who need help, such as a person with a drinking problem or a student needing academic help, will not be helped or will be neglected if their problem is seen as due to their own intentional and volitional behavior. An intentional aggressive act usually generates anger and some kind of retaliation (see Figure 3.5).

In contrast, the emotional and behavioral dynamics are quite different when the problem is seen as uncontrollable and the individual is not judged as responsible, as shown in the bottom half of Figure 3.5. A student who fails because of a lack of aptitude or some special problem (a learning disability, a physical problem) not under their own control usually elicits sympathy from teachers and parents, not anger, and is usually not punished, but rather helped. In the 1980s, a very popular television show that starred Bill Cosby as a father of a middle-class African American family did a series of shows on the academic difficulties of the son, Theo, which illustrated these motivational and attributional dynamics quite clearly. Theo was doing poorly in school. His father was angry, did not understand why Theo was not trying hard, and constantly reprimanded him for his lack of effort and poor grades. Theo was upset because he claimed he was studying hard, but he just could not get it. Finally, Theo was tested by a school psychologist who determined that Theo had a learning disability. When Theo told his parents this news, the change in their expressions, affect, and behavior was quite dramatic. Suddenly, it was not Theo's fault that he was getting bad grades in school; it was his "learning disability" that was the problem and this disability was clearly not under his control. It was something with his brain, not his volition, that was the problem. Needless to say, Theo received a lot of support from his parents from then on, as well as extra help in school, and went on to do well in high school and college. The writers of this television show may not have known anything about attributional theory or the supporting empirical evidence, but the story line and the characters' thoughts, feelings, and behaviors followed an attributional analysis of the problem perfectly. This reflects the strong "naïve psychology" or commonsense psychology of attributional theory that lay people can understand easily.

The other events listed in the bottom half of Figure 3.5 also show a similar dynamic as a function of responsibility judgments. Weiner (1995) has shown that individuals who have AIDS as a function of a blood transfusion, or are obese due to a medical problem, or need help due to an illness are judged to be not responsible for their problem and usually elicit sympathy from others. In addition, if the individuals are held to be not responsible, they are less likely to be punished or condemned and more likely to be helped. Also, in an aggression situation, if the act is perceived as unintentional, there is usually no retaliation (see Figure 3.5).

The integration of personal achievement dynamics with social behavior and conduct dynamics represents an outstanding achievement for attributional theory. It brings together under one theoretical and conceptual framework quite disparate events and people's reactions to them. It helps us understand how individuals might think about their own personal successes and failures and how some people can recover from failures and move on to adaptive and productive ways of coping and achievement, while others seem to flounder and spiral downward in a less adaptive manner with resulting poor achievement. In addition, it gives us insight into our own emotional and behavioral reactions to other's problems as teachers and parents and should serve as a guide in how we think about others and our willingness to help them. Application 3.1, later in the chapter, suggests some strategies for teachers based on these principles. At the same time, some of these general principles and insights may vary for different groups of individuals.

DEVELOPMENTAL AND GROUP DIFFERENCES IN ATTRIBUTIONS

Research on developmental and group differences in attribution theory has focused on two general questions. First, are there differences in the way young children and adults or males and females or minority and nonminority students use the various informational cues or information-processing strategies to make attributional inferences? Second, are there developmental or group differences in the content and dimensional "meaning" of attributions and their links to expectancy for success (see Blumenfeld et al., 1982)?

Developmental Differences

Research from a developmental perspective (see Blumenfeld et al., 1982; Kassin & Pryor, 1985; Nicholls, 1990) suggests that the findings for attribution theory may differ by age. There are a number of ways in which attribution theory can differ given developmental differences. First, there may be developmental differences in the ways younger children use informational cues, content knowledge, and reasoning schemas to form attributions (columns 1 and 2 in Figure 3.1). Second, there seem to be developmental differences in the psychological meaning of different attributions in terms of their dimensional analysis (columns 3 and 4 in Figure 3.1). These two differences represent differences in the internal, psychological, and cognitive mechanisms of attribution theory. Finally, the contexts exposed to younger children may vary, creating differences in the attributional process.

Differences in information processing of cues are related to young children's ability to follow the six general principles of causality discussed earlier in this chapter. Kassin & Pryor (1985) suggest that even very young children (about 3 years old) do follow the ordinal priority rule that causes must precede effects when making inferences about causality. Children as young as 3 years also follow the principle of spatio-temporal contiguity, in which causes and effects must coincide in time and space. The third principle discussed earlier was that salient stimuli were more likely to be perceived as causes than other stimuli in the background. Of course, adults are very susceptible to this salience principle, but Kassin & Pryor (1985) suggest that young children are even more susceptible to it and may ignore other, more relevant and logical information about covariation between events to focus on the salient cues that can lead to an inaccurate attribution.

Besides these differences in the use of general information-processing strategies, children may differ in their content-specific beliefs about attributions (see Table 3.3). A great deal of research suggests that young children do not hold the same "definitions" of different attributions as adults (Blumenfeld et al., 1982; Blumenfeld, Pintrich, & Hamilton, 1986; Dweck & Leggett, 1988; Nicholls, 1990). This research suggests that the normative classification of different attributions such as ability, effort, luck, and task difficulty into the three general dimensions of locus, control, and stability may not hold for younger children. In effect, the psychological meanings of the attributions are different

Table 3.3 Developmental Differences in Children's Concepts of Ability, Effort, Difficulty, and Luck

Differentiating Ability and Effort	Differentiating Ability and Difficulty	Differentiating Ability and Luck
1. *Effort or outcome is ability* (3–5 years) People who try harder are smarter. People who get a higher score try harder and are smarter.	1. *Egocentric* (3–5 years) Task difficulty is relative to individuals' ability to succeed. "Hard" means "hard for me," which also means "I'm not good at it."	1. *Luck and skill are undifferentiated* (3–5 years) Luck or chance tasks are seen as easier or requiring less effort than skills tasks.
2. *Effort is the cause of outcomes* (6–8 years) People who try equally hard should have the same outcome, regardless of ability.	2. *Objective* (5–6 years) Levels of difficulty of tasks are recognized as independent of individuals' ability to succeed. Attributions for failure, however, still confound low ability and high task difficulty such that "it's hard" still means "it's hard for me," which means "I'm not smart at it."	2. *Skill and luck are partially differentiated, but basis unclear* (6–8 years) Effort is still expected to improve performance on both tasks, but a skill task is seen as more amenable to effort.
3. *Effort and ability are partially differentiated* (9–10 years) People who try equally hard may not have the same outcome because of ability, but do not follow this principle systematically.	3. *Normative* (by age 7) Ability and task difficulty are differentiated in terms of success rates of others. Tasks that fewer people succeed on are harder and require more ability, so "it's hard" is different from "it's hard for me."	3. *Skill and luck are partially differentiated, but basis is not explicit* (9–10 years) Effort is still expected to improve performance on both tasks, but a skill task is seen as more amenable to effort because individuals can compare stimuli on skill task.
4. *Ability is capacity* (12–13 years) Ability and effort are separate and can covary. Ability level acts as a capacity limitation and can constrain effort. If ability is low, there is some limit to outcome, regardless of effort level. Also, if outcome is equal, then lower effort implies higher ability.		4. *Skill and luck are fully differentiated* (12–13 years) Effort can't affect outcome on luck tasks, whereas effort can influence performance on skill tasks.

Adapted from Nicholls (1990).

129

and will have different consequences in terms of expectancy-for-success beliefs and affect. These studies have involved in-depth interviews with children and experimental studies of their reactions to different vignettes.

Nicholls (1990) summarizes much of the research on the developmental differences in children's understanding of effort and ability and their covariation. The normative, adult understanding of effort and ability in Western cultures involves two distinct relations. First, most adults understand that effort and ability covary inversely. If you need to try hard at a task, it generally implies less ability for that task, and, conversely, if you have high ability, you do not need to try as hard. Second, most adults have an "ability-as-capacity" belief that suggests that the exertion of effort will help improve performance up to a certain point, but effort will not help beyond that point because their ability has set an upper limit on performance. This belief represents ability as a stable, unchanging, and uncontrollable aptitude of the individual and results in the dimensional classification as internal, stable, and uncontrollable. Young children, however, do not seem to have this belief. They tend to see ability as more incremental and changeable (Dweck & Leggett, 1988).

Nicholls and his colleagues have documented a four-level developmental pattern in the beliefs between effort and ability (see Nicholls, 1978, 1990). The first level reflects children's beliefs before the age of 6 and equates effort and outcome as ability. In this case, children do not differentiate among ability, effort, and outcomes. Success at a task means that you tried hard and you are able. In addition, if you tried hard but did not do as well as others, you are still smarter than someone who did not try as hard. The second level emerges at about the age of 6 (the beginning of school for most children) when children begin to differentiate effort and outcome. Here, children expect effort and outcome to covary positively, with individuals who try harder being more successful than those who don't try as hard. If individuals try equally hard, they should receive equal outcomes. When they have equal outcomes but unequal effort, children explain this pattern by noting that the individual who worked less hard but had an equal outcome must have compensated by working really hard for awhile; those who worked harder must have misapplied their effort (worked hard and quickly but made mistakes). In the third level, which emerges at about age 9, children begin to differentiate effort and ability and believe that students who try less hard but have equal outcomes must be smarter or better. However, children at this level do not systematically follow this differentiation and still may claim that students who try equally hard may achieve the same outcome, regardless of ability. Finally, level four, which emerges at about age 13, represents the adult conception of ability as capacity, and effort and ability are clearly differentiated. Low ability can limit the effect of high effort on the outcome, and high ability combined with high effort can readily increase performance (Nicholls, 1990).

Nicholls and Miller (1983, 1985) have also shown that children's understanding of the relations between ability and task difficulty and between ability and luck change with age (see Table 3.3). The differentiation of task difficulty from ability seems to follow a developmental sequence from egocentric to objective to normative (Nicholls & Miller, 1983). In the egocentric level, approximately age 3–5 years, children see task difficulty as being relative to their ability to succeed at a task. If they can do the task, it is "easy"; if they can't do the task, it is "hard." Moreover, if the task is easy, they are "smart" or good at the task, and if the task is hard, they are not smart or not good at the task.

This egocentric perspective does not take into account any normative data from other children who may or may not be able to do the task. The confounding of task difficulty and ability results from children's egocentric focus on their own level of performance without taking into account what others might be able to do on the task. The objective level emerges by about 5 or 6 years old when children are able to understand that different tasks might be harder or easier depending on task characteristics (e.g., in much of this research, different puzzles are used; objectively difficult tasks are those puzzles with more pieces). However, children in the objective level still believe that their failure is due to the task being hard and that they have no ability for the task, in effect still confounding ability and task difficulty. By about age 7, children seem to be able to differentiate ability from task difficulty and also use normative information from social comparisons with other children to understand that some tasks are hard for everyone, and some tasks are hard for certain individuals. In addition, they also come to realize that if a task is harder because many people cannot do it, it will require more ability.

The differentiation of luck and skill also seems to follow a general developmental pattern (Nicholls, 1990; Nicholls & Miller, 1985; Weisz, 1984). This research has presented children with tasks that require skill (i.e., present a standard drawing and ask children to pick from six other drawings the one that matches the standard) and those that are based on luck or chance (i.e., same task as skill task, except in the luck condition, the six drawings are turned over, so the children cannot see the drawings as they make their pick). This work shows that at the first level, children do not distinguish luck and skill tasks and believe that effort can make a difference on both tasks. At the second level, children start to differentiate the tasks and believe that effort can help more on the skill task, but the basis for this belief is not explained in terms of the ease of comparing the six figures to the standard figure. At the third level, the children articulate that effort can help more on the skill tasks because the six figures can be visually compared to the standard figure, but they still believe that effort can help on the luck task. At the final, fourth level, which emerges at about 12 or 13 years, children clearly differentiate luck from skill tasks and do not believe that effort can make a difference on the luck tasks. It is interesting to note that this capability to differentiate luck from skill tasks emerges in early adolescence, yet many adults who play the lottery or other games of chance (slot machines) still believe that effort or strategy can make a difference in winning. As a result, adults develop very elaborate strategies for picking winning lottery numbers or pulling the handle on a slot machine. Media reports about the big winners in lottery games often reveal the winner's "strategy" for picking numbers. This developmental regression by adults to a more immature and childlike theory regarding luck tasks highlights the distinction between competence and performance that is important to keep in mind when interpreting developmental findings.

In addition to these developmental differences in children's strategies for processing information and their different definitions and dimensional classification of attributions, the third general factor that can result in developmental differences is changes in the nature of the environment. Classrooms can influence students' perceptions and attributions directly, and if features of classrooms are changing, it may be difficult to determine if the developmental differences are due to changes in the children's internal psychological mechanisms or changes in the classroom context (see Blumenfeld et al., 1982; Rosenholtz & Simpson, 1984). For example, research on the nature of middle schools (see Eccles & Midgley, 1989; Eccles, Midgley, Wigfield, Reuman et al., 1993) suggests that the organization and structure of these schools can have a dramatic influence on children's motivational beliefs. Most of this research suggests that middle schools are organized and structured in ways that stress social comparison and the normative nature of ability, and offer less opportunity for student control and autonomy than do elementary schools (Eccles et al., 1993). It is not surprising, then, that the developmental levels in the nature of children's beliefs about ability, effort, luck, and task difficulty show the most adultlike perceptions emerging when children are in middle schools. Obviously, it is some combination of both internal, psychological changes and external, environmental changes that interacts to create these developmental differences in children's attributions. It is important to keep in mind that these developmental differences are not solely the children's own construction or a function of maturational differences, as might be predicted by a stage model of cognitive development.

There are several implications of these developmental differences in children's beliefs about ability, effort, difficulty, and luck for attribution theory. First, these differences suggest that the normative classification of attributions along the dimensions of locus, controllability, and stability may not hold for younger children. In particular, ability is not seen as stable, which fits with a general, experiential perspective on development. Young children are constantly engaging in new tasks (not just school-related ones) and, in most cases, improving their ability to do the tasks (tying shoes, drawing, riding a bike, etc.). Accordingly, it is not surprising that they perceive their abilities as incremental and changing, not entity-like (Dweck & Leggett, 1988). This difference in the stability perception of ability results in a second implication for attribution theory. If ability is not stable, but rather changeable and able to improve with time, an attribution to ability for failure at a task does not need to have detrimental consequences for young children's future expectancies for success. In this case, ability as an unstable, controllable, and internal cause is conceptually equivalent to an attribution to lack of effort for failure (e.g., level 1 in Nicholls's model where effort and ability are equated). Young children can make an attribution to low ability for failure, but because they expect to get better with age and time, they can still expect to succeed in the future.

Gender and Ethnic Differences

In comparison to the developmental literature, there has been much less research on gender and ethnic differences. In addition, much of the research on these topics does not examine the potential interactions between gender and ethnicity. There is some research emerging (see Pollard, 1993) that suggests that minority females may not be as adversely affected as minority males. Even more important, most of the studies of ethnicity do not disentangle the effects of socioeconomic status from ethnicity. In many cases, low-income minorities are compared to middle-class white students, confounding the effects of ethnicity and class, making inferences and generalizations difficult.

The area of gender differences has a long history in psychology, and research on motivation is no exception. Differences between males and females in their motivation for achievement has often been proposed as an explanation for gender differences in achievement and, more recently, as an explanation for the smaller number of women in math and science careers in comparison to men (Meece & Eccles, 1993). One area that has been of research interest is gender differences in attributional patterns. This research, however, has produced very mixed and conflicting results. A number of studies have found gender differences in attributional patterns, with women more likely to show maladaptive patterns of attributing success to external causes (luck, ease of task) or unstable causes (effort, trying hard) and attributing failure to internal and stable causes such as lack of ability. In contrast, other studies have not found these gender differences (see Diener & Dweck, 1978; Dweck & Repucci, 1973; Dweck, Davidson, Nelson, & Enna, 1978; Eccles et al., 1998; Meece, Parsons, Kaczala, Goff, & Futterman, 1982; Ruble & Martin, 1998; Sohn, 1982). Eccles and colleagues (e.g., Eccles, 1983; Eccles et al., 1998; Meece et al., 1982) conclude that it is difficult to summarize this research because of the methodological differences in the instruments used to measure attributions, the differences between tasks in lab and classroom studies, the time when measures of attributions where taken (e.g., before or after feedback about success/failure in experimental studies), and the homogeneity of samples used (high versus low achievers). Accordingly, as pointed out in chapter 2, females in general do have somewhat inaccurate and lower expectancies and perceptions of their competence (Eccles et al., 1998), but it is not clear that attributions mediate this difference.

Graham (1991, 1994) has summarized the research on ethnic differences in African American students' attributions. She notes that there has been relatively little research on this topic and that there is a need for more theoretically based research. First, in terms of differences in the use of informational cues, early research seemed to suggest that African Americans and whites did differ, with African Americans using information about effort less often or less systematically than whites when they evaluate hypothetical others (see Lipton & Garza, 1977; McMillan, 1980; Weiner & Peter, 1973). However, Graham (1994) notes that more recent research on this issue has not shown these ethnic differences (Whitehead, Smith, & Eichorn, 1982; Wong, Derlaga & Colson, 1988).

In terms of ethnic differences in the actual attributions students make for their achievement, there have been two strands of research. First, there has been research on the construct of locus of control, which, as we have seen, emanates more from a personality tradition but is conceptually similar to the locus and controllability dimensions of attribution theory. In the locus-of-control research, the general assumption is that having more internal beliefs (believing one is in control and responsible for outcomes) is a more adaptive motivational pattern than an external pattern. Early research on locus of control suggested that African Americans were more likely to have scores toward the external side of the internal-external continuum, paralleling some of the research showing that females have more external patterns of attributions and locus of control. Graham (1994) summarizes the results from 63 studies of ethnic differences in locus of control in both children and adults by noting that there are more studies that find a pattern of externality among African Americans than studies that find no differences, and very few studies report that African Americans show more internality than other groups. Graham (1994), however, goes on to note that studies that examine locus of control and its relations with other achievement-related variables find no negative effect of this tendency toward externality in African Americans. Given these findings, she suggests that this pattern of externality and perceived uncontrollability may actually be adaptive, not maladaptive, for African Americans, but that the research in the locus-of-control tradition has not addressed this issue.

In research from the more situational perspective of attributional theory, in which students generate attributions for their own behavior based on their success or failure at an achievement task, Graham (1994) again notes that early studies seemed to suggest that whites were more likely to rate internal attributions (effort, ability) as more likely causes, whereas African Americans rated external attributions (luck, task difficulty) higher (see Friend & Neale, 1972). More recent studies suggest that this pattern of externality among African American students has not been replicated. Current studies either find no differences between African American and white students (e.g., Graham & Long, 1986; Hall, Howe, Merkel, & Lederman, 1986) in attributional patterns or that middle-class African Americans have a very adaptive attributional pattern of attributing failure to effort in comparison to white students (Graham, 1984). Accordingly, from a situational and attributional perspective, there seems to be more similarity in the types of attributions African Americans and white students make. However, as Graham (1991, 1994) points out, most of this research on ethnic differences has concentrated on the content of attributions, but there is a great need for more research on ethnic differences in the complete attributional model, in particular, the linkages among the constructs of attributions, dimensions of attributions, expectancy, and affect.

APPLICATION 3.1

Applying Attribution Theory in the Classroom

Attribution theory offers teachers a specific theoretical model of how students' perceptions of the reasons for their success or failure (attributions) can influence their expectancy for success, their self-efficacy, and their actual achievement behavior. This model has been validated empirically in both laboratory and field studies and has important implications for teacher practice. The following items are some suggestions for teacher practice based on attribution theory.

1. *Become a "scientist" of student behavior.* In keeping with the general metaphor of attribution theory that suggests that the individual is a scientist trying to determine the causes of events, teachers should endeavor to adopt this general perspective. They should try to assess the reasons for students' behavior in a scientific manner that involves the collection and use of a variety of information. For example, teachers should use a number of environmental cues as they make attributions for the behavior of their students. Teachers should seek out a variety of information about the students and attempt to examine the distinctiveness, consensus, and consistency of the information before making a final determination of the causes of the behavior. For example, if a teacher is trying to determine why a student continually acts out in her classroom, she should seek information about the specificity of the behavior in her own classroom: Does it only occur on certain types of tasks or for certain types of activities (use of distinctiveness cues)? The teacher also should look for the consistency of the student's behavior across different classrooms (ask other teachers about the child's behavior in their classrooms) as well as the consensus of different teachers' attributions for the student's problem behavior.

Another example of this general scientific perspective is the current popularity of portfolio assessment. Although often couched in more "artistic" or "humanistic" terms, the use of portfolios allows the student to present to the teacher a variety of information about his or her mastery of the course material. The teacher can examine the portfolio materials, and the diversity of the products can provide the teacher with distinctiveness, consistency, and consensus information about the student's performance. For example, the teacher might see that the student does consistently well on more structured assignments and has difficulty in reports or essays that are more open-ended. In addition, all of the information in the portfolio is presented to the teacher at the same time, so she can examine all of the student's work at once and avoid bias in assessment due to recency effects.

2. *Avoid attributional biases.* Related to the first item, attribution research has also shown that all individuals have a propensity to make biased attributions. As shown in Table 3.1, teachers could make a variety of attributions that may not be accurate. In particular, teachers should be careful about making the fundamental attribution error and attributing students' behavior or performance to a disposition or trait. By assuming that most student behavior is a function of traits, teachers will be less likely to believe that they can change the behavior or have an influence on it. This belief could keep teachers from trying new or different management or instructional strategies that could lead to changes in students' behavior. It is difficult to avoid the fundamental attribution error, but one of the most basic strategies is to collect as much data as possible as often as possible about the student, rather than relying on initial perceptions of the student based on only a few interactions.

For example, Mr. Jackson teaches seventh-grade math in a junior high school. He has five minority, low-SES students in his sixth-period class who are not doing well. At first, he wants to attribute their failure to their lack of stable effort and what he believes are the low value and support for school by their parents. However, at parents' night, parents of two of the five students come to him and express their concern. They note that their children are not studying very hard. The parents think math is very important and want to work with Mr. Jackson to help the students do better in math. This surprises Mr. Jackson and makes him rethink his attributions for all five of the students. He takes each one aside separately to talk about his or her performance in math. He finds out that two of the other three students whose parents did not come are actually working fairly hard but are having some real difficulties understanding the material. Again, this information makes him reconsider his initial attributions. He works out a plan for helping the two who are having conceptual difficulties by staying after school and working with them. For the other three, who are not having conceptual difficulties but seem to be putting forth low effort, he works out a new accountability system (in consultation with their parents), whereby the students have their homework checked every night by their parents and turn in their notebook every day to him.

Another important aspect of avoiding biased attributions is maintaining positive beliefs about students' capabilities. Teachers should attempt to maintain their beliefs that all students can learn the knowledge and skills that are the teacher's responsibility to teach. This basically is a belief that students' capabilities are changeable. Some students will naturally take longer to reach mastery than others, but in most

K–12 classrooms, the vast majority of children can learn the material. Of course, maintaining positive beliefs does not mean maintaining inaccurate ones. For example, it does not mean that the teacher should believe that all children are learning when there are clearly children who are not mastering the appropriate knowledge and skills. Rather, it suggests that teachers continue to attribute any student failure to controllable and unstable causes, such as lack of effort (on either the teacher's or student's part) or a need for reteaching, rather than a dispositional trait attribution to student "stupidity." Teachers can communicate expectations through attributional statements about the students and the tasks. Obviously, teachers can lower expectations for task performance by introducing tasks with comments like, "I know that most of you will not be able to do this task, but you should try hard anyway" (an attribution to the student), in comparison to providing tasks that most students can do through effort and communicating this to students, for example, "This task may be tricky, but I think you will find it challenging" (an attribution to the task).

3. *The important role of teacher feedback.* There are a number of factors that can influence students' attributions, but teacher feedback can be crucial. The implications for success and failure conditions are somewhat different and further complicated by the possibility that students may not interpret the same objective event in the same way. For example, for some students, getting a B on a paper may be a success, given their past lower grades. In contrast, for other students, including many high achievers and college students, getting a B is a failure situation. Given the importance of students' perceptions of events in attribution theory, it is suggested that teachers attempt to give *accurate* feedback to the students, rather than "false" feedback designed to encourage them and maintain their self-esteem (Blumenfeld et al., 1982). In this sense, teachers will help students to make accurate attributions for their own behavior that, in the long run, will be more adaptive.

In failure situations, teachers should strive to provide accurate feedback to students about the reasons for their failure. Some researchers have suggested that teachers should attribute all failure situations to low effort and encourage students to make this low effort attribution. In many cases, this is generally good advice because it communicates to students that they can do better in future situations because effort is an unstable, internal, and controllable cause that students can change. However, there are occasions when students actually do try hard and still do poorly because they lack the skills or knowledge for the task. In these situations, the student knows he tried hard, and to be told by the teacher to keep trying harder can be frustrating and lead to a discounting of the teacher's feedback. It would be more accurate to point out to the student the skills or knowledge he lacks, communicate to him that these skills/knowledge are unstable factors, that he can learn them, and, perhaps, even teach him the skills/knowledge he needs to do well on the task. The attribution to lack of skills/knowledge is an important addition to the original attributional idea of ability as aptitude, which leads to the basic contrast between effort and ability. In the case of ability as aptitude that is stable, uncontrollable, and internal, the teacher should avoid aptitude attributions for failure situations.

When students fail, attribute it to an unstable cause that can be changed (controllability). For example, Mr. Herther is teaching reading to a second-grade class. Fernando is having some difficulty learning to recognize words and pronounce them correctly. Mr. Herther asks Fernando to come to his desk and read to him, just the two of them. As Fernando reads, he keeps making mistakes and says, "I can't do this, it is too hard. I wish it was in Spanish. It would be easier for me, and then my parents could teach me."

Mr. Herther responds, "Yes, it might be. It certainly is easier when your parents can help you, but you know you are still very young and you are just learning English. There are a lot of children in this room who are still learning English. The important thing is to keep trying and working at it. Every day I learn new words in English, too. It takes time. You can't give up, but you can't expect to know everything right away. If you keep trying and working with me, we can learn together. Learning takes hard work, but everyone can learn."

In the same fashion, teachers should not attribute student success to effort unless the teacher is confident that the student did actually exert effort. If students do well on a task, it may not be due to effort, but rather to an easy task. If this is the case, it would be better for the teacher to recognize this and provide more challenging tasks to the students in the future. Students who are told they tried hard on an easy task may then infer they have low ability, or they may learn to discount teacher feedback given this type of inaccuracy and, often, insincerity. On the other hand, if the task was fairly difficult and students did try hard, attributions to effort and knowledge/skill are appropriate.

When students succeed, attribute their success to a stable cause. Mrs. Sugrue teaches fifth grade and her class is working on a science project. Kathy has just completed her project and shows it to Mrs. Sugrue.

"That is excellent, Kathy. You did a very nice job on this project and it shows a lot of work. How long did you work on it?"

"Well, not too long," replies Kathy. "It only took me 2 days."

"Really? That's not long at all. You must have a talent for science."

Here, Mrs. Sugrue responds to a successful performance by first determining the amount of effort put forth and then makes an ability attribution. If the student had worked hard, an attribution to stable effort ("You are always a hard worker") would have been appropriate. This illustrates another important principle regarding teacher attributions: It is important for them to be accurate. Students will not believe teacher attributions that are not credible (e.g., praising students for hard work when they did not work hard at all). Accordingly, although attributing success to a stable cause is important, it is even more important for teachers to make accurate and valid attributions.

4. *The role of attributional retraining.* In addition to the effect of general teacher feedback on students' everyday attributions, there has been research on the effectiveness of formal interventions designed to change students' maladaptive attributional patterns. Much of this research assumes that students have stable attributional patterns or schemas that they invoke and use over and over again across a number of different situations. This research has developed from the learned helplessness personality tradition, rather than the general attributional model that stresses the situational nature of attributions. Given the focus on stable individual differences in attributions, the learned helplessness "change" research (see Diener & Dweck, 1978; Dweck, 1975; Dweck & Repucci, 1973) and the attributional

retraining research (see Foersterling, 1985) have developed treatments to help individuals change their maladaptive attributional patterns.

The major thrust of these treatments (in both experimental studies as well as field studies) has been to have students change their attributions for success and failure to effort, but especially in the case of failure (see Foersterling, 1985). The treatment usually involves a teacher (or experimenter) working with students individually on a task and providing effort attributions to the student after success or failure on a number of trials or attempts at a task. It is important to note that most of these treatments do not assume that a student's attributional pattern can be changed as a function of just one statement to the student (cf., however, Wilson & Linville, 1982, 1985), but that more involved interactions and repeated attributional feedback are necessary to have students change their attributional pattern, such as that involved in scaffolded instruction. Accordingly, it may be difficult for regular classroom teachers to develop individual attributional retraining interventions for the many students in their classrooms. However, for some individual students, an attributional retraining intervention may be very useful. For example, in the area of special education, this type of attributional retraining has become fairly popular (see Borkowski, Weyhing, & Carr, 1988) because it is assumed that students with learning disabilities have a long history of academic failure in schools and have developed maladaptive attributional patterns. In these cases, where there are more resources available to work individually with students, attributional retraining may be a very effective technique for teachers and special educators to use.

SUMMARY

This chapter discussed the role of attributions in the formation of expectancy and efficacy beliefs. The development of attribution theory in achievement contexts has been led by Weiner. He and his colleagues have been most responsible for the explication, testing, and refinement of one of the most sophisticated and relevant models for understanding students' motivation in the classroom. In the 1980s, inspired by the work of Weiner, attribution theory was used by many educational psychologists in their own research and was probably the dominant model in research on student motivation and achievement. The research bearing on the theory has used both experimental and correlational designs and has been performed in both laboratory and classroom settings. Finally, attribution theory has relevance for understanding teacher behavior and motivation as well as student motivation.

Attributional processes are one of the most important influences for the formation of students' expectancy and beliefs. The model assumes that individuals are motivated to understand and master their world. One outcome of this goal is that individuals will try to determine the causes of events. In an achievement context, the most important event is a success or failure, and attribution theory proposes that individuals' perceptions of the causes of their successes or failures (their attributions) will have important consequences for the formation of their expectancy beliefs and their behavior. The theory developed two general streams of research: one that focuses on the antecedents of attributions and one that focuses on the consequences of attributions.

The antecedents of students' attributions for success and failure fall into two general categories: environmental and personal factors. Environmental factors that can influence the type of attributions that individuals make are specific information, social norms, and other situational features. Specific information can consist of a teacher's direct attribution to students for their performance (e.g., "You did not try hard enough"). Other types of environmental information can include norms about the difficulty of the task (e.g., all the other students got an A on the test, which suggests that the test was easy). Situational features include the amount of consensus, consistency, and distinctiveness of the cues presented to students as they attempt to make attributions. Consensus occurs when there is high agreement across different people about the event (e.g., "This teacher's math tests are always hard"). Distinctiveness occurs when individuals discriminate between different situations in their reactions to the situation (e.g., a student thinks math is hard and English is easy). These features provide differential information to students that they can use to form their own attributions for their own performance on a task.

The personal factors that can influence the content of an attribution are causal schemata, attributional biases, prior knowledge, and individual differences. All of these factors concern the individuals' cognition and beliefs about themselves or about the task that can influence the type of attribution that is made. Causal schemata refer to the basic knowledge structures that people have for understanding and inferring causality from events. Attributional biases include a number of heuristics that individuals may use to infer causality from a situation that can result in misleading and incorrect attributions. Prior knowledge includes both knowledge about the self in terms of past performance on the task and general knowledge about the task. Individual differences include various styles of making attributions that are consistent across many situations. For example, there is evidence that some individuals have a consistent explanatory or attributional style whereby they always make attributions to internal, stable, and global causes.

Besides the general contextual and personal features that can influence the content of an attribution, there is some research on when students are more likely to actually make an attribution. The theory does not predict that students will make an attribution for every event that happens to them. There are many occasions when attributions are not necessary and students' motivation is more a function of their efficacy and value beliefs for the task. However, if the situation is a novel one for students, the probability increases that they will be more likely to make attributions for their performance. A second factor that increases attributional search is when the outcome is unexpected. If a student has usually done well on a task and suddenly fails, an attributional search is generally instigated. If the outcome is negative, there is also a higher probability that an attributional search will be generated than if the unexpected event is a positive one. Finally, a fourth factor that can influence the attributional search process is whether the event is important to the individual. Events of high personal importance are more likely to foster an attributional search than are events of low importance.

In terms of the actual content of an attribution, there are an infinite number of specific reasons that individuals can use to explain why they succeeded or failed. In many studies in achievement situations, however, the two most frequently used attributions are some form of ability and effort. Other common reasons include task difficulty, luck, teacher help, mood, and health. The important contribution of attributional theory, and its theoretical linchpin, is that these diverse attributions can be grouped along three basic dimensions of locus, stability, and controllability. It is these dimensions, which are implicitly activated once the individual has generated the attribution, that provide the psychological and motivational force in attribution theory.

The locus dimension refers to whether a cause is seen as internal or external to the person. The stability dimension concerns the changeability of the cause over time and situations that range from being very stable to unstable. The controllability dimension involves the perception of control and can vary from uncontrollable to controllable. Given both logical and empirical analyses, it appears that attributions can be analyzed along these dimensions and fit into one of the eight cells generated by a locus-by-stability-by-controllability matrix. It is important to note, however, that although there is a normative classification of attributions into these eight cells based on the research in Western countries, there can be cultural, developmental, and individual differences in how the attributions are classified in terms of the three dimensions.

Nevertheless, once classified along the three dimensions, the research is very consistent across cultures and ages about the implications of these dimensions for expectancy beliefs, affect, and behavior. The findings for the stability dimension are the most consistent and clear-cut, and Weiner proposes a general expectancy principle that reflects the findings. The general expectancy principle states that expectancy beliefs are related to the stability of a cause such that an attribution to a stable cause will increase the expectancy that the event will occur again, whereas an attribution to an unstable cause will result in the expectancy belief staying the same or decreasing. Attribution theory and research show that the dimensions of locus, stability, and controllability are linked to different emotions such as pride, shame, and guilt. In addition, the dimension of controllability and responsibility judgments are linked to anger and sympathy emotions as well as behaviors toward others.

Finally, attribution theory has a number of implications for teachers both in terms of understanding their students' and their own behavior. Attribution theory can help teachers understand why some students form adaptive patterns of self-related beliefs but others use a more maladaptive pattern of attributions for their classroom performance. Teacher feedback can have an important influence on students' attributions and expectancy beliefs, so teachers must be careful to provide accurate and credible feedback to students. Teachers also must realize the potential for attributional biases to influence their thinking about students' and their own behavior. Teachers need to become aware of the types of attributions they make for students' behavior, how these beliefs are formed, and how to best gather information to make appropriate attributions for student behavior.

CHAPTER

4

Social Cognitive Theory

Ms. Teasdale stayed late after school to set up an aquarium in an activity center at the back of her fifth-grade classroom. The next morning, the first few students to enter the room immediately spotted it and went over to investigate. As more children entered the room, they went over to the aquarium, too, and soon it was completely surrounded by children and blocked from view. When Tim, Maria, and Robert entered the room, they saw all the other children in the back of the room but did not know why they were there. Maria said, "I wonder what's going on there. Let's go look." So they joined the group at the aquarium.

At 8:30, Ms. Teasdale announced that the students could look at the aquarium later, but they should go to their seats now because school was ready to begin. After some introductory activities, Ms. Teasdale began a new math lesson on subtracting fractions with unlike denominators and finding lowest common denominators. Ms. Teasdale explained and demonstrated the operations while the children followed along. Afterward they practiced solving problems as a group (guided practice); Ms. Teasdale wrote problems on the board and asked different children to tell her what to do to solve them. She then asked different children to go to the board to solve problems. After a few minutes, she asked children to work alone solving problems (independent practice). She circulated among students and monitored their work, providing corrective instruction to individual students as necessary. By the end of the period, Ms. Teasdale felt the children were making good progress. Derek—a student who often had trouble in math—even remarked to her, "I really think I know how to do these!"

During the independent practice time, Lisa and Patrick began to talk to each other. Ms. Teasdale noticed this but said nothing to these students because she figured it would stop. Ms. Teasdale then began to provide some corrective instruction to Paul. The other students realized that Ms. Teasdale was busy and was letting the conversation go on. Soon the noise level in the classroom increased as more children began talking with one another. Suddenly, Ms. Teasdale stood up and said loudly, "Kerry, you know you are supposed to be working quietly. Please stop talking and get back to work." Kerry became silent, and the rest of the class quickly stopped talking as well.

Later that morning, it was time to line up to go to a computer class. The children were noisy and were pushing and shoving. Michael, a popular boy in the class, stepped out of line and said in a loud voice, "Hey, let's cut this out. You know Ms. Teasdale said if we can't line up quietly we don't get to go to the computer room. I want to go, so let's stop now." The others followed Michael's lead and the line became quiet and orderly.

These examples highlight the importance of social influences on behavior, which is the domain of social cognitive theory. People acquire knowledge, rules, skills, strategies, beliefs, and emotions by observing others. People also learn about the appropriateness of modeled actions by observing their consequences. In contrast to conditioning theories that stress the consequences of behavior, social cognitive theory contends that individuals act based on their thoughts, goals, beliefs, and values.

This chapter focuses on Bandura's (1986) social cognitive theory. Bandura, who was influenced by Miller and Dollard's (1941) work (discussed later), conducted a series of seminal studies on modeling processes that helped to establish the theory's conceptual foundation (Bandura & Walters, 1963). Bandura felt that conditioning theories offered incomplete explanations of behavior because they did not address the influence of social models on behavior, concentrating instead on animal learning and human behavior in one-person situations. Although social cognitive theory contains elements of the mechanistic and organismic metatheoretical models (see chapter 1), its overall orientation is contextual because it posits that behavior represents an interaction of people with their environments.

Social cognitive theory distinguishes learning from performance of previously learned actions. By observing models, people learn skills and strategies that they may not demonstrate at the time of learning but rather later, when they are motivated to do so and believe it would be appropriate. There are countless examples of this phenomenon. A few years ago, one of us read a newspaper article detailing how a 5-year-old boy saved a choking 6-year-old girl by applying the Heimlich maneuver (i.e., applying sudden pressure to the victim's abdomen just below the rib cage to dislodge an object caught in the throat). The boy never performed this life-saving technique previously, but learned it when he watched a TV show in which an individual applied it to someone who was choking. The 45-pound hero became motivated to use the technique when confronted with a situation in which he felt it would prove useful.

Social cognitive theory postulates that motivational processes influence both learning and performance (Schunk, 1989b), unlike some historical theories (chapter 1) that considered motivation to be a performance variable. Bandura expanded social cognitive theory's scope to encompass learning and performance of cognitive, social, and motor skills, strategies, and behaviors. **Self-efficacy**, or one's perceived capabilities to learn or perform actions at designated levels (Bandura, 1993, 1997), is a key variable. Bandura also integrated motivational processes with self-regulation (Bandura, 1986, 1988), which we discuss later in this chapter. This expansion of the theory increases its explanatory potential and has important implications for classrooms.

Initially, we describe some historical influences on social cognitive theory. We then explicate the key assumptions and principles of Bandura's theory, and follow this with an in-depth analysis of modeling processes. We discuss the two key motivational processes—self-efficacy and goals—and show how they fit in a model of motivated learning. A section on social comparison follows. We conclude by discussing self-regulation, in which we describe its development and the role of volition, and social motivation.

After studying this chapter, you should be able to:

1. Describe the various ways that imitation has been construed in psychological theories.
2. Exemplify the reciprocal interaction model of Bandura's social cognitive theory.

3. Exemplify the various functions of modeling.

4. Discuss how model characteristics may affect motivation and learning.

5. Define self-efficacy and its role in motivated learning.

6. Discuss how goal properties, choice, and commitment affect motivation.

7. Define social comparison and explain its relation to motivation.

8. Define self-regulation and discuss how motivation plays a role during its various phases.

9. Using social cognitive theory, explain the important processes involved in group motivation, collective efficacy, conformity, and compliance.

HISTORICAL INFLUENCES

Theorists prior to Bandura recognized the importance of the social environment on motivation or included in their theories processes similar to those emphasized by Bandura. In chapter 1, we discussed Tolman's theory of purposive behaviorism to include latent learning experiments. Here we address theories of imitation and Rotter's social learning theory.

Theories of Imitation

From the time of the ancient Greeks, imitation has been thought of as an important influence on behavior (Rosenthal & Zimmerman, 1978). The Greek word **mimesis** refers to learning through observing the actions of others and abstract models exemplifying literary and moral styles. Theories of imitation conceptualize it as an instinct, a developmental phenomenon, a generalized response class, or instrumental behavior.

Instinct

At the start of the twentieth century, a popular idea was that people possessed a natural instinct to imitate the actions of others (Tarde, 1903). James (1890) believed that imitation was an instinct:

> But the instinct of *imitating gestures* develops earlier than that of imitating sounds . . . The various accomplishments of infancy, making "pat-a-cake," saying "bye-bye," "blowing out the candle," etc., usually fall well inside the limits of the first year. Later come all the various imitative games in which childhood revels, playing "horse," "soldiers," etc., etc. And from this time onward man is essentially *the* imitative animal. His whole educability and in fact the whole history of civilization depend on this trait. (p. 408)

James believed that the imitative instinct was pervasive and included gestures, language, motor skills, and overt behaviors. He felt that imitation was a powerful socialization influence but offered a vague explanation of why people imitate:

> A successful piece of mimicry gives to both bystanders and mimic a peculiar kind of aesthetic pleasure. The dramatic impulse, the tendency to pretend one is someone else,

contains this pleasure of mimicry as one of its elements. Another element seems to be a peculiar sense of power in stretching one's own personality so as to include that of the strange person. (James, 1890, p. 409)

McDougall (1926) believed that all behavior was instinctive (chapter 1). McDougall restricted the scope of imitation to the "copying by one individual of the actions, the bodily movements, of another" (p. 106). Imitation could involve expressive actions sympathetically excited (e.g., children cry upon seeing their mothers cry), simple ideo-motor actions (children copy the motor actions of another), and actions and gestures of someone admired. McDougall felt that imitation was an important influence on social-ization, but he provided the vague explanation that observed actions of another elicit an instinct to copy them. Thorndike (1912) also considered imitation to be an instinct and believed that it was centrally important in education.

The instinct notion is conceptually fuzzy and difficult to verify. Conditioning theo-rists rejected this idea because it assumed the existence of a drive or mental image that intervened between a stimulus (actions of another person) and a response (imitating the actions). Watson (1924) contended that what people labeled as instincts were actually learned behaviors.

Developmental Phenomenon

The developmental psychologist Jean Piaget (1962) postulated that human development is characterized by the acquisition and modification of **schemas,** or cognitive structures that underlie and make possible organized thoughts and actions. Schemas determine how people react to events, reflect individuals' total knowledge, and develop through maturation and experiences slightly more advanced than individuals' existing cognitive structures. Imitation is restricted to activities corresponding to existing schemas. Chil-dren may imitate actions they understand but should not imitate actions that are far ad-vanced from existing schemas. This view that development precedes imitation severely restricts imitation's scope and explanatory potential as a means for learning new actions.

Research has not uniformly supported Piaget's position. There is evidence that chil-dren at one stage of cognitive functioning can imitate modeled actions indicative of a higher stage of functioning, even though they never have displayed any behaviors typi-cal of the higher stage (Rosenthal & Zimmerman, 1978). Imitation and modeling are more potent ways to influence learning and behavior than Piaget's position suggests.

Generalized Response Class

Conditioning theorists construed imitation in associationist terms. Humphrey (1921) believed that imitation was a circular reaction in which each response served as a stim-ulus for the next response. Through conditioning, small reflex units formed progres-sively more complex response chains.

Skinner (1953) viewed imitation in the same fashion as other behaviors and contended that it was a generalized response class (see chapter 1). A modeled act served as a discriminative stimulus. Imitation occurred when an observer performed the re-sponse and was reinforced. Imitation became established when children were reinforced for imitating adults. Once established, an imitative response class was maintained with intermittent reinforcement. Children will imitate the behaviors of models (e.g., parents, peers) as long as the models remained discriminative stimuli for reinforcement.

This view limits imitation to performance of previously learned behaviors because the imitator must be able to perform the response; however, research shows that diverse types of skills and behaviors can be learned through observation (Rosenthal & Zimmerman, 1978). Another limitation concerns the necessity of reinforcement for imitated behaviors. Observers learn from models in the absence of reinforcement to models or observers. Reinforcement primarily affects observers' performance rather than original learning (Bandura, 1986).

Instrumental Behavior

Miller and Dollard (1941) developed an elaborate theory of imitation that generated much research on modeling. They defined imitation as, "A process by which 'matched,' or similar, acts are evoked in two people and connected to appropriate cues" (Miller & Dollard, 1941, p. 10). They rejected the idea that imitation represented mimicking cues and being reinforced. Instead, they adopted a Hullian framework (chapter 1) and proposed that imitation was instrumental behavior triggered in response to a cue and aimed at drive reduction. Imitation was instrumental because it led to reinforcement.

There are different types of imitation. For our purposes, the most important type is **matched-dependent behavior**, which occurs when the model is older, smarter, or more skilled than the imitator. The imitator's behavior is dependent on (elicited by) behavioral cues of the model. The imitator attempts to match behavior to that of the model and need not be aware of whether the action represents a match; the model may provide feedback on the behavior's acceptability. Much classroom activity has the look of matched-dependent behavior: students gradually pattern their behaviors after those of teachers, aides, and peers. Miller and Dollard believed that repeated reinforcement of imitated behavior established imitation as a secondary (acquired) drive, which can generalize to new situations.

Miller and Dollard's conception of imitation as learned instrumental behavior was an important advance in the study of imitation, but this view contains problems. New responses cannot be created through imitation; imitation represents performance of learned behaviors. This theory also does not account for delayed imitation in which imitators perform matching responses some time after they are displayed by models or for imitated behaviors that are not reinforced (Bandura & Walters, 1963). Imitation as learned instrumental behavior is a narrow conception that restricts its usefulness to motivating observers to perform behaviors corresponding closely to those portrayed by models. As we discuss later, modeling is a much more powerful phenomenon that has implications for motivation and learning.

Social Learning Theory

Rotter (1954) formulated a theory that integrated learning and personality theories. A key point is that, "The major or basic modes of behaving are learned in social situations and are inextricably fused with needs requiring for their satisfaction the mediation of other persons" (Rotter, 1954, p. 84). The theory comprises four basic variables: behavior potential, expectancy, reinforcement value, and the psychological situation (Rotter, Chance, & Phares, 1972).

Behavior potential refers to the probability that an individual will act in a certain fashion relative to alternatives. In any given situation, people may perform different actions. Behavior potential denotes the likelihood of these possibilities. Behavior includes observable and nonobservable acts (e.g., thinking, planning) that can manifest themselves in behavior.

Expectancy is an individual's belief concerning the likelihood that a particular reinforcement will occur following a specific behavior. This is not exactly the same construct as expectancy for success, which we discussed in chapter 2, but it is related. Various outcomes may occur following an action, and each outcome has a probability of occurrence. Expectancy is subjective and need not correspond to reality. Students may believe that if they get an A on a term paper, they will make an A in the course, even though they have made low grades on every other course assignment.

Reinforcement value refers to how much individuals value a particular outcome relative to other potential outcomes. Expectancy and reinforcement value are independent; the outcome considered most likely may or may not be most valued. This construct is similar to the value component of expectancy-value theory (see chapter 2).

The psychological situation highlights the importance of the context of behavior. How individuals view situations affects reinforcement value and expectancy. In unpleasant situations, all potential outcomes might be viewed as negative and the least negative one as the most desirable. This is a contextual theory because behavior is situationally specific, but expectancies for reinforcement can generalize to similar situations.

In essence, Rotter's theory says that people form expectations about the likely outcomes of behaviors and act in accordance with these expectations and the value they place on potential outcomes. Individuals will act in a given fashion if they believe that a reinforcing outcome will occur and if they value that outcome. Students may volunteer for a difficult project if they expect teacher praise and peer approval as outcomes and value them.

Rotter's theory offers important insights into the influences on motivation. Many of Rotter's ideas are found in Bandura's theory, but Bandura has significantly expanded Rotter's position to include self-efficacy and self-regulatory processes.

THEORETICAL FRAMEWORK

Bandura's (1986, 1997) theory is based on several key assumptions: (a) reciprocal interactions among personal, behavioral, and environmental factors; (b) the relation of learning to motivation; and (c) enactive and vicarious learning.

Reciprocal Interactions

Bandura (1986) describes his framework of **triadic reciprocality** as follows:

> In the social cognitive view people are neither driven by inner forces nor automatically shaped and controlled by external stimuli. Rather, human functioning is explained in terms of a model of triadic reciprocality in which behavior, cognitive and other personal factors, and environmental events all operate as interacting determinants of each other. (p. 18)

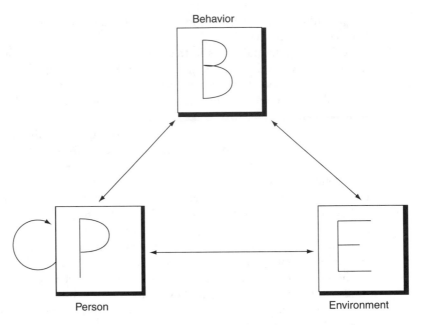

Figure 4.1 Model of triadic reciprocality

This model is shown in Figure 4.1. The behavioral-environmental link is exemplified by an instructional sequence in which a teacher presents information and directs students' attention to instructional aids. Environmental influence on behavior occurs when the teacher says, "Look here," and students automatically direct their attention. That students' behaviors alter the instructional environment can be seen when the teacher asks a question and students give wrong answers. The teacher reteaches the material instead of presenting new information.

The behavioral-personal factor interaction can be exemplified using self-efficacy. Research shows that self-efficacy (a personal factor) influences such achievement behaviors as choice of tasks, persistence, and effort (Schunk, 1989c, 1995). In turn, students' behaviors modify self-efficacy. As students work on tasks, they observe their progress toward their goals (e.g., acquiring skills, completing material). These progress indicators convey that students are capable of learning and performing well, which enhances their self-efficacy for further learning.

An example of the personal-environmental factor interaction is found in students with learning disabilities, many of whom hold a low sense of self-efficacy for performing well (Licht & Kistner, 1986). That personal factors can influence the environment is shown with individuals who react to students with learning disabilities based on attributes typically associated with them rather than on what the students actually do. Some teachers may judge these students as being less capable than nondisabled students and hold lower academic expectations for them, even in content areas where the former students are performing adequately (Bryan & Bryan, 1983). In turn, teacher feedback (environmental factor) influences self-efficacy (personal factor). The teacher statement, "You're doing great!" will have a better effect on self-efficacy than the pronouncement, "I doubt you can learn this."

The direction of influence among the three factors is not always the same; typically, one or two factors predominate. Environmental factors take precedence when classroom life is highly regimented and there are many rules and procedures. Personal factors predominate when environmental influences are weak. Students who must write a term paper and can select a topic from a list will choose one they enjoy or have an interest in.

The three factors typically interact in classrooms. As a teacher presents a lesson to the class, students reflect on what the teacher is saying (environment influences cognition—a personal factor). Students who do not understand a point raise their hands to ask a question (cognition influences behavior). The teacher reviews the point (behavior influences environment). Eventually, the teacher gives students work to accomplish (environment influences cognition, which influences behavior). As students work on the task, they believe they are performing it well (behavior influences cognition) and decide to ask the teacher if they can continue to work on it (cognition influences behavior).

The small loop emanating from the person factor shown in Figure 4.1 means that personal factors influence one another (Zimmerman, 1989). Thus, use of an effective learning strategy will promote acquisition of skills and can lead students to feel more confident about learning because they understand and can apply the strategy. In turn, higher self-efficacy may affect students' choices of strategies. Such within-person interaction is critical for self-regulation (discussed later).

Learning and Motivation

Social cognitive theory distinguishes learning from performance of previously learned actions. People learn much by observing models, but the knowledge and skills they acquire may not be demonstrated at the time of learning (Rosenthal & Zimmerman, 1978). People will not demonstrate skills until they are motivated to display them. This motivation to perform previously learned skills may stem from the belief that the skills are appropriate in the situation and that the consequences will be positive. The learning-performance distinction is apparent in the story recounted earlier about the boy who saved his choking companion by applying the Heimlich maneuver. Social cognitive theory postulates that competence can be acquired without being displayed and addresses how the use of competence is affected by personal and situational factors.

Motivation affects performance and learning. Later we present a social cognitive model of motivated learning that postulates strong links between motivation and learning. Although motivation can affect learning, the two are separable, which is evident in latent learning (see chapter 1), in which motivational inducements that are weak or absent during learning become powerful later.

Enactive and Vicarious Learning

In social cognitive theory, "Learning is largely an information-processing activity in which information about the structure of behavior and about environmental events is transformed into symbolic representations that serve as guides for action" (Bandura, 1986, p. 51). **Enactive learning** is learning by doing and experiencing the consequences of one's actions. Successful actions are retained; those that lead to failure are discarded.

Vicarious learning occurs in the absence of overt performance by learners and derives from observing models that are live (in person), symbolic or nonhuman (e.g., talking animals, cartoon characters), on electronic sources (e.g., television, videotape, computer), or in print. Vicarious learning accelerates learning beyond what occurs when students perform every action at the time it is learned and saves students from personally experiencing negative consequences. Complex-skill learning typically occurs enactively and vicariously. Students observe teachers explain and demonstrate skills. Through observation, students may learn some components of a skill and not others. Practice allows teachers to provide corrective feedback to help students refine their skills.

Bandura (1986) contends that behavioral consequences, whether experienced personally or modeled, inform and motivate students rather than strengthen behaviors, as postulated by Skinner (1953). Consequences inform students of the likely outcomes of actions. If students fail or observe models fail, they learn that something is wrong and they may take steps to correct the problem. From a motivational perspective, students learn behaviors that they value and believe will have desirable consequences. The belief that modeled behaviors will prove useful leads people to attend to and learn from models.

MODELING PROCESSES

One of the primary contributions of social cognitive theory is its explication of modeling processes. We next discuss modeling and highlight its relevance to education.

Functions of Modeling

Modeling refers to behavioral, cognitive, and affective changes that result from observing one or more models (Bandura, 1969, 1989; Rosenthal & Bandura, 1978; Schunk, 1987). Modeling serves different functions: inhibition/disinhibition, response facilitation, and observational learning (Table 4.1).

Inhibition/Disinhibition

Observing a model can strengthen or weaken inhibitions. When models perform threatening or prohibited activities without negative consequences, observers may perform the behaviors themselves. Models who are punished may inhibit observers' responding. Inhibitory and disinhibitory effects result from observers' beliefs that similar consequences are apt to occur should they act accordingly. Inhibited and disinhibited behaviors have been learned previously by observers; motivation makes them more or less likely.

Table 4.1 Functions of Modeling

Function	Effect on Observers
Inhibition/disinhibition	Creates expectations of similar consequences for modeled action
Response facilitation	Social prompt causes similar behavior
Observational learning	New skills and behaviors are acquired

In the example at the beginning of this chapter, student talking during independent practice became disinhibited because Ms. Teasdale did not stop it. When Ms. Teasdale disciplined Kerry, talking among other class members ceased. Although the effects are not automatic, unpunished misbehavior can lead observers to start misbehaving themselves. Misbehavior stops when the teacher disciplines one student for misbehaving. Observers are likely to believe that they, too, will be disciplined if they continue to misbehave.

Response Facilitation

Response facilitation occurs when modeled actions serve as social prompts for observers to behave accordingly. In the earlier example, response facilitation occurs when Tim, Maria, and Robert go to the back of the classroom where they see the other students gathered. The congregation of children serves as a social prompt for these three students to join them. Response facilitation is a motivational phenomenon because the behaviors reflect actions that students have learned. Unlike inhibitory and disinhibitory effects, response facilitation behaviors are socially acceptable and not accompanied by potential restraints (Bandura, 1986).

Observational Learning

Observational learning through modeling occurs when observers display new behaviors that prior to modeling had a zero probability of occurrence, even with motivational inducements in effect (Bandura, 1969; Rosenthal & Zimmerman, 1978). Observational learning expands the range and rate of learning over what could occur if each response had to be performed and reinforced for it to be learned. The students in Ms. Teasdale's class displayed observational learning when they performed fraction skills after observing her modeled demonstration. **Cognitive modeling** incorporates modeled explanations and demonstrations with verbalizations of the model's thoughts and reasons for performing actions (Meichenbaum, 1977).

Observational learning comprises four subprocesses: attention, retention, production, and motivation (Table 4.2). Rather than discuss motivation separately, we show how motivation interacts with the other three subprocesses.

Table 4.2 Processes of Observational Learning

Process	Activities
Attention	Attending to distinctive features of modeled displays
Retention	Coding and transforming modeled information for storage; rehearsing information
Production	Translating visual and symbolic conceptions of modeled events into behavior
Motivation	Performing valued activities and those with expected positive consequences

Observer attention is necessary for modeled acts to be perceived meaningfully. At any time, there are countless cues to which one can attend. Distinctive features command attention (e.g., size, shape, color, sound, unusual location). Teachers apply this principle when they use brightly colored displays and large cutouts.

Motivation affects observer attention through the perceived functional value of modeled acts. Actions judged by observers as important and likely to lead to valued outcomes command greater attention. Students attend to teachers because of anticipated negative consequences if they do not, but also because teachers' actions are viewed as highly functional and students are expected to learn the modeled behaviors. In addition, students generally view teachers as competent, and people attend to models they believe are knowledgeable.

Retention includes coding and transforming modeled information for storage in memory and mentally rehearsing information. Observers store modeled displays in imaginal and verbal form. Imaginal coding is especially important for activities not easily described in words, such as motor skills performed so rapidly that individual movements are part of a smooth, larger sequence (e.g., a tennis serve). Much cognitive skill learning relies upon verbal coding of procedures or strategies.

As with attention, motivational processes influence the activities that observers retain. Modeled actions that observers believe are important are more likely to be retained; those for which observers see little value will not be learned. Retention activities clearly show the interaction of learning and motivation.

Production involves translating visual and symbolic conceptions of modeled events into behavior. Problems in production arise because information is inadequately coded or because learners experience difficulty translating coded information into behavior. Most complex skills are learned through modeling, guided practice, and corrective feedback. Learners may acquire an approximation of a complex skill by observing models and then refine their skills through practice and corrective feedback.

Individuals never demonstrate all the knowledge, skills, and behaviors they acquire through observation. Motivation to act results from direct, vicarious, and self-produced experiences. People perform actions that previously have been successful for themselves or for models. They also perform activities they value and avoid those that are dissatisfying (Schunk, 1987). People forego money, prestige, and power when they judge the activities they must engage in to receive these rewards as unacceptable (e.g., questionable business practices). Classroom applications of modeling are given in Application 4.1.

APPLICATION 4.1

Applying Modeling in the Classroom

1. *Use inhibition functions of modeling.* Mrs. East told her students several times if they did not finish their work they could not go to recess. It was time for recess and Mrs. East said, "Class, it is time to line up for recess." She immediately tapped on a student's desk and said, "James, you may not line up, you did not finish your work." Several other students who also had not finished their work did not line up with the class.

Mr. Taylor was checking to see if the band parade lines were straight. He was walking along the first line and adjusting students who were not in line. The students in the other parade lines began to straighten themselves.

2. *Use disinhibition functions of modeling.* Mrs. Jenkins told one kindergarten student several times not to pour the sand from the sand table onto the floor and that if he did it again, he would have to go to another center area. She then walked away. The little boy continued to pour sand onto the floor, but Mrs. Jenkins did nothing. Soon all the children at the sand table were pouring sand onto the floor.

   A social studies teacher told his class that late work would receive a lower grade. Several students continually turned in late work, but their grade on the work was never lowered. Soon, over half of the class was submitting late work.

3. *Using response facilitation functions of modeling.* A physical education teacher asked the first three students who entered class to start running laps around the gym. As other students arrived, they automatically started running around the gym with the first three students.

   Mr. Laird, a science teacher, brought several homemade robots to share with his class during a unit on mechanics. He had the robots operating at the back of the room when the students arrived. As the students entered, they all immediately went to the back of the room to watch the robots rather than going to their desks.

4. *Using observational learning.* Ms. Sims, a first-grade teacher, used math manipulatives to show her students how to subtract. After explaining each problem, she had the students perform the same operations with the manipulatives at their desks.

   Mr. Moore, a tennis coach, demonstrated different types of tennis swings several times. After demonstrating each type, he had his students practice the swing with their rackets.

Characteristics of Effective Models

Modeling does not occur automatically when observer and model are paired. Observers must attend to models and be motivated to learn from them. In addition, theory and research have identified characteristics of models that are important influences on modeling: competence, perceived similarity, credibility, and enthusiasm.

Competence

Perceived model competence aids observational learning because students are more likely to attend to and pattern their actions after models who perform successfully than after those less competent (Schunk, 1987). Competent models also display skills correctly, which diminishes the likelihood that students will learn erroneously. This is not to suggest that models of superior competence to observers always make the best teachers. When adult models perform poorly, children may be swayed by status and try to learn anyway because they assume that the adults are not entirely at fault. Children are more likely to detect errors by peers than by teachers, especially if children are less familiar with the content demonstrated by teachers. Perceived superior competence also may not affect motivation positively. Some students who observe teachers flawlessly demonstrate complex skills may believe that they never will become that competent.

For self-evaluative purposes, the best models may be students who are equal to or slightly more competent than observers. France-Kaatrude and Smith (1985) had first and fourth graders perform a task. Children could compare their performances with a peer of higher, lower, or equal competence. Children allowed to compare with similarly performing peers compared most often and demonstrated the greatest persistence. Younger children compared more often with similar peers than did older children.

In forming self-evaluations, children routinely compare their performances with those of their peers (Schunk, 1987). Social comparisons with peers whom children judge as similar in ability can be highly motivating. When model age and competence conflict (e.g., same age but lower competence), children are swayed more by competence information. This suggests that teachers could use younger children to model skills, assuming that students believe the models are competent. Use of younger child models also could enhance observers' self-efficacy; observers may believe that if younger children can learn, they can too.

Observers often pattern their actions after those displayed by models of high status as defined by position, job responsibility, or social standing. In the example at the beginning of this chapter, Michael is a high-status model, as shown by the class following his directions to line up properly. Patterning one's actions after high-status models is functional and should lead to improvement so long as the models are competent and are displaying behaviors in their areas of expertise. Status becomes problematic when people model behaviors that lie outside of their areas of expertise (e.g., athletes advertising personal care products).

Perceived Similarity

Similarity to models constitutes an important source of information and can be motivating (Bandura, 1986). Similarity helps observers gauge behavioral appropriateness and form outcome expectations (i.e., beliefs about the consequences of actions). The more alike observers are to models, the greater the probability that similar actions by observers are socially appropriate and will produce comparable results (Bandura, 1986; Schunk, 1987). Model attributes often predict the functional value of behavior. Similarity is especially influential when observers have little information about functional value; for example, unfamiliar tasks or those not immediately followed by consequences (Akamatsu & Thelen, 1974).

Model similarity also affects observers' self-efficacy. Observing similar others succeed can raise observers' self-efficacy and motivate them to try the task if they believe that if others can succeed, they can as well. Observing others fail can lead people to believe they lack the competence to succeed and dissuade them from attempting the task. Similarity is particularly important when students are uncertain about their performance capabilities, such as when they lack task familiarity and have little information to use in judging self-efficacy or when they previously experienced difficulties and possess self-doubts (Bandura, 1986; Schunk, 1987).

Research examining the effects of perceived similarity on students' achievement behaviors shows that children generally are not more inclined to model peers' behaviors rather than adults' (Schunk, 1987); however, model-observer similarity is a reliable cue for behavioral appropriateness. When children are unsure about what to do, they observe what peers are doing and act accordingly. Similarity in age is less important for learning of skills, rules, and novel responses than the perceived value of the learning. Competence is important. To the extent that peers are viewed as equally competent as adults, the behaviors of each are likely to be modeled. Children model adults when peers' competence is questioned. Peers are often more effective models when children hold self-doubts about their competence. In a learning situation, viewing a peer successfully perform a task may raise children's self-efficacy more than observing an adult (Schunk & Hanson, 1985). Children may wonder if the adult possesses such a high level of competence that they will never attain it.

An important distinction is between **mastery models** who perform faultlessly and **coping models** who initially demonstrate the typical fears and deficiencies of observers, but gradually improve their performances and gain confidence (Thelen, Fry, Fehrenbach, & Frautschi, 1979). Coping models demonstrate how determined effort and positive thoughts overcome difficulties. Coping models may be especially beneficial with learners who previously encountered difficulties. To the extent that children view a coping model's initial difficulties but gradual progress as more similar to their typical performances than rapid mastery, observation of coping models might raise self-efficacy more than mastery models.

Schunk and Hanson (1985) compared the effects of peer mastery and coping models with those of adult (teacher) models and no models. Peer mastery models solved subtraction-with-regrouping problems correctly and verbalized statements reflecting high self-efficacy and ability, low task difficulty, and positive attitudes. Peer coping models initially made errors and verbalized negative statements, but then verbalized coping statements (e.g., "I need to pay attention to what I'm doing") and eventually verbalized positive statements and performed as well as mastery models.

Observing a peer model increased efficacy and achievement better than did observing a teacher model or not observing a model. Students who watched the teacher model outperformed students who watched no model. Observing models also enhanced motivation during problem solving. No differences were obtained between mastery and coping models. Although children's prior subtraction successes were limited to problems without regrouping, they might have drawn on these and felt that if the models could learn, they could too.

Schunk, Hanson, and Cox (1987) used a task (fractions) on which children had experienced few successes. The researchers found that observing multiple models—coping or mastery—promoted outcomes as well as observing a single coping model, and better than observing a single mastery model. Children who observed single models judged themselves more similar in competence to coping than to mastery models. Observation of multiple models apparently exerted a strong vicarious influence on children's self-efficacy.

Research also has addressed **self-modeling**, or cognitive and behavioral changes stemming from observing one's own performances. Schunk and Hanson (1989b) videotaped children solving problems and showed them their tapes. Self-modeling students displayed higher self-efficacy and motivation than did children who had been videotaped but did not observe their tapes and those who had not been taped. Self-model tapes may highlight progress in skill acquisition, which enhances self-efficacy and motivation.

Research on similarity in gender supports the idea that similarity is beneficial when it provides information on task appropriateness (Schunk, 1987). Seeing a same-sex child play with a toy provides the observer with sex-appropriateness information, which can have motivational effects. When children are uncertain about the gender appropriateness of behavior, they may model same-sex peers because they have been rewarded for doing so and believe the models to be good examples of their sex role. Teachers who employ peer models of both sexes to portray classroom learning activities may help alter students' preconceived ideas on sex-role appropriateness (e.g., boys are good in math, girls are good in reading).

Credibility

Model credibility can affect the observers' motivation to model actions. Models who act consistently with the behaviors they model are more likely to be judged by observers as credible and to be emulated than are models who display one action but behave differently (Bandura, 1986). Models who practice what they preach validate their claim that the behavior is appropriate and useful. In contrast, when models say one thing and do another, they are conveying to observers that a behavior is fine for observers but not for them, and observers may wonder why.

In a classic study, Bryan and Walbek (1970) exposed elementary school children to an adult model who played a bowling game and won gift certificates, after which children played the game and won certificates. A collection box for certificates was placed on a table so that certificates won could be donated to poor children. While playing, the model preached generosity ("If I win any money today, I am going to give some to those poor children") or selfishness ("If I win any money today, I am not going to give any to the poor children"), after which the model did or did not donate some certificates. The model's actions motivated children better than did the model's verbalizations. Children exposed to a generous model were more likely to donate than those who observed a selfish model; children who heard exhortations for generosity were no more likely to donate than those who heard verbalized selfishness.

Enthusiasm

Models who present their message enthusiastically enhance observers' learning and motivational processes (e.g., self-efficacy, attributions) better than do less enthusiastic models (Perry, 1985). There are numerous real-life examples of model enthusiasm ranging from TV personalities to motivational speakers. These models hope to motivate observers to act in ways they advocate.

Model enthusiasm might affect observers because people may pay better attention to enthusiastic models, which should enhance learning. Enthusiasm also might motivate observers to retain the skills and strategies being modeled. Enthusiastic models could promote observers' perceptions of task value, especially if the models practice what they preach. Enthusiasm could raise observers' self-efficacy because verbal persuasion is a source of efficacy information (discussed in the next section). To the extent that an enthusiastic model conveys a "you-can-do-it" attitude, observers' self-efficacy and motivation for improving their skills should increase.

Classroom research has identified a teacher expressiveness factor that includes such attributes as enthusiasm, rapport, dynamism, and charisma (Abrami, Leventhal, & Perry,

1982; Perry, 1985). In a seminal study, Naftulin, Ware, and Donnelly (1973) had Dr. Myron L. Fox, who unbeknownst to listeners was a professional actor, give a lecture on mathematics as applied to human behavior to audiences of educators and mental health professionals. Dr. Fox delivered his talk in a distinguished and enthusiastic fashion, replete with gestures and humor; however, it made little sense and included unrelated content, double-talk, non sequiturs, neologisms, and contradictions. Afterward, the listeners judged Dr. Fox's presentation positively and felt it was thought provoking. Naftulin and colleagues suggested that a speaker's presumed authority and a charming personality can lead students to believe they have learned in the absence of educational content, a process known as **educational seduction**. In a replication study, Ware and Williams (1975) found that high-expressive instructors received better ratings than low-expressive ones and also produced higher student achievement.

Neither of these studies directly addressed motivation, but Perry and his colleagues (Perry & Dickens, 1984; Perry, Magnusson, Parsonson, & Dickens, 1986) found that expressive instructors enhanced students' perceptions of control, internal attributions (ability, effort), self-confidence, and achievement more than did low-expressive instructors. The instructors were portrayed on videotape and expressiveness was varied along the dimensions of physical movement, voice inflection, eye contact, and humor.

These findings support the idea that enthusiastic teachers help foster students' interest and motivation in learning. Of course, students can learn from unenthusiastic teachers, and overly enthusiastic teachers might be so distracting that they retard student learning. There is a need for research with young children because Perry's studies were conducted with older students. In proper amount, model enthusiasm seems to be an important way to enhance student motivation and thereby increase learning. Applications of this and other model characteristics are provided in Application 4.2.

APPLICATION 4.2

Applying Model Characteristics in the Classroom

1. *Have models display skills correctly (competence)*. Ms. Allen, an algebra teacher, was introducing a new concept in class. She used the overhead projector to demonstrate the process for working the problems, after which she had the students work several problems along with her. She saw that Alex was working the problems correctly, so she asked him to go to the board and solve one while the class observed.

2. *Use high-status models when appropriate (competence)*. Mr. Peterson, a fourth-grade teacher, was introducing a unit on map making to his class. He arranged for Mrs. Alvarez, who worked in the map section at the university library, to come to class and talk about maps. He and Mrs. Alvarez showed the students how to create a key and draw a map.

3. *Use models of equal or slightly greater competence than observers (perceived similarity)*. Ms. Willis introduced a new math concept to her class and had students work a few problems. She then formed small groups of students; each group was composed of students who were experiencing the same level of success or difficulty in mastering

the concept. She circulated among the groups and worked with them on an individual basis. Within each group, as some students mastered the concept, she asked them to work with the others in the group to ensure that they also learned.

4. *Employ coping models with students who previously have experienced difficulties (perceived similarity).* Mr. Ankler was working with some of his students with learning problems who were having difficulty adding fractions. Mr. Ankler showed them places where it was easy to make mistakes. He said, "When I was first learning to add fractions, sometimes I would do this. It's a mistake lots of people make, but you can learn some things to help you remember the right way to work the problems. Let's work on these together and I'll show you."

5. *Have students serve as their own models and gauge progress (perceived similarity).* Ms. Clayton frequently videotaped Ali, one of her remedial reading students, as he worked on a social studies assignment. Afterward, she and Ali would watch the tape together and compare his work with that portrayed on earlier tapes. They then would talk about areas in which he had made progress. Ali experienced higher self-efficacy after watching the tapes and realizing that he was learning in Ms. Clayton's class.

6. *Use multiple models (perceived similarity).* A seventh-grade teacher did a lot of creative writing with her students. After students worked on a writing assignment, she would pair them to discuss and edit their work. She paired students differently throughout the writing process—pairing like abilities and then pairing differing abilities—so that various perspectives would be shared during their discussions. She also met with students individually to discuss their progress and provide feedback.

7. *Ensure that models act consistent with behaviors they model (credibility).* Mr. Parks insisted that his students add columns of numbers without using calculators. Then one day when he was figuring an average for a chart they were making in class, Mr. Parks pulled out his calculator to add a column of numbers. The students commented about him using a calculator. He told them that once they had mastered the addition of a long column of numbers, they could start using calculators. Later in the spring when the class had become proficient in addition, he provided calculators for the class to use.

8. *Show interest and enthusiasm in the content you are teaching and interact with students in an expressive manner (enthusiasm).* Ms. Ball, a kindergarten teacher, bubbled with enthusiasm for every activity that was done in her classroom. She was always saying something like, "Oh, children, you are going to just love what we are going to do next. It is going to be so much fun!" When interacting with the students, she would act out all the silly animals with them, laugh with them, and shout, "Wow! You are all doing such a super job!" Her children were excited about being in school and told their principal that they were the "smartest" class in the school.

Functions of Modeled Consequences

Modeled consequences inform and motivate observers (Schunk, 1987). Observers learn the functional value of behaviors. Observing competent models perform successful actions informs observers of the sequence of actions they should use. Most social situations are structured so that the appropriateness of behaviors depends on such factors as age, gender, or status. By observing modeled behaviors and consequences, people formulate expectations concerning which behaviors are likely to be rewarded and which may be punished.

Vicarious consequences affect observers' motivation. Observing the successes, failures, rewards, and punishments of others creates expectations in observers that they are likely to experience similar outcomes for performing the same behaviors. People perform behaviors they believe will be successful and avoid those they think will not. Students who observe another student praised for working productively are apt to believe that they also will be praised for working diligently. Assuming the students value teacher praise, this expectation may motivate them to work.

Motivational effects of vicarious consequences may not automatically follow from outcomes but also depend on self-efficacy (Bandura, 1986). This was shown by Zimmerman and Ringle (1981). Children observed a model verbalize statements of confidence or pessimism while unsuccessfully attempting to solve a puzzle for a long or short time; then the children attempted the puzzle themselves. Despite the modeled failure, observation of a model exhibiting high persistence and confidence promoted children's motivation (persistence). Observing a low-persistence, high-confidence model raised self-efficacy; observing a high-persistence, high-pessimism model lowered children's efficacy. These results suggest that teachers may need to integrate into their modeled displays statements designed to raise students' self-efficacy.

Reciprocal Teaching

Reciprocal teaching is an example of an instructional procedure that employs extensive use of teacher and peer models. In this approach, teacher and students take turns serving as teacher. Comprehension occurs through teacher-student and student-student dialogue (Palincsar, 1986; Palincsar & Brown, 1984; Rosenshine & Meister, 1994). In a typical small-group reading comprehension procedure, the teacher initially models the strategies to be learned (e.g., summarizing, questioning). The teacher and students read the passage, after which the teacher asks a question, summarizes the content, clarifies troublesome points, and predicts future content. Following the teacher's modeled demonstration, the teacher and students take turns being the teacher. If at first the students have difficulty assuming the role of teacher, the teacher might construct paraphrases and questions for them. As students become more familiar with the procedure, they can implement the strategies with less teacher assistance.

Research has shown that reciprocal teaching leads to greater comprehension gains, better maintenance of skills and strategies over time, and better generalization to classroom comprehension tasks, compared with traditional instruction (Palincsar, 1986; Palincsar & Brown, 1984). Students exposed to reciprocal teaching also demonstrate greater improvements in quality of summaries and questions asked. Palincsar and Brown (1984) reported the following dialogue between a teacher (*T*) and student (*S*) in response to the text about a snake's skeleton:

The snake's skeleton and parts of its body are very flexible—something like a rubber hose with bones. A snake's backbone can have as many as 300 vertebrae, almost 10 times as many as a human's. These vertebrae are connected by loose and rubbery tissues that allow easy movement. Because of this bendable, twistable spinal construction, a snake can turn its body in almost any direction at almost any point.

> *S:* Like, if a snake is turning around, he wouldn't break any bones because he is flexible.
>
> *T:* And the reason he is so flexible is . . .
>
> *S:* If someone stepped on his tail, he wouldn't be able to move unless he was flexible.
>
> *T:* O.K. That explains why it would be helpful to be so flexible, but what makes a snake so flexible? I think that is an important part of the summary.
>
> *S:* So he can move faster?
>
> *T:* That is another reason for being flexible. Let me do a summary for you. Sara [the student] is right. The most important thing we have learned is that the snake is very flexible. The reason they can bend so easily is that they have so many little bones in their backbones and each of them can move separately, making the snake very flexible. Does that make sense? (p. 142)

Reciprocal teaching reflects Vygotsky's (1978) **zone of proximal development (ZPD)**, or the difference between one's performance while working alone and while working with a more competent person. More generally, the ZPD denotes the amount of learning possible by a student given proper instructional support. As long as the teacher and peer teachers are operating in the ZPD, learning is facilitated. Teachers and peers provide **scaffolding** (assistance) that helps support learners until they become competent and it can be removed.

The ZPD also is closely aligned with Vygotsky's (1962) ideas about the role of **private speech,** or self-directed speech that is self-regulatory but not socially communicative (Berk, 1986, 1992). Vygotsky believed that private speech helps develop thought through its role in behavioral self-regulation. The capacity of speech to influence thought and behavior develops during the preschool years when children give themselves many self-regulatory, verbal instructions. Initially such speech follows thought and behavior but develops such that it precedes them. Such private speech often is overt (aloud), but increasingly becomes covert (subvocal), although it can re-emerge in overt form at any time. Vygotsky believed that private speech was an intermediate step between a child's behavior being regulated overtly by others (e.g., parents) and covertly by inner speech (thought) (Behrend, Rosengren, & Perlmutter, 1992).

If private speech represents an intermediate step between regulation by others and covert self-regulation, and if the ZPD represents tasks that a child is capable of mastering, we should expect private speech to occur commonly while the child works in the ZPD (Behrend et al., 1992). This idea is captured in Meichenbaum's (1977) **self-instructional training** procedure. Meichenbaum and Goodman (1971) used the following five-step procedure to train impulsive second graders in a special education class:

1. *Cognitive modeling:* Adult tells child what to do while adult performs the task.
2. *Overt guidance:* Child performs under direction of adult instruction.
3. *Overt self-guidance:* Child performs while instructing him- or herself aloud.
4. *Faded overt self-guidance:* Child whispers instructions while performing task.
5. *Covert self-instruction:* Child performs task while guided by inner silent speech.

Self-instructional training has been used to teach various tasks and is especially useful for teaching students to work strategically (Fish & Pervan, 1985). In the Meichenbaum and Goodman (1971) study, the following sample statements were made by an adult model for a line-drawing task to slow down students' performances:

> Okay, what is it I have to do? You want me to copy the picture with the different lines. I have to go slow and be careful. Okay, draw the line down, good; then to the right, that's it; now down some more and to the left. Good, I'm doing fine so far. Remember go slow. Now back up again. No, I was supposed to go down. That's okay, just erase the line carefully . . . Good. Even if I make an error I can go on slowly and carefully. Okay, I have to go down now. Finished. I did it. (p. 117)

MOTIVATIONAL PROCESSES

In Bandura's (1986, 1993, 1997) theory, motivation is goal-directed behavior instigated and sustained by expectations concerning the anticipated outcomes of actions and self-efficacy for performing those actions. Self-efficacy and goals are discussed in the next sections, after which we describe a model of motivated learning.

Outcome expectations are the expected outcomes of one's actions (Bandura, 1986; Locke & Latham, 1990; Weiner, 1985b). From a motivational perspective, outcome expectations are important because students think about potential outcomes of various actions and act in ways they believe will attain the outcomes they value. Academically motivated students believe if they study diligently, they will make good grades. Given that they value high grades, we should expect them to study hard and thereby validate their expectations.

Self-Efficacy

Self-efficacy is defined as, "People's judgments of their capabilities to organize and execute courses of action required to attain designated types of performances" (Bandura, 1986, p. 391). Self-efficacy affects choice of activities, effort, and persistence. People holding low self-efficacy for accomplishing a task may avoid it; those who believe they are capable are likely to participate. Especially when they encounter difficulties, efficacious students work harder and persist longer than those with doubts. People acquire information to appraise self-efficacy from their actual performances, vicarious (observational) experiences, forms of persuasion, and physiological symptoms.

Self-efficacy bears some similarity to task-specific self-concept and self-perceptions of competence (see chapter 2). Self-efficacy represents people's judgments of their capabilities in the same way that Eccles and Wigfield represent task-specific self-concept and Harter represents self-perceptions of competence. There are, however, some important differences. First, the definition of self-efficacy includes "organize and execute courses of action," which represents the theory's more specific and situational view of perceived competence in terms of including the behavioral actions or cognitive skills that are necessary for competent performance in a given domain (Bong & Clark, 1999; Pajares, 1996; Pajares & Miller, 1995). For example, self-efficacy would not be merely a self-recognition of being good in school, but rather explicit judgments of having the skills for finding main ideas in passages of varying levels of difficulty, correctly subtracting fractions in different problems, composing different types of paragraphs, and so forth.

In assessing self-efficacy, researchers often show students sets of sample tasks and ask them to rate their confidence for successfully performing those types of tasks. Self-efficacy ratings are then averaged across the set to form a measure of self-efficacy for performing the task (e.g., finding main ideas, solving fractions, composing paragraphs).

A second aspect that distinguishes self-efficacy from self-concept and self-competence is that it is used in reference to some type of goal ("attain designated types of performance"). Again, this reflects the more situational perspective of self-efficacy in contrast to the personality and developmental heritage of expectancy-value and perceptions-of-competence research. In support of this perspective, Smith and Fouad (1999) found that self-efficacy, goals, and outcome expectations are specific to subject areas and show little generalization across areas.

One implication of the inclusion of a specific goal is that self-efficacy judgments for similar tasks may vary as a function of personal or environmental differences. For example, experienced runners may lower their self-efficacy for maintaining their usual time for a 10-kilometer run because of a nagging muscle pull. A student's self-efficacy for learning a particular topic in mathematics may be lower because of the difficulty of the material to be learned in contrast to material covered earlier in the course. In colloquial terms, these individuals have lower than usual "self-confidence" in their capabilities to perform a specific task at a certain level of competence.

As noted earlier, outcome expectations form a second construct related to motivational behavior and affect. The outcome expectation notion of a contingency between a response and its outcome is similar to Rotter's (1966) construct of locus of control regarding the contingency between behavior and reinforcement. An outcome expectation is also related to the expectancy for success construct from expectancy-value theories. As Bandura (1986) explained, "The belief that one can high jump six feet is an efficacy judgment; the anticipated social recognition, applause, trophies, and self-satisfactions for such a performance constitute the outcome expectations" (p. 391). In the academic domain, students would have efficacy judgments of their capabilities, skills, and knowledge to master school-related tasks, but also have outcome expectations about what grades they might receive on the tasks.

Although efficacy beliefs and outcome expectations are usually related, it is possible for a student to have relatively high self-efficacy for a task but a negative outcome expectation. For example, a college student in an organic chemistry class might feel efficacious for mastering the material but hold negative outcome expectations about grades on the exams due to the high competition among the students and the grading curve instituted by the professor to separate the weaker from the stronger students.

Although both efficacy and outcome judgments are best thought of as continuums, Bandura (1982) suggested that a simple high/low efficacy by high/low outcome expectation comparison provides insight into behavior and affect. Figure 4.2 shows the expected behavioral and affective reactions for individuals who vary in self-efficacy and outcome expectations. Naturally it is desirable to be high in both. These individuals are confident and assured in their performance, show high levels of effort, persist, and have high cognitive engagement in academic tasks. Students high in efficacy but low in outcome expectations are likely to study hard and be engaged but also may protest and lobby for changes in the grading system. They may leave the environment by dropping out, not because of low self-efficacy but rather because they perceive no contingency between their learning and the outcomes (e.g., grades).

Self Efficacy	**Outcome Expectation**	
	Low outcome expectation	*High outcome expectation*
High self–efficacy	Social activism Protest Grievance Milieu change	Assured, opportune action High cognitive engagement
Low self–efficacy	Resignation Apathy Withdrawal	Self–devaluation Depression

Figure 4.2 Behavioral and affective reactions as a function of different levels of self-efficacy and outcome expectations

From "Self-Efficacy Mechanism in Human Agency" by A. Bandura, 1982, *American Psychologist, 37,* p. 140. Copyright © 1982 by the American Psychological Association. Adapted by permission.

Individuals low in self-efficacy and outcome expectations may show resignation and apathy and an unwillingness or inability to exert much effort. In the academic domain, this cell would represent students who have given up on learning and are unwilling to try. They are similar to learned helpless students (Peterson, Maier, & Seligman, 1993; see chapter 3). The final cell includes students who have low self-efficacy but high outcome expectations. These students believe they cannot do the task but are aware—such as from seeing others rewarded—that if they were able to perform, the environment would be responsive and they would be rewarded appropriately. They tend to evaluate themselves negatively and blame themselves for failure, in contrast to students low in self-efficacy and outcome expectations who also focus on the lack of environmental responsiveness.

Although outcome expectations and self-efficacy need not be related, the former often are dependent on the latter: "If you control for how well people judge they can perform, you account for much of the variance in the kinds of outcomes they expect" (Bandura, 1986, p. 393). How one behaves largely determines the actual outcome and, in the same way, beliefs about outcome expectations are dependent on self-efficacy judgments. Bandura gives the example of drivers who are not confident in their ability to negotiate a winding mountain road (low efficacy). They will conjure up images of wreckage and injuries (one type of outcome expectation), whereas those confident in their ability will anticipate the grand views from the mountains. Teachers who are not confident about their capability to foster student learning may dwell on negative images about their classrooms; those with greater confidence are apt to think of their students as motivated to learn.

In the academic domain, students' self-efficacy beliefs are likely to be highly related to their outcome expectations, as shown in the top right and bottom left cells in Figure 4.2. At the same time, structural constraints (e.g., the chemistry example) can cause mismatches. The high efficacy–low outcome expectation pattern might also occur due to institutional discrimination on the basis of race, ethnicity, or gender. Students in the affected group (e.g., minorities in any school or classroom where they are discriminated against and women in math and science classes) might feel that they can master the material (high efficacy) but cannot succeed due to the discriminatory practices in the setting. We will note that because outcome expectations are beliefs, the fact that students hold negative outcome expectations due to discrimination does not automatically imply that discrimination exists in the setting.

The motivational impact of self-efficacy can be dramatic. When self-efficacy perceptions are high, individuals will engage in tasks that foster the development of their skills and capabilities. When self-efficacy is low, however, people will not engage in new tasks that might help them learn new skills (Bandura, 1997). In addition, by avoiding these tasks, an individual will not receive any corrective feedback to counter the negative self-efficacy perceptions. In general, it is most adaptive to have self-efficacy that slightly exceeds actual skills at any given time. Grossly optimistic efficacy beliefs can lead people to attempt tasks that are far beyond their skills and result in aversive consequences. An overly confident novice mountain climber who attempts a very difficult climb may experience serious injury or death. In the academic domain, students who choose academic tasks that greatly exceed their skill levels can suffer needless failures and subsequent debilitating efficacy beliefs. Individuals who grossly underestimate their efficacy limit their potential for learning. If they do undertake the tasks, they may suffer from unnecessary anxiety and self-doubts and quit easily when they encounter difficulties, which further debilitates self-efficacy (Bandura, 1997).

Self-efficacy is related to task choice as well as career choices. Betz and Hackett (1981, 1983; Hackett & Betz, 1981) found that although there are structural and social influences on career choices, self-efficacy is an important mediator of these external influences and has a direct bearing on career choice. In addition, gender differences that emerge in vocational choices are due to differences in self-efficacy; men are efficacious for all careers, whereas women are efficacious only for careers traditionally held by women and feel inefficacious for careers traditionally held by men.

Self-efficacy is strongly related to effort and task persistence (Bandura & Cervone, 1983, 1986; Schunk, 1995). Individuals with high self-efficacy beliefs are likely to exert effort in the face of difficulty and persist at a task when they have the requisite skills. There is, however, some evidence that self-doubts may foster learning when students have not previously acquired the skills. As Bandura (1986) notes, "Self-doubt creates the impetus for learning but hinders adept use of previously established skills" (p. 394). Salomon (1984) found that students high in efficacy were more likely to be cognitively engaged in learning when the task was perceived as difficult but less likely to be effortful and less cognitively engaged when the task was deemed easy.

Besides the quantity of effort, the quality of effort in terms of the use of deeper processing strategies and general cognitive engagement of learning has been strongly linked to self-efficacy (Pintrich & Schrauben, 1992). Pintrich and De Groot (1990a) found that junior high students high in efficacy were more likely to report using various cognitive and self-regulatory learning strategies. In a series of experimental studies, Schunk (1982, 1983a, 1983b, 1983c, 1983d, 1984, 1987, 1996) found that students with self-efficacy mastered various academic tasks better than did students with weaker self-efficacy. In addition, these studies showed that efficacy was a significant predictor of learning and achievement, even after prior achievement and cognitive skills were taken into consideration.

In sum, self-efficacy has been shown to be an important mediator of all types of achievement behavior as well as many other types of behavior. Self-efficacy is similar to task-specific self-concept and self-perceptions of competence because each represents individuals' judgments of their capabilities. At the same time, self-efficacy is more situation specific than are the other expectancy constructs. This assumption has led researchers to measure self-efficacy in a situationally sensitive fashion and at a microanalytic level (e.g., efficacy for very specific academic problems such as two-digit subtraction problems with regrouping). Related to this situational specificity, self-efficacy beliefs are assumed to be more dynamic, fluctuating, and changeable than the more static and stable self-concept and self-competence beliefs. One's self-efficacy for a specific task on a given day might fluctuate due to the individual's preparation, physical condition (sickness, fatigue), and affective mood, as well as external conditions such as the nature of the task (length, difficulty) and social milieu (general classroom conditions). In contrast, other views of self-competence view it more globally (e.g., math competence) and are less concerned with microlevel instability of beliefs.

Goals

Goal setting refers to establishing quantitative or qualitative standards of performance (Locke & Latham, 1990). Goal setting is an important motivational process (Bandura, 1988, 1997; Schunk, 1989a). Students with a goal are apt to experience a sense of self-efficacy for attaining it and engage in activities they believe will lead to attainment: attend to instruction, rehearse information to be remembered, expend effort, and persist. Self-efficacy is substantiated as learners observe goal progress, which conveys they are becoming skillful (Elliott & Dweck, 1988). Providing students with feedback on goal progress also raises self-efficacy (Schunk & Swartz, 1993). Heightened self-efficacy sustains motivation and improves skills. Goal setting and self-efficacy are especially powerful influences on academic attainments (Zimmerman, Bandura, & Martinez-Pons, 1992).

The motivational benefits of goals depend on learners making a commitment to attain the goals (discussed next) and on the goal properties of *proximity*, *specificity*, and *difficulty*. *Proximal* (close-at-hand) goals promote self-efficacy and motivation better than distant goals because it is easier to judge progress toward the former. For the same reason, goals incorporating *specific* performance standards raise efficacy and motivation better than general goals (e.g., "Do your best"). From a motivational perspective, goals of moderate *difficulty*—those learners perceive as challenging but attainable—are most effective, although for instructional purposes teachers may establish easy goals in the initial stages of learning and gradually increase goal difficulty as skills develop. Progress toward difficult goals raises efficacy because it conveys that students are improving.

Locke and Latham (1990) proposed a goal-setting theory in which two important aspects of goals are goal choice and goal commitment. Goal choice refers to the actual goal that individuals are trying to obtain and the level at which they are trying to attain it.

Goal commitment represents how strongly individuals are attached to the goal, how enthusiastic they are about the goal, or how determined they are to achieve it.

Goal commitment may be assessed through behavior and action because the simple selection of a goal is often not enough to spur action. There must be a volitional element (discussed later in this chapter) to goal commitment. As Locke and Latham (1990) state:

> *Believing* that a goal is desirable and reachable does not automatically force an individual to act. The individual must *choose* to put his or her judgment in action. Individuals who simply wait for their conscious and subconscious estimates of a situation to "turn them on," more often than not find themselves doing nothing or drifting without any sustained purpose. (p. 127)

A partial list of the factors that Locke and Latham have identified as influencing goal choice and commitment is shown in Table 4.3. The first category includes a number of personal factors. Most importantly, previous performance and actual ability/skill level will influence goal choice and commitment. Individuals are most likely to try to attain goals that they have had some success at previously (e.g., good students trying to attain high grades), whereas it is unlikely that people will try to attain goals that are very much beyond their actual skill level or previous performances (e.g., a student with a long history of very poor grades setting a goal of earning all A's). In Locke and Latham's theory, self-

Table 4.3   Factors Influencing Goal Choice and Goal Commitment

Personal-individual factors
    Previous performance
    Actual ability/skill level
    Self-efficacy
    Causal attributions
    Valence/values
    Mood
Social-environmental factors
    Group factors
        Group norms, normative information
        Group goals
        Peer group
    Role modeling
    Reward structure
        Nature of rewards
        Competition
    Nature of authority and goal assignment
        Authority is legitimate
        Authority is knowledgeable
    Nature of feedback
        Conveys efficacy information
        Fosters sense of achievement and mastery
        Implies opportunities for self-development

Locke & Latham (1990).

efficacy is one of the most important positive influences on personal goal setting. People with higher self-efficacy set higher goals. Self-efficacy also bears a positive relation to goal commitment, with commitment being stronger when efficacy is high. Causal attributions (see chapter 3) can play a role in goal setting; for example, attributing failure to unstable causes (bad luck, low effort) leads to setting higher goals on subsequent tasks.

Two other personal factors that can influence goal setting are valence/values and mood. Valence refers to individuals' personal value beliefs about the importance of the goal, which may be based on interest, utility, monetary, or attainment value beliefs (see value beliefs in chapter 2). Mood can be related to goal choice, with positive moods leading to higher goals (Locke & Latham, 1990).

Locke and Latham's model was developed and tested in organizational and work settings; thus, it places greater emphasis on the importance of external factors than do many other motivational models. Group norms and normative information seem to have a generally positive effect on goal setting; higher group norms lead individuals to set higher goals for themselves. However, when people are assigned very high, almost unreachable, goals by someone else and are told that very few people reach these goals (normative information), then personal goals are likely to be lowered (Locke & Latham, 1990).

Group goals (a goal for the group or a two-person partnership) also can have a positive effect on personal goals. Peer groups can exert pressure on members of the group, which may result in the raising or lowering of goals, depending on the group support. For example, if the group does not support the assigned goal (the teacher-assigned or task-explicit goal), individuals in the group will be less personally committed to the goal. This can happen in cooperative groups in classrooms when the small group undermines the teacher's goal for the task, with the subsequent detrimental effect on the task engagement of group members. In contrast, if the group supports the goal and exerts pressure or encourages members of the group to work at the assigned goal, personal commitment to the goal should be higher. One of the positive effects of cooperative groups in classrooms occurs when a small group of students helps a recalcitrant member become engaged in the task through encouragement and peer pressure.

Positive role modeling of goal setting by others influences individuals to set higher goals for themselves. In the classroom, this might involve children watching or hearing other children set high but attainable goals (e.g., "I'm going to read the next two stories in this book and then write a report about them") and then trying to set similar goals for themselves. Positive role models can influence both goal setting and self-efficacy to attain them.

Another external factor that can affect the goals that individuals adopt is the reward structure, although the relation is complex and may depend on goal difficulty. When assigned goals are very difficult or almost impossible, offering incentives may not increase performance. When goals are easy to moderate, however, extra incentives can influence performance positively. Besides the actual rewards, Locke and Latham suggested that competition can positively influence the level of goals set but not the commitment to the goals.

The two final factors listed in Table 4.3 regarding the influences on goal level and goal commitment concern the role of an authority figure and the type of feedback. Characteristics of an authority figure (e.g., a supervisor or manager in business, whose role is not unlike that of a classroom teacher) can influence both goal level and goal commitment. Participatively or self-set goals that allow for individual control do not necessarily have a positive effect over and above assigned goals; however, the manner in which goals are assigned by the authority figure is most important. Individuals are more committed to goals when the authority figure is legitimate, supportive, physically present, trustworthy, knowledgeable, and likable, provides a convincing rationale for the goal, and exerts reasonable pressure. In addition, the nature of the feedback is crucial. Most important are the provision of positive self-efficacy information and feedback that stresses challenge, mastery, self-improvement, and achievement. When presented in this manner, assigned goals and the accompanying feedback can have positive results. Self-efficacy to reach the goal is a crucial mediator: If feedback (including rewards) provides positive efficacy information, there should be a positive effect of using this type of feedback.

In sum, goal level and goal commitment can be influenced by a number of personal and environmental factors. Many of these factors work in a fashion similar to that predicted by social cognitive theory (Bandura, 1986, 1988) or attribution theory (Weiner, 1986; see chapter 3). Locke and Latham (1990) proposed that several external factors, most notably competition, assigned goals, and the use of rewards, can have positive influences on goal level and goal commitment. We will revisit these topics later when we discuss goal orientation theory (see chapter 5) and intrinsic motivation (chapter 6). Some applications of goal setting in classrooms are given in Application 4.3.

APPLICATION 4.3

Applying Goal Setting in the Classroom

1. *Set clear and specific goals.* Teachers should specify clear and unambiguous goals for all students in the class. Locke and Latham's work shows that having this type of goal is much more beneficial than setting no goals or encouraging individuals to do their best.

   Ms. Shapiro asks her high school English students to read four books each semester. The students may choose their four books from a large reading list that Ms. Shapiro provides.

2. *Goals should be challenging and difficult, but not outside the range of students' capabilities.* Students should spend most of their time working on tasks that challenge them but are not so far beyond their skill level that the tasks frustrate them.

   Mr. Washington, an elementary school teacher, pushes his students hard in math. Over the years, he has built up a very clear idea about what his fifth-graders can do. He presents them with many different kinds of problems to work on, but he does not give them any problems they can't master.

3. *Set both proximal and distal goals for students.* Setting proximal goals can have positive effects on self-efficacy and performance. Teachers can help students set proximal goals by designing contracts with them that specify a series of subgoals that lead to larger, distal goals.

   Ms. Yu, a junior high science teacher, requires lab reports and science term papers. However, she divides large reports and projects into a series of subgoals, giving students a due date for an outline, a due date for research notes, a due date for the first draft, and so on, thereby helping her students set proximal goals.

4. *Provide feedback that increases students' self-efficacy for obtaining the goal.* Rewards or verbal feedback given contingent on performance provides efficacy information to individuals and encourages them to continue working toward goal attainment. Teachers should not be afraid to use extrinsic rewards, but should use them in a way that makes them contingent on actual academic performance, not as ways to control general behavior or as bribes to comply with the teacher.

Mr. Larkin's fifth graders periodically work on a self-paced reading program. Students keep a written record of their progress. Mr. Larkin reviews each student's progress every 2 weeks and awards students free time based on the amount of progress they have made in the past 2 weeks.

Model of Motivated Learning

Motivated learning is motivation to acquire skills and strategies rather than to perform tasks (Corno & Mandinach, 1983). Schunk (1989c, 1995) presented a model of motivated learning that highlights the role of self-efficacy (Figure 4.3). At the start of an activity, students differ in their self-efficacy for learning or performing actions as a function of personal qualities (e.g., abilities, attitudes), prior experiences at the same or similar activities, and social support from significant persons in their environments. Regarding the latter, students differ in the extent that parents and teachers encourage them to develop skills, facilitate their access to resources necessary for learning (e.g., materials,

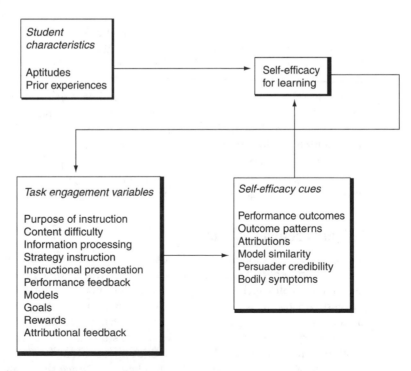

Figure 4.3   Model of motivated learning

facilities), and teach them self-regulatory strategies that enhance skill acquisition and refinement (Ericsson, Krampe, & Tesch-Romer, 1993).

As students engage in activities, they are affected by such personal influences as goal setting and information processing, along with situational factors (e.g., rewards, teacher feedback). From these factors, students derive cues signaling how well they are performing. Motivation and self-efficacy are enhanced when people perceive they are performing skillfully or becoming more competent. Lack of success or slow progress will not necessarily lower self-efficacy and motivation if students believe they can perform better by adjusting their approach (e.g., expend more effort, use effective task strategies) (Schunk, 1995).

Influences on Pretask Self-Efficacy

Students enter tasks with differing personal qualities, prior experiences, and social support, which influence their initial sense of self-efficacy for learning. Personal qualities include general abilities, task-specific skills, interests, attitudes, and personality characteristics (Cronbach & Snow, 1977). Students also differ in their prior educational experiences (e.g., schools attended, number and types of teachers, amount of time spent on various subjects), and how much support they receive from others (e.g., parents, teachers, peers). These factors are interdependent. For example, mathematical ability and interest contribute to students' classroom successes, and encouragement from parents and teachers helps develop positive attitudes and interest (Schunk, 1995).

These factors also affect students' self-efficacy for learning. Students with high mathematical ability, who previously have performed well on mathematical tasks and whose parents support this interest, ought to hold higher self-efficacy for learning a new math skill than learners with lower mathematical ability, who have experienced learning difficulties and whose parents are less supportive. An initial sense of self-efficacy motivates students and promotes learning.

At the same time, self-efficacy is not completely determined by personal factors. Collins (1982) administered standardized tests to students and identified those with high, average, and low mathematical ability. Within each ability level, she identified students of high and low mathematical efficacy and gave all students problems to solve and opportunities to rework those they missed. Ability was positively related to skillful performance; regardless of ability level, students with higher self-efficacy solved more problems correctly and chose to rework more problems they missed.

Task Engagement Variables

Task engagement variables include those factors that come into play during instruction and while students are engaged in academic activities. Some important personal and situational variables include the purpose of instruction, content difficulty, information processing, strategy instruction, instructional presentation, performance feedback, models, goals, rewards, and attributional feedback (Schunk, 1989c).

The purpose of instruction, or what uses students are expected to make of the material to be learned (Marx, 1983), provides information about task value and can influence efficacy and motivation. When teachers announce that material will be on a test, students who have performed poorly on tests may experience anxiety, which could lead to low efficacy. Students who have earned good grades on tests previously should react with high self-efficacy.

Content difficulty is also relevant. Subject matter perceived as difficult to learn may lead to low motivation and low self-efficacy for learning. Many students have qualms about solving algebraic equations. Those who believe they are competent in the component skills (multiplication, subtraction) will feel more efficacious about learning than students who doubt their capabilities.

The type of information processing required affects self-efficacy and motivation. Students who have difficulty processing information required by a task may conclude they have low ability and feel less certain about learning than those who believe they can process the material. Salomon (1984) found that students perceive learning from TV easier than learning from print, hold higher self-efficacy about learning from TV, and invest less mental effort in learning. For print materials, higher self-efficacy was associated with greater expended effort.

Strategy instruction can foster self-efficacy for learning. The belief that one understands and can effectively apply a strategy that aids learning leads to a greater sense of control over learning outcomes, which promotes self-efficacy and motivation to apply the strategy.

Instructional presentation affects motivation and learning. Teachers who present material in ways that students can understand engender high efficacy for learning. When assessing efficacy, students take into account how well they learn from various instructional methods. If they believe they learn best when they work in small groups and the teacher uses small groups often, they should feel more efficacious and motivated than students who believe they learn best in large groups. Brophy (1985) identified differences in how teachers introduce content. Teachers may cue positive/negative expectations by asserting that students will/will not enjoy the task and do well/poorly on it. Assuming that students view the teacher as a credible judge of their capabilities, these statements will affect their self-efficacy.

The role of **performance feedback** is minimal when students can obtain feedback on their own (e.g., mathematical problems for which students check their answers). When students cannot reliably determine how well they are learning, teacher feedback that highlights progress (e.g., "That's right. You're getting better at this") raises self-efficacy. At the same time, teachers who provide excessive assistance to students may improve their skills but not their self-efficacy because students may believe they cannot succeed on their own.

Models are important influences on self-efficacy. Although students attend to and emulate teachers despite being dissimilar in attributes and competence, observation of successful peers may exert stronger effects on efficacy, especially among learners who doubt they can attain the teacher's level of competence (Schunk, 1989c). The latter students may not feel efficacious about learning after observing a flawless teacher model, but seeing similar peers master the task may make them feel more capable and motivate them to attempt to learn.

When students set goals, they are apt to experience a sense of efficacy for goal attainment and higher motivation. Self-efficacy is substantiated as students make goal progress. Progress is easy to gauge with short-term and specific goals (Bandura & Schunk, 1981). Although students may initially doubt their capabilities to attain goals they believe are difficult, these goals build high efficacy because they offer more information about learning capabilities than easier goals.

Rewards are likely to enhance efficacy when they are tied to students' accomplishments and provide information to them about their own capabilities. Telling students they can earn rewards (e.g., free time) based on what they accomplish instills a sense of efficacy for performing well, which is validated as they work and note their progress. Receipt of the reward further validates efficacy because it symbolizes progress. Rewards for participation regardless of performance level may motivate students, but also convey that students are not expected to learn much, which negatively affects self-efficacy.

Attributional feedback that links successes and failures with causes is a persuasive source of efficacy information (see chapter 3). Linking successes with high ability and effort and failure with low effort enhances self-efficacy and motivation (Schunk, 1989b). It is imperative that learners view the feedback as being credible. Providing ability feedback ("You're good at this") when students have to struggle to succeed will not raise self-efficacy. When students believe a task is easy, teacher praise combined with effort information ("That's good. You've been working hard") signals low ability (Weiner, Graham, Taylor, & Meyer, 1983). Students who believe that the teacher does not expect much of them will doubt their capabilities.

Self-Efficacy Cues

Efficacy cues are derived during task engagement. Some important cues include performance outcomes (successes, failures), outcome patterns, attributions, model similarity, persuader credibility, and bodily symptoms.

Successes generally raise self-efficacy and failures lower it. With respect to outcome patterns, early learning often is fraught with failures and the perception of progress promotes efficacy. Self-efficacy is not aided much if students believe their progress is slow or their skills have stabilized at low levels.

Success attributed to great effort should raise efficacy less than if minimal effort is required, because the former implies that skills are not well developed. Self-efficacy remains high as long as learners believe they can maintain the level of effort needed to succeed. As students develop skills, ability attributions for successes enhance efficacy better than effort attributions.

Observing similar peers improving their skills conveys that students can learn as well; observed failures cast doubt on students' capability to succeed. Model similarity can be based on perceived competence or personal attributes (e.g., age, gender, ethnic background), even when the attributes have little bearing on the modeled behaviors (Rosenthal & Bandura, 1978).

Students feel efficacious when persuaded by a trustworthy source (e.g., the teacher) that they are capable of learning, whereas they may discount the advice of less credible sources. Students also may discount otherwise credible sources if they believe the sources do not understand the task demands (e.g., difficult for students to comprehend).

Bodily symptoms serve as physiological cues. Sweating and trembling may signal that students are not capable of learning. Students who notice they are reacting in less-agitated fashion to tasks feel more efficacious about learning. Application 4.4 illustrates classroom applications of this model of motivated learning.

APPLICATION 4.4

Applying Principles of Motivated Learning in the Classroom

1. *Make it clear that students are competent enough to learn the material being taught.* A second-grade teacher has each student work with her in a small group to demonstrate how to subtract with regrouping before she assigns the student a worksheet with the same type of mathematical problems.

2. *Point out how the learning will be useful in students' lives.* Mr. Cristopolous, a high school science teacher, links the subject matter being taught with material that students understand. For example, prior to beginning a unit on electricity, he has students discuss all the ways they use electricity in their lives. While teaching, he shows how electricity operates in these applications. The students enjoy learning about something that affects them in so many ways.

3. *Teach students learning strategies and show them how their performance has improved as a result of strategy use.* Several students in Mr. Wilson's fourth-grade class were having difficulty with long division. Mr. Wilson worked with these students in a small group and taught them to ask the question, "*Does mom serve cheese burgers?*" and then perform those steps (*divide, multiply, subtract, check, bring* down) to solve a long division problem. He then had students repeat the strategy aloud as they worked problems and provided positive feedback as they solved each problem.

4. *Present content in ways students understand and tailor instructional presentations to individual differences in learning.* Mrs. Stein explained a social studies assignment to her class. Some of the students were having difficulty understanding and remembering all the tasks in the assignment. Mrs. Stein outlined the activity and wrote the various tasks on the board.

5. *Have students work toward learning goals.* Mr. Seagroves told his class that he wants them to learn their 8's multiplication tables by the end of the week. He said they will practice in class each day and he wants them to study at home. Each day in class the students complete a sheet with the multiplication facts for 8 and record their progress.

6. *Ensure that attributional feedback is credible.* Ms. Sanchez, a third-grade teacher, has in her class Neal, a boy with emotional and behavioral disorders. He is having difficulty concentrating and paying attention during lessons. Other teachers told Ms. Sanchez to continually praise him or he would get mad and act up. Ms. Sanchez decided to take a more realistic approach. She met with Neal and told him, "Neal, you are smart enough to learn in here, but you have to work harder and pay attention and concentrate."

   Neal remarked, "Ms. Sanchez, I can't believe that you really talked to me about this. Lots of others say I'm too dumb to learn. Maybe I can try to listen better."

7. *Provide feedback on progress in learning and link rewards with progress.* Ms. Burns has been working with Amy to teach her colors. Amy loves to work on computer games. Ms. Burns told Amy that if she learns her colors she can have extra time on the computer. Each time Amy learned a color, she and Ms. Burns colored a block

on the extra-computer-time ticket (using the color just learned). After Amy learned five colors, she was given extra time at the computer.

8. *Use models that build self-efficacy and enhance motivation.* Mr. Prescott was working with his fifth-grade class on reducing fractions. As they worked through each problem, Mr. Prescott let several volunteers demonstrate how to complete the problem at the board. By the end of the class period, all the students in the room felt comfortable demonstrating the process on the board.

SOCIAL COMPARISON

Social cognitive theory stresses the influence of **social comparison,** or comparing ourselves with others, on motivation. Social comparison is an important means for learning about the appropriateness of behavior as well as understanding our capabilities and, in turn, our self-efficacy. When absolute standards of behavior are ambiguous or nonexistent, acceptability of behavior is gauged relative to what is practiced by others. Further, seeing others act in a particular way and receive praise or recognition can motivate observers to act in similar fashion because they believe they will be rewarded.

We now consider social comparison theory, how social comparison changes with development, and the role of social comparison in motivation and achievement.

Festinger's Theory

Festinger (1954) proposed that people are inherently motivated to evaluate their abilities and opinions and they often do this by comparing themselves with others: "To the extent that objective, nonsocial means are not available, people evaluate their opinions and abilities by comparison respectively with the opinions and abilities of others" (p. 118). He also postulated that the most accurate self-evaluations derive from comparisons with individuals similar in the ability or characteristic being evaluated. In choosing people for comparison, individuals are apt to select those who are similar on the characteristics or related attributes most predictive of performance in the domain in question (Goethals & Darley, 1977). Thus, to evaluate personal math ability, an individual ought to choose others who are similar in attributes relevant to math performance: age, prior math courses, math grades.

This similarity hypothesis is supported by research (Suls & Sanders, 1982) and predictions of social cognitive theory. The more alike observers are to models, the greater the probability that similar actions by observers are socially appropriate and will produce comparable results (Bandura, 1986; Schunk, 1987). Anticipating rewarding consequences for acting in a given fashion can motivate observers to act accordingly.

At the same time, Festinger's theory does not fully explain the motivational effects of perceived similarity because these effects depend largely on self-efficacy. Children who observe similar others accomplish a task are apt to try it themselves because they believe they will be successful. Interestingly, research also shows that perceived dissimilarity can motivate. Schunk and Hanson (1989a) found that average-achieving children who observed coping models learn judged their self-efficacy for learning the skills higher than did students who observed mastery models. The former children judged themselves more competent than the coping models, whereas the latter students perceived themselves similar in competence to the mastery models. The belief that one is more competent than a model enhances self-efficacy and motivation.

Development of Social Comparison

Adults employ social comparison regularly for self-evaluation, but the ability to use comparative information depends on higher levels of cognitive development and experience in making comparative evaluations (Veroff, 1969). Festinger's hypotheses may not apply to young children. Children younger than age 5 or 6 tend not to relate two or more elements in thought and are egocentric in that their "self" dominates their cognitive focus (Higgins, 1981). These characteristics do not mean that young children cannot evaluate themselves relative to others, but rather that they do not do so automatically. Children become increasingly interested in comparative information in elementary school. The behaviors of young children are affected by direct adult social evaluation (e.g., You're good at this; you could do better) but by fourth grade, children regularly use peer comparisons to evaluate their competence (Ruble, Boggiano, Feldman, & Loebl, 1980).

The meaning and function of comparative information change with development and especially after children enter school. Preschoolers actively compare physical characteristics (e.g., rewards they and others receive) (Ruble et al., 1980). Their comparisons determine how they are similar to and different from others (e.g., "I'm 4 1/2, you're 4"; "We both had a birthday") and seem to be based on a desire to be better than others without involving self-evaluation (e.g., "I'm the general; that's higher than the captain") (Mosatche & Bragonier, 1981). Less frequently, young children engage in comparison to evaluate their qualifications ("I can do it, too").

Ruble and her colleagues discussed the development of social comparison in children as a multistep process (Ruble, 1983; Ruble, Parsons, & Ross, 1976). The earliest comparisons primarily involve similarities and differences but then shift to a concern for how to perform tasks. Feldman & Ruble (1977) found that first graders engaged in much peer comparison, but primarily to obtain correct answers. Providing comparative information to young children may raise their motivation more for practical reasons (e.g., to finish a task) than for acquiring information about capabilities. Knowing that others are performing better will not necessarily motivate young children, and telling those who fail at a task that most other children also do poorly may not alleviate the negative impact of failure (Ruble, Parsons, & Ross, 1976). After first grade, children's interest increases in determining how well peers are doing; they use comparative information more often to evaluate competence.

The capability to compare one's current and prior performance (temporal comparison) to evaluate progress is present in young children, although they may not employ it. R. Butler (1998) found among children ages 4 to 8 that temporal comparisons increased with age but children most often attended only to their last outcome. In contrast, children frequently employed social comparisons and evaluated their performances higher if they exceeded those of peers. Butler's results suggest that teachers need to assist children in making temporal comparisons, such as by showing children their prior work and pointing out areas of improvement.

Ruble and Frey (1991) suggested that social comparison processes may vary not just by age, but by experience with a task. They postulated a four-phase model with social comparison playing different roles, depending on the phase. The first phase involves initial task assessment for a new task (e.g., learning to play golf) in which the learner does not have much experience. In this phase, Ruble and Frey contend that the focus is on acquiring information about the task (e.g., how to hit the ball into the air), not on performance relative to others. In addition, comparison in this phase is likely to be with the self, relative to previous performance (e.g., "I hit the ball better this time than last"). In the second phase, there is a shift from task mastery to competitive assessment via social comparison with others or with absolute standards (e.g., "I can score under 100 for 18 holes of golf"). The third stage involves the confirmation or maintenance of the behavior and can include changing subgoals (getting a par on a hole) or competing with others (beating your friends). Finally, the last phase is a reassessment of overall goals and continuation of activity. Social comparison can play a role in all four phases, but the nature and function of social comparison processes may be very different.

With respect to gender differences, Ruble, Feldman, and Boggiano (1976) found that among children in kindergarten through second grade, boys showed greater interest in comparison than did girls. Spear and Armstrong (1978) found that comparative information exerted motivational effects on boys' performances on easier tasks, but not on difficult ones; no differences due to type of task were obtained for girls. Ruble, Parsons, and Ross (1976) suggested that there may be more societal pressure on boys than girls to evaluate themselves relative to others. Although much social comparison research has not yielded gender differences, the issue is important for schooling and deserves further attention.

Motivation and Achievement

Social comparison can motivate students in achievement contexts, although its effect on motivation is not automatic. Among elementary school children, Schunk (1983b) found that social comparative information promoted task motivation, academic goals enhanced self-efficacy, and goals plus comparative information led to the highest learning. In a similar study, Schunk (1983c) obtained evidence showing that difficult goals raised children's academic motivation more than did easier goals, persuasive information ("You can work 25 problems") increased self-efficacy more than did social comparative information, and difficult goals plus persuasive information led to the highest achievement.

In summary, comparative information can enhance motivation but not necessarily self-efficacy or learning. Social comparative information that focuses students on the accomplishments of similar (and average) others makes salient that they are average and therefore have no reason to feel overly competent. Direct attainment information conveys nothing about others' accomplishments; students are likely to focus on how their present performance surpasses prior attainments. The perception that one is improving is hypothesized to build self-efficacy.

SELF-REGULATION AND VOLITION

The topic of self-regulation is intimately linked with motivation. **Self-regulation** is the process whereby students activate and sustain cognitions, behaviors, and affects that are systematically oriented toward attainment of their goals (Zimmerman, 1989). Students motivated to attain a goal engage in self-regulatory activities they believe will help them (e.g., rehearse material to be learned, clarify unclear information). In turn, self-regulation promotes learning, and the perception of greater competence sustains motivation and self-regulation to attain new goals (Schunk, 1991a). Research on self-regulation and self-regulated learning has blossomed since the first edition of this book (see Boekaerts, Pintrich, & Zeidner, 2000).

Volition is one aspect of self-regulation that is drawing increased research attention. In chapter 1, we discussed early work in volition. This section describes contemporary views and links volition with self-regulation.

Self-Regulation

Dimensions of Self-Regulation

To address the question of what constitutes self-regulation, Zimmerman (1994, 1998) developed a conceptual framework. This framework can be characterized in terms of six key questions, which are shown in Table 4.4 along with their critical self-regulation processes.

A critical element of self-regulation, and one that makes it distinctive, is that learners have some choice available in at least one aspect and perhaps in others. This does not imply that learners will always take advantage of the available choices; they may be uncertain how to proceed and ask the teacher what to do. But as long as not all task aspects are externally controlled, we can speak of self-regulation. When all aspects are controlled, we might say that behavior is externally controlled or other-regulated (by others or by conditions). This type of situation results when teachers give students no latitude in why, how, when, what, where, and with whom to complete a task. The possibilities for self-regulation can vary from low to high depending on how much choice learners have.

For example, suppose a teacher told students to write a term paper on a specified topic, that it was to be 10 pages long, typewritten, double spaced, that it had to contain references, that it was due in 3 weeks, that it had to be written individually, and that it was to be done in the library and at home. The teacher has dictated this assignment, so little self-regulation is possible. In contrast, suppose the teacher left the topic unspecified, told students that they could work individually or in pairs, and said that they had to give a class presentation but they could choose from alternative formats (e.g., poster, lecture, role play). In this instance, much more self-regulation is possible.

Table 4.4   Dimensions of Self-Regulation

Learning Issues	Self-Regulation Subprocesses
Why	Self-efficacy and self-goals
How	Strategy use or routinized performance
When	Time management
What	Self-observation, self-judgment, self-reaction
Where	Environmental structuring
With Whom	Selective help seeking

Thus, it is sensible to speak of self-regulation in terms of degree rather than in absolute terms (i.e., whether one is or is not self-regulated). The various processes shown in Table 4.4 are those that students can self-regulate. We have discussed some of these and address others in this chapter.

Self-regulation is often confused with motivation. Although the two concepts share some elements, there are some important differences. In some definitions of motivation, choice does not have to be central to the construct (cf. Deci & Ryan, 1985, however). Students may be motivated out of personal choice or because of a perceived necessity or even motivated in implicit or unconscious ways (Bargh & Ferguson, 2000). In contrast, self-regulation requires some degree of choice or intentional selection of strategies or behavior that are designed to help attain some goal. Motivational theories also focus on how motivation may be elicited or wax and wane as a function of both personal and contextual factors, but there is little focus on how to control or intentionally regulate motivation. In contrast, self-regulation models usually discuss issues of how the individual can come to control their own motivation, their own cognition, and their own behavior (Pintrich, 2000d).

Social Cognitive Processes

Social cognitive theory views self-regulation as comprising three processes: self-observation (-monitoring), self-judgment, and self-reaction (Bandura, 1986; Kanfer & Gaelick, 1986; Schunk, 1994; Zimmerman, 1990). **Self-observation** refers to deliberate attention to aspects of one's behavior (Mace, Belfiore, & Shea, 1989). People cannot regulate their performances if they do not know what they do. Self-observation is often accompanied by recording the frequency, intensity, or quality of behavior. Self-observation is critical to determine progress at an activity. Without it, selective memory of successes and failure come into play. Often our beliefs about outcomes do not faithfully reflect actual outcomes. Self-recording can yield surprising results. Students having difficulty studying who keep a written record of their activities may learn they are wasting more than half of their study time on nonacademic tasks.

Self-observation can result in motivational enhancements because when people realize what they do, they may react to this knowledge and alter their behavior. Typically, however, self-judgment and self-reaction also are required.

Self-judgment refers to comparing current performance level with one's goal. Self-judgment depends on the type of self-evaluative standards employed, goal properties, importance of goal attainment, and attributions. The latter three topics were discussed in chapter 3 or earlier in this chapter; thus, they will be treated briefly here.

Goal properties (specificity, proximity, difficulty) affect self-regulation and motivation. These properties enhance comparisons of progress, so that students can maintain or alter their self-regulatory strategies depending on the judgment of progress. Self-judgments also reflect the importance of goal attainment. When people care little about how they perform, they may not assess their performance or expend effort to improve it (Bandura, 1986). People judge progress in learning for goals they value. Attributions are important because students who believe they are not making good goal progress may attribute their performances to low ability, which negatively impacts self-efficacy and performance. Students who attribute poor progress to lackadaisical effort or an inadequate strategy may believe they will perform better if they work harder or switch strategies.

Standards may be absolute (fixed) or normative (relative to the performances of others). Standards inform and motivate. Comparing performance with standards indicates goal progress, and the belief that one is making progress enhances self-efficacy and motivation. Standards are often acquired from social comparisons with models, especially when absolute standards are nonexistent or ambiguous. Davidson and Smith (1982) had children observe a superior adult, equal peer, or inferior younger child set stringent or lenient standards while performing a task. Children who observed a lenient model rewarded themselves more often for lower scores than did those who observed a stringent model. Children's self-reward standards were lower than those of the adult, equal to those of the peer, and higher than those of the younger child. Model-observer similarity in age might have led children to believe that what was appropriate for the peer was appropriate for them. On ability-related tasks, children take relative estimates of ability into account for formulating standards.

Self-reactions are behavioral, cognitive, and affective responses to self-judgments. Self-reactions motivate; the belief that one is making acceptable progress, along with the anticipated satisfaction of accomplishing the goal, enhances self-efficacy. Negative evaluations do not decrease motivation if people believe they can improve. Motivation will not improve if students believe they lack ability and will not succeed no matter how hard they work or which strategy they employ.

Instructions to people to respond evaluatively to their performances promote motivation; people who think they can perform better persist longer and work harder (Kanfer & Gaelick, 1986). People also may make tangible incentives contingent on performance. Social cognitive theory postulates that the anticipated consequences of behavior—rather than the actual ones—enhance motivation (Bandura, 1986). Making free time and nights off from studying contingent on good grades can motivate students to study diligently.

External rewards tied to actual accomplishments enhance self-efficacy and motivation. Telling students that they will earn rewards based on what they accomplish instills a sense of self-efficacy for learning. Self-efficacy is validated as students work on the task, note their progress, and receive the reward that symbolizes progress. Rewards not tied to actual performances (e.g., given for time spent) may actually convey negative efficacy information; students might infer they are not expected to learn much because they are not capable (Schunk, 1983d).

Cyclical Nature of Self-Regulation

Social cognitive theory emphasizes the interaction of personal, behavioral, and environmental factors (Bandura, 1986, 1997; Zimmerman, 1994). Self-regulation is a cyclical process because these factors typically change during learning and must be monitored. Such monitoring leads to changes in an individual's strategies, cognitions, affects, and behaviors.

This cyclical nature is captured in Zimmerman's (1998) three-phase self-regulation model (Figure 4.4). The *forethought phase* precedes actual performance and refers to processes that set the stage for action. The *performance (volitional) control phase* involves processes that occur during learning and affect attention and action. During the *self-reflection phase*, which occurs after performance, people respond to their efforts.

Various self-regulatory processes come into play during the different phases. Thus, learners enter learning situations with goals and varying degrees of self-efficacy for

Figure 4.4   Self-regulation cycle phases
Zimmerman (1998).

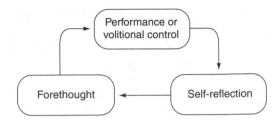

attaining them. During performance control they implement learning strategies that affect motivation and learning. During periods of self-reflection learners engage in self-evaluation of progress and reactions to this evaluation.

Effective self-regulation requires having goals and the motivation to attain them (Bandura, 1986; Kanfer & Kanfer, 1991; Pintrich, 2000d; Zimmerman, 1989). Students must regulate not only their actions but also their underlying achievement-related cognitions, behaviors, intentions, and affects. An increasing body of research substantiates the prediction that **self-monitoring** of achievement beliefs sustains learning efforts and promotes achievement (Schunk & Zimmerman, 1994, 1998; Zimmerman & Martinez-Pons, 1992).

Effective self-regulation depends on students developing a sense of self-efficacy for self-regulating their learning and for performing well (Bouffard-Bouchard, Parent, & Larivee, 1991; Zimmerman et al., 1992). The process of **self-evaluation** of capabilities and progress in skill acquisition is of critical importance. Students may not spontaneously self-evaluate. One means of highlighting progress is to have them periodically assess their progress. By making performance improvements salient, such monitoring should raise self-efficacy, sustain self-regulation, and promote skills. White, Kjelgaard, and Harkins (1995) noted that self-evaluation enhances goal-setting effects on performance when goals are informative of one's capabilities.

Schunk (1996) explored how goals and self-evaluation affected achievement outcomes. Children received instruction and practice on fractions over sessions. Students worked under conditions involving either a goal of learning how to solve problems (learning goal) or a goal of merely solving them (performance goal). In Study 1, half of the students in each goal condition evaluated their capabilities. The learning goal (with or without self-evaluation) and the performance goal with self-evaluation led to higher self-efficacy, achievement, and motivation, then did the performance goal without self-evaluation. In Study 2, all students in each goal condition evaluated their progress in skill acquisition. The learning goal led to higher motivation and achievement outcomes than did the performance goal.

Schunk and Ertmer (1999) examined how goals and self-evaluation affected self-efficacy, achievement, and self-reported competence and use of self-regulatory strategies. College undergraduates worked on computer projects over sessions. Students received a process goal of learning computer applications or a product goal of performing them. In Study 1, half of the students in each goal condition evaluated their learning progress midway through the instructional program. The process goal led to higher self-efficacy, self-judged progress, and self-regulatory competence and strategy use; the opportunity for self-evaluation promoted self-efficacy. In Study 2, self-evaluation students assessed their progress after each session. Frequent self-evaluation produced comparable results when coupled with a process or product goal. Collectively, these results suggest that infrequent self-evaluation complements learning process goals, but multiple self-evaluations outweigh the benefits of process goals and raise achievement outcomes.

This research has implications for teaching. Students may not normally evaluate their skills or learning progress, instead relying on the teacher to do that. Thus, they may require instruction in self-evaluation and frequent opportunities for practice.

Social and Self-Origins of Competence

Schunk and Zimmerman (1996, 1997) formulated a model of how self-regulatory competence develops initially from social sources of academic skill and subsequently shifts to self-sources in a series of levels (Table 4.5). At the outset, novice learners acquire learning strategies most rapidly from teaching, modeling, task structuring, and encouragement (Zimmerman & Rosenthal, 1974). At this observational level, many learners can induce the major features of learning strategies from observing models; however, most also need practice to incorporate the skill. During **participant modeling** (Bandura, 1977), models repeat aspects of the strategy and guide enactment based on learners' imitative accuracy.

Learners attain an emulative level of skill when their performances approximate the general form of the model's. At this point, observers are not directly copying the model, but rather are emulating only general patterns or styles. Thus, they may emulate the type of question the model asks but do not mimic the model's words.

The source of learning is primarily social for the first two levels but shifts to self-influences at advanced levels. The third, self-controlled level, is characterized by learners' ability to use strategies independently while performing transfer tasks. Students' use of strategies becomes internalized but is affected by representational standards of modeled performances (e.g., covert images, verbal meanings) and self-reward processes.

Socialization agents expect a higher level of self-functioning when students reach adolescence. Learners need to attain the self-regulated level of academic skill so they can systematically adapt strategies to changes in personal and situational conditions (Bandura, 1986). At this level, learners initiate use of strategies, incorporate adjustments based on features of situations, and are motivated to achieve by goals and self-efficacy. Learners choose when to use particular strategies and adapt them to changing conditions with little or no guidance from models.

In summary, this four-level analysis of self-regulatory development extends from acquiring knowledge of learning skills (observation), to using these skills (emulation), to internalizing them (self-control), and finally to using them adaptively (self-regulation). Although this conceptualization results from socialization research, it is useful in guiding

Table 4.5   Social and Self Influences on Self-Regulation

Level of Development	Social Influences	Self Influences
Observational	Modeling, verbal description	
Emulative	Social guidance and feedback	
Self-controlled		Internal standards, self-reinforcement
Self-regulated		Self-regulatory processes, self-efficacy beliefs

instruction to teach students how to self-regulate academic learning (Schunk & Zimmerman, 1994, 1996, 1997, 1998).

Volition

Many current researchers define volition as part of a larger self-regulatory system that includes motivation and other cognitive processes (Corno, 1993, 1994; Pintrich, 1999a; Snow, 1989).

> Volition can be characterized as a dynamic system of psychological control processes that protect concentration and directed effort in the face of personal and/or environmental distractions, and so aid learning and performance. (Corno, 1993, p. 16)

The conceptual basis for this current emphasis derives largely from work in action control theory by Heckhausen (1991) and Kuhl (1984). These theorists proposed a differentiation between *predecisional processing,* which refers to cognitive activity involved in making decisions and setting goals, and *postdecisional processing,* which denotes those activities engaged in subsequent to goal setting. In this view, predecisional analyses involve decision making and goal-setting, which are motivational, whereas postdecisional analyses deal with goal implementation and attainment, which are volitional. Volitional processes mediate the relation between one's goals and actions to accomplish them. Once students move from planning and goal setting to implementation of plans, they cross a metaphorical Rubicon in which goals are protected by self-regulatory activities rather than reconsidered or changed (Corno, 1993). This "Crossing the Rubicon" model highlights the distinction between motivation and volitional or control processes.

There is considerable debate whether motivation and volition are separate constructs or if they are part of a larger self-regulatory system (Pintrich, 1999a, 2000d). This point notwithstanding, separating pre- from postdecisional processes can be useful at some levels. Some motivational indexes that have been used in studies of performance are not appropriate for school learning. Choice of activities is a common motivational index, yet in school, students typically do not choose which activities to engage in. There is often little predecisional activity by students in school. Postdecisional activity, however, is important because there may be multiple ways to accomplish a task or many distractions to deal with while trying to perform the task. Volitional or self-regulatory activities presumably direct and control information processing, affects, and behaviors directed toward accomplishing goals (Corno, 1993; Pintrich, 1999a).

Kuhl (1985) proposed a taxonomy of volitional strategies as has Pintrich (1999a). Corno (1993) discussed two such strategies with educational examples (Table 4.6). **Motivation control** involves strategies that students can use to regulate their motivation. **Emotion control** concerns strategies that students can use to control and regulate their emotions. One problem with this volitional view is whether it is justifiable to separate goal setting from implementation when, in fact, research shows that individuals often adjust or set new goals during task performance (Locke & Latham, 1990). Another concern is how important processes such as self-efficacy and attributions relate to volition during task implementation. Future research undoubtedly will address these and other concerns (Pintrich, 1999).

Table 4.6　Examples of Volitional Control Strategies

Motivation Control	Emotion Control
Set contingencies for performance that can be carried out mentally (e.g., self-reward)	Count to 10 in your head
Escalate goals by prioritizing and imagining their value	Control breathing so it is slow, steady, and deep
Visualize doing the work successfully	Generate useful diversions (e.g., sing to yourself)
Uncover ways to make the work more fun or challenging	Visualize doing the work successfully and feeling good about that (change the way you respond emotionally to the task)
Immerse yourself in plans for achieving goals	Recall your strengths and your available resources
Self-instruct	Consider any negative feelings about the experience and ways to make it more reassuring
Analyze failures to direct a second try	

Material drawn from Corno (1993).

SOCIAL MOTIVATION

Students spend much time interacting with others. Social cognitive theory emphasizes the motivational impact of these interactions. This section discusses three topics relevant to social motivation: group motivation, collective efficacy, and conformity and compliance.

Group Motivation

For instructional purposes, teachers routinely group students heterogeneously or according to the ability or skill required for the content. The teacher's job is to understand how to instigate and maintain group motivation at an optimal level.

Group motivation operates according to the same principles that apply to individual motivation. Factors that optimize group motivation include having a goal to attain; feeling efficacious about performing well; holding positive outcome expectations; attributing success to such factors as ability, effort, and strategy use; and receiving feedback indicating goal progress.

What distinguishes motivation in groups from individual motivation is how the task is structured and how members are rewarded. When individuals work on a task alone, they do all the work and receive all the rewards. Much work on academic group motivation has examined **cooperative learning**, in which two or more students work together to complete a task (Slavin, 1983a, 1983b). Types of task structures used in cooperative learning arrangements are task specialization and group study. In task specialization, each group member is responsible for completing one part of the overall task; group study refers to the situation in which group members work together and do not have separate tasks. With respect to how members are rewarded, rewards may be based on the overall group product or on the total of each individual's performance.

Reviews of research lead to several conclusions (Slavin, 1983a, 1983b). First, cooperative learning is usually effective and students often perform better in groups than when working alone. Second, it is imperative that an incentive structure be in effect. In the absence of incentives, there is no evidence that group study results in higher motivation or learning compared with working alone. Third, individual accountability is necessary: Each individual's best efforts must be put forth for the group to succeed and the contribution of each member must be identifiable. Without individual accountability, one or two members can do all the work. In short, cooperative structures are ideally designed to improve performance by increasing helping and encouraging one another to work. Group methods are needed that foster these outcomes.

Another important point is whether the group succeeds or fails. Most research on cooperative groups has looked at group success in which students experience higher perceptions of ability and motivation. As Ames (1984) has shown, however, when cooperative groups fail, there is the tendency to fix blame, and the weaker group members typically receive the blame. This situation adversely affects self-efficacy and motivation. When establishing small groups, teachers should: (a) select tasks at which they are relatively confident the group can succeed with diligent work (b) ensure that each group member has a defined role in the group; and (c) hold each individual accountable for learning. Application 4.5 discusses implications of theory and research on cooperative groups for teaching and learning.

APPLICATION 4.5

Applying Principles of Cooperative Groups in the Classroom

1. *Design tasks at which the group can succeed if the members work diligently. Group success enhances self-efficacy and motivation.* Ms. Kush used recipes to help teach measurement to her fourth-grade students. After she was sure that all the students were successful with measurement activities, she divided the class into cooperative groups and gave each group recipes and ingredients to prepare an item on its own. She made sure that there were enough ingredients in each recipe so that each child would have an opportunity to measure and add something to the item their group was preparing.

   Ms. Myers, a history teacher, assigned a mobile activity to each small group during the study of early U.S. presidents. In selecting the students for the groups, she made sure that each group had a good researcher, a good reader, a good writer, someone who printed well, an artist, and so on. She also gave each group a self-evaluation form to complete and return when the group completed its mobile.

2. *Ensure that each group member has some responsibility and that individual performance can be accounted for. Refocus the group if it becomes apparent that a few members are doing all the work.* A homemaking teacher divided her class into four cooperative groups for each project activity. She mixed the students so that abilities and talents were equally divided. For each project, she also made sure that each student in each

group had some aspect of the project to complete. As the groups worked, she observed them and rated the members on their participation.

At the beginning of the year, Mr. Harrigan assigned several social studies projects to small groups. It became apparent after the completion of the second project that some students were doing the majority of the work, whereas others were doing little or nothing. Before Mr. Harrigan introduced the third project, he regrouped the students. Then he met with each group to help students select an aspect of the project they would like to do and checked with the students periodically to assess progress. At the end of the project, he met with each group to discuss participation and help students assess the quality of their project.

3. *Make sure that the group has a goal and an incentive to work toward the goal.* Mr. Love, a high school drama teacher, assigned each group in his senior class the task of writing a skit that would portray some of the students' high school experiences. Each student was to contribute to the skit through role—writing, acting, designing props, and so on. Each successful skit would be performed at the last senior class meeting.

Ms. O'Brien, a fifth-grade teacher, gave each small group the opportunity to select a science project related to a recent unit on electricity. Guidelines for selecting and completing the project were listed on each project. She met with each group after the group selected a project to discuss how the guidelines applied to what the group had chosen. All groups that did a good job on their projects were allowed to take their projects to the systemwide science fair.

4. *Frequently check on group progress. Provide progress and corrective feedback.* Ms. Harris, an elementary art teacher, divided one of her classes into small groups to make piñatas to correlate with a unit the class was doing on Mexico. She demonstrated how to make a piñata, letting all the children assist before the groups worked on their own piñatas. Once the groups started on their projects, she circulated around the room each day to provide input regarding their progress and success.

Mr. Washbourne worked with a group of his resource students to complete a science project on creating a spring garden for their school. Before the students began, Mr. Washbourne met with them to create a chart that included all the tasks that needed to be done to produce a good garden. He helped the students select activities they wanted to do. Then he checked with the group each day to see what tasks had been completed and helped the students rate the success of the garden project.

Collective Efficacy

Collective efficacy refers to the self-efficacy of a group, team, or larger social entity or system (Bandura, 1997). Collective efficacy is not a simple average of the self-efficacy of the individual participants. Rather, collective efficacy includes both the perceived capabilities of the individual members and group members' perceptions of the effectiveness of the links among tasks, skills, and roles. As Bandura (1997) noted:

Belief of collective efficacy affects the sense of mission and purpose of a system, the strength of common commitment to what it seeks to achieve, how well its members work together to produce results, and the group's resiliency in the face of difficulties (p. 469).

There is little research on collective efficacy, and the existing research has been concentrated in corporate and industrial settings. Clearly, educational research is needed in this area, but a program of educational research on collective efficacy (Goddard, in press; Goddard, Hoy, & Woolfolk Hoy, 2000) is beginning. We should expect that teachers' beliefs about their self-efficacy to influence student learning (teacher self-efficacy is discussed in chapter 8) will be affected by their self-efficacy for what teachers in their school might be able to accomplish. Further, we should expect that students' self-efficacy for performing well in class will depend on their collective efficacy for performing well in group situations. A demoralizing situation could occur for students who feel self-efficacious individually but whose teacher uses lots of group work and does not ensure that groups operate properly, thereby leading to low collective efficacy among students in the groups.

Bandura (1993) reported research showing that the collective efficacy of school professional staff influenced the academic achievement of students. In this study, collective efficacy was affected by both student characteristics (prior academic achievement, socioeconomic status, student body stability) and teacher factors (longevity). More recently, Goddard, Hoy, and Woolfolk Hoy (2000) examined collective teacher efficacy and developed a measure of it. Using multi-level modeling, they found that collective teacher efficacy, as a school-level construct, accounted for between one half and two thirds of the variance in student achievement in reading and math, even controlling for demographic characteristics such as SES levels. Goddard (in press) also found similar results in terms of the relation of collective efficacy to student achievement. In addition, he found that, consistent with Bandura's theory, mastery experience was a predictor of school-wide collective efficacy. Additional research is needed to determine how these effects of collective efficacy operate in classrooms and schools, but the construct seems to be a very useful and powerful one.

Conformity and Compliance

Conformity and compliance often are used interchangeably to mean obedience. Although there are exceptions, we distinguish conformity and compliance as follows: **Conformity** involves willful obedience to a group's behaviors or mannerisms when the individual and group members are roughly equal in stature (peers); **compliance** denotes obedience emanating from another's command when a difference in power or stature exists (subordinate, superior). We consider these in turn.

Conformity

Groups have rules, expectations, and pressures that, whether explicit or implicit, affect individuals' motivation. Conformity represents the desire to go along with the group regardless of one's beliefs. All of us conform to group standards on the job, in school, at home, and at social functions.

From a social cognitive perspective, conformity represents modeling of group behaviors (Bandura, 1986). Conformity may reflect any of the three forms of modeling discussed earlier. Behavior occurring in response to a prompt is response facilitation. The classroom example at the beginning of this chapter illustrates response facilitation when the children enter the room and go over to where the others are. If the chairperson of a volunteer group passes a basket for donations and each member puts in a dollar, that is a social cue for new members that a dollar is an acceptable contribution. Conformity can also represent inhibition and disinhibition. Some groups expect that members will not criticize senior members. Junior members conform to this standard by inhibiting their tendency to openly disagree with senior members. Disinhibition may occur when adolescents discard traditional dress and adopt an outlandish dress style to conform to that of a social group. In the example at the start of this chapter, talking was disinhibited initially because the teacher did not punish it, but then was inhibited when the teacher disciplined one student. Finally, conformity may represent observational learning. Customs and traditions of groups have to be learned. Observational learning occurs when new members demonstrate actions that they acquire from observing older members.

The power of conformity was convincingly demonstrated by Asch (1955, 1958). Asch formed groups of seven to nine adults, only one of whom was a naive participant (the others were confederates of the experimenter). Adults were told the experiment involved visual judgments and that they would be comparing lengths of lines. They were shown a standard line and three comparison lines, one of which was an exact match; the others differed from the standard by 3/4 to 1 3/4 inches. They responded individually with the line that they chose to match the standard; the naive participant responded next to last. On the first two trials, everyone agreed. Beginning on the third trial and on several subsequent ones, however, everyone up to the naive subject purposely picked a wrong line.

Under normal circumstances, participants made mistakes less than 1% of the time, but Asch obtained an overall conformity rate of 37%. Asch also found that the size of the group giving erroneous judgments was important. When only one person gave a wrong answer, the naive individual answered independently. When two people gave wrong answers, conformity among naive individuals increased to 14%; and with three incorrect judgments, it increased to 32%. After that, conformity changed very little with increasing group size.

Teachers continually see the motivation to conform in students. Adolescents, especially, usually do not want to appear to be different and this can be a problem. High-ability students who do not want to be viewed by others as studious, but rather want to be socially accepted, may neglect their coursework and their grades may drop.

Compliance

We introduce compliance with a famous psychological experiment by Milgram (1963), who recruited individuals for a study on the effect of punishment on learning. As each naive person reported for the experiment, he (all participants were men) met another person, who actually was an experimental confederate. The naive individual was the teacher and the confederate the learner. The learner was strapped into a chair and had electrodes attached to him, after which the experimenter and teacher moved to another room. The teacher was shown the (simulated) shock generator with levels ranging from "slight" through "intense" to "XXX." The learning task was explained to the teacher and he was told to shock the learner each time he made a mistake and to increase the shock level each time. The confederate responded incorrectly much of the time and was "shocked" each time. In fact, the switches delivered no shock, but participants did not know that. The confederate began to pound on the wall midway through the shock series and then later quit responding. Teachers were aware of the learner's plight and were visibly nervous. Many turned to the experimenter and asked what to do. The experimenter requested them to continue, although they were free to leave at any time.

Prior to the experiment, Milgram questioned colleagues and students about how far they felt participants would go in obeying the experimenter. Most felt that participants would not obey the experimenter once the shocks presumably became painful and that only 1 to 2% of them might deliver the most painful shock. In fact, 65% delivered the most painful shock. Of the 35% who did not, none stopped prior to when the victim began pounding on the wall. These results were replicated by Milgram (1974) and others using different participants and settings.

These results show that people have strong social motivation to comply with authority figures. Some obedience to authority is necessary because without it a society cannot function effectively. At the same time, blanket compliance with orders results in dehumanization and diffusion of responsibility. The mentality displayed in Milgram's studies is similar (albeit on a much lesser scale) to that displayed by persons responsible for the World War II concentration camps and the My Lai massacre in Vietnam. In Milgram's studies, there undoubtedly were several reasons why people complied, including scientific respectability, anonymity, protection against retaliation, desire to please the experimenter, assigning responsibility to the experimenter, and believing that a qualified experimenter would not allow dangerous events.

Students must behave properly, complete their assignments, and obey rules and procedures. In fact, there is evidence that when students accept responsibility for their social behavior, they also achieve better (Wentzel, 1991a). From a social cognitive perspective, other important influences on compliance are students' expectations concerning the outcomes of their actions and the value they place on those outcomes. We want students to comply with rules because they expect and value the positive outcomes that result from complying. Hamilton, Blumenfeld, Akoh, and Miura (1989) found that Japanese students were highly likely to accept these responsibilities. Teachers who involve students in decision making can help to foster these beliefs. The relations among social responsibility, achievement motivation, and actual achievement in schools will be an area of increased research in the future.

SUMMARY

Social cognitive theory focuses on how people acquire knowledge, rules, skills, strategies, beliefs, and emotions through their interactions with and observations of others. Social cognitive theory is a contextual view because it posits that behavior represents an interaction of the individual with the environment. Important historical influences on social cognitive theory include theories of imitation and Rotter's social learning theory. Although some historical ideas bear similarity to principles of social cognitive theory, each historical view has limitations that preclude its being able to explain the scope and complexity of human motivation.

Bandura's social cognitive theory assumes triadic reciprocality among personal factors, behaviors, and environmental influences as they interact with and affect one another. The theory distinguishes learning from performance because people learn many behaviors that they do not demonstrate at the time of learning. Although learning occurs enactively (by doing), the range of human learning is greatly expanded by the capacity to learn vicariously, whereby individuals are exposed to modeled influences but do not perform the modeled behaviors.

Modeling refers to behavioral, cognitive, and affective changes that result from observing one or more models. Observing models can strengthen or weaken inhibitions (inhibition/disinhibition), serve as social prompts for observers to act accordingly (response facilitation), and lead observers to display new behaviors that prior to modeling had a zero probability of occurrence (observational learning). The latter comprises four subprocesses: attention, retention, production, and motivation. Characteristics of effective models include competence, perceived similarity, credibility, and enthusiasm. Modeled consequences of behaviors inform observers about successful sequences of actions and the likely outcomes of behaviors. Consequences also motivate observers to behave accordingly through their effects on self-efficacy and outcome expectations.

Bandura believes motivation is goal-directed behavior instigated and sustained by expectations concerning anticipated outcomes of actions and self-efficacy for performing those actions. Self-efficacy, or one's perceived capabilities for learning or performing a given task, is a key motivational process that affects students' task choices, effort, persistence, and achievement. The motivational effects of goal setting depend on goal properties, choice, and commitment. Motivated learning is motivation to acquire skills and strategies rather than to perform tasks. At the start of a learning activity, students differ in their self-efficacy for learning, which depends on personal factors, prior experiences, and social support. While working on the task, students are affected by task engagement variables that make salient how well they are learning and cues that students use to appraise efficacy for continued learning. Self-evaluations of progress enhance self-efficacy and sustain motivation for continued learning.

Social comparison is the process of comparing ourselves with others. Festinger proposed an elaborate theory of social comparison. Researchers have identified changes in social comparison that occur with development. Social comparison is pervasive in schools and can motivate achievement behavior.

Social cognitive theory has been applied to the area of self-regulation, or the process whereby students activate and sustain cognitions, behaviors, and affects, systematically oriented toward attainment of their goals. Self-regulation assumes that students have some choice available during task engagement. A topic assuming increasing importance in the field of self-regulation is volition. Many researchers see volitional processes as mediating the relation between goals and actions to accomplish them.

Social cognitive processes also are influential in social situations. Group motivation operates according to many of the same principles that apply to individual motivation: having goals and receiving feedback indicating goal progress, feeling efficacious about performing well, holding positive outcome expectations, and attributing success to such factors as ability, effort, and strategy use. In schools, cooperative learning, in which two or more students work together to complete a task, is common. Collective efficacy is self-efficacy of a group or social system, and comprises both individuals' capabilities and effectiveness of the interdependent links. Collective efficacy of school professional staff may be a key factor affecting students' motivation and achievement. Conformity (modeling of group behaviors and standards) and compliance (obedience to others' commands) are powerful processes. Conformity and compliance are needed in school, and it is important that teachers use positive role models and involve students in decisions.

The Role of Goals and Goal Orientation

*F*our teachers are talking about their students. They all teach at different levels and are fascinated by the differences in their students. Karen is a kindergarten teacher, Bill is a fourth-grade teacher, Lucy teaches science at the junior high, and Mal teaches tenth-grade English.

Karen: *All my children have a high need for physical activity so I have to build in time for active playing either outside or inside. They just can't sit still for 3 or 4 hours at a time. If you don't take their needs into account, you'll miss the boat.*

Bill: *Well, some of my boys are still like that, but I see many more individual differences. I think each child is unique. Some of my kids just have this real need to be the best. They are very competitive, and it is not just the boys. I have a couple of girls who always want to get the highest grades. Other kids want everyone to like them; they have a high need for approval. I have one girl who is always asking me to approve of her work before she does it and this same one worries about everyone liking her.*

Lucy: *You guys have it easy. At least you don't have to deal with the raging hormones of my adolescents. These kids in junior high are off the wall because of their hormones. One day they are calm and normal, the next day they are all over the place, hyper, and teasing and fretting about the opposite sex. It drives me crazy. Sometimes I think junior high is just baby-sitting them until they calm down in high school and then you can go back to teaching them something.*

Mal: *Well, it's not any easier at the high school. Yeah, the kids are not totally off the wall like in junior high, but they all have different goals. Some of them are only concerned about finding a boyfriend or girlfriend, others are thinking about their part-time jobs and making some money to buy a car, others are only concerned about their grades and getting into college, others couldn't care less about school and just want to finish and go to work. It's not easy to motivate all these kids when they have such different goals.*

These comments all demonstrate that an approach to motivation that is concerned with personal needs or goals reflects an intuitive and layperson account of motivation. However, there also have been a number of more formal motivational theories that have been based on the idea that people have different needs and goals and it is the search to satisfy these needs and goals that motivates behavior. In this chapter, we first review several needs-based models of motivation and then move on to more current goal theory models of motivation.

After studying this chapter, you should be able to:

1. Distinguish between the constructs of needs and goals and the different theoretical models that use these constructs.

2. Understand how many of the ideas of both Murray and Maslow about needs reappear in more current cognitive theories of goals.

3. Distinguish between goal content theory and goal orientation theory in terms of their application to classroom learning and development.

4. Apply some of the principles of goal content theory to classroom instruction.

5. Understand the distinction between mastery and performance goals and the implications of these goals for student motivation, affect, cognition, and behavior.

6. Analyze a classroom using the TARGET framework to understand how different features and structures in a classroom might influence student motivation and goal adoption.

HISTORICAL PERSPECTIVE ON NEEDS AND GOALS

Goals are the current cognitive representations of a general "energy" construct that has a long-standing history in psychology, especially motivational psychology. The Latin root of the word motive means "to move," and most motivational theories propose a construct such as instinct, drive, habit, needs, or goals that provide the "engine" to move organisms to act, as noted in chapter 1 in our discussion of various historical perspectives on motivation. Needs and goals also provide the direction in which to act; that is, needs or goals can guide the individual to approach or to avoid certain objects in the environment in order to satisfy the needs or attain the goals.

Murray's Taxonomy of Needs

Although the construct of **needs** has fallen into disfavor given the current cognitive zeitgeist, needs served the same energizing and directional functions in earlier theories of motivation as goals do in current cognitive models. In earlier motivational theories, researchers spent a great deal of time trying to develop a taxonomy of instincts (McDougall, 1923; see chapter 1) or needs (Murray, 1938). This taxonomic strategy is a general strategy used in biology (e.g., classification of plants and animals) as well as psychology (see chapter 3 on classification of attributions and their dimensions and Weiner, 1986) to determine the nature of the basic elements under study, followed by research to examine the relations among the basic elements. Although McDougall's list of instincts is interesting, Murray's taxonomy of needs and his general theory show a great deal of overlap with some current models of goals, so we concentrate on his theory of needs.

Given the biological flavor of needs and instincts, it is interesting to note that Murray had a doctorate in biochemistry, not psychology. Nevertheless, during his doctoral studies in biochemistry in England, he spent some time in Zurich with Carl Jung and became very interested in psychology and psychoanalysis. Upon his return to the United States, he spent a year at the Rockefeller Institute before he was recruited to Harvard to head the Psychological Clinic. The clinic was started with the purpose of studying abnormal psychology and psychoanalytic psychology, and Murray began a series of investigations to test empirically some of the ideas of psychoanalytic psychology, most often using case studies and intensive interviewing techniques. However, given his interest in a general theory of behavior, he concentrated on normal individuals in natural settings, unlike most clinical work in the psychoanalytic tradition (Hall & Lindzey, 1978). Given this background, it is not surprising to find that his theory has a biological flavor and that many of his needs have a decidedly psychoanalytic cast (e.g., his taxonomy of needs).

Murray believed needs have two aspects: a directional or qualitative aspect that specifies the objects that will satisfy the need, and an energetic or quantitative aspect that influences the frequency, intensity, and duration of behavior. According to Murray (1938),

> A need is a construct (a convenient fiction or hypothetical construct) which stands for a force (the physico-chemical nature of which is unknown) in the brain region, a force which organizes perception, apperception, intellection, conation, and action in such a way as to transform in a certain direction an existing, unsatisfying situation. A need is sometimes provoked by internal processes of a certain kind . . . but, more frequently (when in a state of readiness) by the occurrence of one of a few commonly effective press (or by anticipatory images of such a press). Thus it manifests itself by leading the organism to search for or to avoid encountering or, when encountered, to attend and respond to certain kinds of press. (p. 123–124)

There are several important points to note about the theory given this definition. First, all needs are based in the physiological substrate of the brain, but are not just the viscerogenic needs for air, water, and food. More importantly, however, from a motivational point of view, needs provide the "force" for all behavior, including perception, thinking, regulation and will (**conation** in Murray's terms), and action. Needs are assumed to operate on the classic homeostatic principle that unfulfilled needs generate tension (the unsatisfying situation noted in the quote), which leads to some approach or avoidance behavior to release the tension and satisfy the need.

Table 5.1 lists Murray's taxonomy of 20 needs that are assumed to drive all human behavior across the life span. In addition, in comparison to Hull and the other drive theorists, Murray assumed that these needs comprised stable, personal characteristics that extend beyond the physical realm and involve psychological dispositions to pursue certain types of goals or activities. In a schooling context, the **needs for achievement** and understanding would be most relevant. Other researchers who developed models of motivation based on needs (e.g., Atkinson, 1964; McClelland, 1961; McClelland, Atkinson, Clark, & Lowell, 1953) focused on Murray's needs for achievement, **affiliation**, and dominance (see Table 5.1), although they renamed the dominance need as the **need for power**. Winter et al. (1998) state that the three motives of achievement, affiliation, and power "can be seen as the fundamental dimensions underlying Murray's list" (p. 232).

As noted in the definition of needs, Murray's model proposed that needs can be evoked by internal processes in the individual, but are more likely to be linked to the environmental press of the situation. Murray was one of the first to stress the concept

Table 5.1   Murray's Taxonomy of 20 Needs, Listed in Alphabetical Order

1. *Abasement* (nAba)—to submit passively to external force, to admit inferiority, to seek pain, punishment, misfortune

2. *Achievement* (nAch)—to accomplish something difficult, to master, to excel, to rival and surpass others, to overcome obstacles and attain a high standard

3. *Affiliation* (nAff)—to draw near and enjoyably cooperate or reciprocate with an allied other, to adhere and remain loyal to a friend

4. *Aggression* (nAgg)—to overcome opposition forcefully, to fight, to revenge an injury, to attack, injure or kill another, to oppose forcefully

5. *Autonomy* (nAuto)—to get free, to resist coercion and restriction, to be independent and free to act, to avoid or quit activities prescribed by domineering authorities

6. *Counteraction* (nCnt)—to master or make up for a failure by restriving, to maintain self-respect and pride on a high level

7. *Defendance* (nDfd)—to defend the self against assault, criticism, and blame, to conceal or justify a misdeed, failure, or humiliation

8. *Deference* (nDef)—to admire and support a superior, to yield eagerly to the influence of an allied other, to emulate an exemplar, to conform to custom

9. *Dominance* (nDom)—to control one's human environment, to influence or direct the behaviors of others by suggestion, seduction, persuasion, or command

10. *Exhibition* (nExh)—to make an impression, to be seen and heard, to excite, amaze, fascinate, entertain, amuse, or entice others

11. *Harmavoidance* (nHarm)—to avoid pain, physical injury, illness, and death, to take precautionary measures, to escape from a dangerous situation

12. *Infavoidance* (nInf)—to avoid humiliation, to quit embarrassing situations that may lead to belittlement from others, to refrain from action because of fear of failure

13. *Nurturance* (nNur)—to give sympathy and gratify the needs of a helpless object such as an infant or any object that is weak, disabled, tired, lonely, sick, dejected; to feed, help, support, console, protect, comfort others

14. *Order* (nOrd)—to put things in order, to achieve cleanliness, arrangement, organization, balance, neatness, tidiness, and precision

15. *Play* (nPlay)—to act for fun without further purpose, to seek enjoyable relaxation of stress, to like to laugh and make jokes, to participate in games and sports

16. *Rejection* (nRej)—to separate oneself from an object, to exclude, abandon, expel, or remain indifferent to an inferior object

17. *Sentience* (nSen)—to seek and enjoy sensuous impressions

18. *Sex* (nSex)—to form and further an erotic relationship, to have sexual intercourse

19. *Succorance* (nSuc)—to have one's needs gratified by the sympathetic aid of an allied object, to be nursed, supported, protected, loved, advised, to always have a supporter

20. *Understanding* (nUnd)—to ask or answer general questions, to be interested in theory, to speculate, formulate, analyze, and generalize

of environmental presses and the idea that these features of the context can evoke and shape needs. In addition, he emphasized the importance of not only mapping the needs of an individual, but also the environmental presses in which the individual lives (Hall & Lindzey, 1978). This latter focus on the person-situation interaction is very uncharacteristic for his era, given the tendency for most psychological theories to focus either on the individual, as in psychodynamic models, or the environment, as in behavioral models.

Moreover, Murray proposed that there were alpha and beta environmental presses. **Alpha presses** represented the "objective reality" of the environmental context as would be defined by others, including researchers. **Beta presses** represented the individual's own idiosyncratic perception and construction of the context. For example, a course might have a very strict grading curve that everyone could agree was operating (the alpha press). However, there still could be differential perceptions of this grading curve by different individuals (the beta presses), with some students seeing this curve as something to strive to overcome and do well at (an activation of the need for achievement) and others seeing it as something to avoid and try to break out of (an activation of the need for autonomy). This distinction between actual and perceived contexts foreshadows current social cognitive and constructivist perspectives on motivation, such as goal theory (Ames, 1992b) and classroom learning and cognition (e.g., the student-mediating paradigm; Winne & Marx, 1982). Recently, Linnenbrink and Pintrich (in press) have applied this idea of alpha and beta presses to the goal stresses in the environment and how they interact with the personal goals of individuals in the environment.

In keeping with the organismic tradition of focusing on the individual but also being sensitive to the importance of embedding the individual in the situation, Murray proposed that individual needs and environmental presses were always interacting and that a larger, more molar unit of analysis was required that linked needs and presses together in order to have a less fragmented view of behavior. He saw needs and presses integrated in a unit of analysis that he called a **thema**. This thema represented the individual's needs, the situational presses that evoked them, and the outcomes that resulted from the interaction of needs and presses (Hall & Lindzey, 1978). It is important to note that the thema construct is remarkably similar to current views of the person-in-situation construct of interactional psychology (Magnusson, 1990; Pintrich, 2000b), behavior episode schemas in goal theory (M. Ford, 1992), and the person-operating-with-mediational-tools notions (Wertsch & Tulviste, 1992) from a Vygotskian perspective. All of these views attempt to create a larger unit of analysis by embedding the individual in the context.

According to Murray, the psychologist's task was to describe and understand the themas that defined an individual's life. To accomplish this task, Murray developed the Thematic Apperception Test (TAT), which asked individuals to react to a series of ambiguous pictures by telling a story about what they thought was going on in each picture. These stories were then analyzed in terms of the needs expressed in the stories, the presses seen operating (beta presses in this case because it is the individual's perceptions), and themas that characterized the interactions of needs and presses. The TAT was probably the most used instrument to measure motivation up through the 1970s, although it was adapted and most often used to measure just three needs—for achievement, for affiliation, and for power—as McClelland's and Atkinson's theories of motivation superseded Murray's theory.

Maslow's Hierarchy of Needs

Another theory that stressed needs that have since been reformulated as goals in current cognitive goal theories is Maslow's hierarchy of needs. Maslow's theory (Maslow, 1954) grew out of his interest in developing a "third force" in psychology that was not based in clinical studies of neuroses and psychopathology (psychodynamic psychology) or studies of infrahuman subjects (behavioral psychology), but rather focused on normal human growth and development. Although there were a number of aspects of his humanistic theory, the one that generated the most attention and is still relevant today is his hierarchy of needs (see Table 5.2). Maslow believed that the classification of individual motives and the attempts to develop comprehensive taxonomies of all the needs (as Murray and McDougall had done) was of little theoretical value (Heckhausen, 1991). He developed a list of needs that classified all needs into five general groups, and, most importantly, asserted that there was a hierarchy of these five groups of needs in terms of their importance for human development. The higher, or growth, needs at the top of the hierarchy shown in Table 5.2, such as self-actualization, were most important for the development of personality. However, these higher needs could not be satisfied until the lower needs (or deficiency needs), such as the physiological needs and safety needs (see Table 5.2), were satisfied. If two different needs were in conflict, the lower need would dominate. In addition, the hierarchy of needs paralleled developmental tasks in life-span development (Erikson, 1963), with the physiological needs most important for infants, safety needs for young children, followed by the belongingness and esteem needs in later childhood, and the need for self-actualization not becoming prepotent until adolescence and adulthood (Heckhausen, 1991).

These needs function in much the same way that Murray's needs operate to influence behavior. A need that is unsatisfied generates behavior that is designed to satisfy the need. The same general, homeostatic tension-release model is followed, whereby a need creates the behavior to satisfy the need. Once the need is satisfied, there is homeostasis and the behavior is no longer required. Of course, Maslow also noted that the environment played a role, although his model of needs was not as interactionist as Murray's needs-press-

Table 5.2   Maslow's Hierarchy of Needs

Higher needs (growth needs)	5. Self-actualization needs—growth through the realization of one's potential and capacities; the need for comprehension and insight
	4. Esteem needs—need to achieve, to gain approval and recognition
	3. Needs for belongingness and love—need for love, affection, security, social acceptance; need for identity
	2. Safety needs—need for security and protection from pain, fear, anxiety, and disorganization; need for sheltering, dependency, order, lawfulness, and rules of behavior
Lower needs (deficiency needs)	1. Physiological needs—hunger, thirst, sexuality, and so on, as homeostatic and organismic needs

thema interaction model. For Maslow, the environment provided the opportunities for satisfaction of the needs. If the environment did not allow the needs to be satisfied, growth and development would not occur in the most propaedeutic fashion. For example, a family environment that did not provide for the basic physiological and safety needs for a child would not foster the most positive development. Although Maslow's hierarchy of needs may not be cited explicitly, many of the school reform plans that now offer a full range of social and health services to school children including not just lunch, but breakfast, after-school care, health care, dental care, and the like, are implicitly based on this general idea that if children are hungry and in poor health, it is unlikely they will be able to learn. Of course, the importance of dealing with problems of school violence that threaten not just children's safety, but also the faculty and staff of schools, would fit into Maslow's hierarchy, as safety needs are the second level of needs. Without those being met, higher levels such as esteem and self-actualization needs cannot be satisfied.

Deficiencies of Murray's and Maslow's Needs Models

There are some serious conceptual problems with the construct of needs as it has been used in these models. First, it seems to be difficult to develop a manageable list of needs that provides both predictive power and parsimony. Murray's list seems rather long and unparsimonious, whereas McClelland's and Maslow's lists seem to be rather short to be used to explain all behavior. This same problem plagued research on "instincts," whereby instincts represent unlearned wants or urges that all people have (Weiner, 1992). Freud, of course, was one of the most important psychologists to propose that these urges (such as the son's desire to sleep with his mother) drove behavior. As noted in chapter 1, McDougall (1923) also proposed an elaborate theory of instincts that propelled all behavior. As the idea was elaborated, however, it became clear that there was no scientifically acceptable way to determine what an instinct was and how it was linked to behavior. Instinct theory was eventually discarded when the list of instincts became so large (one researcher put it at over 2,500) that researchers recognized the construct did not have much scientific utility.

Moreover, the logic of using constructs like needs and instincts to explain behavior eventually becomes tautological. The most common use of the construct as an explanatory mechanism is to observe a behavior and then infer that the person must have a need to do that behavior. For example, a child acts out in a classroom and ends up hitting the teacher. A simple explanation is that the child has an aggressive urge or need that is being expressed in this behavior. Another student is quiet, not too social, and seems to enjoy spending time alone, while yet another child is very social and talks to everyone and tries to make as many friends as possible. The former child would be said to have a need to be alone, whereas the latter student would be high in social or belongingness needs. At this point, almost any behavior can be referenced to a need as the cause of the behavior and, in turn, when someone has these needs, the needs cause the behavior. The logic is circular and does not provide any real explanation of the behavior. Given these serious problems with needs, especially long lists like Murray's, the need construct is not used much in current research. However, there are more social cognitive theories that recast needs as goals that do represent an improvement on traditional needs models. We turn to those cognitive models now.

CURRENT SOCIAL COGNITIVE PERSPECTIVES ON GOALS

There are a number of goal theories (see Austin & Vancouver, 1996)that reflect a general social cognitive model of motivation, but we will focus on two general models. The social cognitive theory of goal-setting (Locke & Latham, 1990) was discussed in chapter 4. In the next section of this chapter, we discuss the goal content theory of Ford and Wentzel. In the last part of this chapter, we present the various goal orientation theories that have been used most often in developmental and educational psychology to examine motivation in achievement contexts (e.g., Ames, 1992b; Dweck & Leggett, 1988; Nicholls, 1984).

The Role of Goals in M. Ford's Motivational Systems Theory

M. Ford (see M. Ford, 1992; M. Ford & D. Ford, 1987; M. Ford & Nichols, 1991) has proposed his Motivational Systems Theory (MST) as a comprehensive model of motivation for all human behavior, not just achievement in classroom contexts. As M. Ford (1992) notes, MST is an integrative theory that attempts to organize the various motivational constructs from different theories into one model and is "generally compatible with existing theories of motivation and does not try to replace them" (p. 11). The model is based in the living systems framework of D. Ford (D. Ford, 1987; M. Ford & D. Ford, 1987), which represents an organismic–contextual model of human development (see Lerner, 1986). This framework focuses on the individual as the unit of analysis, but it embeds the individual in the biological, social, and environmental contexts that are crucial for development. Following a biological metaphor, it attempts to describe the development of the whole person-in-context, much the same way a biologist might describe an individual plant and its relation to its immediate ecological niche as well as the larger ecosystems in which it resides.

Following this metaphor, M. Ford proposes a simple mathematical formula that attempts to represent all of these factors in one model. The formula for effective person-in-context functioning is:

$$\text{Achievement or competence} = (\text{Motivation} \times \text{Skill})/\text{Biology} \times \text{Responsive environment}$$

This formula proposes that actual "achievement and competence are the result of a motivated, skillful, and biologically capable person interacting with a responsive environment" (M. Ford, 1992, p. 70). We will describe motivation in more detail later, but skill represents the various cognitive and information-processing functions as well as the actual behaviors necessary for competent action. Biology is defined in terms of the person's physical and biological capabilities that can enhance or constrain performance. Responsive environment includes the various contexts (home, school, community, etc.) that individuals move through that must provide positive opportunities for development.

As an example of how these components work together, consider that a highly motivated and skilled basketball player with excellent coaching (the responsive environment) will probably not be able to play professional basketball if he is only 5 feet tall (the biological component acts as a constraint). In the same way, another individual may actually have much better physical capabilities (height, speed, good eye-hand coordination) to play basketball well, but if not provided with a responsive environment in terms of good coaching and opportunities to play, he may not achieve his potential either. This scenario can also apply to academic learning. If students are not provided with a responsive school environment, even when they are motivated, have the prerequisite cognitive skills, and no physical constraints are operating, they will usually not achieve as well as they could in a more responsive context.

The model attempts to provide a comprehensive theory of motivation and proposes that motivation is a "psychological, future-oriented (anticipatory) and evaluative (rather than instrumental) phenomenon" (M. Ford, 1992, p. 248). This means that motivation provides the energy and direction for behavior (the future-oriented function) as well as the evaluation of behavior in terms of whether to continue or stop (persistence), whereas other cognitive and behavioral components actually provide the means for action (the instrumental function that is represented by skill in the preceding formula). There are three main components of motivation such that:

$$\text{Motivation} = \text{Goals} \times \text{Emotions} \times \text{Personal agency beliefs}$$

This triarchic model of motivation assumes that goals, emotions, and personal agency beliefs interact to determine motivation. The mathematical formula with multiplicative terms also implies that if any of these three components is missing, individuals will not be motivated in that situation. That is, if they do not have a goal activated or have very negative inhibitory affect or have a very low belief in their personal capabilities, motivation will be very low and the behavior will likely be terminated for that situation (M. Ford, 1992).

In our summary of the theory, we will concentrate on the goals component. However, personal agency beliefs in M. Ford's model are basically the same construct as self-efficacy beliefs that were discussed in chapter 4. Emotions are the various affects that are generated through interactions with the context and serve to energize behavior as well as provide evaluative information in order to regulate behavior. Affect is discussed more fully in chapter 7.

Goal Content

In M. Ford's theory, there are two important aspects of goals: goal content and goal processes. **Goal content** refers to the desired or undesired consequences of a particular goal. Goal content would be assessed by asking people what they want, what they are trying to accomplish, and why they did something (M. Ford, 1992). M. Ford has classified the contents of goals into a taxonomy that has 24 general categories (see Table 5.3). This taxonomy was developed through both empirical and clinical work with students, clients, and professionals. These 24 goal categories are assumed to represent classes of goals at a fairly abstract level of analysis. Individuals may conceive of their own personal goals in a myriad of idiosyncratic ways, but at an abstract level, the idiographic goals of an individual should fit into the 24 categories. All of the goals or needs that the four teachers discussed at the beginning of this chapter can be found in Table 5.3. The taxonomy of goals has a great deal of overlap with Murray's taxonomy of needs (see Table 5.1 and notes in Table 5.3 that attempt to match Murray's needs and M. Ford's goals), but Ford suggests that his taxonomy is not as tautological as Murray's because he attempts to distinguish between goals and the behavior patterns that might be generated by the goals. In addition,

Ford's taxonomy has a more social cognitive emphasis than the psychodynamic flavor of Murray's taxonomy. Finally, Ford suggests that his taxonomy and the goals listed in it are more specific and less global than Murray's taxonomy, yet also represent a more comprehensive list of goals than Maslow's five needs (see Table 5.2) or McClelland's three needs (need for achievement, power, and affiliation).

There are several other aspects to note about the taxonomy. First, M. Ford does not propose that there is a hierarchy to the goals in the taxonomy, unlike Maslow. Ford does not assume that any of the 24 goals is more important or more fundamental than any of the other goals. He notes that some goals may end up being more important or more compelling than others (e.g., happiness, physical well-being, belongingness), but that this is an empirical question, not a theoretical assumption of the model (M. Ford, 1992). Second, Ford assumes that behavior is usually guided by multiple goals simultaneously, so that the activation of one goal does not preclude the activation of other goals. Finally, the 24 goals may combine into larger units or "themes" (cf. Murray's themas) that represent the merging of several goal categories. For example, Ford suggests that friendship goals may reflect belonging, resource acquisition, and resource provision concerns and that need for achievement may represent both mastery and superiority goals (M. Ford, 1992). Refer to Table 5.3 as you read the following text discussion. Specific goals as listed in the table are referenced by the number in parentheses.

Table 5.3   M. Ford and Nichols's Taxonomy of Human Goals

I. Desired Within-Person Consequences
   A. Affective goals
      1. *Entertainment*—experiencing excitement, arousal; avoiding boredom, stressful inactivity (cf. Murray's 15. nPlay in Table 5.1)
      2. *Tranquility*—feeling relaxed and at ease; avoiding stressful overarousal
      3. *Happiness*—experiencing joy, satisfaction; avoiding emotional distress
      4. *Bodily sensations*—experiencing pleasure associated with physical sensations, movement, or body contact; avoiding unpleasant bodily sensations (cf. Murray's 17. nSen and 18. nSex in Table 5.1)
      5. *Physical well-being*—feeling healthy, energetic; avoiding feelings of lethargy, weakness, or ill-health
   B. Cognitive goals
      6. *Exploration*—satisfying curiosity about personally meaningful events; avoiding a sense of being uninformed
      7. *Understanding*—gaining knowledge; avoiding misconceptions (cf. Murray's 20. nUnd in Table 5.1)
      8. *Intellectual creativity*—engaging in original thinking, using novel ideas; avoiding mindless or familiar way of thinking
      9. *Positive self-evaluations*—maintaining a sense of self-confidence, pride, or self-worth; avoiding feelings of failure, guilt, or incompetence (cf. Murray's 6. nCnt and 12. nInf in Table 5.1)
   C. Subjective organization goals
      10. *Unity*—experiencing a profound or spiritual sense of connectedness, harmony with people, nature, or a greater power; avoiding feelings of psychological disunity or disorganization
      11. *Transcendence*—experiencing optimal or ordinary states of functioning; avoiding feeling trapped within the boundaries of ordinary experience

Table 5.3   M. Ford and Nichols's Taxonomy of Human Goals *(Continued)*

II. Desired Person-Environment Consequences
   A. Self-assertive social relationship goals
      12. *Individuality*—feeling unique, special, or different; avoiding similarity or conformity with others
      13. *Self-determination*—experiencing freedom to make choices; avoiding feelings of being pressured, constrained, or coerced (cf. Murray's 5. nAuto in Table 5.1)
      14. *Superiority*—comparing favorably to others in terms of winning, status, or success; avoiding unfavorable comparisons
      15. *Resource acquisition*—obtaining approval, support, advice, or validation from others; avoiding social disapproval and rejection (cf. Murray's 19. nSuc in Table 5.1)
   B. Integrative social relationship goals
      16. *Belongingness*—building and maintaining attachments, friendships, intimacy, or a sense of community; avoiding feelings of social isolation (cf. Murray's 3. nAff in Table 5.1)
      17. *Social responsibility*—keeping interpersonal commitments, meeting social role obligations, conforming to social and moral rules; avoiding social transgressions and unethical and illegal conduct (cf. Murray's 8. nDef in Table 5.1)
      18. *Equity*—promoting fairness, justice, or equality; avoiding unjust or unfair actions
      19. *Resource provision*—giving approval, support, advice, or validation to others; avoiding selfish or uncaring behavior (cf. Murray's 13. nNur in Table 5.1)
   C. Task goals
      20. *Mastery*—meeting a challenging standard of achievement or improvement; avoiding incompetence, mediocrity, or decrements in performance (cf. Murray's 2. nAch in Table 5.1)
      21. *Task creativity*—engaging in activities involving artistic or creative expression; avoiding tasks that do not provide opportunities for creative action
      22. *Management*—maintaining order, organization, or productivity in daily life tasks; avoiding sloppiness, inefficiency, or disorganization (cf. Murray's 14. nOrd in Table 5.1)
      23. *Material gain*—increasing amount of money or tangible goods one has; avoiding loss of money or material possessions
      24. *Safety*—being unharmed, physically secure, safe from risk; avoiding threatening, depriving, or harmful circumstances (cf. Murray's 11. nHarm in Table 5.1)

From *Motivating Humans: Goals, Emotions, and Personal Agency Beliefs* by M. Ford, 1992, Newbury Park, CA: Sage Publications. Copyright© 1992 by Sage Publications, Inc. Adapted by permission of Sage Publications, Inc.

The taxonomy (see Table 5.3) has two main categories: goals that are intrapersonal and reflect desired within-person consequences, and goals that represent desired outcomes of a person's interactions with the environment. In terms of the intrapersonal goals, there are three main categories: affective, cognitive, and subjective organization. Affective goals are feelings and emotions that individuals want to experience or avoid. For example, entertainment goals (1) reflect our desire to be aroused and stimulated and to avoid repetitive, boring activities, whereas tranquility goals (2) represent our need to avoid very stressful stimulation. The equilibrium between these two goals of entertainment and tranquility would be similar to Berlyne's (1960) notion of optimal arousal (M. Ford, 1992). In terms of the classroom, this would suggest that students would like to have activities that are interesting and spark their curiosity, but not so different or difficult as to be overly stressful. Happiness (3) is usually high in most individuals' goal hierarchies and can also play a regulatory function as an indicator of progress toward other goals (most people are satisfied when they reach a personal goal). The final two affective goals (4 and 5) have to do with physical sensations in terms of specific or transitory physical states ("I wish I could take a nice, hot shower now"—a bodily sensation goal) and with longer term physical goals ("I want to be in good shape aerobically so I can have more energy and live longer"—a physical well-being goal) (M. Ford, 1992).

The cognitive goals include four kinds of goals (see Table 5.3), with the first three representing three different levels of cognitive engagement. The first level is exploration (6) and reflects a person's desire to "change the unknown into the known by acquiring new information" (M. Ford, 1992, p. 90) through attention to relevant information in the environment (e.g., what's going on in the news today). In the classroom context, students operating with this goal would seek out new information in books, worksheets, lectures, and labs and attempt to remember it for later use. In contrast, an understanding goal (7) represents a desire for a deeper level of comprehension that goes beyond just the discovery and observation processes that might accompany an exploration goal, to the use of reasoning, thinking, interpretation, and analysis processes to help the individual create a meaningful understanding (e.g., wondering why people think a certain way). This type of goal is the goal most often proposed as being important for conceptual change learning and constructivist classroom teaching (Pintrich, Marx, & Boyle, 1993). Most teachers want students to go beyond just an exploration goal and to attempt to gain a deep understanding of the content area. M. Ford (1992) also notes that this understanding goal is often attractive to scholars, philosophers, highly educated people, and people who prefer reading to watching television. Finally, the third level, intellectual creativity (8), reflects a desire to engage in mental activities or create mental products that are evaluated in terms of their novelty, cleverness, or elegance, in contrast to the understanding goals that are usually evaluated in terms of truth, accuracy, validity, or persuasiveness. Intellectually creative goals would be pursued by creative writers, humorists, or musicians in contrast to the task creativity goals (see goal 21 in Table 5.3), which would be pursued by artists and architects as well as young children (M. Ford, 1992). Teachers would want to encourage all three of these goals, but certainly the first two would seem to be essential for learning. In fact, Pintrich, Marx, and Boyle (1993) suggest that students often do not pursue understanding goals in the classroom, and this hinders conceptual change learning and instruction. The final cognitive goal is the protection of self-worth or the self in general (9). This is the same goal proposed by many other motivational theorists and includes the motive to protect self-worth or self-esteem (see Covington, 1992; Harter, 1990).

Subjective organization goals represent a complex mix of both affective and cognitive states. Unity goals (10) refer to feelings of being connected to a larger power or force in nature (e.g., God), not just a feeling of belongingness to a group or community (goal 16) and avoiding a sense of psychological disunity ("I'm too fragmented, I've got to get myself together"). Transcendence goals (11) involve feelings of optimal functioning that is quite out of the ordinary. This would be similar to a high level of self-actualization in Maslow's theory or the "flow" state in Csikszentmihalyi's (Csikszentmihalyi & Rathunde, 1993) theory of optimal experience (see chapter 7). In more colloquial sports terms, it is often referred to as "being in the zone" where distractions are gone, time seems to slow down, and the individual is able to focus completely and very competently on the task at hand. It is important to keep in mind that in M. Ford's theory, this feeling of flow is a transcendent goal that a person strives to attain; it is not the actual behaviors that might lead to this feeling. This is true for all of the goals in Ford's theory. They represent something the person is trying to attain, not the actual behaviors, although descriptions of them may explain the behaviors used to attain the goals as well.

The second large set of goals is the desired person-environment consequences. The first eight goals in this set (12–19) include self-assertive goals (12–15) in which the individual is most prominent, and integrative goals (16–19) in which the group or others are more prominent. Each of the self-assertive goals is paired with an integrative goal to reflect the general tension between individuality and the group. Goal 12, individuality, reflects the person's desire to be unique and different from others, whereas goal 16, belongingness, represents a need to be part of a larger group or community. During adolescence, these two goals are often quite high in students' goal hierarchies as they struggle with their own identity as well as with becoming accepted into a peer group. The next two goals, self-determination (13) and social responsibility (17), reflect our desires to experience freedom in making choices, which parallels the need for self-determination in intrinsic motivation theory (Deci & Ryan, 1985). These goals also reflect our need to conform to certain rules and social obligations in general and in the classroom (cf. Blumenfeld et al., 1983; Blumenfeld, Pintrich, & Hamilton, 1987; Hamilton, Blumenfeld, Akoh, & Miura, 1989).

Superiority goals (14) represent individuals' needs to best others, to win, to achieve success at a level better than others (positive social comparison) as well as avoid negative social comparisons with others. This would be similar to a general ego orientation in Nicholls's (1984) goal theory, a performance orientation in Dweck's model (Dweck & Leggett, 1988), and an ability focus in Ames's (1992b) goal model. The countervailing goal in M. Ford's model would be an equity goal (18), in which the emphasis is on justice, equality, and fairness. The last two goals, resource acquisition (15) and resource provision (19), represent our need to acquire help and support from others (recall the supportive environment aspect of the theory) as well as to provide help and mentoring to others. Both goals should be related reciprocally. Teachers should be high in resource provision goals in order to support their students' optimal development.

The final category of goals outlined in Table 5.3 is task goals, which refer to how we choose to relate to different types of tasks we confront in our lives. Mastery goals (20) reflect a desire to meet challenging standards or to show personal improvement. This goal is similar to the mastery goals of Dweck, the task goals of Ames, and the task-involved goals of Nicholls. Task creativity goals (21) represent a goal to engage in activities in which creative expression can be evoked and to avoid tasks that do not allow for creativity. M. Ford notes that mastery and task creativity goals are in the same relation to each other as understanding and intellectual creativity goals, discussed earlier. Mastery goals are usually evaluated in terms of more objective standards of excellence and/or personal improvement, whereas task creativity goals are more likely to be evaluated in subjective terms. Management goals (22) reflect people's desire to maintain order and organization in their daily life and tasks. Material gain (23) is a goal of accumulating wealth or material goods and avoiding the loss of these goods. Finally, safety goals (24) are the same as Maslow's safety goals and represent our need to be secure from harm and deprivation.

These 24 goals represent the broad, general categories of goals, but individuals will always have personalized representations of these goals depending on both the individual and the contexts the individual encounters over time. Accordingly, M. Ford points out that it is important to assess the nature of goals within an individual using idiographic methods that allow for comparison between the different types of goals that might be pursued, but the comparisons are made within the individual. For example, within this individual, does he rate belongingness or individuality goals as more important, not comparing his ratings of these two goals with those of other people (see M. Ford & Nichols, 1991). The model also allows for people to pursue multiple goals simultaneously. In fact, this model is one of the few current goal theories that highlights the idea that people can and do pursue multiple goals within any one situation (cf., Shah & Kruglanski, 2000). Most goal theories stress the importance of pursuing intrinsic or mastery goals instead of extrinsic or performance goals (see chapter 6 and the next section in this chapter on goal orientation).

Given this notion of multiple goals, M. Ford proposes that there are **goal hierarchies** that help the individual set priorities and coordinate the multiple goals that might be evoked in any situation. Ford proposes that within any one situation, there might be a larger overall goal (e.g., to obtain an A in the course, a mastery goal in Ford's theory) as well as many subgoals or proximal goals (to get an A on the midterm, final exam, term paper, etc.; see chapter 4) that help the individual evaluate her progress and maintain her overall direction to the larger target goal. In addition, Ford notes that there may be goal conflict and goal alignment within these hierarchies. For example, the student who wants to obtain an A in the course and has subgoals of getting A's on the various tests and papers in the course, has these goals in alignment and her motivation should be fairly high. However, another student might have goals that conflict with one another, such as wanting to get an A (a mastery goal) and also wanting to be with friends (a belongingness goal). To the extent that the behaviors and subgoals that serve the overall goal of wanting to be with friends (e.g., talking with them during class; getting together with them to study for the course, but spending most of the time talking about other things) conflict with the goal of getting an A, the student's motivation will be diverted into these multiple goals and performance will suffer. Wentzel (1989, 1991a) has shown that high school students with low GPAs (D$^+$ or lower) report having fun and making friends as being more important goals for them than mastery/learning goals in comparison to high achievers.

M. Ford has used his theory to explain behavior in many domains, not just school and achievement contexts. Wentzel (1989, 1991a, 1991b, 1991c, 1992, 1993, 1994, 1996, 1999, 2000) has been the individual most responsible for discussing how a goal-content approach can be applied to understand student performance and achievement in school and classroom settings. Wentzel (1999, 2000) notes that a goal-content approach focuses on the content of what individuals are trying to accomplish, which serves to direct their behavior toward outcomes. In contrast, she notes that the social cognitive goal-setting theories (i.e., Locke & Latham, 1990) focus on levels of challenge, proximity, and specificity, which orient individuals toward certain standards or definitions of performance, while goal orientation models (to be discussed later in this chapter) define specific ways to regulate effort and behavior in order to achieve. Wentzel (1999, 2000) also notes that a goal-content approach assumes that goals can emanate from the individual or the context, and that even though some individuals may tend to pursue certain goals over time, goals are also defined by the social context. In fact, in classrooms, individuals often have to set aside their own personal goals and pursue the goals of others, such as the teacher or other students, or at least try to manage their own personal goals at the same time that they work with group goals. This highlights the fact that a goal-content approach emphasizes the important idea that individuals can pursue multiple goals within the same context. As Wentzel (1999, 2000) points out, in the classroom students can try to achieve and learn, try to make friends, and try to conform to the classroom and school rules all at the same time.

Wentzel has examined the role of different social goals in classroom achievement. She has shown that students endorse a number of social goals in the classroom, such as being responsible and dependable (goal 17 in Table 5.3), seeking approval from others (goal 15 in Table 5.3), and making friends (goal 16 in Table 5.3), besides some of the other goals listed in Table 5.3 such as having fun, seeking mastery, and gaining knowledge or exploring (Wentzel, 1989, 1991a, 1991b, 1991c, 1993, 1996). More importantly, she has shown that students with a high GPA endorsed goals of academic mastery and learning, but also reported frequent pursuit of the social goals of being responsible and seeking approval from others. In contrast, the low GPA students did not differ from the high GPA students on their level of endorsement of the academic goals, but reported much lower levels of the social goals of being responsible and seeking approval (Wentzel, 1989, 1991a, 1991b, 1991c, 1993). She also has shown that academic and social responsibility goals predict more classroom effort (Wentzel, 1996). Accordingly, students who adopt or endorse social responsibility goals, not just academic goals, seem to achieve at higher levels than students who do not seem to be pursuing goals of being responsible and dependable.

Wentzel has been concerned with how the pursuit of other nonachievement goals (e.g., making friends, being responsible) can influence learning and achievement outcomes. In contrast, Urdan and Maehr (1995) have discussed how students may pursue achievement goals (doing well in class, getting good grades, doing better than others) for social reasons. They have argued for the need to expand goal theory beyond a focus on mastery and performance achievement goals to consider the social goals that might lead to achievement goals. They have suggested that students may pursue achievement goals for social reasons such as seeking approval from parents or trying to make friends. In their model, these social goals provide the impetus for achievement and also the manner in which the students may try to approach or avoid achievement. For example, some students may approach achievement goals in a positive manner at the same time they are making friends. Other students, however, may see their social goal of making friends as being antithetical to succeeding at achievement goals and may avoid trying to achieve academically in order to maintain their friendships. The issue of how students coordinate these multiple goals and how the coordination can facilitate or constrain achievement and learning is a key issue for future research (Urdan & Maehr, 1995; Wentzel, 1999, 2000).

Wentzel (1999, 2000) has suggested three models for how the pursuit of social goals may be related to academic goals and accomplishments. The first model is one of complementary relations between social and academic goals whereby the goals are pursued in relatively independent fashion with independent effects. For example, the pursuit of social goals leads to positive social interactions with teachers and peers, which leads to academic achievement, independent of the pursuit of academic goals. Under this model, academic goals lead to task engagement, which also has an independent influence on achievement, separate from the effect of positive social relations that are engendered by social goals.

In the second model, the relations are developmental, with social goals fostering academic goals, which then lead to achievement. In this case, the early development of social goals and their attainment are important precursors to the development of academic goals. In many early childhood programs and in the early years of elementary school, teachers often talk of the need to socialize their students and to meet the social and emotional needs of the children first, before pursuing more academic goals and achievement. In this model, the development of social competence is an important precursor to academic achievement (Wentzel, 1991b, c). Patrick (1997) has proposed that the link between social competence and academic achievement is a function of the ability to regulate social goals, social knowledge, and strategies for social interactions. She suggests that the early development of social regulatory skills and resources can provide the foundation for the later development of academic regulatory skills. This general model and the predictions derived from it will be the focus of research in the future on the development of social and academic competence.

Finally, the third model is hierarchical, with social goals leading to academic goals and, at the same time, academic goals leading to social goals (Wentzel, 1999, 2000). For example, students could strive to attain social goals of approval from others like the teacher, but over time this goal of pleasing the teacher results in academic engagement and better achievement. In the same fashion, the student who is trying to achieve comes to see that by achieving at high levels, this pleases his or her teacher, and so the seeking of this academic goal can help to satisfy a social goal of approval from others. The development and interaction of these goal hierarchies will be an important focus of future research as we continue to explore how academic and social goals are linked in classroom settings.

Goal Processes

The 24 categories of goals represent the content of the goals that individuals are trying to achieve in different situations. Besides the content of a goal, M. Ford (1992) also proposes that there are different methods or styles that individuals use to conceptualize a goal. Within any one situation, what he calls a behavior episode, there are various goal-setting strategies that individuals might use to actually represent the content of the 24 goals. These goal-setting strategies in Ford's model are basically the same as those discussed in the research of Locke and Latham presented in chapter 4. These strategies include setting very specific goals that can help guide and regulate cognition and action better than a vague or do-your-best goal (see Locke & Latham, 1990). Ford also notes that the strategy of setting a difficult but attainable goal has positive consequences (cf. Csikszentmihalyi, 1975; Deci & Ryan, 1985; Locke & Latham, 1990). Finally, M. Ford (1992) notes that a goal-setting strategy that aligns a mastery goal (performance on a specific task) with other goals such as material gain, social responsibility, or resource acquisition can facilitate performance. For example, a student who has a mastery goal for a math exam but also has other nonconflicting goals for that task, such as obtaining a reward from parents, might do better on the exam. The basic notion is that if multiple goals are aligned and do not conflict with one another, they can have a synergistic effect on behavior (Wentzel, 1999, 2000).

Besides the goal-setting processes that work within a specific behavior episode, M. Ford (1992) also proposes that there are goal orientations that are more general, personality-like styles that cut across different situations and behavior episodes. There are a number of different types of goal orientations in his model. For example, M. Ford and Nichols (1991) have shown that there are three general dimensions along which individuals might differ in terms of their orientation to goals.

The first dimension is an *active-reactive style* whereby an active orientation refers to an individual being more involved in initiating, directing, and planning behavior, in contrast to a reactive style whereby behavior is more a function of the situational features of the context. The active style tends to be associated with more personal meaning and coherence because individuals are directing their behavior and are not as subject to the whims of situational constraints and influences. In the classroom, students with an active style would show more self-initiative and self-directed learning, whereas those with a more reactive style would be more passive and wait for the teacher to tell them what to do.

The approach avoidance style describes individuals who tend to conceptualize goal content (see Table 5.3) in terms of approaching desired consequences (e.g., for the mastery goal in Table 5.3, seeking and meeting a challenge) instead of avoiding undesired consequences (e.g., for the mastery goal, avoiding incompetence). This is not unlike the difference in McClelland's (1961) theory between those individuals who have a motive for success in contrast to those who have a motive to avoid failure (M. Ford, 1992). More recently, Covington and Roberts (1994) have suggested that this approach avoidance orientation can be crossed with success-failure to form a matrix of four types of orientations to achievement. Obviously, students with an approach style would seek out new tasks, be more likely to take risks, and not be afraid of failure, in contrast to the avoidance style students who would be anxious about trying new tasks and always seek to avoid failure. This approach avoidance distinction has also become important in goal orientation theory (Elliot, 1997).

The final style of M. Ford and Nichols (1991) is maintenance-change, which refers to people actively seeking to maintain their general goals and behavior in contrast to those individuals who are continually seeking to change and improve their goal levels and themselves. Students with a maintenance style would be self-satisfied with their level of performance, whereas change-orientated individuals would be interested in learning new things and increasing their level of achievement.

M. Ford (1992) notes that other researchers have discussed three other types of goal orientation styles. First, Winell (1987) and many clinical psychologists have distinguished a coping-thriving orientation. Ford sees this pattern as being a more global orientation that combines his (M. Ford & Nichols, 1991) three dimensions into one pattern. Individuals with a general coping orientation would be reactive, avoidant, and focused on maintenance. In contrast, those with a thriving orientation would be active, focused on approaching goals, and seeking positive change. A second, general orientation is the action versus state orientation of Kuhl (1985, 1992). Kuhl has investigated this general style in a number of studies in academic, organizational, and clinical settings. Generally, a state orientation is a way of thinking about goals that interferes with action, such as ruminating about potential negative events, procrastinating before starting the task, difficulty in concentrating on the task while doing it, and having a more passive, reactive style. In contrast, an action orientation describes individuals who work in a directive, active, and self-regulatory fashion toward their goals. The final type of goal orientation that Ford mentions is the general mastery-task-learning orientation as opposed to the ego-performance-ability orientations (see Ames, 1992b; Dweck & Leggett, 1988; Nicholls, 1984). Given that this construct has been the focus of a great deal of research in educational settings, we will discuss it in detail in the next section.

In sum, a goal-content approach offers a comprehensive model of human motivation when personal agency beliefs and emotions are included in the model. Goals are one of the three components that we have focused on here; personal agency beliefs and emotions are similar to constructs we have covered or will discuss in other chapters. The theory has been applied in educational, work, and clinical settings and does have implications for teachers. Application 5.1 lists some strategies for teachers.

APPLICATION 5.1

Applying Goal Content Theory in the Classroom

M. Ford (1992) has proposed a series of principles for motivating people based on his theory. There are 17 general principles that apply to all situations, including motivating students in classrooms, but his theory also can be used to motivate individuals in work settings, to promote social responsibility and caring, and to lead a generally healthy and emotionally satisfying life. These principles are not unlike the general design principles that cognitive psychologists have developed to improve instruction (see Brown, 1997), except, of course, these principles are based in motivational theory and research, not in the cognitive and learning sciences. One general assumption underlies all of these principles. The assumption is that facilitation, not control, should be the guiding idea in attempts to motivate people. Facilitation should focus on the individuals' goals, personal agency, and emotions and not on direct control of individuals' behavior. Accordingly, highly controlling strategies such as threats, strong punishments, controlling (not informational) rewards, and forced competition can have immediate, short-term, positive effects (they increase wanted behavior, decrease unwanted behavior), but in the long run, when used repeatedly or continuously, these types of direct control strategies can have negative consequences. They can adversely affect people's goals, agency beliefs, and emotions, which, in turn, will mediate future behavior. M. Ford (1992) suggests that motivational strategies that can facilitate the attainment of individuals' goals, increase their agency beliefs, and engender positive emotions will have more positive long-term and more durable effects.

1. *The Principle of Unitary Functioning.* This principle, in keeping with the organismic perspective of the theory, states that the unit of analysis is always the *whole person.* Motivational interventions will always need to take into account what the individual brings to the situation in terms of prior personal and developmental history. The situation and the person will interact in complex ways to influence behavior patterns. Given this principle, M. Ford (1992) notes that it is important to keep in mind that each individual is unique and that all motivational interventions will not work in similar ways with all individuals. This implication is the same basic idea behind aptitude-treatment interaction (ATI) research (see Corno & Snow, 1986). Ford also notes that another implication of this unitary functioning principle is that changes in one motivational parameter can produce changes in other parts of the person-in-context system. For example, using cooperative groups may help to motivate children because it allows them to meet their belongingness goal, but it also can result in some poor instructional practices, as may be the case when students who know very little about a topic or have misconceptions attempt to teach their misconceptions to others. This type of outcome (increased motivation, but perhaps sharing of misinformation) is an example of Ford's third implication of this principle that sometimes motivational changes can have unanticipated consequences.

2. *The Motivational Triumvirate Principle.* This principle refers to the idea that behavior is influenced by all three motivational constructs—goals, personal agency beliefs, and emotions—as they interact with each other. Accordingly, interventions to improve individuals' motivation must consider all three of these constructs at

the same time instead of just focusing on one of the three. For example, because Mr. Huang wants to encourage more females to continue in math, he concentrates not only on improving their efficacy beliefs (which are often lower than those of males even though they get higher grades; see Eccles, 1983), but also tries to get them to adopt goals that encourage them to continue in math as well as increase their positive affect toward math (see Eccles, 1983; Miura, 1987).

3. *The Responsive Environment Principle.* This principle concerns the nature of the environment that is created by a teacher—an environment that should be responsive to the individual. M. Ford (1992) suggests that there are four dimensions that can be used to judge the responsiveness of the environment. First, he believes that there should be an alignment between the individual student's personal goals and the general goals that are part of the classroom environment. For example, if a student has mainly task creativity goals and a teacher has mainly management goals (see Table 5.3), there is not much alignment, and that student's motivation will probably suffer. However, aligning goals for all students in a class of 20 to 30 children may be very difficult for a teacher. There would have to be some type of assessment of the students' goals and, given the diversity that would probably emerge, there would probably have to be a great deal of individualized instruction, which is not always the easiest type of instruction to implement with the fairly large class sizes and one-teacher arrangement commonly found in schools.

   The other dimensions are probably somewhat more easily attained in classrooms. The second is the idea that the environment must be responsive to the students' biological, transactional, and cognitive capabilities; that is, the physical space, the curriculum, and the nature of instruction should take into account the students' capabilities. For example, the nature of instruction to teach first graders early reading skills should take into account their developmental cognitive level and will most likely be different from instruction for high school students in a social studies class, given their cognitive capabilities. The third dimension is that the objectives for the tasks to be accomplished are realistic and appropriate given both the materials and resources available. Essentially, the second and third dimensions parallel the general principle of the ZPD from Vygotskian theory, whereby the environment is challenging but supportive by providing activities still within the range of the individual's competence. The final dimension of a supportive environment is that the emotional climate of the classroom be supportive and foster a feeling of trust between the students and teacher.

4. *The Principle of Goal Activation.* This principle is basic to any goal theory (cf. Locke & Latham, 1990; Maehr & Braskamp, 1986) and refers to the necessity of activating a relevant goal for the completion of a task. In terms of implications, it means that the task to be accomplished must provide opportunities for attainment of personally relevant goals. For example, Keisha is high in belongingness goals and may benefit from cooperative learning groups because the activity allows her to work with other students and may help her attain her goal of building friendships. A classroom that has a variety of tasks and activities and allows students different procedures for accomplishing them will increase the probability that personally relevant goals will be activated by this diversity, as opposed to a classroom that does not allow for much diversity in tasks or procedures.

5. *The Principle of Goal Salience.* Beyond simply activating relevant goals, teachers should try to ensure that the goals that are activated are clear, compelling, and presented in such a way that students understand what they need to do to accomplish them. Strategies for accomplishing this goal include setting very specific "targets" for performance (see Harackiewicz & Sansone, 1991; Locke & Latham, 1990) and setting proximal subgoals that help students monitor their progress (Bandura & Schunk, 1981). As noted in the previous section, teachers use these strategies when they help students break up a large task, like a major paper or report, into subparts (outline, research notes, first draft, final draft, etc.) that have specific due dates. Dividing the larger task into smaller subparts makes the task seem more manageable for the students. The specific due dates help the teacher to monitor progress and the students to self-regulate their behavior toward completion of the task.

6. *The Multiple Goals Principle.* This principle invokes the idea that behavior can be related to multiple goals and, in fact, students who are most successful in classroom settings (at least in terms of a high GPA) are more likely to pursue multiple goals, particularly social responsibility goals (Wentzel, 1989, 1991a, 1991b). Accordingly, teachers should try to activate multiple goals for students. For example, Ms. McEvoy provides a number of rationales for why doing a particular task is important (mastery of the task, to obtain rewards, to avoid punishment) (cf. Brophy, 1983) in the hope that these rationales will activate multiple goals within any one student as well as increase the possibility that one of these goals will be activated in all students.

7. *The Principle of Goal Alignment.* This principle complements the principle of multiple goals and concerns the importance of having goals that are aligned, not conflicting with each other. It may be good to have multiple goals, but they also need to be coordinated so that by trying to achieve one goal, other goals are not short-circuited. For example, a proximal goal of completing a section of a report or paper by a certain date (a management goal) may conflict with the more distal goal of intellectual creativity in terms of expressing one's ideas in new or different ways. Teachers also may want to encourage or facilitate intellectual or task creativity goals, but they have management goals as well in terms of classroom order. If the management goal is implemented in too strict or rigid a fashion, it can inhibit the attainment of the creativity goals.

8. *The Feedback Principle.* This principle, basic to all motivational and most general psychological theories, purports that relevant feedback is crucial for continued progress toward a goal. Feedback provides information that can be used to judge progress, repair mistakes, and redirect efforts. It also can influence personal agency beliefs and emotions in positive ways that can facilitate motivation. There are a number of guidelines for effective feedback for teachers, including those put forth by Brophy (1981). Chapters 4 and 8 also offer some suggestions.

9. *The Flexible Standards Principle.* This principle refers to the idea that individuals should have flexible and adaptive standards when evaluating their work or progress. For example, a college student who does poorly on a midterm, thereby eliminating the possibility of attaining an overall A for the course (the original standard), should not become completely discouraged, anxious, and self-doubting, which can lead to withdrawal of effort. The student should instead adjust his standard from getting an A in the course to something more attainable or make his new

standard simply an improvement in grade from the midterm. This flexibility and adaptability will help to maintain his motivation because his personal agency beliefs about being able to attain the new standard will be higher and his affect will be less depressed. In addition, Ford notes that it is important to remember that this flexible standard principle does *not* mean that standards should be vague or "loose." Rather, the standards should be flexible enough to change given the context, but the new standard should be just as clear, attainable, and challenging as any goal (cf. Locke and Latham, 1990).

10. *The Optimal Challenge Principle.* This principle is also well-represented in most motivation theories (see Bandura, 1986; Berlyne, 1960; Csikszentmihalyi, 1975; Deci & Ryan, 1985; White, 1959) and concerns the importance of providing tasks that are difficult and challenging, but not beyond the individual's range of competence (cf. the ZPD from Vygotsky). Implementation of this principle is often difficult in classrooms because of the heterogeneity in levels of competence, even when children are in age-graded classrooms. Of course, one avenue around this problem is to individualize the curriculum for groups of children who share the same levels of competence. This can be very time-consuming and fraught with problems, both ethical (e.g., within-classroom grouping or tracking) and practical (how to assess the levels of competence). Nevertheless, this principle is a general goal for teachers to strive for as they think about the general level of tasks that they will present to all students in their classrooms.

11. *The Principle of Direct Evidence.* This principle is one of the most interesting and important for teachers to consider, given the current interest in school programs to increase general self-esteem. Basically, the principle suggests that interventions should be focused directly on a specific problem of personal agency rather than being vague and general platitudes about building self-esteem, creating trust, or boosting confidence. M. Ford (1992) suggests that many of these self-esteem programs are too broad and general to have a direct impact on specific problems that students may have (e.g., inability to read, difficulty in math, lack of cognitive and regulatory strategies). He suggests that efforts should be targeted at the specific problems and opportunities should be provided for the students to experience success at real academic tasks, rather than just chanting a mantra like, "I'm a good person," without learning the actual academic skills required in schools. The actual success that comes from learning a specific skill and being able to overcome a problem will provide the direct evidence that the student has learned the appropriate skills and will do much more to increase personal agency than will empty platitudes. Bandura (1986) has shown that this type of guided instruction can be very helpful in the treatment of a number of psychological problems from phobias to depression. Schunk (1991b) has shown that this type of direct and targeted intervention can be very successful in academic settings.

12. *The Reality Principle.* This principle follows directly from this last point. M. Ford (1992) suggests that in many cases, a motivational intervention that is targeted at personal agency, goals, or emotions may not be sufficient to change behavior. In these instances, it may be more realistic to actually try to change the problem behavior directly rather than try to change the motivation for the behavior. For example, for children with low efficacy for academic skills, rather than encouraging them to change their efficacy perceptions, teachers should teach them the skills

they need, and efficacy perceptions will change as a function of this increase in skilled behavior. These two principles (11 and 12) stress the need to consider both motivational and cognitive/behavioral components of school learning in any intervention designed to help students academically (cf. Pintrich, 1989, 1991, 1994; Pintrich & Garcia, 1991).

13. *The Principle of Emotional Activation.* Just as the other principles discuss the importance of activating relevant goals and personal agency beliefs, this principle suggests that activating appropriate emotions will facilitate motivation. Teachers can do this by providing simulations that emotionally involve students in an experience. For example, Mrs. Kempler, a junior high teacher, uses a role-playing activity when teaching about medieval history and the relations between royalty and serfs. One student is appointed king; this student then selects other students to be knights and other royalty. Other students are then assigned to be serfs and peasants. The role play progresses as the royalty actors are given a great deal of freedom and control of resources, while the serfs are restricted greatly in their movements and access to resources. The affect and emotions that are generated in this role play are quite intense as the serfs become increasingly angry with the undemocratic system. All of the students are involved in the role play and it seems to be a motivating experience. Nevertheless, as Ford cautions, the activation of emotions can be delicate and there is always the possibility that they can get out of control. The medieval role play resulted in some very heightened emotions for some of the students and must be used with care.

14. *The "Do It" Principle.* This idea is not borrowed from a Nike shoe advertisement, but it does stress the importance of having people actually engage in the desired behavior, especially when they are having a great deal of difficulty beginning the activity. The idea is supported by the general notion from cognitive behavioral research (see Bandura, 1986; Meichenbaum, 1977) that suggests that people's negative cognitions and motivational beliefs are often so inhibiting that they never attempt the desired behavior. If an individual can engage in the behavior and not suffer the expected negative consequences but instead has a positive experience, this type of feedback and engagement will increase the probability that the behavior will be attempted again. Teachers use this strategy quite often when they work individually with students to help them engage in a task.

15. *The Principle of Incremental versus Transformational Change.* This principle suggests that change is more likely to come in small, incremental steps—a more classic evolutionary pattern—than in large, dramatic, or revolutionary steps (a more punctuated equilibrium view). Accordingly, teachers should not attempt large, dramatic changes in the environment or in their teaching strategies unless absolutely necessary. Instead, smaller, more incremental changes will be easier for the students to adapt to and may lead to more change in the long run.

16. *The Equifinality Principle.* This principle is based on the idea that there are multiple pathways to a goal—that there is no one best or right answer to the problems of motivating students. In addition, different students will require different motivational strategies. Teachers should be wary and skeptical of any instructional, management, or motivational program that offers to solve all of their problems

with a simple plan or system. Education is not a deterministic science; it is a probabilistic human endeavor. Consequently, teachers need to be active decision makers as they use different kinds of information about students' motivation, including these 17 principles, to make informed choices about what they will do in their own classrooms to motivate their own students.

17. *The Principle of Human Respect.* This final principle in M. Ford's (1992) theory is the one he considers the most important and basic. He feels that people should always be treated with respect and as unique individuals who possess a variety of skills and goals. This principle parallels the basic ideas of humanistic psychology from Rogers and Maslow and can be particularly important in classrooms. Teachers are often overwhelmed with large numbers of students, especially secondary school teachers who often have over 100–150 students to teach every day, and it can be difficult to act on this principle. Ford is simply reminding all of us about the importance of respect in our interactions with others.

GOAL ORIENTATION THEORIES

In comparison to the goal-content approach that is concerned with human behavior more broadly, goal-orientation theories, for the most part, were developed specifically to explain achievement behavior. They were created by developmental, motivational, and educational psychologists to explain children's learning and performance on academic tasks and in school settings. As such, they are the most relevant and applicable goal theory for understanding and improving learning and instruction. In addition, since the earlier edition of this book, one of the most active areas of achievement motivation research, if not the most active, has been studies of the role of academic goals and goal orientations.

We first define goal orientations and discuss their different definitions, including how they have been measured. We then discuss how these different goals can lead to adaptive and maladaptive patterns of motivational, cognitive, affective, and behavioral outcomes. Given the importance of goals in promoting achievement, we then turn to the personal (e.g., age, gender) and contextual antecedents of goals. Finally, we discuss the implications of goal theory for teachers in the application section.

Definition and Measurement of Goal Orientation

There are a number of different variants of goal orientation theories for achievement behavior, but the main construct that is involved is **goal orientation**, which concerns the purposes for engaging in achievement behavior. In contrast to Locke and Latham's (1990) goal setting theory, which focuses on specific and proximal goals (e.g., get 10 problems correct), goal orientation theory is concerned with why individuals want to get 10 problems correct and how they approach and engage in this task. The goal-content approach discussed in the previous sections focuses on many different possible goals (see Table 5.3) that can guide behavior, while goal orientation remains focused on the goals and purposes for achievement tasks.

Goal orientation represents an integrated pattern of beliefs that leads to "different ways of approaching, engaging in, and responding to achievement situations" (Ames, 1992b, p. 261). Urdan (1997) notes that goal orientations are the reasons why we pursue achievement tasks, not just the performance objectives (i.e., get an A in the course). Goal orientation includes not just the purposes or reasons for achievement, but reflects a type of standard by which individuals judge their performance and success or failure in reaching that goal (Pintrich, 2000a, 2000c, 2000d). As Elliot (1997) has pointed out, goal orientation reflects a way that individuals come to define and evaluate their competence in terms of some standards of excellence. Given that the definition focuses on the nature of the reasons and purposes for doing a task, integrated with the standards to evaluate task performance, the term goal orientation is used, rather than just goals, to signal the integrated nature of the beliefs and the patterns they can generate. However, "goal" is also used as a shorthand term in this research for goal orientation, but it should be clear that the goals discussed in goal-orientation research are different from the goals in goal setting or goal-content theories.

There may be a number of different goal orientations, but the two that are always represented in the different goal-orientation theories have been labeled learning and performance goals (Dweck & Leggett, 1988; Elliott & Dweck, 1988), or task-involved and ego-involved goals (Nicholls, 1984), or mastery and performance goals (Ames, 1992b; Ames & Archer, 1987, 1988), or task-focused and ability-focused goals (Maehr & Midgley, 1991). There is some disagreement among these researchers about whether all of these goal pairs represent the same constructs (see Nicholls, 1990), but there is enough conceptual overlap to treat them in similar ways in a textbook such as this one. Accordingly, we will use the terms mastery and performance goals to refer to the two general goal orientations.

The distinction between mastery and performance goals parallels, to some extent, the distinction between intrinsic and extrinsic motivation. Mastery goals share some of the characteristics of intrinsic motivation and performance goals are similar, in some ways, to certain aspects of extrinsic motivation (see chapter 6). The focus in goal-orientation theories, however, is on a more specific cognitive goal that is more situational and context dependent than the general, global, and more traitlike intrinsic and extrinsic motivation constructs that come from a more organismic, not contextual, perspective.

A **mastery goal** orientation is defined in terms of a focus on learning, mastering the task according to self-set standards or self-improvement, developing new skills, improving or developing competence, trying to accomplish something challenging, and trying to gain understanding or insight (see Ames, 1992b; Dweck & Leggett, 1988; Maehr & Midgley, 1991; Midgley et al., 1998; Nicholls, 1984; and cf. Harter, 1981b). Table 5.4 shows how this construct of mastery goal orientation has actually been operationalized by different researchers. Most often, both mastery and performance goals have been measured with self-report instruments that ask students to rate on a Likert-type scale (from 1 to 4, from 1 to 5, from 1 to 7) how much they agree or disagree with a particular description. It seems clear from Table 5.4 that there is quite a bit of overlap, at least in terms of measurement, between the different labels of mastery, learning, and task orientation.

A **performance goal** orientation, in contrast to a mastery orientation, represents a focus on demonstrating competence or ability and how ability will be judged relative to others, for example, trying to surpass normative performance standards, attempting to best others, using social comparative standards, striving to be the best in the group or

Table 5.4 Different Items Used to Assess Mastery and Performance Goal Orientations

Dweck	Ames	Midgley and Colleagues	Nicholls
Learning goal I like problems that I'll learn something from, even if they're so hard that I'll get a lot wrong.	*Mastery goal* I work hard to learn. Making mistakes is part of learning.	*Task-focused* I like school work that I'll learn from, even if I make a lot of mistakes. An important reason why I do my school work is because I like to learn new things. An important reason why I do my school work is because I want to get better at it.	*Task orientation* I feel successful when I learn something interesting. I feel successful when something I learn makes me want to find out more. I feel successful when something I learn makes me think about things.
Performance goal I like problems that aren't too hard, so I don't get too many wrong. I like problems that are hard enough to show that I'm smart.	*Performance goal* I work hard to get a high grade. I really don't like to make mistakes.	*Performance-approach* I'd like to show my teachers I'm smarter than other students in my classes. I want to do better than the other students in my classes. I would feel really good if I were the only one who could answer the teacher's question in class.	*Ego orientation* I feel successful when I'm the smartest. I feel successful when I know more than other people. I feel successful when I have the highest test scores.
		Performance-avoid It's very important to me that I don't look stupid in my classes. The reason I do my work is so others won't think I'm dumb. One of my main goals is to avoid looking like I can't do my work.	

class on a task, avoiding judgements of low ability or appearing dumb, and seeking public recognition of high performance levels (Ames, 1992b; Dweck & Leggett,1988; Midgley et al., 1998). In some measures of performance orientation, the term "relative ability orientation" is used instead of performance orientation or ego orientation (see Urdan, 1997 for review). However, as seen in Table 5.4, the measures of performance and ego goal orientation also overlap as they do for the different mastery goals. It is important to note that early work in this area did not distinguish between the approach and avoid performance goal orientations as in current measures (e.g., Midgley et al., 1998; Table 5.4).

In addition to the basic distinction between mastery and performance goals, other types of goal orientations have been studied in the literature. For example, Pintrich and his colleagues (Pintrich, 1989; Pintrich & De Groot, 1990a, Pintrich & Garcia, 1991; Pintrich, Roeser, & De Groot, 1994; Pintrich, Smith, Garcia, & McKeachie, 1993; Wolters, Yu, & Pintrich, 1996) measured an extrinsic goal orientation in which the focus was on getting good grades, doing schoolwork to get rewards and special privileges, or to avoid getting into trouble. Urdan (1997) also has discussed the role of an extrinsic goal orientation in learning and achievement. This extrinsic goal orientation is most similar to the extrinsic motivation in self-determination theory (Deci & Ryan, 1985). Nicholls and his colleagues have found two other goals, beyond ego- and task-involved goals, which they labeled work avoidance and academic alienation (Nicholls, 1989; Nicholls et al., 1989). Work avoidant goals concerned feeling successful when work or tasks were easy, while academic alienation goals were defined in terms of feeling successful when the students felt they could fool around and not do their schoolwork and get away with it. Meece et al. (1988) also discussed work avoidant goals in terms of a desire to complete schoolwork without putting forth much effort, a goal of reducing effort. As noted in the previous section, Urdan and Maehr (1995) have discussed the social goals that students might invoke while they pursue achievement tasks.

Given all of these different goals and orientations, which share some similar and some different features, future research needs to clarify the relations among these goals and their links to various outcomes (Pintrich, 2000a, 2000c, 2000d). At the same time, the most important aspect of goal theory is the distinction between mastery and performance goals and how these goals are linked to student outcomes. The remainder of this chapter will focus on the role of mastery and performance goals and their approach and avoidance forms, which seems appropriate given that most of the research has addressed these two general goals. There is clearly a role for extrinsic, work avoidant, and social goals, but the details of the roles of these goals are beyond the scope of this textbook.

As can be seen in Table 5.4, there is a great deal of overlap in how mastery and performance goal-orientation constructs have been measured (see also Jagacinski & Duda, in press). There are some differences, however. First, Dweck, Ames, and Maehr and Midgley all attempt to measure students' general approach to tasks, their reasons for doing a task, or their general purpose when doing a task. Nicholls, in contrast, begins all of his items with the stem, "I feel most successful when," and then adds descriptors that are very similar to the other items listed in Table 5.4. Nevertheless, Nicholls's approach asks students at what point they feel most successful when doing a task, a somewhat different perspective on goals. This perspective reflects a concern with students' general theories of classroom success. As part of his research, Nicholls also included measures of students' beliefs about what causes success, which are basically attributions for the causes of success (see chapter 3). In his model, Nicholls proposed that individuals' goal orientation will be related to their beliefs about the causes of success. Moreover, Nicholls assumed that the goal orientation an individual adopts will become the general standard for judging success and, therefore, goal orientation should predict beliefs about the causes of success (the attributions that are made). For example, students who adopt a task-involved orientation focused on learning will be more likely to give as a cause for student success responses such as, "They try to understand instead of just memorizing" or "They try to figure things out." Students who adopt an ego-involved goal orientation will be concerned with their ability and besting others and will be more likely to cite as reasons for success in school that, "They are better than others at taking tests" or "They try to beat others" (see Duda & Nicholls, 1992).

In contrast to this position, Dweck and her colleagues (e.g., Dweck, 1999; Dweck & Elliott, 1983; Dweck & Leggett, 1988; see Table 5.5) suggest that goal orientation is a function of different theories about the nature of intelligence. In this model, theories of intelligence are defined as students' perceptions about how ability and intelligence change over time. In essence, this belief is isomorphic with the stability dimension for the classification of ability attributions in attribution theory (see chapter 3). This stability dimension of attributions is not at the same conceptual level as the construct Nicholls is concerned with—beliefs/attributions for the causes of success or failure—but as we saw in chapter 3, attributions can be classified into these higher-order dimensions, such as stability, that have motivational implications.

In Dweck's model, these theories about the stability of intelligence and ability create a schema for interpreting and evaluating information about the self. In effect, they become the criteria and standards by which goals, outcomes, and behavior are judged. Dweck assumes, therefore, that these theories of intelligence drive the type of goal

Table 5.5   Dweck's Model of Goal Orientation

Theory of Intelligence	Goal Orientation	Confidence in Intelligence	Behavior Pattern
Entity theory (intelligence is fixed)	Performance goal (to gain positive judgments of competence)	If High ⟶ but If Low ⟶	Mastery oriented Seek challenge High persistence Helpless Avoid challenge Low persistence
Incremental theory (intelligence is malleable)	Learning goal (to increase competence)	If High or Low ⟶	Mastery oriented Seek challenge (fosters learning) High persistence

From "A Social-Cognitive Approach to Motivation and Personality" by C. Dweck and E. Leggett, 1988, *Psychological Review,* 95(2), p. 259. Copyright© 1988 by the American Psychological Association. Adapted by permission.

orientation that students will adopt (see Table 5.5), and her empirical research seems to support this view (e.g., Dweck, 1999; Dweck & Leggett, 1988). Although they are examining somewhat different constructs, this causal link between theories of intelligence and goal orientation in Dweck's model is just the opposite causal relation proposed by Nicholls, who assumes goal orientation influences beliefs and attributions about success. In Dweck's model, if a student has an entity theory of intelligence and believes that his ability is generally stable, he will most likely adopt a performance goal when engaged in a task. This student, because of the stable conception of ability, will be most concerned with how his performance is evaluated, how it compares to others, and with trying to best others. In contrast, the incrementalist theorist believes that ability can be increased; she is more likely to be focused on mastery goals such as trying to increase her competence and judging her success at reaching this goal by using criteria focused on self-improvement, not social comparison with others. Accordingly, although they use somewhat similar terms such as learning goals/task orientation and performance goals/ego orientation, Dweck and Nicholls have very different models about the causal relations between beliefs about ability/intelligence and goal orientation.

Besides these basic differences between the models, more recent research on goals has developed an important distinction within performance goals between approach and avoidance performance goals. For example, Elliot and Harackiewiez and their colleagues (e.g., Elliot, 1997; Elliot & Church, 1997; Elliot & Harackiewicz, 1996; Harackiewicz et al., 1998) make a distinction between two different types of performance goals: an **approach performance** goal and an **avoidance performance** goal. They suggest that individuals can be positively motivated to try to outperform others and to demonstrate their competence and superiority, reflecting an approach orientation to the general performance goal. In contrast, individuals can also be negatively motivated to try to avoid failure and to avoid looking dumb or stupid or incompetent, what they label an avoidance orientation to the performance goal.

In the same vein, Midgley and her colleagues (Middleton & Midgley, 1997; Midgley et al., 1998; see Table 5.4) have separated out both approach and avoid performance goals. Finally, Skaalvik and his colleagues (Skaalvik, 1997; Skaalvik, Valas, & Sletta, 1994) have also proposed two dimensions of performance or ego goals: a *self-enhancing ego orientation,* where the emphasis is on besting others and demonstrating superior ability, as in the approach performance goal; and *self-defeating ego orientation,* where the goal is to avoid looking dumb or to avoid negative judgments, as in the avoidance performance orientation. The approach performance orientation focuses on besting others and superior performance relative to peers. This is similar to the performance and ego orientation in the models of Dweck, Ames, and Nicholls. In addition, although not formally separated out as two distinct performance or ego goals in the models of Dweck and Nicholls, both of those models did include concerns of avoiding judgments of incompetence or feeling dumb or stupid in their conceptualizations of performance and ego orientations, similar to the avoidance-performance orientation of Elliot and Midgley or the self-defeating ego orientation of Skaalvik.

To organize the literature on mastery and performance goals, it seems helpful to propose a general framework that allows for the classification of the two goals and their approach and avoidance versions. Both Elliot (1999) and Pintrich (2000a, 2000d) have proposed a two-dimenisional matrix that represents one attempt at such a taxonomy.

The columns in Table 5.6 reflect the general approach avoidance distinction that has been a hallmark of achievement motivation research (Atkinson, 1957; Elliot, 1997; Mc-Clelland, Atkinson, Clark, & Lowell, 1953) since its inception as well as more recent social cognitive perspectives on approaching and avoiding a task (e.g., Covington & Roberts, 1994; Harackiewicz et al., 1998; Higgins, 1997). In particular, recent social cognitive models of self-regulation such as Higgins (1997) explicitly use this distinction of approach avoidance (or promotion-prevention focus in Higgins's terms) to discuss different self-regulatory processes. An approach or promotion focus leads individuals to move toward positive or desired end-states, to try to promote them to occur, while an avoidance or prevention focus leads individuals to move away from negative or undesired end-states, to prevent them from occurring (Higgins, 1997). As such, there should be some important distinctions between approaching and avoiding certain goals with concomitant influences on student outcomes. For example, a promotion or approach orientation might be expected to have some generally positive relations with cognition, motivation, and behavior, while a prevention or avoidance orientation should be negatively related to various outcomes.

The rows in Table 5.6 reflect two general goals that students might be striving for and represent the general goals of mastery and performance that have been proposed by every one of the different models discussed here. The cells in Table 5.6 include in parentheses some of the different labels that have been proposed for the two main goal orientations in the different models. All of the models agree that mastery goals (learning, task, task-involved) are represented by attempts to improve or promote competence, knowledge, skills, and learning and that standards are self-set or self-referential with a focus on progress and understanding. In all of the models discussed, mastery goals have only been discussed and researched in terms of an approach orientation; that is, that students were trying to approach or attain this goal, not avoid it. As such, most models have only

Table 5.6   Two Goal Orientations and Their Approach and Avoidance Forms

	Approach Focus	Avoidance Focus
Mastery orientation	Focus on mastering task, learning, understanding Use of standards of self-improvement, progress, deep understanding of task (learning goal, task goal, task-involved goal)	Focus on avoiding misunderstanding, avoiding not learning or not mastering task Use of standards of not being wrong, not doing it incorrectly relative to task
Performance orientation	Focus on being superior, besting others, being the smartest, best at task in comparison to others Use of normative standards such as getting best or highest grades, being top or best performer in class (performance goal, ego-involved goal, self-enhancing ego orientation, relative ability goal)	Focus on avoiding inferiority, not looking stupid or dumb in comparison to others Use of normative standards of not getting the worst grades, being lowest performer in class (performance goal, ego-involved goal, self-defeating ego orientation)

proposed the first cell in the first row in Table 5.6; it is not clear if there is an "avoidance mastery" goal theoretically, and there has been little empirical research on an avoidance mastery goal (see, however, Elliot & McGregor, 2001).

On the other hand, there may be occasions when students are focused on avoiding misunderstanding or avoiding not mastering the task (Elliott, 1999; Pintrich 2000a, 2000d). A **mastery avoid goal** may sound counterintuitive, but it seems possible that it could be operating in some achievement contexts. For example, some students that are more "perfectionistic" may use standards of not getting it wrong or doing it incorrectly relative to the task. These students would not be concerned about doing it wrong because of comparisons with others (an avoidance-performance goal), but rather in terms of their own high standards for themselves. For example, one of the author's nieces was in a whole language elementary reading class in which the teacher told the children to just spell their words anyway they wanted to, that it did not matter if they spelled them correctly or not. In this case, however, the niece was quite concerned about "not spelling the words wrong" and this focus led her to become upset and frustrated by the lack of guidance from the teacher. It seemed clear that she was not concerned about others; she just knew there were correct and incorrect spellings, and had a goal of not misspelling the words. Elliot (1999) has discussed a mastery avoidance goal in terms of an aging athlete like Michael Jordan who does not want to fall short of his past outstanding performances and so adopts a mastery avoidance goal that leads him to avoid certain types of activities, and may lead to retirement. Elliot (1999) also notes that aging individuals, in general, may be concerned with not being able to master or do tasks they were able to do quite well in their youth, and that this general mastery avoid goal could lead them to avoid trying these tasks or activities. Elliot and McGregor (2001), using a self-report instrument, operationalized a mastery avoid goal in an academic context in terms of three items including, "I worry I may not learn all that I possibly could in this class", "Sometimes I'm afraid that I may not understand the content of this class as thoroughly as I'd like", and "I am often concerned that I may not learn all that there is to learn in this class." In addition, Elliot and McGregor (2001) found empirical support for the four goals listed in Table 5.6 in terms of factor analyses generating four separable and distinct factors.

The second row in Table 5.6 reflects the general performance goal orientation that all of the models propose, but the approach and avoidance columns allow for the separation of the goal of trying to outperform or best others using normative standards from the goal of avoiding looking stupid, dumb, or incompetent relative to others. This distinction has been formally made in the work of Harackiewicz, Elliot, Midgley, Skaalvik, and their colleagues, and all of the empirical studies have shown that there are differential relations between other motivational and cognitive outcomes and an approach performance goal and an avoidance performance goal (Harackiewicz et al., 1998; Middleton & Midgley, 1997; Midgley et al., 1998: Skaalvik, 1997). In Dweck's model the performance orientation included both trying to gain positive judgments of the self as well as trying to avoid negative judgments (Dweck & Leggett, 1988). In Nicholls' model, ego-involved or ego orientation also included both feeling successful when doing better than others or avoiding looking incompetent (Nicholls, 1984; Thorkildsen & Nicholls, 1998). Accordingly, most of the earlier models did recognize the possibility that students could be seeking to gain positive judgments of the self by besting or outperforming others as well as trying to avoid looking stupid, dumb, or incompetent, although Dweck and Nicholls did not separate them conceptually or empirically as did Elliot, Midgley, and Skaalvik. In this case, within this performance row in Table 5.6, in contrast to the mastery row in Table 5.6, there is no doubt that both approach and avoidance goal orientations are possible, that students can adopt them, and that they can have differential relations to other motivational or cognitive outcomes. In addition, in the empirical work on these two performance goals (e.g., Elliot & Church, 1997; Elliot & McGregor, 2001; Midgley et al., 1998), approach and avoid performance goals have separated empirically in factor analyses.

Goal Orientation and Relations with Other Motivational and Cognitive Outcomes

Goal orientations are an important and meaningful way to describe individual achievement goals as well as classroom contexts, but they also are important because they influence a number of motivational, cognitive, and behavioral outcomes. Table 5.7 summarizes the definitions of the two basic mastery and performance goal orientations and their relations to other motivational and cognitive variables. Much of the early research on goal theory did not distinguish between approach and avoid mastery and performance goals, so the results summarized here focus on the main distinction between mastery and performance goals. Cases in which there is empirical evidence for the differential relations between approach and avoid forms of the goals and other outcomes will be discussed in the text (see also Pintrich, 2000d).

Goals and Links to Attributions and Efficacy

When research on goal theory began, attributional theory (see chapter 3) was one of the most active and productive approaches to the study of achievement motivation. Goal theorists were interested in why some seemingly competent and skilled students would approach academic tasks in a less than adaptive manner and often had negative reactions to failure and made maladaptive attributions for their performance. Accordingly, much of the early work on goal orientations focused on how these different goals were related to attributional patterns, learned helplessness, and beliefs about success and failure. In general, the research shows that a mastery goal orientation is linked to a positive, adaptive pattern of attributions, whereas a performance goal orientation is linked to a maladaptive, helpless pattern of attributions (Ames, 1992b; Dweck & Leggett, 1988).

When operating under a mastery goal orientation, students are concerned with learning and mastery of a task and increasing their competence. This schema or orientation seems to lead students to interpret outcome feedback in different ways than those students following a performance goal orientation, with the focus on maintaining or enhancing their ability and a concern with how ability is assessed. Under a mastery goal orientation, students are more likely to see a strong link between their effort and the outcome and make more effort attributions for both success and failure. In addition, students with a mastery goal orientation see effort linked in a positive manner with ability; that is, more effort means more ability.

In contrast, a performance goal orientation seems to lead to using ability attributions for both success and failure. It is well known that ability attributions for failure (when ability is conceived of as stable) are maladaptive and can lead to learned helpless patterns of behavior (Dweck & Leggett, 1988; Weiner, 1986; see chapter 3). In addition, students with

Table 5.7 Goal Orientation and Other Motivational and Cognitive Outcomes

Definitions/Outcomes	Mastery Goals	Performance Goals
Goal definitions Success defined as	Improvement, progress, mastery, creativity, innovation, learning	High grades, better performance than others, higher achievement on standardized tests, winning at all costs
Value placed on	Effort, attempting challenging tasks	Avoiding failure
Reasons for effort	Intrinsic and personal meaning of activity	Demonstrating one's worth
Evaluation criteria	Absolute criteria, evidence of progress	Norms, social comparison with others
Errors viewed as	Informational, part of learning	Failure, evidence of lack of ability or worth
Outcomes associated with different goals		
Attributional patterns	Adaptive, failure attributed to lack of effort, outcome is seen as contingent on personal effort	Maladaptive, failure attributed to lack of stable ability
Affect	Pride and satisfaction for effortful success Guilt associated with lack of effort Positive attitudes toward learning Intrinsic interest in learning	Negative affect following failure
Cognition	Use of "deeper" processing strategies Use of self-regulatory strategies including planning, awareness, and self-monitoring	Use of more surface or rote learning strategies
Behavior	Choice of more personally challenging tasks More risk-taking, open to new tasks More willing to seek adaptive help	Choice of easier tasks Less willing to take risks, try new tasks Less willing to seek adaptive help

Material drawn from Anderman and Maehr (1994), Ames (1992b), and Maehr and Midgley (1991).

a performance goal tend to see effort and ability as inversely related, as opposed to the positive relation under a mastery goal. The performance-oriented students tend to think that the harder they try, the less ability they have. This belief can lead them to be at risk for avoiding effort in order to protect their ability and self-worth (Covington & Omelich, 1979). It is important to note that in Dweck and Leggett's model (see Table 5.5), this helpless pattern will emerge if students have a performance orientation and low confidence or efficacy in their intelligence. If students have a performance orientation but high confidence in their intelligence, a performance orientation can lead to a mastery pattern of adaptive attributions and adaptive behavior, like seeking challenges and persistence.

Besides these attributional patterns, the links between mastery goals and judgments of self-efficacy and competence are generally positive. In one of the original formulations of mastery goals, Dweck and Leggett (1988) summarized mainly laboratory research that showed that students who were oriented to mastery and learning were able to maintain positive and adaptive efficacy beliefs and perceptions of competence in the face of difficult tasks. Other more correlational classroom research has also shown the same general pattern (e.g., Ames, 1992b; Kaplan & Midgley, 1997; Middleton & Midgley, 1997; Pintrich & De Groot, 1990a, b; Pintrich & Garcia, 1991; Pintrich, Marx, & Boyle, 1993; Thorkildsen & Nicholls, 1998; Wolters et al., 1996). Students who are focused on improving and learning would be more likely to interpret feedback in terms of the progress they have made, thereby supporting their efficacy beliefs.

Correlational studies have revealed a mixture of findings with regard to the linear relations between performance goals and self-efficacy. For example, Anderman and Midgley (1997) showed that approach performance goals were positively related to perceptions of competence for sixth graders, but unrelated to perceptions of competence for fifth graders. Wolters et al. (1996) found that approach performance goals were positively related to self-efficacy for junior high students. In contrast, Middleton and Midgley (1997) found in another sample of junior high students that approach performance goals were unrelated to efficacy, but avoid-performance goals were negatively related to efficacy. In two studies of junior high students, Skaalvik (1997) showed that approach performance goals were positively related to efficacy and avoid-performance goals were negatively related to efficacy.

It seems possible that students who are focused on approach performance goals would have higher perceptions of efficacy as long as they are relatively successful in besting others and demonstrating their high ability. Some of the conflicting findings might be due to differences in the samples and who is represented in the approach performance groups (e.g., actual high versus low achievers). In contrast, students oriented to avoiding looking incompetent or stupid would seem likely to have lower perceptions of self-efficacy. In fact, these students seem to have some consistent self-doubts or concerns about their own competence, reflecting a schema that should generate low efficacy judgments. In addition, it may be that this relation can be moderated by the classroom context. In many of the studies, the positive relations are found in junior high classrooms, but not in elementary classrooms. The literature suggests that junior high classrooms are more performance oriented than elementary classrooms, which are generally more mastery oriented (see review by Midgley, 1993). In this case, in junior high classrooms, there may be good reasons for efficacy to be positively related to approach performance goals, but not in elementary classrooms, which are generally more mastery oriented (Anderman & Midgley, 1997).

Goals and Links to Affective Outcomes

Mastery goals have also been associated with various affective outcomes (see Table 5.7). Given the attribution-affect link specified in attributional theory, it is not surprising that mastery goals seem to lead to pride and satisfaction when successful, and guilt when not successful (Ames, 1992b; Jagacinski & Nicholls, 1984, 1987). These affective outcomes are usually generated by attributions that stress the controllability of behavior (such as effort), and if mastery goals lead to more effort attributions, these emotions would be expected to be generated under attribution theory principles (Weiner, 1986). Mastery goals have also been associated with reports of more intrinsic interest in and positive attitudes toward learning tasks such as higher task value beliefs (e.g., Ames, 1992b; Butler, 1987; Harackiewicz et al., 1998; Meece et al., 1988; Rawsthorne & Elliot, 1999; Stipek & Kowalski, 1989; Wolters et al., 1996). Many of these studies are correlational, so it is difficult to determine causality, but in a meta-analysis of 23 experimental studies of the effect of mastery and performance goals on intrinsic motivation, Rawsthorne & Elliot (1999) showed that mastery goals were positively related to both self-reports of interest and enjoyment as well as behavioral measures of free choice (a classic measure of intrinsic motivation; see chapter 6).

In terms of intrinsic interest or value, the results for performance goals are mixed, paralleling the results for efficacy. Harackiewicz and Elliot and their colleagues have shown in both experimental and correlational studies that approach performance goals do not necessarily lead to less interest, intrinsic motivation, or task involvement, in comparison to mastery goals (Harackiewicz et al., 1998). In their experimental studies of college students playing pinball games or solving puzzles, an approach performance orientation did increase intrinsic motivation and task involvement, especially for students high in achievement motivation (a traditional personality measure of nAch) or in more competitive contexts (a situational variable). They suggest that both mastery and approach performance goals can draw students into an activity, depending on their personal characteristics and the context in which they are doing the task. At the same time, the researchers do note that avoidance performance goals generally have negative effects on intrinsic motivation and performance (e.g., Elliot, 1997). In their meta-analysis of performance goals and interest, Rawsthorne and Elliot (1999) found that only avoid performance goals showed the negative relation to interest, enjoyment, and free choice, but that approach performance goals did not undermine intrinsic motivation in terms of self-reported interest or behavioral choice.

Some of the correlational studies generally support this view of the positive relations between approach performance goals and interest, intrinsic motivation, and task value and the negative relations between avoidance performance goals and these outcomes (e.g., Skaalvik, 1997; Wolters et al., 1996). In addition, work that has examined affective reactions shows that students who are oriented to avoiding negative judgments of their competence are clearly more anxious about tests and their performance (Middleton & Midgley, 1997; Skaalvik, 1997), in line with the original goal theory research on a general performance orientation (Ames, 1992b; Dweck & Leggett, 1988). In contrast, approach performance goals are either uncorrelated with anxiety (Wolters, 1996), or show relatively low negative relations with anxiety (Middleton & Midgley, 1997; Skaalvik, 1997). It seems clear that avoid performance goals are negatively related to intrinsic interest and value, but the research for approach performance goals is much less straightforward. There is a clear need for more research on the relations between approach performance goals and affective outcomes as well as the potential moderators of the relation (Midgley, Kaplan & Middleton, 2001; Rawsthorne & Elliot, 1999).

Goals and Links to Cognitive Outcomes

The next category of outcomes associated with mastery goals includes various types of cognition (see Table 5.7). This includes the use of strategies that promote deeper processing of the material as well as various **metacognitive** and self-regulatory strategies (Pintrich, 2000d). Much of this research is based on self-report data from correlational classroom studies, although Dweck and Leggett (1988) summarize data from experimental studies. The classroom studies typically assess students' goal orientations and then measure students' reported use of different strategies for learning either at the same time or longitudinally. Although there are some problems with the use of self-report instruments for measuring self-regulatory strategies (see Pintrich et al., 2000), these instruments do display reasonable psychometric qualities. Moreover, the research results are overwhelmingly consistent in terms of mastery goals, accounting for between 10 to 30% of the variance in the cognitive outcomes. Studies have been done with almost all age groups from elementary to college students and have assessed students goals for school in general as well as in the content areas of English, math, science, and social studies.

The studies have found that students who endorse a mastery goal are more likely to report attempts to self-monitor their cognition and to seek ways to become aware of their understanding and learning, such as checking for understanding and comprehension monitoring (e.g., Ames & Archer, 1988; Dweck & Leggett, 1988; Meece et al., 1988; Meece & Holt, 1993; Middleton & Midgley, 1997; Nolen, 1988; Pintrich, 1999b; Pintrich & De Groot, 1990a, b; Pintrich & Garcia, 1991; Pintrich & Schrauben, 1992; Pintrich et al., 1994; Wolters et al., 1996). In addition, this research has consistently shown that students' use of various cognitive strategies for learning is positively related to mastery goals. In particular, this research has shown that students' reported use of deeper processing strategies, such as the use of elaboration strategies (i.e., paraphrasing, summarizing) and organizational strategies (networking, outlining), is positively correlated with the endorsement of mastery goals (Ames & Archer, 1988; Bouffard, Boisvert, Vezeau, & Larouche, 1995; Graham & Golan, 1991; Kaplan & Midgley, 1997; Meece et al., 1988; Pintrich, 1999b; Pintrich & De Groot, 1990a, b; Pintrich & Garcia, 1991; Pintrich et al., 1993; Pintrich et al., 1994; Wolters et al., 1996). Finally, in some of this research, mastery goals have been negatively correlated with the use of less effective or surface processing strategies (i.e., rehearsal), especially in older students (Anderman & Young, 1994; Kaplan & Midgley, 1997; Pintrich & Garcia, 1991; Pintrich et al., 1993). In contrast to this research on the use of various self-regulatory and learning strategies, there has not been much research on how mastery goals are linked to the use of other problem-solving or thinking strategies. This is clearly an area that will be investigated in the future.

The research on performance goals and cognitive outcomes is not as easily summarized as the results for mastery goals. The original goal theory research generally found negative relations between performance goals and various cognitive and behavioral outcomes (Ames, 1992b; Dweck & Leggett, 1988), although it did not discriminate empirically between approach and avoidance performance goals. The more recent research that has made the distinction between approach and avoidance performance goals does show some differential relations between approaching a task focused on besting others and approaching a task focused on trying not to look stupid or incompetent. In particular, the general distinction between an approach and an avoidance orientation suggests that there could be some positive aspects of an approach performance orientation. If students are approaching a task trying to promote certain goals and strategies, this might lead them to be more involved in the task than students who are trying to avoid certain goals, which could lead to more withdrawal and less engagement in the task (Harackiewicz et al., 1998; Higgins, 1997; Pintrich, 2000c).

Most of the research on performance goals that did *not* distinguish between approach and avoidance versions finds that performance goals are negatively related to students' use of deeper cognitive strategies (e.g., Meece et al., 1988; Nolen, 1988; cf., however, Bouffard, Boisvert, Vezeau, & Larouche, 1995). This would be expected—performance goals that include items about besting others as well as avoiding looking incompetent would guide students away from the use of deeper strategies. Students focused on besting others may be less likely to exert the time and effort needed to use deeper processing strategies because the effort needed to use these strategies could show to others that they lack the ability, given that the inverse relation between effort-ability is usually operative under performance goals, and trying hard in terms of strategy use may signify low ability. For students who want to avoid looking incompetent, the same self-worth protection mechanism (Covington, 1992) may be operating, whereby students do not exert effort in terms of strategy use in order to have an excuse for doing poorly, which can be attributed to lack of effort or poor strategy use.

However, more recent research with measures that reflect only an approach or avoidance performance goals suggests that there may be differential relations between these two versions of performance goals. For example, Wolters et al. (1996), in a correlational study of junior high students, found that, independent of the positive main effect of mastery goals, an approach performance goal focused on besting others was positively related to the use of deeper cognitive strategies and more regulatory strategy use. However, Kaplan and Midgley (1997), in a correlational study of junior high students, found no relation between an approach performance goal and adaptive learning strategies, but approach performance goals were positively related to more surface processing or maladaptive learning strategies. These two studies did not include separate measures of avoid performance goals. In contrast, Middleton and Midgley (1997), in a correlational study of junior high students, found no relation between either approach or avoidance performance goals and cognitive self-regulation. Some of the differences in the results of these studies stem from the use of different measures, classroom contexts, and participants, making it difficult to synthesize the results. Clearly, there is a need for more theoretical development in this area and empirical work that goes beyond correlational self-report survey studies to clarify these relations.

One factor that adds to the complexity of the results in discussing approach and avoidance performance goals is that in Dweck's original model (Dweck & Leggett, 1988), the links between performance goals and other cognitive and achievement outcomes were assumed to be moderated by efficacy beliefs (see Table 5.5). That is, if students had high perceptions of their competence to do the task, performance goals should not be detrimental for cognition, motivation, and achievement. These students should show the same basic pattern as mastery-oriented students. Performance goals were assumed to have negative effects only when efficacy was low. Students who believed they were unable and were concerned with besting others or wanted to avoid looking incompetent did seem to show the maladaptive pattern of cognition, motivation, and behavior (Dweck & Leggett, 1988).

Other, more correlational research that followed this work did not always test explicitly for the predicted interaction between performance goals and efficacy or did not replicate the predicted moderator effect. For example, both Kaplan and Midgley (1997) and Miller, Behrens, Greene, and Newman (1993) did not find an interaction between approach performance goals and efficacy on cognitive outcomes such as strategy use. Harackiewicz and Elliot and their colleagues (Harackiewicz et al., 1998), using both experimental and correlational designs, did not find moderator or mediator effects of efficacy in relation to the effects of approach mastery or approach performance goals on other outcomes such as actual performance.

Nevertheless, it may be that approach performance goals could lead to deeper strategy use and cognitive self-regulation, as suggested by Wolters et al. (1996), when students are confronted with overlearned classroom tasks that do not challenge or interest them or offer opportunities for much self-improvement. In this case, the focus on an external criterion of "besting others" or being the best in the class could lead them to be more involved in these boring tasks and try to use more self-regulatory cognitive strategies to accomplish this goal. On the other hand, it may be that approach performance goals are not that strongly related to cognitive self-regulation in either a positive or negative way, as suggested by the results of Kaplan and Midgley (1997) and Middleton and Midgley (1997). Taken together, the conflicting results suggest that approach performance goals do not have to be negatively related to cognitive self-regulatory activities in comparison to avoidance performance goals. This conclusion suggests that there may be multiple pathways between approach and avoidance performance goals, cognitive strategy use and self-regulation, and eventual achievement. Future research should attempt to map out these multiple pathways and determine how approach and avoidance performance goals may differentially relate to cognitive self-regulation activities (Barron & Harackiewicz 2001; Pintrich, 2000c, 2000d).

Goals and Links to Behavioral Outcomes

In terms of the last category listed in Table 5.7, behavioral outcomes, studies have shown that mastery goals are more positively related to college students' attempts to manage their time and effort (Pintrich, 1989; Pintrich & Garcia, 1991; Pintrich et al., 1993), an important aspect of behavioral self-regulation. Research on help-seeking has consistently shown that adopting a personal mastery goal is positively associated with adaptive help-seeking (Newman, 1994; 1998a, 1998b; Ryan & Pintrich, 1997; 1998; Ryan, Pintrich & Midgley, 2001). Students who approach a task with a mastery orientation focused on learning would not see help-seeking as reflecting negatively on their ability (e.g., showing others that they are unable). They would be more likely to see help-seeking as a strategy to help them learn (Newman, 1994, 1998a). In contrast, students who adopt a performance goal are less likely to seek adaptive help. Classroom research also shows that contexts that foster a mastery orientation in the classroom climate and structure lead to more adaptive help-seeking (Newman, 1998b; Ryan, Gheen, & Midgley, 1998). In addition, students operating under a mastery goal seem to be more willing to try to undertake challenging tasks or to take more risks (Dweck, 1999; Dweck & Leggett, 1988).

One of the most important behavioral outcomes is actual achievement or performance. Goals may promote different patterns of motivation, affect, and cognition, but they should also be linked to actual classroom achievement. The more experimental research on mastery goals has shown that students in mastery conditions usually achieve or perform at higher levels (Dweck & Leggett, 1988). In fact, given all the positive motivational, affective, and cognitive outcomes associated with mastery goals, it would be expected that mastery goals would also lead to higher levels of achievement. However, in some of the correlational classroom studies, this does not seem to be the case (e.g., Elliot, McGregor, & Gable, 1999; Harackiewicz et al., 1998; Harackiewicz, Barron, Carter, Lehto, & Elliot, 1997; Pintrich, 2000c; VanderStoep, Pintrich & Fagerlin, 1996). The pattern that seems to emerge is that mastery goals are unrelated to performance or achievement in the classroom, usually indexed by grades or GPA. In contrast, in some of these studies, approach performance goals (trying to be better than others) are associated with better grades or higher GPAs (Elliot et al., 1999; Harackiewicz et al., 1997, 1998).

This newer research on the role of performance goals has led some researchers to develop a revised multiple goal theory perspective (e.g., Elliot, 1997; Harackiewicz et al., 1998; Pintrich, 2000c). They have suggested that there is a need to move beyond the simple dichotomy of "mastery goals are good/adaptive versus performance goals are bad/maladaptive" to a conceptualization of the different goals as being adaptive or maladaptive for different types of cognitive, motivational, affective, and behavioral outcomes. In other words, depending on what outcome is under consideration, goals may be adaptive or maladaptive; for example, with mastery goals leading to more interest and intrinsic motivation, but approach performance goals leading to better performance (Harackiewicz et al., 1998). It is important to note that a revised multiple goal perspective and the normative perspective are in complete agreement about the detrimental effects of avoid performance goals. The main revision proposed is that approach performance goals may be adaptive for some outcomes. In addition, the concept of equifinality, or the idea that there are multiple means to accomplish a goal, suggests there may be multiple pathways or trajectories of development that are set in motion by different goals, and these different pathways can lead to similar outcomes overall (Barron & Harackiewicz, 2001; Pintrich 2000c; Shah & Kruglanski, 2000). Finally, interactions between multiple goals and these interactions may lead to different patterns of outcomes that are more complex than the simple linear relations suggested by normative goal theory under the mastery/good and performance/bad generalization (Barron & Harackiewicz, 2001; Pintrich, 2000c).

In contrast, Midgley, Kaplan, and Middleton (2001) have argued that there is no need to revise goal theory and that the basic assumption that mastery goals are adaptive and performance goals are maladaptive is still the best overall generalization from goal theory. They suggest that most of the research on the positive effects of approach performance goals are for special cases, such as students high in self-efficacy (Dweck & Leggett, 1988), or students high in mastery goals as well approach performance goals (Pintrich, 2000c), or in contexts, such as competitive college classrooms (Harackiewicz et al., 1998) where there may be an advantage to adopting performance goals. Moreover, they note that classrooms and schools are often inherently performance-oriented and competitive to begin with, and that any suggestion by researchers that approach performance goals are adaptive would encourage teachers and school personnel to continue to stress the competitive nature of schooling, with the continued many detrimental effects for many school children. This issue is currently a very active area of research and there will, no doubt, be continued research and clarification of these issues as the field progresses.

Personal and Contextual Predictors of Goals

If goal orientations are so important in terms of their relations with various motivational, affective, cognitive, and behavioral outcomes, it is also important to understand what factors lead to the adoption of the different goals. Of course, there are many different potential factors, but in this textbook, we concentrate on a few personal and contextual factors. We first describe the role of personal factors such as age, gender, and ethnicity, and then the contextual factors that might influence the adoption of different goals. One of the hallmarks of goal orientation theory is that it is a contextual model of motivation that assumes that the personal goals an individual adopts are very sensitive to contextual features. As such, the nature of the context can have a very large influence on the goals that students adopt in classrooms. In this manner, goal theory is much more useful to classroom teachers because it assumes that goals are not just stable personal characteristics of the individual, but can be shaped by what teachers do in the classroom and how the classroom is organized and structured.

One personal characteristic that has been linked to the adoption of different goals is age. The work on development differences has proposed that younger and older children have different ways of conceptualizing ability, intelligence, effort, and achievement that relate to their goals. For example, Dweck and her colleagues (e.g., Dweck, 1999; Dweck & Elliott, 1983) suggest that younger children generally have an incremental theory of intelligence, whereas older children (about 10–12 years old) will start to develop more entity-like theories of intelligence. Dweck proposes that there are two basic implicit theories of intelligence: incremental and entity theories. **Incremental theories of intelligence** reflect students' beliefs that their intelligence and ability can change and can increase with time and experience. In contrast, **entity theories of intelligence** represent the belief that ability is fixed, stable, and unchanging. Under this theory, students think they will not be able to increase their ability or intelligence over time.

In Dweck's research, these two beliefs are usually operationalized as opposite sides of a dichotomous variable and students should have one or the other implicit theory. The model, however, suggests that there may be a continuum between entity and incremental beliefs and that individuals may show mixed theories of beliefs about intelligence. These beliefs should be somewhat stable over time once the students are older than 12 or 13 years. Accordingly, these theories of intelligence are more traitlike than many other more contextual models of goals, although theories of ability/intelligence may vary by domain. For example, you may have an entity belief about your ability in mathematics, but you may have an incremental theory of ability for English coursework. This does not just apply to academic domains, however. Individuals may have an entity theory of ability to play basketball because of their short height, but may be incrementalists in terms of their ability to play tennis or to learn how to do their job.

In Dweck's model, these two different theories of intelligence would then lead to different goal orientations, with the younger children more likely to adopt a mastery goal orientation and the older children a performance orientation (see Table 5.5). Eccles and her colleagues (e.g., Eccles & Midgley, 1989) suggest that as children make the transition to junior high school, they tend to endorse an entity theory of ability and intelligence. This research suggests that most adults have entity views of general intelligence, although they also may have incremental theories of ability for certain domains. For example, most adults may have a view of general intelligence as consisting of verbal ability, general thinking and problem-solving skills, and social competence (see Sternberg, 1990) but only think that the verbal ability and problem-solving components are actually entity-like, whereas social competence (ability to get along with others, be on time for appointments, etc.) can be more incremental. If teachers have a more entity-like view of intelligence and ability, they would be more likely to believe that children who are achieving at lower levels would be less able to change their performance. This could result in teachers having lower expectations for these children and subsequently treating them differentially (see Brophy & Good, 1974; Eccles & Wigfield, 1985).

Nicholls and his colleagues (see Nicholls, 1978, 1990; Nicholls & Miller, 1983, 1984a, 1984b, 1985) have also shown that there are developmental differences in students' theories of ability, in particular what ability is and how it is related to beliefs about luck, skill, difficulty, and effort (see chapter 3). Nicholls has followed a developmental perspective in these studies and his work has revealed that there are general levels of development in students' understandings of these concepts. Although Nicholls discusses the development of these concepts in terms of age-related levels of development, he is not advocating a strong stage model of development in a Piagetian or structuralist manner. These levels are descriptive of children's thinking about ability and are age related, but they are context sensitive and not necessarily dependent on larger shifts in cognitive development (e.g., a shift from preoperational to concrete operational thinking).

In this research, Nicholls and his colleagues have found that young children, about 5 years old or younger, generally do not differentiate the concepts of luck, skill, ability, and effort in the same way that adults do. For example, young children do not distinguish luck from skill and believe that effort can make a difference on tasks that are essentially determined by chance. It is not until children are about 12 years old that they fully distinguish luck from skill and realize that effort will not make any difference on tasks determined by chance, but effort can make a difference on skill tasks. Of course, adults may suspend this belief about effort being unrelated to chance tasks. As anyone who has ever watched people playing slot machines knows, the players often expend a great deal of effort and have a number of strategies they use to help them win, no matter how illusory the link is between their effort and their winnings.

Nicholls and his colleagues also have found that young children (preschoolers) have different conceptions of the relations between task difficulty and ability than older children. There seem to be three levels in terms of this relation: the egocentric, objective, and normative levels (see Table 3.3 in chapter 3). At the first level, labeled egocentric by Nicholls, all judgments about task difficulty are in reference to the child's own competence, so that a hard task is one that is hard for the child, not necessarily for anyone else. The second level, called the objective level, occurs when the child can recognize that there is a continuum of difficulty levels that requires different levels of ability. However, the child still cannot distinguish between low ability or high difficulty in a failure situation. In the final level, the normative level, which occurs at about 6 or 7 years old, children can distinguish between a task that is hard for everyone, which is a hard task, and a task that is hard just for them, which means they have low ability. This differentiation may come about because children at this age start to become aware of and actually use social comparison and normative information from peers to make ability, effort, and difficulty judgments (Ruble & Frey, 1991).

Finally, Nicholls also has shown that young children confound ability and effort or, at least, do not share the normative, adultlike definitions of ability and effort. This relation appears to be divided into four levels. Again, children age 5 years and younger tend to merge the concepts of ability, effort, and outcome together, so that a person who tries hard is automatically smarter and someone who is smart also tries hard, regardless of actual outcome. At the second level, which emerges at about 6 or 7 years old, while they begin to develop the normative conception of ability and task difficulty, children begin to differentiate effort from outcome but think effort should determine outcome. They believe that equal effort should lead to equal outcomes. In cases in which the outcome is the same and effort differs, the children will have difficulty reconciling this and invent reasons for why those who did not try as hard still did as well (they tried really hard for a short time) or for those who tried harder but still achieved at the same level (they went too fast and made mistakes). In the third level, the notion that ability can interact with effort to influence outcome begins to develop, although it is not applied systematically. Children at this level will begin to understand that if they try hard but do not do as well as others, they may lack some ability. However, children at this level may still state that equal effort should lead to equal outcomes. The fourth and final level, achieved at about 12 or 13 years of age, reflects the normative adult conception of ability and effort as distinct and often covarying. In particular, ability is conceived of as capacity and ability can therefore limit the effect of effort. For example, students at this level believe that if they have low ability, high effort will only be able to improve their performance to a certain level. Conversely, if students have high ability and combine that with high effort, they should be able to achieve at a very high level. In addition, students at this level will likely believe that effort and ability covary, such that if an individual has high ability, lower effort is required for most tasks.

These developmental differences in children's beliefs about intelligence, ability, skill, effort, difficulty, and luck imply that younger children, particularly preschool and early elementary age children, will likely be more mastery oriented than older children. As students begin to see that ability is capacity or that intelligence is entity-like, they will become concerned about their ability and how their performance reflects on their ability. This focus on ability is in line with a performance orientation, not a mastery goal orientation. The source of these developmental differences appears to be both cognitive-developmental as well as contextual. Nicholls (1990) and Ruble and Frey (1991) both argue that these developmental differences come about because of changes in young children's cognitive capabilities in understanding and using a variety of sources of information in the environment. In contrast, Rosenholtz and Simpson (1984) and Marshall and Weinstein (1984) argue that cognitive/structural changes are not the cause of these differences, but rather the nature of the contexts the children move through, in particular, the classroom context. Eccles and her colleagues (e.g., Eccles & Midgley, 1989) as well as Maehr and his colleagues (e.g., Anderman & Maehr, 1994; Maehr & Midgley, 1991) suggest that the organization and structure of junior high schools influence students' motivational beliefs, rather than developmental differences alone. It seems likely that it is an interaction of both developmental and contextual factors that lead to the adoption of different goal orientations.

In terms of gender and ethnic differences, there is very little empirical research on differences in goal orientation by gender or ethnicity (Eccles et al., 1998). Although Graham (1994) notes the dire need for more research on ethnic differences in attributions and self-perceptions of ability (see chapters 2 and 3), there are some empirical studies on ethnic differences and those motivational constructs in contrast to the void in research on ethnicity and goal orientation. Clearly, given the importance of goal orientation to a variety of other motivational and cognitive outcomes, we need research that examines goal orientation beliefs and their relations to these outcomes for diverse groups of students.

In terms of gender differences, some of the original research by Dweck on learned helplessness (Dweck et al., 1978) showed gender differences, with females having a less adaptive pattern of attributions. It was this early research that led Dweck to reformulate her ideas in terms of theories of intelligence and goal orientation beliefs (Dweck & Leggett, 1988) in which theories of intelligence and goals are the causal determinants of attributions, affect, and behavior. Following the logic of this model and working backward from the early findings of gender differences in attributions, it might be predicted that females would be more performance oriented and more likely to endorse entity theories of ability (Henderson & Dweck, 1990). That is, if entity theories lead to performance goals, and these goals lead to more maladaptive patterns of attributions, the reverse should hold as well for individuals who use more maladaptive patterns of attributions (see Table 5.5). However, the research on gender differences in attribution patterns is not clear at all; many studies do not find maladaptive patterns among females (Eccles, 1983; Eccles, et al., 1998), so it is not clear that females would be less mastery oriented and more performance oriented. Henderson & Dweck (1990) do report on one study that showed that bright females were twice as likely to endorse an entity theory as opposed to bright males. In most of the empirical studies on goal orientation, however, gender differences have not been reported as significant, so there may not be large differences in goal orientation associated with gender. In fact, it might also be proposed that males are more performance oriented. If the stereotypical pattern of males being more competitive than females is assumed, males might be more likely to adopt goals of besting others and trying to achieve the highest grades. Again, there is a need for more research on gender differences in these motivational beliefs about ability, goal orientation, and subsequent attributional, affect, and behavioral patterns before any strong conclusions can be drawn about the role of gender in students' goal orientation.

Moving beyond the role of personal factors, how does the classroom context shape students' goal orientation? The research on goal orientation has often conceptualized students' goal orientation as a context-dependent or classroom-situated construct that is very amenable to change, depending on the environmental cues and presses. This research has used both experimental designs in which goal orientations are induced through certain kinds of instructions to the participants and correlational field studies in which characteristics of the classroom are observed (or reported on) and then linked to students' goal orientations. There are a number of different ways to organize the classroom literature, but the acronym **TARGET** represents a useful way to structure the research. Epstein (1989) identified six dimensions of classrooms that affect motivation and that are modifiable: task design, distribution of authority, recognition of students, grouping arrangements, evaluation practices, and time allocation. The acronym TAR-

GET has been used to represent these dimensions (*task, authority, recognition, group-ing, evaluation, time*). Ames (1992b) and Maehr and Midgley (1996) have used aspects of this structure to summarize research on how classroom characteristics can influence the adoption of different goals. It should be noted that, although these three dimensions are discussed individually in terms of different features that can facilitate the adoption of a mastery or performance orientation, given the reality of classrooms, these features are not orthogonal to one another; they will overlap and interact in the classroom. Ap-plication 5.2, later in the chapter, discusses strategies to make classrooms more mastery focused.

Task

The task dimension concerns the design of learning activities and assignments. Tasks and learning activities are important influences on student motivation and cognition (Blumenfeld, Mergendoller, & Swarthout, 1987; Doyle, 1983). There are several features of classroom tasks that can encourage students to adopt a mastery orientation, accord-ing to Ames (1992a, 1992b). First, the amount of variety and diversity in tasks can help maintain student interest and, by decreasing the amount of public comparability and op-portunities for social comparison regarding performance, help students adopt a mastery goal orientation (Marshall & Weinstein, 1984; Nicholls, 1989; Rosenholtz & Simpson, 1984). A second feature of tasks concerns how they are introduced and presented to stu-dents. If the teacher can help students see the personal relevance and the meaningful-ness of the content for their own learning, this can facilitate an adoption of a mastery goal orientation (Brophy, 1987, 1999; Meece, 1991).

A third feature concerns the level of difficulty of the task. Like most motivational theories we have discussed previously (and those in chapter 6 on intrinsic motivation), goal orientation theory suggests that tasks that offer an optimal level of challenge for students—tasks that can be mastered with effort but are neither easy enough to produce boredom nor hard enough to produce anxiety—can facilitate a mastery goal orientation (Ames, 1992b; Lepper & Hodell, 1989; Malone & Lepper, 1987). Finally, Ames (1992b) notes that tasks that are structured to highlight specific, short-term, or proximal goals can help students marshal their efforts toward these goals and feel efficacious as they ac-complish these goals. This latter feature represents the same implication regarding task design that would be derived from self-efficacy theory (Schunk, 1991b) as well as goal-setting theory (see chapter 4).

There are various classroom motivational strategies to structure tasks to develop a mastery goal orientation in students. These strategies include making learning interest-ing, using variety and personal challenges, helping students set realistic goals, and de-veloping in students organizational and management skills and effective task strategies (Ames, 1992a, 1992b). Task structure helps to distinguish unidimensional from multi-dimensional classes (e.g., Rosenholtz & Simpson, 1984). In unidimensional classes, stu-dents use the same materials and have the same assignments, so ability differences have motivational impact. For example, social comparisons are much easier to make in uni-dimensional classrooms because everyone is working on the same tasks. In multidi-mensional structures, students work on different tasks and there is less opportunity for negative social comparisons.

Authority

This dimension involves the degree of opportunity that students have to take leadership roles and develop a sense of independence and control over learning activities (Ames, 1992b). The general principle is that students should be given some choice and control in the classroom setting, the same principle that intrinsic motivation theorists (Deci & Ryan, 1985) propose as important for intrinsic motivation (see chapter 6). Research from both goal theory and intrinsic motivation theory suggests that the provision of some control and choice for students increases their interest in the task and their cognitive engagement in the task (Ames, 1992b). This can include having students participate in the decision making for the classroom, such as setting priorities for *when* work will be done, not *what* work will be done; that is, the content of the curriculum is still under the teacher's control.

Other aspects can include giving students opportunities to set the pace of learning or how the task will be accomplished. These types of opportunities can provide students with real choices and encourage them to develop personal responsibility for their own learning. At the same time, as Corno and Rohrkemper (1985) point out, students must have the necessary cognitive and self-regulatory skills to be able to cope with this type of responsibility. It may be that very young children or students with learning problems may not have the self-regulatory skills that would enable them to adapt to a classroom situation that allows a great deal of choice. If the students are unable or unwilling to regulate their own behavior in line with classroom opportunities for choice and control, it is unlikely that these opportunities will have a positive influence on students' motivation and achievement (Ames, 1992b).

Recognition

Recognition relates to the formal and informal use of rewards, incentives, and praise, which have important consequences for students' motivation to learn. To develop a mastery goal orientation, Ames (1992a, b) recommends that teachers recognize student effort, progress, and accomplishments. In this way, any use of rewards or recognition is based on individual learning and progress, not normative comparisons, and can provide important informational feedback to the student. The role of rewards is also discussed in more detail in chapter 6, but one important principle to keep in mind is that rewards can be useful when they provide informational feedback to students about their progress or their competence (Deci & Ryan, 1985; Deci, Koestner, & Ryan, 1999; Lepper & Henderlong, 2000; Morgan, 1984). Ames (1992a, b) also suggested that giving all students opportunities to earn rewards will be helpful in promoting a mastery orientation. If some students feel that they can never obtain rewards or recognition, they will be less interested and motivated for the task. This implies that rewards or recognition may be based not just on overall achievement or performance, but on progress and effort (Brophy, 1998). Finally, Ames (1992a, b) suggested the use of private forms of recognition and reward so that their value is not derived at the expense of others. Maehr and Midgley (1996) note how public recognition of athletic accomplishments in secondary schools can overshadow academic activities and can communicate the importance of competition and performance goals.

Grouping

The grouping dimension focuses on students' ability to work effectively with others. To develop an atmosphere where differences in ability do not translate into differences in motivation, teachers should provide opportunities for heterogeneous cooperative groups and peer interaction (Ames, 1992a, b; Brophy, 1998). Small-group work is especially useful for low achievers who share in the group success and feel more efficacious about performing well. Group work allows students to assume more responsibility for their learning. Individual work also is important, however, because it allows for a clear portrayal of individual progress.

Besides the use of small groups, the overall classroom culture can be designed to foster a "community of learners" (e.g., Bransford, Brown, & Cocking, 1999; Brown, 1997; Maehr & Midgley, 1996) where the emphasis in the classroom as a whole (or even the school as a whole) is on learning together. This type of classroom culture would include norms and expectations about collaboration among students and teachers, not competition (Brophy, 1998), as well as structures that foster collaboration. This type of classroom and school culture should foster the adoption of mastery goals and a focus on learning (Maehr & Midgley, 1996).

Evaluation

Evaluation involves methods used to monitor and assess student learning. In terms of the evaluation practices and reward systems, goal orientation theory suggests that there are several factors that can facilitate a mastery goal (Ames, 1992b). First, the publicness of the evaluation practices can increase the salience of social comparison information, which can foster a performance orientation on the part of students. For example, disclosing students' grades for all classwork on bulletin boards, displaying only a select group of papers or tests in public spaces, or calling out test grades in public can provide social comparison information to all students about their relative performance and ability and can foster a performance orientation (Ames, 1992b; Marshall & Weinstein, 1984; Rosenholtz & Simpson, 1984). The use of within-classroom ability grouping that is made salient to students can also influence students' social comparison behavior and their perceptions of ability (Reuman, 1989), although the relation can be mediated by the degree of heterogeneity of student ability levels in the classroom (Mac Iver, 1988).

A third factor concerns the general type of feedback that is provided to students about their performance and what criteria are used to evaluate the students' performance. Ames (1992b) suggests that feedback that communicates that mistakes are a part of learning and that effort is important will help students adopt a mastery goal orientation. In addition, she notes that when evaluation criteria allow for assessment of individual improvement, progress, and mastery rather than normative comparisons, students will be more likely to focus on learning and mastery than on competition and performance goals. In addition, the use of standardized tests or other more conventional classroom assessment methods such as multiple choice tests provide some students opportunities to succeed, but not all students demonstrate their best work in these formats. Some diversity in assessment methods and criteria for grading allows for more diversity and offers all students an opportunity to show their competence and improvement (Brophy, 1998). Some evaluation strategies that effectively enhance motivation are to evaluate students for individual progress and mastery, give students opportunities to improve their work (e.g., revise compositions for a higher grade), vary methods of evaluation (e.g., use portfolios, not just multiple choice exams), and use private evaluation. Teachers must be careful about normative grading systems that compare students to one another; such normative comparisons can lower feelings of efficacy among students who do not compare favorably to their peers.

Time

Time encompasses the appropriateness of workload, the pace of instruction, and the time allotted for completing work (Epstein, 1989). Time relates closely to design of tasks. Effective strategies for enhancing mastery goal orientation are to adjust time or task requirements for students having trouble completing work and to allow students to plan their work schedules and timetables for progress. For example, the use of projects and other larger tasks (reports, design assignments) allow students some autonomy and choice in planning their own work, rather than the timeline being completely determined by the teacher. The provision of some autonomy and choice should foster a mastery orientation. These effective strategies also may allay student anxiety about learning, which can raise perceptions of competence and motivation.

These three general dimensions often overlap; classrooms may have some or all of the positive features to facilitate a mastery orientation. It is possible that classrooms may have some task structure features (interesting tasks) that will facilitate a mastery orientation but have evaluation (public display of grades) or authority structures (little student choice or control) that are not very mastery oriented. As both Ames (1992b) and Blumenfeld (1992) point out, there is very little research on how students perceive and react to this type of diversity in classroom structures. It could be that certain dimensions are more salient to all of the students in terms of their perceptions of classroom mastery orientation. For example, in a classroom where there is a great deal of emphasis on public evaluation and social comparison, this evaluation dimension may result in students perceiving the classroom as being more performance oriented, even if the task and authority structures are more mastery oriented. A second possibility is that there may be individual differences in students in terms of what they perceive as being more salient, with some focusing on the evaluation structures and others focusing on the task or authority structures. This is an important, unresolved issue in goal theory and there is a need for more classroom-based research to investigate these and other possibilities.

This matter regarding how students perceive and react to differential classroom structures also brings up several other, unresolved issues in goal orientation theory. First, as noted earlier, there is disagreement among goal orientation theorists about the conceptual definitions of mastery and performance goal orientations. Different researchers espouse different labels for these two general goals, different definitions, and, of course, different ways of measuring the goals. Second, beyond the definitions of the two goals, there are varying models regarding the issue of whether goal orientation is more situated and contextual or is more of a personal predisposition or individual difference variable. If one adopts a more situated view, classrooms can have a stronger influence on students' goal orientation. This is a more optimistic view of student motivation because it suggests that teachers can structure classrooms in such a way to increase the mastery orientation of all students. In contrast, a more individual difference perspective on goal orientation suggests that it may be harder for teachers to change students' goal orientation. It may be that the solution to this matter regarding the stability of goal orientation will involve the adoption of a strategy used in social and personality psychology that assumes that both situational and personal conceptualizations are important and the issue is to specify how they interact (Mischel, 1990; Pintrich, 2000a). There may be personal dispositions for certain types of goal orientations that situational features can override. For example, it may be that when the situational features and cues in a classroom stress a performance orientation, most students may adopt this orientation regardless of their initial level of a mastery orientation. In the absence of strong environmental cues, personal goal orientations may take precedence. In addition, there may be developmental differences such that younger elementary students may not have formed stable goal orientations and are more susceptible to the classroom context, whereas older students in secondary classrooms have formed more stable goal orientations and are less likely to be influenced by the classroom context (Pintrich, 2000a).

Related to the idea that goal orientations may be somewhat stable over individuals is a third issue concerning multiple goals (Barron & Harackiewicz, 2001; Midgley et al., 2001; Pintrich, 2000c). The goal theories of Locke and Latham (1990; see chapter 4) and M. Ford (1992) both assume that individuals can adopt and pursue multiple goals at the same time. Goal orientation theorists have not been clear about this issue. Some propose that mastery and performance goals are at opposite ends of one continuum, thereby suggesting that individuals are basically pursuing either a mastery or a performance goal (Dweck & Leggett, 1988). Others (Meece & Holt, 1993; Nicholls et al., 1989) find that these goals can be orthogonal to one another and that it is possible for individuals to have a mixture of different goals that they report they are pursuing at the same time. In addition to this issue of the theoretical relations between the two types of goals, goal orientation researchers are still struggling with the best way to operationalize these multiple goals in their research. One strategy would be to specify the multiple goals in terms of orthogonal dimensions (e.g., a classification of individuals into a two-by-two matrix of high–low mastery and high–low performance goals) and another strategy would be to examine the intraindividual patterns of goals using cluster analysis (see Meece & Holt, 1993).

Beyond this specification of multiple goals, there is still a need for more research on how these multiple patterns of goals then influence motivation, affect, cognition, and actual achievement (Barron & Harackiewicz 2001). As noted earlier, there is a controversy regarding the relative adaptiveness of approach performance goals. Some researchers have suggested that approach performance goals can be adaptive for certain outcomes (Harackiewicz et al., 1998; Pintrich, 2000c, 2000d). Others (Midgley et al., 2001) have suggested that there is no need to revise goal theory's main generalization regarding the adaptive nature of mastery goals and the maladaptive nature of performance goals. This issue and how it is related to the nature of multiple goals will continue to be an important issue for future research in goal theory (Barron & Harackiewicz, 2001; Pintrich, 2000a).

APPLICATION 5.2

Applying Goal Orientation Theory in the Classroom

Mastery and performance goals have been conceptualized as both individual difference constructs and more contextually sensitive beliefs. It appears that students will adopt the goal orientations that are stressed in their classroom (Ames, 1992b; Ames & Archer, 1988; Maehr & Midgley, 1991). Given that the research is very clear that approach mastery goal orientations are related to better motivational outcomes as well as cognitive outcomes, what can teachers do to facilitate the adoption of mastery goals? Ames (1992b) and Maehr and Midgley (1991) have suggested a number of strategies that teachers might use in their classroom. These strategies cut across the six TARGET dimensions, although they clearly reflect attempts to change these dimensions to facilitate the adoption of mastery goals. Given the debate and unresolved issues regarding the adaptive nature of approach performance goals, we do not offer any strategies to foster performance goals.

1. *Focus on meaningful aspects of learning activities.* Teachers should stress how the academic tasks that are done in the classroom are relevant and "authentic" tasks that have meaning in the real world. For example, Mr. Alvarez, a tenth-grade biology teacher, has students involved in a project on local water quality. Students go out into the field and take samples of water from local streams and the main river in the area, perform tests for water quality, and then discuss the implications of their findings for water use in terms of drinking, sanitation, and overall water pollution.

2. *Design tasks for novelty, variety, diversity, and interest.* Teachers should attempt to provide a wide variety of tasks for students to engage in and ensure that the tasks have some novel, interesting, or surprising features that will engage the students. Ms. Donovan, a third-grade teacher, uses her one classroom computer to help students practice their math skills. She has acquired a number of different math software programs that embed arithmetic skills in games and fantasy-like environments. Even though they are basically drill-and-practice activities on a computer, she finds that her children, especially some of the low achievers, really enjoy working on the computer rather than doing math worksheets.

3. *Design tasks that are challenging but reasonable in terms of students' capabilities.* Again, Ames (1992b) suggests the same basic principle as Locke and Latham (1990) and M. Ford (1992) as well as the general Vygotskian principle regarding the ZPD. Given the diversity of student capabilities in the classroom, this suggestion to individualize instruction is often difficult to implement. However, it does not mean that every individual student needs to have unique types of tasks, but that a range of tasks is offered to students. For example, Ms. Nelson, a sixth-grade English teacher in a middle school, teaches the whole class certain aspects of literacy in terms of reading and writing. All of the students have some core projects, papers, and assignments that have to be in their individual portfolios. However, she does individualize by providing a range of extra required assignments that must be included in the students' portfolios. These extra assignments include creative writing tasks as well as basic grammar and spelling assignments. Students can choose which of these extra tasks they are going to engage in, but Ms. Nelson

guides students to work on areas where they can improve. Accordingly, some children have more grammar assignments in their portfolios, whereas others have more reading comprehension assignments. This system also allows Ms. Nelson to give reading and writing tasks that are at different grade levels without using highly public within-classroom grouping practices.

4. *Provide opportunities for students to have some choice and control over the activities in the classroom.* This does not mean that the teacher should give up all decision making about the curriculum or tasks. In fact, it is probably shirking professional responsibility and ethics for a teacher to turn over the curriculum to the students. Teachers are in their role because they supposedly have some knowledge and skills about their content areas and instruction in general that can help students to learn. However, it is possible for teachers to provide opportunities for students to do different activities within a range of activities that fit the curriculum. For example, Mr. Wolters, a junior high social studies teacher, allows students some choice in topics for reports or papers. He constrains the general topic (e.g., the era of the American Revolution) and students' papers have to fit within one of the general themes of the unit (e.g., military, economic, political, social, cultural, geographical), but the students are allowed to pursue their own interests within these constraints.

5. *Focus on individual improvement, learning, progress, and mastery.* Teachers in both their daily verbal feedback and in the rewards they give should focus students on their improvement. Ms. Vekiri, a fourth-grade teacher, provides individual feedback to students on worksheets and their daily work that focuses on how the students are mastering the skills or knowledge required and their improvement from previous days or weeks. In addition, she has students compile their work in folders that she periodically reviews with them individually. In these conferences with the students, she tries to help the students see how they are progressing in terms of growth in their own skills and knowledge.

6. *Strive to make evaluation private, not public.* Although it is impossible to make all evaluation private (after all, classrooms are public places), teachers can minimize public evaluations. Mr. Martin, a seventh-grade English teacher, used to have students call out their spelling test scores to save time, but he eventually found that it promoted a lot of social comparison and contests among students because it provided very public information about who is doing well and who is not doing well. The students who did well seemed to thrive on the competition, but after a while, the students who did not perform well consistently began to resist taking the spelling tests. They would be slow to get ready for the test, they would often drift off and stare out the window when Mr. Martin was calling out the words, and they would not even try to write them down. He also used a big bulletin board to display all of the students' grades on all assignments, tests, and papers that everyone in the class could see. Although these management procedures were helpful to him, Mr. Martin found that they led to some very negative feedback and teasing from the higher achieving students toward the students who were not doing so well. At the end of the first marking period, he stopped using both of these procedures and had students turn in their papers to him. He kept all grades in a record-keeping spreadsheet on his computer. This took some time to set up and enter students' grades, but it allowed him to keep evaluations more private and did not

foster as much negative social comparison. In addition, the spreadsheet program allowed him to print out individual student records, so he could give each student a copy of his or her own performance over the term.

7. *Recognize student effort.* Although effort cannot and should not be the sole criterion for judgments regarding the quality of work, there are ways to build effort into the evaluation. Ms. Danos, a high school English teacher, gives separate scores or grades for content and effort on major papers. She tries to help her students see that the effort they put in is linked to the overall quality of the paper, but also recognizes that there still may be differences in content due to knowledge and skill differences. Nevertheless, she wants to encourage students who are trying hard by giving them a high mark for effort, although they may need more work on their grammar and overall writing skills.

8. *Help students see mistakes as opportunities for learning.* Teachers, through their feedback and grading practices, can encourage the view that mistakes are indicators of a student's ability or that mistakes happen to everyone regardless of ability and really represent an opportunity to learn. How teachers treat wrong answers in a class recitation can send strong messages about the nature of mistakes and their role in learning. In order to foster a mastery orientation, teachers need to be careful to recognize mistakes (that is, don't just let mistakes go by without comment) but treat them in a way that encourages students to see them as positive and fruitful for learning. For example, Ms. Garcia, a high school algebra teacher, has students work problems on the board. She sends up teams of two or three students to work on different problems and the whole class works at the board during this time. When the students are done, they return to their seats, then each team goes up individually and explains how the team worked the problem. Ms. Garcia and the students can ask the teams questions about their methods to see if there are difficulties and where they are in the problem solution. Errors are treated as a way to learn as the class sees and discusses the process by which the team came to use the method the team chose for the problem. In addition, because the students work in teams of two or three, no one student ever feels that he or she is solely responsible for the problem.

9. *Use heterogeneous cooperative groups to foster peer interaction; use individual work to convey progress.* Mr. Myers, a fifth-grade teacher, uses cooperative grouping for all of his social studies and science units. He changes groups with each unit, making an effort to group students according to abilities and talents related to the skills and creativity needed to complete the selected activities. Students are encouraged to participate actively by being given responsibilities. At the conclusion of each unit, students are graded on their performance on the mastery test and their participation in group activities.

10. *Adjust time on task requirements for students having trouble completing work; allow students to plan work schedules and time lines for progress.* Ms. Chambers had several students with learning problems in her class. Initially, the students had difficulty completing assigned work in the allotted time. Ms. Chambers met with each student and together they adjusted the amount of work to complete for each assignment. She told students that she expected them to eventually be able to complete all of the work. She met with each student and allowed each of them to set goals for

the amount of work to complete each day, with the overall goal being total completion at the end of 6 weeks.

These are just a few of the strategies that different goal theorists have suggested to foster a mastery goal orientation in the classroom. In addition, Maehr and Midgley (1991) suggest that schools, not just classrooms, can adopt many of these same strategies. In fact, their work suggests that it is difficult for one teacher in a school to adopt many of these mastery strategies without support from other teachers in the building and the school principal. They have worked with whole school buildings to incorporate these strategies schoolwide in order to ensure that there is consistency throughout the building.

SUMMARY

This chapter reviewed a number of different need and goal theories that have been proposed to explain personal motivation. The early need theories of Murray and Maslow were much more global and encompassing theories of human motivation. These theories were designed to explain all of human behavior, not just the achievement motivation of students in classrooms. Both theories developed a taxonomy of needs that were assumed to provide the instigation for action as well as the direction of action. Murray's list of needs included 20 needs, whereas Maslow's hierarchy of needs included 5 different levels of needs. Although needs have an intuitive appeal for explaining motivated behavior, there are serious conceptual and theoretical problems associated with the construct, particularly difficulties in avoiding a tautological argument between needs and behavior and in specifying a parsimonious number of needs.

Most current research on motivation has focused on goals, a more social cognitive construct that does not have some of the same conceptual difficulties as needs. We discussed two general goal theories and their implications for student motivation and achievement in the classroom. The goal content theory presented was M. Ford's (1992) Motivational Systems Theory (MST). This theory represents an attempt to synthesize a number of different motivational theories into one comprehensive system. As such, it includes goals, personal agency beliefs (efficacy and control), and emotions as the three defining motivational constructs. The functions of agency beliefs and emotions are similar to those in other motivational theories such as self-efficacy theory, but the definition of goals is somewhat different from that in other goal theories. Ford proposes that there are 24 general goals that individuals can strive to attain. The taxonomy of 24 goals is derived from empirical work with individuals not only in school settings, but in many other institutional settings such as work organizations and clinical settings. These goals are much more global and psychological in nature than the very specific task goals that are central to Locke and Latham's goal-setting theory (see chapter 4) or the goal orientations in achievement goal theory. These 24 goals are similar in many ways to Murray's 20 needs, but they are more specific and less psychodynamic than Murray's and they are not assumed to be hierarchical as in Maslow's theory. In addition, these 24 goals can be combined in a number of ways, which allows individuals to pursue multiple goals. The theory has been developed to explain human motivation in many settings, and it does have relevance for educational settings. MST proposes 17 general principles for the facilitation of motivation that are directly applicable to classrooms and schools.

The final goal theory discussed in this chapter is goal orientation theory. Of all the current goal theories, this one has the most direct applicability to classrooms and student motivation. It was developed to explain achievement behavior specifically and has been tested in many experimental and classroom field studies with both children and adults as they perform various learning tasks. Currently, it is probably the most active area of research on student motivation in classrooms and it has direct implications for students and teachers. The theory proposes that there are two general goal orientations that students can adopt toward their academic work: a mastery orientation with the focus on learning and mastery of the content and a performance orientation with the focus on demonstrating ability, getting good grades or rewards, or besting other students. More recently, there have been proposals to split apart both of these goals into approach and avoidance forms. There is clear empirical support for distinguishing between approach and avoidance performance goals, while the idea of mastery avoid goals awaits further theoretical and empirical support. Goal orientations have been linked to a number of cognitive, affective, and behavioral outcomes in a number of empirical studies. Generally, the research suggests that a mastery goal orientation leads to adaptive attributional patterns, positive affect and interest, higher levels of cognitive engagement, more effort and persistence, and adaptive help-seeking and risk-taking. In contrast, an avoid performance goal orientation (avoiding looking dumb or stupid) often leads to maladaptive patterns of attribution, higher levels of anxiety, lower value for tasks, less cognitive engagement, withdrawal of effort and failure to persist, and lower levels of performance. The results for approach performance goals are more mixed, showing both adaptive and maladaptive outcomes in different studies. In addition to these links to student outcomes, goal orientation theory and research have shown that the task, authority, recognition, grouping, evaluation, and time dimensions of classrooms can help to create mastery and performance orientations in students. Given these findings, there are a number of instructional strategies that teachers can use in their classrooms to make changes in the task, authority, and evaluation structures to make classrooms more mastery oriented.

Intrinsic Motivation

*J*on Crocker, a high school English teacher, sat at home planning his week's lessons. His students were studying nineteenth-century American writers (e.g., Emerson, Hawthorne, Poe, Thoreau), and their assignment was to write a critical analysis of a literary work by one of the figures of the period. Jon was planning whole-class, small-group, and individual activities, including time to do library research on the students' topics.

Jon loved literature and teaching. He recalled how excited he became when he was in high school and studied great literature. He had a couple of dynamic teachers who made literature come alive and showed how issues and events of long ago related to contemporary happenings. For Jon, class was only the beginning. He read more books and did more work in his English classes than was required because of his love for learning literature rather than because it was something to be done. He always earned good grades, but they were less important to him than the excitement he derived from studying literature.

Jon's challenge was to try to recreate that excitement among his students. So far the results were disappointing; the students seemed interested in everything but literature. For example, Todd talked with Jon the other day and said that he really needed to make an A in the course to improve his grade point average so he could get admitted to college. Todd asked what he could do to ensure that he would get an A in the class. Kai complained about having to take the class and hoped that he could stay awake in there. Tina announced in front of the class that all of this "literature stuff" seemed like a waste of time because it didn't pertain to living in today's world. Mark was less candid but made the same point when he said that he hoped more time could be spent on authors who understand young people better. Lilia was an exception. She seemed truly interested in literature and displayed some of the excitement that Jon felt. A couple of other students seemed similarly intrinsically motivated, but Jon thought that only 3 highly interested students out of 23 seemed pretty dismal.

Jon considered the problems he faced. His course was required; students needed it to graduate. They had no control over who taught the course, the topics were pretty well set, and the assignments did not offer much latitude. Many students were concerned about their grades. At a minimum, they did not want to appear to be stupid. They also likely did have a legitimate problem relating historical material to their own lives.

Jon thought about some ways he might enhance intrinsic motivation for literature among the students. The term papers were a good start because students could choose their own topics and pursue a format mutually agreed upon by themselves and by him. He decided to spend more time relating themes and events in literature to contemporary happenings. He knew the students enjoyed small-group work and discussions, so he decided to plan more of those. Some *discussion time could focus on how literature related to current events and students' own lives. He decided to try some role playing; students would assume the role of characters and act out scenes. He planned one session in which he would come to class dressed as Poe and talk about his life and writings. Jon realized that he could not change many things (e.g., students' concern about grades), but he believed that collectively these activities would make the class more interesting and that maybe students would feel more of a sense of personal involvement.*

Like most teachers, Jon is concerned about his students' intrinsic motivation for learning. **Intrinsic motivation** refers to motivation to engage in an activity for its own sake. People who are intrinsically motivated work on tasks because they find them enjoyable. Task participation is its own reward and does not depend on explicit rewards or other external constraints. In contrast, **extrinsic motivation** is motivation to engage in an activity as a means to an end. Individuals who are extrinsically motivated work on tasks because they believe that participation will result in desirable outcomes such as a reward, teacher praise, or avoidance of punishment.

It is tempting to think of intrinsic and extrinsic motivation as two ends of a continuum such that the higher the intrinsic motivation, the lower the extrinsic motivation, but, in fact, there is no automatic relation between intrinsic and extrinsic motivation. For any given activity, an individual may be high on both, low on both, medium on both, high on one and medium on the other, and so forth. It is more accurate to think of intrinsic and extrinsic motivation as separate continuums, each ranging from high to low.

Intrinsic and extrinsic motivation are time and context dependent. They characterize people at a given point in time in relation to a particular activity. The same activity can be intrinsically or extrinsically motivating for different people. Jon's English class is extrinsically motivating for Todd but intrinsically motivating for Lilia. As another example, assume that Scott and Rhonda play the banjo. Scott's intrinsic motivation is high because he plays for enjoyment, whereas his extrinsic motivation is low. In contrast, Rhonda's extrinsic motivation is high because she plays largely as a means to the end of playing well enough to earn money in a Dixieland band. Rarely does she play for intrinsic reasons.

Because intrinsic motivation is contextual, it can change over time. Many things that young children find interesting (e.g., "Sesame Street") gradually lose their appeal as children become older. Sudden changes in level of intrinsic motivation are not uncommon. Scott may become extrinsically motivated to play the banjo well if he experiences financial problems and decides to play the banjo to earn money. Doing something because one wants to can easily become doing it because one has to.

Aside from the fun that people have while engaging in activities they enjoy, we can ask whether intrinsic motivation bears any relation to learning. Do students learn better when they enjoy the content, or can they learn just as well if their goal is to please the teacher, earn good grades, or stay out of trouble with parents? We can all remember times when we were intrinsically and extrinsically motivated to learn. Students can learn for intrinsic or extrinsic reasons. Nonetheless, working on a task for intrinsic reasons is not only more enjoyable, there also is evidence that across grade levels, intrinsic motivation relates positively to learning, achievement, and perceptions of competence, and negatively to anxiety (Gottfried, 1985, 1990).

These benefits presumably occur because students who are intrinsically motivated engage in activities that enhance learning; they attend to instruction, rehearse new information, organize knowledge and relate it to what they already know, and apply skills and knowledge in different contexts. They also feel efficacious about learning and are not burdened down with anxiety. In turn, learning promotes intrinsic motivation. As students develop skills, they perceive their progress and feel more efficacious about learning. Heightened self-efficacy and positive outcome expectations (see chapter 4) raise intrinsic motivation and lead to further learning (Bandura, 1986, 1993).

In this chapter, we examine intrinsic motivation from several perspectives: effectance motivation, incongruity, mastery motivation, personal causation and control, self-determination, self-perception and overjustification. We also examine how various conditions, such as extrinsic rewards, may affect intrinsic motivation. Despite some differences, there are common themes running through these views. Lepper and Hodell (1989) identify four major sources of intrinsic motivation: challenge, curiosity, control, and fantasy. Intrinsic motivation may depend on students finding activities challenging, as when goals are of intermediate difficulty and success is uncertain. Intrinsic motivation also may depend on learners' curiosity being piqued by activities that are surprising, incongruous, or discrepant with their existing ideas. Intrinsic motivation derives in part from students experiencing a sense of control over their learning and task participation. And, finally, activities that help learners become involved in make-believe and fantasy may enhance intrinsic motivation.

After studying this chapter, you should be able to:

1. Define intrinsic motivation and contrast it with extrinsic motivation.
2. Explain White's theory of effectance motivation and other views emphasizing incongruity.
3. Discuss the major variables in Harter's theory including the role of the social environment.
4. Describe the primary features of locus of control and personal causation.
5. Explain the role of self-determination in intrinsic motivation.
6. Explain the overjustification phenomenon and use it, along with cognitive evaluation theory, to explain why offering extrinsic rewards for performing an intrinsically interesting task can decrease intrinsic motivation.
7. Describe the conditions under which rewards may enhance learning and motivation.

EARLY VIEWS OF INTRINSIC MOTIVATION

Early work on intrinsic motivation explained it in terms of a developmental phenomenon or as dependent upon arousal and incongruity. We discuss these perspectives, then turn our attention to contemporary views.

Effectance Motivation

In a classic paper, White (1959) discussed **effectance motivation** as:

> Fitness or ability, and the suggested synonyms capability, capacity, efficiency, proficiency, and skill. It is therefore a suitable word to describe such things as grasping and exploring, crawling and walking, attention and perception, language and thinking, manipulating and changing the surroundings, all of which promote an effective—a competent—interaction with the environment . . . The behavior . . . is directed, selective, and persistent, and it is continued not because it serves primary drives . . . but because it satisfies an intrinsic need to deal with the environment. (pp. 317–318)

White argued that people have an inherent need to feel competent and interact effectively with the environment. The goal of effectance motivation is a feeling of personal mastery or efficacy. This need is present early in life, as seen in babies who grab objects that catch their attention. As children get older, they examine objects, turn them over, push them away, and pull them back—all of which are part of their efforts to control the environment. The effectance motive does not include reflexes or well-learned behaviors and it exerts itself only when such homeostatic motives as the need for food, air, and water are satisfied. The effectance motive has evolutionary value because it helps organisms deal competently with environmental forces. It may also contribute to learning, although that is not its primary function. A child who opens a kitchen cupboard learns there are cookies inside, and this knowledge eventually may be used to satisfy hunger.

White suggested that effectance motivation is undifferentiated in young children; that is, it is global and directed toward environmental features that capture their attention. Toddlers may engage in the same action repeatedly (turning a light switch on and off). Parents may not understand such actions, but they serve an important developmental function. With development, effectance motivation becomes specialized. Once students enter school, they may direct effectance motivation toward mastery of certain school subjects. School achievement and other outcomes (e.g., mastery in art and music) are hypothesized to derive from effectance motivation. In adults the motive is further specialized and manifested in mastery of job skills.

White's contention—people possess an effectance motive that propels them toward competence and is satisfied by feelings of mastery—is intuitively appealing. Although it is tempting to say that a global construct of effectance motivation explains diverse phenomena, the construct's generality limits its ability to explain and predict events. Specification and assessment of the construct are needed to determine the circumstances in which it is valid and the types of factors that might affect it. The idea of effectance motivation is found in many other perspectives on intrinsic motivation and most clearly in work on mastery motivation (discussed later).

Arousal and Incongruity

Recall Berlyne's (1960, 1963) (see chapter 1) contention that an optimal level of physiological arousal (stimulation to the nervous system) was adaptive. If it became too low, individuals were intrinsically motivated to increase arousal. Conversely, if arousal became too great, they were motivated to reduce it. Berlyne also felt that collative properties of stimuli involving their novelty, ambiguity, incongruity, and surprise affected arousal and motivated people to explore the objects.

Hunt (1963) argued that intrinsic motivation gave rise to exploratory behavior and curiosity and stemmed from **incongruity** between prior experiences and new information. People extracted information from the environment and compared it with memory. When incongruity existed between inputs and knowledge, people became intrinsically motivated to reduce the incongruity (a notion somewhat akin to cognitive dissonance; see chapter 1). Hunt believed that individuals required an optimal level of incongruity. Too much incongruity was frustrating and triggered a drive to reduce it.

Hunt's incongruity is conceptually similar to Berlyne's arousal. Although Hunt's and Berlyne's ideas seem intuitively sensible, the notion of optimal level of incongruity or arousal is vague and it is not clear how much is needed to stimulate intrinsic motivation (Deci, 1975). From a practical perspective, we know that use of novelty, surprise, and incongruity in the classroom are popular ways to enhance student interest in learning. But the notion of an optimal level is important. When arousal or incongruity becomes too great, people may become frustrated and attempt to escape from the situation or diminish level of arousal.

MASTERY MOTIVATION

Contemporary perspectives on effectance motivation stress the individual's goals and attempts to master environmental challenges. Here we discuss the views of Harter and her colleagues.

Harter's Theory

Theoretical Predictions

Harter (1978, 1981a) attempted to specify the antecedents and consequences of effectance motivation. She assumed that effectance motivation was best viewed in a developmental framework where the content and operation of the motive change with development. Although White focused on the effects of success on effectance motivation, Harter believed that the effects of failure also are relevant. Further, the degree of challenge of tasks is a potentially important mediator of the effects of outcomes. The roles of socializing agents and rewards in the environment also need to be considered. How children internalize mastery goals and develop a self-reward system is relevant as well. Finally, the important correlates of effectance motivation (e.g., perceived competence, perceived control) need to be identified.

Harter's model of effectance motivation is shown in Figure 6.1. The left side portrays success experiences and is similar to White's original formulation. Beginning at the top, we see that effectance motivation can trigger mastery attempts. White postulated that the motive is generic, but Harter suggested differentiating it according to domain (school performance, peer relationships, athletic accomplishments). Most behaviors are likely to involve optimally challenging tasks (not too easy and not too hard), that also should yield maximum pleasure. Successes should produce intrinsic pleasure and perceptions of competence and control; in turn, these strengthen effectance motivation.

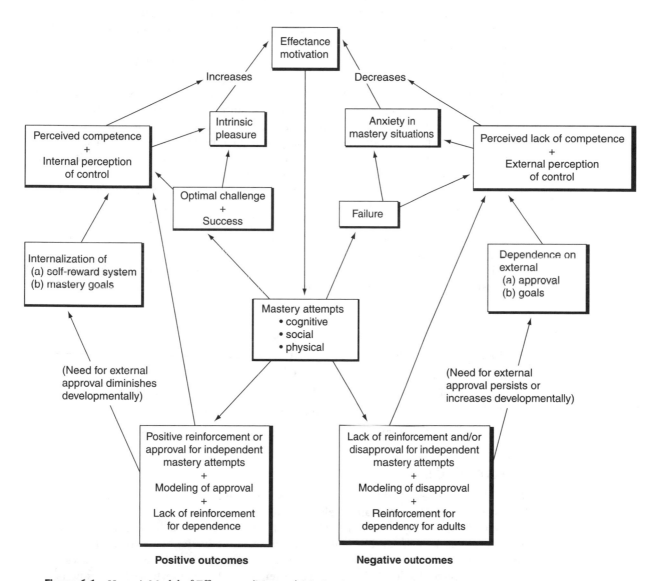

Figure 6.1 Harter's Model of Effectance (Mastery) Motivation

From "A Model of Mastery Motivation in Children" by S. Harter in *Aspects on the Development of Competence: The Minnesota Symposia on Child Psychology* (Vol. 14, p. 218) edited by W. A. Collins, 1981, Hillsdale, NJ: Lawrence Erlbaum Associates. Copyright © 1981 by Lawrence Erlbaum Associates, Inc. Reprinted by permission.

The bottom-left part of Figure 6.1 highlights the role played by socializing agents. Harter believed that some positive reinforcement for mastery attempts is necessary for children to develop and maintain effectance motivation. Much of this reinforcement presumably comes from primary caregivers in the child's early years. With sufficient reinforcement, children gradually internalize a self-reward system and mastery goals. The self-reward system allows children to reinforce themselves for mastery attempts. Through observational learning and reinforcement, children acquire mastery goals from caregivers. With development comes greater internalization and less dependence on others as models and reinforcing agents.

The left side of Figure 6.1 portrays the positive outcomes that might result when children's social environments cooperate with their natural desires. In contrast, the right side of the figure portrays negative outcomes, or what might lead to extrinsically oriented individuals. Mastery attempts that result in failure, coupled with an environment that does not model or reward mastery, can result in children with low perceptions of competence who perceive outcomes as being controlled by external agents and are anxious in achievement situations. Effectance motivation is diminished as children increasingly depend on others to set their goals and reinforce their efforts.

Perceived competence, which Harter felt applied to specific areas rather than being generic in nature, is a critical variable in the model. She developed the Perceived Competence Scale for Children (Harter, 1982), which assesses perceptions of competence in three areas (cognitive, social, physical) and includes a fourth scale to measure self-worth (see chapter 2). Harter (1981b) also developed a measure of intrinsic and extrinsic classroom motivational orientation, which assesses such dimensions as curiosity, challenge, and mastery. The latter scale is based on the assumption that intrinsic motivation includes the following five aspects (Harter & Connell, 1984):

1. Preference for challenge rather than for easy work.
2. Incentive to work to satisfy one's own interest and curiosity rather than working to please the teacher and obtain good grades.
3. Independent mastery attempts rather than dependence on the teacher.
4. Independent judgment rather than reliance on the teacher's judgment.
5. Internal criteria for success and failure rather than external criteria.

Research Evidence

Research supports many of the hypothesized relations among variables in Harter's model. For example, intrinsic motivation relates positively to perceived competence and internal control (Harter, 1981a; Harter & Connell, 1984). Students who believe they are competent enjoy tasks more and display greater intrinsic motivation than do students who judge their competence as being lower (Boggiano, Main, & Katz, 1988; Gottfried, 1985, 1990). With respect to level of difficulty, children judge their competence higher and obtain greater pleasure from succeeding on more difficult tasks compared with easier tasks (Harter, 1978, 1981a). Models and reinforcement affect children's mastery attempts and internalization of mastery goals and self-rewards (Bandura, 1986). On the negative side, students with learning problems often fail and believe they lack the competence to do well, which lowers their intrinsic motivation (Licht & Kistner, 1986; Schunk, 1989b). Such children may be held in low esteem by peers, and their parents may have low academic expectations for them (Bryan & Bryan, 1983). Motivation suffers when families do not reward mastery attempts and students do not associate with mastery-oriented peers.

Harter postulated that the effectance motive should operate across different developmental levels but that its corresponding behaviors may change with development (Harter, 1978). In one study (Harter, 1975), 4-year-old and 10-year-old children participated in a discrimination task in which they were presented with colored disks and had to choose one; a marble was released if they chose the correct disk. The results showed that older children were motivated to succeed to obtain correct answers, whereas younger children were motivated for sensorimotor reasons (e.g., pushing buttons that made lights go on and off, causing marbles to be released). This point supports White's (1959) contention that effectance motivation becomes more focused with development.

Harter (1981b) reported an overall decline in intrinsic motivation in children from elementary through middle school/junior high. A number of factors have been postulated to account for this decline, including the corresponding increase in ability-related social comparisons that children make with development and greater use of norm-referenced grading and extrinsic rewards for academic attainment in school. A question arises, though, of whether the intrinsic motivation decline is accompanied by a corresponding increase in extrinsic motivation.

Lepper, Sethi, Dialdin, and Drake (1997) replicated and clarified Harter's results. These authors also found a steady decline in children's intrinsic motivation with age and grade level; however, they obtained no evidence of an accompanying increase in extrinsic motivation. The latter remained steady over development. This supports the idea that the two constructs can operate independently (as we noted at the outset of this chapter). These results suggest that some forms of extrinsic motivation may become internalized—a point to which we return later in our discussion of self-determination theory.

Harter's theory addresses the development of intrinsic motivation and its links to other variables. The model has generated much research and many hypotheses have been supported. Application 6.1 provides some suggestions for how to create mastery motivation in classrooms. At the same time, Harter relies on models and rewards from socializing agents as primary influences on students' internalization of mastery goals and development of self-reward systems. These are key influences, but motivational research shows that there are other ways to foster mastery behavior, including setting learning goals, providing attributional feedback linking outcomes to effort and strategy use, and teaching self-regulatory activities (Ames, 1992a; Pintrich & Schrauben, 1992; Schunk, 1995; Zimmerman, 1989). Another potential concern is that little attention has been paid to the educational implications of the theory. We might ask whether and how students can be taught to adopt an intrinsic orientation toward school learning. In chapters 2 and 4, for example, we discussed ways to enhance students' perceptions of self-efficacy and control. It appears that Harter's theory needs to be broadened to include the role of these educational influences.

APPLICATION 6.1

Applying Mastery Motivation in the Classroom

1. *Foster in students a preference for challenging assignments rather than for easy work.* A kindergarten teacher said to Avi, "Why don't you work on this puzzle today? You put those easy ones together so quickly yesterday. I know you can work this harder one."

   Mr. Hopkins, an eighth-grade social studies teacher, was assigning student projects. He listed several activities that could be done with each project. The more activities that students selected to complete, the higher the grade they could earn.

2. *Develop in students an incentive to satisfy interests and curiosity rather than to please the teacher and obtain good grades.* Ms. Burns, a fifth-grade teacher, was working with a group of students in selecting topics for a research paper. She told the students she wanted them to pick a topic they really wanted to learn something about. She worked with each student throughout the research, compiling, and writing processes. When the paper was complete, she met with them to assign a grade based on effort, how much they felt they learned, and quality of the completed product.

   Every Friday a third-grade teacher set up various activity centers (math, writing, reading, science, social studies, art, music) in the classroom. The students selected one or more activities to participate in for the entire morning.

3. *Encourage independent mastery attempts rather than dependence on the teacher.* Mr. Metcalf worked with each of his fourth-grade math students at the beginning of each 6 weeks to select five learning goals. The students then kept their own records on mastering the skills and concepts to accomplish the goals. Each student met with Mr. Petersen periodically to discuss progress.

   A high school science teacher gave her students a list of objectives and activities for each unit of study. Students completed the tasks independently and took written and laboratory tests to demonstrate mastery of the unit objectives.

4. *Have students exercise independent judgment rather than relying on the teacher's judgment.* Mr. Sampson, a seventh-grade language arts teacher, had his students work through the writing process for each writing assignment. Students used a checklist to assess progress and improvement over previous drafts. During the final phase of each assignment, he met with students individually and discussed the process, improvement, and final grade.

   Ms. Chambers, a second-grade teacher, listed six to eight independent activities on the board each morning. She then had students individually decide which four of the activities they wanted to do and the order in which they wanted to complete them.

5. *Get students to apply internal criteria for success and failure rather than external criteria.* Mr. Beck, a basketball coach, continually worked with his team members on mastery of various skills. While reviewing game videotapes with the team, he asked the members to evaluate their performances and the reasons for their successes and failures. They talked about what they did and what they might have done differently.

   Ms. Appleton, a high school civics teacher, planned various units throughout the year that included different activities and independent and group projects. For each unit, she had students write a couple of paragraphs that expressed what they had learned from the unit, what contributed to their success or failure on the unit, and how their new knowledge and insights would affect their lives.

PERCEIVED CONTROL

The concept of **perceived control** over task engagement and outcomes is central to many views of intrinsic motivation. In the introductory scenario, Jon felt that a lack of perceived control by students may be contributing to their low intrinsic motivation. We discuss two important perspectives on control: locus of control and personal causation.

Locus of Control

Rotter (1966) expanded his social learning theory (see chapters 3 and 4) to include locus of control, which is a generalized belief about the extent to which behaviors influence outcomes (successes, failures). People with an external locus of control believe their actions have little impact on outcomes and there is little they can do to alter them. Those with an internal locus of control believe that outcomes are contingent on their actions and largely under their control. As Rotter (1966) states,

> When a reinforcement is perceived by the subject as following some action of his own but not being entirely contingent upon his action, then, in our culture, it is typically perceived as the result of luck, chance, fate, as under the control of powerful others, or as unpredictable because of the great complexity of the forces surrounding him. When the event is interpreted in this way by an individual, we have labeled this a belief in *external control*. If the person perceives that the event is contingent upon his own behavior or his own relatively permanent characteristics, we have termed this a belief in *internal control*. (p. 1)

Locus of control is postulated to affect learning, motivation, and behavior. Students who believe they have control over whether they succeed or fail should be more motivated to engage in academic tasks, expend effort, and persist on difficult material than students who believe their actions have little effect on outcomes. In turn, these motivational effects should raise learning. Research supports the hypothesized positive relation between internal locus of control and motivation and achievement in school (Phares, 1976).

Internal locus of control bears some similarity to White's (1959) effectance motive. Individuals with an internal locus of control make greater efforts to attain mastery over their environment (Phares, 1976), which is indicative of intrinsic motivation. Locus of control presumably is a generalized expectancy that affects behavior across different settings, but other investigators have noted that locus of control varies with the situation (Phares, 1976). For example, a student may hold an internal locus in math class and an external locus in English. Although locus of control is important, there is a need to specify the conditions that can affect it and the extent to which it generalizes across tasks and settings. Moreover, as we noted in chapter 3, attributional theory has reformulated locus of control into two separate dimensions of locus and control, which can have different influences on motivation and achievement.

Personal Causation

Origins and Pawns

The role of personal causation in intrinsic motivation was highlighted by de Charms (1968, 1984). **Personal causation** is an individual's initiation of behavior intended to alter the environment. de Charms postulated that people strive to be causal agents and that a primary motivation is to produce changes in the environment. As Rotter distinguished internal from external locus of control, de Charms (1968) differentiated origins and pawns in terms of personal causation:

> We shall use the terms "Origin" and "Pawn" as shorthand terms to connote the distinction between forced and free. An Origin is a person who perceives his behavior as determined by his own choosing; a Pawn is a person who perceives his behavior as determined by external forces beyond his control. We hypothesize . . . that feeling like an Origin has strong effects on behavior as compared to feeling like a Pawn. The distinction is continuous, not discrete—a person feels *more* like an Origin under some circumstances and *more* like a Pawn under others. (pp. 273–274)

Origins have strong feelings of personal causation and attribute changes in their environments to their actions. They believe they are responsible for their behavior, and feedback showing they have produced effects substantiates these feelings. The perception of personal causation motivates behavior. Origins engage in activities they value, and they believe that outcomes will be consistent with their expectations. In contrast, pawns believe that causes of behavior are beyond their control and reside in external forces or the behaviors of others. Pawns typically have feelings of powerlessness and ineffectiveness and perceive situations as threatening. A low perception of personal causation inhibits behavior. Pawn feelings are self-fulfilling; low motivation leads to avoidance of activities; the lack of involvement retards development of skills that help people deal better with environmental events.

Similar to Rotter's internal-external distinction, origin feelings reflect intrinsically motivated behavior, whereas pawn perceptions place the locus of causality outside of oneself. Origins set realistic goals for themselves, know their strengths and weaknesses, determine actions that they can take to accomplish their goals, and assess their goal progress. One problem with the origin-pawn distinction is that it oversimplifies the explanation of intrinsic motivation. People typically are not wholly one or the other, but rather may shift their perceptions depending on the context. This point notwithstanding, de Charms's principles are highly germane to classrooms. We now discuss some programs that have been used to help people develop origin beliefs.

Personal Causation Training

de Charms (1976) described a longitudinal program in which teachers were trained in ways to foster origin behaviors in students. Teacher training included self-study of academic motivation, realistic goal setting, development of concrete plans to accomplish goals, and evaluation of goal progress. Following the training, teachers worked with students. Methods to induce origin behaviors were integrated with academic activities. Classroom exercises were designed to enhance achievement motivation, self-concept, realistic goal setting, and personal responsibility. For example, teachers taught realistic goal setting by having students choose easy, moderate, or difficult words to learn to spell. To teach personal responsibility, teachers had students write imaginative achievement motivation stories from supplied skeleton plots (e.g., write a story about a hero trying to do something better than she or he did it before).

Students demonstrated significant increases in origin behaviors as a consequence of the training and maintained this increase over time. In contrast, control students who received the regular curriculum from nontrained teachers demonstrated no change in origin behaviors. Over a 2-year period, training stopped the trend among low achievers to fall increasingly behind peers in school achievement. The training also reduced student absenteeism and tardiness and positively affected teachers' motivation. de Charms (1984) reported similar results from other efforts to enhance origin behaviors in students.

Alderman (1985) applied goal setting and self-evaluation to a senior high girls' physical education class. Students evaluated their health, physical fitness status, competence, and interest in different activities, and also set fitness goals. Weekly self-tests were given in aerobics, flexibility, strength, and posture. At the end of the first grading period, students set goals for the final exam. Students had some choices of ways to accomplish the aerobic goal (running, walking, jumping rope). The teacher met with students to assess goals and made suggestions if these did not seem realistic. Students established practice schedules of at least three times a week for 9 weeks and kept a record of practices. Following the final exam, students completed a self-evaluation of what they had learned.

Several points can be gleaned from these interventions. First, fostering origin behaviors in students requires that teachers believe that they are origins and can stimulate similar behaviors in students (de Charms, 1984). Another point is that origin training requires teacher structure. Teachers need to present students with possibilities and have students make choices, but teachers must decide what the range of choices will be. An origin classroom is not an unstructured classroom where students decide what they will work on and when they will do it. A third point is that personal responsibility must be developed. Once students make a choice, they must live with the consequences of that choice. One means of teaching personal responsibility is by helping students place greater emphasis on effort as a cause of outcomes and not to blame others when they fail or to believe they were lucky when they succeed. As students experience success, they should develop higher self-efficacy and believe they have control over the attainment of their academic goals (see chapters 3 and 4). Some applications of these points to classrooms are presented in Application 6.2.

APPLICATION 6.2

Applying Personal Responsibility Ideas in the Classroom

1. *Model personal responsibility and believe you can develop it in students.* Ms. Cortez always organizes books and materials, cleans the board, picks up trash, and straightens her desk at the end of each class period. Her room looks neat and it is easy for students to find books and materials that are needed for each activity. She also works with her students to straighten and organize their own materials for each activity.

Mr. Cardotta was working with his debate class to foster open, active group discussions. He wanted to encourage a free exchange of ideas and eliminate the need to raise hands. He never interrupted a student who was sharing and he accepted each student's response as a valuable contribution.

2. *Provide students with options to choose from and have them consider the consequences of each choice.* A high school counselor was working with small groups of students on course selections for the next semester. She explained the demands of each class and reviewed grade points and unit totals necessary for graduation. She had each student select three possible class loads. She then met with each student to discuss the pros and cons of each option.

Mr. Elledge, a middle school principal, was working with Dewitt to develop a program to help him with his aggressive behavior. First, Mr. Elledge asked Dewitt to share some of the problems he was having in the classroom. Then they discussed various ways to handle those situations and what the consequences of each solution might be.

3. *Foster internal attributions. Do not allow students to blame others for their failures or attribute successes to luck.* Mr. Keio meets with his students individually to go over the results of each unit test. While looking at each section of the test, he discussed with the students why they felt they had done well or poorly and what they might have done differently to have prepared and performed better.

Ms. Valentine had R. B. in her kindergarten class. R. B. loved to work with blocks, but when he built something and it fell over he always started crying and told her someone had knocked it down. Ms. Valentine had R. B. talk to her while he was building. If the structure fell over, she would ask him why he thought it fell and help him figure out how he might build it next time to keep it from falling. When R. B. succeeded with a structure, she praised him, letting him know his hard work and persistence had helped him.

4. *Have students set goals, periodically evaluate their progress, and decide if a change in strategy is necessary.* Mr. Rhoads, a high school geometry teacher, uses small-group instruction, computer programs, and activity packets in his classroom. At the beginning of each geometry unit, Mr. Rhoads has each student list areas that need to be worked on from the previous unit and the new goals for the current unit. The last activity for each class period is for all students to complete an individual checklist that includes the progress they are making and how well they are doing with each computer assignment or class activity. Mr. Rhoads reviews the checklists each afternoon, makes comments related to progress, and sets up individual meetings with students who are having difficulty and need additional assistance or a change in activities.

Ms. Long has been working with Jill, one of her first-grade students, to help Jill complete her work during the allotted time. Before Jill starts on her independent work each day, Ms. Long talks with her and they decide how much of each written assignment Jill thinks she can complete (trying to increase the amount every few days). Toward the end of each working period, Ms. Long checks with Jill to see how much she has done and if adjustments to the amount to be completed are needed. At the end of each period, Jill and Ms. Long record the goal and accomplishment for the day.

SELF-DETERMINATION THEORY

The views of de Charms (1968), Rotter (1966), White (1959), and Harter (1978) stress that motivation derives in part from the belief that individuals can exert control over their environment. A related perspective, which has been advanced by Deci, Ryan, Connell, Skinner, and their colleagues postulates that humans have a need to be autonomous and engage in activities because they want to. In this section, we discuss this self-determination (autonomy) view of intrinsic motivation. This perspective is one of the most comprehensive and empirically supported theories of motivation available today. In some ways, it incorporates the other theories and models discussed in this chapter in terms of the focus on both internal control (Rotter, de Charms) as well as mastery or intrinsic motivation (Harter). Although we will discuss it in terms of achievement and learning in this book, the theory has been applied to other domains such as work, athletic, health, and social arenas of live. At one point in time, Deci, Ryan, Connell, and Skinner were all colleagues at the University of Rochester. Their perspective on intrinsic motivation and self-determination is sometimes referred to as the "Rochester School" or perspective on motivation.

Assumptions

Deci and his colleagues (Deci, 1980; Deci & Ryan, 1985, 1991) distinguish self-determination from will. Will is "the capacity of the human organism to choose how to satisfy its needs" (Deci, 1980, p. 26). **Self-determination** is "the process of utilizing one's will" (Deci, 1980, p. 26). Self-determination requires that people accept their strengths and limitations, be cognizant of forces acting on them, make choices, and determine ways to satisfy needs. Will and self-determination are linked: To be self-determining, people have to decide how to act on their environment. Individuals would not be content if all of their needs were automatically satisfied without them having choices and deciding how to attain those choices.

Deci and Ryan propose that there are three basic innate psychological needs that underlie behavior. These include the need for competence, autonomy, and relatedness. The need for competence is similar to the need for mastery of the environment in White's (1959) writings. It is also similar to the need for understanding and mastery that is assumed in attributional theory (Weiner, 1986). Individuals need to feel and to be competent in their interactions with others, with tasks and activities, and with the larger context. At some very basic level, if an organism cannot master interactions in the environment, then from an evolutionary perspective, it is unlikely to survive. The need for autonomy refers to the need to feel a sense of control, agency, or autonomy in interactions in the environment, or from an attributional point of view, a perceived internal locus of causality (Ryan & Deci, 2000). That is, Ryan and Deci propose that individuals have a basic psychological need to have feelings of autonomy and control. The last basic need, relatedness, refers to a need to belong to a group, and is sometimes called a need for belongingness. The three needs of competence, autonomy, and relatedness also share some similarities with the need for achievement, the need for power, and the need for affiliation from classic achievement motivation theory (Atkinson, 1958; Winter et al., 1998). The need for affiliation is very similar to the need for relatedness. The need for achievement overlaps, to some extent, with the need for competence. The need for power and the need for autonomy are the most different, with the need for power reflecting desires or wishes for impressing or dominating or controlling others, while the need for autonomy is more inward-focused and represents desires or needs for feeling a sense of internal control and freedom for choices and actions.

Intrinsic motivation is "the human need to be competent and self-determining in relation to the environment" (Deci, 1980, p. 27). The need for intrinsic motivation energizes people's wills, and the will uses the energy of intrinsic motivation to satisfy needs, resolve conflicts among competing needs, and hold needs in check. Intrinsic motivation is satisfied when an individual acts willfully. It is the process of self-determination that is intrinsically motivating rather than the underlying need of the manifested behavior. A person may have an inherent need to learn and may manifest it by reading books. Intrinsic motivation is satisfied when that person decides which books to read and when to read them, although the actual reading may provide further satisfaction. Deci's position reflects an organismic perspective (see chapter 1) because it postulates that these needs are present at birth and evolve with development.

Motivational Processes

The focus on intrinsic motivation within self-determination theory is covered by a subtheory, labeled **Cognitive Evaluation Theory** (CET) by Deci and Ryan (see Deci & Ryan, 1985; Ryan & Deci, 2000). Self-determination theory attempts to cover the range of all human behavior, but recognizes that only a subset of all behaviors is actually intrinsically motivated. CET theory was developed to explain the intrinsic motivation side of human behavior. Intrinsic motivation leads people to seek out and master challenges, which satisfies their needs to be competent and self-determining (Deci & Porac, 1978). Challenges ideally are within students' reach. If challenges are too easy, learners will seek more difficult ones; if too difficult, they may abandon their efforts. Intrinsic motivation will suffer when individuals cannot exercise self-determination. They want to feel responsible for their actions and free to make choices (see the section on self-regulation in chapter 4). Unfortunately, in many classrooms, students have few choices about what to do and when and how to do it. Self-determination theory also predicts that intrinsic motivation will be diminished when individuals believe their actions are extrinsically determined (i.e., they are engaging in the activity as a means to an end).

As noted in all of the theories discussed in this chapter, perceived control is an important determinant of intrinsic motivation. Skinner, Wellborn, and Connell (1990) distinguish three types of beliefs that contribute to perceived control and are important in school. These three beliefs can be organized around the relations between an agent, the means or strategies an agent might use, and the ends or goals that the agent is trying to attain through the means or strategies (Skinner, 1995, 1996; see Figure 6.2). **Capacity beliefs** refer to an individual's beliefs about his or her personal capabilities with respect to ability, effort, others, and luck (e.g., "I can't seem to try very hard in school"). These beliefs reflect the person's beliefs that he or she has the means to accomplish something, and are similar to efficacy judgments (Bandura, 1997) or agency beliefs (Skinner, 1995, 1996; Skinner, Chapman, & Baltes, 1988a, 1988b, see Figure 6.2). **Strategy beliefs** are expectations or perceptions about factors that influence success in school, such as abil-

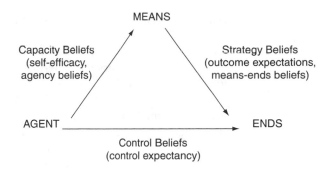

Figure 6.2 Three types of perceived control
Adapted from Skinner, 1995, 1996.

ity, effort, others, luck, or unknown factors (e.g., "The best way for me to get good grades is to work hard"). These beliefs refer to the perception that the means are linked to the ends—that if one uses the strategies, the goal will be attained. They also have been called outcome expectations (Bandura, 1997) and means-ends beliefs (Skinner, 1995, 1996). **Control beliefs** are expectations about an individual's likelihood of doing well in school without reference to specific means (e.g., "I can do well in school if I want to"). These beliefs refer to the relation between the agent and the ends or goals (see Figure 6.2) and also have been called control expectancy beliefs (Skinner, 1995, 1996). Skinner and colleagues (Skinner, 1995; Skinner et al., 1990) found that perceived control influenced academic performance by promoting or decreasing active engagement in learning. Teachers contributed to students' perceptions of control when they provided clear and consistent guidelines and feedback, stimulated students' interest in learning, and assisted them with resources.

Research Evidence

Research has explored the relation of self-determination to intrinsic motivation (Ryan, 1993). Ryan and Grolnick (1986) had children complete de Charms's (1976) Origin Climate Questionnaire and measures of perceived competence, perceived control, and mastery motivation. The de Charms instrument measures perceptions of the origin (autonomy) versus pawn (control) orientation of the teacher and classroom. Children perceiving the environment as more origin-like reported greater internal control over outcomes and higher perceived competence and mastery motivation.

Research shows that choice affects intrinsic motivation (Swann & Pittman, 1977; Zuckerman, Porac, Lathin, Smith, & Deci, 1978). In the Zuckerman et al. study, college students either chose puzzles to solve or were assigned puzzles that had been selected by others. Students who chose puzzles displayed greater intrinsic motivation than did those not given choices. Swann and Pittman (1977) found that leading children to believe they had choice over play activities increased their intrinsic motivation.

Glass and Singer (1972) reported experiments showing that when individuals feel they have control over their environment, they tolerate aversive stimuli better and perform at a higher level. Adults worked on tasks and periodically were exposed to a loud irritating noise. No-control participants could not control the sound. Perceived direct-control adults were told they could terminate the noise by pressing a button, but were advised not to press the button unless they needed to. Perceived indirect-control participants were told that pressing a button would signal someone who could terminate the noise. The experimenter also advised these participants not to press the button unless they needed to. Perceived control (direct or indirect) led to significantly longer persistence and fewer errors compared with no perceived control. Perceived-control adults judged the noise as less aversive than did no-control adults. In an interesting study, Rodin, Solomon, and Metcalf (1978) found that people who stood in front of an elevator's control panel reported feeling less crowded than those who stood away from the control panel, even though the elevator was equally crowded in the two conditions.

Deci and Ryan (1987) summarized the research on contextual features that support or curtail self-determination and intrinsic motivation. These features include the element of providing rewards that are controlling, such as rewards given to merely engage in an activity, which seem to decrease self-determination. Threats and deadlines can also curtail self-determination because people feel compelled to act by the threat or deadline rather than by interest in the activity. A third negative feature is evaluation and surveillance. Although both common in classrooms, experiments have shown that evaluation and surveillance decrease interest and intrinsic motivation (Deci & Ryan, 1987). Two positive features that support self-determination are the amount of choice allowed and positive feedback regarding competence and self-efficacy. The preceding contextual features are part of everyday life in classrooms and teachers should be sensitive to how they can affect students' self-determination and intrinsic motivation, although it is unlikely that teachers can remove them completely.

Development of Self-Determination

Intrinsic motivation is an innate human need and begins in infants as an undifferentiated need for competence and self-determination (Deci & Porac, 1978). This organismic position (see chapter 1) is quite similar to White's (1959). As children develop, the need differentiates into specific areas such as the need to achieve in academics, athletics, or manual activities. Which activities assume children's interest will depend on environmental interactions. "A child who is surrounded by artist-painters and is supported for engaging in various art endeavors is more likely to become intrinsically motivated toward art than is a person who has had no exposure to art until college" (Deci & Porac, 1978, p. 153).

At the same time, Deci and Ryan are quite aware that not all behavior is intrinsically motivated. In fact, an important aspect of development concerns the internalization of social values and mores (Deci & Ryan, 1991; Ryan, Connell, & Deci, 1985). In school, there are extrinsic structures, controls, and rewards that may not fit with the child's quest for self-determination and intrinsic motivation but help to produce good behavior and desirable social functioning. Eventually, these extrinsic motivators may become internalized and part of the self-regulation process. In recognition that not all important behaviors are intrinsically motivated, Deci and Ryan and their colleagues have developed a second subtheory within the larger self-determination theory, which they have labeled, **Organismic Integration Theory** (OIT), to deal with extrinsically motivated behaviors (Deci & Ryan, 1985; Ryan & Deci, 2000). Figure 6.3 displays the taxonomy of motivation according to this theory and subtheory.

As shown in Figure 6.3, Deci and Ryan and their colleagues (Deci & Ryan, 1985; Rigby, Deci, Patrick, & Ryan, 1992; Ryan & Deci, 2000) have conceptualized motivation

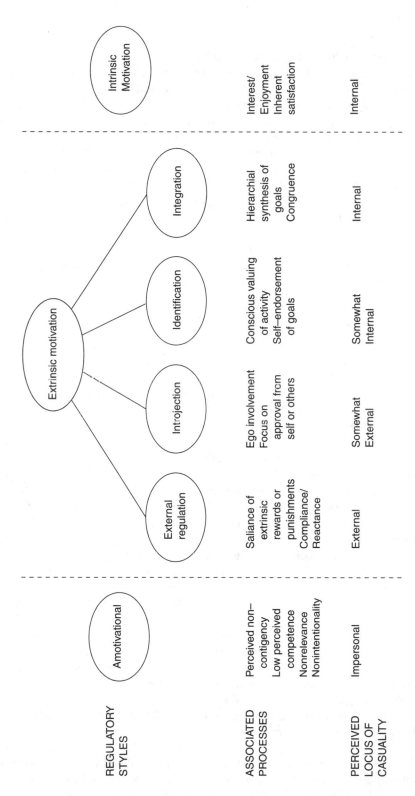

Figure 6.3 Types of motivation in self-determination theory
Reprinted with permission from Ryan & Deci (2000), Academic Press.

from amotivation or unmotivated to extrinsic motivation to intrinsic motivation, as represented by the dotted lines in the figure. They have labeled these three separate types of motivational patterns "regulatory styles," but it should be noted that they are discussing ways of being motivated, not strategies for self-regulation of cognition (see Pintrich, 2000d). As noted previously, intrinsic motivation concerns activities that are autotelic—engaged in for their own sake and enjoyment. The individual has freely chosen these activities and they are, by definition, self-determined (the far right side of Figure 6.3). This is the focus of Cognitive Evaluation Theory (CET), which was discussed in the previous section. Extrinsic motivation involves a set of four different types of extrinsically motivated behaviors from behaviors that originally were completely extrinsically motivated but became internalized and now are self-determined, albeit they are not intrinsically motivated by definition (Figure 6.3).

The far left side of the figure represents behaviors that are amotivated. The individual does not feel competent (low efficacy, low capacity beliefs), there is a perceived noncontingency between behaviors and outcomes (low strategy and control beliefs; Skinner, 1995, 1996) or a sense of learned helplessness (Peterson et al., 1993), as well as low value for the task or perceptions of irrelevance of the task (see chapter 2 on expectancy-value theory). Individuals with this pattern of motivation (or regulatory style, in Deci and Ryan's terms) also do not feel intentional or self-determined in their actions. Students with this motivational style would be very unmotivated for school due to the low value, efficacy, and internal control they feel for school activities. These students would be those about whom teachers often say, "Nothing motivates them, nothing interests them, I can't even threaten to punish them to get them to do their work."

The middle of the figure represents four extrinsic motivational or self-regulatory styles in which the individual is motivated, in contrast to being amotivated (hence, the dotted line in the figure to distinguish the qualitative differences between amotivation and extrinsic motivation). The first level includes what Deci and his colleagues call **external regulation**. For example, students initially may not want to work on math but do so to obtain teacher rewards and avoid punishment. These students would react well to threats of punishment or the offer of extrinsic rewards and would tend to be compliant. They would not be intrinsically motivated or show high interest, but they would tend to behave well and try to do the work to obtain rewards or avoid punishment. Obviously, the control is external in this case and there is no self-determination on the part of the students.

At the next level of extrinsic motivation, students may engage in a task because they think they should and may feel guilty if they don't do the task (e.g., study for an exam). Deci and his colleagues call this **introjected regulation** because the source of motivation is internal (feelings of "should," "ought," guilt) to the person but not self-determined because these feelings seem to be controlling the person. These students are not doing it solely for the rewards or to avoid punishment; the feelings of guilt or "should" are actually internal to the person, but the source is still somewhat external because they may be doing it to please others (teacher, parents).

The third level or style is called **identified regulation**. Individuals engage in the activity because it is personally important to them. For example, a student may study hours for tests in order to get good grades to be accepted into college. This behavior represents the student's own goal, although the goal has more utility value (Wigfield & Eccles, 1992; see chapter 2) than does intrinsic value such as learning. The goal is chosen consciously by the student and, in this sense, the locus of causality is somewhat more internal to the person as he or she feels it is personally very important, not just important to others such as teachers or parents. In this case, the student wants to do the task because it is important to him or her, even if it is more out of utilitarian reasons, rather than intrinsic interest in the task.

The final level of extrinsic motivation is **integrated regulation,** whereby individuals integrate various internal and external sources of information into their own self-schema and engage in behavior because of its importance to their sense of self. This final level is still instrumental, rather than autotelic as in intrinsic motivation, but integrated regulation does represent a form of self-determination and autonomy. As such, both intrinsic motivation and integrated regulation will result in more cognitive engagement and learning than will external or introjected regulation (Rigby et al., 1992; Ryan & Deci, 2000).

Deci and his colleagues' position is thought-provoking, has generated much research, and has important implications for educational practice. Many points in the self-determination model are not clearly specified and the model is continually evolving, but researchers increasingly are conducting studies that are adding to our understanding of how this theory can be applied in the classroom as well as other domains. We now continue our discussion of intrinsic and extrinsic motivation by examining the theory and research on the role of rewards.

REWARDS AND INTRINSIC MOTIVATION

Earlier we mentioned four sources of intrinsic motivation (Lepper & Hodell, 1989): challenge, curiosity, control, and fantasy. The perspectives on intrinsic motivation we have discussed support the importance of these sources. Despite their differences, the various perspectives contend that intrinsic motivation is a strong and positive force in people's lives.

We typically think of intrinsic motivation as growing and developing, but it also can diminish. Much research has shown that engaging in an intrinsically interesting activity to obtain an extrinsic reward can undermine intrinsic motivation (Lepper & Greene, 1978). This finding is distressing and has important implications for education because of the prevalence of rewards in classrooms and schools. We now consider theory and research on rewards and intrinsic motivation and discuss ways that rewards can be used productively to enhance and maintain student motivation.

Experimental Findings

An early study by Lepper, Greene, and Nisbett (1973) provided evidence for the detrimental effects of rewards on intrinsic motivation. The participants were preschool children who spent a high percentage of time drawing during free play. The experimenter took children individually and asked them to draw. Expected-award children were shown a "good player certificate" and told they could win one by drawing. After they drew, they were told they had done well and were given the certificate. Unexpected-award children were not informed about the certificate in advance, but after they drew they were given the same feedback and certificate. This condition controlled for any effect due to receiving a reward. No-award children drew with no mention of a certificate and were not given one at the end, which controlled for any effect due to drawing. Two weeks later, children again were observed during free play to determine the percentage of time spent drawing.

Expected-award children spent less time drawing during the postexperimental phase compared with the pretest baseline phase; pretest-to-posttest changes of the other groups were nonsignificant. Compared with the other conditions, expected-award children spent less time drawing during the postexperimental phase. The investigators also rated the quality of the drawings children made during the experimental session. The three conditions did not differ in number of pictures drawn, but the quality of expected-award children's pictures was lower than the quality of pictures drawn by children in the other conditions. Similar results have been obtained in several studies using different research populations (children, adolescents, adults), types of rewards (monetary, social), and target activities (Lepper & Greene, 1978).

The conclusion from this research is that offering people rewards for doing things they enjoy may undermine their intrinsic motivation and lead to less interest in the tasks. This conclusion is often misinterpreted to mean that rewarding people for doing things they enjoy decreases their interest. This conclusion is erroneous. The critical component is the offer of the reward, not the actual receipt of the reward. Indeed, if rewarding people for doing things they enjoy diminished interest, we would expect to see high-salaried sports stars retire after 1 year, "A" students quickly drop out of school, and people who receive large raises suddenly quit their jobs. These types of occurrences are rare. As we discuss next, there are many conditions that determine the effects of rewards on subsequent intrinsic motivation.

One such condition is the salience of the reward. Ross (1975) offered preschoolers a prize for playing a drum (an intrinsically interesting activity). For some children, no further mention was made of the reward, whereas for others (salient reward condition) the reward was in a nearby box and children were told that they could have it at the conclusion of the study. Children assigned to a control condition were not offered or given a reward. Salient-reward children displayed less subsequent interest in playing the drum compared with the other two conditions. In a second study, preschoolers were promised a reward for playing with drums. Some were told to think about the reward as they engaged in the activity (salient condition), others were told to think about something else (distraction condition), and those in a control condition were not given thinking instructions. Relative to the salient and control conditions, distraction children showed more interest in playing with drums.

Overjustification

To explain the preceding findings and other similar ones, Lepper and his colleagues advanced the **overjustification** hypothesis: Working at an intrinsically interesting task under conditions that make it clear that the activity is a means to an end can diminish subsequent intrinsic motivation (Lepper, 1981, 1983; Lepper & Greene, 1978; Lepper & Hodell, 1989). When people work on a task to obtain a reward, they are likely to view their actions as extrinsically motivated. Offering people a reward to work on a task they enjoy provides more than adequate justification for (overjustifies) their participation. When the reward contingency is no longer in effect, people lose their justification and motivation for working on the task. When people work in the absence of external conditions that could explain their participation, they should believe their actions reflect their interests. They engage in the task because they want to, not because they have to. Rather than being a means to an end, the task is an end by itself. Such intrinsic motivation is likely to sustain itself in the future.

This overjustification explanation derives from cognitive dissonance theory (see chapter 1). Cognitive dissonance research often explored reactions of people who were led to act in ways that contradicted their beliefs. Studies showed that the less clear or powerful the external pressures put on individuals to behave contrary to their beliefs, the more likely they were to internalize the contrary behavior and alter their beliefs (Lepper & Greene, 1978). Cognitive dissonance research findings were reinterpreted by Bem (1967, 1972), who emphasized self-perception (or self-attribution; see chapter 3). Bem postulated that people's attitudes toward an activity are determined in part by their perceptions of why they are engaging in it. Individuals are likely to attribute their actions to external factors when those factors are clear and sufficient to explain the actions and to internal factors when external forces are unclear or insufficient to explain actions. From an attributional standpoint, students attribute their actions to rewards offered for performing a task and to their own desires when extrinsic rewards are absent or too weak to justify task participation.

Controlling and Informational Aspects of Rewards

Whether the overjustification hypothesis best explains the negative effects of offering rewards on intrinsic motivation is debatable. An alternative explanation, which overlaps somewhat with the overjustification view, derives from cognitive evaluation theory (Deci, 1975; Deci & Porac, 1978). According to Deci (1975):

> Every reward (including feedback) has two aspects, a controlling aspect and an informational aspect that provides the recipient with information about his competence and self-determination. The relative salience of the two aspects determines which process will be operative. If the controlling aspect is more salient, it will initiate the change in perceived locus of causality process. If the informational aspect is more salient, the change in feelings of competence and self-determination process will be initiated. (p. 142)

All rewards have the potential to control and to inform. The relative salience or weight of each aspect determines the effect on intrinsic motivation. Rewards control behavior when they are given contingent on individuals accomplishing a given task or performing at a certain level. Thus, teachers tell students they can have free time after they finish their work, supervisors tell employees they will get a pay raise if they boost company profits, and parents tell children they can have dessert after they eat all of their dinner. When people view rewards as controlling their behavior (they believe they are acting the way they are in order to earn the reward), they attribute their actions to factors outside of themselves (e.g., the reward) and they lose a sense of self-determination. Once the reward contingency is no longer in effect, there is nothing compelling them to work at the activity, so their interest declines.

Rewards also convey information about one's skills or competence when they are linked to actual performance or progress, such as when teachers praise students for learning new skills or acquiring new knowledge, supervisors give workers merit raises for performing better than others, and parents buy children toys for keeping their room neat. People who derive such performance information from rewards feel efficacious and experience self-determination. Interest is sustained even when the reward contingency is removed because people place the locus of causality of behavior inside themselves (e.g., desire to learn).

Research studies have shown that such factors as task-contingent rewards (rewards given for working on tasks regardless of level of performance), offers to receive good player awards, deadlines, imposed goals, avoidance of unpleasant stimuli, surveillance, and social evaluation can diminish intrinsic motivation (Cameron & Pierce, 1994; Deci & Ryan, 1991; Morgan, 1984). In contrast, intrinsic motivation is maintained or enhanced when people are offered choices or allowed to work in an environment perceived as supporting autonomy rather than as controlling (Deci & Ryan, 1991). Positive feedback that enhances perceived competence also raises intrinsic motivation (Deci, Vallerand, Pelletier, & Ryan, 1991).

Schunk (1983d) tested the idea that reward structure affects self-efficacy, motivation, and skill acquisition. Some children were offered rewards based on their level of problem solving (performance-contingent rewards), others were offered rewards for working on the task regardless of level of performance (task-contingent rewards), and children in a control group were not offered rewards. Performance-contingent rewards led to the highest skill, motivation, and self-efficacy. Task-contingent rewards resulted in no benefits compared with not offering rewards.

These effects are not confined to learning. Research shows that rewards given contingent on novel, creative efforts promote creativity and that intrinsic motivation for creative performance suffers when rewards are offered for performance regardless of level of creativity (Eisenberger & Armeli, 1997; Eisenberger, Armeli, & Pretz, 1998).

Despite the robustness of the research base showing that offering rewards can undermine intrinsic motivation, the debate on the effects of rewards continues. In fact, since the earlier edition of this book, the debate has been reinvigorated, mainly due to several recent meta-analyses by Cameron, Eisenberger and their colleagues (Cameron & Pierce, 1994; Eisenberger & Cameron, 1996, 1998). Cameron and Pierce (1994) reviewed 96 experimental studies on the topic and concluded that overall rewards did not diminish intrinsic motivation. The only negative effect they obtained was when expected tangible rewards were given to people simply for working on a task. Eisenberger and Cameron (1996, 1998) also suggested a similar conclusion.

As might be expected, these articles received a negative response from the scientific community in motivation, who criticized it on both conceptual and methodological grounds (e.g., Deci, Koestner, & Ryan, 1999; Kohn, 1996; Lepper, Henderlong, & Gingras, 1999; Lepper, Keavney, & Drake, 1996; Ryan & Deci, 1996). In fact, this renewed debate even generated an edited book (Sansone & Harackiewicz, 2000) in which many of the chapters addressed the key issue of the role of rewards in undermining intrinsic motivation. The debate is complicated partially by disagreements about how to use meta-analytic procedures to summarize across diverse studies (e.g., Lepper & Henderlong, 2000) as well as more conceptual issues regarding the nature of rewards and the definition and measurement of intrinsic and extrinsic motivation (Sansone & Harackiewicz, 2000).

Although complicated, for the purpose of this book, the best summary of the issue revolves around the controlling versus informational aspects of the reward. A reward given simply for working on a task conveys nothing about skills or competence and is unlikely to raise self-efficacy or intrinsic motivation. Further, this type of reward could even convey negative efficacy information. Learners might conclude that they are receiving a reward for working because they are not expected to learn or accomplish much. This negative belief can lead people to view the reward as controlling and the task as uninteresting. Maximal benefits of rewards on self-efficacy and motivation should be expected when being told of the contingency leads students to believe they can learn and receiving the reward signifies progress in learning. In this way, the reward provides information to the students about their own competence, their progress, or their learning, and so may increase their efficacy and their future performance. Applications of these ideas to classrooms are given in Application 6.3.

APPLICATION 6.3

Using Rewards in the Classroom

Using rewards in the classroom to foster motivation requires that they be linked with students' progress, skill improvement, learning, and competence. When rewards are contingent on these outcomes, they convey to students that they are learning, which builds self-efficacy and sustains motivation. Rewards linked only with spending time on a task regardless of performance level do not have this motivational effect.

1. Ms. Allison, a kindergarten teacher, uses lots of praise to motivate her students to learn the letters of the alphabet and the sounds they make. Working individually with each student, she has the student say the letters of the alphabet to her and tell her about the sounds. While working with Susan, Ms. Allison said, "Susan, do you realize that the last time we went over your letters you knew only 14 and today you know 21? Not only do you know 21, but you can tell me their sounds. I am so proud of you for working so hard to learn your letters and keep getting better."

2. Mrs. Stone, a fourth-grade teacher, is working with her students on multiplication and division facts. Based on their progress, she rewards them with extra time to play math games on the computer. Students take a timed test each day on math facts. Students earn 1 additional minute of computer time for each additional fact they have learned. Thus, if Joe completes 52 facts on Monday and 54 facts on Tuesday, he earns 2 extra minutes of computer time. At the end of 2 weeks, Joe can use the time earned or continue to accumulate minutes.

3. Mr. Kent, a tenth-grade science teacher, uses extra enrichment activities that reinforce learning as an incentive to raise a student's final grade. He creates a list of experiments to be completed that correlate with the regular studies in class. The experiments have data sheets to complete that force the student to record procedures and reactions throughout the experiment and to formulate a conclusion. Each student decides how many of the experiments to complete. For each experiment completed, Mr. Kent adds 3 points to that student's final grade.

4. Dr. Lowe, a psychology professor, works with his students to develop a more comprehensive, research-based term paper. He organizes the components of completing the paper into various tasks. Dr. Lowe meets individually with students every other week to assess progress toward completion. For each successful completion of the various tasks, the student can earn up to 5 points. If a student earns as many as 20 points, the student is exempt from one of the quizzes during the semester.

Enhancing Intrinsic Motivation

The preceding discussion focuses on the detrimental effects of offering rewards on high intrinsic motivation, but in school there are many students who have low intrinsic motivation. An important goal for teachers is to raise motivation. If rewards are used, it is critical that they be linked with the development of students' competencies to enhance intrinsic motivation. Rewards tied to skill acquisition (e.g., points given based on mastery of skills) inform students that they are developing competence and skills and can raise their self-efficacy (Cameron & Pierce, 1994; Morgan, 1984; Schunk, 1995).

Other classroom factors such as goals and attributional feedback also convey information about capabilities and raise self-efficacy and motivation, as we discussed in preceding chapters. Investigators increasingly are exploring how to structure instructional and social factors to optimize intrinsic motivation. To enhance intrinsic motivation, attention must be given to the four sources mentioned at the beginning of this chapter and shown in Table 6.1: challenge, curiosity, control, and fantasy (Lepper & Hodell, 1989).

Challenge

Activities that challenge students' skills may be intrinsically motivating (Deci, 1975; Harter, 1978; White, 1959). Challenging activities should be intermediate in level of difficulty, and as students develop skills, difficulty level must be adjusted upward to maintain this intermediate level. Attainment of challenging goals conveys to learners that they are becoming more competent, which raises self-efficacy and perceived control over outcomes. In turn, learners are apt to set new, challenging goals, which serves to maintain intrinsic motivation.

Curiosity

Curiosity is prompted by activities that present students with information or ideas that are discrepant from their present knowledge or beliefs and that appear surprising or incongruous (Berlyne, 1960, 1963; Hunt, 1963; Lepper & Hodell, 1989). Such incongruities motivate students to seek information and resolve the discrepancy. As with challenge, moderate discrepancies are most effective because they are easily incorporated into an individual's mental framework; large discrepancies may be rapidly discounted.

Table 6.1 Sources of Intrinsic Motivation

Source	Implications
Challenge	Present learners with tasks of intermediate difficulty that they feel efficacious about accomplishing
Curiosity	Present students with surprising or incongruous information that will motivate them to close a gap in their knowledge
Control	Provide learners with choices and a sense of control over their learning outcomes
Fantasy	Involve learners in fantasy and make-believe through simulations and games

Lowenstein (1994) proposed that curiosity is a feeling of cognitive deprivation that occurs when one becomes aware of a gap in information. It is necessary, however, for students to have a pre-existing knowledge base so that they will be aware of a gap. In the absence of prerequisite knowledge, prompting students to ask questions—a technique often advised to raise curiosity—should not have much effect. Students also must believe that the gap is manageable, which can be fostered through moderate discrepancies. Curious learners who believe that the gap is attainable should feel efficacious and motivated to manage the gap and learn.

Control

Activities that provide students with a sense of control over their academic outcomes may enhance intrinsic motivation (de Charms, 1968; Deci, 1980). Boggiano, Main, and Katz (1988) found that children's perceived competence and personal control related positively to their academic intrinsic motivation and preference for challenge. Allowing students choices in activities and a role in establishing rules and procedures fosters perceptions of control. Perceived control also can engender a sense of self-efficacy for performing well (Schunk, 1995). In contrast, students are not motivated to engage in activities when they believe their actions bear little relationship to outcomes. A perceived lack of control is associated with learned helplessness (see chapter 3).

Fantasy

Intrinsic motivation can be promoted with activities that involve learners in fantasy and make-believe through simulations and games that present them with situations that are not actually present (Lepper & Hodell, 1989). By identifying with fictional characters, students can derive vicarious pleasure not ordinarily available to them. As shown in Figure 6.4, gamelike elements can add meaning to what might otherwise be a boring activity. Fantasy may portray out-of-school situations to which school learning can be applied and thereby reinforce teachers' instructions to students about the usefulness of learning. Students who place greater value on learning are likely to be more intrinsically motivated in the activity.

There also is evidence that fantasy can enhance learning compared with instruction presented without fantasy elements. Parker and Lepper (1992) conducted two studies with third- and fourth-grade students. In one study, students were taught computer graphics programming whereby they received instruction both in straightforward fashion and embellished with fantasy contexts involving pirates, detectives, or astronauts. Students preferred the fantasy to the traditional context. In a second study, children received computer instruction and were assigned to an individualized-fantasy, assigned-fantasy, or no-fantasy condition. The two fantasy conditions had fantasy elements incorporated into instruction. Individualized-fantasy students selected their fantasy context; assigned-fantasy students had their contexts assigned by the experimenter in the same proportion as fantasies chosen by children in the individualized group. The results showed greater learning by students in the fantasy conditions compared with children assigned to the no-fantasy condition. Fantasy contexts also produced generalization; these students showed better general understanding of geometric concepts.

Lepper and Malone (1987) discussed mechanisms whereby greater interest in learning activities may translate into better learning. These mechanisms involve focusing the

Note: Player 1 dribbles ball from end to mid-court and passes ball to player 2. Player 2 dribbles ball to where player 3 is and passes to player 3, who shoots basket. Down what fraction of the court did the players dribble?

Figure 6.4   Fractions task presented in traditional format (top) and gamelike format (bottom)

learner's attention on relevant features of the learning context and increasing cognitive effort in the learning activity. By their very nature, many fantasy elements ought to focus learners' attention and increase mental effort. During elementary school children's participation at computer activities, Cordova and Lepper (1996) found that children's cognitive engagement during learning, perceived competence, and intrinsic motivation were enhanced by personalizing the material to be learned, situating it in meaningful contexts, and offering students some choices during learning.

A caveat is in order, however, because it is imperative that motivational embellishments be relevant to the task and not overly distracting (Lepper & Hodell, 1989). Nonrelevant features or those that distract will not enhance students' mental effort in relevant task features and may convey that students lack control over outcomes, both of which do not enhance intrinsic motivation. Computer learning programs with such motivational enhancements as lights and noises that are only loosely linked to what learners do quickly lose their motivational appeal and are distracting. If the enhancements are contingent on learner progress in skill acquisition, they convey that learners are developing competence, which builds intrinsic motivation. Some strategies for incorporating these sources of intrinsic motivation into classroom activities are given in Application 6.4.

APPLICATION 6.4

Applying Sources of Intrinsic Motivation in the Classroom

1. *Challenge: Challenge students' skills with activities of intermediate difficulty. Ensure that students do not become bored with easy tasks or reluctant to work on tasks perceived as overly difficult.* Ms. Logan, a middle school math teacher, pretests all of her students at the beginning of each unit. After analyzing the results of the test, she plans small-group and individual activities that will challenge each student but are attainable.

   Mr. Armstrong uses cooperative groups often in his sixth-grade social studies class. When he places students in groups and works with each group to assign tasks, he makes sure that each child is involved and responsible for a challenging yet attainable task.

2. *Curiosity: Present ideas slightly discrepant from learners' existing knowledge and beliefs.* Incorporate surprise and incongruity into classroom activities. Mrs. Watkins, a high school teacher, told her history class that she wants them to develop their own test for the next unit. As they read through the assigned reading for the unit, they are to develop relevant activities and make a list of possible questions for the end-of-unit test. Each student contributes to developing the unit and the test, working individually, in small groups, and as a whole class.

   Mr. Jacobs, a sixth-grade science teacher, had each group of students in his class build a replica of a volcano out of clay, mud, and twigs. Then he gave each group the correct proportions of baking soda and vinegar to simulate the eruption. After the groups experimented with their volcanoes, he introduced a unit on mixing and reactions of various substances and chemicals. At the end of the unit, each group repeated the project and explained why the volcano had erupted.

3. *Control: Allow students choices in activities and a voice in formulating rules and procedures. Foster attributions to causes over which they have some control.* At the beginning of each school year, Mr. Tilley helps his fourth-grade class develop the classroom rules and create a list of rewards and consequences for following or breaking the rules.

   Mrs. Hicks, a middle school assistant principal, involves the student council to develop extracurricular spectator rules of conduct. She lets council members work in small groups to brainstorm areas that each group feels should be addressed. The entire student council then evaluates each group's suggestions and develops overall guidelines and consequences.

4. *Fantasy: Engage students in make-believe activities, games, and simulations. Ensure that the motivational embellishments are task relevant and not too distracting.* Mr. Hopkins, a fifth-grade teacher, portrays presidents from the past with costume and voice. He periodically dresses as one of the former presidents (e.g., Washington, Lincoln) and tells about his life as if he were that president. He makes sure that he does an outstanding job of portraying the character so that the students learn about the life of the individual and are not just fascinated with the costume and voice.

   Mrs. Littlejohn directs the computer laboratory in an elementary school. She teaches the students keyboarding, word processing, and other skills, but she also includes a fair number of computer simulations in her teaching. She tries to link these to what the children are studying in their regular classes. When the fifth graders were studying a unit on marine life in science, Mrs. Littlejohn allowed them to work on a computer simulation of an underwater environment.

SUMMARY

Intrinsic motivation is motivation to engage in an activity for its own sake; extrinsic motivation is motivation to engage in an activity as a means to an end. Intrinsic motivation is contextual; it refers to how people view activities and can vary over time and with changes in circumstances. Different levels of intrinsic and extrinsic motivation can exist within individuals at a given time. The constructs are not conceptually distinct and each may range on separate continuums from high to low. There is evidence that intrinsic motivation can promote learning and achievement better than can extrinsic motivation.

Early views of intrinsic motivation explained it in terms of a developmental phenomenon or as being dependent upon arousal and incongruity. White discussed effectance motivation to feel competent and interact productively with the environment. The effectance motive presumably was undifferentiated in young children but became specialized with development. Berlyne believed that people were intrinsically motivated to maintain an optimal level of arousal. Hunt felt that intrinsic motivation stemmed from incongruity between prior and new experiences. These views are important but are too general in nature to be applicable to school settings.

Harter formulated a theory of mastery motivation that refined the effectance motivation construct and specified its antecedents and consequences. Harter believed that the content and operation of the mastery motive change with development. Harter's model also considers success and failure experiences. Important variables are degree of challenge of tasks, rewards, socializing agents, need for approval, perceived competence, and internalization of mastery goals. Harter believes that intrinsic motivation comprises a preference for challenge, incentive to work to satisfy one's curiosity, independent mastery attempts, independent judgment, and internal criteria for success and failure.

Many perspectives stress the role of perceived control over outcomes as an integral component of intrinsic motivation. Rotter proposed that people differed in locus of control, or whether they believed that outcomes generally occur independently of how they behave (external control) or usually were contingent on their behaviors (internal control). de Charms discussed personal causation, or an individual's initiation of behavior intended to alter the environment. According to de Charms, people can act like origins and perceive their behavior as determined by their own choosing, or as pawns and believe that behavior is determined by external forces beyond their control.

A related perspective postulates that humans have a need to be autonomous and engage in activities they desire. This self-determination view of Deci and Ryan and their colleagues postulates that individuals have a need to make decisions about how to act. Intrinsic motivation leads them to seek and master challenges that are optimal given their capabilities. Motivation suffers when people cannot exercise self-determination. Perceived control—comprised of strategy, capacity, and control beliefs—is an important determinant of intrinsic motivation. Intrinsic motivation is an innate need and differentiates with development through internalization of values and self-regulatory influences.

Much educational research has explored the role of extrinsic rewards on intrinsic motivation. Although there are exceptions, a common finding is that the offer of a reward to perform an intrinsically interesting task leads to a decrease in intrinsic motivation. Lepper and his colleagues formulated the overjustification hypothesis: Engaging in an intrinsically interesting activity under conditions that make it obvious that the activity is a means to an end can diminish subsequent intrinsic interest because offering a reward justifies task participation. When the reward contingency is no longer in effect, people lose their motivation. Deci and Ryan postulated that every reward has controlling and informational aspects. Rewards control behavior when they are given contingent on individuals accomplishing a given task or performing at a certain level. Controlling rewards lead people to attribute their behaviors to external factors and to lose a sense of self-determination. Rewards are informational when they are linked to actual level of performance or progress. Informational rewards lead to feelings of self-efficacy and a sense of self-determination, both of which enhance intrinsic motivation.

Students' intrinsic motivation can be affected by four sources: challenge, curiosity, control, and fantasy. Activities are intrinsically motivating when they challenge students' skills, present information or ideas that are discrepant from students' present knowledge and beliefs and that appear surprising or incongruous, provide students with a sense of control over outcomes, and involve learners in fantasy and make-believe through simulations and games that present situations not actually present.

The Role of Interest and Affect in Achievement Motivation

*S*everal high school teachers are talking in the lunch room about one of their favorite topics—student motivation. The teachers have somewhat different views about motivation, but all are concerned that their students just do not have much interest in schoolwork.

Ms. Duncan:　　*I'm really worried. None of my students have any interest in math. They just don't care about anything to do with school. They just don't have the right values. All they care about are their girlfriends or boyfriends, MTV, and having a good time partying. I really think that song about sex, drugs, and rock and roll describes kids pretty accurately when they get to the high school.*

Mr. Anderman:　　*Well, I don't know. I have some kids who at least are interested in learning. They do get involved in learning and I try to make the work meaningful to them and get them involved in the class. They have to talk and discuss things, at least some of them seem to like it. And sometimes, very rarely, but on those really great days, the class discussion really gets going and some of the kids are so into it, you can see that they are so involved they are not really thinking of anything else. You know I live for those days, that is what makes teaching worthwhile.*

Mr. Lopez:　　*Well, at least you have those high-track kids. They do get turned on to some academic things. The kids I have in the lower track math classes are not interested and don't think it's that important. But, I do try to do some puzzles and games with them. When we have "game" day they do get interested for at least a little while. I also try to teach them some skills in these classes. They are going to need them when they get in the real world, so I try to hold them to some standards.*

Mr. Anderman:　　*Yes, or at least when they go to college, that is always a good thing to try to motivate them, the threat of college. But, you know, sometimes some of my kids get so wound up about going on to college and making sure they get into the best one, that they get so nervous they bomb the test. You can just see them getting all anxious before the test, and then during the test, you can see them wriggling around, sweating, looking all panicky. Some of them make themselves sick with nerves. Some of my best students have trouble on the tests. They will do great on the homework but then really blow it on the test. I don't know what to do with them.*

Ms. Duncan: *Well, I have some like that, too. They don't seem too interested in the math, but they do get anxious for a test. I just try to make them feel good about themselves. You know that is the biggest thing for all adolescents—they need all the positive strokes and positive feedback and self-esteem we can give them. They are dealing with so many things, it's no wonder they have self-esteem problems. I just wish they would get more interested in school.*

Mr. Lopez: *Well, I don't know if that's all there is to it. I think self-esteem is important, but there is more to motivation than that. I used to be really nervous before tests, too. I would think I was prepared because I could do the problems correctly on homework assignments, but then once I started on the test, it seemed like I couldn't do the problems. I would start to think, "Oh no, I'm going to fail this test, I'm going to flunk out, my parents will really be ashamed because I'm doing so badly." I would look around and everyone else seemed to be just working away, doing fine, which would just make me more nervous. It was so hard to concentrate. Eventually, I had a teacher who helped me. He showed me some tricks to help me control my nerves. He also helped me see that if I did do poorly, it was not due to being a stupid Latino, like some of the other teachers used to say. He helped me see that I did have the ability to do math. In fact, he's probably the reason I went on to be a math teacher. Now, I try to help my students the same way he helped me and it is not just by giving them positive strokes, or warm fuzzies, or trying to raise their self-esteem. I have high standards and try to make sure my students have the skills to meet them. They will feel better about themselves if they can actually do the math problems than if I just tell them how great they are. They can spot a phony right away and they think, just like Holden Caulfield, that most adults are phonies, so they don't need their teachers to be that way.*

The research discussed in this chapter concerns a variety of more affective or emotional constructs that have been linked to student learning and achievement. Given the diversity of constructs, this chapter is not organized around one theoretical perspective like most of the preceding chapters in this book, but it includes some of the most relevant and common constructs and models. We begin with a short summary of some of the general issues in research on emotions and affect, followed by a discussion of one of the most well-known models of motivation and interest—the research and theory on emergent motivation and flow by Csikszentmihalyi. We then move on to what is probably the most commonly cited description and explanation of motivation by laypeople: the role of interest in learning and achievement. In contrast to the positive emotions of flow and interest, we then discuss one of the most researched constructs in achievement motivation research, test anxiety, and how it can constrain learning and performance. Finally, we conclude with a brief discussion of another popular construct: self-esteem or self-worth.

After studying this chapter, you should be able to:

1. Distinguish between emotions and moods as well as all the potential emotional responses that could be generated in a classroom context.

2. Understand the nature of the "flow" experience and how it is linked to student motivation as well as contextual characteristics.

3. Distinguish between situational and personal interest and explain how both are related to student motivation and learning in classroom contexts.

4. Define text anxiety and explain how it operates to influence student learning as well as how classroom contexts can increase or decrease anxiety.

5. Recognize the difference between self-esteem and other self constructs such as self-concept, self-efficacy, and other judgments of self-competence and explain how they are differentially related to learning and achievement.

GENERAL ISSUES IN EMOTIONS AND AFFECT RESEARCH

As noted in chapter 1, some of the earliest work in psychology was focused on aspects of emotions. Freudian and psychodynamic theories, in particular, stressed the importance of unconscious wishes or desires giving rise to various emotions and behaviors. However, as behaviorism came to dominate psychology, or at least American psychology, questions regarding the role of emotions and affect became less central to mainstream academic and research psychology. Finally, with the ascent of the general cognitive paradigm, cognitive models and computer metaphors came to guide much of the research on cognition, learning, and performance. Although these cognitive models were not intentionally designed to ignore affect, they did emphasize rational and cognitive processes, not affective or emotional processes. After all, if the guiding metaphors for cognition and learning are the computer and information processing, it is fairly easy to see why psychologists did not tend to investigate emotions or to give them a central role in their theories.

This is not to say that there wasn't research on emotions and affect. Of course, there was research on emotional development (see Saarni, Mumme, & Campos, 1998) in developmental psychology as well as research on attitudes and emotions in social psychology (e.g., Eagly & Chaiken, 1998; Schwarz & Clore, 1996; Zajonc, 1998), but research on cognition and learning did not necessarily integrate this work. In fact, in the 1983 *Handbook of Child Psychology,* Brown, Bransford, Ferrara, and Campione, in their classic and oft-cited chapter on learning, remembering, and understanding stated, "Bleak though it may sound, academic cognition is relatively effortful, isolated, and cold . . . Academic cognition is cold, in that the principal concern is with the knowledge and strategies necessary for efficiency, with little emphasis placed on the emotional factors that might promote or impede that efficiency" (p. 78). It is unlikely that this statement would be made today, but it does reflect the general zeitgeist of cognitive and developmental research on cognition and learning in the heyday of pure cognitive models.

In addition, much of the research on achievement motivation has been dominated by social cognitive models such as expectancy-value theory, attributional theory, self-efficacy theory, goal theory, and self-determination theory, all of which include emotions, but tend to focus on the central role of cognitions like attributions, judgments of efficacy and competence, goals, and value beliefs. Attributional theory (see chapter 3) did address emotions the most directly of all these social cognitive models, but as we saw in chapter 3, under attributional theory, emotions are the direct outcome of a cognitive-attributional analysis of success or failure. In this case, cognitions (i.e., attributions) are still the most important construct in the model and emotions flow from the nature of the attributions made in a situation (Weiner, 1986, 1995). Accordingly, cognition is still the dominant construct, not emotions.

In contrast to these motivational models that have highlighted the role of cognition, this chapter discusses models that give equal weight to the role of emotions and affect, and attempts to integrate affect and cognition and their links to learning and performance. As a first step, we discuss some general definitional issues related to emotions and present a taxonomy of emotions that provides a useful framework for classifying different emotions. Of course, there are a number of different taxonomies or ways of defining emotions that have been used by personality and social psychologists (cf., Frijda, 1986; Plutchik, 1980; Russell & Barrett, 1999; Watson & Tellegen, 1985; Watson, Wiese, Vaidya, & Tellegen, 1999), but we use a taxonomy that has been related to issues of student motivation, learning, and performance (Pekrun, 1992; Pekrun & Frese, 1992). Before describing the taxonomy, it will help to clarify a few terms.

As Forgas (2000) has recently pointed out, the definition of terms such as affect, feelings, emotions, and mood is difficult because there is a lack of broad agreement among researchers about their meaning. This is not unusual in research on motivation (see Murphy & Alexander, 2000), but it is a particular problem in doing research on emotions and moods. Forgas (2000) notes that **affect** can be considered the broadest and most inclusive term that refers to both specific emotions and general moods. He then suggests that **mood** can be defined in terms of relatively low-intensity, diffuse, and enduring affective states that have no salient antecedent cause and little cognitive content. That is, people can feel good or bad, be in a good or bad mood, without any salient antecedent event or without really knowing why (the cognitive antecedent) they feel the way they do. In contrast, Forgas (2000) suggests that emotions are more short-lived, intense phenomena that usually have a salient cause (e.g., failing an exam) and that the person is usually aware of this cause of the emotion. In addition, he notes that emotions usually have some clear cognitive content or referent. Specific emotions such as pride, anger, pity, fear, shame, and guilt are often the target of emotions research in contrast to the general and more diffuse good and bad moods that mood researchers examine.

Pekrun (1992; Pekrun & Frese, 1992) has proposed a general taxonomy of emotions that are relevant to student motivation, learning, and achievement. Table 7.1 displays a summary of his model. The columns reflect the common dimension of the positivity/negativity of the emotions (also labeled pleasantness/unpleasantness; see Russell & Barrett, 1999; Watson et al., 1999). In other emotions research, there is often a second dimension of activation/deactivation (or engagement/disengagement; see Russell & Barrett, 1999; Watson et al., 1999), but that is not reflected in the taxonomy in Table 7.1. In contrast, the taxonomy divides up emotions into two general categories: task-related emotions and social emotions. Task-related emotions would be expected to be relevant when a student en-

Table 7.1   Taxonomy of Student Emotions

	Positive	Negative
Task-related		
Process-related	Enjoyment	Boredom
Prospective	Hope	Anxiety
	Anticipatory joy	Hopelessness
		(Resignation/despair)
Retrospective	Relief	—
	Outcome-related joy	Sadness
	Pride	Disappointment
		Shame/guilt
Social		
	Gratitude	Anger
	Empathy	Jealousy/envy
	Admiration	Contempt
	Sympathy/love	Antipathy/hate

Adapted from Pekrun, 1992.

gages in any type of achievement or learning task in school or other settings, as well as work-related tasks in the business world (Pekrun & Frese, 1992). Social emotions refer to potential emotions that could be generated from social interactions with other individuals.

Within the task-related section of Table 7.1, a distinction is made between emotions that are experienced when actually engaged in the task, which includes the process-related emotions of enjoyment and boredom. The second main category reflects prospective relations that students might experience as they approach a task or think about engaging in a task and the expected outcomes. These prospective emotions include hope or anticipatory joy as well as anxiety about the task or hopelessness or despair. Finally, the third category includes retrospective emotions that a student might experience after the task is completed, such as relief, joy, and pride as well as more negative emotions such as sadness, disappointment, and shame or guilt. Of course, many of these retrospective emotions are the same as those discussed in chapter 3 as outcomes of attributional processes. It is likely that many of these retrospective emotions like pride, shame, and guilt are linked closely with the type and nature of the attributions that individuals make for their performance on the task (Weiner, 1986, 1995).

The taxonomy in Table 7.1 displays the specific emotions that might be engendered in school achievement contexts. It is clear that these emotions are much more specific than general good or bad moods. In addition, many of these emotions have a cognitive component in terms of some type of referent for the emotion. That is, moods are more diffuse and do not have any specific content associated with them, while emotions such as pride or shame or guilt are usually in reference to some specific task or behavior or achievement. Individuals can just be in a bad mood, without much thinking. If they feel pride or shame, however, they are usually thinking about a particular event such as succeeding or failing on an exam, doing well in a competition or game, etc. Of course, individuals might have "free-floating" anxiety or anger that is not tied to any specific cognitive content or event, but most likely there also will be cognitive rumination or thinking about why they are anxious or angry.

Forgas (2000) also notes that the distinction between mood and emotions parallels, to some extent, the research on the interplay of affect and cognition. For example, emotions researchers tend to focus on the contextual and cognitive antecedents of emotional reactions, including various appraisal strategies like attributions. That is, they are trying to understand how and why people come to experience the specific emotions that are generated in different situations (such as those outlined in Table 7.1). In contrast, mood researchers are usually interested in the consequences of mood on cognition and cognitive processing, so mood becomes the independent variable. In contrast, for emotion researchers, the emotions are often the dependent variable that flows from various cognitive and appraisal processes.

There has been a long history of research on the causal ordering of cognition and affect (cf., Smith & Kirby, 2000; Weiner, 1985; Zajonc, 1980, 2000) and like many of these disagreements (i.e., the debate over the causal precedence of self-concept versus achievement; Wigfield & Karpathian, 1991), the current and most sensible perspective is that the influence is bi-directional. It is not clear that we need to continue to argue over whether cognition precedes affect or vice versa, but rather to develop models that help us understand how, why, and when (under what conditions) does cognition precede and influence affect and how, why, and when affect precedes and influences cognition. Chapter 3 on attributional theory outlined some of the ways that cognitive appraisals and attributions can influence emotions. This chapter focuses more on the links that go from affect to cognition. In terms of the relations between affect and subsequent cognition, learning, and performance, Pekrun (1992) has suggested that there are four general routes by which emotions or mood might influence various outcomes (see also Linnenbrink & Pintrich, 2000). Three of these routes are through cognitive mediators and the fourth is through a motivational pathway. The different models and constructs discussed in this chapter illustrate all four of these routes quite well; we provide a brief overview of the four pathways as an advance organizer.

The first route by which emotions or mood might influence learning and performance is through memory processes such as retrieval and storage of information (Pekrun, 1992). There is quite a bit of research on mood-dependent memory. The general idea is that affective states such as mood get encoded at the same time as other information and that the affect and information are intimately linked in an associative network (Bower, 1981; Forgas, 2000). This leads to findings such as affect-state dependent retrieval, in which retrieval of information is enhanced if the person's mood at the retrieval task matches the person's mood at the encoding phase (Forgas, 2000). Forgas (2000) also notes that there are findings that show that mood or affective state facilitates the recall of affectively congruent material, such that people in a good mood are more likely to recall positive information and people in a bad mood are more likely to recall negative information. In other work, Linnenbrink and Pintrich (2000) and Linnenbrink, Ryan, and Pintrich (1999) suggest that negative affect might influence working memory by mediating the effects of different goal orientations. In this work, it appears that negative affect might have a detrimental effect on working memory, but positive affect was unrelated to working memory. This general explanation for the integration of encoding, retrieval, and affective processes is one of the main thrusts of the personal and situational interest research that will be discussed later in this chapter.

The second mediational pathway that Pekrun (1992) suggests is that affect influences the use of different cognitive, regulatory, and thinking strategies (cf., Forgas, 2000), which could then lead to different types of achievement of performance outcomes. For example, some of the original research suggested that positive mood produced more rapid, less detailed and less systematic processing of information, while negative mood resulted in more systematic, analytic, or detailed processing of information (Forgas, 2000; Pekrun, 1992). However, recent work suggests that this is too simplistic a position and more complex proposals have been made. For example, Fiedler (2000) has suggested that positive affect as a general approach orientation facilitates more assimilation processes including generative, top-down, and creative processes, including seeking out novelty. In contrast, he suggests that negative mood reflects a more aversive or avoidance orientation and can result in more accommodation, including a focus more on external information and details, as well as being more stimulus-bound and less willing to make mistakes.

Other research on the use of cognitive and self-regulatory strategies in school settings has not addressed the role of affect in great detail, but the few studies do show that negative affect decreases the probability that students will use cognitive strategies that result in deeper, more elaborate processing of the information (Linnenbrink & Pintrich, 2000). For example, Turner, Thorpe, and Meyer (1998) found that negative affect was negatively related to elementary students' deeper strategy use. Moreover, negative affect mediated the negative relation between performance goals and strategy use. If negative affect or emotion is a generally aversive state, it makes sense that students who experience negative affect are less likely to use deeper processing strategies, as these require much more engagement and a positive approach to the academic task. In contrast, positive affect should result in more engagement and deeper strategy use. This latter argument is also similar to some of the findings from the personal and situational interest research that we will discuss later in this chapter.

The third cognitive pathway that Pekrun (1992) suggests is that affect can increase or decrease the attentional resources that are available to students. Linnenbrink and Pintrich (2000) make a similar argument. As Pekrun (1992) notes, emotions can take up space in working memory and increase the cognitive load for individuals. For example, if a student is trying to do an academic task and at the same time is having feelings of fear or anxiety, these feelings (and their accompanying cognitions about worry and self-doubt) can take up the limited working memory resources and can interfere with the cognitive processing needed to do the academic task (Hembree, 1988; Wine, 1971; Zeidner, 1998). In fact, this general interference or cognitive load explanation is a hallmark of work on test anxiety that will be discussed in more detail later in this chapter. Under this general cognitive load hypothesis, it might be expected that any emotion, positive or negative, would take up attentional resources and result in reduced cognitive processing or performance. However, this does not seem to be the case, given the differential and asymmetric findings for positive and negative affect (Forgas, 2000), so it is clear there is a need for further exploration of how emotions and mood can influence attentional resources and ultimately performance.

The fourth and final general pathway that Pekrun (1992) suggests is that emotions can work through their effect on intrinsic and extrinsic motivational processes. Linnenbrink and Pintrich (2000) have also suggested that motivational and affective processes can interact to influence cognitive and behavioral outcomes. Under this general assumption, positive emotions, such as the experience of enjoyment in doing a task, or even the anticipatory or outcome-related joy of a task (see Table 7.1), may lead to intrinsic motivation for the task. Of course, as we have seen in this book, there are many different definitions of intrinsic motivation (see chapter 6). The idea that the experience of enjoyment and deep engagement in a task is reflective of intrinsic motivation is represented in the next section of this chapter on emergent motivation and flow. Of course, negative emotions such as boredom or sadness or fear should decrease intrinsic motivation for doing the task, albeit some of them (e.g., fear) might increase the extrinsic motivation for the task. It seems clear that affective and motivational processes can interact and, through these interactions, can influence cognition, learning, and performance (Linnenbrink & Pintrich, 2000). At the same time, there is a need for much more research on how to effectively integrate affective processes with the motivational and cognitive processes that have been examined in much more detail. This is sure to be one of the major areas of future research in achievement motivation research. We now turn to some of the specific theories and models that have integrated affective processes with motivational and cognitive processes to better explain learning and achievement.

RESEARCH ON EMERGENT MOTIVATION AND FLOW

Perspectives on intrinsic motivation emphasize such qualities as perceived control, the desire for autonomy, and the need to master the environment (see chapter 6). A perspective on intrinsic motivation closely aligned with these others has been advanced by Csikszentmihalyi and his colleagues (1975, 1978, 1985, 1990, 1996, 1997, 1999; Csikszentmihalyi & Csikszentmihalyi, 1988; Csikszentmihalyi & Rathunde, 1993, 1998). This perspective, referred to as **emergent motivation,** denotes motivation stemming from the discovery of new goals and rewards as a consequence of interacting with the environment. As Csikszentmihalyi (1978) states,

> When small children begin to play with building blocks, they rarely have a plan or a goal to guide their actions. They will place the blocks more or less randomly next to or on top of each other until some combination of shapes suggests a particular form that the children will then seek to approximate—at this point we might say that they have a "goal" or plan to direct their actions. This goal will typically change with every new block they place along the others, as new possibilities are suggested by the developing structure. The reward that keeps the children going is the feedback that tells how closely they are able to match what they do with what they want to do. . . . Neither the goal nor the rewards could be specified in advance, because both emerge out of the interaction. (p. 207)

Csikszentmihalyi believes that behavior is governed by intrinsic and extrinsic motivational forces. Extrinsic forces are preprogrammed biologically (e.g., food, sleep) or derive from the reward structure in which the individual is socialized (money, prestige, grades, approval of others, etc). Intrinsic forces grow out of the individual's belief that a given activity or outcome is worth striving toward for its own sake. He calls this type of activity autotelic, as it becomes an experience that is so engrossing and enjoyable that it is worth doing for its own sake. He notes that many creative activities, music, sports, games, and religious rituals are often resources for this type of autotelic experience (Csikszentmihalyi, 1999). This autotelic activity is similar to the intrinsically motivated or self-determined activity discussed in Deci and Ryan's (1985) theory of intrinsic motivation (see chapter 6).

Intrinsic Rewards and Flow

Csikszentmihalyi (1985) studied individuals who engaged in intrinsically motivating activities and found that their experiences reflected complete involvement with the activities. This involvement, or **flow,** is defined as "the holistic sensation that people feel when they act with total involvement" (Csikszentmihalyi, 1985, p. 36). In the beginning of the chapter, Mr. Anderman mentions that this sometimes happens in his class and that it is one of the most rewarding aspects of teaching. The relation of flow to other human motives is shown in Figure 7.1. The dimensions in this two-by-two classification are closed-versus open-system goals and intra- versus interindividual processes. Closed goals are those determined by genetics (needs) or socialization; open goals develop as a result of experience and cannot be explained by pre-existing factors. Interindividual processes are social in nature, whereas intraindividual processes refer to the person. Flow is a personal process and reflects open systemic goals. It is analogous to Maslow's growth motivation and Rogers's concept of the fully functioning individual (see chapters 1 and 5).

Individuals experiencing flow are so intensely involved with a task that they may lose awareness of time and space. They also seek a flow experience for itself rather than for anticipated rewards. Although flow can be experienced with any activity, it is more likely to occur with activities that allow for free expression and creativity such as games, play, and art. De Charms's (1968) origin state shares many elements with flow. The following quotes are from interviews with individuals who describe the state of flow as they are involved in their work. These quotes help to give a sense of the intense involvement in the activity that the individual feels when in the flow state.

	Primarily intraindividual processes	*Primarily interindividual processes*
Primarily closed systemic goals	*Needs* Hunger Thirst Safety Optimal activation, etc.	*Socialization* Sex Affiliation Achievement Presented life theme
Primarily open systemic goals	*Emergent Motives* Intrinsic motivation Flow Self-development Discovered life theme	*Cultivation* Values Social goals Identification Ideologies, etc.

Figure 7.1   Relation of emergent motivation to other motives
Adapted from Csikszentmihalyi, 1985.

A music composer described flow when composing music in the following manner: "You are in an ecstatic state to such a point that you feel as though you almost don't exist. I have experienced this time and time again. My hand seems devoid of myself, and I have nothing to do with what is happening. I just sit there watching in a state of awe and wonderment. And the music flows out by itself" (Csikszentmihalyi, 1975, p. 44). Csikszentmihalyi (1999) also picked out two other quotes—one by a poet and the other by a mother interacting with her daughter—to illustrate the feeling and experience of flow. In terms of his writing, a poet notes: "You lose your sense of time, you're completely enraptured, you are completely caught up in what you're doing, and you are sort of swayed by the possibilities you see in this work" (Csikszentmihalyi, 1996, p. 121). The following quote by a mother shows that flow is not just limited to creative activities such as creating music or poetry (Csikszentmihalyi, 1999). "I am working with my daughter, when she's discovered something new. A new cookie recipe that she has accomplished, that she has made herself, an artistic work that she has done and she is proud of. Her reading is something that she is really into, and we read together. She reads to me and I read to her, and that's a time when I sort of lose touch with the rest of the world. I am totally absorbed in what I am doing" (Allison & Duncan, 1988, p. 129).

All of these quotes show how people can become completely involved in an activity and lose a sense of themselves as well as a sense of time when in flow. It is important to note that in most of these cases, the underlying skills and knowledge are so practiced and automatized that it makes it easy for the composer or poet to experience flow. If the novice composer or poet is struggling with basic composition skills, it would be less likely that he or she would experience flow in the same manner. Athletes also talk about their experience of flow during a game, such as "getting into the zone" and "time slows down and everything seems to move in slow motion." As Csikszentmihalyi (1999) notes, the type of effortless performance that is a part of flow comes about because the skills and techniques are so well-learned and practiced that they are automatic. He also suggests that this is one of the paradoxes of flow in the sense that the person has to be in control of the activity to experience it, but not try to consciously control the activity or one's behavior. Finally, it is important to note that experiencing flow in this model of motivation is not the same as the cliché of "going with the flow," which tends to connote giving oneself over to a situation that feels good, natural, and spontaneous (Csikszentmihalyi, 1999). Csikszentmihalyi is very careful to point out that in his model of motivation, the flow experience requires skill, expertise, concentration, and perseverance, not just hanging out and feeling good.

Figure 7.2 portrays a model of the flow state. Flow represents a state of equilibrium between the amount of challenge in activities and an individual's capabilities. People feel bored when their perceived skills exceed their opportunities for using them; they become anxious when they believe that challenges exceed capabilities. Flow can vary in intensity, with the critical variable being the ratio of challenge to skill. The portrayed relations presumably hold for peak as well as everyday experiences. As we have noted throughout this book, one of the most optimal patterns of motivation comes when the relation between skill or knowledge levels is matched to the challenge or difficulty of the task. Flow theory has shown that people's affective reactions are related to their expertise and the difficulty of the task. As noted previously, if a novice composer or poet is struggling with basic composition skills, he or she would be unlikely to feel flow if attempting to create great

Figure 7.2   The flow state

From "Toward a Psychology of Optimal Experience" by M. Csikszentmihalyi in *Review of Personality and Social Psychology* (Vol. 3, p. 17) edited by L. Wheeler, 1982, Beverly Hills, CA: Sage Publications. Copyright © 1982 by Sage Publications, Inc. Reprinted by permission of Sage Publications, Inc.

new pieces of music or poetry. On the other hand, a less dramatically challenging task, such as mastering certain traditional forms of music or poetry, might be a task at the appropriate level of difficulty to allow for a flow experience. The important issue for student learning and achievement is to try to help create the conditions in which tasks match student expertise levels and to increase the probability that they will experience positive affect and enjoyment in school, not boredom or anxiety.

Research on Flow

Despite being nebulous, the notion of flow makes intuitive sense. Csikszentmihalyi (1982) describes a research study in which the **Experience Sampling Method** (ESM) was employed (a self-report measure; see chapter 1). Adults carried beepers (which is why the ESM is often called the "beeper methodology") that sounded several times a week, at which time subjects rated themselves on two dependent variables: affect (comprising items "happy," "cheerful," "sociable") and activation (comprising "active," "alert," "strong"). Subjects also judged the situation for challenges present in the activity and the skills available to them. The amount of time individuals judged themselves to be in flow (defined as challenges and skills present and equal to one another) was related positively to affect and activation.

Mayers (reported in Csikszentmihalyi, 1982) had high school students rate school subjects and activities on challenge and skill (Figure 7.3). Favorite activities fell into the flow area where challenges equal skills: TV and music listening (low on each); friends (moderate); and arts, such as drama or ballet, and sports (high on each). Skills were judged to exceed challenges in humanities and social sciences, resulting in boredom. Challenges were rated as exceeding skills in mathematics and the sciences, resulting in anxiety. It seems clear that in many cases, school subjects and courses are not generating positive emotions, let alone flow, but seem to result in more boredom and anxiety for students.

Other research compared the flow experiences of three groups of adolescents. One group attended a select public school in Italy, a second group attended a typical suburban high school near Chicago, and a third group was comprised of talented math students from a top Chicago public school (Csikszentmihalyi, 1985). Students used the Experience Sampling Method. The Italian teens reported more flow experiences than did

Figure 7.3 Ratings of school subjects and activities on challenges and skills

From "Toward a Psychology of Optimal Experience" by M. Csikszentmihalyi in *Review of Personality and Social Psychology* (Vol. 3, p. 18) edited by L. Wheeler, 1982, Beverly Hills, CA: Sage Publications. Copyright © 1982 by Sage Publications, Inc. Reprinted by permission of Sage Publications, Inc.

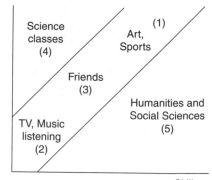

U.S. teens, especially those talented in math. Among U.S. teens, those attending the typical school reported more time in flow than did the talented ones. The talented U.S. sample reported the most amounts of boredom (skills exceed challenges) and anxiety (challenges exceed skills). Interestingly, the talented group scored significantly lower than the other two samples in apathy, defined as skills and challenges in sync but below average (e.g., watching TV, listening to music). In sum, experiences are comparable for average and above average students across cultures, whereas for talented U.S. teens, flow and apathy are rarer and boredom and anxiety more common.

These findings have implications for teaching and learning because they highlight the importance of ensuring that challenges and skills are in balance and sufficiently high to counter apathy. Unfortunately, many school activities do not challenge students. The suggestions given in the previous chapter and this chapter for ways to enhance students' choices, challenges, and perceived capabilities are relevant to increasing flow. Flow will suffer when students have few opportunities to structure their environments in ways that might maximize flow, such as by establishing challenging goals and mastering difficult tasks that build beliefs in their capabilities.

The theory of emergent motivation and flow represents a good example of how the investigation of emotional reactions can lead to a unique and interesting theory of motivation. The theory and research starts with trying to understand how adults and students experience daily life in terms of their affect and emotions. The methodology used, ESM, is quite an innovation and has been used by a number of other researchers in other areas. From the description of emotional experience, the theory then links experiences to involvement in activities and actual achievements. It seems clear that when students are enjoying and engaged in their school activities, they will be more likely to do well and learn more. Accordingly, this theory is a good exemplar of the role that emotions can play in motivation, learning, and achievement. At the same time, it does not give much attention to other social cognitive constructs such as efficacy judgments or goals, which are also important, as we have seen in other chapters in this book. The theory reminds us of the importance of affect and emotions in life, but there is a need for integrating other motivational constructs as well.

Application 7.1 suggests some potential ways that emergent motivation and flow theory can be applied to the classroom.

APPLICATION 7.1

Applying Flow Theory in the Classroom

1. *Match task challenges to student expertise.* Flow emerges from an interaction of the person's capabilities and the challenges in the task or context. In some ways, it is difficult to design instruction to facilitate flow because it is so idiosyncratic to the individual. However, the general idea of increasing the probability of students having positive emotions (enjoyment) and decreasing the probability of negative ones such as boredom or fear by providing a optimal match between task challenges and expertise is one that should help to motivate students.

    Ms. Rhee is a high school English teacher. She has the students reading and analyzing the play Hamlet. The unit on Hamlet takes place over a number of weeks and it includes mini-lectures, reading aloud parts of the play and discussing, students acting out parts of it, watching and discussing various film versions of it, etc. One activity that she finds works well is to have the students attempt to re-write scenes from the play but place the characters in a modern-day context. She assigns students to different parts of the play, with some students getting harder scenes to rewrite, and others somewhat easier parts (helping to match skill level to the task). She then has the re-written parts of the play acted out with the authors serving as director of their own scenes. The students really seem to enjoy this activity and get very involved in writing and acting out the new scenes as well as discussing the connections between the play and modern life. Even students who are not acting out parts of the play seem to be very engaged and there is very little boredom.

2. *Provide opportunities for control and action.* Another important aspect of flow theory, as in most intrinsic motivation and interest theories (see the Applications in chapter 6 as well Application 7.2 in this chapter), is the sense of choice and control. In addition, it seems to be important that individuals have opportunities to make choices and decisions, and to be actively doing something.

    Mr. Sims is a middle school science teacher who uses computer simulations in his inquiry-driven classroom. These computer simulations allow students to design experiments and run them, collecting as well as analyzing the data (the software provides support for graphing of data, etc.). The students are placed in small groups of about two to three people for the 10 computers in the class and then asked to design experiments to test different ideas. The students get quite engaged in making changes to the design of the experiment, running different versions of the experiment, and then comparing the data from their own experiments, as well as the data from other small groups. The students are quite involved and excited about the chance to use the computer and to actually see the results of their experiments fairly quickly and compare with other groups.

3. *Create a positive emotional climate in the classroom.* Given the focus on positive emotions in flow theory, it is important that the general classroom climate is free from fear, anxiety, and other potential negative emotions. Ms. Zusho, a fifth-grade elementary school teacher, maintains an atmosphere of trust, respect, and caring in her classroom. She treats all of her children with care and concern, shows interest in

their personal lives, and generally makes the classroom a warm and welcoming place. She is careful to teach the students the importance of respect for others and their ideas. She also models this behavior in her own teaching and interactions with others. There are classroom rules and norms about how to talk to others, how to respond to other students in class discussions, how to work together in small groups, etc. Ms. Zusho takes the time to teach these rules to the students and is careful to monitor and enforce them throughout the year. In general, the children seem happy and like to come to her classroom. It is a place where they feel at home, safe, and secure, and a place to have fun as well as to explore new ideas.

4. *Provide tasks that have some structured goals.* Flow theory presumes that part of the involvement in the task comes from the fact that the goals for the task are clear. For example, in sport activities, there is usually a fairly clear goal—get the ball (puck) in the goal (soccer, field hockey, ice hockey), in the basket (basketball), over the goal line (football), over the net and in bounds (tennis), etc. These clear goals help people focus their efforts. At the same time, there are multiple ways to accomplish these sports goals that allow for individual choice and control.

Ms. Linnenbrink is a high school music teacher and band director. When she sets up tasks and activities for her different classes, she makes it clear what the goals are for the different tasks. Practice sessions are not just times to play the same piece over and over; she sets goals for the different sessions that help guide the students while working or practicing. In addition, she allows some flexibility in ways of meeting the goals. She allows the different sections of the band to work out the ways they will meet the goals of the practice sessions.

5. *Use tasks that have built-in opportunities for feedback and provide multiple opportunities for feedback.* Tasks with structured goals also usually provide some built-in mechanisms for feedback. To use the sports example again, it is usually clear if you are making progress toward your goal. You (or your team) are advancing the ball, scoring, winning, etc. This type of feedback makes it easier for individuals to adjust their cognition and behavior to increase the probability of doing well. In many computer games, the same types of feedback opportunities are offered. As you play the game, you get feedback on how you are doing, and this helps you with your engagement and progress. As any parent watching his or her children play games on a home computer, or taking a casual stroll through an arcade full of children playing computer games will tell you, children can get engrossed in computer games and become so involved that they lose track of time and seem to be in flow. It may be difficult to design classroom tasks that have these features, but there should be plenty of opportunities for feedback during a task, not just after the task is completed.

Ms. Hruda is a middle school math teacher who uses computer games and computer math activities with her students quite frequently. She finds that the computer activities help the students greatly in terms of their learning and it seems to motivate them to take on other noncomputer activities. She also is careful to be available for frequent consultation and feedback when students are working on seatwork or group work. She does not sit at her desk grading homework when students are doing seatwork or small-group work, but is constantly roving around the room, asking questions, giving feedback, and guiding and directing the students as they work.

RESEARCH ON SITUATIONAL AND PERSONAL INTEREST

If you asked most laypersons and teachers for their definition of motivation, they would probably provide an answer that refers to some aspect of interest. That is, the common generalization is that people will learn or do well if they are interested, and they will not learn or perform if they are uninterested. For example, at the beginning of this chapter, Ms. Duncan talks about how her students are just not interested in learning. Many parents will explain their children's lack of motivation and poor performance in school as due to a lack of interest. Students will say they don't learn because school and classes are boring and they can't get interested in the work. These intuitive views of motivation and general folk psychology usually propose interest as an important aspect of motivation that causally influences attention, learning, thinking, and performance. In addition, most people believe that they know what interest is and that they understand how it operates to influence learning. The popularity of these intuitive notions about interest has sometimes hindered the development of careful psychological research on interest.

As noted in chapter 2, the construct of interest is similar to the construct that Eccles and Wigfield have called intrinsic interest. However, research on interest, broadly defined, has been pursued by researchers from a number of different perspectives, beyond specific expectancy-value models and motivational theories in general. As pointed out by Krapp, Hidi, and Renninger (1992), interest in the construct of interest has waxed and waned in psychology and education over the years. Krapp and colleagues (Krapp et al., 1992) note that early in the nineteenth century, Herbart developed a model of interest and that both James and Dewey also discussed the role of interest in learning early in the twentieth century (e.g., see Dewey, 1913). These models usually owed more to philosophical perspectives than to psychological theories and there was often little empirical research to support the models. Of course, during the heyday of behaviorism, there was very little research on interest in the United States, although related concepts such as curiosity (Berlyne, 1960) and attitudes (Evans, 1971) were examined (Krapp et al., 1992). However, with the development of cognitive and constructivist models of learning and development, research on interest became more popular in the 1980s and 1990s. Currently, there are a number of active programs of research on the role of interest in learning and development that include researchers from around the world. The book on interest edited by Renninger, Hidi, and Krapp (1992) still represents the best introduction to this burgeoning area of research. Nevertheless, current theoretical and empirical work on the construct of interest is still rather young in comparison with the traditions of expectancy-value theory, attribution theory, self-efficacy theory, and intrinsic motivation theory.

Three Perspectives on Interest

One of the issues that has plagued research on interest is the theoretical and conceptual definition of the construct. There has been recent research on interest by motivational psychologists, developmental psychologists, educational psychologists, and reading and literacy researchers, all of whom have used somewhat different definitions of interest. However, Krapp, Hidi, and Renninger (1992) have proposed that there are three general perspectives on interest that can help us understand this diverse body of research (see Figure 7.4). The three approaches cover personal interest (an individual disposition),

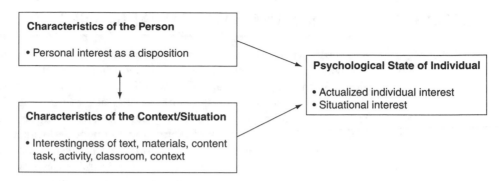

Figure 7.4   Three approaches to interest research
Adapted from Krapp et al., 1992.

interestingness (an aspect of the context), and interest as a psychological state (including situational interest). Each of these three perspectives is explained in the following text along with its relations to the other two general definitions of interest. It is clear from these definitions that interest in this research tradition includes both an affective component that is similar in some ways to the joy and positive affect that is experienced during flow, but it also includes cognitive components such as knowledge and values. In this way, it is important to note that interest refers to more than just the positive feelings (enjoyment) when doing a task, but also includes cognition (Krapp, 1999).

Personal Interest

Researchers who have investigated **personal interest** have conceptualized it as a personality trait or a personal characteristic of the individual that is a relatively stable, enduring disposition of the individual (Krapp et al., 1992). In addition, this personal interest is usually assumed to be directed toward some specific activity or topic (a particular interest in sports, science, music, dance, computers, etc.) in contrast to curiosity, which is assumed to be a characteristic of the person that is more diffusely directed (e.g., someone who is generally curious about many things). For example, much of the vocational education and career choice literature is based on assessing individuals' interests in different activities and careers. Eccles and Wigfield's concept of intrinsic interest (see chapter 2) would be conceptually similar to personal interest. Other researchers (see review by Schiefele, Krapp, & Winteler, 1992) have measured personal interest as a preference for certain topics (e.g., "I prefer math to science"), a general liking for the subject area (e.g., "I like math"), personal enjoyment (e.g., "I enjoy working on math problems"), and sometimes importance or personal significance of the topic (e.g., "Math is important to me"). Of course, in Eccles and Wigfield's model, this last aspect would be a separate construct of importance or attainment value, not interest (see chapter 2). Given these definitions, this work has focused on individual differences in personal interest and how these individual differences are related to learning and performance. It is important to note, however, that in all of these definitions, personal interest—the personal liking or positive attitude or affect—is directed toward a specific content or activity that is somewhat stable over time. In contrast, in the general models of affect and flow, the positive affect or emotions can come up in many different situations and for many different activities.

Interestingness as a Contextual Factor that Leads to Situational Interest

In contrast to the more personality or trait-like characteristic of personal interest, another approach has been to study the contextual features that make some text or task or activity interesting (see Figure 7.4); in other words, the interestingness of the context (Krapp et al., 1992). In this work, the interestingness of the context should result in the generation of **situational interest** (Krapp et al., 1992), which is the psychological state of being interested in the task or activity (see Figure 7.4). The researchers who have studied situational interest have often been reading researchers who investigated text-based interest, trying to understand how different aspects of texts can generate and sustain interest on the part of readers. There are many different features of texts that can generate interest, such as novelty, surprise, complexity, ambiguity, and inclusion of certain types of themes (e.g., death, sex). Given this situated perspective, researchers have tended to ignore individual differences and have looked for general principles to describe how the features of the environment (classrooms, media, computers, textbooks) can generate situational interest. Brophy (1999) and Bergin (1999) discuss many of the factors in classrooms that can generate student interest.

Hidi and Anderson (1992) note, however, that situational interest is different from just arousal or curiosity (cf. Berlyne, 1960) because situational interest may be tied to very specific content (e.g., a story about space travel), not only structural features (novelty, surprise) of the text or environment, and it may last longer than simple arousal and may develop into a personal interest. Although situational interest is more context-dependent than personal interest, it is still usually tied to specific features of the text or context, not just general positive affect or arousal or positive emotions, as in general affect theories or as in flow theory. Hidi (2000) has suggested that situational interest involves both an affective component of positive affect as well as increased attention or automatic attention to the task as a function of the affective involvement. In addition, she has noted that there may be two phases of situational interest. In the first phase, situational interest is triggered or activated. In the second, interest is further maintained (Hidi, 2000; Hidi & Baird, 1986; Hidi & Harackiewicz, 2000). Mitchell (1993) has used the phrases "catching" and "holding" interest, following a distinction by Dewey (1913), which is similar to the triggering versus maintaining situational interest distinction. However, Hidi (2000) does suggest that catching refers to the direction or diversion of already activated situational interest, while triggering suggests the initial activation of situational interest.

Interest as a Psychological State

As shown in Figure 7.4, situational interest is one type of interest as a psychological state. The previous section noted that situational interest is aroused or activated as a function of interestingness of the context. Some texts (a novel versus a dry textbook) are more interesting than others, some content areas generate more interest than others, and some teachers or lecturers are very good at making their classrooms or lectures interesting, generating at least situational interest on the part of their students. In these cases, the individual person is feeling situational interest as a psychological state, but it is more a function of the contextual features that he or she is in, than his or her own personal interest.

In addition to situational interest as a psychological state, there can be actualized individual interest, which reflects an interactive and relational perspective on interest. An individual's personal interest interacts with the interesting environmental features to produce the psychological state of interest in the person (Krapp et al., 1992). For example, a student may have a fairly high level of personal interest in science-related topics and, in her reading class, she occasionally gets to read expository texts about science topics. On these occasions, she experiences a heightened psychological state of interest in contrast to other occasions during reading class when she reads about other topics. In this case, however, her personal interest in science is activated in the science class and she experiences actualized individual interest.

Renninger (1990, 1992; Renninger & Wozniak, 1985) has been one of the researchers most involved with developing a research program on interest that reflects this relational construct of interest as a psychological state. She has conceptualized interest not just in terms of a personal preference or liking for an activity or topic, but as occurring only when the individual has both high value for an activity (choosing to do it, thinking it is important) and high stored knowledge about the activity or topic (a very obvious cognitive component). It is only under these conditions that Renninger would label the state as interest (see Figure 7.5). The argument is that if individuals have very little knowledge of an activity or topic, it is hard for them to judge their interest in it. In addition, individuals usually have more knowledge about activities that have a high level of interest and value for them. Accordingly, if a person has a high value for an activity but low knowledge of the activity, Renninger does not consider this interest; she labels this state as attraction. Noninterests are defined by high stored knowledge for an activity but low value for the activity. Renninger (1992) does not label the fourth cell in this two-by-two matrix of knowledge and value, which would represent the low value and low knowledge cell, but the psychological state would be unconcern, indifference, and ignorance about the topic (see Figure 7.5).

This position that interest is evoked only when an individual has both high value and high knowledge of an activity or topic has not been accepted by all interest researchers. For example, Alexander, Kulikowich, and Jetton (1994) and Tobias (1994) have argued that interest/value is orthogonal to prior knowledge. They assume that individuals can have high interest and high knowledge (cell 4 in Figure 7.5), which would be similar to Renninger's interest cell. However, these researchers assume that individuals can have high interest in a topic even though they may have low knowledge about it (cell 2 in Figure 7.5). Tobias (1994) does not label his cells explicitly, but notes that the low knowledge–high personal interest cell (cell 2) may not be found often in adults, but that there could be domains where children would be interested in the content but have little knowledge or expertise in that domain. Accordingly, Tobias (1994) suggests that this state of high interest–low knowledge (cell 2) would be transitory over the course of development. He notes that cells 1 and 3 would be similar to the ignorance and noninterest cells in Renninger's matrix. It seems intuitively possible that individuals could have high interest and low knowledge, but Renninger's (1992) logic about this state representing only attraction also seems plausible. This controversy over the relation between prior knowledge and interest/value reflects the theoretical and conceptual difficulties in research on interest. At the same time, it makes it clear that interest and cognition (knowledge) are inseparably linked in these models, unlike many models of

Figure 7.5 Contrasting models of the relations between interest and knowledge

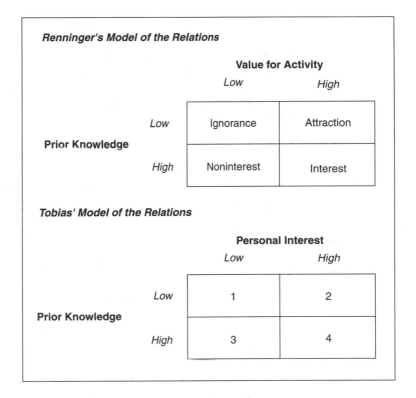

motivation and affect that keep them quite separate. We need better theoretical models and more empirical research on the construct of interest. Fortunately, this work is currently under way and promises to be an important area of research in motivation theory.

Measures of Interest and Research Findings

Related to the fact that there are various definitions and theories of interest, there have been a number of different methods used to measure student interest. In contrast to the research on students' perceptions of ability and efficacy, which has mainly used self-reports (see chapters 2 and 4), the research on interest has used self-reports and other measures. Research on personal interest has often used self-report instruments like questionnaires that ask students to rate various topics or activities on Likert-scaled items. Items are rated in a number of different ways, depending on the theoretical framework for personal interest, including general attitude toward the activity, specific preference for or liking the activity, enjoyment of the activity, personal importance or significance of the activity to the individual, intrinsic interest in the content of the activity, and reported choice of or participation in the activity (see Schiefele et al., 1992; Wigfield, 1994; Wigfield & Eccles, 1992). Students' responses to these various aspects of interest are then used to create scales that reflect different levels of interest in different activities (e.g., math versus English, academics versus sports). These scales represent individual differences in interest (i.e., some people will have high interest for academics, others will have high interest for sports) that are then used to predict various outcomes such as choice to do an activity in the future, persistence, level of effort or engagement in the activity, and actual performance. Although these self-reports of interest can be used quite easily and efficiently, there remain validity problems with using them because they require some metacognition or self-awareness on the part of individuals responding to them. This is not just a problem with interest self-report items; it may be difficult for some individuals (young children) to accurately report on their interests.

Interest has also been measured through the use of ESM methods (Experience Sampling Method, or "beeper" studies, described in the previous section). For example, Krapp and his colleagues (Wild, Krapp, Schreyer, & Lewalter, 1998) have used the ESM-beeper method to ask students about their interests, moods, motivation, and cognition during both school and work activities and settings. These studies still use self-reports in that students are asked to report on their affect, interest, and cognition on some questionnaire format, but they are "beeped" and asked to fill out the self-report forms at that specific time point. This allows for a much more situation-specific measure of interest than provided by general self-report questionnaires that ask students to report on their interest for a course in general. In the latter case, students are essentially "summing" up their experience over many occasions, and it is not clear how students actually do this cognitive calculation, or if they work off specific salient examples of being interested or bored. In contrast, the ESM method asks for a self-report at a specific time and should be a better indicator of students' experience of interest. Of course, the ESM data are usually summed over time or settings across individuals, but this method does provide a rich dataset that can be used to more accurately estimate the experience of interest in comparison to general questionnaires.

Besides self-report measures, Renninger (1990, 1992; Renninger & Wozniak, 1985) has used actual observations of the play of young children to measure interest as a psychological state. Students were observed during 240 minutes of free play and interest was coded for objects that the children (a) returned to play with repeatedly, (b) spent more time with than other objects, (c) played with in solitary play, and (d) played with in other than manipulative play (Renninger, 1992). Objects could then be classified as high or low interest in relation to the individual child's actual behavior with the object. This allowed for a very sensitive measure of interest for each individual, rather than just assuming, for example, that all boys are interested in trucks and all girls are interested in dolls. The results clearly showed that play objects that were of high interest to some children were not of much interest to other children (e.g., some boys had a high interest in trucks, but other boys did not). This type of behavioral measure also allowed Renninger to examine interest without having to ask children specifically about their own interests. Accordingly, this type of measure does not assume that individuals have to be metacognitively aware of their interests as do explicit questionnaire items that ask about personal interest. Actual observations allow for the investigation of interest in young children who may be lacking in the verbal, cognitive, or metacognitive skills to answer questionnaire items. Moreover, by focusing on behavior, observational measures do not introduce the term interest and avoid the validity problems associated with invoking participants' prior conceptions of interest that they then might use to interpret questionnaire items differently than the researcher intended.

Finally, the situational interest researchers, who have been concerned mainly with the influence of text-based interest on students' learning, have used a number of different measures of interest (Alexander et al., 1994). They have used self-report questionnaires of students' interest in the general domain of the reading (e.g., science) and the specific topic of the reading (space travel) in much the same way as noted in the research on personal interest. These researchers have also used students' personal ratings of the interestingness of the text (e.g., text on space travel written in an interesting style) as well as specific details of the text (e.g., walking on the moon or living in outer space). More recently, Ainley and Hidi (in press) have developed a computer methodology that allows for the assessment of interest as students read a text. Boekaerts (in press) also has developed and validated an "On-line Motivation Questionnaire" (OMQ) that is not computer-based, but can be used before and after students engage in classroom tasks or activities and generates situational measures of motivation, positive and negative affect, and interest.

The research on text-based interest also has used ratings of the text by others (other students, adults, teachers, experts) in terms of interest and then assigned students to high- and low-interest groups based on these ratings by others (e.g., Hidi & Anderson, 1992). Of course, this strategy assumes that one can normatively classify a text as generally interesting or uninteresting without considering how an individual student will perceive the text. This methodology also raises questions of validity concerning the normative and idiographic measurement of interest, another problem that will have to be resolved in future research.

Although there are problems in both the theoretical conceptions of interest and in the measurement of interest, the research has revealed fairly consistent results regarding how interest is related to other cognitive and achievement outcomes. First, in terms of cognitive outcomes, both situational interest and actualized personal interest are generally related positively to measures of memory, attention, comprehension, deeper cognitive engagement, thinking, and achievement (Hidi, 2000; Hidi & Harackiewicz, 2000; Schiefele, 1991, 1992; Schiefele & Krapp, 1996; Schiefele, Krapp, & Winteler, 1992; Tobias, 1994), as suggested in most lay or folk psychology theories on the role of interest in learning. For example, Renninger and Wozniak (1985) have shown that preschoolers' interest in different activities predicts their attention, recognition, and recall memory for these objects at a later point in time. Schiefele (1991), using both experimental and correlational designs, has shown that college students' personal interest was positively related to the use of deeper cognitive processing strategies such as elaboration, seeking information when confronted with a problem, engagement in critical thinking, and self-reported time and effort investment. In addition, Schiefele (1991) reported that personal interest was negatively related to the use of a more surface processing strategy—rehearsal. Pintrich and his colleagues (Pintrich, 1989; Pintrich & De Groot, 1990a; Pintrich & Garcia, 1991) have shown that personal interest and task value measures are correlated positively with deeper processing strategies such as the use of elaboration and organizational strategies as well as reports of critical thinking and time and effort regulation strategies in both college and junior high samples. The research on situational interest and text-based learning shows basically the same pattern of relations (Alexander et al., 1994; Hidi, 2000; Hidi & Anderson, 1992; Hidi & Harackiewicz, 2000; Tobias, 1994), although the findings are somewhat more complicated by the type of text involved (narrative versus expository text, linear versus nonlinear text) and levels of student prior knowledge.

Given these generally consistent, positive findings on the role of interest in learning, future research will probably be more likely to address the issue of *how* interest has an influence on learning, not *whether* it has an effect (Hidi, Renninger, & Krapp, 1992). In this sense, it will continue to broaden our understanding of the four general pathways by which affect can influence learning and performance that were described in the beginning of this chapter. As noted in that section, the third pathway deals with attentional resources and interest. Research has generally hypothesized that interest has an effect on learning through attention. Higher levels of interest are supposed to lead to greater attention to the task, which in turn would lead to better memory or learning. Although this selective attention explanation does have empirical support (see Shirey, 1992), others (e.g., Hidi, 1990) have argued that interest may actually result in less conscious attention given to the task. Hidi (1990; Hidi & Anderson, 1992) suggests that when interest is high, there does not have to be as much effortful selective attention; that, in fact, interest could result in more spontaneous attention and less cognitive effort, but still have a positive influence on learning. Tobias (1994) also suggests that high interest might make it easier for students to activate a richer network of prior knowledge about the topic or activity that would make memory and learning easier (the first pathway mentioned in the beginning of this chapter). High levels of personal interest might also decrease the demands for self-regulation of time and effort (i.e., students trying to maintain their effort level in the face of a boring task) and thereby free up more cognitive capacity for actual learning of the task content, rather than self-regulation. Current research is examining these and other possibilities to help us understand just how interest can influence learning.

Developmental and Individual Differences in Interest

In comparison to the research on some motivational constructs, there has been less research on developmental and group differences in interest. First, in terms of developmental issues, the research suggests that even fairly young (3–4 years old) preschool children have relatively stable personal interests and that these interests are related to their choice of activities and their learning (Renninger, 1992). There has been little research, however, on how interests develop over time and experience. Second, interest may play a larger role in directing and guiding the behavior of younger children for a larger number of tasks than it does for older children and adults. Older children and adults very often have to engage in tasks that do not really interest them and they often have no choice over these tasks (e.g., tasks in school, job-related tasks). In these situations, interest may have a more differential effect, depending on the task and content area, than the diverse effect it has for younger children on many tasks (Krapp et al., 1992). For example, Hidi and Anderson (1992) found that situational interest had a stronger effect in reading tasks for upper elementary school children than it did in writing tasks. It seems that the functional role of interest in learning may vary depending on the age of the child. Finally, in terms of developmental differences in levels of interest, research clearly shows that students' interest in school and school tasks does decline with age and that interest in math and science may drop the most (see Eccles et al., 1998; Kahle et al., 1993; Wigfield, 1994; Wigfield & Eccles, 1992). Clearly, there is a need for more research on the domain and developmental differences in the role of interest in learning and development.

The development of situational interest is often seen as one pathway to the development of more stable personal interests. The general idea is that teachers should try to create situational interest in their courses with the hope that over time this situational interest will help students develop more personal interest in the content or topics of the course. In addition, by attempting to generate situational interest in all students, teachers do not have to deal with the problems of trying to ascertain all the personal interests of their students (which will obviously vary a great deal) and then trying to structure the course to fit all of these different personal interests (Hidi & Harackiewicz, 2000). Following a distinction suggested by Hidi and Baird (1986) between factors that stimulate situational versus those that maintain interest, Mitchell (1993) found that in secondary math classrooms, certain classroom factors catch student interest, while others hold it. He found that group work, puzzles, and the use of computers helped to activate interest, but did not hold student interest. In contrast, the use of meaningful work and the active involvement of students as learners were related to the maintenance of situational interest. In the vignette at the start of this chapter, Mr. Anderman and Mr. Lopez both talk about ways they try to catch and hold student interest using games and puzzles as well as meaningfulness and involvement. Harackiewicz and her colleagues (Harackiewicz, Barron, Tauer, Carter, & Elliot, 2000) have found similar results in a college classroom setting. The simple experience of enjoyment of the course and the lectures, similar to the catch aspect, was not related to continued interest over time or to performance. However, a measure of interest in course content that reflected perceptions of meaningfulness of the content and intrinsic interest (similar to the hold component) was related to continued interest over time and short-term performance. Accordingly, the long-term development of interest seems to be served better by the use of meaningful tasks and student involvement in active learning, than by a "bells and whistles" approach to make the class interesting and stimulating.

In terms of ethnic differences, there is very little research, but gender differences in interest have been found in the research. For example, Renninger (1992) found gender differences in the nature of preschool boys' and girls' play with objects of interest to them. Girls were more likely to use their interest objects in a number of different ways in their play, whereas boys showed more play actions only when using their objects to mimic the real-world use of the object. In addition, Renninger (1992) found gender differences in the role of interest in elementary school students' solution of arithmetic problems. Boys were more likely to make errors on uninteresting math problems, whereas the girls made more errors when they worked on interesting math problems. Renninger interprets this gender-by-interest interaction by suggesting that interest facilitates boys' problem solving because it helps them to understand and work on the interesting problems. In contrast, interest seems to interfere and becomes a distraction for girls on the interesting math problems. Schiefele, Krapp, and Winteler (1992) also found that the interest-achievement linkage was stronger for males; about 12% of the variance in achievement for males was accounted for by interest, whereas the variance was only 6% for females. There is a need for much more research on the potential gender and ethnic differences in both situational and personal interest.

Application 7.2 suggests some possible strategies that teachers might use to increase both situational and personal interest in their classrooms.

APPLICATION 7.2

Applying Situational and Personal Interest Research in the Classroom

Given the difficulties in adapting instruction to diverse personal interests, it may be easier for teachers to attempt to create situational interest, but many of these strategies also may stimulate personal interest. Alderman (1999), Bergin (1999), Brophy

(1998), and Stipek (1998) also provide a number of good, concrete suggestions for increasing interest.

1. *Use original source materials.* These materials often have interesting content or details that get left out of more generic texts and can help spark some situational interest. Mr. Urdan, a high school American history teacher, uses a number of different texts and sources in his class, not just the textbook. These texts include more detailed, scholarly books as well as original source material. The students find these materials more interesting than the rather dry textbook.

2. *Model your own enthusiasm and interest for the content.* By modeling interest in the material, the teacher can communicate that the content is interesting.

   Ms. Ryan, a high school biology and chemistry teacher, consciously tries to model her own interest in the science material she is teaching by talking about her own learning of it and how it interests her.

3. *Create surprise and disequilibrium in the classroom.* Creating surprise by presenting material that goes against expectations or prior knowledge can create some cognitive disequilibrium on the part of students. They then may be drawn to the material to attempt to figure out why their beliefs or knowledge are discrepant and become more engaged or involved.

   Ms. Patrick attempts to create surprise and disequilibrium by having students predict what will happen in different science experiments and then showing that the students' predictions are wrong when she does the model experiment. She then spends the remainder of the class talking about how the students derived their predictions and how the experiment and related theory disprove their predictions.

4. *Use variety and novelty.* As common sense, as well as interest research, tells us, if students are doing the same activity day in and day out, boredom will inevitably set in. It is useful to have a variety of activities throughout the week, month, and school year. In addition, the introduction of novel ideas, content, tasks, and activities may facilitate situational interest.

   Ms. Blazevski is a third-grade elementary school teacher who uses a wide variety of activity and task formats to keep her children engaged. The class has a regular structure and organization, so the novelty is not overwhelming, but within the structure. The students do many different activities for reading, math, science, and social studies. Moreover, the same activities are not just used within one content area domain (e.g., plays in reading) but are used across the different content domains. Students enjoy the diversity of activities and are always waiting to see the next new thing that Ms. Blazevski will bring to the class.

5. *Provide some choice of topics based on personal interest.* As almost all motivation theories suggest (not just interest or intrinsic motivation theories), the provision of some choice increases motivation. In this case, the focus is on building on individual's personal interest in a particular topic.

   Mr. Kaplan, a middle school social studies teacher, assigns geography projects every year to his students. However, students are allowed to choose their own topic or area of study based on their own personal interests. Some students want to investigate Alaska because their parents visited there once. Others are very interested in Africa because of their heritage. Still others want to explore the Caribbean because they take spring vacations there every year. Although there is quite a bit of diversity in the topics, Mr. Kaplan finds that the students are much more engaged because they end up working on something that connects to their own lives and personal interests.

6. *Build on and integrate student personal interest in designing lessons.* Although there is clearly a diversity of personal interests, many students do share some common interests. When teachers connect the lesson content to personal interests or common interests of the students, it can facilitate attention and situational interest.

Ms. Hofer is a sixth-grade elementary school teacher who was having difficulty getting a group of Latino boys in her class interested in some review of basic arithmetic principles. Although the rest of the class was quite engaged in the games she designed to make the review fun, this group of boys just thought it was boring. However, she did notice that the boys spent many sessions discussing baseball and the different star Latino baseball players in the major leagues. She then designed a set of math activities around computing various baseball statistics like batting average, earned run average, and slugging percentage. She found that although some other students did not like this homework activity, the group of Latino boys got quite engaged in this and actually came to ask for more math homework so they could get better at computing these statistics.

RESEARCH ON TEST ANXIETY

At the beginning of this chapter, both Mr. Anderman and Mr. Lopez discussed the problem of test anxiety and how it can have a negative influence on student performance on tests. Mr. Lopez even talked about how he suffered from it when he was a student. Test anxiety can be a major problem in the classroom at all levels, from elementary through postsecondary classrooms. It represents a type of emotion that can have a negative effect on learning, in contrast to the positive affect that is generated by flow or personal and situational interest. In addition, unlike the recent resurgence of empirical research on interest, test anxiety research has been ongoing since at least the 1950s (Tryon, 1980). In fact, there is a professional organization devoted to research on test anxiety (International Society for Test Anxiety Research), separate journals that are devoted to research on test anxiety (*Anxiety, Stress, and Coping: An International Journal*), and a number of edited books on the problems of anxiety and stress (e.g., Hagtvet & Johnsen, 1992; Schwarzer, van der Ploeg, & Spielberger, 1989). More recently, Zeidner (1998) has provided an excellent and comprehensive state-of-the-art review of the research on test anxiety. Anyone interested in more detail on the role of test anxiety needs to start with the Zeidner text. Given all the research on test anxiety and the all-encompassing text by Zeidner (1998), we do not attempt to provide a detailed discussion of the construct and how it can influence classroom performance, but will highlight some important issues about test anxiety.

Defining Test Anxiety

In terms of the definition of test anxiety, there are a number of important issues to consider. First, a general definition of anxiety is "an unpleasant feeling or emotional state that has physiological and behavioral concomitants, and that is experienced in formal testing or other evaluative situations" (Dusek, 1980, p. 88). Test anxiety is a more specific form of this generalized evaluative anxiety in reference to specific test situations. Zeidner (1998) defines **test anxiety** as a set of phenomenological, physiological, and behavioral responses that accompany concern about possible negative consequences or failure on an exam or similar evaluative situation. The phenomenological aspect of the construct usually includes cognitive and emotional components. The cognitive component is usually called the worry component, and the emotional component is usually labeled as the emotionality, or affective, component (Liebert & Morris, 1967; Wigfield & Eccles, 1989; Zeidner, 1998). The cognitive, or worry, component refers to the cognitions that accompany anxiety, such as worrying about flunking the test, thinking about the consequences of failing the test (parents being upset, having to drop out of college), worrying about being unable to finish the test, thinking about items that one cannot answer, and thinking about being embarrassed because of a low grade (see Mr. Lopez's comments at the start of this chapter). These are just some of the thoughts that can run through a highly test-anxious person's mind as he or she tries to take a test.

The emotionality component refers to the actual emotional arousal that individuals experience as they take a test, such as fear, general unease, or general uncomfortableness (Zeidner, 1998). This arousal can become a classically conditioned affective reaction to evaluation situations (Wigfield & Eccles, 1989). It should be noted that most people do feel some anxiety when put in a performance situation. For test-anxious individuals, however, the anxiety becomes overwhelming and interferes with their ability to actually perform a task they have mastered in another nonevaluative situation. In the example at the beginning of this chapter, Mr. Lopez recalled how he could do the math problems on the homework (nonevaluative situation) but had difficulties during tests. Many performers (musicians, actors) and athletes may show debilitating effects of anxiety during a performance in contrast to rehearsals or practice. Zeidner (1998) also notes that the physiological aspect can include physiological arousal symptoms like sweaty palms, upset stomach, and faster than usual heartbeat.

In Zeidner's (1998) model of test anxiety, these three components are the most central to test anxiety. However, the behavioral aspect of anxiety can include the various coping mechanisms that people use to deal with their anxiety as well as the ultimate behavioral and cognitive outcomes like task-related thinking, cognition, attention, and actual performance. He also notes that there are both contextual and personal factors that influence the activation of test anxiety. The nature of the testing situation can create cues that can arouse anxiety. In addition, there are a number of personal characteristics (e.g., personal traits, self-efficacy, actual ability, self-regulatory skills, expertise, etc.) that can lead individuals to appraise the same objective "testing" situation in different ways. For some individuals, tests can be seen as a challenge; for others, it is just a very anxiety-arousing situation (Zeidner, 1998).

A second issue related to the definition of test anxiety concerns the stability of test anxiety. Most models of test anxiety propose that there is both a trait of test anxiety and a state of test anxiety (Covington, 1992; Spielberger, 1972; Zeidner, 1998). This dichotomy parallels the distinction between personal interest as a relatively enduring trait of the individual and a more situational interest fostered by external conditions. Trait test anxiety represents a stable, traitlike individual difference; some individuals are much higher on test anxiety across many different situations in comparison with those low on test anxiety. Highly test-anxious individuals tend to experience anxiety in most testing or evaluative situations. These individuals are likely to come into an evaluative situation primed to interpret it and appraise it in an anxiety-arousing manner. Those low in trait anxiety are less likely to appraise the same evaluative situation in such a threatening manner. In contrast, state test anxiety is more situation specific and may be experienced by many or most people in certain stressful situations. For example, taking a college or graduate school admissions test (i.e., the SAT , the ACT, the GRE, the medical or law school exam), which has high importance for most people, will probably generate state test anxiety in many of the test-takers. Besides these high-stakes testing situations, some classrooms (see Hill & Wigfield, 1984) in which testing, grading, and competition are emphasized can generate high levels of state test anxiety in many students. Of course, most test anxiety models also predict that people who are high in trait test anxiety will be even more anxious in these types of anxiety-arousing situations.

Effects on Learning and Performance

The empirical research on the negative effects of anxiety on academic performance is quite large and consistent (Zeidner, 1998). Hembree (1988), in a meta-analysis of 562 studies that related test anxiety and academic achievement, found that test anxiety does cause poor performance, is negatively related to self-esteem, and is directly related to students' defensiveness and fear of negative evaluation. Hill and Wigfield (1984) report that studies have found correlations up to $-.60$ between test anxiety and achievement, suggesting that anxiety and achievement share significance variance. Moreover, Hill and Wigfield estimate that in most classrooms, about 10% of the children will have a relatively high level of trait anxiety, which translates into about two to three children per classroom. By their estimates, between 4 and 5 million children in elementary and secondary schools in the United States will have to cope with high test anxiety. Hill and Wigfield also suggest that another 10–15% of the children in any classroom, although not in the top 10% of the population in test anxiety, will experience some anxiety. Taken together, this resulting estimate that 25% of the children in classrooms will have some problems with anxiety means that approximately 10 million children in the United States could be affected by test anxiety. Accordingly, there is a need to understand how test anxiety works and what can be done about it in classrooms (Wigfield & Eccles, 1989).

A number of mechanisms or models have been suggested by researchers to explain how anxiety influences learning and performance (Zeidner, 1998). Given that many empirical studies have shown that the worry component is more closely linked to performance decrements than the emotionality component (Covington, 1992; Tryon, 1980), explanations have tended to focus on the role of the worry component. Tobias (1985) has provided a model that integrates two explanations of the effects of test anxiety. One explanation has been that anxiety interferes with attention (see Wine, 1971; Zeidner, 1998) because all of the negative thoughts and worry distract the individual from the task. Given the limited capacity of working memory, these distracting thoughts take up cognitive/attentional resources that could be used to work on the task at hand (the test). In some ways, these students would suffer at the retrieval phase in an information-processing model because they would not be able to recall needed information in order to do well on the test, even if they knew it before the test (Zeidner, 1998). This explanation includes the first and third pathways on how affect might influence learning that were presented in the first section of this chapter (Pekrun, 1992).

The other explanation has been that highly test-anxious students have deficits in general cognitive learning strategies or test-taking strategies; that is, they don't know how to study very well, don't know how to take a test strategically, and often are not well-prepared for the test. This explanation parallels the second pathway for the effect of emotion on cognition (Pekrun, 1992). This lack of skill can result in retrieval problems. More importantly, this model suggests that the problem is really an encoding problem at the time of learning the material originally. It is not that students just can't remember it well on the exam, it is that these students never learned it very well in the first place (Zeidner, 1998). Tobias (1985) has suggested that these two models are complementary given our limited cognitive capacity. He suggests that when students do have good study skills and test-taking strategies, more working memory capacity will be freed up to cope with any negative thoughts and worry generated by high test anxiety. In contrast, if students don't have those skills, the worry generated by high test anxiety does interfere with attention and cognitive processing and there is a concomitant drop in performance. Much research needs to be done to tease apart these different explanations, but research that focuses on the interactive nature of anxiety and cognition, learning and coping strategies, and self-regulation is promising. In fact, the most recent models of test anxiety are based in self-regulation theory or coping/appraisal models that combine both explanations and focus on how strategies, including cognitive and metacognitive strategies, as well as motivational and emotional coping strategies, are used (or not used) in testing situations (Zeidner, 1998). For example, Schutz and Davis (2000) present a detailed model of how emotions, including test anxiety, are related to the use of various cognitive and emotional regulatory strategies in a classroom context. This type of model will be in the vanguard of future research on not only test anxiety, but all emotions and affect in the classroom.

In terms of how the classroom situation can create state anxiety, Hill and Wigfield (1984) and Wigfield and Eccles (1989) discuss a number of features of the classroom that can heighten anxiety for children. First, they note that many classroom and standardized achievement tests have time limits that create pressure on students to finish within a certain amount of time. The lack of time (or perceived lack of time) can increase students' anxiety, particularly if anxious students spend part of the testing time worrying about their performance. This distraction will not only reduce cognitive attentional capacity, it will reduce the amount of overall time spent thinking about the test. In addition, these tests are often introduced or discussed in terms of students' relative ability, which can heighten social comparison and anxiety. Finally, Hill and Wigfield (1984) note that the format and mechanics of the tests can be unfamiliar to students or more difficult than their usual schoolwork.

Wigfield and Eccles (1989) note that classrooms that have overly high standards for evaluation are associated with higher levels of anxiety (cf. Helmke, 1988; Zatz & Chassin, 1985). Research on aptitude-treatment interactions (ATIs) suggests that organized instruction and fairly easy tasks can help anxious students learn better, whereas less organized and student-centered instruction may not work as well with anxious students (Cronbach & Snow, 1977; Tobias, 1980; Wigfield & Eccles, 1989). Moreover, general changes in grading practices as students move into secondary schools, where grading systems are more normative and strict, can increase student anxiety over testing and evaluation. Finally, standardized testing and grades do become more salient and have greater real consequences in later grades in secondary schools, thereby increasing anxiety (Wigfield & Eccles, 1989). Important as all of these contextual factors are in increasing the probability that students might feel anxious, Zeidner (1998) also points out that current models of anxiety stress that the most important factor is how the context is perceived and appraised by the individual student. That is, it is not just the "objective" classroom environment that is important, but how students perceive and judge the classroom in terms of how anxiety-arousing it will be to different students. This general perception-mediating model is in line with all of the models of motivation discussed in this book.

Interventions

Hill and Wigfield (1984) summarize a number of studies that attempted to change school or classroom use of tests and report cards. These studies suggest that very simple things like removing time constraints from classroom tests can help anxious students perform better. Of course, this may not be easy when classes are only 45–50 minutes long, as in secondary classrooms compared to elementary classrooms. However, teachers can develop creative ways to change their test format to ensure that all students have enough time to demonstrate their mastery. If demonstrating mastery of the material is the most important aspect of the assessment, the amount of time taken to do so should not be an issue, particularly given individual differences in students' speed and ability to perform. In addition, Hill and Wigfield suggest that reducing the amount of importance that teachers place on tests as a sign of ability and decreasing the opportunities for social comparison of report card grades and test grades (no public displays of grades) can help to create a less anxious classroom climate.

In addition to changing the classroom climate and structure, a large number of studies that have attempted to change students' coping strategies for dealing with anxiety (Wigfield & Eccles, 1989; Zeidner, 1998). These interventions would include the "tricks" that Mr. Lopez said that his math teacher taught him. Some of these intervention or treatment studies have mainly addressed the emotionality component, others have addressed the cognitive or worry component, and some have attempted to address both components (Tryon, 1980; Zeidner, 1998). Treatments aimed at the emotionality component usually attempt some type of desensitization to the negative affect generated in the situation, similar to what is done with desensitization of phobics in behavioral therapy. Some studies have also used self-directed relaxation techniques to help students cope with the negative affect and anxiety (Zeidner, 1998). Tryon (1980) suggests that these studies have had mixed success, and it may be due to the fact that by addressing only the emotionality component, they are not considering the worry component, which is more closely associated with actual decrements in performance.

Interventions that have been aimed at the worry component have included direct study and strategy skills training, cognitive behavioral self-regulation to control the unwanted and distracting thoughts, and motivational or attributional training to help students control and manage their anxiety (Zeidner, 1998). These more cognitive treatments have shown somewhat stronger positive effects on reducing anxiety and improving performance, but most researchers (e.g., Hill & Wigfield, 1984; Tryon, 1980; Zeidner, 1998) suggest that interventions need to address both emotionality and worry components through a diversity of methods. For example, Hill and Wigfield outline a school-based anxiety reduction program that includes training in both study and test-taking skills as well as motivational and attributional training. It seems likely that these types of ecologically valid programs that address the multiple aspects of anxiety in the classroom will be more successful than single treatment or simpler interventions. Wigfield and Eccles (1989) note that these anxiety intervention programs need to become more integrated into the school curriculum, be sensitive to developmental differences, and develop strategies targeted to help the diverse problems that different types of test-anxious students have (skills training versus anxiety control).

Application 7.3 provides some specific suggestions for decreasing test anxiety in the classroom.

APPLICATION 7.3

Applying Test Anxiety Research in the Classroom

There are a large number of strategies that can be used to reduce test anxiety in the classroom. Zeidner (1998) provides a good listing of many strategies. We provide a few here.

1. *Provide more time to complete the test.* The loosening of time requirements seems to help many text-anxious students. Mr. Wolters, an eighth-grade math teacher, makes arrangements for some students to have a longer period of time to complete his end-of-unit tests. He knows his tests usually take about 40–45 minutes of his 50-minute period for most students. However, several students need more time to take the tests because of their test anxiety. He allows them to continue to work on the test into the next class period. His next class is not disrupted because they also are taking the same end-of-unit test. Mr. Wolters always explains to the other teachers why some of the students will be a little late to their next class.

2. *Modify test item difficulty and order.* As noted throughout this book, tasks (including tests) should be matched closely to student expertise—challenging, but not overwhelmingly difficult. This principle also applies to anxiety. Tasks that are too difficult create anxiety; test items that are too difficult create test anxiety. It helps to not only have items that are matched to student skill level, but also to have items progress in difficulty level, from easier items at the start of the test to harder items later in the test.

   Mr. Middleton, a high school history teacher, designs his multiple choice tests so that easier items are at the beginning and harder items are at the end. He finds this helps all students "warm up" to the task, and especially those who are very nervous. As they start the test, they have some success and thus feel more comfortable. Their anxiety dissipates and they can then progress more easily through the test.

3. *Provide students opportunities to comment on test or test items.* When some students can write comments on test items, particularly ambiguous ones or difficult ones, it seems to help them perform better.

   Ms. Bien always provides space on the test for students to make comments about their thoughts about the items, their difficulty, etc. Students like this and seem to feel less anxiety because of it.

4. *Reduce social comparison and public display of test scores.* When teachers and students have public access to test scores (i.e., through listing on public bulletin boards, by the public calling out of scores in front of whole class), it can create many opportunities

for social comparison among students. In this case, students know how others did and they may begin to make negative and maladaptive comparisons and attributions for their own or others' performance. Teachers should strive to reduce social comparison and have students make appropriate attributions for test performance.

Ms. Knieper does not post student scores on bulletin boards and he always talks about test performance as a function of effort and actual skill, not general ability.

5. *Reduce the performance-oriented nature of testing situations to focus on mastery and formative assessment purposes.* If teachers discuss tests as ways of beating out others, as a competition that only a few can win (grading on a strict curve), this can create anxiety for all students, let alone high-anxious students.

Mr. Carlisle is careful to discuss tests as opportunities for all students to demonstrate what they have learned and as a way for him to evaluate his teaching. He also notes how the information from tests can help students go back and relearn what they have not mastered. The evaluation also provides him with information that he might need to reteach certain concepts if most of the students are not mastering them on the test.

RESEARCH ON SELF-WORTH

The construct of **self-worth,** or as it is more often called in popular views, **self-esteem,** concerns individuals' affect or emotions toward or evaluation of themselves. We have discussed emergent motivation and situational and personal interest models that focus on affect that is directed toward tasks or activities. Self-worth or self-esteem concerns the feelings we have about ourselves. At the beginning of this chapter, Ms. Duncan invokes self-esteem as an explanation for some students' motivational problems. Although it is often confounded in popular views with self-perceptions of ability, self-esteem should *not* be confused with individuals' perceptions of their own competence or efficacy, which are more cognitive appraisals or beliefs about the self (see chapters 2 and 4). In contrast, the research on self-esteem usually suggests that self-esteem is a more affective or emotional reaction to the self. It can mean taking pride in yourself and your behavior, feeling good about yourself and accomplishments, and having a general positive image of yourself. In addition, self-esteem is usually a more diffuse and less specific reaction to the self than a specific appraisal of personal ability to do a specific task or of competence in a specific domain (Harter, 1985a, 1990). Accordingly, a person could believe that he is not very good at tennis (a low perception of tennis competence), but this would not necessarily influence his overall positive or negative feeling toward himself as a person, as long as tennis is not that important to him. Harter (1985a, 1990) has proposed that self-worth can be linked differentially to a number of different domains across the life span rather than linked to all domains in a global and diffuse fashion.

This distinction is often lost in the popular views of self-esteem, not just in schools but in many domains of life, much to the detriment of our understanding of motivation and how self-beliefs can play a role in influencing behavior. For example, on many TV talk shows or in popular self-help books, high self-esteem is offered as the major panacea for all individual problems. The basic argument is that poor or low self-esteem is the root of all problems, whether they be child abuse, spousal abuse, substance abuse, weight or body image problems, marital infidelity, delinquency, personal unemployment, criminality, learning problems, or just personal unhappiness and depression. Given this assumption, it then follows that increasing self-esteem will result in the remediation of these problems. As Lazarus (1991) notes, this logic leads people to believe that they will avoid these problems by rehearsing simple positive statements about the self (i.e., "I'm a good person, student, or worker") or having others give them the same type of non-contingent positive feedback. Of course, any view this simplistic is absurd in the face of the complexity of these problems (see Crocker & Wolfe, 2001).

The difficulty is that in U.S. schools today, many teachers do subscribe to this simplistic view, reflecting the emphasis it receives in our popular culture. Teachers are often afraid to say anything negative to students about their performance because they believe it will hurt the students' self-esteem. There are schools and classrooms that engage in self-esteem programs whereby children are asked to chant positive statements about themselves in order to enhance self-esteem (cf. Ms. Duncan's comments at the beginning of this chapter) or teachers are directed to give unconditional positive feedback to all students. In contrast to these popular but misleading views of self-esteem, Covington (see Covington, 1992, 1998; Covington & Beery, 1976) has proposed a model of self-worth that is based on current theoretical views of student motivation. He has developed a program of empirical research that helps us understand self-worth in school contexts.

Covington (1992) proposes that the need for self-worth is a basic need of all individuals. This need is represented in the universal search for self-acceptance. Covington notes that in our society, worth for school-age children is often determined by their academic achievements, and is often assessed in competitive ways (i.e., doing better than other students). To the extent that children internalize or accept this general societal value, their self-worth will depend on their school achievement. Covington then suggests that the need for self-worth will generate a number of different patterns of motivational beliefs and behaviors. First, Covington (1992) shows that children and adults will often want to make attributions to ability for their successes because they increase self-worth more than do attributions to hard work. In this case, the need for self-worth is driving the types of attributions individuals make in a situation, an important addition to the standard model of attribution theory, which does not really include the possibility that personal needs can influence the attribution process (see chapter 3). In fact, Covington suggests that individuals will often try to hide how much effort they put forth on a task so that others will think they simply have high ability. For example, some students will not tell their peers that they studied hard for a test. If they then do well, the usual attributional logic is that they must have high ability because they did not study hard (Covington, 1992, 1998).

In addition, Covington (1992, 1998) has shown that students will often engage in self-handicapping patterns of behavior in order to protect their self-worth. For example, students will often procrastinate on studying for an exam or doing a paper or project for a class. If they wait until the last minute to do the work, it is likely that they will not be as successful as they could be. Over the long run, this behavior is self-handicapping because performance is lower than possible. However, from a self-worth and attributional perspective, procrastination can have a positive motivational effect. If the students do poorly, they can attribute their performance to lack of effort, thereby protecting their self-worth because they do not have to conclude they lack ability. At the same time, if they end up doing well, even with the procrastination, they can make an attribution that they must have high ability. Otherwise, how could they explain success with a low level of effort? On the other hand, if they do try hard and don't procrastinate and still do poorly, it is likely that the students will conclude they lack ability and their self-worth will suffer. By combining his self-worth perspective with constructs from attribution theory, Covington shows us that the dynamics of self-worth are much more complicated than simple self-esteem models would have us believe.

Moreover, the issue is not that self-esteem is not an important outcome of schooling. Harter (1998, 1999) has reviewed the research on self-concept and self-esteem and it is clear that these concepts are correlated, albeit they are not the same construct. More importantly, it is clear from developmental research that self-esteem or self-worth often declines over the course of development, and in particular in adolescence (Harter, 1998, 1999). This decline is often accompanied by an increase in depression and other mental health problems (Harter, 1998, 1999). Of course, this decline in self-esteem is not just a function of personal cognitive-developmental changes or contextual changes (transition to middle schools/high schools), but an interaction between the personal and contextual factors. Nevertheless, the fact that self-esteem does decline with age, and it appears that it may decline more for females than for males (see Harter, 1998, 1999), is an important issue. Interestingly, Harter, Waters, and Whitesell (1997) suggest that some of the decline may be a function not of gender status per se, but rather of the individual's endorsement of masculinity-femininity values, with more feminine individuals showing a bigger drop in self-esteem over time.

Accordingly, although schools should be sensitive to these issues of self-esteem and more general issues of mental health (Roeser, 1998; Roeser, Eccles, & Strobel, 1998), the simple, causal linkage of self-esteem to school achievement is questionable. Many laypeople and teachers automatically assume that if self-esteem is important and should be encouraged, they should work on it directly, often by praising the students indiscriminately. By working on increasing self-esteem, they assume that learning, motivation, and achievement will be automatically improved. The causal ordering in this simple model is most likely incorrect, as self-esteem tends to flow from actual accomplishments and achievements, not vice versa. As Damon (1995) points out (and as stated by Mr. Lopez in the opening vignette of this chapter) praising students noncontingently can be detrimental. It leads students to think they should be praised for just being, not for their actual accomplishments and skills. Moreover, in the long run, students will not benefit from this type of empty praise; they will not get feedback on the development of their actual skills and expertise. Without accurate feedback about the development of their skills, it is difficult for students to actually try to change or regulate their behavior. For example, praising students indiscriminately for their reading, even when many of them cannot read very well, to protect their self-esteem, can lead to students who think they can read when they can't. At some point in their lives, they will have to confront the fact they can't read well, and it is better to have them work on improving their reading early in their education, than to find out in adolescence that they lack basic literacy skills. In addition, although the causal direction is certainly bi-directional (Blumenfeld et al., 1982; Wigfield & Karpathian, 1991), it may be easier to actually help students learn the skills and knowledge they need to be successful academically, than to try to boost their self-esteem noncontingently.

SUMMARY

This chapter has covered a great deal of material from a number of different theories and models on the role of affect and interest in motivation, learning, and performance. We began with a description of the different kinds of affective experiences, including the emotions and moods that individuals might experience in classroom situations. We then discussed four general pathways by which affect might lead to differential learning and performance: (1) affective experiences influence how information is encoded and recalled, (2) affective experiences influence the types of cognitive and self-regulatory strategies used, (3) affective experiences influence attention and working memory resources, and (4) affective experiences influence intrinsic and extrinsic motivation.

The first formal model discussed was Csikszentmihalyi's theory and research on emergent motivation and flow. This model proposes that individuals will experience flow, an intense involvement in an activity, when the challenges of a task are equal to the skills and expertise of the individual. Flow includes both positive affect and emotions as well as deep cognitive involvement. Flow and the positive affect generated in the situation are linked to more engagement, more intrinsic motivation, and generally better performance over time.

Personal and situational interest are two different types of interest that can influence learning and performance. Personal interest is a more stable personality or individual difference variable. Personal interests are directed at specific activities or topics but there is a great deal of variability in what activities or topics will become of personal interest to any one individual. In contrast, situational interest is a more situated view of interest, whereby interest is generated by the features of the immediate environment. Situational interest can be increased by the use of interesting texts, media, presentations, and the like, and is generally assumed to be relatively consistent across individuals. Both personal and situational interest are positively related to choice of future activities, memory, attention, deeper cognitive processing, and actual achievement and performance.

Test anxiety has several components, but the two most important are worry and emotionality components. The worry component refers to the cognitions or thoughts that individuals have when they worry during a test-taking situation. The emotionality component involves the emotional arousal (fear and negative affect) that is often generated in evaluative situations. Paralleling the distinction between personal and situational interest, test anxiety is often divided into trait and state anxiety. Trait anxiety represents a more stable personality characteristic of an individual, whereas state anxiety is a more situational arousal of anxiety due to stressful testing circumstances. Test anxiety has been consistently shown to have a negative effect on academic learning and performance through effects on attention, memory, and strategy use.

Self-esteem and self-worth are emotional reactions to the self. Self-worth refers to emotional reactions or feelings about the self. Popular views of self-esteem are too simplistic to offer much help in our attempts to understand student achievement in the classroom. Covington's (1992) self-worth theory represents an important discussion of the role of self-worth in school learning because of his use of current theoretical models of motivation, such as attribution theory. In addition, his research is based on empirical research with students, not just popular opinions about the role of self-esteem. Self-worth is an important outcome of schooling, but the popular notion that increasing self-esteem will lead to better learning and achievement is not a useful perspective on the relations between self-esteem and school learning.

Teacher and Classroom Influences

L isa McMahan was beginning her sixth year of teaching and she had never felt so discouraged. After 2 months of school, she was ready to give up on her fourth-grade class.
Part of her problem undoubtedly stemmed from her move this past summer to a new community and going to work at an unfamiliar school. But a larger part was due to her interactions—
or lack thereof—with her students. She thought she might be experiencing burnout.

Lisa recalled the day she was at school about a week before classes started to get her room
ready for her children. Betty, an experienced teacher, came by to see how things were going.
She sat down and proceeded to give Lisa the rundown on the students she would have in her
class, and it was quite a cast. Betty told her that Preston was caught stealing over the summer,
Mike had an abusive father, Doris's mother was a drug addict, Kip's brother was in prison,
Lele's father was an alcoholic, Todd ran with an older crowd that some people thought were
gang members, and so forth. Betty said, "You really can't expect much from them. Do your best
but don't go out of your way because they have too many problems to do well in school. No one
will blame you." Betty also told Lisa the names of a few good students worth working with.

When Lisa finally met each of the children, all she could think about was what Betty had
told her. During the first few weeks of school, Lisa acted in accordance with her expectations
for the students created by what Betty had said. She had previously taught average classes; now
in her lesson planning she "dumbed down" the instruction to a level she thought students could
handle. She introduced lessons by noting that the material was tough and some students might
have trouble learning it. When she interacted with students, she asked harder questions of those
who she felt were brighter and easier ones of students whom she thought would have trouble
learning. When she grouped students, she separated the slower ones from the brighter ones.

Not surprisingly, the scenario played out according to her expectations. The students she
expected would learn did learn, the ones she expected would not learn did not. As her low
achievers fell further behind, Lisa felt less motivated to try to help them improve. Discipline
problems increased. No wonder she felt discouraged!

Lisa was enrolled in a master's degree program at a local university. One of the classes
she was taking had a unit on motivation. Included in that unit was a discussion of the role
that teacher expectations and classroom factors play in student motivation. Lisa read with
fascination how research showed that teachers' expectations for students can become self-
fulfilling prophecies: If teachers expect little, students perform worse than when teachers
expect more from them. Lisa shared her teaching experiences with her university class and a
lively discussion ensued. She became so interested in the topic that she chose to write a term
paper on it for the class.

Lisa decided to make some changes in her own teaching. First, she stopped differentiating students and instead assumed that they all could learn. She planned lessons around this new, higher standard of achievement. She introduced units by stating that all students could learn the material if they were willing to work diligently. When she grouped students, she mixed students of different ability levels and ensured that each student in the group had some responsibility for the group's success. She challenged all students based on her perceptions of what would motivate them.

Changes in the class became readily apparent. Some of the students who Betty said could not learn in fact were quite bright and learned easily. Students were more motivated to learn and there were fewer discipline problems in class. Students who had fallen behind began to catch up. Lisa decided not to give up on the class, felt more capable of helping them learn, and realized that this year might not be so bad after all!

Few people would argue with the contention that teachers can affect student motivation. Lisa McMahan's story illustrates some of the ways this can happen. In their planning of instruction and interactions with students, teachers can structure classroom events to have different effects on student motivation. Despite this seemingly powerful influence of teachers, however, only recently have researchers identified the many ways that teachers can affect student motivation. Historically, the function of teachers as motivators was viewed in a narrow sense. Their primary means to motivate students was to dispense such rewards as grades, privileges, praise, prizes, and stickers. This view, which derived from operant conditioning theory (see chapter 1), placed the locus of motivation in the environment. The ultimate goal of an operant system was to have students engage in much independent learning. The teacher arranged materials and students responded and received reinforcement. Learning could occur with little interaction with teachers (Keller, 1968).

Evidence from various sources has altered this role of the teacher. Virtually everything the teacher does has potential motivational impact on students (Stipek, 1996). This includes not only the obvious motivational actions by teachers (e.g., setting goals, rewarding good performances) but also activities typically associated with instruction (e.g., grouping students, questioning strategies) and teacher attempts at classroom management and methods for minimizing and dealing with disciplinary problems. Previous chapters suggested ways that teacher behaviors can influence student motivation.

Another development is increasing recognition of the reciprocal influence between teachers and students. Many early studies of teaching effectiveness assumed that teachers' actions affected student motivation, but there was little effort to determine how students' behaviors influenced teachers (Dunkin & Biddle, 1974). In recent years, research evidence has shown that students influence teachers' thoughts and actions. Teachers' planning and instructional activities affect student cognitions and learning and, in turn, teachers' thoughts and behaviors are influenced by how students react to classroom activities. This point brings to mind Bandura's (1986) emphasis on reciprocal interactions among cognitions, behaviors, and environmental factors (see chapter 4).

We begin this chapter by discussing motivational processes associated with traditional teacher functions of planning and instruction. We then discuss teacher-student interactions and the influence of teacher beliefs. The next area covered, which is receiving increased research emphasis, is how teacher expectations for student learning and performance affect student motivation. As part of this discussion we cover the role of teacher self-efficacy. We conclude by discussing the motivational impact of classroom management practices.

After studying this chapter, you should be able to:

1. Explain the type of planning and decision-making process that teachers seem to employ most often.

2. Describe the key differences among competitive, cooperative, and individualistic grouping structures.

3. State several effective instructional functions and explain why they promote motivation and achievement.

4. Explain how different forms of teacher feedback (performance, motivational, attributional, strategy) affect student motivation.

5. Describe authoritarian, democratic, and laissez-faire leadership styles and their potential consequences for student motivation.

6. Explain how teachers form expectations about students and how expectations may manifest themselves in teacher behaviors to influence student motivation.

7. Define teacher self-efficacy and explain how it relates to student motivation and achievement.

8. Define key variables of classroom management investigated by Kounin (withitness, overlapping, movement management, group focus) and explain why they enhance classroom productivity.

9. Discuss the key differences between unidimensional and multidimensional classrooms and explain their effects on student motivation.

10. Understand the utility of 10 principles of constructivist teaching and explain how they may relate to student cognition and motivation.

TEACHER PLANNING AND DECISION MAKING

Planning and decision making are integral components of teaching. Instructional models incorporate these aspects and relate them to student achievement. Planning and decision making also are relevant to motivation. We discuss models of planning and decision making, followed by the important topic of grouping for instruction.

Models of Planning and Decision Making

Many models of teacher planning are prescriptive and spell out what teachers should do to foster student learning (Clark & Yinger, 1979). They include such steps as specifying learning objectives, selecting teacher and student activities, organizing activities, and delineating evaluation methods. These models are linear and rational in the sense that they assume that planning requires orderly thinking concerning ways to attain objectives. A second type of planning model conceives of planning as beginning with teacher decisions about the types of learning activities to be used. Within this context, objectives arise and are integrated with activities. The means and ends of teaching become integrated, so goals are not specified initially.

Current advances in learning theory and research methodology have led some researchers away from these types of models and toward exploring teachers' thought processes prior to, during, and after teaching (Gagné, Yekovich, & Yekovich, 1993). In this view, planning and decision making are not confined to the preinstructional aspects of teaching but rather occur during all phases of teaching, including while lessons are being conducted. This view is based on information-processing and cognitive theories, which stress the reception, organization, and encoding of information in memory (Anderson, 1990; Gagné et al., 1993). To explore teachers' thought processes, researchers rely on such methods as self-reports through interviews and questionnaires, think-aloud protocols whereby teachers verbalize while planning, and stimulated recall procedures in which teachers comment on their thought processes while planning and teaching as they watch videotapes of their performances (see chapter 1).

Teachers' planning is strongly influenced by the characteristics of their students, such as needs, abilities, and motivation (Clark & Peterson, 1986; Clark & Yinger, 1979). Teachers are concerned with not only how to foster attainment of objectives given the abilities and competence of the students, but also how much the instruction and activities will appeal to students' interests. When teachers take interest into account, it is often the case that student activities do not follow logically from specification of objectives and that the latter is not always an important component of planning (Zahorik, 1975).

Motivational concerns are important in teachers' decision making. Clark and Yinger (1979) reported a study in which elementary school teachers rated potential language arts teaching activities in terms of how likely they were to use each activity in their classrooms. For those activities rated highly, teachers listed features that contributed to their decisions. The most frequently mentioned category involved students—especially their motivation and involvement.

Similar importance of motivation is found in studies examining teachers' decisions while they are engaged in instruction. In one study (Clark & Yinger, 1979), teachers viewed videotaped segments of their teaching and were asked to recall what they were thinking about at that particular time. Some important findings were that teachers considered using alternative teaching strategies only when the instruction was not working well and that the main cue teachers used to determine how well instruction was proceeding was the involvement and participation of their students. Thus, teachers considered changing approaches when they noticed that student motivation was lagging. Other research supports the point that teachers' decisions during teaching are heavily influenced by their inferences about students' cognitive and affective processes relevant to motivation (Clark & Yinger, 1979).

In sum, teachers often do not follow a rational planning model because they do not begin planning in relation to specific objectives or goals (Clark & Yinger, 1979). Teachers often begin planning by considering the setting and the content to be taught, after which they shift their attention to motivational concerns (i.e., student participation and involvement). With respect to decisions during teaching, teachers typically deviate little from their plans, but when they do, it is often because of motivational concerns (student interest is lagging).

There exists a reciprocal influence between teachers and students. Teachers affect student motivation and learning through their planning and instruction, but student reactions to instruction cause teachers to take stock of the situation and implement strategies that they believe will have a better effect on motivation and learning.

Instructional Grouping

A critical component of planning is deciding what activities students will work on, which also involves deciding how students will be grouped. Much research has examined the effects of grouping on student motivation (Webb & Palincsar, 1996). Three types of grouping structures are competitive, cooperative, and individualistic.

Competitive situations are those in which the goals of individuals are linked negatively such that if one person attains his or her goal, the chances of others attaining theirs are lessened. *Cooperative* situations are those in which the goals of the group members are linked positively such that one individual can attain his or her goal only if others attain theirs. In *individualistic* situations, there is no link between the goals of individuals; accomplishment or nonaccomplishment of one person's goal has no effect on goal attainment of others (Deutsch, 1949; Johnson & Johnson, 1974; Slavin, 1983a). Table 8.1 presents descriptions and examples of the three types of grouping.

Structures affect student motivation in large part by providing cues that inform students about their capabilities (Ames, 1984; Johnson & Johnson, 1985). Competitive structures accentuate the importance of ability and social comparisons of one person's work with that of others. Motivation is enhanced when students believe they are performing better than others but is weakened for those students who perceive their work as inferior to that of others. In competitive situations, it commonly happens that a few students receive the rewards most of the time. These situations may not motivate many students in the class. In individualistic structures, rewards are based on self-improvement (Ames, 1984). Rather than comparing personal performance with that of others, students compare their present outcomes with their prior performances. Students who notice that they are improving are apt to feel a sense of self-efficacy for

Table 8.1   Instructional Grouping

Arrangement	Description	Example
Competitive	Students' goals negatively linked: One attains one's goal only if others do not attain their's.	Teachers grades "on the curve" and gives 15% of the students A's, 25% of the students B's, and so on.
Cooperative	Students' goals positively linked: One attains one's goal only if others attain their's.	Teacher forms small group to work on project; each student is responsible for completing a part and all students put parts together to form final product.
Individualistic	Students' goals not linked: Attainment or nonattainment has no effect on goal attainment by others.	Students work on computer software programs individually and record completion on their progress sheets.

learning and to be motivated to continue to improve (Schunk, 1989c). In cooperative structures, students share in the successes or failures as a function of their collective performance. The group outcome affects students' perceptions of their capabilities.

Ames (1981) compared competitive and cooperative structures for their effects on children's self-evaluations. In the competitive condition, students were paired and told that the winner would receive a prize; in the cooperative condition, both group members were informed that they would receive prizes if they attained a specific performance goal. Performance outcome was manipulated such that one child in each pair outperformed the other; within the cooperative condition, groups either did or did not attain their goal. The results showed that in cooperative groups, the group outcome had a direct effect on students' perceptions of their ability and feelings of satisfaction. Group success also alleviated negative self-perceptions resulting from poor individual performance, and group failure lowered positive self-perceptions of students who performed well.

This and other research (Ames, 1984) shows that failure in competitive settings has more deleterious effects on self-perceptions than does failure in noncompetitive ones. In cooperative groups, low achievers share in the group success as much as do high achievers. At the same time, however, when cooperative groups fail, dissatisfaction can run high regardless of one's individual performance. For low achievers, successful cooperative groups can help to build self-efficacy, but unsuccessful groups can have the same type of negative effect on self-efficacy as does failure under competitive conditions (Ames & Felker, 1979).

INSTRUCTIONAL PRACTICES

In addition to their planning efforts, how teachers deliver instruction and monitor student performance has an important impact on student motivation. In this section, we review the literature on the influence of teaching practices on student motivation.

Effective Teaching

Research has investigated how teaching practices affect student achievement. In several studies, some teachers were trained to implement various instructional practices in their classrooms and others were not trained and continued to teach in their regular manner. Research, in general, is consistent in showing that teachers trained to implement effective teaching practices raise student achievement more so than untrained teachers (Brophy & Good, 1986).

Rosenshine and Stevens (1986) reviewed research on how effective teachers teach structured content whereby the objectives are to attain knowledge or master skills that can be taught in step-by-step fashion or to acquire general rules that students might apply to new problems or content. Examples are arithmetic facts and computation, decoding skills, grammar and vocabulary, musical notation, map reading, solving algebraic equations, mechanics of letter writing, and factual aspects of history and science. These findings are summarized in Table 8.2.

The results are consistent with principles of contemporary cognitive theories of learning (Anderson, 1990; Gagné et al., 1993). For example, by beginning lessons with short reviews of prior relevant material and stating learning objectives, teachers help to

Table 8.2   Effective Teaching Practices for Structured Content

---

- Begin lessons with a short review of prerequisite learning and a statement of goals.
- Present new material in small steps and give students practice after each step.
- Give clear, detailed instructions and explanations.
- Provide students with high levels of active practice.
- Ask questions, check for student understanding, and obtain responses from all students.
- Guide students during initial practice.
- Provide systematic feedback and corrective instruction.
- Provide explicit instruction and practice for seatwork exercises; monitor students during seatwork.

Material drawn from Rosenshine and Stevens (1986).

activate information in students' long-term memory and provide them with a cognitive structure for encoding the new material. Information processing is easier for students as they integrate new information with the prior learning and thereby build better organized mental networks of knowledge. Presenting material in small steps and allowing student practice ensures that students' information-processing capabilities are not overloaded and that the students can effectively process information and store it in memory before more material is presented. Practice is a form of rehearsal that helps to organize and store information in memory. With repeated practice, material is learned and skills can be executed with little conscious attention, which frees space in working memory for new learning. Clear explanations and demonstrations ensure that students understand the content and do not engage in complex mental processing to determine what the teacher has said. Asking students questions, checking for understanding, monitoring students' work, and providing corrective feedback ensure that learning has occurred properly and serve to correct errors before faulty knowledge is acquired.

Some steps are more important for certain learners and types of content (Rosenshine & Stevens, 1986). For example, use of small steps helps students with learning problems, all learners during the early stages of learning, and young children who have developmental limitations in information-processing capabilities. Presenting material in small steps ensures that students are not mentally overloaded with information, which could result in faulty learning. Younger students may need more practice and feedback. With development, the amount of presentation time can increase relative to practice because older students rehearse and encode information more effectively. All of these points apply best to material that is hierarchically ordered, such that more advanced skills build on mastery of basic skills, and to difficult material for which a small-step approach and much student practice facilitate learning.

By integrating learning research with research on teaching, Rosenshine and Stevens (1986) developed the following list of fundamental instructional functions:

1. Review; check previous day's work; reteach as necessary.
2. Present new material.
3. Give students guided practice; check for understanding.
4. Provide feedback; reteach if needed.

5. Give students independent practice.

6. Review at spaced (weekly, monthly) intervals.

These instructional procedures should promote student motivation and achievement. The review of previous material helps prepare students for new learning and creates an initial sense of self-efficacy for learning. Students are apt to believe that if they understand prerequisite material, they will be able to learn the new material. Presenting new material, especially in small steps, allows them to be successful, and successful performances constitute an important means for sustaining student motivation to learn (Schunk, 1991a, 1995). Teacher feedback is another source of self-efficacy information. Teachers who tell students they are performing well or give corrective information help substantiate students' self-efficacy for learning. Independent practice increases efficacy; students who can succeed on their own feel efficacious about learning and are motivated to continue to improve. Periodic reviews in which students perform well convey that students have learned and retained the information, which enhances motivation for further learning because it validates students' beliefs about their competence (Schunk, 1989c).

Use of Models

Models are important influences on student motivation (Bandura, 1986; Schunk, 1987; see chapter 4). Teachers-as-models provide a vicarious source of self-efficacy information for students. Students who observe teachers explain and demonstrate concepts and skills are apt to believe that they are capable of learning. As students follow teacher explanations and mentally rehearse operations, they may believe that they are learning the material, especially if teachers present material in manageable units and provide clear explanations.

Teachers also provide persuasive information to students. Consider the following example of how a teacher might introduce a lesson:

Today we are going to learn how to add fractions with like denominators. For the past few days, we have been discussing fractions and you all know how to add numbers. We will see that adding fractions with like denominators requires you to do things that you already can do. So I know that everyone will be able to learn how to add fractions.

This introduction should lead students to believe they are capable of learning. Their self-efficacy is validated as they work on the task and experience success. Teachers also enhance motivation through the use of interesting displays and presentations that capture and hold student attention. Attention is a critical component of learning and the interest generated is motivational. Finally, teachers often provide information about why learning is important. Teachers who inform students about why learning is important and how it will help them on different tasks, motivate students to attend to material, organize and rehearse information to be remembered, and use the material as needed.

Peers as models also impact student motivation (Schunk, 1987; see chapter 4). Observing a similar peer performing a task well instates a sense of self-efficacy. Students believe that if peers can succeed, they can as well. This sense of self-efficacy motivates students to work on the task productively and is validated as students experience success. The number of models used is an important variable in modeling (Schunk et al., 1987). Compared with a single model, multiple models increase the probability that observers will perceive themselves as similar to at least one of the models (Thelen et al., 1979). Students who might discount the successes of a single model due to dissimilarity in important characteristics (e.g., abilities) may be influenced by observing several peers accomplishing a task.

Another way to raise efficacy is to use *coping* models, who initially demonstrate the typical fears and deficiencies of observers but gradually improve their performance and gain confidence. Coping models show how effort and positive self-thoughts overcome difficulties. In contrast, *mastery* models demonstrate faultless performance and high confidence from the outset (Schunk, 1987). Coping models enhance perceived similarity and self-efficacy among students who view the coping models' initial difficulties and gradual progress as more similar to their typical performances than the rapid learning of mastery models.

TEACHER-STUDENT INTERACTIONS

Classrooms are active places where teachers and students constantly interact with one another. Teachers ask questions, provide feedback, administer rewards and punishments, praise and criticize, respond to students' questions and requests for help, and offer assistance when students experience difficulties. In this section, we discuss how these interactions affect student motivation.

Teacher Feedback

Teacher feedback is a major teaching function (Rosenshine & Stevens, 1986). Various types of teacher feedback are summarized in Table 8.3.

Performance Feedback

Performance feedback is feedback on the accuracy of work and may include corrective information. Performance feedback is an important influence on student learning.

Table 8.3 Teacher Feedback

Type	Description	Examples
Performance	Provides information on accuracy of work; may include corrective information	"That's correct." "The first part is right but you need to bring down the next number."
Motivational	Provides information on progress and competence; may include social comparisons and persuasion	"You've gotten much better at this. You are doing a great job." "I know you can do this."
Attributional	Links student performance with one or more attributions	"You're good at this." "You've been working hard and you're doing well."
Strategy	Informs students about how well they are applying a strategy and how strategy use is improving their work	"You got it right because you used the steps in the right order." "The five-step method is helping you do better."

Teachers give performance feedback following four types of student responses (Rosen-shine & Stevens, 1986): (1) a correct answer given quickly and firmly; (2) a correct answer given hesitantly; (3) an incorrect answer reflecting a careless error; and (4) an incorrect answer suggesting lack of knowledge of facts or a process.

Students are likely to respond correctly in a quick and firm fashion during the later stages of learning and during reviews. Teacher feedback conveying accuracy of the response (e.g., "Right") is informative. Research suggests that teachers should then ask a new question and maintain the momentum of the lesson. Student responses that are correct but hesitant are more likely during the earlier stages of learning—during guided or independent practice and when teachers check for understanding. Teachers need to provide confirmatory feedback ("Correct" "Good"), and may need to provide feedback covering the process used to arrive at the correct answer. This process feedback also informs other students who may be unsure of what they are doing (Rosenshine & Stevens, 1986).

When students make careless errors, teachers should provide corrective feedback but not explain the process again (Rosenshine & Stevens, 1986). Student errors indicating lack of knowledge of facts or the process are likely during the early stages of learning. In this circumstance, teachers can either provide students with prompts to lead them to the correct answer or reteach the material to the students who do not understand. If the teacher is leading the class, it seems helpful to attempt to lead the student to the correct answer with hints or simple questions; however, such interactions are most effective if they remain brief (30 seconds or less). Longer personal contacts tend to lose the attention of the rest of the class. If the student cannot be guided to a correct answer through a brief contact, it is necessary to reteach the content to that student and others who do not understand, for example, when the other students engage in independent practice.

Reteaching and leading students to the correct answer are effective ways to promote learning (Rosenshine & Stevens, 1986). Asking simpler questions and giving hints are useful when the contact can be kept short (Anderson, Evertson, & Brophy, 1979). Reteaching is helpful when errors are made by many students during a lesson (Good & Grouws, 1979). With a small group, the teacher will reteach the entire group. With a large group when only some of the students require assistance, the teacher should reteach when the others are engaged with the material (Arlin & Webster, 1983). Alternatively, reteaching can be scheduled during breaks (lunch, recess), and peers can reteach the material in groups.

Feedback informing students that answers are correct motivates because it indicates that the students are becoming more competent and are capable of further learning (Schunk, 1989c). Feedback indicating an error can also build motivation and efficacy if followed by corrective information showing the student how to perform better. Such feedback engenders the belief that students will perform better by using the method demonstrated by the teacher. The belief of individuals that they are capable of learning raises motivation and leads to better skill acquisition.

Motivational Feedback

Teachers often provide students with feedback designed to motivate rather than to inform about accuracy of answers. One type of **motivational feedback** provides social comparative information about capabilities of other students. A teacher might remark to Kevin, "See how well Mark is doing. Why don't you try to work like that?" Another common type of motivational feedback is persuasive and takes the form of such statements as, "I know you can do this," and, "Keep up the good work." Although both forms of feedback indirectly convey information about competence, their primary function is to get students to work on tasks and maintain productive task engagement.

The vicarious information provided with social comparisons and persuasive feedback is an important source of self-efficacy information (Bandura, 1986; Schunk, 1989c; see chapter 4). Observing similar others succeed raises observers' self-efficacy and motivates them to persevere at the task. Once students become engaged in the task and experience success, this initial sense of efficacy is substantiated and motivation improves. Similarity is especially influential in situations in which individuals have experienced difficulties and hold doubts about performing well. Positive persuasive feedback also creates feelings of efficacy. Students experience high efficacy when told they are capable of learning by a trustworthy source such as the teacher but may discount the advice of less credible sources. Students also may discount otherwise trustworthy sources if they believe the sources do not fully understand the task demands (e.g., difficult for students to comprehend) or contextual factors (room is too noisy or too warm).

The effects of vicarious and persuasive sources on self-efficacy are generally weaker than those due to actual performances, so it is imperative that increases in self-efficacy derived from vicarious and persuasive sources be confirmed by subsequent performance successes. Information derived from these sources that is not confirmed loses its impact.

Attributional Feedback

Attributional feedback links student performance with one or more attributions (perceived causes of outcomes) in an attempt to facilitate motivation (Schunk, 1989c; see chapter 3). Some students who have difficulty during the early stages of learning attribute the difficulty to low ability. Students who believe they lack the ability to perform well may work in a lackadaisical fashion and give up readily. These negative motivational effects retard learning. Teachers may train students to attribute their difficulties instead to controllable factors (e.g., low effort, improper strategy use).

The role of effort has received special attention. If students believe they failed in the past because of low ability, they may not expend much effort to succeed in the future. If they attribute failure to low effort, however, they may work harder because effort is controllable and they may believe that more effort will lead to better outcomes. Several research studies show that students can be taught to attribute outcomes to effort and that effort feedback produces beneficial effects on self-efficacy, motivation, and skills (Andrews & Debus, 1978; Dweck, 1975; Relich, Debus, & Walker, 1986; Schunk, 1982; Schunk & Cox, 1986; Schunk & Rice, 1986). Linking children's prior achievements with effort (e.g., "You've been working hard") enhances motivation, self-efficacy, and skills better than linking future achievement with effort ("You need to work hard") or not providing effort feedback (see chapters 3 and 4). Effort feedback must be perceived by recipients as credible; that is, students realistically need to work hard to succeed, as in the early stages of learning or when working on difficult material.

Effort feedback may be especially useful for students with learning problems. When students generally must work hard to succeed, effort feedback for success is credible and likely to raise self-efficacy for skill acquisition (Schunk & Cox, 1986). Effort feedback is also highly credible and motivating for young children, who tend to attribute successes to effort. Around the age of 9, however, they begin to form a distinct conception of ability (Nicholls, 1978, 1979; see chapter 3). Ability attributions become increasingly important with development, whereas the influence of effort declines (Harari & Covington, 1981). Schunk (1983a) found that among average-achieving elementary school children, ability feedback for prior successes ("You're good at this") enhanced self-efficacy and skill better than did effort feedback or effort-plus-ability feedback. Combining the two types of feedback may lead children to discount some of the ability information in favor of effort. Children may think that their ability cannot be too high if they have to work hard to succeed. Schunk (1984) found that ability feedback given for initial learning successes raised achievement outcomes better than did effort feedback regardless of whether ability feedback is continued later on.

Strategy Feedback

Strategy feedback informs learners about how well they are applying a strategy and how strategy use improves their performance (Pressley et al., 1990). Strategies help learners attend to tasks, focus on important features, organize material, and maintain a productive psychological climate for learning (Weinstein & Mayer, 1986). Because it leads to better performance, strategy use raises self-efficacy and motivation. Use of strategies relates positively to achievement and self-efficacy (Borkowski, Carr, Rellinger, & Pressley, 1990; Pintrich & De Groot, 1990a; Zimmerman & Martinez-Pons, 1992).

Of course, simply teaching students a strategy does not ensure that they will use it. Failure to employ a strategy may result from the belief that the strategy, although useful, is not as important as such other factors as time available or effort expended. Strategy value information is information about the usefulness of a strategy as an aid to performance (Paris, Lipson, & Wixson, 1983; Pressley et al., 1990). Teachers who provide students with strategy value feedback help engender the belief that they are learning a useful strategy, which can raise self-efficacy and motivate learners to continue applying it (Schunk, 1989c). Strategy value feedback promotes achievement outcomes and strategy use better than instruction alone (Borkowski et al., 1988; Kurtz & Borkowski, 1987; Paris, Newman, & McVey, 1982).

Schunk and Rice (1987) taught a reading comprehension strategy to children with low reading skills. Children given multiple forms of strategy value information stressing both the general usefulness of the strategy as an aid to performance and its specific value for the task at hand developed higher self-efficacy and skill than did students who received either type of information alone. Schunk and Rice (1987) also found that combining specific strategy value information with feedback linking students' improved performance with strategy use (e.g., "You got it right because you followed the steps in the right order") led to higher self-efficacy and skill compared with providing either specific information or strategy feedback. Schunk and Swartz (1993) found that strategy feedback benefited students' self-efficacy and writing skills.

Strategy feedback is actually a type of attributional feedback because it conveys strategy attributions by linking outcomes with use of the strategy's steps. Strategy feedback can be combined effectively with effort feedback (e.g., "That's correct. You're working hard and using the steps properly").

Rewards

Teachers dispense a variety of rewards to students for exemplary behavior and academic performance: grades, privileges, honors, free time, points or tokens exchangeable for other things, stickers, and stars. Rewards occupy a prominent place in motivation theory and research (see the discussion in chapter 6 regarding rewards and intrinsic motivation). In Skinner's (1953) operant conditioning theory (see chapter 1), rewarding (reinforcing) the consequences of behavior may strengthen the behavior and increase its likelihood of occurring in the future. Responses to stimuli that are reinforced will be repeated; those that are punished will not.

Bandura (1986) challenged this view as an incomplete perspective on how rewards affect motivation. It is not the reward itself that is important, but rather the individual's belief about the consequences of behavior. Based on their personal experiences and observations of models, people develop beliefs about likely outcomes of actions (see chapter 4). Rewards are motivating because people expect that behaving in a given fashion will be rewarded. This belief, coupled with perceived importance or value of the reward, leads people to act in ways they believe will result in reward attainment.

Perceived similarity can enhance motivational effects. Observers who see models rewarded become motivated to act accordingly. These motivational effects depend in part on self-efficacy (see chapter 4). Observing similar others succeed raises observers' self-efficacy and motivates them to perform the task. Such motivational effects are common in classrooms. Students who observe other students performing a task well may become motivated to try their best.

Rewards can also inform learners about their progress in skill acquisition and thereby sustain motivation (see chapter 6). Rewards that are contingent on students' actual accomplishments are likely to enhance self-efficacy. Telling students that they can earn rewards based on what they accomplish instills a sense of self-efficacy for performing well, which is validated as they work on the task and perceive they are making progress. Receipt of the reward further validates self-efficacy because it symbolizes progress. When teachers reward students for time spent working regardless of how well they perform, rewards may convey negative efficacy information and be detrimental to motivation (Morgan, 1984). Students might infer that they are not expected to learn much because they lack the ability. During mathematics instruction, Schunk (1983d) found that giving students rewards commensurate with their skillful performances enhanced motivation, self-efficacy, and achievement, whereas offering rewards for task participation regardless of the level of performance led to no benefits.

In chapter 6, we discussed the potential deleterious effect on intrinsic interest of offering students rewards for performing tasks they enjoy (Lepper & Greene, 1978). Less has been written about ways to help students develop interest. The development of interest depends in part on an enhanced sense of competence for the activity (Lepper & Hodell, 1989). Performance-contingent rewards may raise interest when they promote students' perceptions of learning progress and self-efficacy (Schunk, 1989c).

Classroom Climate

Classroom climate refers to the atmosphere of the classroom—its social, psychological, and emotional characteristics (Dunkin & Biddle, 1974). The importance of classroom climate as it relates to motivation derives from the notion that teaching is leadership intended to affect classroom behavior. Classroom climate is often described using such terms as "warm," "cold," "permissive," "democratic," "autocratic," and "learner-centered." The climate in the classroom is largely established through teacher-student interactions.

A classic study by Lewin, Lippitt, and White (1939) showed how different forms of leadership affect motivation and behavior. Although this study was not conducted in a school, the results have classroom implications. Adult leaders supervised 10-year-old boys as they worked on group construction projects (e.g., making masks). The boys were exposed to three different forms of leadership. The authoritarian (autocratic) leader was cold and harsh, took control and told the boys what to do, assumed full responsibility, and did not allow the boys to make contributions. The democratic (collaborative) leader worked with the boys cooperatively, stimulated them about how to complete the projects, posed questions, and had them share ideas. Although the leader assumed ultimate responsibility for the outcomes, he encouraged problem solving and decision making by the boys. The laissez-faire (permissive) leader used a hands-off approach and let the boys work on tasks with minimal supervision. He did not take responsibility for the tasks and did not provide structure, suggestions, or assistance in completing the projects.

Group productivity was highest with the authoritarian and democratic styles. Under the authoritarian leader, the boys followed the instructions and completed the tasks. Although effective, this group was characterized by anxiety and tension, submission, and overt rebellion. When the leader was present, productivity was high, but when the leader was absent, productivity dropped and aggression and destructive behavior resulted. The laissez-faire group showed the lowest productivity because it was essentially leaderless. The boys did not achieve consensus on their goals and worked individually without being organized. They seemed to enjoy their work but there was hostility and scapegoating and little was accomplished.

The boys preferred the democratic style of leadership. The democratic leader produced a group that was task oriented, cooperative, and friendly. The boys displayed a high degree of independence and initiative, continued to work productively in the leader's absence, and endured frustration well. They showed a slight loss in efficiency compared with the authoritarian group—probably due to the time spent solving problems and seeking consensus—but this was minor and more than compensated for by the improvement in group atmosphere. This leadership style produced the benefits of the other two styles without the negative features.

The classroom implications are clear. Laissez-faire leadership creates chaos and uncertainty; authoritarian leadership leads to high performance but also to frustration, aggression, and a negative group atmosphere; democratic leadership allows learners to reach their goals without producing frustration and aggression. Democratic leadership has the added benefit of teaching the group to collaborate on projects and function independently in the leader's absence.

These styles are quite general and include many qualities, making it difficult to determine the critical variables. In applying these findings to classrooms, researchers have suggested that one critical variable is the degree of emotional support or warmth provided by the leader (Dunkin & Biddle, 1974). A second critical dimension may be the extent to which the leader directs the group's activities, with the middle ground being preferred. Application 8.1 contains suggested ways to apply democratic leadership principles in the classroom.

APPLICATION 8.1

Applying Democratic Leadership Principles in the Classroom

1. *Foster collaborative relationships through cooperative groups.* When Mr. Schutz divides his students into cooperative groups for social studies, he groups students with varying abilities and talents. He tries to rotate students so that the same students do not continually end up in the same groups.

   Ms. Linklater, a high school drama teacher, forms three-student groups to write and perform a television ad. The students select their own product and write and produce their ad. All three students in each group receive grade points based on their average score. Each student is encouraged to help his or her teammates complete difficult portions of the assignment.

2. *Question students and have them share ideas on ways to complete projects.* While introducing a history unit, a teacher has his students brainstorm ideas about projects that would be appropriate for the unit. The class then selects three projects to complete and each student chooses one of the three to do individually. Each student is able to generate his or her own list of activities that will be included in the project. The project grade is based on originality and completion of the activities.

   Ms. Henessey asked her second-grade students to identify what geometric shapes they saw in various objects in the room. After the students played with the objects and were able to identify all of the shapes, she gave each student copies of the same shapes made out of construction paper, which the students then used to make a picture.

3. *Encourage problem solving and decision making by students.* Mr. Mesa, a math teacher, started each unit with a different "teaser" (a question for students to solve that required using the math skills to be taught in the new unit). Students were able to work in pairs the last 10 minutes of each class to make decisions about how to solve the problem. The students kept notes on the steps they used to solve the teaser.

   Ms. Vaughn, an elementary teacher, was introducing a review unit on linear measurement. She divided her students into groups of three and gave each group a 12-inch ruler, a yardstick, a ball of string, a notepad, and pencils. She asked each group to find three objects in the school building that they could measure with these items. The students were to sketch the objects and label their measurements. At the end of the activity, each group shared its sketches with the entire class and explained how the items were selected and measured.

4. *Make sure students understand that the teacher bears the ultimate responsibility for classroom activities.* Mr. Kerr, a high school teacher, let his students select their own science projects. After each student selected a project, he or she completed a proposal sheet defining and outlining the project. Mr. Kerr then met with each student individually to discuss the project. At that time, Mr. Kerr accepted or revised the student's proposal or worked with the student to develop a new proposal.

   Mrs. Patrick, a third-grade teacher, worked with her students to establish classroom rules. Before they began setting rules and consequences, she discussed one rule that she said must be included in the list and stated that she must approve all rules and consequences that the class formulated.

Praise and Criticism

Teacher-student interactions often include praise and criticism for students. There is an extensive literature on the effects of these variables on student behavior. We examine next the relation of praise and criticism to student motivation.

Praise

Praise is positive feedback that expresses approval or commendation. It goes beyond simple feedback indicating that behavior is appropriate or that answers are correct because it conveys positive teacher affect and provides information about the worth of students' behaviors (Brophy, 1981). When a teacher says to a student, "That's correct. You're doing so well," the first part of the statement ("That's correct") is feedback on performance, whereas the last part is praise. As a type of positive reinforcer, praise given following a student behavior should make that behavior more likely to be repeated (Skinner, 1953). O'Leary and O'Leary (1977) noted that for praise to be effective as a reinforcer, it must be delivered contingent on performance of the behavior to be reinforced, be specific about which aspects of the behavior are being reinforced, and be viewed by students as sincere and credible. Teachers praise students when they display good classroom behavior and progress in learning in the hope that the praise will reinforce the desirable behavior and students will repeat it.

Brophy (1981) reviewed research on teacher praise and found that praise did not always function as a reinforcer because it frequently was not delivered following student responses. It often was infrequent, noncontingent, general in nature rather than linked to specific behavior, and dependent more on teachers' perceptions of students' need for praise than on students' actual behaviors (Wittrock, 1986). There also is evidence that praise does not relate well to student achievement (Brophy, 1981). Correlations between praise and student achievement are weak and mixed in direction (Dunkin & Biddle, 1974). The effects of praise may be moderated by such variables as grade level, socioeconomic status, and ability. At the early elementary level, praise correlates weakly but positively with achievement among low-socioeconomic and low-ability students and correlates weakly but negatively or not at all with achievement among high-socioeconomic and high-ability students (Brophy, 1981).

Bandura (1986) disputed Skinner's notion that reinforcers operate as response strengtheners. Rather, reinforcement serves to inform and motivate. Reinforcement informs individuals about the desirability and accuracy of responses. It also can motivate; students who expect and value reinforcement for acting in a given fashion are likely to behave accordingly. Wittrock (1986) noted that these informational and motivational functions also pertain to teacher praise. Overall, the evidence suggests that praise is a weak reinforcer, especially after the first few grades in school (Brophy, 1981). Up to around age 8, children desire to please adults, so the effects of praise on behavior can be powerful. But praise may have unintended effects. Because praise conveys information to students about teachers' beliefs, teachers who praise students for success at easy tasks may send the message that they do not expect the students to learn much. Students believe the teacher thinks they have low ability, which negatively affects motivation (Weiner et al., 1983).

From an attributional perspective (see chapter 3), praise conveys information to students about the teacher's beliefs about their ability (Pintrich & Blumenfeld, 1985). Praise

Table 8.4 Guidelines for Using Praise Effectively

- Make praise simple and direct, deliver it in a natural voice, and avoid theatrics.
- Use straightforward, declarative sentences rather than gushy exclamations and rhetorical questions.
- Specify the accomplishment being praised and recognize noteworthy effort, care, and persistence. Call attention to progress and the development of skills.
- Use a variety of phrases in praising students.
- Back up verbal praise with nonverbal communication of approval.
- Avoid ambiguous statements (e.g., "You were really good today") and make it clear that praise is for learning rather than for compliance.
- Praise individual students privately to avoid public embarrassment.

Material drawn from Good and Brophy (1987).

given for success and progress in learning substantiates students' beliefs that they are learning and raises self-efficacy for learning. Praise used indiscriminately carries no information about capabilities and has little effect on behavior. Good and Brophy (1987; see also Brophy, 1981; Brophy & Good, 1986) present guidelines for using praise effectively (Table 8.4). As these guidelines make clear, effective praise is contingent on successful performances and is aimed at boosting students' perceived competencies and motivation for learning.

Criticism

Criticism refers to teacher disapproval of student behavior through verbal feedback or gestures. Criticism is distinguished from performance feedback because it provides information about undesirability of students' behaviors. The statement, "Alex, that's wrong. I'm disappointed that you didn't do better," contains performance feedback (first part) and criticism (second part).

We intuitively might expect that criticizing students is bad and lowers performance and motivation; however, the research evidence is mixed. Studies have shown that criticism is unrelated to student achievement, that it relates negatively to achievement, and that it relates to achievement in a curvilinear fashion such that moderate criticism may be motivating but effects diminish as criticism increases and decreases (Dunkin & Biddle, 1974). The effects of criticism on performance are tempered by other variables. Observational studies show that criticism is more frequently given to boys than to girls, to African American students than to Caucasian students, to students for whom teachers hold low expectations than to those for whom they hold high expectations, and to students of lower social status (primarily boys) than to higher status students (Brophy & Good, 1974). Clearly, the reasons are complex as to why teachers criticize some students more often than others.

Whether criticism increases, decreases, or has no effect on student motivation should depend on the extent that it involves motivational processes. Thus, criticism should motivate students when it conveys they are competent and can perform better with more effort or better use of strategies, informs students about the value of the learning, provides information on progress toward goals, and so forth. The statement, "I'm disappointed in you. I know that you can perform better," is critical and encouraging: It contains persuasive self-efficacy information and may motivate students to try harder. Conversely, the statement,

"I'm disappointed in you. You will probably never figure this out," may lower self-efficacy and motivation in students. Teachers who use criticism should try to incorporate positive motivational features and use it judiciously in situations in which other motivational techniques have been ineffective and they believe that the student might respond.

Unsolicited Help

Providing unsolicited help is another way that teachers interact with students. Unsolicited help is best viewed against the background of classroom life in which teachers routinely provide assistance to students in the form of corrective feedback and instruction. During guided and independent practice, teachers stay on the lookout for student problems and attempt to correct them. Students also ask for help when they are baffled about what to do. Research shows that seeking help is an important self-regulatory strategy that relates positively to motivation and achievement (Newman & Schwager, 1992). Although such help is well intended and generally serves to enhance learning, under certain conditions, it can have an undesirable effect on motivation.

First, let us consider the benefits of providing help. Teachers who provide corrective feedback to students having difficulty are likely to help students learn. As a consequence of such assistance, students should observe that they are making progress in learning, which raises self-efficacy and motivates them to continue to improve. While providing assistance, teachers may also praise correct performance (e.g., "You're doing great on this part") and persuasive efficacy information ("I know that you can learn to do this"). These comments also raise efficacy and motivation.

The downside to unsolicited assistance is that it conveys information about the recipient's ability. According to attribution theory (see chapter 3), unsolicited assistance reflects the perceived cause of the recipient's problems (Weiner, 1985a). Help is most likely forthcoming when the perceived cause is a factor beyond the recipient's control, such as low ability (Weiner et al., 1983). If the causal factors appear to be within the recipient's control (e.g., low effort), the recipient is held personally responsible and help is not given. As a consequence of helping, the recipient may infer the help-giver's intentions. The recipient may believe that help was provided because the help-giver felt the recipient's ability was low. The recipient may attribute difficulty to low ability, which negatively affects perceptions of competence and motivation.

Teachers can alleviate potential negative effects of assistance by casting it in a positive light. Comment on what the student is doing well, what needs improvement, and what the student needs to do to perform better. Giving help with words of encouragement ("I know that you can do this") should benefit motivation.

TEACHER EXPECTATIONS

An important process influencing student motivation involves the expectations that teachers hold for student learning and performance. For over 30 years, research on **teacher expectations** has addressed such issues as how teachers form expectations, how they communicate them to students, and how these expectations affect student outcomes (Braun, 1976; Cooper & Good, 1983; Cooper & Tom, 1984; Dusek, 1985; Jussim, 1986,

1991; Stipek, 1996). Practitioners are equally concerned about expectation effects; recall the story of Lisa McMahan at the beginning of this chapter.

We begin by discussing a famous study that instigated interest in the role of teacher expectations. We then present models that explain how expectations are formulated, how teachers communicate them to students, and how they might influence students. A section on teacher self-efficacy follows, which is a type of teacher expectation. We conclude by providing a critique of teacher expectation effects and offering suggestions for employing them productively in classrooms.

The Pygmalion Study

In 1968, Rosenthal and Jacobson conducted the classic study *Pygmalion in the Classroom* (Rosenthal & Jacobson, 1968) which gave rise to the term the **Pygmalion effect**. The researchers gave elementary school children (grades 1 through 6) a test of nonverbal intelligence at the start of the academic year. Teachers were told that this test predicted which students would bloom intellectually during the year. Actually, the researchers randomly identified 20% of the school population as intellectual bloomers and gave the names of these students to their teachers. Teachers were not aware of the deception: The test did not predict intellectual blooming and the names they were given bore no relation to test scores. Teachers taught in their usual fashion and students were retested after 1 semester, 1 year, and 2 years. For the first two tests, students were in the classes of teachers who had been given the names of the bloomers; for the last test, students were in new classes with different teachers who had not been given the bloomers' names.

After the first year, significant differences in intelligence occurred between the bloomers and the control students (students who had not been identified as bloomers). The differences were greater among students in grades 1 and 2. During the subsequent year, these younger bloomers lost their advantage, but bloomers in the upper grades showed an increasing advantage over control students. Differences were greater among average achievers than they were among high and low achievers. Bloomers gained significantly more than control students in their grades in reading; these differences were greater among average and younger students. Overall, the differences between bloomers and control students were small both in reading and on the intelligence test.

Rosenthal and Jacobson concluded that teacher expectations can act as self-fulfilling prophecies because student achievement comes to reflect the expectations. (The name *Pygmalion* comes from George Bernard Shaw's play, in which others' expectations concerning the heroine influence how they perceive and treat her.) With regard to the grade-level differences, the researchers suggested that younger children's advantage may stem from their close personal contact with teachers and that the advantage disappears when students lose this contact with the influencing teacher. Older students may function better autonomously after they move to a new teacher.

These conclusions about the Pygmalion effect are controversial. The Rosenthal and Jacobson study has been criticized on conceptual and methodological grounds (Elashoff & Snow, 1971; Jensen, 1969). There have been several attempts to replicate the Pygmalion study and not all have been successful (Cooper & Good, 1983). In an interesting series of studies, Schrank (1968, 1970) told some teachers that they had students of high learning potential and other teachers that their classes had low learning potential, when in fact the groups had been randomly assigned to conditions. Students of teachers in the high-potential condition learned more than students of teachers in the low-potential group. In a follow-up replication study, teachers knew that students had been grouped randomly rather than by ability level but Schrank asked teachers to teach the groups as if they had been grouped by ability. No differences in learning between the groups were obtained. Collectively, these two studies highlight the potential influence of teacher beliefs on student learning.

Models of Teacher Expectation Effects

Various explanations have been proposed for teacher expectation effects. Brophy and Good (1974) described a process whereby teacher expectations may be formed, conveyed to students, and affect student behavior. Early in the school year, teachers form expectations based on initial interactions with students and information from school records. Teachers then begin to treat students differently consistent with their expectations. Teacher behaviors are reciprocated; for example, teachers who show warm interaction with students are likely to have that warmth returned. Thus, student behaviors begin to complement and reinforce teacher behaviors and expectations. The differential teacher behaviors may spread to other areas, such as opportunities for learning, type of feedback provided, and leadership roles assumed. Effects will be most pronounced for expectations that are rigid and inappropriate. When expectations are appropriate, or inappropriate but flexible, student behavior may substantiate or redefine expectations. But when expectations are inappropriate and not easily changed, student performance may decline and become consistent with expectations.

Another model was described by Cooper and Tom (1984). Students enter learning settings with different abilities and backgrounds and teachers have initial beliefs for individual students that are formed based on prior experiences with students and knowledge of their intelligence and abilities from school records. A critical variable is the teacher's perception of control over student performance. Control refers to the teacher's ability to influence the content, timing, and duration of interaction with students. Control beliefs vary with the context; some settings allow the teacher greater control than others. Control beliefs influence teachers' decisions about providing student feedback (e.g., praise, criticism) and the type of socioemotional climate to create for the student. Different climates and types of feedback affect students' beliefs about their performance capabilities and the value of effort in producing good performance. Capability and effort beliefs, in turn, affect student motivation and achievement.

Braun (1976) developed a model to explain the origin of teacher expectations. Some possible sources of expectations are intelligence and ability scores, gender, information from previous teachers, medical and psychological information on records, ethnic background, knowledge about older siblings, physical characteristics, prior achievement, socioeconomic status, and actual behaviors of the students. Research supports the potential influence of these factors (Brophy & Good, 1974). Teachers often hold higher expectations for students of higher intelligence or ability compared with students of lower ability. Teachers expect fewer behavior problems from girls and, at least at the elementary level, expect girls to perform better academically; however, beginning in middle school, many teachers expect girls to perform worse than boys in mathematics and the sciences (Eccles, 1983). Teachers generally hold higher expectations for upper- and middle-class students than for lower-class students, as well as for Caucasian compared with African American students (Brophy & Good, 1974). Expectations also vary according to achievement level, with teachers expecting more from students who have demonstrated high achievement in the past.

Other research shows that teachers may believe physically attractive students are more intelligent than unattractive students and hold correspondingly higher expectations for them (Brophy & Good, 1974). Teachers' expectations also are influenced by information they obtain from records and previous teachers and by their knowledge of older siblings. To Braun's (1976) list of sources of expectations, we might add speech characteristics. Children who speak in nonstandard English tend to be perceived negatively by teachers who hold lower expectations for their performances (Brophy & Good, 1974).

Differential Teacher Behaviors

Once teachers form expectations, how are they communicated to students and translated into teacher behaviors? Expectations may translate into behaviors in four areas: socioemotional climate, verbal input, verbal output, and feedback (Rosenthal, 1974). Socioemotional climate includes such verbal and nonverbal behaviors as smiles, head nods, eye contact, and supportive and friendly actions. In general, teachers provide a warmer socioemotional climate for students for whom they hold high expectations than for those for whom expectations are lower (Cooper & Tom, 1984). Verbal input denotes opportunities to learn new material and the difficulty of material. High-expectation students may have more opportunities to interact with and learn new material and be exposed to more difficult material compared with low-expectation learners (Cooper & Tom, 1984).

Verbal output refers to the number and length of academic interactions. Research shows that teachers engage in more academic interchanges with high- than with low-expectation students (Brophy & Good, 1974). High-expectation students (highs) initiate more contacts with teachers compared with low-expectation students (lows). Teachers have more public interactions with highs and more private or individual interactions with lows (Cooper & Tom, 1984). They also are more persistent with highs; if highs fail to answer a question, teachers are apt to repeat or rephrase the question or provide prompts. Teachers may devote more time to brighter students, allow them more time to respond before redirecting questions, and pay closer attention to their answers compared with slower students. Feedback refers to use of academic praise and criticism. Teachers praise highs more and criticize lows more (Cooper & Tom, 1984).

Each of these factors is genuine and operates in classrooms (Cooper & Tom, 1984). At the same time, there are differences among teachers. Few teachers will behave consistently in all four areas, and some teachers may not treat students differently at all. The best conclusion is that many teachers occasionally act in accordance with one of these factors.

In addition to these direct effects of teacher differential treatment on motivation and behavior, students perceive teacher treatment in different ways. The work of Weinstein and her colleagues (Brattesani, Weinstein, & Marshall, 1984; Weinstein, 1985, 1989, 1993; Weinstein & Middlestadt, 1979) has shown that students can and do perceive differential teacher treatment in the classroom, with high achievers often treated more positively, given more privileges, allowed more choice and control over their learning, and provided more opportunities to talk in class and answer questions than low achievers. Some evidence suggests that teachers have different expectations and treat boys and girls differently, especially in math and science classrooms (e.g., Becker, 1981; Leinhardt, Seewald, & Engel, 1979; Parsons, Kaczala, & Meece, 1982). At the same time, much of this teacher behavior may be reactive and based on real differences in student behavior, not gender per se (Brophy, 1985; Jussim, 1991). Finally, there may be differences in how boys and girls react to the same teacher behavior (Eccles & Blumenfeld, 1985; Stipek, 1998), making it difficult to develop any broad generalizations about how different expectations and differential teacher behavior relate to student motivation and achievement. The most important point is that teachers should focus on developing accurate perceptions of students based on actual student behavior and performance in the classroom (not just on teacher expectations, as with Lisa in the beginning of this chapter) and then use this information to plan their instruction accordingly (Jussim, 1991).

Teacher Self-Efficacy

Teacher self-efficacy is increasingly being shown to relate to various student achievement outcomes and to affect student motivation (Pajares, 1996; Tschannen-Moran, Hoy, & Hoy, 1998). **Teacher self-efficacy** (or **instructional self-efficacy**) refers to personal beliefs about one's capabilities to help students learn. Teacher self-efficacy should influence the same types of activities that student self-efficacy affects: choice of activities, effort, persistence, achievement (Ashton, 1985; Ashton & Webb, 1986). Teachers with low self-efficacy may avoid planning activities they believe exceed their capabilities, not persist with students having difficulties, expend little effort to find materials, and not reteach in ways that students might understand better. Teachers with higher self-efficacy are more apt to develop challenging activities, help students succeed, and persist with students who have problems. Such teachers may encourage student learning better through planning of activities and in their interactions with students (e.g., as they help students persist on tasks and cope with academic demands). These motivational effects on teachers can enhance student achievement. Ashton and Webb (1986) found that teachers with higher self-efficacy were likely to have a positive classroom environment, support students' ideas, and address students' needs. Teacher self-efficacy was a significant predictor of student achievement. Woolfolk and Hoy (1990) obtained comparable results with preservice teachers.

In addition to its effects on teachers' activities prior to and during instruction, teacher self-efficacy also can affect teachers' activities following instruction (Tschannen-Moran, Woolfolk Hoy, & Hoy, 1998). Teacher self-efficacy should rise when students display learning progress. Further, efficacious teachers may not necessarily find little student progress discouraging if the teachers believe that different teaching strategies may produce better results.

Researchers have investigated the dimensions of teacher self-efficacy that relate best to student learning (Gibson & Dembo, 1984; Woolfolk & Hoy, 1990). Ashton and Webb (1986) distinguished *teaching efficacy,* or outcome expectations about the consequences of teaching in general, from *personal efficacy,* defined as self-efficacy to perform particular behaviors to bring about given outcomes. As mentioned in chapter 4, self-efficacy and outcome expectations are often related but need not be. A teacher might have a high sense of personal efficacy but lower teaching efficacy if he or she believes that most student learning is due to home and environmental factors outside of the teacher's control.

Support for this idea was obtained by Guskey (1987). Teachers' self-efficacy was differentially affected depending on whether poor performance was demonstrated by a single student or by a group of students. When a single student performed poorly, teachers expressed little personal responsibility and self-efficacy was relatively unaffected. Conversely, when a large group of students performed poorly, teachers assumed greater responsibility for the outcome and their self-efficacy was lower. Other research suggests that instructional efficacy reflects an internal-external distinction: Internal factors represent perceptions of personal influence and power, whereas external factors relate to perceptions of influence and power of elements that lie outside the classroom (Guskey & Passaro, 1994).

An important challenge for pre- and inservice teacher education programs is to develop methods for increasing teachers' instructional self-efficacy by incorporating Bandura's (1997) efficacy-building sources (i.e., actual performance, vicarious experiences, persuasion, physiological indexes). Benz, Bradley, Alderman, and Flowers (1992) found that classroom teachers generally held a lower sense of self-efficacy than did preservice teachers. Perhaps after working in classrooms for a time, teachers placed greater emphasis on factors outside of their control as being responsible for student learning. Only with respect to planning and evaluation did classroom teachers judge self-efficacy higher than did preservice teachers. As discussed in chapter 4, observing models (a vicarious source of efficacy information) can promote observers' learning and self-efficacy. For example, when students observe teacher models demonstrate how to work successfully with students having learning problems or those not motivated to learn, the students acquire specific skills and experience a higher sense of self-efficacy for succeeding with such students in their classrooms. Suggestions for raising teachers' self-efficacy are given in Application 8.2.

APPLICATION 8.2

Applying Self-Efficacy in the Classroom

Bandura (1997) listed four sources of self-efficacy information: performance accomplishments, vicarious experiences, social persuasion, and physiological indicators. Each of these can be employed to enhance self-efficacy among preservice and practicing teachers.

Performance Accomplishments

1. Ms. Hutton, an undergraduate student, is enrolled in an early field experience as part of her teacher education program. This semester she is helping her supervising teacher plan small-group activities and she works on these with children. Through her actual teaching and working with the small groups, Ms. Hutton is developing instructional self-efficacy.

2. Mr. Hannum is teaching an American government high school class for the first time. During the semester he reflects on his performance each day to determine how well the students are understanding the material and enjoying the course. By realizing that he is helping students learn, Mr. Hannum feels more efficacious about continuing to succeed.

Vicarious Experiences

1. Professor Martin teaches an undergraduate course in elementary mathematical methods. During the course he often shows his students videotapes of teachers practicing effective teaching methods. Observing successful teacher models raises preservice teachers' self-efficacy.

2. Ms. Whitlock attended an inservice program on classroom management. As part of the program, various teachers shared their experiences on how they handled difficult classroom situations. As a result of listening to these teachers, Ms. Whitlock experienced increased self-efficacy for successfully managing difficult situations.

Social Persuasion

1. Ms. Critchon is doing her student teaching in a fifth-grade classroom. Her supervising teacher, Mr. Cooper, discusses planning and teacher activities with her daily. Ms. Critchon occasionally expresses a lack of confidence for teaching well. Mr. Cooper encourages her by saying, "You've been doing great so far. I know you'll be able to handle this."

2. A group of seventh-grade teachers met to plan an interdisciplinary unit on America's role during World War II. One of the teachers, Mr. Kenmore, had never worked on an interdisciplinary team before. The other teachers encouraged him and offered persuasive efficacy information by stating, "You can do it, Jim. Just ask us if you're not sure of what to do—we'll help you."

Physiological Indicators

1. Ms. Janko felt very anxious prior to starting her student teaching. As the semester progressed, she noticed that she experienced less anxiety and she looked forward to working with students each day. Her university supervisor told her, "You're feeling more confident; that should help you work with the students better."

2. Mr. Ambrose attended a workshop on stress management. He learned relaxation and breathing activities to use when he felt tense. Realizing that he knew how to handle stress on the job raised Mr. Ambrose's self-efficacy for teaching because he was confident that he could control stress and focus on student learning.

Critique

Expectations are normal, usually reasonable, and based upon observations. Most beliefs that teachers hold about students are accurate because they are based on multiple observations of performance (Jussim, 1991). Because teacher expectations generally reflect actual student behaviors, the effects of teacher expectations on student performances typically are weak and affect student achievement minimally (Jussim, 1991). When effects are found, they are usually negative; holding positive expectations for students does not seem to raise performance as much as holding negative expectations lowers it (Brophy & Good, 1974; Cooper & Tom, 1984; Good & Brophy, 1987).

Rosenthal and Jacobson (1968) found that expectation effects were stronger among young children and became weaker with development. The stronger effects among early elementary children may be due to the close teacher-student interactions that are typically found in those grades. Such close interactions allow ample opportunities for teachers to behave differently in the preceding areas (Rosenthal, 1974). As students progress through grades, teacher-student interactions become less frequent and more impersonal.

Some expectations are appropriate and instructionally sound. Because expectations usually result from student performance rather than cause it (Brophy & Good, 1974), teachers typically hold higher expectations for students who perform better. It may make instructional sense to present high achievers with more difficult material, question them more extensively about it, and move them through a sequence of instruction more quickly. In short, expectations may have instructional benefits when they are appropriate (based on student performances) and flexible (capable of changing to reflect changes in student performances). Expectations become a problem when they are inappropriate and rigid such that teachers hold firm beliefs about what students can and cannot do that bear little relation to students' actual behaviors (Brophy & Good, 1974).

Expectation effects do not always occur. Smith (1980) found that expectation effects were stronger in reading than in mathematics. This may result because reading is typically taught in small groups with much teacher-student interaction, whereas mathematics is usually a large-group and individual activity and the frequency of teacher-student interactions is less.

Expectation effects are typically not obtained when expectations are highly inaccurate. Teachers who hold low expectations for bright students are unlikely to lower these students' expectations (Cooper & Tom, 1984). Grossly distorted expectations are not credible. Mild self-fulfilling prophecies reflecting a small distortion between expectations and student behavior may be more common, which helps explain why expectation effects are typically small and in a negative direction. Although teacher expectation effects are real and can affect student performance, the scope and size of their effects have probably been distorted, which has led to more concern than warranted (Jussim, 1991). Some applications of these points to classrooms are given in Application 8.3.

APPLICATION 8.3

Teacher Expectations in the Classroom

1. *Enforce rules fairly and consistently.* Ms. Tom, a new kindergarten teacher, worked with her students at the beginning of the year on classroom rules. She reviewed the rules and consequences and made sure she enforced the rules fairly and consistently. She corrected each child who did not follow one of the rules so that all of the children were aware that the rules applied to everyone.

   Mr. Adams was having discipline problems in his second-period physical education class. He asked a department member, Ms. Lourcey, to observe the class and give him feedback. After observing, Ms. Lourcey told Mr. Adams that he always corrected the same five boys for not following the classroom rules but did not say anything to other students who were doing the same thing. She suggested that he try harder to apply the rules to everyone. After Mr. Adams worked on being more consistent, student misbehavior became less frequent.

2. *Assume that all students can learn and convey that expectation to them.* Ms. Bird, a kindergarten teacher, told her class that she was very excited because they had learned their colors. Ms. Bird said, "I am so proud of you. I knew that you could do it. Now we are all going to learn our shapes. I know we can."

    A high school English teacher greeted his new class by stating, "I look forward to getting to know all of you. We are going to have a great time in this class as we improve our writing, and we all can improve it if we try. I am going to work with each of you, and I know by the end of the semester, each of you will be writing well."

    One student replied, "I can hardly write a sentence. I don't know how you'll make a writer out of me."

    "Well, sentences are a great place to start," countered the teacher.

3. *Do not form differential student expectations based on qualities (e.g., gender, ethnicity, parents' background) unrelated to performance.* Mr. Willett, a special education resource teacher, was always quick to defend his students. He had several boys who were from a rough neighborhood and were known to be involved in gang activities. Some teachers ignored the boys in their classes and did not try to help them when they had difficulty learning. Mr. Willett worked with these boys and did everything he could to help them succeed.

    A sixth-grade teacher planned several projects that included activities for her students to do with their parents. There were two students whose parents never participated in school activities or did anything with their children. She met with these students privately and told them she would be glad to work with them on the parent activities after school each day. This would allow them to complete as many activities as the others in the class.

4. *Do not accept excuses for poor performance.* Justin kept telling Ms. Osgood that he could not complete his social studies assignment because he could not read as well as the other students. "After all, I'm in reading resource," said Justin.

    Ms. Osgood said, "I know you are in reading resource, but you also are a very good social studies student. You are always sharing in the class and can answer all the questions during discussion time." Ms. Osgood offered to help Justin read any of the words or selections that he felt were too difficult.

    Mr. Leeland assigned homework in his history class every evening. Kyle, a capable but lazy student, usually complained about completing homework. He said he did not have any supplies at home. Mr. Leeland gathered up several items (paper, pens, pencils, resource books) and sent them home with Kyle. Mr. Leeland told Kyle he expected him to complete all of his homework from now on.

5. *Realize that upper limits of student ability are unknown and not relevant to school learning.* Mr. Willis, a third-grade teacher, was helping one of his students with her math.

    "Alice, let's try some regrouping in subtraction since you have been doing such a wonderful job with all of your other subtraction problems. It's time for you to try something harder."

    Alice said, "I'm not smart enough to try those. They're too hard."

    "That's not true, Alice. I know you can do them, just give it a try," replied Mr. Willis.

Ms. Harlow, a university English teacher, introduced a poetry unit to her class. She told the students at the end of the unit they were going to write their own poetry. Denzel said, "I can't write poetry, I'm not smart enough to do that."

Ms. Harlow replied, "Denzel, I know that with my help you will be able to write at least one poem. There are many different styles of poetry and I know that one of those styles will be something you can build on."

CLASSROOM MANAGEMENT AND ORGANIZATION

Among the more important classroom processes are those involving classroom management (Levin & Nolan, 2000). **Classroom management** refers to the ways that teachers maintain order in their classrooms (Doyle, 1986). Order denotes the extent that students are acting acceptably such that classroom events can occur. Order does not necessarily mean quiet and passive students, although it may depending on which events need to occur. Rather, there typically are acceptable limits to order. Order is defined according to the type of environment needed given the instructional demands placed on students.

Few would dispute that how teachers manage students' behaviors affects learning. Teachers who are effective classroom managers establish rules and procedures and organize activities to help keep students productively engaged. These teacher activities prevent discipline problems. When problems occur, effective teachers deal with them quickly and fairly so they are stopped and do not interfere with other students (Doyle, 1986). Collectively, these efforts make the classroom more productive for learning (Levin & Nolan, 2000). Teacher activities designed to prevent, minimize, and deal with problems also influence student motivation. Even bright, task-oriented students who enjoy learning are not motivated to work diligently in noisy and disruptive environments. Students who engage in misbehavior and receive punishment are likewise not motivated to concentrate on academic material. Student motivation to learn is optimal in well-managed classes (Doyle, 1986; Stipek, 1996).

In this section, we consider the role of classroom management in motivation. We distinguish between proactive and reactive teacher processes. *Proactive* processes are those teacher activities designed to prevent disciplinary problems from occurring; *reactive* processes are designed to deal with problems when they occur and attempt to quickly return misbehaving students to academic work and minimize disruption to others. Both processes are critical to good classroom management and student motivation. Initially, we discuss Kounin's (1977) research on effective classroom management. We then consider the role of classroom organization in student motivation.

Kounin's Research

Kounin (1977) conducted an extensive analysis of dimensions of group management in elementary school classrooms to determine what factors contributed to student work involvement and diminished misbehavior. The research done by Kounin (1977) was prompted by a fortuitous incident:

I was teaching a course in Mental Hygiene . . . While lecturing, I glanced around the room and noticed a student in the back row intently reading a newspaper that he was holding completely unfolded in front of himself. Contrary to what I advocated in the course, I angrily reprimanded him without diagnosis or understanding . . . The reprimand succeeded. He stopped reading the newspaper, or at least did not hold it completely unfolded in midair. But, the major observable impact seemed to be upon *other* members of the class. Side glances to others ceased, whispers stopped, eyes went from windows or the instructor to notebooks on the desks. The silence was heavy, as if the students were closing out the classroom and escaping to the safety of a notebook. I believe that if I had sneezed they would have written the sound in their notes. (p. 1)

What Kounin observed was a **ripple effect,** or how a teacher's handling of misbehavior by one student affects the behaviors of other students who are witnesses to, but not participants in, the event. The ripple effect is actually a form of modeling (see chapter 4); this incident illustrates inhibition of student misbehavior brought about by disciplining one offender.

Desists

In Kounin's system, the term **desist** refers to the teacher's actions to stop misbehavior. In the preceding incident, the teacher's desist had a ripple effect. In four settings (kindergarten, high school, college, summer camp with children ages 7 to 13), Kounin tested the hypothesis that a teacher's desist would have a ripple effect. Support was obtained in all four settings, although the most powerful effects were obtained with the kindergartners. The ripple effect was more pronounced early in the school year and diminished as the year progressed.

In the kindergarten study, Kounin (1977) explored whether the qualities of desists—clarity, firmness, and roughness—made a difference among observing children. Clarity is the extent to which the desist names the misbehaving student, specifies the unacceptable behavior, and gives the reasons for the desist. Firmness refers to how well the desist conveys an "I-mean-it" attitude with follow-through until the misbehavior ceased. Roughness is the extent to which the desist includes threats, anger, physical handling, and punishment. Greater clarity increased conformity among observing students, firmness increased compliance only in students who were also misbehaving or were inclined toward misbehavior, and roughness did not improve behavior and tended to promote emotional upset among observers. Examples of these qualities are given in Table 8.5.

Interestingly, Kounin (1977) found no relationship between these qualities of desists and success in handling a deviancy.

For any one teacher, neither the degree of clarity, firmness, or intensity of her desist effort; nor whether she focuses on the misbehavior; . . . nor whether she treats the child positively, negatively, or neutrally; makes any difference for how readily a child stops his deviancy or gets with the prescribed task. (p. 70)

Thus, qualities of desists influenced observing students' behaviors but not the behaviors of misbehaving students. Kounin (1977) concluded that the techniques of dealing with misbehavior are not good predictors of how well children behave in classrooms or whether misbehavior spreads to other students. Intuitively, it seems puzzling that how teachers react to misbehavior makes little difference in the overall work involvement of

Table 8.5 Qualities of Desists

Quality	Description	Example
Clarity	Extent that desist names the misbehaving student, states the unacceptable behavior, and gives the reason for the desist	"Karen, stop bothering Alex. You know that you are to be working alone. Please get back to work on your math."
Firmness	Extent that desist conveys an "I-mean-it" attitude with follow-through until misbehavior ceases	"Luis, we do not push in the line. If you cannot behave in line you will not go to recess."
Roughness	Extent that desist includes threats, anger, physical handling, punishment	"A.J., you are so lazy. You're worse than your brother and look where he ended up. You make me furious. I wish you weren't in this class."

the classroom. We need to consider this in light of the earlier distinction between proactive and reactive disciplinary techniques. Teachers' efforts to prevent disciplinary problems are more important than techniques for handling problems. Kounin (1977) identified some proactive teacher activities, which we will discuss separately, that relate positively to group management:

Withitness—demonstration by teachers that they know what is going on at all times; having "eyes in the back of their heads"

Overlapping—ability of teachers to attend to more than one issue simultaneously

Movement management—strategies designed by teachers to initiate, sustain, and alter activity flow in the classroom

Group focus—extent to which teachers keep students attentive to the learning task

Programming to avoid satiation—how well teachers minimize boredom due to repetition of material

Withitness

Withitness is "a teacher's communicating to the children by her actual behavior (rather than by simple verbal announcing: 'I know what's going on') that she knows what the children are doing, or has the proverbial 'eyes in back of her head' " (Kounin, 1977, pp. 80–81). For example, a teacher may be writing on the board with his or her back to the class, yet observe a child misbehaving. The teacher may remark (perhaps without turning around), "Shawn, stop bothering your neighbor and pay attention to what I'm doing." Shawn will probably be surprised that his teacher knew about his misbehavior even without looking at him. This teacher action communicates the teacher's withitness to Shawn.

Kounin identified two types of errors that teachers sometimes make when they utter desists that are designed to convey withitness. Target errors occur when the teacher identifies the wrong student for a desist (e.g., teacher utters a desist to Shawn even though Shawn's neighbor Kim is bothering Shawn and Shawn is trying to get Kim to stop). Another type of target error occurs when the teacher overlooks a more serious deviancy and utters a desist designed to stop a less serious one. For example, a teacher tells two children to stop talking while in another part of the room two students are pushing and shoving one another. Timing errors are those in which the deviancy spreads to more students or becomes more serious before the teacher intervenes.

Kounin found that withitness was a significant predictor of good classroom management. Studies showed that withitness correlates positively with student work involvement and with freedom from deviancy, both during student recitation periods and while students are engaged in seatwork. Although these results do not imply causality, they do show that the higher the level of a teacher's withitness, the better that teacher's classroom is managed and the more productive the learning environment and the student motivation to learn.

Overlapping

Overlapping, a second important teacher characteristic, is defined as what teachers do when they have two matters to deal with simultaneously (Kounin, 1977). Overlapping occurs when teachers are occupied with students at a task at the same time a deviancy occurs. For example, a teacher may be working with a small group of students on reading while the rest of the class is engaged in seatwork. Suddenly, two students in the class start talking to one another and become distracted from their work. These are overlapping situations: attending to the reading group and issuing a desist to stop the talking. In some cases, a teacher might exit the reading group, move over to the talking students, and utter a desist. In other cases, the teacher might stay with the reading group and keep them on task while simultaneously uttering a desist to the offending students. Teachers overlap well when they attend to two issues at once.

Overlapping correlates positively with work involvement and freedom from deviancy both during recitation and seatwork, although its correlations are stronger with freedom from deviancy than with encouraging work involvement. Interpreting these results is difficult; some correlations of overlapping may result from withitness because the two often occur together. Highly with-it teachers generally can attend to two issues simultaneously. There is some evidence that withitness alone correlates more strongly with managerial success than does overlapping alone in both recitation and seatwork settings.

Movement Management

A third important attribute, **movement management**, reflects how smoothly teachers keep lessons moving and make transitions between activities. It is important to keep a smooth classroom pace, maintain momentum, and avoid jerkiness in transitions. Two kinds of mistakes that teachers make involve jerkiness and slowdowns. Jerkiness occurs when teachers suddenly announce a change in activities that catches the students by surprise, or when a teacher temporarily or permanently leaves one activity unfinished and moves to another. Slowdowns (delays that waste time) occur when teachers spend too much time giving directions and explanations or when they unnecessarily fragment a task by breaking it into many small tasks when it could be accomplished easily as a whole.

Kounin (1977) found that momentum (the absence of slowdowns) correlated positively with work involvement and freedom from deviancy during recitation but less so during seatwork. It seems that momentum is more highly related to students' behaviors during recitation. Smoothness correlates positively with both indexes during recitation and seatwork. In addition, momentum and smoothness correlated positively with each other.

Group Focus

Group focus, which refers to the teacher's efforts to keep students on task, consists of three dimensions. The first, group alerting, refers to the extent that the teacher maintains student attention during a group activity. For example, a teacher may call on students in random order. Accountability, the second dimension, means that each student in the group is responsible for learning the concepts being taught. Thus, a teacher may not let students move to new material until they have mastered basic concepts. The third dimension of group focus—format—involves grouping students in such a way to facilitate active participation by all students. For example, during a recitation lesson when one student is reciting, what does the teacher do to keep the other students involved?

Of these three dimensions of group focus, accountability and group alerting correlated positively with each other and with dimensions of classroom behavior. Accountability was correlated with work involvement and freedom from deviancy in recitation settings only; it is important during recitations for teachers to ensure that all students are learning the material. In recitations, alerting correlated in recitations with work involvement and freedom from deviancy, and weakly but positively with freedom from deviancy during seatwork. Keeping children alert and focused on the task is important during recitations. Format did not relate to any outcome, suggesting that how teachers conduct classes with different formats is more important for classroom management and motivation than the formats themselves.

Programming to Avoid Satiation

Kounin (1977) examined teachers' efforts to minimize satiation, defined as the change of value of an activity due to repetition. Repetition creates boredom and changes activities from being positively valued (liked) to disliked. Kounin found that satiation did not occur, or occurred slowly, when students experienced feelings of progress and did not believe that the work was repetitious. Other variables that minimized satiation and boosted motivation were variety and challenge. Variety means greater numbers or types of activities per unit of time. Challenge derives from the teacher showing enthusiasm, remarking about the positive valence of the activity (e.g., "This next one will be fun. I know you'll like it"), and discussing the challenge (e.g., "This is a tough one but I know you can figure it out").

Summary

Kounin (1977) found that classroom management did not depend on how teachers reacted to disciplinary problems. What distinguished classrooms with few problems and where students were involved in academic work from classrooms with more problems and less work involvement were techniques teachers used to prevent problems. Effective classroom managers are with-it, attend to more than one issue at a time, keep classroom activities moving well, keep students focused on the task, and minimize boredom. Effective managers make the work environment more productive and give students little opportunity to misbehave. It is little wonder that student (and teacher) motivation is higher in these settings! Some classroom applications of the variables in Kounin's system are provided in Application 8.4.

APPLICATION 8.4

Applying Kounin's Ideas in the Classroom

Withitness

1. Mrs. Sharpe is taking her kindergarten class to lunch and hears quite a commotion behind her. She stops, without turning around, and says, "We need to straighten our line. John and Susie, you need to stop talking so loudly. Thanks, I know we can all move quietly the rest of the way to the lunchroom."

2. Mrs. Renning, a music teacher, is working with one of her fifth-grade classes on a song for the spring musical. There are three students who are quietly trying to sing a totally different tune to throw the other students off. Mrs. Renning is able to tell which students are singing the inappropriate song. She stops the song and calls out the names of the three students. For the next verse, she asks those students to come to the front of the room and lead the rest of the class.

3. Mrs. Applegate was late for her third-period English class because of a meeting with the counselor and another student. When she approached her classroom, she heard several of her students shouting comments about the assistant principal. She stood outside her door for a few seconds to make sure she recognized the shouting voices. Mrs. Applegate walked into her classroom, greeted the class, and apologized for being late. She then walked over to the board and wrote the names of five students on the board. She turned around and said, "I would like to see these five students immediately after class." Then Mrs. Applegate started the lesson for the day.

Overlapping

1. In Mrs. Frens's first-grade class, she has several activities going on at a time. She is working with a small group at a table in one part of the room. Some students are working at their desks on morning assignments, while other students are busy working at activity centers. At the computer center, two students begin arguing about who gets to do the computer math game next. Mrs. Frens asks one of the students in the small group to start reading and she walks over to the computer area, turns off the computer, and asks the two students to go to their desks and put their heads down. Mrs. Frens returns to the small group before the student finishes reading the paragraph. When Mrs. Frens finishes with the small group, she goes over to talk to the students who were having a problem at the computer center and reviews the classroom rules about working at activity stations.

2. Mr. Fowler, a sixth-grade teacher, was busy working with a small group at the front of the room. He was facing away from the rest of the students, who were working on assignments at their desks. Suddenly, Maggie and Bobby started laughing and giggling. Mr. Fowler recognized their laughs immediately, and without turning around he wrote a quick note and asked a student who was sitting close to the small group to take the note to Maggie and Bobby. The note read: "Maggie and Bobby—you are keeping the rest of the class from concentrating. I know that you want to finish your work as much as everyone else. If you choose to play now you will lose your free time later."

Movement Management

1. In circle time each morning, Mrs. Phillips goes over the schedule for the day with her second-grade class. Today as she began reading she told her students the following:

    "This morning, boys and girls, we will be reading a new story. I am going to give you about 5 minutes to look over the story at your seats and then we are going to read the story together. After we have read the story I will go over the workbook pages that you are to do. Then I will call small groups over to the reading table to work with me, while the rest of you work on the workbook pages that go with the story. If you finish your work before you are called to work with me, remember you may go to one of the activity centers to work. You can tell what small group you are going to be in today by finding your name on the board. Your names are listed under the name of one of the characters in today's story. Now please get your reading book, workbook, and a pencil out on your desks. Turn in your reading books to page 87. The name of our story today is Mr. Figglebom Finds Something Mysterious in His Backyard. Please read pages 87 to 96 silently to yourself."

    In about 5 minutes Mrs. Phillips asks all of the students to look at her and begins discussing the story. Then the students take turns reading the story. After they finish with the story, Mrs. Phillips says, "Now please put down your reading books and open your workbooks to page 54. We will be doing pages 54, 55, and 56 today."

    Mrs. Phillips explains how to complete the workbook pages and asks the students if they have any questions about the workbook pages or anything else they will be doing during reading. Then she says, "I would like for the students whose names are listed under Mr. Figglebom to join me at the reading table. I would like to thank the rest of you for working so quietly and responsibly. Remember, if you have a question on something you are doing, quietly ask a neighbor. If that doesn't help, come quietly over to me."

2. Mr. Statton always lists the activities for his eleventh-grade history class on the board before each class period. The students then know the order of the activities and also know what materials to have ready. Today the students are going to be working in small groups after the lesson is introduced. At the beginning of the lesson Mr. Statton said, "Students, since we will be spending most of the class time today in small groups, I would like for us to get in those groups before we begin the lesson. While we are moving our chairs I would also like for you to get your history book, some paper, and a pencil out on your desk." Arranging the students in the groups before the lesson begins eliminates the need to rearrange chairs during the middle of the lesson and does not interrupt the lesson flow.

During the introduction of the lesson Mr. Statton told the class, "We are going to spend about 10 minutes discussing the chapter you were to read last night and then we will work on some activities that go with that chapter in our small groups. Who would like to tell us what were the main events in chapter 8?"

At the end of the discussion Mr. Statton said, "Thank you for doing such a great job reviewing the main events in chapter 8. Now if you will arrange your chairs in each group so that you are facing the other group members and have your paper and pencil handy for writing down ideas, I will explain to you what each group is to work on."

Group Focus

1. In Mrs. Sanders's fourth-grade class, the students are encouraged to read and then complete book reports. The book reports are to include not only telling about the book's characters and events but also a project that is related to the book (e.g., poster, map, shadow box). After students complete a report they present it to the class. The student presenting is usually excited about sharing, but sometimes the other students are not so excited about listening.

   Mrs. Sanders developed a form that students use to critique reports. The students list their favorite character, their favorite part of the book, what they liked about the way the presenter reported on the book, and what they liked about the presenter's project. The items call for positive comments; improvement comments come from the teacher. Students also must list one question that they want to ask the presenter. At the end of the report, different students are called on by the presenter to share their feedback and to ask questions. Then the students give their forms to the presenter.

2. Alice, a seventh-grade student, never liked classes in which different students were selected to read part of the chapter because she found it boring. In Mrs. Johnson's social studies class, Mrs. Johnson breaks the students into groups of three to review chapters. Each student in a group quietly reads one paragraph until the section is read. If a group finishes before the other groups, the students are to discuss with each other the main idea of the section. During this time Mrs. Johnson moves around the room to determine if all of the students are reading and participating. At the end of reading each section, Mrs. Johnson leads the class in a discussion of what they read. Mrs. Johnson makes sure that every student answers at least one question. Then they read the remainder of the pages assigned for the day. Alice really likes this approach because more students read and participate.

Programming to Avoid Satiation

1. Mrs. Fretton loves teaching math to her first-grade students. Today Mrs. Fretton is working on place value and looking at how adding 1 to 9 moves you to the ten's place and adding 1 to 99 moves you to the hundred's place. First Mrs. Fretton uses magnet pieces at the board and has different students group the magnets to show the changes from the one's to the ten's place and from the ten's to the hundred's place. Then Mrs. Fretton passes out small discs for students to use at their desks. They group and regroup together to see what happens when 1 is added to 9 or 99. During the lesson Mrs. Fretton says, "I know this looks difficult, but you are such a sharp class I know we can learn this."

2. Professor Lane plans a variety of activities for each meeting of his biology class. One day he may begin with a short lecture and then break students into small groups to discuss questions he distributed to the groups. In another class period he may begin with a lecture, but then have students work on an activity at the lab tables. On another day, Professor Lane may have the students complete charts on animal groups and then work in groups to compare the material on the charts. He feels that variety will keep the students as interested in the topics as he is. He also encourages and challenges the students. On a day they worked with lots of scientific names of animals he said, "These scientific names are crazy sounding and hard to learn, but I know you can do it. If you can memorize them and list them on a sheet I pass out at the beginning of the next class, I will add 3 extra points to your grade at the end of the semester."

Expectations and Rules

Effective teachers establish a good classroom environment. The beginning of the school year is the time to establish this environment, because it is then that students learn rules and procedures to follow for the year. A major goal is to obtain student cooperation in following rules and procedures and successfully completing assignments. Teacher expectations for student behavior are conveyed to students through rules and procedures that need to be taught. Emmer, Evertson, and Worsham (2000) and Evertson, Emmer, and Worsham (2000) recommend a three-step sequence for doing so: (a) describe and demonstrate desired behaviors to students, (b) have students practice behaviors repeatedly, and (c) provide students with feedback on whether they performed behaviors correctly and suggest improvement where needed.

These ideas are supported by a series of studies that examined third-grade classrooms (Emmer, Evertson, & Anderson, 1980). Researchers observed classrooms at the start of the school year and at other times during the year. They then compared what teachers did during the first 3 weeks of school to determine what distinguished good classroom managers from poor ones. A major difference was how teachers handled rules and routines. Effective classroom managers established clear rules for conduct (e.g., "Be prepared for class"). They also set up routines for conducting tasks (e.g., going to the bathroom). An important priority was to teach students rules and procedures during the first few days of the year. In contrast, ineffective managers did not have clear rules and procedures. In some cases, they had none; in others, the rules were vague (e.g., "Be in the right place at the right time"). They often introduced rules casually without clear explanations.

This research highlights the importance of teachers establishing high expectations for classroom behavior and conveying those expectations to students. They expect students to obey rules and do not tolerate excuses for disobeying them. Research substantiates Kounin's finding that the teacher's proactive efforts to create a productive classroom are critical in establishing good management (Emmer et al., 2000; Evertson et al., 2000; Levin & Nolan, 2000). Rules, procedures, and expectations are proactive techniques designed to prevent problems. Teachers who use them wisely and devote adequate time at the start of the year to instill them in students will not regret the time spent, but rather will find that they benefit student motivation.

Classroom Organization

The preceding discussion makes it clear that teachers can influence student motivation through their planning, scheduling, organization, management, and interactions. That is not surprising, but only recently have researchers examined how classroom factors influence motivation and the process whereby these effects occur. A particularly intriguing area of research addresses the role of classroom structure and organization (Stipek, 1996); specifically, how activities are set up, how students are grouped, how work is evaluated and rewarded, how authority is established, and how time is scheduled. Marshall and Weinstein (1984) contend that classrooms are complex places, that to understand student motivation one must consider many factors, and that factors interact such that one factor may enhance or lessen the impact of another factor. Thus, a democratic classroom may have its motivational impact negated by a system of strict ability grouping. Much has been written about how social comparisons with students of higher ability can have a negative effect on other students' self-efficacy. Such social comparisons, however, also identify who is competent in an area and tells students whom to seek out for help in completing work (Marshall & Weinstein, 1984).

An important aspect of classroom organization is **dimensionality** (Rosenholtz & Simpson, 1984), a basic distinction being between unidimensional and multidimensional classrooms. **Unidimensional classrooms** have a few classroom activities that tap a limited range of student abilities. Classrooms become **multidimensional** when there are more activities that allow for diversity in student abilities and performances. There are four specific characteristics of classrooms that indicate dimensionality (Table 8.6): differentiation of task structure, student autonomy, grouping patterns, and salience of formal performance evaluations.

Unidimensional classrooms have undifferentiated task structures; all students work on similar tasks and a small number of qualitatively similar materials and methods are used during instruction (Rosenholtz & Simpson, 1984). The more undifferentiated the structure, the more likely the daily work will produce consistent performances from each student and the greater the opportunities for social comparisons for students to determine how well they are performing. Negative comparisons can have deleterious

Table 8.6 Dimensionality Characteristics of Classrooms

Characteristic	Unidimensional Class	Multidimensional Class
Differentiation of task structure	Undifferentiated: Students work on same task simultaneously	Differentiated: Students work on different tasks simultaneously
Student autonomy	Low: Students have little choice about what to do, when, and how to do it	High: Students have greater choice of activities, time, place, and method used to complete them
Grouping patterns	Whole-class activities; small groups formed based on ability	Individual work; small groups formed not based on ability
Performance evaluations	Students graded on same assignments; grades are public; much social comparison	Students graded on different assignments; social comparisons less likely because grades reflect progress

effects on the low-performing students. Structures become more differentiated (classrooms become multidimensional) as students work on different tasks at the same time. Social comparisons are less likely to occur and student motivation may be greater.

Student autonomy refers to the degree of choice that students have about tasks and when and how to perform them (see the sections on self-regulation in chapter 4 and intrinsic motivation theory in chapter 6). Classrooms can be unidimensional to the extent that autonomy is low, which can stifle student motivation. Multidimensional classrooms motivate by giving students choices of work and times and places to perform it. Greater autonomy can also enhance intrinsic motivation because it takes individuality into account and provides students with a measure of control (see chapter 6).

Unidimensional classrooms are characterized by social comparisons among students, which become more likely when students work in whole-class activities or are grouped by ability. Comparisons are not as straightforward when students work individually or in groups not formed on the basis of ability. Grouping patterns contribute to the multidimensionality of the classroom and have profound implications for motivation. Grouping also has long-term effects if groups remain intact and students realize they are bound to those groups regardless of their level of performance.

Salience of formal performance evaluations refers to the public nature of grading. Unidimensional classrooms are characterized by students being graded on the same assignments and grades being made public, so students know the grades of others. Those who receive low grades are not motivated to improve. As grading becomes less formal or as grades are assigned for different projects (as in multidimensional classes), grading can motivate more students, especially if they are making progress and grades are improving.

Unidimensional classrooms are also characterized by high visibility of performance (Rosenholtz & Rosenholtz, 1981). This situation may motivate the high achievers but often has negative effects on students who typically perform worse. Multidimensional classrooms motivate more students because they introduce greater differentiation, increase student autonomy, minimize ability grouping, and reduce the extent of public grading of assignments. The work on unidimensional and multidimensional classrooms shares many of the same dimensions as the TARGET framework discussed in chapter 5.

TEACHING IN CONSTRUCTIVIST CLASSROOMS

The research on classroom management and teacher-student interactions helps us understand certain general aspects of the classroom and how they might influence student motivation. This work was mainly based in a process-product tradition of classroom research that attempted to link classroom processes, such as teacher feedback, to student outcomes such as achievement (Dunkin & Biddle, 1974). However, since the cognitive revolution and the development of constructivist and social constructivist perspectives on learning and instruction, there has been an explosion in new ways of thinking about classroom instruction and the development of a movement for classroom and school reform. It is beyond the scope of this book to summarize all of this new theory and research, but it does offer different perspectives on student motivation and learning. In particular, these newer perspectives change the orientation of research and theory from a focus on controlling or managing student learning and behavior to facilitating or encouraging student learning and development.

Much of this work on constructivist classrooms has been focused more on the cognitive side of learning and achievement and has not directly addressed student motivation theoretically or empirically (Hickey, 1997). In addition, a great deal of this work on constructivist classrooms has been motivated and guided by the use of new and powerful technologies to improve instruction (Cognition and Technology Group at Vanderbilt, 1996). These reform efforts to develop constructivist classrooms have been based in elementary, middle, and high schools and have been focused on literacy, math, science, and social studies instruction (Bruer, 1993; McGilly, 1994). Although an important principle of most of these constructivist efforts is that instruction must be deeply embedded in disciplinary content, there have attempts to summarize some general design principles to guide instructional improvement and reform efforts (e.g., Blumenfeld, Fishman, Krajcik, Marx, & Soloway, 2000; Blumenfeld, Soloway, Marx, Krajcik, Guzdial, & Palincsar, 1991; Bransford, Brown, & Cocking, 1999; Brown, 1994, 1997; Brown & Campione, 1994; Greeno, Collins, & Resnick, 1996; Singer, Marx, Krajcik, & Chambers, 2000).

We will discuss some of these design principles here and link them to potential motivational and achievement outcomes. In most of this work, there has been very little empirical evidence for how these different classroom reforms actually influence student motivation, so our discussion is mainly based on theoretical predictions, not necessarily empirical evidence. Some of these design principles overlap with the TARGET framework discussed in chapter 5. In addition, the principles tend to overlap and support one another; that is, there is no assumption that these principles represent orthogonal dimensions of a classroom. Finally, our list cuts across many of the different perspectives and writings on instructional design principles. Some of the principles discussed here may be on all of the different lists, others on only a few of the lists.

1. *Create agency for learning.* This design principle (e.g., Brown, 1997) is just a restatement of motivational theory and research regarding the importance of self-efficacy (see chapter 4), control beliefs (see chapters 3 and 6) and expectancy beliefs (see chapter 2). Basically, the suggestion is that teachers organize their classroom to allow students to experience agency in their own learning, often by providing them with some choice and control, as well as tasks that require them to be active, not passive, learners. As we have pointed out throughout this book, classrooms that help students experience agency should increase their motivation for learning.

2. *Provide opportunities for reflection.* Given the importance of metacognition and self-regulation in learning (Bransford et al., 1999), students need to be provided with opportunities for reflection and thinking about their own thinking, learning, and classroom behaviors. There are numerous ways to provide these opportunities, from teacher modeling of his or her own thinking and reflection, to the use of small groups that facilitate sharing of ideas and questioning other students, to the use of technology that prompts students to think about their answers and their methods of obtaining them. This principle should lead to classroom activities that have a direct effect on student metacognition and self-regulation of cognition. However, the links to student motivation are less clear. It may be that through self-reflection, efficacy perceptions are better calibrated; that is, students who believe they are quite capable or know all the answers are led to see that perhaps they do not yet have all of the answers. There is a clear need for more research on these types of questions.

3. *Organize the classroom for collaboration and cooperation among students, teachers, and others.* One of the hallmarks of social constructivist perspectives on learning is the assumption that learning is inherently a social activity (Hickey, 1997). Given the social nature of learning, it is important to organize classrooms to allow for sustained and coherent collaboration among the members of the classroom. Brown and her colleagues (Brown, 1994, 1997; Brown & Campione, 1994) have labeled their reform effort, "Fostering Communities of Learners" (FCL), to stress the importance of building and sustaining a community in the classroom that is focused on learning and understanding disciplinary knowledge. The creation of a community of learners can certainly help socialize learning and create new opportunities for shared cognitive activity, but how it is linked to student motivation is not clear. At one level, in terms of self-determination theory (see chapter 6), the creation of a community would help to satisfy the basic need of relatedness or belongingness that is assumed to be operating in all individuals. A classroom community where the focus is on all individuals learning—including the teacher, not just the students—may help to decrease social comparison and may facilitate a general mastery goal orientation whereby students are focused on learning and understanding, not trying to outperform one another (adopting a performance goal; see chapter 5).

4. *Use authentic tasks, problems, and assessments.* Both cognitive and motivational researchers have suggested the importance of using authentic tasks, problems, and assessments in classrooms (e.g., Blumenfeld et al., 1991; Brown, Collins, & Duguid, 1989; Greeno et al., 1996; Hickey, 1997). The general idea is that tasks and problems that are more authentic will be more meaningful to students, will increase their interest, and will lead to better learning. Of course, there is disagreement about what types of tasks are truly authentic. For some researchers and teachers, tasks are only authentic if they are based or grounded in the knowledge and frameworks of the disciplines. In this case, in science classes for example, students should be working on tasks that are similar to the tasks that biologists, chemists, or physicists undertake in their own disciplinary scientific research. In the same way, math classes should focus on helping students to think mathematically, to become "mathematicians," and to mathematize everyday problems. Others have suggested that K–12 school subject areas are somewhat different and should have different educational goals than the disciplines and should not strive to make everyone a little scientist or mathematician. In contrast, the emphasis is still on disciplinary content, but the focus may be on real-life applications or content that has some utility beyond the classroom. Regardless of this debate, the use of authentic tasks is deemed to be useful cognitively because they should facilitate transfer of learning outside the classroom context. From a motivational perspective, the usual assumption is that authentic tasks will engage student interest, intrinsic motivation, or utility value (see chapters 2, 6, and 7) which will lead to better learning and achievement.

5. *Create and sustain classroom discourse on learning and knowledge.* As part of collaborating around authentic tasks, the teachers and students should develop a mode of talking, listening, questioning, and discussing issues related to the content knowledge of the class as well as the general topic of how to learn and understand. This can happen through class discussions or student presentations, through reciprocal teaching activities (Brown, 1997; Palincsar & Brown, 1984), in the discussion of experiments, and the use of technology. Again, this design principle may be more focused on cognition, but it would be assumed to help maintain student interest as well as perhaps student efficacy

as students can come to see that most members of the classroom community are trying to learn and understand the content.

6. *Provide opportunities for practice of ways of thinking and learning.* This design principle is similar to the guided practice principle suggested by Rosenshine and Stevens (1986) and discussed in an earlier section of this chapter. In constructivist classrooms, however, this principle refers not just to simple drill and practice exercises, but to the creation of a community of practice and inquiry (Brown, 1994; Greeno et al., 1996; Singer et al., 2000). In these contexts, students have opportunities to actually engage in and practice some of the same activities that disciplinary experts engage in when they are doing their work. For example, students in science classrooms would engage in real experiments and inquiry around a particular problem or driving question that involves deep science content and application to real-world problems (Blumenfeld et al., 1991; Singer et al., 2000). This would include the design of data-collection activities, the analysis and presentation of the data, and making correct inferences and conclusions from the evidence. This should foster interest and value, as well as self-efficacy.

7. *Provide learning tools that support student learning when working on challenging tasks.* The kinds of authentic tasks and the nature of inquiry and learning in these constructivist classrooms often involve projects, experiments, papers, presentations, etc. that are much harder for students to manage. In addition, they unfold over longer periods of time—they are not just done in a short period of time like worksheets or other simple academic tasks. These tasks and activities require self-regulation and often push students beyond their normal range of skills and knowledge. As such, various tools, particularly those available through the use of powerful technologies, can help students manage these tasks (Cognition and Technology Group at Vanderbilt, 1996; Edelson, Gordin, & Pea, 1999; Singer et al., 2000). These tools can reduce the cognitive load on students and allow them to think and learn more effectively than if they were trying to do all of the cognitive activities associated with such complex and challenging tasks. Of course, from a motivational point of view, these learning tools are often fun and interesting for the students to use, thereby increasing the interest and value beliefs (see chapters 2, 6, and 7). The tools also support skill development which should lead to better self-efficacy.

8. *Have students create and use various artifacts.* The sharing of ideas and knowledge in constructivist classrooms can be a challenging task because it is often difficult for students to talk about their ideas and to communicate them to others clearly. The creation of artifacts, such as reports, concept maps, physical models, charts, graphs, figures, etc., can help students put into concrete form some of their ideas. In addition, other students can readily see these artifacts and discuss them and their meaning with all of the members of the classroom. This can help to support and sustain the discourse and inquiry in these classrooms. In addition, by making "cognition" concrete, it may help students reflect on their own and others' thinking. The production of artifacts may help students increase their efficacy for learning as well as increase their interest in the academic content and tasks.

9. *Provide scaffolding to support student learning.* Although the phrase "scaffolding of learning" has almost become a cliché, it does reflect an important principle of Vygotskian and social constructivist perspectives on instruction (Hogan & Pressley, 1997). The basic idea is that teachers (or other students, parents) provide support to a student as that student is learning a new task. These supports help students perform at a level that would be unattainable without the assistance. By working within this zone of proximal development

(ZPD) between what the student can do without help and with help, the student comes to learn how to do the task. The supports can then be faded or taken away (just as building scaffolding is taken down after construction is complete). Teachers and other competent individuals can provide scaffolding by providing models or different representations, by thinking aloud, by giving hints, by providing useful feedback, by guiding students through the first part of a task, etc. Of course, the idea of scaffolding through modeling and feedback is also present in other theories such as self-efficacy theory. As such, these types of scaffolding would be expected to support and develop positive self-efficacy judgments as the student comes to be able to accomplish tasks that he or she would not be able to accomplish alone.

10. *Create a culture of learning and respect for others.* In some ways, this last principle is the sum of all of the previous principles. As noted at the beginning of this section, the principles do overlap; to engage in one of them usually requires engaging in some of the other principles as well. Creating a culture of learning requires many of the other principles mentioned. However, one aspect that has not been mentioned specifically in the previous nine principles is the importance of norms and expectations about respecting others in terms of their knowledge, beliefs, and individual differences (Brown, 1994). Classrooms are social situations with anywhere from 10–40 students and at least one teacher, all of whom have somewhat different levels of knowledge, skills, beliefs, and attitudes. If the other principles regarding sharing ideas, collaborating on projects, and engaging in discourse, inquiry, and practice are to be implemented smoothly, there must be respect for other people's ideas and beliefs. A classroom where students are afraid to express their ideas for fear of ridicule or embarrassment will not be conducive to the use of the other constructivist principles. Accordingly, teachers must help to set these norms and expectations clearly with the students. Of course, this should enable the use of the other principles, but it also will help in terms of student motivation. It is certainly in line with the goal-content theory principles outlined in chapter 5, and it should help relieve student anxiety (see chapter 7) as well as foster general feelings of self-worth (see chapter 7).

These 10 principles are suggested as starting points in the development of constructivist classrooms. Because they are general, they will have to be modified and adapted to fit with the disciplinary knowledge being taught and with other classroom factors (e.g., class size, types of students), as well the classroom and school constraints (e.g., availability of technology) that are always operating in schools. Much of the theory and research on these ideas and principles has been focused on how they help improve student cognition, but has not specifically examined how they might facilitate student motivation. We look forward to more sustained and careful research on these issues in the future.

SUMMARY

Teachers can affect student motivation in many ways. An important means is through planning and decision making. Some models of teacher planning are prescriptive and state what teachers should do to foster student learning. Other models conceive of planning as beginning with teacher decisions about the types of learning activities to be used. Objectives are formulated and integrated with activities. Currently, many researchers are exploring teachers' thought processes prior to, during, and after teaching. In this view, planning and decision making are not confined to the preinstructional phase of teaching but instead occur throughout all phases of teaching. Teachers often do not use a rational planning model, but instead begin by considering the setting and content to be taught. Teacher planning is strongly influenced by student characteristics, and motivational concerns are important in decision making.

A critical component of planning is deciding on what activities students will work, which involves decisions about grouping. Types of grouping structures are competitive, cooperative, and individualistic. Structures affect student motivation largely by the cues they provide that inform learners about their capabilities. Competitive structures highlight the importance of ability and increase the likelihood of social comparisons with others. In individualistic structures, rewards are based on self-improvement. Cooperative structures allow students to share the rewards as a function of the group's collective performance.

Research exploring the effects of teaching practices on student achievement shows that when teachers teach well-structured content, they engage in practices that are consistent with principles of contemporary cognitive theories of learning (e.g., begin with a short review of prior relevant material, present material in small steps). These practices are also likely to enhance motivation and facilitate success because they help to ensure that students learn. Another important influence on student motivation is the use of models. Models provide vicarious information for learners to use in appraising their self-efficacy and motivate them to try the task themselves. Multiple models and peer models can impact student motivation; for some students, portraying behaviors designed to cope with difficulties is useful.

Teacher-student interactions are critical influences on motivation. A major teaching function is providing different forms of feedback: performance, motivational, attributional, and strategy. Another function involves dispensing rewards. Rewards enhance motivation when they are linked to progress in learning and thereby inform learners about their competencies. Classroom climate affects motivation. The best effects on motivation and performance derive from the democratic (collaborative) classroom leader, who works with students cooperatively and encourages their problem solving and decision making. Laissez-faire (permissive) leadership creates chaos and uncertainty; authoritarian (autocratic) leadership leads to high performance but also to frustration, aggression, and a negative group atmosphere.

Teacher-student interactions often involve praise and criticism. Praise is a type of positive reinforcer. Although praise usually facilitates motivation, teachers often do not deliver praise contingent on good performance, but rather give it infrequently and noncontingently. Beyond the early grades in school, praise is often a weak reinforcer. Moderate criticism may motivate but the effects diminish when criticism is high. Providing unsolicited help is another way that teachers interact with students. Help can correct problems and inform students of their progress, which raises motivation.

Much research has examined the influence of teacher expectations on student learning and performance. The Pygmalion study found that teacher expectancies acted as self-fulfilling prophecies because student achievement came to reflect the expectations. This conclusion is controversial and research has not always demonstrated expectation effects. Various explanations have been proposed for how teachers form expectations and convey them to students and how, in turn, student motivation and achievement are affected. Much of the time expectations are realistic and based upon observations. They become problematic when they are inappropriate and inflexible.

An important type of teacher expectation is teacher self-efficacy, or teachers' beliefs about their capabilities to help students learn. Efficacious teachers are more likely to plan challenging activities, persist in helping students learn and overcome difficulties, and facilitate motivation and achievement in their students. Teacher self-efficacy can be developed through performance successes and through observation of models displaying effective teaching practices.

Teacher activities relating to classroom management, which are designed to prevent, minimize, and deal with problems, also affect student motivation. Kounin identified several key variables, including the ripple effect—the qualities of desists, withitness, overlapping, movement management, group focus, and programming to avoid satiation. Kounin found that good classroom management depended on the teacher's proactive efforts to prevent disciplinary problems; how teachers reacted to misbehavior and the techniques they used to deal with it made little difference. Productive classrooms in which students are motivated to learn are those with expectations and rules, which are best established at the start of the school year and enforced consistently and fairly.

Much recent work has examined the role of classroom structure and organization in motivation. An important organizational aspect is dimensionality. Unidimensional classrooms have a few activities that tap a limited range of student abilities; multidimensional classrooms have more activities that allow for greater diversity in student abilities and differences in student performances. Unidimensional and multidimensional classrooms differ in task structure, student autonomy, grouping patterns, and salience of formal performance evaluations.

More recently, there have been many suggestions for the development of constructivist classrooms. Ten general principles were discussed that should help to facilitate both student cognition and motivation. They include: creating agency, encouraging reflection, facilitating collaboration, using authentic tasks, engaging in sustained discourse, providing practice, using tools, creating artifacts, providing scaffolding, and creating a culture of respect for others.

CHAPTER

9

The Role of Schools in Motivation

*S*hirley, Chris, and Stasia are students at a big, urban high school. They are talking about their school as they walk to school in the morning.

Shirley: I really hate going to this place. It really gets to me. I mean, you have to show up here every day and all these teachers do is just talk at you. They never listen to you. It's like they just don't care about us, all they really care about is getting through the books and for us to get high scores on the stupid state tests. I don't think some of them even know my name.

Chris: Aw, c'mon, Shirl, it's not that bad. They try hard but they have so many of us and so little time to do anything but teach.

Shirley: Well, they could at least act like they cared about us sometimes.

Stasia: Yeah. Chris, I think you think it's okay because you do well and no one bothers you. You're a guy and they leave you alone. We get picked on all the time. I'm scared half the time when I go to the bathroom. I won't even go to that bathroom on the second floor at the end of the hallway.

Shirley: Oh, yeah, that one. That's where all the losers hang out, those kids in the low track. I'm afraid of them, too. I think they would just as soon beat you up as look at you. I won't go there either.

Chris: What are you talking about? Come to the boys' gym sometime, then you'll see pure fear. Half the kids won't even look at anyone else because they don't want to act like they disrespect anyone. That could be dangerous and it sure makes it hard to play basketball if no one will even look at each other. At least in my neighborhood we know each other. There are fights and all, but we know we belong there. Here you never feel like you belong to anything. I just keep to myself and try to do well in my classes. I can't wait to get out of here and get to college.

Stasia: Yeah, but the thing that gets to me is that these kids never get in trouble. They break the rules all the time, get into fights, and the teachers never do anything about it.

Shirley: Oh, I don't know. I think those kids always get into trouble. The teachers seem to be just waiting for them to screw up and then they nail them. People like Chris who brownnose the teacher, they can get away with murder. Those other kids, they just won't play the game and they get killed.

Chris: Hey, that's not fair! I just do my work and stay out of trouble.

Shirley and Stasia: Yeah, right!

At the same time, several teachers are talking in the faculty lounge, waiting for the day to start.

Ms. Strobel: *Well, another day at the salt mines. It is so hard to keep going. Most of the kids are not motivated, and the rest of the kids are just troublemakers. I think they love to see how far they can push the rules. Then, if you do call them on it, they raise a stink and the principal doesn't even back you up.*

Mr. Lin: *What, are you dreaming? Half the teachers don't even believe in the rules. That's one of the problems around here, the staff can't even agree on what the rules should be, let alone what we should be doing in our classrooms.*

Mr. De Groot: *Yes, I went to this workshop about teaching for conceptual understanding a few weeks ago and thought it would be good to try some of the ideas in my classroom, but most of my colleagues in the math department just laughed when I told them about it. They said, "Who cares about those kinds of things?" The only thing that matters is that the kids do well on the standardized tests. They're not going to change their ways.*

Ms. Strobel: *Well, I'd like to hear about those ideas. It's a big thing in science, this conceptual change stuff, but I don't really understand how you're supposed to do it and still cover the curriculum. I sure could use some new ideas, though. It might motivate me. But when could we do it? You have fourth hour free and I have second hour. There really isn't much time to talk about this.*

Mr. Lin: *There's the bell! Off to another day in the trenches.*

These students and teachers are talking about different aspects of a school's culture and organization. In the previous chapter, we discussed how characteristics of the classroom can influence students' motivation. In this chapter, we turn to a larger unit of analysis, the school level, and show how schools can influence student motivation. A focus on schools as the unit of analysis has not been adopted by many psychologists interested in motivation, but there are a few exceptions (see Maehr & Midgley, 1991, 1996; Mac Iver, Reuman, & Main, 1995; Sarason, 1990). Psychologists, given their disciplinary traditions, have tended to focus on individuals and have been concerned with how individuals' motivational beliefs, perceptions, needs, goals, and so on can influence motivation and behavior. In many ways, the psychological theories and basic and applied research described in chapters 2 through 7 took this perspective. Of course, in chapter 8 specifically, and in most of the other chapters, we have contextualized our discussion of the theories and research in terms of what they mean for student motivation and teacher behavior in classrooms. At the same time, as will become clear in this chapter, many of the psychological ideas regarding individual motivation are relevant to a school-level analysis.

Nevertheless, a move to a discussion of school influences involves a shift from a more psychological perspective to a more sociological and cultural perspective. In fact, much of the research and theory we will draw on in this chapter comes from the sociology of education and school effectiveness literature, rather than the educational and motivational psychology literature. As such, some of this sociological literature has been more concerned with overall student achievement and academic performance on standardized tests, not with student motivation as we have conceptualized it in this book. Moreover, when concerned about social outcomes, this literature has tended to use more broadly defined constructs such as commitment and engagement, not the more specific and narrowly defined motivational constructs used by psychologists. These more global constructs are surely related to the types of motivational beliefs such as expectancies, values, attributions, self-efficacy, goals, intrinsic motivation, and interest that we have been discussing in this book, but the empirical research on school-level effects has not necessarily focused on them. Given this gap in the literature, some of our discussion of school effects on student motivation in this chapter will be more speculative and general than in previous chapters. In addition, most of the research is correlational, so it is difficult to make strong, causal statements. Of course, there are some motivational psychologists (e.g., Eccles & Midgley, 1989; Maehr & Midgley, 1991, 1996) who have been concerned with the effects of school culture and organization on specific motivational beliefs. When relevant, we will rely heavily on their work in this chapter.

After studying this chapter, you should be able to:

1. Organize the different school-level factors into a conceptual model with links to teacher and student outcomes.
2. Understand how different school-level factors can operate to influence teacher and student motivation.
3. Understand how external constraints and opportunities can facilitate or constrain school reform efforts and, by implication, influence teacher and student motivation.
4. Analyze the various strategies for school reform or improvement in terms of their potential teacher or student outcomes as well as the challenges in attempting to implement them.

Figure 9.1 displays the general conceptual framework that we will use as a heuristic to help us organize this chapter. This figure is based on the overview of school effects in Lee, Bryk, and Smith (1993) and Maehr and Midgley (1991). The component at the top of the figure displays the various external constraints and opportunities that can have an influence on school culture and organization as well as on teachers and students. The main focus of discussion in this chapter will be the next component in the figure, school culture and organization. As in chapter 5, the TARGET framework that was developed by Epstein (1989) and has been applied to classrooms and schools (see Maehr & Midgley, 1991, 1996) serves as the main organizer for our treatment of school culture and organization. Finally, Figure 9.1 shows that school culture and organization can have an

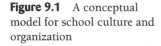

Figure 9.1   A conceptual model for school culture and organization

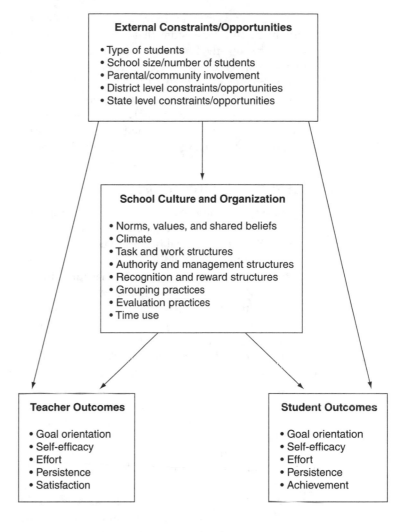

influence on teacher and student motivation and behavior. We will focus on the school culture and organization component first, sketching out how it can influence teacher and student motivation and behavior. Then, paralleling the organization of the previous chapters where we discussed developmental and individual differences, we will discuss how the various external constraints and opportunities might moderate the general relations between school culture and organization and teacher and student outcomes.

SCHOOL CULTURE AND ORGANIZATION

The eight dimensions listed in Figure 9.1 under the school culture and organization component represent various features of schools that can have an influence on teacher and student outcomes. These eight dimensions are listed separately only for expository purposes in this chapter. In the reality of schools, they are overlapping, interdependent, and interactive dimensions that help to create the overall culture of the school building. In many ways, the first two—school norms, values, and shared beliefs and school climate—which are more perceptual and constructive dimensions, will be reflected and instantiated in the other six TARGET dimensions. At the same time, the six TARGET dimensions, which are more directly observable, will help to create the norms and climate of the school. Accordingly, to discuss them as separate dimensions is somewhat misleading given how they combine to constitute school culture, but for the didactic purposes of this chapter, it is a necessary rhetorical strategy.

Norms, Values, and Shared Beliefs

There are any number of ways from psychology, sociology, and anthropology to theoretically define and conceptualize norms, values, and shared beliefs. We will not detail these different theoretical perspectives, but rather for our purposes in this book, we will use a fairly broad and global definition. If one thinks of a school building as having a culture, just as different countries have a culture, then the individuals in the school building will share some common values and core beliefs about the organization, its function, its students, and its teaching and learning practices. These core beliefs and values are constructed by the individuals and can be consciously held, as in the case of a list of school goals, or implicit beliefs that are reflected in the daily practices that guide teacher and student behavior. There should be some tacit consensus among individuals within a school about these beliefs because they are partially created by the school structure and organization, but there is always the possibility that there will be subcultures of individuals within a building that do not necessarily endorse the beliefs of the larger group. In any event, as one talks to individuals in schools and observes the practices and organization of the school, it is possible to come to an understanding of the norms, values, and shared beliefs of a school.

It is important to note that the effects these beliefs might have on students must be mediated through the actual practices that teachers engage in as they interact with the students. Accordingly, whereas it is valuable to acknowledge the role of shared beliefs, it will become even more significant to discuss the actual practices that teachers use, which we do later in this chapter. The shared beliefs become very important, however, when there are efforts made to change teacher or school practices because the beliefs can act as a constraint on the reform efforts (Blumenfeld, Fishman, Krajcik, Marx, & Soloway, 2000). These shared beliefs can be seen as analogous to the entrenched beliefs and knowledge that individual students have about science concepts in the conceptual change literature (Patrick & Pintrich, 2001; Pintrich, Marx, & Boyle, 1993; Woolfolk Hoy & Murphy, 2001). In the same way, the shared beliefs at the school level can act as an ecology of school-level thinking that can accept, adapt to, or resist change. Changing the shared beliefs of a building is analogous to the difficulty of the conceptual change process at the individual level (Maehr & Midgley, 1996).

There are a number of aspects of these shared beliefs that could have an influence on both teachers and students. However, in terms of our interest in motivational outcomes, we will focus on four general beliefs. These four beliefs can influence the types of instructional practices that teachers will engage in and how they will interact with their students. In turn, these practices can influence student motivation and learning. The first general belief concerns a very global belief about the character of human nature. Are students basically good, motivated to learn, and intrinsically interested in schoolwork or are they basically bad, not motivated to learn, and in need of control or coercion to do their schoolwork? At some level, these beliefs hearken back to the general metatheoretical positions and metaphors we discussed in chapter 1 as organizing principles for motivational theories. These very general beliefs will obviously have some influence on the types of discipline and management practices that are put into place at the school (Maehr & Midgley, 1996). In turn, we know from goal orientation theory (see chapter 5) and intrinsic motivation theory (see chapter 6) that certain types of practices whereby students have less control and choice (see chapter 8) may result in students who will be less mastery oriented and less intrinsically motivated.

The second aspect of beliefs concerns the malleability or stability of student learning and ability. At a general school level, teachers can believe that the students can learn and that students can increase their knowledge and ability to do well in school (an incremental belief about learning and intelligence), or the teachers can have an entity belief about student learning and ability that assumes that students have a set amount of ability and that it will not change much (Dweck, 1999; Dweck & Leggett, 1988; Woolfolk Hoy & Murphy, 2001). This belief about the malleability of student ability is related to the idea from the effective schools literature that teachers should have high expectations for all students (Brookover, Beady, Flood, Schweitzer, & Wisenbaker, 1979; Edmonds, 1979; Purkey & Smith, 1983; Rutter, Maughan, Mortimore, Ouston, & Smith, 1979). This literature on school effectiveness has proposed that one of the tenets of an effective school is the shared belief among staff that all students can learn and, therefore, teachers should have high expectations for all students regarding their ability to learn and master the material (see chapter 8). Good and Brophy (1986) point out, however, that it is difficult in many of the school effectiveness studies to assess causality between school practices, such as setting high expectations for everyone in the building, and student achievement given the correlational designs used. Nevertheless, current motivational theories about incremental and entity beliefs and goal orientation (Ames, 1992b; Dweck, 1999; Dweck & Leggett, 1988; Maehr & Midgley, 1991) and the stability of attributions (Weiner, 1986; see chapter 3) suggest that having a general incremental belief about the malleability of student learning at the school level would lead to positive school practices regarding instruction. For example, if teachers believe that all students can learn and that students' ability is not stable, they might be more willing to use instructional practices like reciprocal teaching (see Rosenshine & Meister, 1994) that require more teacher effort and support of students.

A third aspect of the shared beliefs system that could have an influence on teacher practices and, in turn, on student motivation essentially relates to shared beliefs and norms about teaching and instruction. At one level, the content of these beliefs can refer to norms about how instruction is supposed to occur in classrooms. For example, school norms about the need for quiet classrooms where students work silently and individually at their seats as a sign of good instruction or of a good teacher may not be most conducive to student motivation and cognition given current constructivist views of teaching and learning (see chapter 8). Of course, if these are the norms for the building and they are enforced by the principal and other teachers directly (warnings from principal) or indirectly (faculty lounge discussions; see teacher conversation at beginning of this chapter), then it may be difficult to use constructivist teaching practices, cooperative groups, discovery or inquiry learning, or project-based learning, which require more interaction and discussion among students and teachers (see chapter 8).

At a more psychological level, beliefs about teaching can refer to the perceptions of controllability and efficacy that teachers have about instruction (Ashton & Webb, 1986; Goddard, Hoy, & Woolfolk Hoy, 2000; Tschannen-Moran, Woolfolk Hoy, & Hoy, 1998; Woolfolk & Hoy, 1990). That is, do teachers in the building share the belief that their instructional actions can make a difference in student motivation or learning, or do they assume that student change is beyond their control? If these beliefs about lack of control and efficacy of instruction become very rigid and stable, teachers may develop a sense of learned helplessness about their efforts. For example, teachers in a large urban school that serves children with many life stresses may begin to see their instructional efforts as fruitless. Of course, as we have already seen in chapter 3 in our discussion of attribution theory, this type of attributional pattern of helplessness will not be conducive to change in behavior, exertion of effort, or persistence. Teachers with this pattern of beliefs will be unlikely to try to engage in much innovative instruction and, in some cases of severe teacher helplessness and burnout, even much of any kind of instruction. In these cases, it seems clear that student motivation and learning will suffer. In fact, Midgley, Feldlaufer, and Eccles (1989a), in a longitudinal study of the transition from elementary school to middle school, found that students who moved from having high-efficacy elementary math teachers to low-efficacy middle school math teachers had the lowest level of expectancy beliefs for math performance in comparison to other students.

More recently, there has been increased interest and focus on teacher efficacy beliefs and how these beliefs are linked to teacher behavior and student achievement (e.g., Goddard, Hoy, & Woolfolk Hoy, 2000; Tschannen-Moran, Woolfolk Hoy, & Hoy, 1998; Woolfolk & Hoy, 1990). This research has proceeded on a number of different levels, but one that is important to note here is a distinction between teacher efficacy at the individual level and collective teacher efficacy. Teacher efficacy at the individual teacher level maps onto the same definition of student self-efficacy discussed in chapter 4. That is, it refers to the self-efficacy beliefs of the teacher to organize and execute plans of action to attain a goal at some level (see chapter 4; Tschannen-Moran, Woolfolk Hoy, & Hoy, 1998). Teachers high in individual teacher efficacy believe they can enact certain teaching strategies and have an effect on student learning or motivation, while teachers with low efficacy tend to believe they cannot use these strategies or behaviors and doubt whether they can really have an effect on students. Collective teacher efficacy refers to the school level or group level beliefs of teachers about efficacy. It is not an individual teacher's beliefs about his or her own efficacy, it is the school-wide or group's shared belief about its efficacy to enact strategies to reach goals (Goddard et al., 2000). It is assessed at the group level by having teachers respond to items such as, "Teachers in this school are able to get through to difficult students," and then analyzing these responses at the group level through the use of multi-level data analysis (e.g., hierarchical linear modeling) that maps the school-level beliefs to school-level achievement outcomes (Goddard, in press; Goddard et al., 2000). In contrast, teacher efficacy at the individual level would ask the teacher to respond to the same item in terms his or her own behavior such as "I'm confident I can get through to difficult students." This work on both individual and collective teacher efficacy has shown that teachers and schools that have high levels of efficacy are more likely to have students with higher levels of achievement and learning. It seems clear that teacher efficacy and collective efficacy are both important beliefs that can have an impact on student motivation as well as overall achievement.

The fourth, and final, aspect of the belief system that could have an influence on teachers and students concerns the shared goals or purposes of the school. The effective schools literature (Brookover et al., 1979; Good & Brophy, 1986; Edmonds, 1979; Purkey & Smith, 1983; Rutter et al., 1979) has stressed the importance of a school having an agreed upon set of clear goals and purposes (a mission statement for the school). The related literature on the principal as an instructional leader (e.g., Leithwood & Montgomery, 1982; Manassee, 1985) has also stressed the importance of the principal as an instructional leader who helps a school building staff develop and strive for a set of clearly articulated goals. A set of clear and shared goals that is consistently enforced would certainly help guide teachers and students as they make choices about their behavior (recall Ms. Strobel's comment about behavior at the beginning of this chapter). In fact, Good and Brophy (1986) summarize this research by noting that schools with clear goals had higher teacher morale, fewer classroom disruptions, less student misbehavior, more time-on-task, and lower student absenteeism—all positive teacher and student outcomes (see Figure 9.1).

Although clear goals are undoubtedly important for a school, Lee, Bryk, and Smith (1993) have pointed out that much of this research has not examined the content of the goals in an effective school. They note that this research has often used what they call a rational-bureaucratic model to conceptualize school organization. They suggest that it can be misleading to ignore the content of the goals that are put forth by a school. First, they note that there can be multiple goals operating at different levels in a school (e.g., between departments in a secondary school regarding teaching all students versus preparing the academic elite; or teaching to the test versus teaching for conceptual understanding; see Mr. De Groot's comments at the beginning of this chapter) and that the content of these goals may not be compatible. Second, they suggest that even if the organizational goals are clear and shared, there may be some disagreement about the desirability of these goals. Lee and colleagues (Lee et al., 1993) provide examples of two organizations that have very clear and shared goals: a medical school (see Becker, Geer, & Hughes, 1961) and a fundamentalist academy (see Peshkin, 1986), yet point out that the culture in these two organizations may not be the most adaptive or democratic. They note that the medical school had very clear goals and common activities but the result was a very competitive environment with low personal support. The fundamentalist academy also had clearly articulated goals, but the goals did not encourage tolerance of diversity and, hence, were antithetical to some basic democratic values (Lee et al., 1993). Lee and colleagues (Lee et al., 1993) suggest that a communitarian perspective regarding goals, with an emphasis on social and personal relations, on creating a community, and on a shared ethos, may be more adaptive for schools than a rational-bureaucratic model.

Other research on the content of shared beliefs and norms has stressed the academic emphasis of the school (e.g., Goddard, Sweetland, & Hoy, in press; Hoy & Sabo, 1998; Hoy, Tarter, & Kottkamp, 1991). Schools that take as their main goal the quest for academic excellence seem to have higher levels of achievement. These schools are characterized by teachers setting high goals and expectations for all students, the school environment is serious about academic issues, teachers take responsibility for student success, and the teachers and principals pursue and respect academic success (Goddard et al., in press). This is similar in some ways to the effective schools research, but the key idea is that there is a set of shared norms and goals for all staff in the school that is focused on academic achievement and success.

Maehr and Midgley (1996) also raise this issue regarding the importance of the content of the shared goals, not merely having consensus about any goals. Given their work on the role of achievement goals at the school level (Anderman & Maehr, 1994; Maehr & Midgley, 1991; Midgley & Wood, 1993), they suggest that schools should adopt goals that are in line with a general mastery goal orientation. As pointed out in chapter 5, this goal orientation defines success as individual improvement, growth, and mastery. Value is placed on effort, evaluation criteria are absolute and based on progress toward these standards, and errors are viewed as informational and part of learning. In contrast, a performance goal orientation defines success as besting others on tests and grades and winning at all costs. Value is placed on avoiding failure, evaluation criteria are normative and force comparisons between teachers and students, and errors are viewed as failures to be avoided at all costs. At the school level, these different goal orientations would be reflected in the staff position on standardized test scores, the public display of grades and honors (bulletin boards displaying only some students' work), competitions for academic performance (numbers of books read in a month without concern for comprehension), grouping and teaching practices, and differential and salient rewards for winning competitions of academic performance (special field trips awarded to top 10% of students in a schoolwide ranking of performance), all of which can have important influences on student outcomes (Mac Iver et al., 1995).

These school-level beliefs and the practices that are derived from them can, in turn, create individual goal orientations (Anderman & Maehr, 1994; Maehr & Midgley, 1996). As discussed in chapter 5, a personal goal orientation toward mastery, in comparison to performance goals, has a strong link to a number of positive motivational and cognitive outcomes, including better self-efficacy, more effort and persistence, more cognitive engagement, and better achievement. Whereas we stressed the importance of individuals' personal goal orientations in chapter 5, the research on school context suggests that these personal goals are created, supported, and maintained by both the classroom and school context. Accordingly, if a school wishes its students to be mastery oriented at the individual level, the content of the school's goals should reflect the same type of mastery orientation at the building level (Maehr & Midgley, 1996).

Climate

The climate of a school building can also have an influence on teacher and student outcomes. The construct of school climate has been defined in many different ways using a number of different typologies and theories and, not surprisingly, has been researched using a number of different methodologies (Anderson, 1982; Moos, 1979). In some ways, the construct of school climate has been incorporated into research on school culture, reflecting a general shift away from simple psychological models of climate to more complex sociological and anthropological perspectives on school culture. Most of the six TARGET dimensions listed in Figure 9.1 as part of school culture and organization would have been included in various models of school climate as well as the dimension of norms, values, and shared beliefs just discussed (see Anderson, 1982). However, we will single out three affective aspects of school climate and discuss them in this section as part of climate rather than as part of the other seven dimensions listed in Figure 9.1. The three aspects are (a) a sense of community and belongingness, (b) warmth and civility in personal relations, and (c) feelings of safety and security.

A sense of community is a rather vague construct, but it would include individuals' feelings that they belong to the group or organization (recall the comments by Chris at the beginning of the chapter), that they are committed to the organization's goals and values (see preceding discussion), and that there is some reciprocity in the relation such that the representatives of the organization care about and are concerned about the individual group member. Lee and colleagues (Lee et al., 1993) stress the importance of a communitarian perspective on school organization that focuses explicitly on the quality of the social relations among the individuals in the organization. They note that schools where the administration, faculty, and students seem to demonstrate mutual respect and concern for each other are linked to positive outcomes for teachers and students (see Figure 9.1). Noddings (1992) has proposed that caring for others is an important component that should be present in all relations in a school as well as explicitly taught in the curriculum. The student dropout and at-risk student literature also suggests that the absence of teacher concern and care (recall Shirley's comments at the beginning of this chapter) is a major factor mentioned by students who leave school (Bryk, Lee, & Holland, 1993; Calabrese & Poe, 1990; Lee et al., 1993; Natriello, 1986). Deci and Ryan (1985) also propose that all individuals have a basic need to feel a sense of belongingness or relatedness and that organizational structures that support or satisfy this need will result in more intrinsic motivation and engagement (see chapter 6). Skinner and Belmont (1993) have shown that students' feelings of relatedness are sensitive to contextual aspects of the classroom and are connected to their future motivation and involvement. Given these few examples that reflect the results from both sociological and psychological research, it seems important, at least from a motivational perspective, that teachers and students feel a sense of community in their schools.

The second dimension of climate also reflects the affective life of the school in terms of the warmth and civility expressed in the relations among individuals in the building. At the teacher and staff level, Lee and colleagues (Lee et al., 1993) have noted that research from both the rational-bureaucratic and the communitarian perspectives has shown that civil and collegial relations between teachers and administrators are associated with positive outcomes in terms of organizational effectiveness. The effective schools literature also stresses the importance of collegial relations for school effectiveness (Purkey & Smith, 1983). In addition, these researchers (Lee et al., 1993) note that friendly and collegial relations among teachers helps them personally in terms of easing the isolation of teaching and is associated with more teacher satisfaction.

In terms of teacher-student relations, certainly a feeling of concern, care, support, and respect for students and positive teacher-student interactions would be associated with positive motivational outcomes (see Calabrese & Poe, 1990; Eccles, Midgley, Wigfield, Buchanan et al., 1993; Midgley, Feldlaufer, & Eccles, 1989b; Natriello, 1986). Bryk, Lee, and Holland (1993), in their study of Catholic schools, suggest that a concern for the welfare of others or the creation of a caring community can have very positive effects for all students, even those from populations that would be at risk for school failure. The literature on middle schools suggests that they are more bureaucratic, less personal, and engender fewer positive teacher-student interactions than elementary schools. These differences have been linked to declines in student motivation as the students make the transition to middle schools (Eccles, Midgley, Wigfield, Reuman et al., 1993; Midgley et al., 1989b). In their review of the process-product research on teaching, Brophy and Good (1986) note that the emotional climate of the classroom (as defined by teacher criticism and teacher and student negative affect) can be associated with student achievement. However, they note that although a very negative emotional climate can have negative consequences for achievement, a warm emotional climate is not necessarily associated with better achievement. They suggest that neutral climates are just as supportive of achievement as warm climates. At the same time, it should be noted that these classroom studies focused only on student achievement on standardized tests for the most part; motivational constructs were not usually examined. Nevertheless, it seems clear that positive teacher-student interactions at the school level can create a positive climate for all members of the school community.

The last dimension of climate refers to the teachers' and students' feelings of personal safety and security (see students' comments at the beginning of the chapter). In one sense of psychological climate, these perceptions could refer to individuals' feelings about taking risks and feeling secure in expressing different ideas and opinions. However, in many schools today, this aspect of climate refers to feelings of physical safety and being free from the fear and anxiety of physical harm. There is no real need to document the harmful effects and problems that school violence can create in a school building, although the school effectiveness literature has demonstrated the importance of this decision. For example, Lee and Bryk (1989) have shown that schools that offer a safe and orderly environment have higher achievement, especially for minority students. As common sense will tell us, and as Maslow's (1954) hierarchy of needs suggests (see chapter 5), if individuals are concerned about basic survival and safety needs, it is difficult for them to achieve other goals. Accordingly, it is important for schools to offer a safe and secure environment for all staff and students.

Task and Work Structures

The remaining six dimensions of school culture and organization reflect the TARGET dimensions that were introduced in chapter 5 on classroom goal structures. These same dimensions can be applied to the larger unit of school organization in terms of its impact on both students and teachers (Anderman, 1997; Anderman & Maehr, 1994; Anderman, Maehr, & Midgley, 1999; Lee et al., 1993; Maehr, & Midgley, 1991, 1996; Midgley, 1993; Midgley, Anderman, & Hicks, 1995; Midgley & Edelin, 1998). The first dimension, task and work structures, can refer to the nature of the activities and curriculum that students and teachers engage in as they enact the school curriculum in the classroom. Work structures can also refer to how the school is organized in terms of teachers' work and role differentiation. As far as the nature of the curriculum and tasks is concerned, Maehr & Midgley (1991) suggest that a mastery-oriented school will focus the curriculum and academic tasks in such a way to foster student value and interest in learning, rather than merely provide coverage of the curriculum to meet assessment or bureaucratic needs. This can be done by encouraging the use of authentic tasks and meaningful activities that link the content of the curriculum to real-world problems and to the backgrounds and experiences of the students (Blumenfeld et al., 2000; Singer et al., 2000). These tasks also should be challenging to students, but not beyond their level of competence. A mastery-oriented curriculum can also include the use of programs that encourage learning in non-school settings, such as internships in work settings, field experiences, and cocurricular activities (Maehr & Midgley, 1991, 1996). This emphasis on the value of learning along with these types of activities should support the adoption of a personal mastery goal orientation that should have positive outcomes for students.

In terms of the work structures of the school, Lee and colleagues (Lee et al., 1993) note that several work design features of large, bureaucratic schools may act against some of the positive outcomes for teachers and students listed in Figure 9.1, although the actual empirical evidence is limited. For example, departmentalization and specialization of teachers' roles can create the possibility that students' interactions with teachers will be relatively transient; that is, limited to a 45- to 60-minute class period once a day with four to six teachers, as in most large, secondary schools, in contrast to the 4–6 hours per day contact with one teacher possible in elementary schools. This lack of interaction can obviously create barriers to the development of personal relations between teachers and students (see the previous section on climate) as well as increase the problems of student alienation (Lee et al., 1993; Newmann, 1981). In fact, some of the recommendations for the reform of middle schools (e.g., Carnegie Council on Adolescent Development, 1989) have suggested that there be structures set in place that allow for teachers to work with smaller groups of students in order to form more close personal relations. Bryk, Lee, and Holland (1993) found that the small, more communally organized Catholic schools they examined are structured in such a way that there is not as much teacher role specialization and departmentalization, thereby providing more opportunities for the development of personal relations between teachers and students.

Authority and Management Structures

The second dimension in the TARGET framework refers to the authority and management structures that guide both teacher and student participation in school and classroom activities. At the teacher level, there is a great deal of literature on the need for teacher control, teacher empowerment, and teacher participation in shared decision making and school management (e.g., Bolin, 1989; Duke, Showers, & Imber, 1980; Shedd & Bacharach, 1991), although the empirical base for this research is not strong (Lee et al., 1993). From a motivational perspective involving both goal orientation theory (Ames, 1992b; Maehr & Midgley, 1996) and intrinsic motivation theory (Deci & Ryan, 1985), teachers' perceptions of control and autonomy over aspects of their work environment should be associated with positive outcomes.

At the student level, Maehr & Midgley (1991, 1996) suggest that allowing student participation in learning and school decisions will help to develop a mastery orientation. At the classroom level, as discussed in chapter 8, allowing students some autonomy, choice, and control can have beneficial effects on their motivation and learning as well as on their development of self-regulation strategies. Finally, these opportunities for participation in decision making can help students develop responsibility, independence, and leadership skills. Of course, no one is suggesting that school staff and teachers give up their authority to students, but rather that there are some areas where the authority structure can be expanded so that students can exercise some control. For example, school councils can have student members who are allowed to play an active role in school decision making. School discipline can be a matter that is determined by the staff with little input from students, or efforts can be made to include students in the discussion and clarification of the values that guide group and institutional behavior. Students can be given opportunities for some choice in instructional settings, or they can be forced to take certain types of curricula without much control over the decision. Schools can foster choice and participation in cocurricular and extracurricular activities for all students or limit these activities to certain types of students (Maehr & Midgley, 1991, 1996).

Recognition and Reward Structures

This dimension concerns how students are recognized for their work and performance and, given the recognition criteria used, who then gets recognized. Maehr and Midgley (1991, 1996) note that the operation of school-level recognition structures was the first school-level dimension that convinced them they could not simply try to reform schools by acting at the classroom level. They were working with classroom teachers to help the teachers make their classrooms more mastery oriented. A large part of this effort involved building classroom recognition and reward structures that were based on student progress, mastery, individual improvement, and effort, not social comparison, competition, and extrinsic rewards. However, as they worked with the teachers, the teachers noted that the school's honor roll did not recognize these types of mastery-oriented criteria, but in fact recognized normative criteria that could increase social comparison among students and foster an orientation to just "getting good grades" rather than learning. Besides the honor roll, the school also participated in a book-reading program in which the students who read the most books would receive rewards (free pizzas). Maehr and Midgley report that this program often resulted in students reading the greatest number of the easiest and shortest books they could find, without regard for challenge or difficulty level, let alone comprehension and learning. Needless to say, the mismatch between the classroom efforts to increase mastery-based criteria for recognition and the school-level recognition structures did not support the teachers' efforts to change their classroom reward structures.

Accordingly, although it is important to have classroom recognition and reward structures that are focused on mastery, progress, and individual improvement, it is also important that the school-level recognition structures be aligned and support these criteria. In addition, if school recognition structures are based solely on normative and competitive criteria, there is always the chance that only certain types of students will be recognized. For example, the same group of high-achieving students could always be those who win all of the academic awards, suggesting that good academic performance cannot be attained by others and that it is a stable, entity-like trait. These types of messages can discourage other students from even trying to attain reasonable levels of academic performance.

Maehr and Midgley (1991, 1996) suggest that schools provide opportunities for all students to be recognized, such as fostering "personal best" awards and recognition procedures. They suggest that there are schoolwide strategies and policies that can help teachers and students focus on progress in goal attainment, not just comparative levels of achievement. For example, Mac Iver et al. (1995) reviewed several schoolwide programs designed to help teachers implement recognition and reward structures that are based on personal improvement. These programs assume that there may be some students who do need rewards to at least begin their schoolwork. Moreover, if the rewards are informational about their skills and increase their efficacy, they can have a positive influence on the students' behavior (Cameron & Pierce, 1994; Morgan, 1984). Finally, Maehr and Midgley (1991, 1996) note that schools can recognize efforts in a number of domains and learning activities by recognizing and publicizing achievements in different domains (e.g., science fairs, debating clubs, artistic and musical accomplishments, school-community relations), not just overall academic achievement based on GPA.

Grouping Practices

As Maehr and Midgley (1991, 1996) characterize this dimension, it has to do with the structures that allow for certain types of student interaction and the development of social skills in students. At the classroom level, grouping practices can involve the use of within-classroom grouping (e.g., high and low reading groups in first grade) as well as the use of cooperative groups and other alternatives to whole-group instruction. At the school level, one aspect of grouping practices would involve the support for alternatives to whole-group instruction. A wealth of research supports the use of small groups and cooperative groups as long as they are designed and implemented properly, not just used to throw students together and let them interact without guidance and support (see Bossert, 1988; Cohen, 1994; Johnson, Maruyama, Johnson, Nelson, & Skon, 1981; Rosenshine & Meister, 1994; Sharan, 1980; Slavin, 1983a, 1983b, 1995; Webb & Palincsar, 1996). If school policies and practices undermine the appropriate use of small groups at the classroom level, teachers will have a difficult time using them as one of their instructional strategies.

Beyond the use of small-group instruction within the classroom, the grouping dimension at the school level involves the use of between-classroom tracking. The literature on the effects of tracking is extensive and cannot be easily summarized in a chapter of this scope. For more detail, see the articles and books by Alexander, Cook, and McDill (1978); Bowles and Gintis (1976); Gamoran and Berends (1987); Heyns (1974); Jencks and Brown (1975); Lee and Bryk (1988); Mac Iver, Reuman, and Main (1995); Oakes (1985); Rosenbaum (1976, 1980); Sorensen (1987); and Sorensen and Hallinan (1986), to name just a few. Rather, we will focus our comments on some general considerations for school-level policies that can lessen the negative effects of between-classroom tracking.

First, Lee and colleagues (Lee et al., 1993) point to evidence that in many schools in the United States today, there are not the clear and well-defined two or three tracks within a school (i.e., academic, business, vocational) that may have been the norm in earlier research. They note that there is much more flexibility and variance in individual course-taking patterns of students and that there is often a much wider range of course offerings for students to choose from than in earlier times, especially in large, comprehensive high schools. Accordingly, they suggest that it may be more important to examine differential course taking by students and what learning and instructional opportunities and resources are offered in these different courses than to examine the effects of nominal track designations per se.

Mac Iver et al. (1995) point out in a review on the social structures of schools that access to these different types of courses can offer either positive opportunities or negative constraints for students. They note that many schools do not offer equal access to college preparatory courses for all students, even though these courses usually offer more academic content and are necessary for college admission. They do suggest, however, that restrictions in scheduling and resources at the school level and lack of information at the teacher, counselor, or student level can often be responsible for enrollment decisions, not intentional decision making on the part of the school personnel. Nevertheless, the types of courses taken by students (e.g., advanced academic courses) correlate very highly with achievement, holding other student background variables constant and without even taking into account the quality of instruction (Lee et al., 1993).

Second, in addition to access to general college preparatory courses, a number of studies show that access to advanced or accelerated math courses (e.g., algebra in the eighth grade) has very positive effects on student achievement in math. For example, in one study (Lee & Bryk, 1988), the correlation between taking advanced math courses and senior year achievement was 0.65. This relation remained strong even after student background, attitudes, and behaviors were considered (Lee et al., 1993). Finally, Mac Iver and colleagues (Mac Iver et al., 1995) note that access to courses that are focused on teaching for understanding (a current suggestion for quality instruction) is often limited to those upper-level or upper-track courses within a school (cf., Oakes, 1985; Page, 1990; Raudenbush, Rowan, & Cheong, 1993). Although there may not be a great deal of teaching for understanding even in these upper-track courses, it seems clear from current constructivist models of motivation and cognition that this type of instruction can have positive benefits for students (see chapter 8).

Given these findings, it is important for schools to offer opportunities for all students to have access to academic track courses. Lee and colleagues (Lee et al., 1993) note that in their research on Catholic schools (Bryk et al., 1993), a much higher percentage of the students enroll in the academic courses, partially because there are not as many other types of courses offered and partially because it is the general norm of the school that most students will take these academic courses. Beyond the types of classes, equal access to quality instruction is important. Maehr and Midgley (1991, 1996) suggest that schools offer all students opportunities for group learning, problem solving, and decision making of the kind that could be provided when small-group instruction is used. In much the same way, if teaching for understanding is deemed to be an exemplar of quality instruction, all groups and tracks should have access to it. Given that some form of tracking will probably exist in many large high schools for bureaucratic reasons, Maehr and Midgley also encourage the development of subgroups (teams, families, schools within a school) in large schools that will provide more opportunities for positive teacher-student and student-student interaction. They also suggest that there should be encouragement of multiple group membership to increase the range of peer interaction across groups.

Evaluation Practices

Evaluation practices concern the nature and use of student evaluation and assessment procedures. As with the grouping dimension, there can be two levels of school influences on evaluation practices. First, some school buildings might have fairly standard grading policies regarding the distribution of grades. For example, the school policy might be that there should be some distribution of grades from A's to F's in a course, with fewer A's and F's, more B's and D's, and a large number of C's (i.e., an approximation of a normal curve distribution). If this is the policy of the school, mastery-oriented classroom evaluation systems that focus on personal effort, improvement, and progress will be difficult for teachers to implement (Maehr & Midgley, 1991, 1996). Accordingly, general school building policies regarding grades and evaluation can support or undermine what teachers may try to do in their classroom in terms of changing the evaluation practices.

In addition, the evaluation policies of the school can have a direct impact on student motivation. For example, if the evaluation procedures stress normative comparisons among students (e.g., class rankings of students), it is likely that social comparisons will be made and, at least for those who are not doing well, students' perceptions of competence and efficacy may suffer. The types of schoolwide assessment programs can also influence what teachers come to stress in their instruction and what students come to believe is important to learn (Maehr & Midgley, 1991, 1996). Of course, if the assessments are designed to reflect important and valued goals, this may not be a problem. However, many of the assessments that are used at the school, district, or statewide levels mainly represent factual knowledge assessments, not assessments for conceptual understanding or higher-level thinking. In these cases, it is not surprising that many teachers don't teach for conceptual understanding, as we noted in the previous section. Moreover, it is unlikely that students will see the utility or value of these large-scale assessments for their own learning given that they are often not connected to the regular classroom activities or to any meaningful tasks (Paris, Lawton, Turner, & Roth, 1991).

Schools can help decrease these potentially negative influences of evaluation practices by reducing the emphasis on normative social comparisons that are highly public. They also can establish procedures by which students can assess their own progress toward their own goals. For example, portfolios offer one assessment procedure that can help students reflect on their own strengths and weaknesses in a particular course (see Paris & Ayres, 1994). Portfolios also can help teachers to individualize instruction and assessment to meet individual students' needs. They can be used by teachers to gauge student progress and improvement as well. However, portfolios are a fairly new assessment tool for most schools, classrooms, and teachers. Many problems with their reliability and validity need to be resolved. There also are practical implementation problems in terms of time to evaluate and use portfolios across teachers, classes, and grades/year in school. Nevertheless, they do offer one type of assessment that can be used to foster many of the goals suggested by mastery goal orientation researchers (Ames, 1992b; Maehr & Midgley, 1991, 1996).

Time Use

The final TARGET dimension concerns how time is used at the school level. Many of the current suggestions for increasing mastery goals, for improving instruction to facilitate conceptual understanding and critical thinking, and for creating shared norms and a climate of collegiality will require more time from teachers and students or a change in the way time is currently used. Yet in many schools in the United States, teachers do not have time for many of the suggestions we have been making throughout this chapter and in the book as a whole. Stevenson and Stigler (1992) point out that in Japanese schools, teachers usually have much more time set aside for planning, for consulting with colleagues, and for grading and evaluating student work because they do not teach as many hours per school day as do their counterparts in the United States. This time away from teaching, but spent at the school building involved with other teachers, helps to facilitate the collegial climate and consultation among teachers in Japan. It also allows more opportunity for teachers to discuss their goals and their teaching practices, which can help to build a consensus about the norms and goals for the school. Although it is unlikely that there will be a major change in how most U.S. schools structure outside classtime use by teachers due to financial constraints, it seems important to find ways for teachers to work together and to collaborate on school and instructional improvement without making it extra work that is taken on after an entire day of teaching (see Maehr & Midgley, 1996).

In terms of time use by students, there are a number of ways that schools can help students develop appropriate time management skills. For example, some flexibility in when students do their work during the day or during the week can increase student control and responsibility. Of course, students need to be taught and guided in their time management, but these kinds of opportunities can help to increase student intrinsic motivation and mastery goal orientation (Deci & Ryan, 1985; Maehr & Midgley, 1991, 1996). Another strategy is to provide students with opportunities to set proximal and long-term goals (see chapters 4 and 5) regarding the completion of their work. Students will have to be scaffolded and monitored by the teacher at first, but eventually these opportunities can help the students become self-regulating in terms of assessing goal progress, implementing their plans to reach their goals, and monitoring their time use on different goals (Zimmerman, Greenberg, & Weinstein, 1994). Application 9.1, later in the chapter, suggests some strategies to improve schools based on these ideas.

EXTERNAL CONSTRAINTS AND OPPORTUNITIES

Although it has been implicit in our discussion to this point, it seems clear that these eight dimensions of school culture and organization are created, shaped, and exist within a larger context. As shown in Figure 9.1, this context includes a number of different features that can act as constraints to limit the development of the school culture and organization or as opportunities to facilitate the development of an adaptive school culture and organization. There are many different features of the larger school context that can influence school culture and organization, but we focus on a few of the most salient. In general, much of the research on these external features has linked them directly to teacher and student outcomes. However, in this chapter, we focus on how these external features have an indirect effect on these outcomes through their influence on school culture and organization (Lee et al., 1993).

Type of Students

There are many ways to characterize students, but we will focus on general ability or achievement level, race, social class, and age. In terms of ability composition, it appears that effective schools have at least a core group of academically motivated and engaged students (Rutter et al., 1979), a situation that can help facilitate the development of a school culture that is focused on academic learning and mastery. In contrast, if a school has too many students who present serious problems and are alienated from school, it is more difficult to create and maintain an ethos focused on academic concerns. Just as a teacher and a classroom can be constrained by a preponderance of low-achieving and difficult students (Barr & Dreeben, 1983), schools can be constrained in a similar way (Lee et al., 1993). At the same time, most of this data is correlational, so it is possible that positive school and classroom cultures will help to create a core of motivated and engaged students.

In terms of race, there has been a great deal of research on racial composition, school integration, and achievement (see Rossell and Howley, 1983), which is too extensive to be summarized in this chapter. In terms of our analysis of school culture that focuses on shared values and a climate of good social relations, however, there is evidence that intergroup relations were somewhat better in schools that had a higher percentage of minority students (Schofield & Sagar, 1983). Nevertheless, there is also evidence based on case study data (Cusick, 1983; Metz, 1978) that intergroup problems between students of different races in forced integrated schools contributed to a breakdown of community and cohesion with a concomitant drop in the academic focus of the school (Lee et al., 1993). Accordingly, the racial heterogeneity of schools can be an opportunity for multicultural learning, but it can also act as a constraint on building a school culture of shared values and a climate of social community if the groups do not actually interact and work together (Eyler, Cooke, & Ward, 1983; Grant, 1988).

Social class may not act in such a marked manner as race, but Lee and Bryk (1988) have found that the average SES level of a school is related to overall achievement of the school. Moreover, research in the effective schools tradition has found that there are differences in how schools with low and high social class students implement the various tenets of effective schools (Hallinger & Murphy, 1986). For example, principals of effective schools with a mainly lower-class population were likely to exert more direct control and authority than were principals of effective schools with higher SES levels (Lee et al., 1993). Of course, given our analysis of school culture from mastery goal theory, higher levels of direct control by the principal could act as a constraint in the implementation of some of the changes suggested by Maehr and Midgley (1991, 1996).

In terms of age, there may be different school structures and organizations that provide a better fit or match for students of different ages. For example, the literature on the transition to middle schools (Anderman & Maehr, 1994; Anderman, Maehr, & Midgley, 1999; Braddock & McPartland, 1993; Eccles, Lord, & Midgley, 1991; Eccles & Midgley, 1989; Eccles, Midgley, Wigfield, Reuman et al., 1993; Eccles et al., 1998; Midgley et al., 1995) documents large decrements in children's achievement, motivation, and engagement as they make the move from elementary schools to middle schools. Traditionally, psychologists have attributed some of these changes to cognitive-developmental processes such as the increase in metacognition and the ability to use social comparison processes (cf., Anderman & Maehr, 1994; Ruble & Frey, 1991) as well as more physical changes due to puberty (Eccles et al., 1998). However, the most recent research suggests that a portion of this drop may be due to a developmental mismatch between the students' needs and capabilities and the structure and organization of middle schools.

For example, junior high school students are developmentally able to exercise greater choice and control, are better able to engage in more self-regulated learning, and are cognitively able to engage in more critical thinking and metacognition (Eccles & Midgley, 1989; Simmons & Blyth, 1987). However, middle schools are often structured with stricter rules and discipline systems that provide fewer opportunities for these students to have choice and control in comparison to elementary schools. In addition, the classroom tasks and instructional procedures often do not allow for much self-regulation or critical thinking (Anderman & Maehr, 1994; Eccles, Midgley, Wigfield, Reuman et al., 1993; Midgley, Anderman, & Hicks, 1995; Urdan, Midgley, & Wood, 1995). Given these types of developmental mismatches, it is not surprising that many motivated and engaged elementary students become less motivated and engaged middle school students.

These kinds of developmental differences suggest that the effects of the school culture and organizational dimensions on student outcomes may vary depending on the age of the students. Many of the issues we discussed in the previous section may be especially salient and important at the middle school level (Midgley et al., 1995; Urdan et al., 1995). Certainly, they can be important at the high school level, but the salience may not be as great as in the middle schools. Many high school students may have adapted to the bureaucratic structures of middle schools and have an easier time adjusting to a similar culture at the high school level. Nevertheless, given our analysis of school culture, we still believe it is important to work to improve school culture and organization at the high school level. At the elementary level, there may not be as much urgency as at the middle school level because the students are still developing their beliefs, knowledge, skills, and motivation. Moreover, many elementary schools, due to their smaller size and more cohesive norms and structures, may have relatively positive school cultures (Maehr & Midgley, 1996; Midgley et al., 1995).

School Size

As noted previously, school size can operate as a facilitator of changes in school culture and organization or as a constraint in a number of ways. Lee and colleagues (Lee et al., 1993) note three problems that are generated by very large, bureaucratic schools. First, the role differentiation is increased in large schools and there can be a diffusion of responsibility or loyalty to the school in favor of other subunits, especially the academic department in high schools. Second, in a large school, it is harder to communicate with all members of the staff, thereby lowering the opportunities for the development of shared values and a climate of collegial and personal relations. Finally, norms and goals can become more formalized (e.g., written lists of school goals), but given the large size and lack of opportunity to interact among all staff members, members' individual beliefs and goals may not be represented in the formalized mission statement or list of school goals. This can result in individuals holding goals and beliefs that are in opposition to the formalized school goals, hindering any efforts to work toward those goals or to change the school goals.

Maehr and Midgley and their colleagues (Maehr & Midgley, 1991, 1996; Urdan et al., 1995) present a case study of many of these problems as they struggled to reform both an elementary and a middle school to bring them more in line with a mastery goal orientation. They had a fair amount of success at the elementary school level for many of the reasons just enumerated. At the junior high school, however, they were less successful at first. Some of the department chairs formally and forcefully blocked the recommended changes and the principal was not able to develop strategies to involve all of the faculty in the changes. Obviously, size was not the direct cause of the successes and failures of the project, but the smaller, more manageable size of the elementary school allowed for more sustained interaction and the development of a coherent plan for school reform. In contrast, at the junior high school, size operated as a constraint; there were many more individuals involved and it was difficult to build a consensus for reform. Nevertheless, some of the junior high teachers banded together in smaller teams and continued to implement changes. Urdan, Midgley et al. (1995) discuss some of the special constraints and challenges involved in reforming middle schools.

Parental and Community Involvement

There is a wealth of evidence that parental involvement in schools can have a positive influence on the school in general as well as on the students and teachers (Becker & Epstein, 1982; Chubb, 1988; Comer, 1980; Epstein, 1986, 1987, 1995; Lee et al., 1993). Hence, it seems important to involve parents in schools and classrooms. At the same time, however, it should be noted that parental and community involvement or control of schools can increase the probability that there will be conflict between the professional judgment and expertise of school personnel and the parents' and community's interests and goals (Lee et al., 1993). This does not mean that there is necessarily an automatic conflict between school personnel and the community, but suggests that there is a need for negotiation of common interests, values, and goals, just as we have suggested is necessary for school personnel to do within the school building.

For example, in terms of the types of reforms and changes that we discussed in the earlier section on fostering a mastery goal orientation at the school building level, parents may support these changes or they may not see them as compatible with their goals. Some parents may see a mastery goal orientation and the accompanying changes as important and work with the school staff to implement these changes (see Maehr & Midgley, 1996; Urdan et al., 1995). In contrast, other parents may not believe that a general mastery goal orientation will prepare their children for competition in the "real world" and work to block or constrain any changes along these lines. Accordingly, parental and community involvement can act as a moderator of school culture and organization and, in particular, facilitate or constrain school reform efforts.

District- and State-Level Constraints and Opportunities

Schools operate within a community, a state, and, of course, a national context. All of these contexts can influence the dimensions of school culture and organization. We note only a few of the possible influences of the district and state levels. First, there are always fiscal constraints and opportunities. Given the vagaries of local and state school funding practices, some school districts have much more funding than other school districts. This allows the wealthier districts many more opportunities to develop school reforms along some of the lines we have discussed in this chapter. For example, we mentioned time as an important dimension of school organization. Districts with more funds can afford more staff and allow them some flexibility in time use and staffing patterns.

For example, one local district we know of that has a fairly high level of funding has had a middle school staffing arrangement that provides the teachers time to meet individually with students and other teachers. These teachers teach fewer class hours and the nonteaching periods are used to develop closer relations with their students and their colleagues (in line with the 1989 Carnegie report on improving middle schools). However, recent budget cuts have forced the school district administration to cut back on these periods and require the teachers to teach more hours per day. Interestingly, this did not only upset the teachers, but the middle school students were so angry about the changes that they organized strikes at school and demonstrations at the school board meetings. This anecdote serves to illustrate the problems of school finance and how these problems can constrain school reform.

Another type of district or state constraint that can operate on schools concerns assessment practices. Standardized testing at the district or state level can have a great influence on teacher beliefs, the nature of the curriculum, the general goals that a school adopts, and the nature of instruction. If the tests are designed to reflect mainly the acquisition of knowledge, it seems likely that curriculum and instruction decisions will follow from this type of assessment. There could be a focus on coverage of the curriculum and drill-and-practice in factual knowledge, instead of teaching for conceptual understanding or critical thinking. Moreover, if the tests are "high-stakes" tests with funding decisions contingent on performance, assessment can have even a greater impact on the school culture and organization.

APPLICATION 9.1

Applying Motivational Principles to School Reform

The research reviewed in this chapter has a number of implications for school staff. Moreover, any number of suggestions for school reform are being put forth by educational researchers and policymakers (see Muncey & McQuillan, 1993; Perkins, 1992; Sizer, 1992; and just about any recent issue of *Educational Leadership* and *Phi Delta Kappan*). We do not pretend to discuss all of the suggestions or even do justice to the ones we do discuss. School reform is a difficult, time-consuming, and nonalgorithmic task (Blumenfeld et al., 2000). If there were one, simple "magic bullet" of school reform that could be enacted with positive consequences for all, it seems likely that schools would have adopted it and there would be no need for us to make suggestions (Cuban, 1990; Newmann, 1993; Sarason, 1990). However, just as changing a classroom is a difficult task and involves personal judgment, so is school reform. We offer the following suggestions as guidelines for thinking about changes in schools. These guidelines reflect a concern for student motivation first and foremost, in keeping with the focus of the book. Nevertheless, they should also be related to better student achievement and more positive teacher outcomes. In fact, Lee and Smith (1995) have found that schools that were at least attempting some reforms had better achievement levels than those that were not trying to change their culture and organization, even after controlling for various differences in the schools.

1. *Develop common school norms, values, and shared beliefs.* As we have already noted, schools that have shared beliefs and goals seem to function better and are more effective. Although it is difficult and time-consuming, there must be opportunities

for teachers and staff to work together, to collaborate, and to develop a shared vision for their school. For example, Sizer's Coalition of Essential Schools (see Muncey & McQuillan, 1993; Sizer, 1992) proposes nine common principles that should guide school organization, curriculum, and staff. These principles are fairly general and reflect many of the ideas we have discussed in this chapter. At the same time, it is recognized that the nine principles will be adapted and implemented in relation to the local school context, staff, and resources available. Accordingly, there will have to be substantial time available for school staff to discuss how these nine principles can be enacted at their school. Maehr and Midgley and their colleagues (see Maehr & Midgley, 1991, 1996; Urdan et al., 1995) also describe a school reform process in which considerable time, energy, and resources were devoted to the development of a school-level commitment to creating a mastery goal-oriented school. The research on a school's academic emphasis (Goddard et al., in press; Hoy et al., 1991) also suggests the importance of developing norms that focus on academic success.

2. *Develop a school climate of good collegial and personal relations.* Related to the first suggestion, schools seem to work better when the personal relations among staff and students reflect a mutual trust and concern for the school community. Of course, given the various constituencies and personal differences in staff, this type of climate is not easy to create in any school. However, the principal can help model appropriate behavior and, as Sizer (1984, 1992) points out in his anecdotes about teachers and schools, if school staff is engaged in a common task of school reform that is taken seriously and has some chance of making real changes, respectful and trusting relations can develop among the staff.

3. *Design task and work structures to foster engagement.* Students are more likely to be engaged in tasks that take advantage of their backgrounds, interests, and experiences. There are many ways that teachers can develop tasks and activities that provide for authentic and meaningful work. For example, Paris and Ayres (1994) describe how portfolios can be used in elementary classrooms to provide a range of literacy tasks, including journals, letters, self-portraits, peer conferencing, and self-evaluation of artifacts, that can motivate students and facilitate the development of self-regulation. Sizer (1992) also provides a number of suggestions for "exhibitions," which are tasks that require students to demonstrate the products of their learning in meaningful ways. Recent calls for project-based instruction (e.g., Blumenfeld et al., 1991; Singer et al., 2000) also suggest ways that teachers and schools can involve students in meaningful and authentic activities.

4. *Design authority and management structures that allow for some control.* Mastery goal theory and intrinsic motivation theory both suggest that individuals who have some choice and control over their activities within an institution will be more motivated, and engaged, try harder, persist longer, and actually perform better. Almost all of the current school reform efforts stress the importance of involving teachers in the decision making for the school (school-based management or site-based management are the terms often used). This process can take place in many ways, including school reform or restructuring committees headed by and staffed with teachers, school improvement teams made up of teachers who are charged with different

tasks, schools-within-schools that have their own curriculum and planning committees headed by teachers, and university-school collaborations in which teachers play an active role (Blumenfeld et al., 2000). Of course, as we have noted throughout this chapter, merely giving control to teachers or local school staffs is not enough. Close attention must be paid to the content of the goals developed by the teams and committees and how the goals or policies adopted might influence student motivation and learning. Nevertheless, involving school staff, teachers, parents, and students in school decision and policy making can have important benefits for school reform when it is seen as a continuing process, not as an outcome in itself (Midgley & Wood, 1993).

5. *Provide opportunities for all students to be recognized and rewarded.* Schools can develop programs that reward and recognize all students for their progress and improvement, not just for normative achievement. Although it is difficult to envision alternative reward structures, many school improvement programs are implementing different types of grading and recognition practices. Sizer (1992) describes how a school can use exhibitions whereby students actually demonstrate their knowledge and skills. These exhibitions can then be judged in terms of absolute standards that are set by a team of teachers, not norm-referenced comparisons. Portfolios also allow for the development of standards and evaluation criteria that focus on student improvement and effort as well as criterion-referenced standards rather than norm- or group-referenced standards.

6. *Provide grouping arrangements that foster student interaction.* The use of small groups within the classroom can foster student-student interaction. Between-classroom grouping, or tracking, should be minimized. In addition, many schools that are constrained by their large size are instituting schools-within-school arrangements or forming teams of teachers and students. These differential teacher staffing and student grouping structures can promote more and better teacher-student and student-student interactions because they can provide more opportunities for the individuals involved to get to know one another.

7. *Evaluation practices should focus on progress and improvement.* Alternative assessment tools, like portfolios, can help teachers and students judge their progress and evaluate their strengths and weaknesses. This practice might be better implemented at the classroom level than at the school level, but schoolwide grading policies can influence teacher practices. Report cards can be changed to reflect an emphasis on mastery and improvement. Actual letter grades don't have to be used, nor do percentages (e.g., 88%) need to appear on report cards. Of course, letter grades can be used to represent mastery and improvement, but this type of individually referenced system is not usually implied by an A–E letter grading system.

8. *Time use should be managed to facilitate changes in the culture and organization of the school.* Schools can use a number of different strategies for differentiated teaching patterns that can provide the needed time for school reform efforts. Maehr and Midgley and their colleagues (Maehr & Midgley, 1996; Urdan et al., 1995) note that the rigidity of the schedule of the middle school they worked with was an extremely difficult constraint to overcome. Sizer (1992) also notes that time use and

daily schedules can constrain many school reform efforts. However, block scheduling (e.g., two class periods of 45 minutes each are combined into a 90-minute instructional period) can provide more time for teachers and students to work on sustained activities and projects. Schools-within-school structures can allow for more flexible scheduling because the number of teachers and students to coordinate is smaller.

SUMMARY

This chapter discussed the various aspects of a school's culture and organization that can influence student and teacher outcomes. We have relied heavily on the work of both sociologists of education and educational psychologists.

We proposed a model of eight dimensions of school culture and organization. The first two dimensions were more perceptual and constructive dimensions of culture that are reflected in teachers' beliefs about their school. Norms, values, and shared beliefs represent the notions about human nature, the stability of learning, the controllability of teaching, and the extent of the consensus about these beliefs. The climate of the school was defined in terms of the collegial and professional relations among staff as well as the warmth and civility of the building for all staff and students.

The next six dimensions of school culture and organization were taken from the TARGET framework of Epstein (1989) as elaborated by Maehr and Midgley (1991, 1996). Task and work structures concern how the work is designed and accomplished in schools. Authority structures refer to the nature of the relations between teachers and students regarding how much choice and control is allowed. Recognition and reward structures involve the criteria by which rewards are distributed and who actually receives the rewards. Grouping practices refer to both the use of alternative ways of grouping for instruction within classrooms and between-classroom tracking. Evaluation practices relate to how students are evaluated in terms of tests and assignments. Time, the last dimension, involves the use of time in the school building.

These eight dimensions make up the internal culture and organization of schools, which can have a direct influence on teacher and student outcomes. However, there also are external factors that can operate as opportunities or constraints on the school culture. The composition of the school's student body in terms of achievement, race, social class, and age can facilitate the development of a positive school culture or it can act to constrain this development. School size is another external factor; large school size generally has a negative effect on school culture in comparison to smaller school sizes. Parental and community involvement can support or hinder the development of school culture. Finally, district- and state-level factors can have a dramatic influence on school culture and organization.

Sociocultural Influences

*D*ena Carlson had a problem and she did not know what to do about it. Dena was the new principal at Taylor Ridge Elementary School. For the past 5 years, Dena was the principal at a school in a neighboring school district. Prior to that, Dena was an elementary teacher for 14 years. Dena moved to Taylor Ridge because she wanted to serve a larger school population; however, she was doubting the wisdom of her decision.

The student population at Taylor Ridge was racially mixed and primarily lower to middle socioeconomic status. Although the school's student achievement test scores were among the lowest in the district, student discipline problems were no worse than in other schools. The 40-year-old school building needed improvements that would be completed the following year. Inside the building, technology and other equipment were inadequate, but the superintendent assured Dena that additional funding would be forthcoming for technology and that Taylor Ridge would receive priority. Dena felt that she could work with students and staff to make other improvements and raise achievement test scores.

What Dena did not realize in advance was that there was a high level of apathy about the school in the community. Few parents came to the school orientation program conducted before school started in the fall. During the first month of school, Dena rarely saw any parents in the school other than those who had to be there (e.g., to pick up a sick child). Staff members complained that parents did not care about what happened. Teachers told her that when they assigned homework, few students completed it. Getting students to do schoolwork outside of class was next to impossible.

The straw that broke the camel's back for Dena occurred last night when the teachers held meetings for parents. During these hour-long programs, teachers explained the overall goals for the year and the curricula to be covered in different areas (e.g., math, literacy, social studies, science). They also went over rules and procedures, and parents could ask questions. Parent volunteers were sought for various activities.

Despite a lot of publicity and perfect weather, the parents of only 10% of the students came to the meetings. Dena was demoralized. She had wanted to show off the school and the interesting things planned for the year. Why, she asked herself, did so few parents bother to come? Did they not care about what went on in their children's school? And what could be done to improve this?

The next day Dena called a meeting with the teacher team leaders, the school counselor, and other key school personnel. She wanted to discuss reasons for the apathy and possible remedies. The group felt that something needed to be done to stimulate community involvement in the school. Suggestions were made to contact community leaders. One teacher was taking courses at a nearby university; she volunteered to discuss the situation with her professors.

From the conversations that followed, Dena learned that the apathy that pervaded the school was due to various factors. The peer culture in the neighborhood valued things other than school achievement: athletics, hanging out with friends, after-school employment. The elementary children were being influenced by their older brothers and sisters. The working-class community viewed school as something one had to attend rather than a means for promoting the quality of life. Finally, prior administrators at the school had made little attempt to encourage community involvement beyond the usual ways (e.g., parent council).

Dena worked with staff, interested parents, community leaders, and two university professors to develop a plan for enhancing community involvement. A school-wide planning committee composed of school and community individuals was formed. Teachers at each grade level worked with each other and with parents to plan activities. In the early grades, children took walking trips in the community and drew maps. At the later grades, children wrote stories about the history of the community. Rather than busing children long distances for field trips, children visited local restaurants, stores, businesses, and community agencies to learn how they operated. The parent council raised money to charter a boat that gave children rides on a nearby river. Teachers conducted science lessons about rivers and ecology during the trips.

Dena contacted persons who had attended the school and asked them to come to the school to talk to classes about what it was like when they were students at Taylor Ridge. Perhaps the most interesting activity of the year was "occupations night." In the gym and throughout the rooms and corridors tables were set up, each staffed by community members. Signs indicated the occupation of the member: carpenter, roofer, plumber, teacher, banker and so forth. Children and their parents chose which tables to visit and children learned about different occupations and what types of skills they required. Over 90% of the children attended this event. As children and their parents moved up and down the halls, Dena stood by a doorway and smiled, realizing how far the school had come in such a short time.

The first nine chapters in this text discussed motivation for achievement and the personal and situational influences on it. For the most part we have confined our discussion to factors inside schools: students, teachers, classrooms, school environments. These factors clearly are important, and an increasing theoretical and research literature helps us understand their operation. These factors are also sociocultural in nature but have been the focus of much work aimed at understanding individual student motivation.

This chapter addresses another set of factors: sociocultural influences, which emanate from peers, homes, communities, and cultures. Although sometimes neglected in discussions of student motivation, sociocultural factors outside of school influence students in school. Research into the role of these factors will become an important area for future research in motivation.

We begin by discussing the role of peers and peer cultures. Although many researchers and practitioners have felt for years that peers exert a critical influence, it has been only recently that research has substantiated this idea. We next examine the role of home influences, and conclude by discussing community and cultural effects.

After studying this chapter, you should be able to:

1. Give examples of peer modeling effects illustrating response facilitation, inhibition/disinhibition, and observational learning.
2. Explain the ways that peer networks can affect students' academic motivation.
3. Describe how friendships may influence school adjustment.
4. Explain the major influences on school dropout.
5. Discuss how factors associated with socioeconomic status may affect children's academic motivation and achievement.
6. Explain the research evidence on the role of the following home factors on children's motivation: environmental stimulation, mothers' responsiveness and self-efficacy, fathers' involvement.
7. Describe the key principles and components of the School Development Program.
8. Discuss how differences in motivation of people from various cultures and ethnic groups reflect their beliefs, attitudes, and behaviors.

PEERS AND STUDENT MOTIVATION

We initially review some theoretical material on modeling processes from chapter 4, which is critical for understanding how peers affect one another. We then discuss the role of peers in the areas of academic motivation and school adjustment. We conclude by considering the motivational issues involved in school dropout.

Theoretical Background

Modeling and Behavior

Social cognitive theory has described in depth the various functions of modeling (Bandura, 1969, 1989). Modeling refers to behavioral, cognitive, and affective changes that result from observing one or more models (Rosenthal & Bandura, 1978; Schunk, 1987). Three important functions of modeling are inhibition/disinhibition, response facilitation, and observational learning.

Observers' inhibitions about engaging in certain acts can be strengthened and weakened by observing models. When models are punished for their actions, observers' inhibitions may be strengthened and they are unlikely to perform the same actions because they believe if they do, they will be punished. Conversely, when models go unpunished or are even rewarded, observers' inhibitions may be weakened and they may perform the same actions. Note that inhibited and disinhibited behaviors previously were learned. Models convey information about consequences and the modeled effects are motivational.

Response facilitation occurs when modeled actions serve as social prompts for observers to behave accordingly. Again, the actions were learned previously by observers; the models convey information and their actions are motivational. One difference between these two categories is response facilitation behaviors typically are neutral whereas inhibited/disinhibited actions are rule governed or have moral or legal overtones. A student walking down a hall who sees a group of students looking into a classroom might stop and also look into the classroom. This is a response facilitation effect. Recall from chapter 8 the discussion of the ripple effect, whereby a teacher disciplines one misbehaving student and misbehavior in other students is immediately inhibited. Another difference is that, unlike response facilitation, inhibition/disinhibition often involves emotions (e.g., anxiety, exhilaration).

Observational learning through modeling occurs when observers display new behaviors that prior to modeling had a zero probability of occurring, even with motivational inducements in effect (Bandura, 1969; Rosenthal & Bandura, 1978). Observational learning is powerful: It greatly expands the range and rate of learning over what could occur if each response had to be performed and reinforced for it to be learned.

As discussed in chapter 4, observational learning comprises four processes: attention, retention, production, and motivation. Although motivation is a separate process, it affects the other three. Observers who are motivated to learn modeled actions are likely to attend to models, attempt to retain the modeled actions, and perform them when necessary.

These three forms of modeling are easily discerned among students and highlight peer effects. Response facilitation can be seen in forms of dress. Students who aspire to be valued by a certain peer group may wear the same type of clothes as those worn by members of that group. Outlandish behaviors may be disinhibited in those students when they observe members of the group display those behaviors without punishment. Through association with group members, other students learn slang words, expressions, and in-group behaviors.

Modeling and Observers' Beliefs

Models also can affect observers' beliefs. Modeling is both informative and motivational. As discussed in chapter 4, similarity to models in important attributes helps observers gauge behavior appropriateness. The more alike observers are to models, the greater the probability that similar actions by observers are socially appropriate and will produce comparable results (Bandura, 1986; Schunk, 1987). These outcome expectations can motivate observers to act accordingly.

Model similarity affects observers' self-efficacy. Observing similar others succeed can raise observers' self-efficacy and motivate them to perform the task; they believe that if others can succeed, they can as well. Observing others fail can lead students to believe that they lack the competence to succeed and dissuade them from attempting the task. Similarity is most influential when students are uncertain about their performance capabilities, such as when they lack task familiarity and have little information to use in judging self-efficacy or when they previously experienced difficulties and hold self-doubts (Bandura, 1986; Schunk, 1987).

We can see, therefore, that because peers are highly similar to one another in many ways, their potential for modeled influence is great. Further, children and adolescents are unfamiliar with many tasks, so the effects of perceived similarity on outcome expectations and self-efficacy are further heightened.

Goals and Achievement Motivation

The influence of peers on students' goals and achievement motivation has been investigated by several researchers. Research on goal setting has documented that observation of peers can lead students to adopt comparable goals (Bandura, 1986, 1988).

Peer-oriented goals are highly valued by students. Such social goals can be diverse. For example, students may want to be liked and approved by others, to develop social or intimate relationships, to cooperate with others, to win favor from others (e.g., teachers, coaches), or to be sensitive to the needs of others (Dweck, 1996; Wentzel, 1991c). Chapters 4 and 5 discussed how valued goals energize and direct students' choices, effort and persistence.

Academic motivation also depends upon goals being coordinated because, as often happens, two or more goals conflict. Thus, a high school student may want to earn high grades to be accepted at a prestigious university and may want to be accepted by a social clique that values partying more than studying. Trying to "have one's cake and eat it too" causes conflict and anxiety. Students may try to mask their studying and lie about how much they study or do it surreptitiously. They may not discuss their academic record when they are with clique members or may lie about it (e.g., say they made a B on a test instead of the A they really made). Over time, some goals may have to be sacrificed if students realize that they cannot coordinate their attainment (e.g., begin to associate with studious peers and abandon the non-studious clique).

Students' perceptions of competence are affected by peers and, in turn, influence their academic motivation. Eccles and her colleagues (Eccles, Midgley, Adler et al., 1984, 1998; Eccles & Midgley, 1989) have investigated changes that occur after students make the transition from elementary school to junior high (Table 10.1). At the elementary level, students remain with the same peers for much of the school day. Students receive more individual attention, and individual progress is stressed.

The transition brings several changes. Typically, several elementary schools feed into the same junior high. As students change classes, they are exposed to many different peers whom they do not know. Evaluation becomes normative; there is less teacher attention to individual progress. The widely expanded social reference group, coupled

Table 10.1 Changes from Elementary School to Junior High

Variable	Elementary School	Junior High
Peer group	Stable during school	Varies from one class to another
Teacher attention	Much individual	Little individual
Student progress	High emphasis	Less emphasis
Teacher evaluation	Individual progress	Normative
Student self-efficacy	Generally high	Generally declines

with the shift in evaluation standards, necessitates that students reassess their capabilities for succeeding academically. For many, this change is a real jolt that serves to diminish their self-efficacy and motivation. Compared with the sixth grade, perceptions of competence typically decline by the seventh grade (Eccles, et al., 1998; Harter, 1996).

Peer Networks

An increasing amount of research has examined the role of **peer networks**. Unlike close friends, peer networks are much larger groups of peers with whom students associate. Students in peer networks tend to be highly similar to one another (Cairns, Cairns, & Neckerman, 1989), which enhances the likelihood of influence by modeling.

Peer networks can heavily influence members' academic motivation in several ways. Networks help define students' opportunities for interactions, for observing others' interactions, and access to activities (Dweck & Goetz, 1978; Ryan, 2000). Over time, network members become more similar to one another. Researchers have found that discussions among friends influence their choices of activities and that friends often make similar choices (Berndt, 1999; Berndt & Keefe, 1992).

A key issue in this literature is the selectivity versus socialization explanation for peer effects (Ryan, 2000). That is, many parents often attribute the decline in their adolescent's motivation or school performance as a function of "getting in with the wrong group of kids." This is the basic socialization explanation that suggests that the peer group has a negative influence on students and socializes them to adopt less adaptive motivational beliefs and to become less engaged in school. In contrast, the selectivity argument suggests that students select their friends and peer groups, often on the basis of some similarity in values, attitudes, or beliefs, and so similar individuals end up in the same groups. Of course, within these similar groups the values and beliefs are reinforced, which can lead to more or less motivation or engagement in school (Ryan, 2000).

Kindermann and his colleagues (Kindermann, 1993; Kindermann, McCollam, and Gibson, 1996) examined motivation in peer selection and socialization among children (grades 4–5) and adolescents (grades 9–12). Not surprisingly, adolescent peer networks were more complex than children's networks. Most child networks were dyads; average network size was 2.2 students. Large networks were uncommon. Among adolescents there were many dyads and triads, as well as larger networks (average group size was 3.2 students). Among both groups, there were a few students not connected with any network.

There also were gender differences. Among children, groups were composed exclusively of members of the same sex. Among adolescents, there were instances of groups including members of both sexes. The researchers assessed motivation as reported by students and by teachers. A significant decline in motivation was reported by students. Teachers, however, reported comparable levels of student motivation across grades. Older students expressed lower motivation than did younger ones.

Comparisons of individual motivation with peer group motivation scores showed that among ninth graders, students who were more academically motivated had larger peer networks. Adolescents who were less motivated had fewer classmates in their peer networks. Across the school year and grade levels, students' motivation scores remained consistent.

There was clear evidence of motivational selection and socialization through peer groups. Changes in children's motivational engagement across the school year were accurately predicted by their peer group membership at the start of the year. There also were effects due to peer networks containing students from different grades. Students in highly motivated peer groups that contained members from across grades tended to increase in motivation across the school year. Students in low-motivation peer networks that had little grade diversity tended to decrease in motivation across time.

It is interesting that although adolescents' peer groups' members changed often, their motivational compositions remained relatively consistent. Children affiliated with highly motivated groups changed positively across the school year; children in less-motivated groups changed negatively. Among adolescents, the evidence for change was strongest in peer groups that included peers from different grades. Although the Kindermann et al. (1996) study is correlational and does not allow for conclusions about causality, it highlights the important relations between academic motivation and peer socialization processes.

Other studies have examined this issue as well (see review by Ryan, 2000). For example, Ryan (2001) has found that both selectivity and socialization effects seem to be operating in terms of adolescent motivation. Students do end up in peer networks that have similar motivational beliefs to them at the beginning of a school year. However, over course of the year, the peer group does exert an influence on the members of the group, so that group members do become more similar over time. Moreover, Ryan found that peer group socialization influence depended on the nature of the motivational outcome. Student intrinsic interest in school, as well as actual performance in terms of grades, was influenced by the peer group. However, the utility value that students had for school (how useful they think school work is) was not related to peer socialization effects. It seemed to be more a function of selection into certain peer groups from the beginning of the year. It seems clear that both selection and socialization explanations of friend and peer group effects are possible and there is a need for careful research that untangles the relative effects of the two explanations (Ryan, 2000).

These findings are supported by longitudinal research by Steinberg, Brown, and Dornbusch (1996). Over a period of 10 years, these authors surveyed more than 20,000 adolescents from nine high schools in different states, and also interviewed many parents and teachers. Peer relations were categorized into three groups (Table 10.2). Best friends are peers with whom students spend most of their free time. At the next level is the **clique**. Clique members are friends, but friendships are not as intimate as between best friends and relationships may fluctuate in importance over time. Cliques typically comprise 6–10 members, but cliques are likely to share similar values, beliefs, and attitudes. The broadest level is the **crowd**, which is composed of like-minded students who have some attributes

Table 10.2   Peer Networks

Group	Composition
Best friends	Peers with whom students spend most of their free time
Clique	Peers who are friends; friends are not as intimate as best friends and friendships may fluctuate over time
Crowd	Like-minded peers with some common attributes but not friends with everyone else in the crowd (e.g., populars, jocks, druggies, brains, loners, averages)

in common but are not friends with everyone else. Crowd membership is determined by common interests, attitudes, and desired activities, not by close relationships.

Friends and cliques can strongly influence students (friends are discussed in the next section) through the methods discussed previously (modeling, reinforcement). Friends and cliques can also be coercive when they exert pressure on members to engage in certain activities (e.g., "Oh come on, just have a drink with the rest of us").

Crowds also are influential, although their influence tends to be indirect through establishing norms and standards to which members believe they must adhere. Once crowd identification occurs, the adolescent incorporates these standards for conformity into his or her sense of self (Steinberg et al., 1996).

Various types of crowds have been identified by Steinberg and others. The "populars" are concerned about social status and being well liked and have a moderately strong commitment to academics; however, they may also show some involvement in delinquency and illicit drug use. "Jocks" are athletically oriented and otherwise similar to populars but are less involved in drug use except for alcohol. "Druggies" are alienated and delinquent, have heavy involvement in drug use, and display hostility toward teachers and others. "Brains" are highly academically oriented, avoid drugs, and form close relationships with school staff. "Loners" are socially inept and low in social status. Finally there is a large, amorphous crowd ("averages") that is undistinguished in all areas including academics.

Steinberg et al. (1996) found developmental patterns in the influence of peer pressure on many activities including academic motivation and performance. It rises during childhood and peaks around the eighth or ninth grade, but then declines through high school. A key time of influence is roughly from age 12 through 16. Interestingly, it is around this time that parental involvement in children's activities declines. As parents' role declines and peers' roles ascend among adolescents in grades 6 through 10, they become especially vulnerable to peer pressure.

The research by Steinberg et al. (1996) tracked students over 3 years, from the time they entered high school until their senior year. They determined whether students who began high school equivalent academically (in terms of grades), but who became affiliated with different crowds, remained stable academically. These authors found that crowds mattered in academic performance and delinquency. Children in more academically oriented crowds achieved better during high school compared with those in less academically oriented crowds. Students in crowds in which delinquency occurred more often became more delinquent in terms of conduct problems and drug and alcohol use. Students in less-delinquent crowds did not develop the same problems.

We discuss the effects of parents later, but the conclusion by Steinberg et al. (1996) is thought provoking: "At least by high school, the influence of friends on school performance and drug use is more substantial than the influence of parents' practices at home" (p. 148). Steinberg et al. note that parents typically "launch" children onto a particular trajectory by establishing goals for their children and involving them in groups and activities. But what happens afterwards is just as important.

For example, parents who want their child to be academically oriented are likely to involve the child in activities that stress academics. If the peer crowd in those settings is also academically focused, the peer influence complements that of the parents. Conversely, if there are other types of crowds in those settings, the child may come under the influence of a less academically oriented crowd, in line with the socialization explanation.

School Adjustment

Students face many adjustments in school. From year to year, there are changes in teachers, classrooms, school and class rules and procedures, performance expectations, difficulty of the work, and peers. Their successes in negotiating these challenges predict school success.

School adjustment has been construed historically in terms of children's academic progress or achievement (Birch & Ladd, 1996). This outcome is important, but being very narrow, it constricts the search for precursors and events in children's environments that may affect adjustment. On a broader level, we might think of adjustment as involving not only children's progress and achievement but also their attitudes toward school, anxieties, loneliness, social support, and academic motivation (e.g., engagement, avoidance, absences) (Birch & Ladd, 1996; Roeser, 1998; Roeser et al., 1998).

Investigators have argued that interpersonal relationships affect children's academic motivation. Connell and Wellborn (1991) contended that involvement is a powerful motivator—involvement refers to the quality of a student's relationships with peers and teachers. Ryan and Powelson (1991) noted that school learning can be promoted by learning contexts that enhance student involvement with others.

Researchers are increasingly studying the role of **friendships,** or voluntary reciprocal relationships between two children (Berndt, 1999; Birch & Ladd, 1996). Research by Ladd and his colleagues supports the proposition that friendships affect motivation and achievement (Birch & Ladd, 1996; Ladd, 1990; Ladd & Kochenderfer, 1996). Friendships support children in school environment and assist with their adjustment. Students with a friend in the classroom can use that peer as a source of support to deal with problems and avoid becoming lonely.

Berndt (1992, 1999; Berndt & Keefe, 1992, 1996) proposed that friends influence one another in two ways: (1) students are affected by the attitudes, behaviors, and other characteristics of their friends; and (2) students are influenced by the quality of friendships. Both positive friend characteristics and intimate relationships affect school adjustment in constructive fashion.

Four motives affect the influence that friends have on students' school adjustment: need for approval, identification, self-enhancement, and need to be correct. Students want to be liked, so they try to please friends and engage in actions that friends will approve of. Identification denotes the need to think and act like friends. Self-enhancement means that students compare themselves socially with friends and judge their capabilities partly on the basis of these comparisons. Need to be correct refers to a student's desire to hold correct beliefs. Trusted friends are deemed to be important sources of information for confirming beliefs. Students can focus on what their friends are saying and gain a better understanding of the situation, rather than judging the accuracy of the source. Research supports the influence of each of these motives (Berndt & Keefe, 1996).

Berndt and Keefe (1992) found that when peer pressure operated, it often functioned in a positive rather than a negative manner. Friends often discourage negative behavior, drug and alcohol use, and poor academic performance, and encourage prosocial behavior, good studying behaviors, and academic motivation (Berndt & Keefe, 1996). Friendships can relate to students' success in the transition from elementary to junior high school. Berndt, Hawkins, and Jiao (1999) found that students with high-quality friendships that endured across the transition demonstrated increased leadership and sociability. Conversely, students' behavior problems increased across the transition if they had stable friendships with peers high in behavior problems.

With respect to friendship quality, research shows that children and adolescents whose friendships have a positive quality display greater prosocial behavior, are more popular, hold higher self-esteem, have fewer emotional problems, have better attitudes toward school, and achieve at a higher level in school, compared with other students (Berndt & Keefe, 1996). Friendships with negative qualities lead to less student classroom involvement and more disruptive behavior. Interestingly, number of friends is weakly correlated with school adjustment. Thus, relationship quality is more influential than quantity. Although much of this research is correlational, Berndt and Keefe (1996) also report longitudinal data showing that friendships with positive qualities increase academic involvement (motivation). In sum, there is good evidence that peers play a dynamic role in students' school adjustment.

School Dropout

School dropout may represent the ultimate in low student academic motivation. A key motivation index is choice of activities, and dropout represents not choosing to attend school. In the United States, about 11% of students drop out of high school; the figure is much higher among minority students in urban areas (Hymel, Comfort, Schonert-Reichl, & McDougall, 1996).

Most research on school dropout has concentrated on nonsocial factors (e.g., academic, familial, school), but peers also play a role. As postulated by Ryan and Powelson (1991), feelings of relatedness contribute to motivation and learning. Students' relations with peers are part of this influence.

Hymel et al. (1996) suggested that students' involvement and participation in school depend partly on how much the school environment contributes to their perceptions of autonomy and relatedness, which in turn influence perceptions of competence (self-efficacy) and academic achievement. Although parents and teachers contribute to feelings of autonomy and relatedness, peers become highly significant during adolescence. The peer group creates a context that enhances or diminishes students' feelings of relatedness (i.e., belonging, affiliation).

Hymel et al. (1996) identified four critical aspects of peer influence. One is prior social acceptance within a peer group. Students rejected by peers are at a greater risk for adjustment problems than those who are socially accepted (Parker & Asher, 1987). Research also shows that students who are not socially accepted by peers are more likely to drop out of school later than are those with greater social acceptance (Hymel et al., 1996).

A second factor is social isolation versus involvement. It is true that not all socially rejected youth drop out of school. What may be more important is students' perception of rejection or isolation within the peer group. Students who are socially rejected but do not perceive themselves that way are at lower risk for dropping out.

A third factor is the negative influence of peers. Recall the earlier point that the peer crowd can affect students' motivation. Students who quit school are more likely than others to be part of a crowd that is at risk for dropping out (Cairns et al., 1989). Apparently the crowd collectively disengages from school. Even when students are not socially isolated, they are affected by negative peer influence.

Finally, aggression and antisocial behavior contribute to dropping out. Compared with students who graduate, those who drop out are rated by teachers and peers as displaying more aggressive behavior (Hymel et al., 1996). The latter students also have a higher incidence of alcohol and drug use and are more likely to have a criminal record.

We discuss familial influences on motivation in the next section, but it appears that a combination of familial, academic, school, and social factors contribute to school dropout. The peer group becomes especially influential during adolescence (Steinberg et al., 1996), which is the time when dropout occurs. Various influences likely contribute to dropouts' lack of school involvement and feelings of relatedness with the dominant school culture.

FAMILIAL INFLUENCES

It seems intuitive that families affect students' academic motivation. Although some argue that the importance of the family's role on children's development has been overstated (Harris, 1998), researchers are increasingly obtaining support for the critical role of families. Many of the same factors at work with peers also seem to be influential in families; for example, the extent that families encourage school involvement in their children is predictive of motivation. When we look at families, however, we also see key influences due to other factors. We discuss in this section the roles of socioeconomic status, home environment, mothers' beliefs and skills, and fathers' involvement.

Socioeconomic Status

The link between family socioeconomic status and children's academic motivation is well established (Meece, 1997). Children from lower socioeconomic backgrounds typically display lower academic motivation and achievement and are at greater risk for school failure and dropout (Borkowski & Thorpe, 1994).

We must keep in mind that socioeconomic status is a descriptive variable but not an explanatory one. Low socioeconomic status does not cause low motivation. Rather, it is the factors that frequently accompany low socioeconomic status that influence motivation and achievement. Further, the fact that a child comes from a low socioeconomic family does not guarantee that the child will have the preceding problems. There are countless individuals who were raised in poverty but succeeded academically and professionally.

What are some of these factors? Poor families have fewer resources to support their children's learning outside of school compared with families higher in socioeconomic status (Meece, 1997). The resource issue is a critical one, because lower socioeconomic students often display learning problems and require extra assistance. Families that cannot provide that (i.e., parents or tutors who help the child) place the child at a disadvantage.

Socialization influences in lower-class homes often do not match or prepare students for the middle-class orientation of schools and classrooms. This mismatch and lack of proper training can lead to lower socioeconomic students having more behavior and discipline problems in school, which relate negatively to motivation and achievement.

Lower socioeconomic students may not understand the full benefits of schooling (Meece, 1997). They may not comprehend that if they get a good education, they increase their chances of securing college acceptance, good jobs, and financial stability. In addition, they may not want to, or be financially able to, put off the short-term benefits of working now in exchange for the long-term future benefits of schooling. In their present situations, they may have few positive role models who have succeeded and display these attributes. Instead, they may believe that college is out of reach and follow the models they do have, many of whom may have quit school and hold low-paying jobs or are unemployed.

Stipek and Ryan (1997) compared disadvantaged and nondisadvantaged preschoolers and kindergartners on a variety of cognitive and motivational measures. On the cognitive skills tests (e.g., reading, memory, language), the socioeconomic differences were in the expected direction, with disadvantaged children performing poorer. Lower socioeconomic children performed especially poorly on tests of math and reading achievement. In contrast, there were virtually no differences on the motivational measures (e.g., perceived competence, attitude toward school, difficult choice after success or failure). As the authors noted, "Most young children, whatever their family economic situation, enter school with considerable enthusiasm, self-confidence, and willingness to take on learning challenges" (Stipek & Ryan, 1997, p. 721). To the extent that disadvantaged children later in their schooling display motivational deficits, these may result from negative learning experiences in school coupled with a lack of support at home.

The literature on socioeconomic status suggests that programs like Head Start and others that seek to redress skill deficits and remedy potential learning problems are well warranted. An effective way to ensure that children maintain positive motivation is to make sure that they have the cognitive prerequisites to learn. Without these, they are apt to become discouraged with subsequent failures, and their motivation will suffer accordingly. Applications of these ideas to classrooms are given in Application 10.1.

APPLICATION 10.1

Applying Peer and School Support Strategies

Research shows that children are apt to experience learning problems and their motivation may suffer when they lack the requisite cognitive skills and coping strategies. This implies that academic deficiencies should be addressed as quickly as possible.

1. Mr. Katona's classroom has several second graders from lower socioeconomic backgrounds who had problems with beginning reading instruction in first grade. Mr. Katona cannot spend enough time with these students and parent volunteers are lacking. Through a local university, he arranged for some students in teacher preparation programs to come to his classroom to tutor these students individually in basic reading skills. After a few weeks, his children were reading better and feeling more efficacious about continuing to improve.

2. Nikki, a sixth grader in Mrs. Bem's class, had a long bout with a serious illness that required hospitalization and home care. Nikki was an average student prior to the illness but fell far behind in all subjects. Mrs. Bem trained some of Nikki's friends

in the class in tutoring techniques. When Nikki returned to school, Mrs. Bem had her work with these peer tutors for up to 2 hours per day at times when Nikki could not participate with her classmates (e.g., physical education, recess). By the end of the semester, Nikki had caught up with her classmates in her schoolwork and was excited about starting junior high school next year.

3. Dolan is a third grader in Ms. Abraham's class. His parents recently divorced and his home environment is unsettled and often acrimonious. He is living with his mother, who enrolled him in an after-school program. The divorce and unstable home life have affected Dolan's academic motivation and achievement adversely. With his mother's consent, Ms. Abraham keeps Dolan in her room for the first hour after school ends while she stays there to work. Dolan likes using the computer, and Ms. Abraham has Dolan work on software programs that emphasize basic skills in reading, spelling, and mathematics. As Dolan successfully completes the programs, his self-efficacy and motivation for learning are enhanced.

4. Six high school students were caught using drugs on school property and are on juvenile probation. Their grades have suffered and they have little academic motivation. Mr. Livengood, an assistant principal, worked with them and the school counselor to develop a plan for addressing their learning difficulties. For each student, a contract was devised for each subject for the 6-week grading period. The contracts specified the strategies students would use to complete their work. History, for example, has weekly reading and quizzes, a unit test, and a book report. The contract broke each of these into short-term goals specifying a plan for completion (e.g., when and where students would study, when subtasks were to be completed to ensure adequate preparation for the test and quizzes, and timely completion of the reading and report). All of the students showed grade improvements and were motivated to continue working diligently.

Home Environment

We have stressed elsewhere in this text (see chapters 5, 6, 7, and 8) that children are motivated to work on activities and learn new information and skills when their environments are rich in interesting activities that arouse their curiosity and offer moderate challenges.

The same can be said about the home environment. Unfortunately, there is much variability in motivational influences in homes. Some homes have many activities that stimulate children's thinking, as well as computers, books, puzzles, and the like. Parents may be heavily invested in their children's cognitive development, and spend time with them on learning. Other homes do not have these resources and adults in the environment may pay little attention to children's education (Eccles et al., 1998).

What difference can the home environment make on children's academic motivation? As Meece (1997) notes:

> It is generally believed that children's intellectual development is most strongly influenced by the home environment during infancy and early childhood when they are under the direct influence of parents. As children mature, schools and peers may play a more important role than parents in their intellectual socialization. (p. 205)

There is much evidence supporting the hypothesis that the quality of a child's early learning in the home environment relates positively to the development of intelligence. Various home factors have been shown to be important: mother's responsiveness, discipline style, and involvement with the child; organization of the environment; availability of appropriate learning materials; opportunities for daily stimulation. Parents who provide a warm, responsive, and supportive home environment; encourage exploration; stimulate curiosity; and provide play and learning materials accelerate their children's intellectual development (Meece, 1997).

Gottfried, Fleming, and Gottfried (1998) conducted longitudinal research examining the role of cognitive stimulation in the home on children's academic intrinsic motivation. Home environment variables measured included family discussions, attendance at cultural events, library visits, trips taken, importance of reading, provision of private lessons, access to play equipment, and family interest in music, art, and literature. The authors assessed home environment when children were age 8 and academic motivation at ages 9, 10, and 13.

The results showed that children whose homes had greater cognitive stimulation displayed higher academic motivation from ages 9 through 13. The effect of socioeconomic status was indirect: Families of higher socioeconomic status were more likely to provide cognitively stimulating home environments, which in turn directly increased academic motivation. The fact that home environment effects were both short- and long-term suggests that home environment continues to play a role in early adolescence when peer influence becomes more powerful. These results highlight the need for parent awareness programs that teach them how to provide rich learning experiences for their children.

Within the home environment, we must examine both the roles of mothers and fathers, because differential parent behavior has often been implicated as a variable affecting children's development (Eccles et al., 1998; Volling & Elins, 1998). Eccles et al. (1998) list six potential parental beliefs that can influence children's motivational beliefs. They include the parents': (1) attributions for the child's school performance, (2) perceptions of the task difficulty of school work, (3) expectations and confidence in children's abilities, (4) values for school work, (5) actual achievement standards, and (6) beliefs about barriers to success and strategies for overcoming these barriers. We consider the roles of both mothers and fathers in the following sections.

Mothers' Beliefs and Interactions

Our knowledge of the influence of family practices on children's academic motivation is limited by the fact that most research on parent variables has focused on interactions between mothers and their children. There are various reasons for this, including the fact that mothers are often more available to participate in research. A great amount of research substantiates the idea that maternal attachment is critical for children's development. As researchers have begun to explore fathers' influence, it has become clear that both mothers and fathers affect children's achievement and motivation (Eccles et al., 1998; Meece, 1997).

Research has shown that parenting styles can make a difference in children's academic motivation. In general, motivation is enhanced when parents allow children to have input into decisions, state expectations as suggestions rather than as directives, acknowledge children's feelings and needs, and provide children with alternatives and choices (Meece, 1997). Moreover, when mothers make adaptive attributions for their children's performance, have high confidence in the children's abilities, and value school work, their children tend to also have positive motivational beliefs such as attributions, efficacy, and value (Eccles et al., 1998).

Researchers have recently examined the role of mothers' efficacy beliefs about child-rearing competence. We should expect that mothers who feel more efficacious about performing effective child-rearing practices would provide better learning opportunities and expend greater effort to enhance their children's motivation and learning. In turn, children's outcomes should reflect these maternal beliefs.

There is evidence supporting these hypotheses. Brody, Flor, and Gibson (1999) assessed mothers' efficacy beliefs, developmental goals, and parenting practices among rural, single-parent, African American families. Efficacy items covered the areas of education, communication, and general parenting. Mothers' developmental goals for their children included showing respect, becoming well educated, getting along with others, and being well behaved. The researchers also assessed children's self-regulation in the areas of planning, persisting, and paying attention. The results showed that mothers with higher parental efficacy set positive developmental goals for their children and engaged in better parenting practices. Children's self-regulation (which included motivational variables) was influenced by effective parent practices and predicted children's academic competence.

Mothers' responsiveness to their children can also help outweigh powerful peer effects during adolescence. Bogenschneider, Wu, Raffaelli, and Tsay (1998) found that mothers affected adolescents' orientations to peers and substance use. Mothers' responsiveness was defined as the extent that they expressed love and praise, were available when needed, and engaged in discussions. Mothers with higher responsiveness had adolescents with lower orientation to peers and, in turn, lower substance use.

Among divorced mothers, DeGarmo, Forgatch, and Martinez (1999) found that parenting practices resulted in greater skill-building activities by children at home and better school behavior and achievement. The parenting practices of interest in this study were mothers' discipline and family problem-solving processes. In short, there is good evidence that mothers' beliefs and interactions with their children have effects on their parenting practices and children's motivational and academic outcomes.

Father Involvement

Conceptions of fathers have altered dramatically over the years. The old image of doting but wise fathers (e.g., "Father of the Bride," "Father Knows Best") has given way to a negative conception characterized by the "deadbeat" dad and absent parent in single-parent families. Neither conception accurately captures the mainstream attributes of fathers. Currently, family scholars and policymakers have placed fathers in the national spotlight as they debate their importance for children's development.

Types of Father Involvement

Father involvement may be of different forms (Lamb, 1997; see Table 10.3). Most commonly, it is viewed as a form of responsibility: Fathers are responsible for meeting their children's needs, such as providing economic resources and assisting with planning and organizing children's lives. This view goes beyond the narrow father-as-an-economic-provider notion and views that define father involvement strictly in terms of absence or presence, provision of child support, and visitation frequency.

Table 10.3 Types of Father Involvement

Type	Characteristics
Economic provider	Provides economic resources
Presence	Spends times with children; provides some support
Responsibility	Meets children's needs; provides economic resources; helps plan and organize children's lives
Engagement	Has direct contact and shared interactions with children during caretaking, play, and leisure time
Accessibility	Present and available to the child

More in-depth assessment of father involvement can be obtained by using such indexes as engagement and accessibility. Engagement includes the extent that fathers have direct contact and shared interactions with their children during caretaking, play, and leisure. Accessibility involves the father's presence and availability to the child (Tamis-LeMonda & Cabrera, 1999).

Father Involvement and Children's Outcomes

Research has not clearly shown which index of father involvement affects which outcomes in children. As a general construct, father involvement relates to children's development from the first months of life (Tamis-LeMonda & Cabrera, 1999). Young children's well-being and cognitive and social development are positively affected by fathers' provision of resources, attachment, and emotional investment (Lamb, 1997). Some research shows a positive relation between father involvement and children's abilities (Yogman, Kindlon, & Earls, 1995).

Once children are in school, father involvement both in and out of school relates directly to children's school success and achievement (Tamis-LeMonda & Cabrera, 1999). Although fathers are seen less often than mothers at such events as parent-teacher conferences and school meetings, their presence at these activities is important. Perhaps father presence sends a message to the child that school is important because the father is willing to spend part of his time there. Some ways that fathers and mothers can influence children's school motivation are discussed in Application 10.2.

Earlier we noted the tendency of parents to dissociate themselves from children's schooling at the precise time that peers become more important, which can leave children especially vulnerable to peer influence (Steinberg et al., 1996). Interestingly, father involvement during adolescence relates to a lower incidence of adolescent delinquent behavior. Fathers may possibly help to protect their adolescent sons and daughters from the type of negative crowd influence that can lead to problems.

Modes of Influence

In sum, there is evidence that father involvement impacts children's cognitive, social, and affective development, as well as prosocial behavior and academic achievement. These outcomes all likely involve elements of motivation. We might ask how father involvement effects occur.

APPLICATION 10.2

Applying Parental and Familial Support Strategies

Parents can affect their children's motivation both directly (e.g., by giving advice, requiring them to do homework) and indirectly (e.g., by steering them to desirable activities and other people who influence their motivation). Some examples of these follow.

1. During summer vacation, Kara has been laying around the house and watching TV and videos. To stimulate her academic motivation, her parents get her to agree to be part of a summer book club. If she reads 10 books, her parents will take her to the beach for a weekend. This motivates Kara and she makes good progress. After she finished her tenth book, she maintained her motivation for reading and completed five more books before school began.

2. Jack picks up his third-grade daughter Samantha one day each week and takes her out to lunch. Jack always arrives a few minutes early, and before Samantha gets out of class he walks through the halls and greets school staff (e.g., principal, media specialist, office personnel, teachers) and other parents. Samantha likes going to lunch with her dad, and his taking time out of his busy schedule to spend time at the school and with her shows her how important he thinks school is. By midway through the school year, Jack has volunteered to work on three activities, which further increases his involvement in Samantha's school.

3. Twelve-year-old Tad's parents are concerned because two of his friends are part of a crowd that does not value academics. When a summer band camp is advertised, they check with parents of other children to see who will be attending. It becomes clear that many of the students who will attend the camp also earn good grades in school. Tad's parents convince him to attend the camp. Although they cannot control who his friends will be at the camp, they figure that it probably does not matter much who they are because the campers as a group will be students who do well in school.

4. A lot of 14-year-old Jason's friends are hanging out at the mall on weekends. These are not the crowds that his parents want him to be part of. A classmate's parents, who share this concern, own an old building in town. Together with Jason's and other parents, they renovate it and equip it with games and activities for adolescents. When it opens, Jason and many others go there instead of to the mall. Parents take turns supervising. Jason's parents find that the students who come are part of the social and academic crowds at the school.

5. When 10-year-old Laura comes home from school each day, she talks with her mother about what happened at school. Her mom stops what she is doing to devote her attention to Laura during this time. Laura appreciates her mom's responsiveness to her needs. Once this is finished, Laura and her mom decide on a plan for Laura to complete her homework. Positive reports from Laura's teacher help to build her mom's parenting self-efficacy and motivate her to continue to spend time each day with Laura.

Although there is no clear answer, several possibilities emerge. Father involvement may indirectly affect children's outcomes through its direct effect on the mother-child relationship (Tamis-LeMonda & Cabrera, 1999). Higher father involvement is associated with better treatment of mothers by fathers, which positively influences the mother-child interaction. Fathers who have a positive relationship with a child's mother are more likely to be involved in the child's life (Belsky, 1998).

It also is likely that fathers have direct effects on their children. Economic security is a strong influence, given the powerful relation of poverty to low achievement, social problems, and delinquency (Tamis-LeMonda & Cabrera, 1999). Fathers also help teach children skills, especially motor and athletic skills. Although traditions are changing, fathers are turned to more often than mothers for help with mathematics and science problems. Through their advice and guidance, fathers provide a sense of security to children and can bolster their self-confidence for succeeding.

Further research is needed to clarify the direct and indirect ways that fathers can influence their children's academic motivation. We also need data on the influence of fathers who do not live with their children. There is great variability among fathers in their involvement with children who live with their mothers or other family members.

COMMUNITIES AND CULTURES

We now turn to the impact of communities and cultures on children's academic motivation. Although the influence of communities and cultures is typically acknowledged, there has been little systematic research examining their effects until recently.

Communities

Community involvement in children's education is nothing new. Indeed, most schools involve their communities in many ways. Parents serve as volunteers in schools and are active in parent organizations. School teams are often coached by parent volunteers. Students take field trips in their communities. Community members are routinely invited to talk with children and visit classrooms. Apprentice programs with community businesses are often established.

Aside from these activities, there are examples of school-wide involvement of the community. Among the best known is the School Development Program, which we discuss next.

School Development Program

James Comer is probably the best-known advocate of the position that communities should be involved in the planning and implementation of school programs. Comer and his colleagues developed the **School Development Program**, which began in two schools in 1968 and has spread to over 500 schools nation-wide.

The impetus for this program came from Comer's experiences in schools. He related the following tale from his early days of working in a school:

What I saw was almost unbelievable. Children were yelling and screaming, milling around, hitting each other, calling each other names, and calling the teacher names. When

Table 10.4   Principles of the School Development Program

- Children's behaviors are determined by their interactions with the physical, social, and psychological environments.
- Children need positive interactions with adults to develop adequately.
- Child-centered planning and collaboration among adults facilitate positive interactions.
- Planning for child development should be done collaboratively by professional and community members.

Emmons et al., 1996.

the teacher called for order, she was ignored. When I called for order, I was ignored. That had never happened to me before. We headed for the hall, confused and in despair. (Comer, Haynes, & Joyner, 1996, p. 2)

The *SDP* (or **Comer Program** as it is often called) is based on the following principles (Emmons, Comer, & Haynes, 1996; see Table 10.4). Children's behaviors are shaped by their interactions with the physical, social, and psychological environments. Children need positive interactions with adults to develop adequately. Child-centered planning and collaborations with adults enhance positive interactions. Planning for child development should be a collaborative effort between professionals and community members.

What does the SDP include? There are three guiding principles: consensus, collaboration, and no-fault. Decisions are based on consensus, which discourages taking sides to win critical votes. Collaboration requires a willingness to work as part of a team. No-fault means that everyone accepts responsibility for change.

School staff and stakeholders are organized into three teams. The School Planning and Management Team plans and coordinates school activities. The Parent Team involves parents at all levels of school activities. The Student and Staff Support Team addresses school-wide prevention issues and handles individual student cases.

At the core of the program is a comprehensive school plan. Major components include curriculum, instruction, assessment, social and academic climate, and sharing of information between community and school. The School Planning and Management Team includes the building principal, teachers, parents, and support staff. The comprehensive school plan provides a structured set of activities in academics, social climate, staff development, and public relations, which allows the team to establish priorities and to coordinate school improvement (Comer et al., 1996).

After the initial success of the program, it expanded to develop partnerships with university schools of education, state departments of education, and other institutions. Participating schools of education have revised their teacher preparation programs to include greater emphasis on the objectives and processes used in the School Development Program.

Effects on Student Motivation

How do Comer schools affect student motivation? The achievement data reported by Comer and his colleagues are impressive (Haynes, Emmons, Gebreyesus, & Ben-Avie, 1996). Comer schools show gains in student achievement and outperform the school district averages in mathematics, reading, and language skills.

There also is evidence for positive motivational effects (Haynes et al., 1996). Students in Comer schools typically show positive changes in attendance, teacher ratings of classroom behavior, attitude toward authority, and group participation, compared with students not in Comer schools. Comer-school students also display higher scores on self-concept tests compared with control students.

Clearly, more data are necessary to determine how the SDP affects student motivation. We should expect that the greater involvement by school personnel and community members would have a positive impact, given our previous discussion relative to peers and families. Regardless of whether a school adopts the SDP, the principles used and the increased involvement of community members ought to benefit the school. At the beginning of this chapter, we saw how Dena Carlson applied many SDP principles at Taylor Ridge Elementary School. Applications of this program are given in Application 10.3.

APPLICATION 10.3

Applying Community Involvement Strategies

There are many ways that educators can involve community members in their children's schools. Further, people typically are willing to help where needed.

1. Like Dena Carlson, Alex Moravo—principal of Holloman Senior High School—seeks greater community involvement. When the school district's budget was cut, Alex could not obtain funds for a landscaping project. He enlisted parent volunteers to visit community businesses to solicit donations for the project. A nursery donated trees, shrubs, and mulch, a home improvement center donated garden equipment, and many businesses pledged money. Alex organized a parent work team, which did all the planting and landscaping on a Saturday. School pride is high and people are motivated to work to keep improving the school. The makeover was so impressive that a newspaper wrote a feature story on it.

2. A retirement community is within half a mile of Potter Elementary School. Mary Sahakian, the assistant principal, recently addressed a group of residents to solicit volunteers to come to the school and help tutor students in reading. When 30 residents volunteered, Mary organized a tutoring training session for them. Residents came to the school once or twice weekly for 1–2 hours each session and tutored individual students for 30-minute periods. The residents experienced satisfaction from being able to assist, the children increased their skills and motivation for reading, and the teachers were grateful for the support. At the end of the year, Mary held a pizza party for all tutors and their students.

3. Washington and Lincoln Middle School is part of a school district that implemented a site-based management plan. The principal, Carly Berkowitz, explained the plan to members of the parent organization and asked for volunteers for three school committees: Facilities, Curriculum, Long-Range Planning. Several parents volunteered, and Carly formed committees composed of parents, teachers, administrators, staff, and students. In addition to their work at the school, representa-

tives from each committee gave periodic reports at meetings of community organizations (e.g., neighborhood associations, civic clubs). The greater community involvement has enhanced motivation for continual school improvement among school staff, students, and community members.

4. The teachers at Ft. Mason Elementary School wanted to implement a school-wide social studies curriculum on their community. They organized a planning committee that included members of community organizations and long-time residents. The overall learning outcomes for each grade level were established, after which individual units were developed. In the younger grades, students learned about what was in the community: homes, stores, streets, parks, and so forth. Older children learned the history of the community and studied scientific aspects (e.g., rock formations, underground water locations). All students took field trips in the community. Residents and leaders met with students and classes to provide information on such topics as how the community was settled and significant changes over the years. The integration across grades ensured continuity in learning and motivated students to learn more each year.

Cultures

This text discussed cultural differences when appropriate to do so and when research has identified reliable findings. Cultural differences in motivational processes and variables are descriptive rather than explanatory; that is, they indicate the locus, direction, and magnitude of the differences but do not explain what might cause them. To explain cultural differences we must examine the beliefs, attitudes, and behaviors of people, and link these to the observed differences.

Researchers often do not find cultural differences in motivation for various reasons. Culture (and ethnicity) are often treated as control variables; that is, their effects are controlled statistically so that the effects of other variables on motivation can be studied. Cultural identities and differences are often merged and researchers provide general interpretations of data (Portes, 1996).

Glossing over potential cultural differences poses a serious limitation for any theory that seeks to explain human motivation. Expectancy-value theory provides one example. Early work framed the achievement motive in a highly individualistic, competitive sense (Atkinson, 1957; McClelland et al., 1953). One had a high motive to achieve if one sought to perform a task quickly and well (and presumably better than most others).

This motive has been criticized as reflecting a bias toward Western societies and male achievement (Schunk, 2000). There are cultures in the world in which competition and individual achievement are not as highly valued as are cooperation and group achievement. Many also have questioned whether these behaviors are incompatible with the basic (traditional) notion of femininity. Thus, the generality of classic expectancy-value theory seems limited by cultural beliefs and social practices.

A similar problem can be seen in the current focus on the importance of goals in motivation. The contemporary literature on learning and performance goals (see chapter 5), social goals, and multiple goals (Wentzel, 1996), is based heavily on research in Western cultures. We might ask whether students from other cultures are as concerned with appearing competent to others, performing better than peers, and negotiating academic and social goals.

Research evidence on this issue was obtained by McInerney, Hinkley, Dowson, and Van Etten (1998). These researchers assessed mastery, performance, and social goals among three groups of Australian high school students: Anglo Australian, Aboriginal Australian, and immigrant-background Australian. The results showed that the three groups were similar in their goal beliefs. Groups placed greatest emphasis on satisfying mastery needs; satisfying social and performance-goal needs were judged as less important. At the same time, the effects were greatest for the Anglo and immigrant-background Australian students; Aboriginal Australian students were less likely to believe that their success depended on satisfying mastery and performance-goal needs. Overall, the Aboriginal Australian group was more socially oriented and less individually oriented than the other groups.

These findings must be interpreted in light of cultural knowledge. Australian Aboriginal students come from families that emphasize traditional values (e.g., affiliation, social concern). Thus, it is not surprising that they would ascribe greater value to that goal. The implications for education are that for these children and for other groups that might respond similarly, more activities should be incorporated into education that include social links (e.g., cooperative learning). This does not mean that the emphasis on mastery should be abandoned in school. In the McInerney et al. (1998) study, all groups espoused a mastery goal orientation. Rather, the two goal orientations can be linked in creative ways. Future research on other cultures will contribute greatly to the motivation literature and will become an important future direction for research. As we develop some generalizations or principles of motivation, it will be crucial to test their cross-cultural consistency if we are to truly understand motivation in all contexts and cultures.

SUMMARY

Sociocultural influences from peers, families, cultures and communities play an important role in students' development, achievement, and motivation. Many of these factors operate outside of formal schooling, although they impact various aspects of learning and motivation in school.

Modeling is an important process whereby peers influence other students. Three important functions of modeling are inhibition/disinhibition, response facilitation, and observational learning. Models also affect observers' beliefs. Similarity to models enhances their influence. Peers' similarity in background and experiences can affect their outcome expectations and self-efficacy.

Another way that peers exert influence is through choice of goals. Students may desire to attain multiple goals, such as having friends and performing well in school. The desire for peer approval can affect goal choice. When multiple goals conflict, motivation and behaviors may be affected.

Peer networks are large groups of peers with whom students associate. Students in networks tend to be similar in many respects. Peer networks can influence members' academic motivation in several ways. Networks define students' opportunities for social interactions, allow them to observe others' interactions, and provide access to activities. Researchers have found that motivational socialization occurs in networks, as their members tend to become more similar over time.

Peer pressure can emanate from friends, cliques, and crowds. Pressure may be direct but often is indirect through establishing norms and standards to which members believe they must adhere. Pressure tends to rise during childhood and peak around grades 8–9. Unfortunately at the time when peer pressure is highest, parental involvement in children's activities declines, which leaves adolescents even more vulnerable to pressure.

Researchers have investigated factors contributing to school adjustment and school dropout, both of which involve academic motivation. Adjustment is affected by students' need for approval, identification, self-enhancement, and need to be correct. Students who associate with academically inclined peer networks also make a better transition from elementary to junior high school. School dropout is predicted by low involvement in school activities and negative influence from peers.

Families are critical in children's development and motivation. Family involvement in schooling predicts children's motivation. A variable often studied is socioeconomic status. Children from lower socioeconomic backgrounds tend to display lower achievement and motivation. Variables that may contribute to this result include fewer learning resources in the home, poorer preparation for the school regimen, and inadequate understanding of the value of schooling.

Homes that are rich in interesting activities stimulate children's motivation to learn. Home quality is especially influential during the early years and declines somewhat in importance by adolescence. Motivation is also enhanced when parents allow children to have input into decisions, state expectations as suggestions, acknowledge children's feelings, and provide children with choices.

Mothers' beliefs about their parenting efficacy help to predict children's motivation. Mother responsiveness to children's needs is also critical. Father involvement in the academic lives of their children relates positively to motivation. Parental presence in the school sends a clear message that education is to be valued. Part of the effect of fathers on children's motivation may be indirect through providing resources and facilitating a positive mother-child relationship.

Community involvement in education is increasingly being extolled as important. Community members traditionally have been involved in education through such means as participation in school activities and field trips in the community. The School Development Program (SDP), developed by Comer and his colleagues, is based on sound developmental principles. The SDP raised community participation in education to a higher level by involving community members at the planning and curricular levels and stressing collaboration between schools and communities. Research evidence indicates that the SDP has a positive effect on student motivation.

Cultural differences are often found in motivational variables. The attitudes, beliefs, and practices of cultures must be examined to determine the cause of these differences. It is important to control for the effects of extraneous variables (e.g., socioeconomic status). When reliable differences in motivation are obtained among cultural or ethnic groups, students may benefit from programs aimed at enhancing academic motivation.

Glossary

Acquired drives   Drives that are learned, not innate.

Actor-observer bias   The propensity for actors to attribute their behavior to situational factors, whereas observers tend to make dispositional attributions for other's behavior.

Actualizing tendency   Innate motive that is a precursor to other motives and is oriented toward personal growth, autonomy, and freedom from external control.

Affect   A general term that refers to both diffuse moods and specific emotions.

Affective memories   Memories of previous experiences with a task, particularly in terms of the emotions the task arouses.

Alpha press   The "objective reality" of the environment, context, or situation that can influence the person.

Approach performance goal   A performance goal focused on looking smarter than others, on doing better than others, on demonstrating high ability; also called a self-enhancing ego orientation.

Attainment value (or importance)   In expectancy-value theory, one of four task value beliefs regarding the subjective importance of the task to the individual.

Attribution process   Processes whereby environmental and personal factors influence the generation of attributions.

Attributional feedback   Feedback that links successes and failures with one or more attributions.

Attributional process   Processes whereby attributions influence a host of cognitive, affective, and behavioral outcomes.

Attributions   Perceived causes of outcomes.

Avoid performance goal   A performance goal focused on not looking dumb or stupid and on avoiding the appearance of inability; also called a self-defeating ego orientation.

Behavior potential   The probability that a person will act in a certain fashion relative to alternatives.

Behavioral theory   Theory that views motivation as a change in the rate, frequency of occurrence, or form of behavior (response) as a function of environmental events and stimuli.

Beta press   The subjective environment, context or situation, as perceived by the individual, that can influence the individual.

Capacity beliefs   Beliefs that one has the means to accomplish a task, usually in reference to ability, effort, strategies; also known as agency beliefs.

Cell assembly   Brain structure that represents knowledge and that is gradually developed through repeated stimulation.

Classroom management   The ways that teachers maintain order in their classrooms.

Clique   A group of peers who share similar values and beliefs; smaller in size than a crowd, larger than a small group of friends.

Cognitive consistency   Theory assuming that motivation results from relations between cognitions and behaviors.

Cognitive dissonance   Theory that postulates that individuals are motivated to maintain consistent relations among their beliefs, attitudes, and cognitions. Also refers to experience of having discrepant beliefs, attitudes, or cognitions.

Cognitive engagement   The processes by which an individual becomes cognitively involved in a task.

Cognitive Evaluation Theory (CET)   A subtheory within self-determination theory dealing with the role of intrinsic motivational processes.

Cognitive map   Internal plan comprising expectancies for which actions are needed to attain one's goals.

Cognitive modeling   Modeled explanation and demonstration incorporating verbalizations of the model's thoughts and reasons for performing given actions.

Cognitive strategy Strategies used to understand text, to learn new material, and to think and problem solve.

Cognitive theory Theory that views motivation as arising from mental structures or the processing of information and beliefs.

Collective efficacy Self-efficacy of a group, team, or larger social entity or system.

Comer Program See *School Development Program.*

Compliance Obedience emanating from another's command wherein a difference in power or stature exists.

Conation Also called conative component; having to do with the will or volition or striving to attain a goal.

Conditional regard Regard that is contingent on certain actions.

Conditioned response The response elicited by a conditioned stimulus.

Conditioned stimulus A stimulus that, when repeatedly paired with an unconditioned stimulus, elicits a conditioned response similar to the unconditioned response.

Conformity Willful obedience to a group's behaviors or mannerisms wherein the individual and group members are roughly equal in stature.

Connectionism Theory that postulates that learning is accomplished by building associations (connections) between sensory experiences and behavior.

Control beliefs Expectations about the links between an agent and the ends; also called control expectancy beliefs.

Controllability dimension In attributional theory, the dimension that refers to how controllable or uncontrollable a cause is perceived as by an individual.

Cooperative learning Two or more students working together to complete a task.

Coping model Model who initially demonstrates the typical fears and deficiencies of observers but gradually demonstrates improved performance and self-efficacy.

Correlational research Research that investigates the relations that exist between variables.

Cost belief In expectancy-value theory, one of four task value beliefs concerning the negative costs of engaging in a task.

Criticism Feedback that expresses disapproval through verbalizations or gestures.

Crowd A large group of peers who share some similar attributes, interests, and desired activities, but not close friendships.

Desist Teacher actions to stop misbehavior.

Determining tendency Process that allows goals to be translated into action.

Dialogue Conversation between two or more persons.

Dimensionality Classroom organization feature involving the number of activities occurring and how well they address diversity in student abilities and performances.

Direct observations Behavioral instances of motivation.

Drive Internal force that seeks to maintain homeostasis.

Educational seduction Process whereby observers believe they have learned; brought about by a model's presumed authority and charming personality in the absence of educational content.

Effectance motivation Motivation to interact effectively with one's environment and control critical aspects.

Effective reaction potential The likelihood of a behavior occurring.

Efficacy expectations See *Self-efficacy.*

Emergent motivation Motivation that arises from the discovery of new goals or rewards as a consequence of interacting with the environment.

Emotion A feeling that is often short-lived, intense, and specific.

Emotion control strategies Strategies used to control and regulate affect, emotions, and mood.

Enactive learning Learning by doing and experiencing the consequences of one's actions.

Entity theory of intelligence The belief that intelligence or ability is stable, set for life, and does not change with experience or through learning.

Expectancy An individual's belief concerning the likelihood that a particular reinforcement will occur following a specific behavior.

Expectancy component In expectancy-value theory, the constructs related to beliefs about competence to do the task.

Expectancy for success The belief that one will succeed on a task. The term *expectancy* is used more generally to represent the individual's belief about what will happen in the future on an achievement task.

Expectancy principle In attributional theory, the principle that changes in expectancy of success are influenced by the stability of the cause of the event.

Experience sampling method (ESM) A methodology whereby individuals are signalled electronically at certain times and asked to report on their experience, cognitions, and affects at that specific time; also called the "beeper" method.

Experimental research Research in which one or more variables are altered to determine the effects on other variables.

Explanatory style A generalized, habitual way of explaining events and making similar attributions across situations and domains; also called attributional style.

External regulation In self-determination theory, the process by which individuals are motivated and regulated by extrinsic rewards and the avoidance of punishment.

Extinction Decrease in intensity and disappearance of a conditioned response due to repeated presentations of the conditioned stimulus without the unconditioned stimulus; a lack of responding produced by nonreinforcement of a response.

Extrinsic motivation Motivation to engage in an activity as a means to an end.

Facilitator One who establishes a classroom climate oriented toward significant learning and helps students clarify their purposes in learning.

False consensus effect Tendency for individuals to come to see their own behavior and cognition as typical, as representing what "all" people do or think.

Field research Research conducted where participants live, work, or go to school.

Flow The holistic sensation that individuals feel when they act with total engagement in the task, often losing track of time, space, and their self.

Friendship Voluntary reciprocal relationship between two persons.

Fundamental attribution error Attributional bias that leads to dispositional inferences; ignoring situational factors.

Globality dimension In attributional theory, the dimension that refers to how global or situation specific a cause is perceived as by the individual.

Goal The behavior (outcome) that one is consciously trying to perform (attain).

Goal commitment How strongly an individual is attached to, enthusiastic about, or determined to achieve a specific goal.

Goal content The actual substance or domain that a goal is directed toward.

Goal hierarchies Goals that are arranged in some superordinate and subordinate manner, so that some are more important than others, or some subsume others.

Goal orientation The general purposes or reasons for engaging in achievement tasks combined with some general standards for evaluating progress.

Goal setting Process of establishing a standard or objective to serve as the aim of one's actions.

Group focus Extent to which teachers keep students attentive to learning tasks.

Habit strength Strength of a stimulus-response association.

Hedonic bias Propensity to take responsibility for positive outcomes and deny responsibility for negative outcomes; also called self-serving bias, beneffectance bias, self-enhancement bias, ego defensiveness, and self-protective bias.

Homeostasis Optimal levels of physiological states.

Hypothesis An assumption that can be tested empirically.

Id Personality structure devoted to attainment of basic needs.

Identified regulation In self-determination theory, the processes by which individuals are motivated or regulated by internal thoughts regarding how important a task is to them personally.

Incentive motivation Motivation for goal attainment.

Incentive value In Atkinson's model of achievement motivation, the pride in accomplishment, defined as the inverse of the probability of success.

Incongruity Idea that individuals are motivated to reduce discrepancy between prior experience and knowledge and new or conflicting information.

Incremental Theory of Intelligence The belief that intelligence or ability can change, develop, and grow with experience or through learning.

Inhibition Fatigue due to nonresponding and the reinforcement derived from not responding when one is fatigued.

Instinct Innate propensity that manifests itself in behavior.

Instructional self-efficacy See *Teacher self-efficacy*.

Integrated regulation In self-determination theory, the processes by which individuals are motivated or regulated by an integration of external and internal factors that become part of the self.

Interview A type of questionnaire in which questions or points to discuss are presented by an interviewer and the respondent answers orally.

Intrinsic interest or intrinsic value In expectancy value theory, one of four task value beliefs concerning the personal interest the task has for an individual.

Intrinsic motivation Motivation to engage in an activity for its own sake.

Introjected regulation In self-determination theory, the processes by which individuals are motivated or regulated by internal thoughts or feelings of ought, should, or guilt.

Introspection Type of self-analysis in which individuals verbally report their immediate perceptions following exposure to objects or events.

James-Lange Theory of Emotion Emotion is a consequence of behavior rather than an antecedent (cause) and involves perceptions of responses to arousing situations.

Laboratory research Research conducted in a controlled setting.

Latent learning Learning in the absence of a goal or reinforcement.

Law of Effect The strength of a connection is influenced by the consequences of performing the response in the situation: Satisfying consequences strengthen a connection, whereas annoying consequences weaken it. Eventually modified by Thorndike to state that annoying consequences do not weaken a connection.

Law of Readiness When an individual is prepared to act, to do so is satisfying and not to do so is annoying. When one is not prepared to act, forcing action is annoying.

Learned helplessness Pattern of learned cognitions, attributions, and behaviors that lead an individual to see no contingency between the behavior and the outcomes leading to hopelessness, depression, and passivity.

Level of aspiration The goal or standard for judging success or performance on a task set by an individual.

Locus dimension In attributional theory, the dimension that refers to how internal or external a cause is perceived as by the individual.

Locus of control Motivational concept referring to generalized control over outcomes; individuals may believe that outcomes occur independently of how they act (external control) or are highly contingent on their actions (internal control).

Mastery approach goal Goal of trying to learn and master tasks, to learn new skills, to self-improve.

Mastery avoid goal Goal of avoiding making mistakes, of avoiding doing the task incorrectly.

Mastery goal Goal of increasing one's competence through learning skills, mastering tasks, self-improvement, and understanding new material; also called a learning goal, task-involved goal, or task-focused goal.

Mastery model Model who demonstrates faultless performance and high self-efficacy throughout the modeled sequence.

Mastery motivation See *Effectance motivation*.

Matched-dependent behavior Behavior displayed by an imitator that is dependent on (elicited by) behavioral cues of a model.

Metacognition Knowledge about cognition as well as the control and regulation of cognition.

Metacognitive knowledge Knowledge about cognition and cognitive processes.

Metacognitive strategies Strategies used to actually control and regulate cognition.

Metatheoretical model Way to organize theories according to their underlying assumptions.

Mimesis Learning through observing the actions of others and abstract models exemplifying literary and moral styles.

Modeling Behavioral, cognitive, and affective changes deriving from observing one or more models.

Mood A more diffuse, general feeling that often has no specific antecedent.

Motivated learning Motivation to acquire skills and strategies rather than to perform tasks.

Motivation The process whereby goal-directed activity is instigated and sustained.

Motivation control strategies   Strategies used to control and regulate various aspects of motivation.

Motivational feedback   Feedback designed to motivate students rather than to inform them of the accuracy of answers.

Motive for success   To approach or seek out achievement tasks, to strive to be successful.

Motive to avoid failure   The motive to avoid doing poorly in achievement situations.

Motives   Learned but stable individual differences or dispositions to seek or desire particular outcomes; often more implicit than conscious cognitions.

Movement management   Teacher actions that initiate, sustain, and alter activity flow in the classroom.

Multidimensional classroom   Classrooms where there are a diversity of activities and students are evaluated along a large number of criteria.

Multiple necessary schema   Schema that leads to a causal inference only if both causes are present.

Multiple sufficient schema   Schema that leads to a causal inference if either one or another cause is present.

Need   An internal force or drive to attain or to avoid certain states or objects.

Need for achievement   The motive or desire to be successful, to strive for achievement outcomes, such as obtaining high grades.

Need for affiliation   The motive, desire, or striving to affiliate with others, to form close relations with others.

Need for power   The motive, desire, or striving for dominance or power over others.

Negative reinforcement   Procedure in which a negative reinforcer is removed following a response.

Negative reinforcer   A stimulus that, when removed by a response, increases the future likelihood of the response occurring in that situation.

Observational learning   Display of a new pattern of behavior by one who observes a model; prior to the modeling the behavior had a zero probability of occurrence by the observer even with motivational inducements in effect.

Organismic Integration Theory (OIT)   A subtheory within self-determination theory that explains extrinsically motivated behavior.

Origins   In de Charms's theory, individuals who believe that their behavior is under their own control.

Outcome expectations   Beliefs about the consequences of actions.

Overjustification   Decrease in intrinsic interest (motivation) in an activity subsequent to engaging in it under conditions that make task engagement salient as a means to some end (e.g., reward).

Overlapping   Ability of teachers to attend to more than one issue simultaneously.

Paradigm   A particular theoretical or conceptual perspective used to understand and research phenomena, including the models, constructs, and methodology used.

Participant modeling   Therapeutic treatment comprising modeled demonstrations, joint performance between client and therapist, gradual withdrawal of performance aids, and individual mastery performance by the client.

Pawns   In de Charms's theory, persons who do not feel they can control their own behavior; they believe that external factors control their behavior.

Peer networks   Large groups of peers with whom students associate.

Perceived competence   See *Self-perceptions of competence.*

Perceived control   See *Locus of control.*

Performance feedback   Feedback on the accuracy of work that may include corrective information.

Performance goal   Goal to appear smart to others, to do better than others, to avoid appearing to be stupid, and to have others believe one is competent; also called an ego-involved goal, an ability-focused goal, or relative ability goal.

Personal causation   Individual's initiation of behavior intended to alter the environment.

Personal interest   A more stable, individual disposition or personal characteristic to experience an interest in a particular topic or activity.

Positive regard   Feelings such as respect, liking, warmth, sympathy, and acceptance.

Positive reinforcement   Procedure in which a positive reinforcer is presented following a response.

Positive reinforcer   A stimulus that, when presented following a response, increases the future likelihood of the response occurring in that situation.

Positive self-regard   Positive regard that derives from self-experiences.

Praise   Feedback that expresses approval or commendation.

Premack principle   The opportunity to engage in a more valued activity reinforces engaging in a less valued activity.

Primary control   Processes regarding the individual's attempt to control self, others, or events.

Private speech   Self-directed speech that has a self-regulatory function but is not socially communicative.

Probability for success   In Atkinson's model of achievement motivation, the individual's subjective belief about the likelihood of success on a task (see *Expectancy for success*).

Projective test   Test in which individuals' responses to ambiguous pictures are scored to indicate their standing on a motivational construct (e.g., Thematic Apperception Test).

Psychical energy   Internal force responsible for behavior.

Punishment   Withdrawal of a positive reinforcer or presentation of a negative reinforcer following a response, which decreases the future likelihood of the response being made in the presence of the stimulus.

Pygmalion effect   Process whereby expectations by others lead one to behave accordingly.

Qualitative research   Research characterized by intensive study, descriptions of events, and interpretation of meanings.

Reciprocal teaching   Interactive dialogue between teacher and students in which the teacher initially models activities, after which the teacher and students take turns being the teacher.

Reductionism   View that complex events can be reduced to simple phenomena.

Reinforcement   Any stimulus or event that leads to response strengthening.

Reinforcement value   How much individuals value a particular outcome relative to other potential outcomes.

Repress or repression   The resistance of an internal force by an individual; usually an unconscious process whereby there is little awareness that the force is being ignored or avoided by the individual.

Response facilitation   Previously learned behaviors of observers are prompted by the actions of models.

Ripple effect   Behaviors of students are affected by their witnessing a teacher's handling of misbehavior by another student.

Scaffolding   Process of controlling task elements that are beyond learners' capabilities so that they can focus on and master those task features that they can grasp quickly.

Schemas   Cognitive structures that underlie and make possible organized thoughts and actions.

School adjustment   Student index based on progress, achievement, attitudes toward school, anxieties, loneliness, social support, and motivation.

School Development Program   School organization stressing community involvement in the planning and implementation of school programs.

Secondary control   Processes whereby individuals relinquish some personal control to others or to events.

Self-centered bias   Tendency to take more self-responsibility for an outcome.

Self-concept   Individuals' belief about themselves in terms of their academic, social, athletic, and personal capabilities and characteristics.

Self-determination   Motive aimed at developing autonomy, agency, and competence; begins as undifferentiated but eventually differentiates into specific areas.

Self-efficacy   One's perceived capabilities for learning or performing actions at designated levels.

Self-esteem   Global, more affective reaction and evaluation of oneself; similar to self-worth.

Self-evaluation   Process comprising self-judgments of current performance by comparing it to one's goal and self-reactions to these judgments by deeming performance noteworthy, unacceptable, and so forth.

Self-instructional training   Instructional procedure that comprises cognitive modeling, overt guidance, overt self-guidance, faded overt self-guidance, and covert self-instruction.

Self-judgment   Comparing one's current performance level with one's goal.

Self-modeling   Changes in behaviors, thoughts, and affects that derive from observing one's own performances.

Self-monitoring   See *Self-observation*.

Self-observation   Deliberate attention to aspects of one's behavior.

Self-perceptions of competence (ability)   Individuals' evaluative judgments of their competence or ability for a task; also known as perceptions of competence.

Self-reaction   Changes in one's beliefs and behaviors after judging performance against a goal.

Self-regulated learning   See *Self-regulation.*

Self-regulation   The process whereby students personally activate and sustain behaviors, cognitions, and affects that are systematically oriented toward the attainment of goals.

Self-reports   People's judgments and statements about themselves.

Self-schemas   Cognitive or knowledge structures about the self in terms of capabilities, personality, interests, values, etc.

Self-worth   Individuals' global feelings or emotions about themselves as a person; similar to self-esteem.

Situational interest   The experience of interest as a function of contextual features.

Social comparison   Process of comparing one's beliefs and behaviors with those of others.

Stability dimension   In attributional theory, the dimension that refers to how stable or unstable a cause is perceived as by the individual.

Stereotype threat   Psychological process whereby a negative stereotype about a group is activated, leading to a decrease in performance for members of that group.

Stimulated recall   Procedure in which an investigator asks participants to recall their thoughts at different times during performance of a task.

Strategy beliefs   Beliefs about how means are linked to ends; also known as means-ends beliefs.

Strategy feedback   Feedback that informs learners about how well they are applying a strategy and how strategy use is improving their performances.

TARGET   An acronym that stands for six dimensions of classrooms that may influence motivation: task, authority, recognition, grouping, evaluation, and time.

Task value   In expectancy value theory, the subjective beliefs about reasons for doing the task, why the individual wants to do the task.

Teacher expectations   Teachers' beliefs about their students in terms of their achievement, cognition, motivation, and potential to learn.

Teacher self-efficacy   Personal beliefs about one's capabilities to help students learn.

Test anxiety   Feelings of fear, anxiety, stress, and related cognitions of doubt and worry regarding test performance.

Thema   In Murray's theory, the combination of the individual's needs, the environmental presses, and the resulting outcomes.

Theory   A scientifically acceptable set of principles advanced to explain a phenomenon.

Think-aloud   Procedure in which participants verbalize aloud their thoughts, actions, and emotions while performing a task.

Traits   Unique realities within individuals that help to account for the relative consistency of behavior across situations.

Triadic reciprocality   Reciprocal interactions (causal relations) among behaviors, environmental variables, and cognitions and other personal factors.

Unconditional positive regard   Attitudes of worthiness and acceptance with no conditions attached.

Unconditioned response   The response elicited by an unconditioned stimulus.

Unconditioned stimulus   A stimulus that when presented elicits a natural response from an individual.

Unidimensional classroom   Classrooms where there is not much variability in tasks and students are evaluated on a limited set of criteria.

Utility value   In expectancy-value theory, one of four task value beliefs concerning the subjective beliefs about the usefulness of the task to the individual.

Valence   The value or importance that is attached to an object in the environment.

Value component   In expectancy-value theory, beliefs that individuals hold about the reasons they want to do an achievement task.

Vicarious learning   Learning that occurs without overt performance, such as by observing live or symbolic models.

Volition   The act of using the will; the process of dealing with the implementation of actions to attain goals.

Will   The part of the mind that reflects one's desire, want, or purpose.

Withitness Demonstration by teachers that they know what is going on at all times; having "eyes in the back of their heads."

Zone of proximal development The amount of learning possible by a student given the proper instructional conditions.

References

Abrami, P. C., Leventhal, L., & Perry, R. P. (1982). Educational seduction. *Review of Educational Research, 52,* 446–464.

Ach, N. (1910). *Uber den Willensakt und das Temperament.* Leipzig, Germany: Quelle & Meyer.

Ainley, M., & Hidi, S. (in press). Dynamic measures for studying intent and learning. In M. Maehr & P. R. Pintrich (Eds.), *Advances in motivation and achievement: New Directions in Measures and Methods.* Oxford, England. JAI Press-Elsevier.

Akamatsu, T. J., & Thelen, M. H. (1974). A review of the literature on observer characteristics and imitation. *Developmental Psychology, 10,* 38–47.

Alderman, M. K. (1985). Achievement motivation and the preservice teacher. In M. K. Alderman & M. W. Cohen (Eds.), *Motivation theory and practice for preservice teachers* (pp. 37–51). Washington, DC: ERIC Clearinghouse on Teacher Education.

Alderman, M. K. (1999). *Motivation for achievement: Possibilities for teaching and learning.* Mahwah, NJ: Lawrence Erlbaum Associates.

Alexander, K., Cook, M., & McDill, E. (1978). Curriculum tracking and educational stratification: Some further evidence. *American Sociological Review, 43,* 47–66.

Alexander, P., Kulikowich, J., & Jetton, T. (1994). The role of subject-matter knowledge and interest in the processing of linear and nonlinear texts. *Review of Educational Research, 64,* 201–252.

Allison, M., & Duncan, M. (1988). Women, work, and flow: In M. Csikszentmihalyi & I. Csikszentmihalyi (Eds.), *Optimal experience: Psychological studies of flow in consciousness* (pp. 118–137). New York: Cambridge University Press.

Allport, G. W. (1937). *Personality: A psychological interpretation.* New York: Henry Holt.

Ames, C. (1981). Competitive versus cooperative reward structures: The influence of individual and group performance factors on achievement attributions and affect. *American Educational Research Journal, 18,* 273–287.

Ames, C. (1984). Competitive, cooperative, and individualistic goal structures: A cognitive-motivational analysis. In R. Ames & C. Ames (Eds.), *Research on motivation in education* (Vol. 1, pp. 177–207). New York: Academic Press.

Ames, C. (1992a). Achievement goals and the classroom motivational climate. In D. H. Schunk & J. Meece (Eds.), *Student perceptions in the classroom* (pp. 327–348). Hillsdale, NJ: Erlbaum.

Ames, C. (1992b). Classrooms: Goals, structures, and student motivation. *Journal of Educational Psychology, 84,* 261–271.

Ames, C., & Archer, J. (1987). Mothers' beliefs about the role of ability and effort in school learning. *Journal of Educational Psychology, 79,* 409–414.

Ames, C., & Archer, J. (1988). Achievement goals in the classroom: Students' learning strategies and motivation processes. *Journal of Educational Psychology, 80,* 260–267.

Ames, C., & Felker, D. (1979). An examination of children's attributions and achievement-related evaluations in competitive, cooperative, and individualistic reward structures. *Journal of Educational Psychology, 71,* 413–420.

Ames, R. (1975). Teachers' attributions of responsibility: Some unexpected nondefensive effects. *Journal of Educational Psychology, 67,* 668–676.

Anderman, E. (1997). Motivation and school reform. In M. L. Maehr & P. R. Pintrich (Eds.), *Advances in motivation and achievement* (Vol. 10, pp. 303–338). Greenwich, CT: JAI Press.

Anderman, E., & Maehr, M. L. (1994). Motivation and schooling in the middle grades. *Review of Educational Research, 64,* 287–309.

Anderman, E., Maehr, M. L., & Midgley, C. (1999). Declining motivation after the transition to middle school: Schools can make a difference. *Journal of Research and Development in Education, 32,* 131–147.

Anderman, E., & Midgley, E. (1997). Changes in achievement goal orientations, perceived academic competence, and grades across the transition to middle-level schools. *Contemporary Educational Psychology, 22,* 269–298.

Anderman, E., & Young, A. (1994). Motivation and strategy use in science: Individual differences and classroom effects. *Journal of Research in Science Teaching, 31,* 811–831.

Anderson, C. (1982). The search for school climate: A review of the research. *Review of Educational Research, 52,* 368–420.

Anderson, J. R. (1990). *Cognitive psychology and its implications* (3rd ed.). New York: Freeman.

Anderson, L. M., Evertson, C. M., & Brophy, J. E. (1979). An experimental study of effective teaching in first-grade reading groups. *Elementary School Journal, 79,* 193–222.

Andrews, G. R., & Debus, R. L. (1978). Persistence and the causal perception of failure: Modifying cognitive attributions. *Journal of Educational Psychology, 70,* 154–166.

Arlin, M., & Webster, J. (1983). Time costs of mastery learning. *Journal of Educational Psychology, 75,* 187–195.

Arnold, M. B. (1968). *The nature of emotion.* Middlesex, England: Penguin.

Aronson, E. (1966). The psychology of insufficient justification: An analysis of some conflicting data. In S. Feldman (Ed.), *Cognitive consistency: Motivational antecedents and behavioral consequences* (pp. 109–133). New York: Academic Press.

Asch, S. E. (1955). Opinions and social pressure. *Scientific American, 193*(5), 31–35.

Asch, S. E. (1958). Interpersonal influence. In E. E. Maccoby, T. M. Newcomb, & E. L. Hartley (Eds.), *Readings in social psychology* (3rd ed., pp. 174–183). New York: Holt.

Ashton, P. T. (1985). Motivation and the teacher's sense of efficacy. In C. Ames & R. Ames (Eds.), *Research on motivation in education. Vol. 2: The classroom milieu* (pp. 141–171). Orlando, FL: Academic Press.

Ashton, P., & Webb, R. (1986). *Making a difference: Teachers' sense of efficacy and student achievement.* New York: Longman.

Assor, A., & Connell, J. P. (1992). The validity of students' self-reports as measures of performance affecting self-appraisals. In D. H. Schunk & J. L. Meece (Eds.), *Student perceptions in the classroom* (pp. 25–47). Hillsdale, NJ: Erlbaum.

Atkinson, J. W. (1957). Motivational determinants of risk-taking behavior. *Psychological Review, 64,* 359–372.

Atkinson, J. W. (1958). *Motives in fantasy, action, and society.* Princeton, NJ: Van Nostrand.

Atkinson, J. W. (1964). *An introduction to motivation.* Princeton, NJ: Van Nostrand.

Austin, J., & Vancouver, J. (1996). Goal constructs in psychology: Structure, process, and content. *Psychological Bulletin, 120,* 338–375.

Bailey, S. M. (1993). The current status of gender equity research in American schools. *Educational Psychologist, 28,* 321–339.

Bandura, A. (1969). *Principles of behavior modification.* New York: Holt, Rinehart & Winston.

Bandura, A. (1977). Self-efficacy: Toward a unifying theory of behavioral change. *Psychological Review, 84,* 191–215.

Bandura, A. (1982). Self-efficacy mechanism in human agency. *American Psychologist, 37,* 122–147.

Bandura, A. (1986). *Social foundations of thought and action: A social cognitive theory.* Englewood Cliffs, NJ: Prentice-Hall.

Bandura, A. (1988). Self-regulation of motivation and action through goal systems. In V. Hamilton, G. H. Bower, & N. H. Frijda (Eds.), *Cognitive perspectives on emotion and motivation* (pp. 37–61). Dordrecht, The Netherlands: Kluwer.

Bandura, A. (1989). Social cognitive theory. In R. Vasta (Ed.), *Annals of child development* (Vol. 6, pp. 1–60). Greenwich, CT: JAI Press.

Bandura, A. (1993). Perceived self-efficacy in cognitive development and functioning. *Educational Psychologist, 28,* 117–148.

Bandura, A. (1997). *Self-efficacy: The exercise of control.* New York: Freeman.

Bandura, A., & Cervone, D. (1983). Self-evaluative and self-efficacy mechanisms governing the motivational effects of goal systems. *Journal of Personality and Social Psychology, 45,* 1017–1028.

Bandura, A., & Cervone, D. (1986). Differential engagement of self-reactive influences in cognitive motivation. *Organizational Behavior and Human Decision Processes, 38,* 92–133.

Bandura, A., & Schunk, D. H. (1981). Cultivating competence, self-efficacy, and intrinsic interest through proximal self-motivation. *Journal of Personality and Social Psychology, 41,* 586–598.

Bandura, A., & Walters, R. H. (1963). *Social learning and personality development.* New York: Holt, Rinehart & Winston.

Bargh, J. (1997). The automaticity of everyday life. In R. Wyer (Ed.), *The automaticity of everyday life: Advances in social cognition* (Vol. 10, pp. 1–61). Mahweh, NJ: Erlbaum.

Bargh, J., & Ferguson, M. (2000). Beyond behaviorism: On the automaticity of higher mental processes. *Psychological Bulletin, 126,* 925–945.

Barnes, R., Ickes, W., & Kidd, R. (1979). Effects of perceived intentionality and stability of another's dependency on helping behavior. *Personality and Social Psychology Bulletin, 5,* 367–372.

Barr, R., & Dreeben, R. (1983). *How schools work.* Chicago: University of Chicago Press.

Barron, K. & Harackiewicz, J. (2001). Achievement goals and optimal motivation: Testing multiple goal models. *Journal of Personality and Social Psychology, 80,* 706–722.

Battle, E. (1965). Motivational determinants of academic task persistence. *Journal of Personality and Social Psychology, 2,* 209–218.

Battle, E. (1966). Motivational determinants of academic competence. *Journal of Personality and Social Psychology, 4,* 634–642.

Baumeister, R. F., & Scher, S. J. (1988). Self-defeating behavior patterns among normal individuals: Review and analysis of common self-destructive tendencies. *Psychological Bulletin, 104,* 3–22.

Becker, H., & Epstein, J. (1982). Parent involvement: A survey of teacher practices. *Elementary School Journal, 83,* 85–102.

Becker, H., Geer, B., & Hughes, E. (1961). *Boys in white: Student culture in the medical school.* Chicago: University of Chicago Press.

Becker, J. (1981). Differential treatment of females and males in mathematics classes. *Journal for Research in Mathematics Education, 12,* 40–53.

Beckman, L. (1970). Effects of students' performance on teachers' and observers' attributions of causality. *Journal of Educational Psychology, 61,* 76–82.

Behrend, D. A., Rosengren, K. S., & Perlmutter, M. (1992). The relation between private speech and parental interactive style. In R. M. Diaz & L. E. Berk (Eds.), *Private speech: From social interaction to self-regulation* (pp. 85–100). Hillsdale, NJ: Erlbaum.

Belsky, J. (1998). Paternal influence and children's well-being: Limits of and new directions for understanding. In A. Booth & A. C. Crouter (Eds.), *Men in families* (pp. 279–293). Mahwah, NJ: Erlbaum.

Bem, D. J. (1967). Self-perception: An alternative interpretation of cognitive dissonance phenomena. *Psychological Review, 74,* 183–200.

Bem, D. J. (1972). Self-perception theory. In L. Berkowitz (Ed.), *Advances in experimental social psychology* (Vol. 6, pp. 1–62). New York: Academic Press.

Bennett, W. J. (1993). *The book of virtues: A treasury of great moral stories.* New York: Simon & Schuster.

Benz, C. R., Bradley, L., Alderman, M. K., & Flowers, M. A. (1992). Personal teaching efficacy: Developmental relationships in education. *Journal of Educational Research, 85,* 274–285.

Bergin, D. (1999). Influences on classroom interest. *Educational Psychologist, 34,* 87–98.

Berk, L. E. (1986). Relationship of elementary school children's private speech to behavioral accompaniment to task, attention, and task performance. *Developmental Psychology, 22,* 671–680.

Berk, L. E. (1992). Children's private speech: An overview of theory and the status of research. In R. M. Diaz & L. E. Berk (Eds.), *Private speech: From social interaction to self-regulation* (pp. 17–53). Hillsdale, NJ: Erlbaum.

Berlyne, D. E. (1960). *Conflict, arousal, and curiosity.* New York: McGraw-Hill.

Berlyne, D. E. (1963). Motivational problems raised by exploratory and epistemic behavior. In S. Koch (Ed.), *Psychology: A study of a science* (Vol. 5, pp. 284–364). New York: McGraw-Hill.

Berndt, T. J. (1992). Friendship and friends' influence in adolescence. *Current Directions in Psychological Science, 1,* 156–159.

Berndt, T. J. (1999). Friends' influences on students' adjustment to school. *Educational Psychologist, 34,* 15–29.

Berndt, T. J., Hawkins, J. A., & Jiao, Z. (1999). Influences of friends and friendships on adjustment to junior high school. *Merrill-Palmer Quarterly, 45,* 13–41.

Berndt, T. J., & Keefe, K. (1992). Friends' influence on adolescents' perceptions of themselves at school. In D. H. Schunk & J. L. Meece (Eds.), *Student perceptions in the classroom* (pp. 51–73). Hillsdale, NJ: Erlbaum.

Berndt, T. J., & Keefe, K. (1996). Friends' influence on school adjustment: A motivational analysis. In

J. Juvonen & K. R. Wentzel (Eds.), *Social motivation: Understanding children's school adjustment* (pp. 248–278). Cambridge, England: Cambridge University Press.

Betancourt, H., & Lopez, S. (1993). The study of culture, ethnicity, and race in American psychology. *American Psychologist, 48,* 629–637.

Betz, N. E., & Hackett, G. (1981). The relationship of career-related self-efficacy expectations to perceived career options in college women and men. *Journal of Counseling Psychology, 28,* 399–410.

Betz, N. E., & Hackett, G. (1983). The relationship of mathematics self-efficacy expectations to the selection of science-based college majors. *Journal of Vocational Behavior, 23,* 329–345.

Birch, S. H., & Ladd, G. W. (1996). Interpersonal relationships in the school environment and children's early school adjustment: The role of teachers and peers. In J. Juvonen & K. R. Wentzel (Eds.), *Social motivation: Understanding children's school adjustment* (pp. 199–225). Cambridge, England: Cambridge University Press.

Blumenfeld, P. (1992). Classroom learning and motivation: Clarifying and expanding goal theory. *Journal of Educational Psychology, 84,* 272–281.

Blumenfeld, P., Fishman, B., Krajcik, J., Marx, R., & Soloway, E. (2000). Creating usable innovations in systemic reform: Scaling up technology-embedded project-based science in urban schools. *Educational Psychologist, 35,* 149–164.

Blumenfeld, P., Hamilton, V. L., Bossert, S., Wessels, K., & Meece, J. (1983). Teacher talk and student thought: Socialization into the student role. In J. Levine & M. Wang (Eds.), *Teacher and student perceptions: Implications for learning* (pp. 143–192). Hillsdale, NJ: Erlbaum.

Blumenfeld, P., Mergendoller, J., & Swarthout, D. (1987). Task as a heuristic for understanding student learning and motivation. *Journal of Curriculum Studies, 19,* 135–148.

Blumenfeld, P., Pintrich, P. R., & Hamilton, V. L. (1986). Children's concepts of ability, effort and conduct. *American Educational Research Journal, 23,* 95–104.

Blumenfeld, P., Pintrich, P. R., & Hamilton, V. L. (1987). Teacher talk and students' reasoning about morals, conventions, and achievement. *Child Development, 58,* 1389–1401.

Blumenfeld, P., Pintrich, P. R., Meece, J., & Wessels, K. (1982). The formation and role of self-perceptions of ability in the elementary classroom. *Elementary School Journal, 82,* 401–420.

Blumenfeld, P., Soloway, E., Marx, R. W., Krajcik, J. S., Guzdial, M., & Palincsar, A. (1991). Motivating project-based learning: Sustaining the doing, supporting the learning. *Educational Psychologist, 26,* 369–398.

Boekaerts, M. (in press). The on-line motivation questionnaire: A self-report instrument to assess students' context sensitivity. In M. Maehr & P. R. Pintrich (Eds.), *Advances in motivation and achievement: New directions in measures and methods.* Oxford, England: JAI Press-Elsevier.

Boekaerts, M., Pintrich, P. R., & Zeidner, M. (2000). *Handbook of self-regulation.* San Diego, CA: Academic Press.

Bogenschneider, K., Wu, M., Raffaelli, M., & Tsay, J. C. (1998). Parent influences on adolescent peer orientation and substance use: The interface of parenting practices and values. *Child Development, 69,* 1672–1688.

Boggiano, A. K., Main, D. S., & Katz, P. A. (1988). Children's preference for challenge: The role of perceived competence and control. *Journal of Personality and Social Psychology, 54,* 134–141.

Bolin, F. (1989). Empowering leadership. *Teachers College Record, 91,* 81–96.

Bong, M., & Clark, R. E. (1999). Comparison between self-concept and self-efficacy in academic motivation research. *Educational Psychologist, 34,* 139–153.

Borkowski, J. G., Carr, M., Rellinger, E., & Pressley, M. (1990). Self-regulated cognition: Interdependence of metacognition, attributions, and self-esteem. In B. F. Jones & L. Idol (Eds.), *Dimensions of thinking and cognitive instruction* (pp. 53–92). Hillsdale, NJ: Erlbaum.

Borkowski, J. G., & Thorpe, P. K. (1994). Self-regulation and motivation: A life-span perspective on underachievement. In D. H. Schunk & B. J. Zimmerman (Eds.), *Self-regulation of learning and performance: Issues and educational applications* (pp. 45–73). Hillsdale, NJ: Erlbaum.

Borkowski, J. G., Weyhing, R. S., & Carr, M. (1988). Effects of attributional retraining on strategy-based reading comprehension of learning-disabled students. *Journal of Educational Psychology, 80,* 46–53.

Bossert, S. (1988). Cooperative activities in the classroom. In E. Rothkopf (Ed.), *Review of Research in Education* (Vol. 15, pp. 225–250).

Washington, DC: American Educational Research Association.

Bouffard, T., Boisvert, J., Vezeau, C., & Larouche, C. (1995). The impact of goal orientation on self-regulation and performance among college students. *British Journal of Educational Psychology, 65,* 317–329.

Bouffard-Bouchard, T., Parent, S., & Larivee, S. (1991). Influence of self-efficacy on self-regulation and performance among junior and senior high-school age students. *International Journal of Behavioral Development, 14,* 153–164.

Bower, G. (1981). Mood and memory. *American Psychologist, 36,* 129–148.

Bowles, S., & Gintis, H. (1976). *Schooling in capitalist America: Educational reform and the contradictions of economic life.* New York: Basic Books.

Braddock, J., & McPartland, J. (1993). Education of early adolescents. In L. Darling-Hammond (Ed.), *Review of educational research* (Vol. 19, pp. 135–170). Washington, DC: American Educational Research Association.

Brandt, L., Hayden, M., & Brophy, J. (1975). Teachers' attitudes and ascription of causation. *Journal of Educational Psychology, 67,* 677–682.

Bransford, J., Brown, A., & Cocking, R. (1999). *How people learn: Brain, mind, experience, and school.* Washington, DC: National Academy Press.

Brattesani, K., Weinstein, R., & Marshall, H. (1984). Student perceptions of differential teacher treatment as moderators of teacher expectation effects. *Journal of Educational Psychology, 76,* 236–247.

Braun, C. (1976). Teacher expectation: Sociopsychological dynamics. *Review of Educational Research, 46,* 185–213.

Brewer, W. F. (1974). There is no convincing evidence for operant or classical conditioning in adult humans. In W. B. Weimer & D. S. Palermo (Eds.), *Cognition and the symbolic processes* (pp. 1–42). Hillsdale, NJ: Erlbaum.

Broadhurst, P. L. (1957). Emotionality and the Yerkes-Dodson law. *Journal of Experimental Psychology, 54,* 345–352.

Brody, G. H., Flor, D. L., & Gibson, N. M. (1999). Linking maternal efficacy beliefs, developmental goals, parenting practices, and child competence in rural, single-parent, African American families. *Child Development, 70,* 1197–1208.

Brookover, W., Beady, C., Flood, P., Schweitzer, J., & Wisenbaker, J. (1979). *School social systems and student achievement: Schools can make a difference.* New York: Praeger.

Brophy, J. (1981). Teacher praise: A functional analysis. *Review of Educational Research, 51,* 5–32.

Brophy, J. (1983). Conceptualizing student motivation. *Educational Psychologist, 18,* 200–215.

Brophy, J. (1985). Teacher-student interaction. In J. B. Dusek (Ed.), *Teacher expectancies* (pp. 303–328). Hillsdale, NJ: Erlbaum.

Brophy, J. (1987). On motivating students. In D. Berliner & B. Rosenshine (Eds.), *Talks to teachers* (pp. 201–245). New York: Random House.

Brophy, J. (1998). *Motivating students to learn.* New York: McGraw-Hill.

Brophy, J. (1999). Toward a model of the value aspects of motivation in education: Developing appreciation for particular learning domains and activities. *Educational Psychologist, 34,* 75–85.

Brophy, J., & Good, T. L. (1974). *Teacher-student relationships: Causes and consequences.* New York: Holt, Rinehart & Winston.

Brophy, J., & Good, T. L. (1986). Teacher behavior and student achievement. In M. C. Wittrock (Ed.), *Handbook of research on teaching* (3rd ed., pp. 328–375). New York: Macmillan.

Brophy, J., & Rohrkemper, M. (1981). The influence of problem ownership on teachers' perceptions of and strategies for coping with problem students. *Journal of Educational Psychology, 73,* 295–311.

Brown, A. (1994). The advancement of learning. *Educational Researcher, 23,* 4–12.

Brown, A. (1997). Transforming schools into communities of thinking and learning about serious matters. *American Psychologist, 52,* 399–413.

Brown, A., Bransford, J. D., Ferrara, R. A., & Campione, J. C. (1983). Learning, remembering, and understanding. In P. H. Mussen (Series Ed.), and J. H. Flavell and E. M. Markman (Vol. Eds.), *Handbook of child psychology: Vol. 3. Cognitive development* (4th ed., pp. 77–166). New York: Wiley.

Brown, A., & Campione, J. (1994). Guided discovery in a community of learners. In K. McGilly (Ed.), *Classrooms lessons: Integrating cognitive theory and classroom practice* (pp. 229–270). Cambridge, MA: MIT Press.

Brown, J., & Weiner, B. (1984). Affective consequences of ability versus effort ascriptions: Controversies, resolutions, and quandaries. *Journal of Educational Psychology, 76,* 146–158.

Brown, J. S., Collins, A., & Duguid, P. (1989). Situated cognition and the culture of learning. *Educational Researcher, 18,* 32–42.

Bruer, J. (1993). *Schools for thought: A science of learning in the classroom.* Cambridge, MA: MIT Press.

Bryan, J. H., & Bryan, T. H. (1983). The social life of the learning disabled youngster. In J. D. McKinney & L. Feagans (Eds.), *Current topics in learning disabilities* (Vol. 1, pp. 57–85). Norwood, NJ: Ablex.

Bryan, J. H., & Walbek, N. H. (1970). Preaching and practicing generosity: Children's actions and reactions. *Child Development, 41,* 329–353.

Bryk, A., Lee, V., & Holland, P. (1993). *Catholic schools and the common good.* Cambridge, MA: Harvard University Press.

Butler, R. (1987). Task-involving and ego-involving properties of evaluation: Effects of different feedback conditions on motivational perceptions, interest, and performance. *Journal of Educational Psychology, 79,* 474–482.

Butler, R. (1998). Age trends in the use of social and temporal comparison for self-evaluation: Examination of a novel developmental hypothesis. *Child Development, 69,* 1054–1073.

Byrne, B. M. (1984). The general/academic self-concept nomological network: A review of construct validation research. *Review of Educational Research, 54,* 427–456.

Byrne, B. (1996). *Measuring self-concept across the lifespan: Issues and instrumentation.* Washington, DC: American Psychological Association.

Cairns, R. B., Cairns, B. D., & Neckerman, J. J. (1989). Early school dropout: Configurations and determinants. *Child Development, 60,* 1437–1452.

Calabrese, R., & Poe, J. (1990). Alienation: An explanation of high dropout rates among African American and Latino students. *Educational Research Quarterly, 14*(4), 22–26.

Cameron, J., & Pierce, W. D. (1994). Reinforcement, reward, and intrinsic motivation: A meta-analysis. *Review of Educational Research, 64,* 363–423.

Cannon, W. B. (1927). The James-Lange theory of emotion: A critical examination and an alternative theory. *American Journal of Psychology, 39,* 106–124.

Carnegie Council on Adolescent Development. (1989). *Turning points: Preparing American youth for the 21st century.* New York: Carnegie Foundation.

Caslyn, R., & Kenny, D. (1977). Self-concept of ability and perceived evaluations by others: Cause or effect of academic achievement? *Journal of Educational Psychology, 69,* 136–145.

Chen, C., & Stevenson, H. (1995). Motivation and mathematics achievement: A comparative study of Asian-American, Caucasian-American, and East Asian high school students. *Child Development, 66,* 1215–1234.

Chubb, J. (1988). Why the current wave of school reform will fail. *The Public Interest, 90,* 28–49.

Clark, C. M., & Peterson, P. (1986). Teachers' thought processes. In M. C. Wittrock (Ed.), *Handbook of research on teaching* (3rd ed., pp. 255–296). New York: Macmillan.

Clark, C. M., & Yinger, R. J. (1979). Teachers' thinking. In P. L. Peterson & H. J. Walberg (Eds.), *Research on teaching: Concepts, findings, and implications* (pp. 231–263). Berkeley, CA: McCutchan.

Cofer, C. N., & Appley, M. H. (1964). *Motivation: Theory and research.* New York: Wiley.

Cognition and Technology Group at Vanderbilt. (1996). Looking at technology in context: A framework for understanding technology and education research. In D. Berliner & R. Calfee (Eds.), *Handbook of Educational Psychology* (pp. 807–840). New York: Macmillan.

Cohen, E. (1994). Restructuring the classroom: Conditions for productive small groups. *Review of Educational Research, 64,* 1–35.

Collins, J. (1982, March). *Self-efficacy and ability in achievement behavior.* Paper presented at the meeting of the American Educational Research Association, New York.

Comer, J. (1980). *School power: Implications of an intervention project.* New York: Free Press.

Comer, J. P., Haynes, N. M., & Joyner, E. T. (1996). The School Development Program. In J. P. Comer, N. M. Haynes, E. T. Joyner, & M. Ben-Avie (Eds.), *Rallying the whole village: The Comer process for reforming education* (pp. 1–26). New York: Teachers College Press.

Connell, J. P. (1985). A new multidimensional measure of children's perceptions of control. *Child Development, 56,* 1018–1041.

Connell, J. P., & Wellborn, J. G. (1991). Competence, autonomy, and relatedness: A motivational analysis of self-system processes. In M. R. Gunnar & L. A. Sroufe (Eds.), *Minnesota symposium on child psychology* (Vol. 23, pp. 43–77). Hillsdale, NJ: Erlbaum.

Cooper, H. M., & Dorr, N. (1995). Race comparisons on need for achievement: A meta-analytic alternative to Graham's narrative review. *Review of Educational Research, 65,* 483–508.

Cooper, H. M., & Good, T. L. (1983). *Pygmalion grows up: Studies in the expectation communication process.* New York: Longman.

Cooper, H. M., & Tom, D. Y. H. (1984). Teacher expectation research: A review with implications for classroom instruction. *Elementary School Journal, 85,* 77–89.

Cordova, D. I., & Lepper, M. R. (1996). Intrinsic motivation and the process of learning: Beneficial effects of contextualization, personalization, and choice. *Journal of Educational Psychology, 88,* 715–730.

Corno, L. (1993). The best-laid plans: Modern conceptions of volition and educational research. *Educational Researcher, 22*(2), 14–22.

Corno, L. (1994). Student volition and education: Outcomes, influences, and practices. In D. H. Schunk & B. J. Zimmerman (Eds.), *Self-regulation of learning and performance: Issues and educational applications* (pp. 229–251). Hillsdale, NJ: Erlbaum.

Corno, L., & Mandinach, E. B. (1983). The role of cognitive engagement in classroom learning and motivation. *Educational Psychologist, 18,* 88–108.

Corno, L., & Rohrkemper, M. (1985). The intrinsic motivation to learn in the classroom. In C. Ames & R. Ames (Eds.), *Research on motivation in education* (Vol. 2, pp. 53–90). New York: Academic Press.

Corno, L., & Snow, R. (1986). Adapting teaching to individual differences among learners. In M. C. Wittrock (Ed.), *Handbook of research on teaching* (3rd ed., pp. 605–629). New York: Macmillan.

Cotton, J. L. (1981). A review of research on Schachter's theory of emotion and the misattribution of arousal. *European Journal of Social Psychology, 11,* 365–397.

Covington, M. V. (1992). *Making the grade: A self-worth perspective on motivation and school reform.* New York: Cambridge University Press.

Covington, M. V. (1998). *The will to learn: A guide for motivating young people.* New York: Cambridge University Press.

Covington, M. V., & Beery, R. G. (1976). *Self-worth and school learning.* New York: Holt, Rinehart, & Winston.

Covington, M. V., & Omelich, C. L. (1979). Effort: The double-edged sword in school achievement. *Journal of Educational Psychology, 71,* 169–182.

Covington, M. V., & Omelich, C. L. (1991). Need achievement revisited: Verification of Atkinson's original 2 × 2 model. In C. D. Spielberger, I. G. Sarason, Z. Kulcsar, & G. L. Van Heck (Eds.), *Stress and emotion: Anxiety, anger, and curiosity* (Vol. 14, pp. 85–105). Washington, DC: Hemisphere.

Covington, M. V., & Roberts, B. (1994). Self-worth and college achievement: Motivational and personality correlates. In P. R. Pintrich, D. R. Brown, & C. E. Weinstein (Eds.), *Student motivation, cognition, and learning: Essays in honor of Wilbert J. McKeachie* (pp. 157–187). Hillsdale, NJ: Erlbaum.

Crandall, V. C., Katkovsky, W., & Crandall, V. J. (1965). Children's beliefs in their own control of reinforcements in intellectual-academic achievement situations. *Child Development, 36,* 91–109.

Crandall, V. J., Katkovsky, W., & Preston, A. (1962). Motivational and ability determinants of young children's intellectual achievement behavior. *Child Development, 33,* 643–661.

Crespi, L. P. (1942). Quantitative variation of incentive and performance in the white rat. *American Journal of Psychology, 55,* 467–517.

Crocker, J., & Major, B. (1989). Social stigma and self-esteem: The self-protective properties of stigma. *Psychological Review, 96,* 608–630.

Crocker, J., & Wolfe, C. (2001). Contingencies of self-worth. *Psychological Review, 108,* 593–623.

Cronbach, L. J., & Snow, R. (1977). *Aptitudes and instructional methods.* New York: Irvington.

Csikszentmihalyi, M. (1975). *Beyond boredom and anxiety.* San Francisco: Jossey-Bass.

Csikszentmihalyi, M. (1978). Intrinsic rewards and emergent motivation. In M. R. Lepper & D. Greene (Eds.), *The hidden costs of reward: New perspectives on the psychology of human motivation* (pp. 205–216). Hillsdale, NJ: Erlbaum.

Csikszentmihalyi, M. (1982). Toward a psychology of optimal experience. In L. Wheeler (Ed.), *Review of personality and social psychology* (Vol. 3, pp. 13–36). Beverly Hills, CA: Sage.

Csikszentmihalyi, M. (1985). Emergent motivation and the evolution of the self. In D. A. Kleiber & M. L. Maehr (Eds.), *Advances in motivation and achievement* (Vol. 4, pp. 93–119). Greenwich, CT: JAI Press.

Csikszentmihalyi, M. (1990). *Flow.* New York: Harper & Row.

Csikszentmihalyi, M. (1996). *Creativity: Flow and the psychology of discovery and invention.* New York: HarperCollins.

Csikszentmihalyi, M. (1997). *Finding flow.* New York: Basic Books.

Csikszentmihalyi, M. (1999). If we are so rich, why aren't we happy? *American Psychologist, 54,* 821–827.

Csikszentmihalyi, M., & Csikszentmihalyi, I. (1988). *Optimal experience: Psychological studies of flow in consciousness.* New York: Cambridge University Press.

Csikszentmihalyi, M., & Rathunde, K. (1993). The measurement of flow in everyday life: Toward a theory of emergent motivation. In J. E. Jacobs (Ed.), *Nebraska symposium on motivation 1992* (Vol. 40, pp. 57–97). Lincoln: University of Nebraska Press.

Csikszentmihalyi, M., & Rathunde, K. (1998). The development of the person: An experiential perspective on the ontogenesis of psychological complexity. In W. Damon (Series Ed.) & R. Lerner (Vol. Ed.), *Handbook of child psychology: Vol. 1. Theoretical models of human development* (5th ed., pp. 635–684). New York: Wiley.

Cuban, L. (1990). Reforming, again, again, and again. *Educational Researcher, 19,* 3–30.

Cusick, P. (1983). *The egalitarian ideal and the American high school.* New York: Longman.

Damon, W. (1995). *Greater expectations: Overcoming the culture of indulgence in America's homes and schools.* New York: Free Press.

Damon, W., & Hart, D. (1988). *Self-understanding in childhood and adolescence.* Cambridge, England: Cambridge University Press.

Davidson, E. S., & Smith, W. P. (1982). Imitation, social comparison, and self-reward. *Child Development, 53,* 928–932.

de Charms, R. (1968). *Personal causation: The internal affective determinants of behavior.* New York: Academic Press.

de Charms, R. (1976). *Enhancing motivation: Change in the classroom.* New York: Irvington.

de Charms, R. (1984). Motivation enhancement in educational settings. In R. Ames & C. Ames (Eds.), *Research on motivation in education* (Vol. 1, pp. 275–310). New York: Academic Press.

Deci, E. L. (1975). *Intrinsic motivation.* New York: Plenum.

Deci, E. L. (1980). *The psychology of self-determination.* Lexington, MA: D. C. Heath.

Deci, E. L., Koestner, R., & Ryan, R. M. (1999). A meta-analytic review of experiments examining the effects of extrinsic rewards on intrinsic motivation. *Psychological Bulletin, 125,* 627–668.

Deci, E. L., & Porac, J. (1978). Cognitive evaluation theory and the study of human motivation. In

M. R. Lepper & D. Greene (Eds.), *The hidden costs of reward: New perspectives on the psychology of human motivation* (pp. 149–176). Hillsdale, NJ: Erlbaum.

Deci, E. L., & Ryan, R. M. (1985). *Intrinsic motivation and self-determination in human behavior.* New York: Plenum.

Deci, E. L., & Ryan, R. M. (1987). The support of autonomy and the control of behavior. *Journal of Personality and Social Psychology, 53,* 1024–1037.

Deci, E. L., & Ryan, R. M. (1991). A motivational approach to self: Integration in personality. In R. A. Dienstbier (Ed.), *Nebraska symposium on motivation 1990* (Vol. 38, pp. 237–288). Lincoln, NE: University of Nebraska Press.

Deci, E. L., Vallerand, R. J., Pelletier, L. G., & Ryan, R. M. (1991). Motivation and education: The self-determination perspective. *Educational Psychologist, 26,* 325–346.

DeGarmo, D. S., Forgatch, M. S., & Martinez, C. R., Jr. (1999). Parenting of divorced mothers as a link between social status and boys' academic outcomes: Unpacking the effects of socioeconomic status. *Child Development, 70,* 1231–1245.

Deutsch, M. (1949). A theory of cooperation and competition. *Human Relations, 2,* 129–152.

Dewey, J. (1913). *Interest and effort in education.* Boston: Riverside Press.

Diener, C. I., & Dweck, C. S. (1978). An analysis of learned helplessness: Continuous changes in performance, strategy, and achievement cognitions following failure. *Journal of Personality and Social Psychology, 36,* 451–462.

Diener, C. I., & Dweck, C. S. (1980). An analysis of learned helplessness: II. The processing of success. *Journal of Personality and Social Psychology, 39,* 940–952.

Doyle, W. (1983). Academic work. *Review of Educational Research, 53,* 159–199.

Doyle, W. (1986). Classroom management. In M. C. Wittrock (Ed.), *Handbook of research on teaching* (3rd ed., pp. 392–431). New York: Macmillan.

Duda, J., & Nicholls, J. (1992). Dimensions of achievement motivation in schoolwork and sport. *Journal of Educational Psychology, 84,* 290–299.

Duke, D., Showers, B., & Imber, M. (1980). Studying shared decision making in schools. In S. B. Bacharach (Ed.), *Organizational behavior in schools and school districts* (pp. 220–268). New York: Praeger.

Dunkin, M. J., & Biddle, B. J. (1974). *The study of teaching.* New York: Holt, Rinehart & Winston.

Dusek, J. B. (1980). The development of test anxiety in children. In I. G. Sarason (Ed.), *Test anxiety: Theory, research, and applications* (pp. 87–110). Hillsdale, NJ: Erlbaum.

Dusek, J. B. (1985). *Teacher expectancies*. Hillsdale, NJ: Erlbaum.

Dweck, C. S. (1975). The role of expectations and attributions in the alleviation of learned helplessness. *Journal of Personality and Social Psychology, 31,* 674–685.

Dweck, C. S. (1986). Motivational processes affecting learning. *American Psychologist, 41,* 1040–1048.

Dweck, C. S. (1991). Self-theories and goals: Their role in motivation, personality, and development. In R. A. Dienstbier (Ed.), *Nebraska symposium on motivation 1990* (Vol. 38, pp. 199–235). Lincoln, NE: University of Nebraska Press.

Dweck, C. S. (1996). Social motivation: Goals and social-cognitive processes. A comment. In J. Juvonen & K. R. Wentzel (Eds.), *Social motivation: Understanding children's school adjustment* (pp. 181–195). Cambridge, England: Cambridge University Press.

Dweck, C. S. (1999). *Self-theories: Their role in motivation, personality, and development*. Philadelphia: Taylor & Francis

Dweck, C. S., Davidson, W., Nelson, S., & Enna, B. (1978). Sex differences in learned helplessness: II. The contingencies of evaluative feedback in the classroom. III. An experimental analysis. *Developmental Psychology, 14,* 268–276.

Dweck, C. S., & Elliott, E. S. (1983). Achievement motivation. In P. H. Mussen (Series Ed.) & E. M. Heatherington (Vol. Ed.), *Handbook of child psychology: Vol 4. Socialization, personality, and social development* (4th ed., pp. 643–691). New York: Wiley.

Dweck, C. S., & Goetz, T. (1978). Attributions and learned helplessness. In J. Harvey, W. Ickes, & R. Kidd (Eds.), *New directions in attribution research* (pp. 157–179). Hillsdale, NJ: Erlbaum.

Dweck, C. S., & Leggett, E. L. (1988). A social-cognitive approach to motivation and personality. *Psychological Review, 95,* 256–273.

Dweck, C. S., & Repucci, N. (1973). Learned helplessness and reinforcement responsibility in children. *Journal of Personality and Social Psychology, 25,* 109–116.

Eagly, A., & Chaiken, S. (1998). Attitude structure and function. In D. Gilbert, S. Fiske, & G. Lindzey (Eds.), *The handbook of social psychology* (Vol. 1, 4th ed., pp. 269–322). New York: McGraw-Hill.

Eccles, J. (1983). Expectancies, values and academic behaviors. In J. T. Spence (Ed.), *Achievement and achievement motives* (pp. 75–146). San Francisco: Freeman.

Eccles, J. (1987). Gender roles and women's achievement-related decisions. *Psychology of Women Quarterly, 11,* 135–172.

Eccles, J. (1993). School and family effects on the ontogeny of children's interests, self-perceptions, and activity choice. In J. Jacobs (Ed.), *Nebraska symposium on motivation: Developmental perspectives on motivation* (pp. 145–208). Lincoln, NE: University of Nebraska Press.

Eccles, J., Adler, T., & Meece, J. (1984). Sex differences in achievement: A test of alternate theories. *Journal of Personality and Social Psychology, 46,* 26–43.

Eccles, J., & Blumenfeld, P. (1985). Classroom experiences and student gender: Are there differences and do they matter? In L. Wilkinson & C. Marrett (Eds.), *Gender influences in classroom interaction* (pp. 79–114). Hillsdale, NJ: Erlbaum.

Eccles, J., & Harold, R. (1991). Gender differences in sport involvement: Applying the Eccles' expectancy-value model. *Journal of Applied Sport Psychology, 3,* 7–35.

Eccles, J., Lord, S., & Midgley, C. (1991). What are we doing to early adolescents? The impact of educational contexts on early adolescents. *American Journal of Education, 99,* 521–542.

Eccles, J. S., & Midgley, C. (1989). Stage-environment fit: Developmentally appropriate classrooms for young adolescents. In C. Ames & R. Ames (Eds.), *Research on motivation in education* (Vol. 3, pp. 139–186). San Diego, CA: Academic Press.

Eccles, J. S., Midgley, C., & Adler, T. (1984). Grade-related changes in the school environment: Effects on achievement motivation. In J. Nicholls (Ed.), *Advances in motivation and achievement: The development of achievement motivation* (Vol. 3, pp. 283–331). Greenwich, CT: JAI Press.

Eccles, J., Midgley, C., Wigfield, A., Buchanan, C., Reuman, D., Flanagan, C., & Mac Iver, D. (1993). Development during adolescence: The impact of stage-environment fit on young adolescents' experiences in schools and families. *American Psychologist, 48,* 90–101.

Eccles, J., Midgley, C., Wigfield, A., Reuman, D., Mac Iver, D., & Feldlaufer, H. (1993). Negative effects of traditional middle schools on students' motivation. *Elementary School Journal, 93,* 553–574.

Eccles, J., & Wigfield, A. (1985). Teacher expectancies and student motivation. In J. B. Dusek (Ed.), *Teacher expectancies* (pp. 185–226). Hillsdale, NJ: Erlbaum.

Eccles, J., & Wigfield, A. (1995). In the mind of the actor: The structure of adolescents' achievement task values and expectancy-related beliefs. *Personality and Social Psychology Bulletin, 21,* 215–225.

Eccles, J., Wigfield, A., Flanagan, C., Miller, C., Reuman, D., & Yee, D. (1989). Self-concepts, domain values, and self-esteem: Relations and changes at early adolescence. *Journal of Personality, 57,* 283–310.

Eccles, J., Wigfield, A., Harold, R., & Blumenfeld, P. (1993). Age and gender differences in children's self- and task perceptions during elementary school. *Child Development, 64,* 830–847.

Eccles, J., Wigfield, A., & Schiefele, U. (1998). Motivation to succeed. In W. Damon (Series Ed.) & N. Eisenberg (Vol. Ed.), *Handbook of child psychology: Vol. 3. Social, emotional, and personality development* (5th ed., pp. 1017–1095). New York: Wiley.

Edelson, D., Gordin, D., & Pea, R. (1999). Addressing the challenges of inquiry-based learning through technology and curriculum design. *The Journal of the Learning Sciences, 8,* 391–450.

Edmonds, R. (1979). Effective schools for the urban poor. *Educational Leadership, 37,* 15–24.

Eisen, S. V. (1979). Actor-observer differences in information inference and causal attribution. *Journal of Personality and Social Psychology, 37,* 261–272.

Eisenberger, R., & Armeli, S. (1997). Can salient reward increase creative performance without reducing intrinsic creative interest? *Journal of Personality and Social Psychology, 72,* 652–663.

Eisenberger, R., Armeli, S., & Pretz, J. (1998). Can the promise of reward increase creativity? *Journal of Personality and Social Psychology, 74,* 704–714.

Eisenberger, R., & Cameron, J. (1996). Detrimental effects of reward: Reality or myth? *American Psychologist, 51,* 1153–1166.

Eisenberger, R., & Cameron, J. (1998). Reward, intrinsic interest, and creativity: New findings. *American Psychologist, 53,* 676–679.

Elashoff, J. D., & Snow, R. (1971). *Pygmalion reconsidered.* Worthington, OH: Jones.

Elliot, A. J. (1997). Integrating the "classic" and "contemporary" approaches to achievement motivation: A hierarchical model of approach and avoidance achievement motivation. In M. Maehr & P. Pintrich (Eds.), *Advances in motivation and achievement* (Vol. 10, pp. 243–279). Greenwich, CT: JAI Press.

Elliot, A. J. (1999). Approach and avoidance motivation and achievement goals. *Educational Psychologist, 34,* 169–189.

Elliot, A. J., & Church, M. (1997). A hierarchical model of approach and avoidance achievement motivation. *Journal of Personality and Social Psychology, 72,* 218–232.

Elliot, A. J., & Harackiewicz, J. M. (1996). Approach and avoidance achievement goals and intrinsic motivation: A mediational analysis. *Journal of Personality and Social Psychology, 70,* 461–475.

Elliot, A. J., & McGregor, H. (2001). A 2 × 2 achievement goal framework. *Journal of Personality and Social Psychology, 80,* 501–519.

Elliot, A. J., McGregor, H., & Gable, S. (1999). Achievement goals, study strategies, and exam performance: A mediational analysis. *Journal of Educational Psychology, 91,* 549–563.

Elliott, E. S., & Dweck, C. S. (1988). Goals: An approach to motivation and achievement. *Journal of Personality and Social Psychology, 54,* 5–12.

Emmer, E. T., Evertson, C. M., & Anderson, L. M. (1980). Effective classroom management at the beginning of the school year. *Elementary School Journal, 80,* 219–231.

Emmer, E. T., Evertson, C., & Worsham, M. E. (2000). *Classroom management for secondary teachers* (5th ed.). Boston: Allyn & Bacon.

Emmons, C. L., Comer, J. P., & Haynes, N. M. (1996). Translating theory into practice: Comer's theory of school reform. In J. P. Comer, N. M. Haynes, E. T. Joyner, & M. Ben-Avie (Eds.), *Rallying the whole village: The Comer process for reforming education* (pp. 27–41). New York: Teachers College Press.

Entwisle, D. R., & Baker, D. P. (1983). Gender and young children's expectations for performance in arithmetic. *Developmental Psychology, 19,* 200–209.

Epstein, J. (1986). Parents' reactions to teacher practices of parent involvement. *Elementary School Journal, 86,* 277–294.

Epstein, J. (1987). Toward a theory of family-school connections: Teacher practices and parent involvement. In K. Hurrelmann, F. Kaufmann, & F. Losel (Eds.), *Social intervention: Potential and constraints* (pp. 121–136). Hawthorn, NY: Aldine de Gruyter.

Epstein, J. (1989). Family structures and student motivation: A developmental perspective. In C. Ames & R. Ames (Eds.), *Research on motivation in education* (Vol. 3, pp. 259–295). San Diego, CA: Academic Press.

Epstein, J. (1995). School/family/community partnerships: Caring for the children we share. *Phi Delta Kappan, 76,* 701–712.

Erickson, F. (1986). Qualitative methods in research on teaching. In M. C. Wittrock (Ed.), *Handbook of research on teaching* (3rd ed., pp. 119–161). New York: Macmillan.

Ericsson, K., Krampe, R., & Tesch-Roemer, C. (1993). The role of deliberate practice in the acquisition of expert performance. *Psychological Review, 100,* 363–406.

Ericsson, K., & Simon, H. (1993). *Protocol analysis: Verbal reports as data* (2nd ed.). Cambridge, MA: MIT Press.

Erikson, E. (1963). *Childhood and society.* New York: Norton.

Evans, K. (1971). *Attitudes and interests in education.* London: Routledge & Kegan.

Evertson, C., Emmer, E. T., & Worsham, M. E. (2000). *Classroom management for elementary teachers* (5th ed.). Boston: Allyn & Bacon.

Eyler, J., Cooke, V., & Ward, L. (1983). Resegregation: Segregation within desegregated schools. In C. Rossell & W. Howley (Eds.), *The consequences of school desegregation* (pp. 126–162). Philadelphia: Temple University Press.

Feather, N. (1982). Human values and the prediction of action: An expectancy-valence analysis. In N. T. Feather (Ed.), *Expectations and actions: Expectancy-value models in psychology* (pp. 263–289). Hillsdale, NJ: Erlbaum.

Feather, N. (1988). Values, valences, and course enrollment: Testing the role of personal values within an expectancy-value framework. *Journal of Educational Psychology, 80,* 381–391.

Feldman, N. S., & Ruble, D. N. (1977). Awareness of social comparison interest and motivations: A developmental study. *Journal of Educational Psychology, 69,* 579–585.

Festinger, L. (1954). A theory of social comparison processes. *Human Relations, 7,* 117–140.

Festinger, L. (1957). *A theory of cognitive dissonance.* Stanford, CA: Stanford University Press.

Fiedler, K. (2000). Toward an integrative account of affect and cognition phenomena using the BIAS computer algorithm. In J. Forgas (Ed.), *Feeling and thinking: The role of affect in social cognition* (pp. 223–252). New York: Cambridge University Press.

Fish, M. C., & Pervan, R. (1985). Self-instruction training: A potential tool for school psychologists. *Psychology in the Schools, 22,* 83–92.

Fiske, A., Kitayama, S., Markus, H., & Nisbett, R. (1998). The cultural matrix of social psychology. In D. Gilbert, S. Fiske, & G. Lindzey (Eds.), *The handbook of social psychology* (Vol. 2, 4th ed., pp. 915–981). New York: McGraw-Hill.

Fiske, S., & Taylor, S. (1991). *Social cognition.* New York: McGraw-Hill.

Fletcher, G., & Ward, C. (1988). Attribution theory and processes: A cross-cultural perspective. In M. H. Bond (Ed.), *The cross-cultural challenge to social psychology* (pp. 230–244). Newbury Park, CA: Sage.

Foersterling, F. (1985). Attributional retraining: A review. *Psychological Bulletin, 98,* 495–512.

Ford, D. H. (1987). *Humans as self-constructing living systems: A developmental perspective on personality and behavior.* Hillsdale, NJ: Erlbaum.

Ford, D. Y., & Harris, J. (1996). Perceptions and attitudes of Black students toward school, achievement, and other educational variables. *Child Development, 67,* 1141–1152.

Ford, M. (1992). *Motivating humans: Goals, emotions, and personal agency beliefs.* Newbury Park, CA: Sage.

Ford, M., & Ford, D. H. (1987). *Humans as self-constructing living systems: Putting the framework to work.* Hillsdale, NJ: Erlbaum.

Ford, M., & Nichols, C. W. (1991). Using goal assessments to identify motivational patterns and facilitate behavioral regulation and achievement. In M. L. Maehr & P. R. Pintrich (Eds.), *Advances in motivation and achievement: Goals and self-regulation* (Vol. 7, pp. 51–84). Greenwich, CT: JAI Press.

Fordham, S., & Ogbu, J. (1986). Black students' school success: Coping with the burden of "acting white." *Urban Review, 18,* 176–206.

Forgas, J. (2000). The role of affect in social cognition. In J. Forgas (Ed.), *Feeling and thinking: The role of affect in social cognition* (pp. 1–28). New York: Cambridge University Press.

France-Kaatrude, A., & Smith, W. P. (1985). Social comparison, task motivation, and the development of self-evaluative standards in children. *Developmental Psychology, 21,* 1080–1089.

Freud, S. (1966). *The complete introductory lectures on psychoanalysis* (J. Strachey, Trans.). New York: Norton.

Frey, K., & Ruble, D. N. (1987). What children say about classroom performance: Sex and grade differences in perceived competence. *Child Development, 58,* 1066–1078.

Friend, R., & Neale, J. (1972). Children's perceptions of success and failure: An attributional analysis of the effects of race and social class. *Developmental Psychology, 7,* 124–128.

Frijda, N. (1986). *The emotions.* Cambridge, England: Cambridge University Press.

Fuhrer, M. J., & Baer, P. E. (1965). Differential classical conditioning: Verbalization of stimulus contingencies. *Science, 150,* 1479–1481.

Fuligni, A. (1997). The academic achievement of adolescents from immigrant families: The roles of family background, attitudes, and behavior. *Child Development, 68,* 351–363.

Gagné, E. D., Yekovich, C. W., & Yekovich, F. R. (1993). *The cognitive psychology of school learning* (2nd ed.). New York: HarperCollins.

Gagné, R. M. (1985). *The conditions of learning* (4th ed.). New York: Holt, Rinehart, & Winston.

Gamoran, A., & Berends, M. (1987). The effects of stratification in secondary schools: Synthesis of survey and ethnographic research. *Review of Educational Research, 57,* 415–435.

Garcia, T., & Pintrich, P. R. (1994). Regulating motivation and cognition in the classroom: The role of self-schemas and self-regulatory strategies. In D. H. Schunk & B. J. Zimmerman (Eds.), *Self-regulation of learning and performance: Issues and educational applications* (pp. 127–153). Hillsdale, NJ: Erlbaum.

Gibson, S., & Dembo, M. H. (1984). Teacher efficacy: A construct validation. *Journal of Educational Psychology, 76,* 569–582.

Glass, D. C., & Singer, J. E. (1972). *Urban stress: Experiments on noise and social stressors.* New York: Academic Press.

Goddard, R. (in press). Collective efficacy: A neglected construct in the study of schools and student achievement. *Journal of Educational Psychology.*

Goddard, R., Hoy, W., & Woolfolk Hoy, A. (2000). Collective efficacy: Its meaning, measure, and impact on student achievement. *American Educational Research Journal, 37,* 479–507.

Goddard, R., Sweetland, S., & Hoy, W. (in press). Academic emphasis of urban elementary schools and student achievement in reading and mathematics: A multilevel analysis. *Educational Administration Quarterly.*

Goethals, G. R., & Darley, J. M. (1977). Social comparison theory. In J. M. Suls & R. L. Miller (Eds.), *Social comparison processes: Theoretical and empirical perspectives* (pp. 259–278). Washington, DC: Hemisphere.

Good, T., & Brophy, J. (1986). School effects. In M. C. Wittrock (Ed.), *Handbook of research on teaching* (3rd ed., pp. 570–602). New York: Macmillan.

Good, T., & Brophy, J. E. (1987). *Looking in classrooms* (4th ed.). New York: Harper & Row.

Good, T., & Grouws, D. A. (1979). The Missouri mathematics effectiveness project. *Journal of Educational Psychology, 71,* 355–362.

Gottfried, A. E. (1985). Academic intrinsic motivation in elementary and junior high school students. *Journal of Educational Psychology, 77,* 631–645.

Gottfried, A. E. (1990). Academic intrinsic motivation in young elementary school children. *Journal of Educational Psychology, 82,* 525–538.

Gottfried, A. E., Fleming, J. S., & Gottfried, A. W. (1998). Role of cognitively stimulating home environment in children's academic intrinsic motivation: A longitudinal study. *Child Development, 69,* 1448–1460.

Graham, S. (1984). Communicating sympathy and anger to black and white students: The cognitive (attributional) antecedents of affective cues. *Journal of Personality and Social Psychology, 47,* 40–54.

Graham, S. (1991). A review of attribution theory in achievement contexts. *Educational Psychology Review, 3,* 5–39.

Graham, S. (1992). "Most of the subjects were white and middle class": Trends in reported research on African Americans in selected APA Journals, 1970–1989. *American Psychologist, 47,* 629–639.

Graham, S. (1994). Motivation in African Americans. *Review of Educational Research, 64,* 55–117.

Graham, S., Doubleday, C., & Guarino, P. (1984). The development of relations between perceived controllability and the emotions of pity, anger, and guilt. *Child Development, 55,* 561–565.

Graham, S., & Golan, S. (1991). Motivational influences on cognition: Task involvement, ego involvement, and depth of information processing. *Journal of Educational Psychology, 83,* 187–194.

Graham, S., & Hudley, C. (1992). An attributional approach to aggression in African-American children. In D. H. Schunk & J. L. Meece (Eds.), *Student perceptions in the classroom* (pp. 75–94). Hillsdale, NJ: Erlbaum.

Graham, S., & Long, A. (1986). Race, class, and the attributional process. *Journal of Educational Psychology, 78,* 4–13.

Graham, S., Taylor, A. Z., & Hudley, C. (1998). Exploring achievement values among ethnic minority early adolescents. *Journal of Educational Psychology, 90,* 606–620.

Grant, G. (1988). *The world we created at Hamilton High.* Cambridge, MA: Harvard University Press.

Greeno, J., Collins, A., & Resnick, L. (1996). Cognition and learning. In D. Berliner & R. Calfee (Eds.), *Handbook of Educational Psychology* (pp. 15–46). New York: Macmillan.

Guskey, T. R. (1987). Context variables that affect measures of teacher efficacy. *Journal of Educational Research, 81,* 41–47.

Guskey, T. R., & Passaro, P. D. (1994). Teacher efficacy: A study of construct dimensions. *American Educational Research Journal, 31,* 627–643.

Gutman, L. M., & Eccles, J. S. (1999). Financial strain, parenting behaviors, and adolescents' achievement: Testing model equivalence between African American and European American single- and two-parent families. *Child Development, 70,* 1464–1476.

Hackett, G., & Betz, N. E. (1981). A self-efficacy approach to the career development of women. *Journal of Vocational Behavior, 18,* 326–339.

Hagtvet, K., & Johnsen, T. B. (1992). *Advances in test anxiety research* (Vol. 7). Amsterdam: Swets & Zeitlinger.

Hall, C. S., & Lindzey, G. (1978). *Theories of personality.* New York: Wiley.

Hall, V., Howe, A., Merkel, S., & Lederman, N. (1986). Behavior, motivation, and achievement in desegregated junior high school science classes. *Journal of Educational Psychology, 78,* 108–115.

Hallinger, P., & Murphy, J. (1986). The social context of effective schools. *American Journal of Education, 94,* 328–355.

Hamilton, V. L., Blumenfeld, P., Akoh, H., & Miura, K. (1989). Citizenship and scholarship in Japanese and American fifth grades. *American Educational Research Journal, 26,* 44–72.

Hansford, B., & Hattie, J. (1982). The relationship between self and achievement/performance measures. *Review of Educational Research, 52,* 123–142.

Harackiewicz, J., Barron, K., Carter, S., Letho, A., & Elliot, A. (1997). Determinants and consequences of achievement goals in the college classroom: Maintaining interest and making the grade. *Journal of Personality and Social Psychology, 73,* 1284–1295.

Harackiewicz, J., Barron, K., & Elliot, A. (1998). Rethinking achievement goals: When are they adaptive for college students and why? *Educational Psychologist, 33,* 1–21.

Harackiewicz, J., Barron, K., Tauer, J., Carter, S., & Elliot, A. (2000). Short-term and long-term consequences of achievement goals: Predicting interest and performance over time. *Journal of Educational Psychology, 92,* 316–330.

Harackiewicz, J., & Sansone, C. (1991). Goals and intrinsic motivation: You *can* get there from here. In M. L. Maehr & P. R. Pintrich (Eds.), *Advances in motivation and achievement: Goals and self-regulation* (Vol. 7, pp. 21–49). Greenwich, CT: JAI Press.

Harari, O., & Covington, M. V. (1981). Reactions to achievement behavior from a teacher and student perspective: A developmental analysis. *American Educational Research Journal, 18,* 15–28.

Harris, J. R. (1998). *The nurture assumption: Why children turn out the way they do.* New York: Free Press.

Harter, S. (1975). Developmental differences in the manifestation of mastery motivation on problem-solving tasks. *Child Development, 46,* 370–378.

Harter, S. (1978). Effectance motivation reconsidered: Toward a developmental model. *Human Development, 21,* 34–64.

Harter, S. (1981a). A model of mastery motivation in children: Individual differences and developmental change. In W. A. Collins (Ed.), *Aspects on the development of competence: The Minnesota symposia on child psychology* (Vol. 14, pp. 215–255). Hillsdale, NJ: Erlbaum.

Harter, S. (1981b). A new self-report scale of intrinsic versus extrinsic orientation in the classroom: Motivational and informational components. *Developmental Psychology, 17,* 300–312.

Harter, S. (1982). The perceived competence scale for children. *Child Development, 53,* 87–97.

Harter, S. (1983). Developmental perspectives on the self-system. In P. H. Mussen (Series Ed.) & E. M. Heatherington (Vol. Ed.), *Handbook of child psychology: Vol. 4. Socialization, personality, and social development* (4th ed., pp. 275–386). New York: Wiley.

Harter, S. (1985a). Competence as a dimension of self-evaluation: Toward a comprehensive model of self-worth. In R. Leahy (Ed.), *The development of the self* (pp. 55–121). New York: Academic Press.

Harter, S. (1985b). *The self-perception profile for children: Revision of the perceived competence scale for children* (Manual). Denver, CO: University of Denver.

Harter, S. (1986). Processes underlying the construction, maintenance, and enhancement of the self-concept in children. In J. Suls & A. C. Greenwald (Eds.), *Psychological perspectives on the self* (Vol. 3, pp. 137–181). Hillsdale, NJ: Erlbaum.

Harter, S. (1990). Causes, correlates, and the functional role of self-worth: A life-span perspective. In R. J. Sternberg & J. Kolligian (Eds.), *Competence considered* (pp. 67–97). New Haven, CT: Yale University Press.

Harter, S. (1996). Teacher and classmate influences on scholastic motivation, self-esteem, and level of voice in adolescents. In J. Juvonen & K. R. Wentzel (Eds.), *Social motivation: Understanding children's school adjustment* (pp. 11–42). Cambridge, England: Cambridge University Press.

Harter, S. (1998). The development of self-representations. In W. Damon (Series Ed.), and N. Eisenberg (Vol. Ed.), *Handbook of child psychology. Vol. 3. Social, emotional, and personality development* (5th ed., pp. 553–617). New York: Wiley.

Harter, S. (1999). *The construction of the self: A developmental perspective.* New York: Guilford Press.

Harter, S., & Connell, J. P. (1984). A comparison of children's achievement and related self-perceptions of competence, control, and motivational orientation. In J. G. Nicholls (Ed.), *Advances in motivation and achievement: The development of achievement motivation* (Vol. 3, pp. 219–250). Greenwich, CT: JAI Press.

Harter, S., Waters, P., & Whitesell, N. (1997). False self behavior and lack of voice among adolescent males and females. *Educational Psychologist, 32,* 153–173.

Haynes, N. M., Emmons, C. L., Gebreyesus, S., & Ben-Avie, M. (1996). The School Development Program evaluation process. In J. P. Comer, N. M. Haynes, E. T. Joyner, & M. Ben-Avie (Eds.), *Rallying the whole village: The Comer process for reforming education* (pp. 123–146). New York: Teachers College Press.

Hebb, D. O. (1949). *The organization of behavior.* New York: Wiley.

Hebb, D. O. (1966). *A textbook of psychology* (2nd ed.). Philadelphia: Saunders.

Heckhausen, H. (1977). Achievement motivation and its constructs: A cognitive model. *Motivation and Emotion, 1,* 283–329.

Heckhausen, H. (1991). *Motivation and action.* Berlin: Springer-Verlag.

Heidbreder, E. (1933). *Seven psychologies.* Englewood Cliffs, NJ: Prentice-Hall.

Heider, F. (1946). Attitudes and cognitive organization. *Journal of Psychology, 21,* 107–112.

Heider, F. (1958). *The psychology of interpersonal relations.* New York: Wiley.

Helmke, A. (1988). The role of classroom context factors for the achievement-impairing effect of test anxiety. *Anxiety Research, 1,* 37–52.

Hembree, R. (1988). Correlates, causes, effects, and treatment of test anxiety. *Review of Educational Research, 58,* 47–77.

Henderson, V., & Dweck, C. S. (1990). Motivation and achievement. In S. Feldman & G. Elliott (Eds.), *At the threshold: The developing adolescent* (pp. 308–329). Cambridge, MA: Harvard University Press.

Hess, R., Chang, C., & McDevitt, T. (1987). Cultural variations in family beliefs about children's performance in mathematics: Comparisons among People's Republic of China, Chinese-American, and Caucasian-American families. *Journal of Educational Psychology, 79,* 179–188.

Heyns, B. (1974). Social selection and stratification within schools. *American Journal of Sociology, 79,* 1434–1451.

Hickey, D. (1997). Motivation and contemporary socio-constructivist instructional perspectives. *Educational Psychologist, 32,* 175–193.

Hidi, S. (1990). Interest and its contribution as a mental resource for learning. *Review of Educational Research, 60,* 549–571.

Hidi, S. (2000). An interest researcher's perspective: The effects of extrinsic and intrinsic factors on motivation. In C. Sansone & J. Harackiewicz (Eds.), *Intrinsic and extrinsic motivation: The search for optimal motivation and performance* (pp. 309–339). San Diego, CA: Academic Press.

Hidi, S., & Anderson, V. (1992). Situational interest and its impact on reading and expository writing. In K. A. Renninger, S. Hidi, & A. Krapp (Eds.), *The role of interest in learning and development* (pp. 215–238). Hillsdale, NJ: Erlbaum.

Hidi, S., & Baird, W. (1986). Interestingness—a neglected variable in discourse processing. *Cognitive Science, 10,* 179–194.

Hidi, S., & Harackiewicz, J. (2000). Motivating the academically unmotivated: A critical issue for the 21st century. *Review of Educational Research, 70,* 151–179.

Hidi, S., Renninger, K. A., & Krapp, A. (1992). The present state of interest research. In K. A. Renninger, S. Hidi, & A. Krapp (Eds.), *The role of interest in learning and development* (pp. 433–446). Hillsdale, NJ: Erlbaum.

Higgins, E. T. (1981). Role taking and social judgment: Alternative developmental perspectives and processes. In J. H. Flavell & L. Ross (Eds.), *Social cognitive development: Frontiers and possible futures* (pp. 119–153). Cambridge, England: Cambridge University Press.

Higgins, E. T. (1997). Beyond pleasure and pain. *American Psychologist, 52,* 1280–1300.

Hilgard, E. R. (1963). Motivation in learning theory. In S. Koch (Ed.), *Psychology: A study of a science* (Vol. 5, pp. 253–283). New York: McGraw-Hill.

Hill, K. T., & Wigfield, A. (1984). Test anxiety: A major educational problem and what can be done about it. *Elementary School Journal, 85,* 105–126.

Hilton, D. J., & Slugoski, B. R. (1986). Knowledge-based causal attribution: The abnormal conditions focus model. *Psychological Review, 93,* 75–88.

Hogan, K., & Pressley, M. (1997). *Scaffolding student learning: Instructional approaches and issues.* Cambridge, MA: Brookline Books.

Holloway, S. (1988). Concepts of ability and effort in Japan and the United States. *Review of Educational Research, 58,* 327–345.

Hong, Y., Morris, M., Chiu, C., & Benet-Martinez, V. (2000). Multicultural minds: A dynamic constructivist approach to culture and cognition. *American Psychologist, 55,* 709–720.

Hoy, W., & Sabo, D. (1998). *Quality middle schools: Open and healthy.* Thousand Oaks, CA: Corwin.

Hoy, W., Tarter, C., & Kottkamp, R. (1991). *Open schools/healthy schools: Measuring organizational climate.* Thousand Oaks, CA: Corwin.

Hull, C. L. (1943). *Principles of behavior: An introduction to behavior theory.* New York: Appleton-Century-Crofts.

Hull, C. L. (1951). *Essentials of behavior.* New Haven, CT: Yale University Press.

Hull, C. L. (1952). *A behavior system: An introduction to behavior theory concerning the individual organism.* New Haven, CT: Yale University Press.

Humphrey, G. (1921). Imitation and the conditioned reflex. *Pedagogical Seminary, 28,* 1–21.

Hunt, J. McV. (1963). Motivation inherent in information processing and action. In O. J. Harvey (Ed.), *Motivation and social interaction: Cognitive determinants* (pp. 35–94). New York: Ronald.

Hunt, M. (1993). *The story of psychology.* New York: Doubleday.

Hymel, S., Comfort, C., Schonert-Reichl, K., & McDougall, P. (1996). Academic failure and school dropout: The influence of peers. In J. Juvonen & K. R. Wentzel (Eds.), *Social motivation: Understanding children's school adjustment* (pp. 313–345). Cambridge, England: Cambridge University Press.

Jagacinski, C., & Duda, J. (in press). A comparative analysis of contemporary achievement goal orientation measures. *Educational and Psychological Measurement.*

Jagacinski, C., & Nicholls, J. (1984). Conceptions of ability and related affects in task involvement and ego involvement. *Journal of Educational Psychology, 76,* 909–919.

Jagacinski, C., & Nicholls, J. (1987). Competence and affect in task involvement and ego involvement: The impact of social comparison information. *Journal of Educational Psychology, 79,* 107–114.

Jagacinski, C., & Nicholls, J. G. (1990). Reducing effort to protect perceived ability: "They'd do it but I wouldn't." *Journal of Educational Psychology, 82,* 15–21.

James, W. (1884). What is an emotion? *Mind, 9,* 188–205. (Reprinted in K. Dunlap (Ed.), *The emotions* (pp. 11–30). Baltimore, MD: Williams & Wilkins, 1922.)

James, W. (1890). *The principles of psychology* (Vol. 2). New York: Henry Holt.

James, W. (1892). *Psychology: Briefer course.* New York: Henry Holt.

Jencks, C., & Brown, M. (1975). Effects of high schools on their students. *Harvard Educational Review, 45,* 273–324.

Jensen, A. (1969). How much can we boost IQ and achievement? *Harvard Educational Review, 39,* 1–123.

Johnson, D., & Johnson, R. (1974). Instructional goal structure: Cooperative, competitive, or individualistic. *Review of Educational Research, 44,* 213–240.

Johnson, D., & Johnson, R. (1985). Motivational processes in cooperative, competitive, and individualistic learning situations. In C. Ames & R. Ames (Eds.), *Research on motivation in education* (Vol. 2, pp. 249–286). New York: Academic Press.

Johnson, D., Maruyama, G., Johnson, R., Nelson, D., & Skon, L. (1981). Effects of cooperative, competitive, and individualistic goal structures on achievement: A meta-analysis. *Psychological Bulletin, 89,* 47–62.

Johnson, T. J., Feigenbaum, R., & Weiby, M. (1964). Some determinants and consequences of the teacher's perceptions of causation. *Journal of Educational Psychology, 55,* 237–246.

Jones, E. E., & Harris, V. A. (1967). The attribution of attitudes. *Journal of Experimental Social Psychology, 3,* 1–24.

Jones, E. E., & Nisbett, R. (1972). The actor and the observer: Divergent perceptions of the causes of behavior. In E. E. Jones, D. E. Kanouse, H. H. Kelley, R. Nisbett, S. Valins, & B. Weiner (Eds.), *Attribution: Perceiving the causes of behavior* (pp. 79–94). Morristown, NJ: General Learning Press.

Jussim, L. (1986). Self-fulfilling prophecies: A theoretical and integrative review. *Psychological Review, 93,* 429–445.

Jussim, L. (1991). Social perception and social reality: A reflection-construction model. *Psychological Review, 98,* 54–73.

Kahle, J., Parker, L., Rennie, L., & Riley, D. (1993). Gender differences in science education: Building a model. *Educational Psychologist, 28,* 379–404.

Kanfer, F. H., & Gaelick, L. (1986). Self-management methods. In F. H. Kanfer & A. P. Goldstein (Eds.), *Helping people change: A textbook of methods* (3rd ed., pp. 283–345). New York: Pergamon.

Kanfer, R., & Kanfer, F. H. (1991). Goals and self-regulation: Applications of theory to work settings. In M. L. Maehr & P. R. Pintrich (Eds.), *Advances in motivation and achievement* (Vol. 7, pp. 287–326). Greenwich, CT: JAI Press.

Kaplan, A., & Midgley, C. (1997). The effect of achievement goals: Does level of perceived academic competence make a difference? *Contemporary Educational Psychology, 22,* 415–435.

Kassin, S., & Pryor, J. (1985). The development of attribution processes. In J. Pryor & J. Day (Eds.), *The development of social cognition* (pp. 3–34). New York: Springer-Verlag.

Keller, F. S. (1968). Good-bye, teacher. . . . *Journal of Applied Behavior Analysis, 1,* 79–89.

Kelley, H. H. (1967). Attribution theory in social psychology. In D. Levine (Ed.), *Nebraska symposium on motivation* (Vol. 15, pp. 192–238). Lincoln, NE: University of Nebraska Press.

Kelley, H. H. (1971). *Attributions in social interactions.* Morristown, NJ: General Learning Press.

Kelley, H. H. (1972). Causal schemata and the attribution process. In E. E. Jones, D. E. Kanouse, H. H. Kelley, R. Nisbett, S. Valins, & B. Weiner (Eds.), *Attribution: Perceiving the causes of behavior* (pp. 151–174). Morristown, NJ: General Learning Press.

Kelley, H. H., & Michela, J. (1980). Attribution theory and research. *Annual Review of Psychology, 31,* 457–501.

Kihlstrom, J. (1990). The psychological unconscious. In L. Pervin (Ed.), *Handbook of personality: Theory and research* (pp. 445–464). New York: Guilford Press.

Kindermann, T. A. (1993). Natural peer groups as contexts for individual development: The case of children's motivation in school. *Developmental Psychology, 29,* 970–977.

Kindermann, T. A., McCollam, T. L., & Gibson, E., Jr. (1996). Peer networks and students' classroom engagement during childhood and adolescence. In J. Juvonen & K. R. Wentzel (Eds.), *Social motivation: Understanding children's school adjustment* (pp. 279–312). Cambridge, England: Cambridge University Press.

Kohn, A. (1996). By all available means: Cameron and Pierce's defense of extrinsic motivators. *Review of Educational Research, 66,* 1–4.

Kounin, J. S. (1977). *Discipline and group management in classrooms.* Huntington, NY: Krieger.

Krapp, A. (1999). Interest, motivation, and learning: An educational-psychological perspective. *European Journal of Psychology of Education, 14,* 23–40.

Krapp, A., Hidi, S., & Renninger, K. A. (1992). Interest, learning, and development. In K. A. Renninger, S. Hidi, & A. Krapp (Eds.), *The role of interest in learning and development* (pp. 3–25). Hillsdale, NJ: Erlbaum.

Kruglanski, A. (1977). The place of naive contents in a theory of attribution: Reflections on Calder's and Zuckerman's critique of the endogenous-exogenous partition. *Personality and Social Psychology Bulletin, 3,* 592–605.

Kuhl, J. (1984). Volitional aspects of achievement motivation and learned helplessness: Toward a comprehensive theory of action control. In B. A. Maher (Ed.), *Progress in experimental personality research* (Vol. 13, pp. 99–171). New York: Academic Press.

Kuhl, J. (1985). Volitional mediators of cognition-behavior consistency: Self-regulatory processes and action versus state orientation. In J. Kuhl & J. Beckmann (Eds.), *Action control: From cognition to behavior* (pp. 101–128). New York: Springer-Verlag.

Kuhl, J. (1992). A theory of self-regulation: Action versus state orientation, self-discrimination, and some applications. *Applied Psychology: An International Review, 41,* 97–129.

Kun, A., & Weiner, B. (1973). Necessary versus sufficient causal schemata for success and failure. *Journal of Research in Psychology, 7,* 197–207.

Kurtz, B. E., & Borkowski, J. G. (1987). Development of strategic skills in impulsive and reflective children: A longitudinal study of meta-cognition. *Journal of Experimental Child Psychology, 43,* 129–148.

Ladd, G. W. (1990). Having friends, keeping friends, making friends, and being liked by peers in the classroom: Predictors of children's early school adjustment? *Child Development, 61,* 1081–1100.

Ladd, G. W., & Kochenderfer, B. J. (1996). Links between friendship and adjustment during early school transitions. In W. M. Bukowski, A. F. Newcomb, & W. W. Hartup (Eds.), *The company they keep: Friendship in childhood and adolescence* (pp. 322–345). New York: Cambridge University Press.

Lamb, M. (1997). *The role of the father in child development.* New York: Wiley.

Lange, C. G. (1885). One leudsbeveegelser (I. A. Haupt, Trans.). In K. Dunlap (Ed.), *The emotions* (pp. 33–90). Baltimore, MD: Williams & Wilkens, 1922.

Lazarus, R. (1991). *Emotion and adaptation.* Oxford, England: Oxford University Press.

Leary, D. E. (1990). Psyche's muse: The role of metaphor in the history of psychology. In D. E. Leary (Ed.), *Metaphors in the history of psychology* (pp. 1–78). Cambridge, England: Cambridge University Press.

Lee, V., & Bryk, A. (1988). Curriculum tracking as mediating the social distribution of high school achievement. *Sociology of Education, 61,* 78–94.

Lee, V., & Bryk, A. (1989). A multilevel model of the social distribution of high school achievement. *Sociology of Education, 62,* 172–192.

Lee, V., Bryk, A., & Smith, J. (1993). The organization of effective secondary schools. In L. Darling-Hammond (Ed.), *Review of research in education* (Vol. 19, pp. 171–267). Washington, DC: American Educational Research Association.

Lee, V., & Smith, J. (1995). Effects of high school restructuring and size on early gains in achievement and engagement. *Sociology of Education, 68,* 241–270.

Leinhardt, G., Seewald, A., & Engel, M. (1979). Learning what's taught: Sex differences in instruction. *Journal of Educational Psychology, 71,* 432–439.

Leithwood, K., & Montgomery, D. (1982). The role of the elementary school principal in program improvement. *Review of Educational Research, 52,* 309–339.

Lepper, M. R. (1981). Intrinsic and extrinsic motivation in children: Detrimental effects of superfluous social controls. In W. A. Collins (Ed.), *Aspects of the development of competence: The Minnesota symposia on child psychology* (Vol. 14, pp. 155–214). Hillsdale, NJ: Erlbaum.

Lepper, M. R. (1983). Extrinsic reward and intrinsic motivation: Implications for the classroom. In J. M. Levine & M. C. Wang (Eds.), *Teacher and student perceptions: Implications for learning* (pp. 281–317). Hillsdale, NJ: Erlbaum.

Lepper, M. R., & Greene, D. (1978). Overjustification research and beyond: Toward a means-ends analysis of intrinsic and extrinsic motivation. In M. R. Lepper & D. Greene (Eds.), *The hidden costs of reward: New perspectives on the psychology of human motivation* (pp. 109–148). Hillsdale, NJ: Erlbaum.

Lepper, M. R., Greene, D., & Nisbett, R. E. (1973). Undermining children's intrinsic interest with extrinsic reward: A test of the "overjustification" hypothesis. *Journal of Personality and Social Psychology, 28,* 129–137.

Lepper, M., & Henderlong, J. (2000). Turning "play" into "work" and "work" into "play": 25 years of research on intrinsic versus extrinsic motivation. In C. Sansone & J. Harackiewicz (Eds.), *Intrinsic and extrinsic motivation: The search for optimal motivation and performance* (pp. 257–307). San Diego, CA: Academic Press.

Lepper, M., Henderlong, J., & Gingras, I. (1999). Understanding the effects of extrinsic rewards on intrinsic motivation—Uses and abuses of meta-analysis: Comment on Deci, Koestner, and Ryan (1999). *Psychological Bulletin, 125,* 669–676.

Lepper, M. R., & Hodell, M. (1989). Intrinsic motivation in the classroom. In C. Ames & R. Ames (Eds.), *Research on motivation in education* (Vol. 3, pp. 73–105). San Diego, CA: Academic Press.

Lepper, M. R., Keavney, M., & Drake, M. (1996). Intrinsic motivation and extrinsic rewards: A commentary on Cameron and Pierce's meta-analysis. *Review of Educational Research, 66,* 5–32.

Lepper, M. R., & Malone, T. (1987). Intrinsic motivation and instructional effectiveness in computer-based education. In R. E. Snow & M. J. Farr (Eds.), *Aptitude, learning, and instruction* (Vol. 3, pp. 255–296). Hillsdale, NJ: Erlbaum.

Lepper, M. R., Sethi, S., Dialdin, D., & Drake, M. (1997). Intrinsic and extrinsic motivation: A developmental perspective. In S. S. Luthar, J. A. Burack. D. Cicchetti, & J. R. Weisz (Eds.), *Developmental psychopathology: Perspectives on adjustment, risk, and disorder* (pp. 23–50). New York: Cambridge University Press.

Lerner, R. M. (1986). *Concepts and theories of human development* (2nd ed.). New York: Random House.

Levin, J., & Nolan, J. F. (2000). *Principles of classroom management: A professional decision-making model.* Boston: Allyn & Bacon.

Lewin, K. (1935). *A dynamic theory of personality: Selected papers* (D. K. Adams & K. E. Zener, Trans.). New York: McGraw-Hill.

Lewin, K., Dembo, T., Festinger, L., & Sears, P. (1944). Level of aspiration. In J. McV. Hunt (Ed.), *Personality and the behavioral disorders* (Vol. 1). New York: Ronald.

Lewin, K., Lippitt, R., & White, R. K. (1939). Patterns of aggressive behavior in experimentally created "social climates." *Journal of Social Psychology, 10,* 271–299.

Licht, B. G., & Kistner, J. A. (1986). Motivational problems of learning-disabled children: Individual differences and their implications for treatment. In J. K. Torgesen & B. W. L. Wong (Eds.), *Psychological and educational perspectives on learning disabilities* (pp. 225–255). Orlando, FL: Academic Press.

Liebert, R., & Morris, L. (1967). Cognitive and emotional components of test anxiety: A distinction and some initial data. *Psychological Reports, 20,* 975–978.

Lilienfeld, S., Wood, J., & Garb, H. (2000). The scientific status of projective techniques. *Psychological Science in the Public Interest, 1,* 27–66.

Linn, M., & Hyde, J. (1989). Gender, mathematics, and science. *Educational Researcher, 18,* 17–19, 22–27.

Linnenbrink, E., & Pintrich, P. R. (2000). Multiple pathways to learning and achievement: The role of goal orientation in fostering adaptive motivation, affect, and cognition. In C. Sansone & J. Harackiewicz (Eds.), *Intrinsic and extrinsic motivation: The search for optimal motivation and performance* (pp. 195–227). San Diego, CA: Academic Press.

Linnenbrink, E., & Pintrich, P. R. (in press). Multiple goals, multiple contexts: The dynamic interplay between personal goals and contextual goal stresses. In S. Volet & S. Jarvela (Eds.), *Motivation in learning contexts: Theoretical and methodological implications.* Amsterdam: Pergamon.

Linnenbrink, E., Ryan, A., & Pintrich, P. R. (1999). The role of goals and affect in working memory functioning. *Learning and Individual Differences, 11,* 213–230.

Lipton, J. P., & Garza, R. T. (1977). Responsibility attribution among Mexican-American, Black, and Anglo adolescents and adults. *Journal of Cross-Cultural Psychology, 8,* 259–272.

Locke, E. A., & Latham, G. P. (1990). *A theory of goal setting and task performance.* Englewood Cliffs, NJ: Prentice-Hall.

Lowenstein, G. (1994). The psychology of curiosity: A review and reinterpretation. *Psychological Bulletin, 116,* 75–98.

Mac Iver, D. (1988). Classroom environments and the stratification of pupils' ability perceptions. *Journal of Educational Psychology, 80,* 495–505.

Mac Iver, D., Reuman, D., & Main, S. (1995). Social structuring of the school: Studying what is, illuminating what could be. *Annual Review of Psychology, 46,* 375–400.

Mace, F. C., Belfiore, P. J., & Shea, M. C. (1989). Operant theory and research on self-regulation. In B. J. Zimmerman & D. H. Schunk (Eds.), *Self-regulated learning and academic achievement: Theory, research, and practice* (pp. 27–50). New York: Springer-Verlag.

Maehr, M. L., & Braskamp, L. A. (1986). *The motivation factor: A theory of personal investment.* Lexington, MA: Lexington Books, D.C. Heath.

Maehr, M. L., & Midgley, C. (1991). Enhancing student motivation: A schoolwide approach. *Educational Psychologist, 26,* 399–427.

Maehr, M. L., & Midgley, C. (1996). *Transforming school cultures.* Boulder, CO: Westview Press.

Maehr, M. L., & Pintrich, P. R. (1991). *Advances in motivation and achievement: Vol 7. Goals and self-regulatory processes.* Greenwich, CT: JAI Press.

Magnusson, D. (1990). Personality development from an interactional perspective. In L. A. Pervin (Ed.), *Handbook of personality: Theory and research* (pp. 193–222). New York: Guilford Press.

Major, B. (1980). Information acquisition and attribution process. *Journal of Personality and Social Psychology, 39,* 1010–1023.

Malone, T., & Lepper, M. R. (1987). Making learning fun: A taxonomy of intrinsic motivations for learning. In R. Snow & M. Farr (Eds.), *Aptitude, learning, and instruction* (Vol. 3, pp. 223–253). Hillsdale, NJ: Erlbaum.

Manassee, A. (1985). Improving conditions for principal effectiveness: Policy implications of research. *Elementary School Journal, 85,* 439–463.

Mandler, G., & Sarason, S. (1952). A study of anxiety and learning. *Journal of Abnormal and Social Psychology, 47,* 166–173.

Markus, H., & Nurius, P. (1986). Possible selves. *American Psychologist, 41,* 954–969.

Marsh, H. (1984a). Relations among dimensions of self-attribution, dimensions of self-concept, and academic achievements. *Journal of Educational Psychology, 76,* 1291–1308.

Marsh, H. (1984b). The relationship between dimensions of self-attribution and dimensions of self-concept. *Journal of Educational Psychology, 76,* 3–23.

Marsh, H. (1986). Global self-esteem: Its relation to specific facets of self-concept and their importance. *Journal of Personality and Social Psychology, 51,* 1224–1236.

Marsh, H. (1989). Age and sex effects in multiple dimensions of self-concept: Preadolescence to early adulthood. *Journal of Educational Psychology, 81,* 417–430.

Marsh, H. (1990a). Causal ordering of academic self-concept and academic achievement: A multivariate, longitudinal panel analysis. *Journal of Educational Psychology, 82,* 646–656.

Marsh, H. (1990b). The structure of academic self-concept: The Marsh/Shavelson model. *Journal of Educational Psychology, 82,* 623–636.

Marsh, H. (1993). Academic self-concept: Theory, measurement, and research. In J. Suls (Ed.), *Psychological perspectives on the self* (Vol. 4, pp. 59–98). Hillsdale, NJ: Erlbaum.

Marsh, H., Byrne, B., & Shavelson, R. (1992). A multi-dimensional, hierarchical self-concept. In T. Brinthaupt & R. Lipka (Eds.), *The self: Definitional and methodological issues* (pp. 44–95). Albany, NY: State University of New York Press.

Marsh, H., & Hattie, J. (1996). Theoretical perspectives on the structure of self-concept. In B. Bracken (Ed.), *Handbook of self-concept* (pp. 38–90). New York: Wiley.

Marsh, H., & O'Neill, R. (1984). Self-description questionnaire III: The construct validity of multidimensional self-concept ratings by late adolescents. *Journal of Educational Measurement, 21,* 153–174.

Marsh, H., & Shavelson, R. (1985). Self-concept: Its multifaceted hierarchical structure. *Educational Psychologist, 20,* 107–123.

Marshall, H., & Weinstein, R. S. (1984). Classroom factors affecting students' self-evaluations: An interactional model. *Review of Educational Research, 54,* 301–325.

Marx, R. W. (1983). Student perception in classrooms. *Educational Psychologist, 18,* 145–164.

Maslow, A. (1954). *Motivation and personality.* New York: Harper.

McClelland, D. (1961). *The achieving society.* Princeton, NJ: Van Nostrand.

McClelland, D., Atkinson, J. W., Clark, R. A., & Lowell, E. L. (1953). *The achievement motive.* New York: Appleton-Century-Crofts.

McClelland, D., Koestner, R., & Weinberger, J. (1989). How do self-attributed and implicit motives differ? *Psychological Review, 96,* 690–702.

McDougall, W. (1923). *Outline of psychology.* New York: Scribner.

McDougall, W. (1926). *An introduction to social psychology* (Rev. ed.). Boston: John W. Luce.

McGilly, K. (1994). *Classroom lessons: Integrating cognitive theory and classroom practice.* Cambridge, MA: MIT Press.

McInerney, D. M., Hinkley, J., Dowson, M., & Van Etten, S. (1998). Aboriginal, Anglo, and immigrant Australian students' motivational beliefs about personal academic success: Are there cultural differences? *Journal of Educational Psychology, 90,* 621–629.

McMillan, J. H. (1980). Children's causal attributions in achievement situations. *Journal of Social Psychology, 112,* 31–39.

McReynolds, P. (1990). Motives and metaphors: A study in scientific creativity. In D. E. Leary (Ed.), *Metaphors in the history of psychology* (pp. 133–172). Cambridge, England: Cambridge University Press.

Meece, J. (1991). The classroom context and students' motivational goals. In M. L. Maehr & P. R. Pintrich (Eds.), *Advances in motivation and achievement* (Vol. 7, pp. 261–286). Greenwich, CT: JAI Press.

Meece, J. L. (1997). *Child and adolescent development for educators.* New York: McGraw-Hill.

Meece, J., Blumenfeld, P. C., & Hoyle, R. H. (1988). Students' goal orientation and cognitive engagement in classroom activities. *Journal of Educational Psychology, 80,* 514–523.

Meece, J., & Eccles, J. (1993). Introduction: Recent trends in research on gender and education. *Educational Psychologist, 28,* 313–319.

Meece, J., & Holt, K. (1993). A pattern analysis of students' achievement goals. *Journal of Educational Psychology, 85,* 582–590.

Meece, J., Parsons, J., Kaczala, C., Goff, S., & Futterman, R. (1982). Sex differences in math achievement: Toward a model of academic choice. *Psychological Bulletin, 91,* 324–348.

Meece, J., Wigfield, A., & Eccles, J. (1990). Predictors of math anxiety and its influence on young adolescents' course enrollment intentions and performance in mathematics. *Journal of Educational Psychology, 82,* 60–70.

Meichenbaum, D. (1977). *Cognitive behavior modification: An integrative approach.* New York: Plenum.

Meichenbaum, D., & Goodman, J. (1971). Training impulsive children to talk to themselves: A means of developing self-control. *Journal of Abnormal Psychology, 77,* 115–126.

Metz, M. (1978). *Classrooms and corridors: The crisis of authority in desegregated secondary schools.* Berkeley, CA: University of California Press.

Meyer, W., Bachmann, M., Biermann, U., Hempelmann, M., Plöger, F., & Spiller, H. (1979). The informational value of evaluative behavior: Influences of praise and blame in perceptions of ability. *Journal of Educational Psychology, 71,* 259–268.

Mickelson, R. (1990). The attitude-achievement paradox among Black adolescents. *Sociology of Education, 63,* 44–61.

Middleton, M., & Midgley, C. (1997). Avoiding the demonstration of lack of ability: An underexplored aspect of goal theory. *Journal of Educational Psychology, 89,* 710–718.

Midgley, C. (1993). Motivation and middle level schools. In M. Maehr & P. R. Pintrich (Eds.), *Advances in motivation and achievement* (Vol. 8, pp. 217–274). Greenwich, CT: JAI Press.

Midgley, C., Anderman, E., & Hicks, L. (1995). Differences between elementary and middle school teachers and students: A goal theory approach. *Journal of Early Adolescence, 15,* 90–133.

Midgley, C., & Edelin, K. (1998). Middle school reform and early adolescent well-being: The good news and the bad. *Educational Psychologist, 33,* 195–206.

Midgley, C., Feldlaufer, H., & Eccles, J. (1989a). Change in teacher efficacy and student self- and task-related beliefs in mathematics during the transition to junior high school. *Journal of Educational Psychology, 81,* 247–258.

Midgley, C., Feldlaufer, H., & Eccles, J. (1989b). Student/teacher relations and attitudes toward mathematics before and after the transition to junior high school. *Child Development, 60,* 981–992.

Midgley, C., Kaplan, A., & Middleton, M. (2001). Performance-approach goals: Good for what, for whom, under what circumstances, and at what cost? *Journal of Educational Psychology, 93,* 77–86.

Midgley, C., Kaplan, A., Middleton, M., Maehr, M., Urdan, T., Hicks Anderman, L., Anderman, E., & Roeser, R. (1998). The development and validation of scales assessing students' achievement goal orientations. *Contemporary Educational Psychology, 23,* 113–131.

Midgley, C., Maehr, M. L., & Urdan, T. (1993). *Patterns of adaptive learning survey (PALS).* Ann Arbor, MI: University of Michigan, Combined Program in Education and Psychology.

Midgley, C., & Wood, S. (1993). Beyond site-based management: Empowering teachers to reform schools. *Phi Delta Kappan, 75,* 245–252.

Milgram, S. (1963). Behavioral study of obedience. *Journal of Abnormal and Social Psychology, 67,* 371–378.

Milgram, S. (1974). *Obedience to authority: An experimental view.* New York: Harper & Row.

Miller, D. T., & Ross, M. (1975). Self-serving biases in the attribution of causality: Fact or fiction. *Psychological Bulletin, 82,* 213–225.

Miller, J. G. (1984). Culture and the development of everyday social explanation. *Journal of Personality and Social Psychology, 46,* 961–978.

Miller, N. E. (1948). Studies of fear as an acquirable drive: I. Fear as motivation and fear-reduction as reinforcement in the learning of new responses. *Journal of Experimental Psychology, 38,* 89–101.

Miller, N. E. (1963). Some reflections on the law of effect produce a new alternative to drive reduction. In M. R. Jones (Ed.), *Nebraska symposium on motivation* (Vol. 11, pp. 65–112). Lincoln, NE: University of Nebraska Press.

Miller, N. E., & Dollard, J. (1941). *Social learning and imitation.* New Haven, CT: Yale University Press.

Miller, R., Behrens, J., Greene, B., & Newman, D. (1993). Goals and perceived ability: Impact on student valuing, self-regulation, and persistence. *Contemporary Educational Psychology, 18,* 2–14.

Mischel, W. (1968). *Personality and assessment.* New York: Wiley.

Mischel, W. (1990). Personality dispositions revisited and revised: A view after three decades. In L. Pervin (Ed.), *Handbook of personality: Theory and research* (pp. 111–134). New York: Guilford Press.

Mitchell, M. (1993). Situational interest: Its multifaceted structure in the secondary school mathematics classroom. *Journal of Educational Psychology, 85,* 424–436.

Miura, I. T. (1987). A multivariate study of school-aged children's computer interest and use. In M. E. Ford & D. H. Ford (Eds.), *Humans as self-constructing living systems: Putting the framework to work* (pp. 177–197). Hillsdale, NJ: Erlbaum.

Mook, D. G. (1987). *Motivation: The organization of action.* New York: Norton.

Moos, R. (1979). *Evaluating educational environments.* San Francisco: Jossey-Bass.

Morgan, M. (1984). Reward-induced decrements and increments in intrinsic motivation. *Review of Educational Research, 54,* 5–30.

Mosatche, H. S., & Bragonier, P. (1981). An observational study of social comparison in preschoolers. *Child Development, 52,* 376–378.

Mowrer, O. H. (1960). *Learning theory and behavior.* New York: Wiley.

Mullen, R., & Riordan, C. A. (1988). Self-serving attributions for performance in naturalistic settings: A meta-analytic review. *Journal of Applied Social Psychology, 18,* 3–22.

Muncey, D., & McQuillan, P. (1993). Preliminary findings from a five-year study of the Coalition of Essential Schools. *Phi Delta Kappan, 74,* 486–489.

Murphy, P. K., & Alexander, P. (2000). A motivated exploration of motivation terminology. *Contemporary Educational Psychology, 25,* 3–53.

Murray, H. A. (1938). *Explorations in personality.* New York: Oxford University Press.

Naftulin, D. H., Ware, J. E., & Donnelly, F. A. (1973). The Doctor Fox lecture: A paradigm of educational seduction. *Journal of Medical Education, 48,* 630–635.

Natriello, G. (1986). *School dropouts: Patterns and policies.* New York: Teachers College Press.

Newman, R. S. (1994). Adaptive help-seeking: A strategy of self-regulated learning. In D. H. Schunk & B. J. Zimmerman (Eds.), *Self-regulation of learning and performance: Issues and educational applications* (pp. 283–301). Hillsdale, NJ: Erlbaum.

Newman, R. S. (1998a). Adaptive help-seeking: A role of social interaction in self-regulated learning. In S. Karabenick (Ed.), *Strategic help-seeking: Implications for learning and teaching* (pp. 13–37). Hillsdale, NJ: Erlbaum.

Newman, R. S. (1998b). Students' help-seeking during problem solving: Influences of personal and contextual goals. *Journal of Educational Psychology, 90,* 644–658.

Newman, R. S., & Schwager, M. T. (1992). Student perceptions and academic help-seeking. In D. H. Schunk & J. L. Meece (Eds.), *Student perceptions in the classroom* (pp. 123–146). Hillsdale, NJ: Erlbaum.

Newmann, F. (1981). Reducing student alienation in high schools: Implications of theory. *Harvard Educational Review, 51,* 546–564.

Newmann, F. (1993). Beyond common sense in educational restructuring: The issues of content and linkage. *Educational Researcher, 22,* 4–13.

Nicholls, J. (1978). The development of the concepts of effort and ability, perception of academic attainment, and the understanding that difficult tasks require more ability. *Child Development, 49,* 800–814.

Nicholls, J. (1979). Development of perception of own attainment and causal attribution for success and failure in reading. *Journal of Educational Psychology, 71,* 94–99.

Nicholls, J. (1984). Achievement motivation: Conceptions of ability, subjective experience, task choice, and performance. *Psychological Review, 91,* 328–346.

Nicholls, J. (1989). *The competitive ethos and democratic education.* Cambridge, MA: Harvard University Press.

Nicholls, J. (1990). What is ability and why are we mindful of it? A developmental perspective. In R. Sternberg & J. Kolligian (Eds.), *Competence considered* (pp. 11–40). New Haven, CT: Yale University Press.

Nicholls, J., Cheung, P., Lauer, J., & Patashnick, M. (1989). Individual differences in academic motivation: Perceived ability, goals, beliefs, and values. *Learning and Individual Differences, 1,* 63–84.

Nicholls, J., & Miller, A. (1983). The differentiation of the concepts of difficulty and ability. *Child Development, 54,* 951–959.

Nicholls, J., & Miller, A. (1984a). Development and its discontents: The differentiation of the concept of ability. In J. Nicholls (Ed.), *Advances in motivation and achievement: The development of achievement motivation* (Vol. 3, pp. 185–218). Greenwich, CT: JAI Press.

Nicholls, J., & Miller, A. (1984b). Reasoning about the ability of self and others: A developmental study. *Child Development, 55,* 1990–1999.

Nicholls, J., & Miller, A. (1985). Differentiation of the concepts of luck and skill. *Developmental Psychology, 21,* 76–82.

Nisbett, R., & Ross, L. (1980). *Human inference: Strategies and shortcomings of social judgment.* Englewood Cliffs, NJ: Prentice-Hall.

Nisbett, R., & Wilson, T. (1977). Telling more than we can know: Verbal reports on mental processes. *Psychological Review, 84,* 231–259.

Noddings, N. (1992). *The challenge to care in schools.* New York: Teachers College Press.

Nolen, S. (1988). Reasons for studying: Motivational orientations and study strategies. *Cognition and Instruction, 5,* 269–287.

Norem, J. K., & Cantor, N. (1986). Defensive pessimism: Harnessing anxiety as motivation. *Journal of Personality and Social Psychology, 51,* 1208–1217.

Oakes, J. (1985). *Keeping track: How schools structure inequality.* New Haven, CT: Yale University Press.

O'Connor, C. (1997). Dispositions toward (collective) struggle and educational resilience in the inner city: A case analysis of six African-American high school students. *American Educational Research Journal, 34,* 593–629.

Ogbu, J. (1987). Variability in minority school performance: A problem in search of an explanation. *Anthropology and Education Quarterly, 18,* 312–334.

O'Leary, K., & O'Leary, S. (1977). *Classroom management: The successful use of behavior modification* (2nd ed.). New York: Pergamon.

Olson, J., Ellis, R., & Zanna, M. (1983). Validating objective versus subjective judgments: Interest in social comparison and consistency information. *Personality and Social Psychology Bulletin, 9,* 427–436.

Ortony, A., Clore, G., & Collins, A. (1988). *The cognitive structure of emotions.* Cambridge, England: Cambridge University Press.

Overton, W. F. (1984). World views and their influence on psychological theory and research: Kuhn-Lakatos-Laudan. In H. W. Reese (Ed.), *Advances in child development and behavior* (Vol. 18, pp. 191–226). Orlando, FL: Academic Press.

Page, R. (1990). The lower track curriculum in a college-preparatory high school. *Curriculum Inquiry, 20,* 249–282.

Palincsar, A. S. (1986). Metacognitive strategy instruction. *Exceptional Children, 53,* 118–124.

Palincsar, A. S., & Brown, A. L. (1984). Reciprocal teaching of comprehension-fostering and comprehension-monitoring activities. *Cognition and Instruction, 1,* 117–175.

Pajares, F. (1996). Self-efficacy beliefs in achievement settings. *Review of Educational Research, 66,* 543–578.

Pajares, F., & Miller, M. D. (1995). Mathematics self-efficacy and mathematics performances: The need for specificity of assessment. *Journal of Counseling Psychology, 42,* 190–198.

Paris, S., & Ayres, L. (1994). *Becoming reflective students and teachers with portfolios and authentic assessment.* Washington, DC: American Psychological Association.

Paris, S., Lawton, T., Turner, J., & Roth, J. (1991). A developmental perspective on standardized testing. *Educational Researcher, 20,* 12–20.

Paris, S., Lipson, M. Y., & Wixson, K. K. (1983). Becoming a strategic reader. *Contemporary Educational Psychology, 8,* 293–316.

Paris, S., Newman, R. S., & McVey, K. A. (1982). Learning the functional significance of mnemonic actions: A microgenetic study of strategy acquisition. *Journal of Experimental Child Psychology, 34,* 490–509.

Paris, S., & Oka, E. (1986). Children's reading strategies, metacognition, and motivation. *Developmental Review, 6,* 25–56.

Parker, J. G., & Asher, S. R. (1987). Peer relations and later personal adjustment: Are low-accepted children at risk? *Psychological Bulletin, 102,* 357–389.

Parker, L. E., & Lepper, M. R. (1992). Effects of fantasy contexts on children's learning and motivation: Making learning more fun. *Journal of Personality and Social Psychology, 62,* 625–633.

Parsons, J., & Goff, S. (1978). Achievement and motivation: Dual modalities. *Educational Psychologist, 13,* 93–96.

Parsons, J., Kaczala, C., & Meece, J. (1982). Socialization of achievement attitudes and beliefs: Classroom influences. *Child Development, 53,* 322–339.

Parsons, J., & Ruble, D. N. (1977). The development of achievement-related expectancies. *Child Development, 48,* 1075–1079.

Patrick, H. (1997). Social self-regulation: Exploring the relations between children's social relationships, academic self-regulation, and school performance. *Educational Psychologist, 32,* 209–220.

Patrick, H., & Pintrich, P. R. (2001). Conceptual change in teachers' intuitive conceptions of learning, motivation, and instruction: The role of motivational and epistemological beliefs. In B. Torff & R. J. Sternberg (Eds.), *Understanding and teaching the intuitive mind: Student and teacher learning* (pp. 117–143). Mahwah, NJ: Erlbaum.

Pavlov, I. P. (1927). *Conditioned reflexes* (G. V. Anrep, Trans.). London: Oxford University Press.

Pavlov, I. P. (1928). *Lectures on conditioned reflexes* (W. H. Gantt, Trans.). New York: International Publishers.

Pekrun, R. (1992). The impact of emotions on learning and achievement: Towards a theory of cognitive/motivational mediators. *Applied Psychology: An International Review, 41,* 359–376.

Pekrun, R. (1993). Facets of adolescents' academic motivation: A longitudinal expectancy-value approach. In M. L. Maehr & P. R. Pintrich (Eds.), *Advances in motivation and achievement: Motivation in adolescence* (Vol. 8, pp. 139–189). Greenwich, CT: JAI Press.

Pekrun, R., & Frese, M. (1992). Emotions in work and achievement. In C. Cooper & I. Robertson (Eds.), *International review of industrial and organizational psychology* (Vol. 7, pp. 153–200). Chichester, UK: Wiley.

Perkins, D. (1992). *Smart schools: From training memories to educating minds.* New York: The Free Press.

Perry, R. P. (1985). Instructor expressiveness: Implications for improving teaching. In J. G. Donald & A. M. Sullivan (Eds.), *Using research to improve teaching* (pp. 35–49). San Francisco: Jossey-Bass.

Perry, R. P., & Dickens, W. J. (1984). Perceived control in the college classroom: Response-outcome contingency training and instructor expressiveness effects on student achievement and causal attributions. *Journal of Educational Psychology, 76,* 966–981.

Perry, R. P., Magnusson, J. L., Parsonson, K. L., & Dickens, W. J. (1986). Perceived control in the college classroom: Limitations in instructor expressiveness due to noncontingent feedback and lecture content. *Journal of Educational Psychology, 78,* 96–107.

Peshkin, A. (1986). *God's choice: The total world of a fundamental Christian school.* Chicago: University of Chicago Press.

Peterson, C., Maier, S., & Seligman, M. (1993). *Learned helplessness: A theory for the age of personal control.* New York: Oxford University Press.

Peterson, C., & Seligman, M. (1984). Causal explanations as a risk factor for depression: Theory and evidence. *Psychological Review, 91,* 347–374.

Peterson, C., Semmel, A., Von Baeyer, C., Abramson, L. Y., Metalsky, G. I., & Seligman, M. (1982). The attributional style questionnaire. *Cognitive Therapy and Research, 6,* 287–300.

Peterson, P., & Barger, S. (1984). Attribution theory and teacher expectancy. In J. Dusek (Ed.), *Teacher expectancies* (pp. 159–184). Hillsdale, NJ: Erlbaum.

Peterson, P., Swing, S. R., Braverman, M. T., & Buss, R. (1982). Students' aptitudes and their reports of cognitive processes during direct instruction. *Journal of Educational Psychology, 74,* 535–547.

Phares, E. J. (1976). *Locus of control in personality.* Morristown, NJ: General Learning Press.

Phillips, D. (1984). The illusion of incompetence among academically competent children. *Child Development, 55,* 2000–2016.

Phillips, D. (1987). Socialization of perceived academic competence among highly competent children. *Child Development, 58,* 1308–1320.

Phillips, D., & Zimmerman, M. (1990). The developmental course of perceived competence and incompetence among competent children. In R. Sternberg & J. Kolligian (Eds.), *Competence considered* (pp. 41–66). New Haven, CT: Yale University Press.

Piaget, J. (1954/1981). *Intelligence and affectivity.* Palo Alto, CA: Annual Reviews, Inc.

Piaget, J. (1962). *Play, dreams and imitation.* New York: Norton.

Piaget, J. (1985). *The equilibration of cognitive structures.* Chicago: University of Chicago Press.

Pintrich, P. R. (1988a). A process-oriented view of student motivation and cognition. In J. Stark and L. Mets (Eds.), *Improving teaching and learning through research: New directions for institutional research* (Vol. 57, pp. 65–79). San Francisco: Jossey-Bass.

Pintrich, P. R. (1988b). Student learning and college teaching. In R. Young and K. Eble (Eds.), *College teaching and learning: Preparing for new commitments: New directions for teaching and learning.* (Vol. 33. pp. 71–86). San Francisco: Jossey-Bass.

Pintrich, P. R. (1989). The dynamic interplay of student motivation and cognition in the college classroom. In C. Ames & M. L. Maehr (Eds.), *Advances in motivation and achievement: Motivation enhancing environments* (Vol. 6, pp. 117–160). Greenwich, CT: JAI Press.

Pintrich, P. R. (1991). Current issues and new directions in motivational theory and research. *Educational Psychologist, 26,* 199–205.

Pintrich, P. R. (1994). Continuities and discontinuities: Future directions for research in educational psychology. *Educational Psychologist, 29,* 137–148.

Pintrich, P. R. (1999a) Taking control of research on volitional control: Challenges for future theory and research. *Learning and Individual Differences, 11,* 213–230.

Pintrich, P. R. (1999b). The role of motivation in promoting and sustaining self-regulated learning. *International Journal of Educational Research, 31,* 459–470.

Pintrich, P. R. (2000a). An achievement goal theory perspective on issues in motivation terminology, theory, and research. *Contemporary Educational Psychology, 25,* 92–104.

Pintrich, P. R. (2000b). Educational psychology at the millennium: A look back and a look forward. *Educational Psychologist, 35,* 221–226.

Pintrich, P. R. (2000c). Multiple goals, multiple pathways: The role of goal orientation in learning and achievement. *Journal of Educational Psychology. 92,* 544–555.

Pintrich, P. R. (2000d). The role of goal orientation in self-regulated learning. In M. Boekaerts, P. R. Pintrich, & M. Zeidner, (Eds.), *Handbook of self-regulation* (pp. 451–502). San Diego, CA: Academic Press.

Pintrich, P. R., & Blumenfeld, P. (1985). Classroom experience and children's self-perceptions of ability, effort and conduct. *Journal of Educational Psychology, 77,* 646–657.

Pintrich, P. R., Cross, D. R., Kozma, R. B., & McKeachie, W. J. (1986). Instructional psychology. *Annual Review of Psychology, 37,* 611–651.

Pintrich, P. R., & De Groot, E. (1990a). Motivational and self-regulated learning components of classroom academic performance. *Journal of Educational Psychology, 82,* 33–40.

Pintrich, P. R., & De Groot, E. (1990b). *Quantitative and qualitative perspectives on student motivational beliefs and self-regulated learning.* Paper presented at the American Educational Research Association conference, Boston.

Pintrich, P. R., & Garcia, T. (1991). Student goal orientation and self-regulation in the college classroom. In M. L. Maehr & P. R. Pintrich (Eds.), *Advances in motivation and achievement: Goals and self-regulatory processes* (Vol. 7, pp. 371–402). Greenwich, CT: JAI Press.

Pintrich, P. R., & Garcia, T. (1993). Motivation and self-regulation in the college classroom. *Zeitschrift für Pädagogische Psychologie, 7,* 99–107.

Pintrich, P. R., Marx, R. W., & Boyle, R. (1993). Beyond "cold" conceptual change: The role of motivational beliefs and classroom contextual factors in the process of conceptual change. *Review of Educational Research, 63,* 167–199.

Pintrich, P. R., Roeser, R., & De Groot, E. (1994). Classroom and individual differences in early adolescents' motivation and self-regulated learning. *Journal of Early Adolescence, 14,* 139–161.

Pintrich, P. R., & Schrauben, B. (1992). Students' motivational beliefs and their cognitive engagement in classroom tasks. In D. Schunk & J. Meece (Eds.), *Student perceptions in the classroom: Causes and consequences* (pp. 149–183). Hillsdale, NJ: Erlbaum.

Pintrich, P. R., Smith, D. A. F., Garcia, T., & McKeachie, W. J. (1993). Reliability and predictive validity of the Motivated Strategies for Learning Questionnaire (MSLQ). *Educational and Psychological Measurement, 53,* 801–813.

Pintrich, P. R., Wolters, C., & Baxter, G. (2000). Assessing metacognition and self-regulated learning. In G. Schraw & J. Impara (Eds.), *Issues in the measurement of metacognition* (pp. 43–97). Lincoln, NE: Buros Institute of Mental Measurements.

Plutchik, R. (1980). *The emotions: A psychoevolutionary synthesis.* New York: Harper.

Pollard, D. S. (1993). Gender, achievement, and African-American students' perceptions of their school experience. *Educational Psychologist, 28,* 341–356.

Portes, P. R. (1996). Ethnicity and culture in educational psychology. In D. C. Berliner & R. C. Calfee (Eds.), *Handbook of educational psychology* (pp. 331–357). New York: Macmillan.

Premack, D. (1962). Reversibility of the reinforcement relation. *Science, 136,* 255–257.

Premack, D. (1971). Catching up with common sense or two sides of a generalization: Reinforcement and punishment. In R. Glaser (Ed.), *The nature of reinforcement* (pp. 121–150). New York: Academic Press.

Pressley, M., Woloshyn, V., Lysynchuk, L. M., Martin, V., Wood, E., & Willoughby, T. (1990). A primer of research on cognitive strategy instruction: The important issues and how to address them. *Educational Psychology Review, 2,* 1–58.

Purkey, S., & Smith, M. S. (1983). Effective schools: A review. *Elementary School Journal, 83,* 427–452.

Raudenbush, S., Rowan, B., & Cheong, Y. (1993). Higher order instructional goals in secondary schools: Class, teacher, and school influences. *American Educational Research Journal, 30,* 523–553.

Rawsthorne, L., & Elliot, A. J. (1999). Achievement goals and intrinsic motivation: A meta-analytic review. *Personality and Social Psychology Review,* 3, 326–344.

Relich, J. D., Debus, R. L., & Walker, R. (1986). The mediating role of attribution and self-efficacy variables for treatment effects on achievement outcomes. *Contemporary Educational Psychology, 11,* 195–216.

Renninger, K. A. (1990). Children's play interests, representation, and activity. In R. Fivush & J. Hudson (Eds.), *Knowing and remembering in young children* (pp. 127–165). Cambridge, England: Cambridge University Press.

Renninger, K. A. (1992). Individual interest and development: Implications for theory and practice. In K. A. Renninger, S. Hidi, & A. Krapp (Eds.), *The role of interest in learning and development* (pp. 361–395). Hillsdale, NJ: Erlbaum.

Renninger, K. A., Hidi, S., & Krapp, A. (1992). *The role of interest in learning and development.* Hillsdale, NJ: Erlbaum.

Renninger, K. A., & Wozniak, R. H. (1985). Effect of interest on attentional shift, recognition, and recall in young children. *Developmental Psychology, 21,* 624–632.

Rescorla, R. (1972). Informational variables in conditioning. In G. H. Bower (Ed.), *The psychology of learning and motivation* (Vol. 6, pp. 1–46). New York: Academic Press.

Rescorla, R. (1987). A Pavlovian analysis of goal-directed behavior. *American Psychologist, 42,* 119–129.

Reuman, D. (1989). How social comparison mediates the relation between ability-grouping practices and students' achievement expectancies in mathematics. *Journal of Educational Psychology, 81,* 178–189.

Rheinberg, F., Vollmeyer, R., & Rollett, W. (2000). Motivation and action in self-regulated learning. In M. Boekaerts, P. R. Pintrich, & M. Zeidner (Eds.), *Handbook of self-regulation* (pp. 503–529). San Diego, CA: Academic Press.

Rigby, C. S., Deci, E. L., Patrick, B. C., & Ryan, R. M. (1992). Beyond the intrinsic-extrinsic dichotomy: Self-determination in motivation and learning. *Motivation and Emotion, 16,* 165–185.

Rodin, J., Solomon, S. K., & Metcalf, J. (1978). Role of control in mediating perceptions of density. *Journal of Personality and Social Psychology, 36,* 988–999.

Roeser, R. (1998). On schooling and mental health: Introduction to the special issue. *Educational Psychologist, 33,* 129–133.

Roeser, R., Eccles, J., & Strobel, K. (1998). Linking the study of schooling and mental health: Selected issues and empirical illustrations at the level of the individual. *Educational Psychologist, 33,* 153–176.

Rogers, C. R. (1959). A theory of therapy, personality, and interpersonal relationships, as developed in the client-centered framework. In S. Koch (Ed.), *Psychology: A study of a science* (Vol. 3, pp. 184–256). New York: McGraw-Hill.

Rogers, C. R. (1963). The actualizing tendency in relation to "motives" and to consciousness. In M. R. Jones (Ed.), *Nebraska symposium on motivation* (Vol. 11, pp. 1–24). Lincoln, NE: University of Nebraska Press.

Rogers, C. R. (1969). *Freedom to learn.* Columbus, OH: Merrill.

Rokeach, M. (1979). *Understanding human values.* New York: Free Press.

Rosenbaum, J. (1976). *Inequality: The hidden curriculum of high school tracking.* New York: Wiley.

Rosenbaum, J. (1980). Track misperceptions and frustrated college plans: An analysis of the effects of track and track perceptions in the NLS. *Sociology of Education, 53,* 74–88.

Rosenberg, M., & Simmons, R. (1971). *Black and white self-esteem. The urban school child.* Washington, DC: American Sociological Association.

Rosenholtz, S. J., & Rosenholtz, S. H. (1981). Classroom organization and the perception of ability. *Sociology of Education, 54,* 132–140.

Rosenholtz, S. J., & Simpson, C. (1984). The formation of ability conceptions: Developmental trend or social construction? *Review of Educational Research, 54,* 31–63.

Rosenshine, B., & Meister, C. (1994). Reciprocal teaching: A review of the research. *Review of Educational Research, 64,* 479–530.

Rosenshine, B., & Stevens, R. (1986). Teaching functions. In M. C. Wittrock (Ed.), *Handbook of research on teaching* (3rd ed., pp. 376–391). New York: Macmillan.

Rosenthal, R. (1974). *On the social psychology of the self-fulfilling prophecy: Further evidence for Pygmalion effects and their mediating mechanisms.* New York: MSS Modular Publications.

Rosenthal, R., & Jacobson, L. (1968). *Pygmalion in the classroom.* New York: Holt, Rinehart & Winston.

Rosenthal, T. L., & Bandura, A. (1978). Psychological modeling: Theory and practice. In S. L. Garfield & A. E. Bergin (Eds.), *Handbook of psychotherapy and behavior change: An empirical analysis* (2nd ed., pp. 621–658). New York: Wiley.

Rosenthal, T. L., & Zimmerman, B. J. (1978). *Social learning and cognition.* New York: Academic Press.

Ross, L. (1977). The intuitive psychologist and his shortcomings: Distortions in the attribution process. In L. Berkowitz (Ed.), *Advances in experimental social psychology* (Vol. 10, pp. 174–221). New York: Academic Press.

Ross, L., Bierbrauer, G., & Polly, S. (1974). Attribution of educational outcomes by professional and nonprofessional instructors. *Journal of Personality & Social Psychology, 29,* 609–618.

Ross, L., & Nisbett, R. (1991). *The person and the situation.* New York: McGraw-Hill.

Ross, M. (1975). Salience of reward and intrinsic motivation. *Journal of Personality and Social Psychology, 32,* 245–254.

Rossell, C., & Howley, W. (1983). *The consequences of school desegregation.* Philadelphia: Temple University Press.

Rotter, J. B. (1954). *Social learning and clinical psychology.* New York: Prentice-Hall.

Rotter, J. B. (1966). Generalized expectancies for internal versus external control of reinforcement. *Psychological Monographs, 80*(1, Whole No. 609).

Rotter, J. B., Chance, J. E., & Phares, E. J. (1972). *Applications of a social learning theory of personality.* New York: Holt, Rinehart & Winston.

Ruble, D. N. (1983). The development of social-comparison processes and their role in achievement-related self-socialization. In E. T. Higgins, D. N. Ruble, & W. Hartup (Eds.), *Social cognition and social development* (pp. 134–157). New York: Cambridge University Press.

Ruble, D. N., Boggiano, A. K., Feldman, N. S., & Loebl, J. H. (1980). Developmental analysis of the role of social comparison in self-evaluation. *Developmental Psychology, 16,* 105–115.

Ruble, D. N., Feldman, N. S., & Boggiano, A. K. (1976). Social comparison between young children in achievement situations. *Developmental Psychology, 12,* 192–197.

Ruble, D. N., & Frey, K. (1991). Changing patterns of comparative behavior as skills are acquired: A functional model of self-evaluation. In J. Suls & T. Wills (Eds.), *Social comparison: Contemporary theory and research* (pp. 79–113). Hillsdale, NJ: Erlbaum.

Ruble, D., & Martin, C. (1998). Gender development. In W. Damon (Series Ed.) & N. Eisenberg (Vol. Ed.), *Handbook of child psychology: Vol. 3. Social, emotional, and personality development* (5th ed., pp. 933–1016). New York: Wiley.

Ruble, D. N., Parsons, J., & Ross, J. (1976). Self-evaluative responses of children in an achievement setting. *Child Development, 47,* 990–997.

Russell, J., & Barrett, L. (1999). Core affect, prototypical emotional episodes, and other things called emotion: Dissecting the elephant. *Journal of Personality and Social Psychology, 76,* 805–819.

Russell, W. A. (1970). *Milestones in motivation: Contributions to the psychology of drive and purpose.* New York: Appleton-Century-Crofts.

Rutter, M., Maughan, B., Mortimore, P., Ouston, J., & Smith, A. (1979). *Fifteen thousand hours: Secondary schools and their effects on children.* Cambridge, MA: Harvard University Press.

Ryan, A. (2000). Peer groups as a context for the socialization of adolescents' motivation, engagement, and achievement in school. *Educational Psychologist, 35,* 101–111.

Ryan, A. (2001). The peer group as a context for the development of young adolescents' motivation and achievement. *Child Development, 72,* 1135–1150.

Ryan, A., Gheen, M., & Midgley, C. (1998). Why do some students avoid asking for help? An examination of the interplay among students' academic efficacy, teachers' social-emotional role, the classroom goal structure. *Journal of Educational Psychology, 90,* 528–535.

Ryan, A., & Pintrich, P. R. (1997). Should I ask for help? The role of motivation and attitude in adolescents' help seeking in math class. *Journal of Educational Psychology, 89,* 329–341.

Ryan, A., & Pintrich, P. R. (1998). Achievement and social motivational influences on help seeking in the classroom. In S. Karabenick (Ed.), *Strategic help seeking: Implications for learning and teaching* (pp. 117–139). Mahweh, NJ: Erlbaum.

Ryan, A., Pintrich, P. R., & Midgley, C. (2001). Avoiding seeking help in the classroom: Who and why? *Educational Psychology Review, 13,* 93–114.

Ryan, R. M. (1993). Agency and organization: Intrinsic motivation, autonomy, and the self in psychological development. In J. E. Jacobs (Ed.), *Nebraska symposium on motivation* (Vol. 40, pp. 1–56). Lincoln, NE: University of Nebraska Press.

Ryan, R. M., Connell, J. P., & Deci, E. L. (1985). A motivational analysis of self-determination and self-regulation in education. In C. Ames & R. Ames (Eds.), *Research on motivation in education* (Vol. 2, pp. 13–51). New York: Academic Press.

Ryan, R. M., & Deci, E. L. (1996). When paradigms clash: Comments on Cameron and Pierce's claim that rewards do not undermine intrinsic motivation. *Review of Educational Research, 66,* 33–38.

Ryan, R. M., & Deci, E. L. (2000). Intrinsic and extrinsic motivations: Classic definitions and new directions. *Contemporary Educational Psychology, 25,* 54–67

Ryan, R. M., & Grolnick, W. S. (1986). Origins and pawns in the classroom: Self-report and projective assessments of individual differences in children's perceptions. *Journal of Personality and Social Psychology, 50,* 550–558.

Ryan, R. M., & Powelson, C. L. (1991). Autonomy and relatedness as fundamental to motivation and education. *Journal of Experimental Education, 60,* 49–66.

Saarni, C., Mumme, D., & Campos, J. (1998). Emotional development: Action, communication, and understanding. In W. Damon (Series Ed.) & N. Eisenberg (Vol. Ed.), *Handbook of child psychology: Vol. 3. Social, emotional, and personality development* (5th ed., pp. 237–309). New York: Wiley.

Salomon, G. (1984). Television is "easy" and print is "tough": The differential investment of mental effort in learning as a function of perceptions and attributions. *Journal of Educational Psychology, 76,* 647–658.

Sansone, C. & Harackiewicz, J. (2000). *Intrinsic and extrinsic motivation: The search for optimal motivation and performance.* San Diego, CA: Academic Press.

Sarason, S. B. (1990). *The predictable failure of school reform: Can we change course before it's too late?* San Francisco: Jossey-Bass.

Schachter, S. (1964). The interaction of cognitive and physiological determinants of emotional state. In L. Berkowitz (Ed.), *Advances in experimental social psychology* (Vol. 1, pp. 49–80). New York: Academic Press.

Schachter, S., & Singer, J. E. (1962). Cognitive, social, and physiological determinants of emotional state. *Psychological Review, 69,* 379–399.

Scheirer, M. A., & Kraut, R. E. (1979). Increasing educational achievement via self-concept change. *Review of Educational Research, 49,* 131–149.

Schiefele, U. (1991). Interest, learning, and motivation. *Educational Psychologist, 26,* 299–323.

Schiefele, U. (1992). Topic interest and levels of text comprehension. . In K. A. Renninger, S. Hidi, & A. Krapp (Eds.), *The role of interest in learning and development* (pp. 151–182). Hillsdale, NJ: Erlbaum.

Schiefele, U., & Krapp, A. (1996). Topic interest and free recall of expository text. *Learning and Individual Differences, 8,* 141–160.

Schiefele, U., Krapp, A., & Winteler, A. (1992). Interest as a predictor of academic achievement: A meta-analysis of research. In K. A. Renninger, S. Hidi, & A. Krapp (Eds.), *The role of interest in learning and development* (pp. 183–212). Hillsdale, NJ: Erlbaum.

Schofield, J., & Sagar, H. (1983). Desegregation, school practices, and student race relations. In C. Rossell & W. Howley (Eds.), *The consequences of school desegregation* (pp. 58–102). Philadelphia: Temple University Press.

Schrank, W. (1968). The labeling effect of ability grouping. *Journal of Educational Research, 62,* 51–52.

Schrank, W. (1970). A further study of the labeling effect of ability grouping. *Journal of Educational Research, 63,* 358–360.

Schunk, D. H. (1982). Effects of effort attributional feedback on children's perceived self-efficacy and achievement. *Journal of Educational Psychology, 74,* 548–556.

Schunk, D. H. (1983a). Ability versus effort attributional feedback: Differential effects on self-efficacy and achievement. *Journal of Educational Psychology, 75,* 848–856.

Schunk, D. H. (1983b). Developing children's self-efficacy and skills: The roles of social comparative information and goal setting. *Contemporary Educational Psychology, 8,* 76–86.

Schunk, D. H. (1983c). Goal difficulty and attainment information: Effects on children's achievement behaviors. *Human Learning, 2,* 107–117.

Schunk, D. H. (1983d). Reward contingencies and the development of children's skills and self-efficacy. *Journal of Educational Psychology, 75,* 511–518.

Schunk, D. H. (1984). Sequential attributional feedback and children's achievement behaviors. *Journal of Educational Psychology, 76,* 1159–1169.

Schunk, D. H. (1987). Peer models and children's behavioral change. *Review of Educational Research, 57,* 149–174.

Schunk, D. H. (1989a). Self-efficacy and achievement behaviors. *Educational Psychology Review, 1,* 173–208.

Schunk, D. H. (1989b). Self-efficacy and cognitive achievement: Implications for students with learning problems. *Journal of Learning Disabilities, 22,* 14–22.

Schunk, D. H. (1989c). Self-efficacy and cognitive skill learning. In C. Ames & R. Ames (Eds.), *Research on motivation in education* (Vol. 3, pp. 13–44). San Diego, CA: Academic Press.

Schunk, D. H. (1989d). Social cognitive theory and self-regulated learning. In B. J. Zimmerman & D. H. Schunk (Eds.), *Self-regulated learning and academic achievement: Theory, research, and practice* (pp. 83–110). New York: Springer-Verlag.

Schunk, D. H. (1991a). *Learning theories: An educational perspective.* New York: Merrill/Macmillan.

Schunk, D. H. (1991b). Self-efficacy and academic motivation. *Educational Psychologist, 26,* 207–231.

Schunk, D. H. (1994). Self-regulation of self-efficacy and attributions in academic settings. In D. H. Schunk & B. J. Zimmerman (Eds.), *Self-regulation of learning and performance: Issues and educational applications* (pp. 75–99). Hillsdale, NJ: Erlbaum.

Schunk, D. H. (1995). Self-efficacy and education and instruction. In J. E. Maddux (Ed.), *Self-efficacy, adaptation, and adjustment: Theory, research, and application* (pp. 281–303). New York: Plenum Press.

Schunk, D. H. (1996). Goal and self-evaluative influences during children's cognitive skill learning. *American Educational Research Journal, 33,* 359–382.

Schunk, D. H. (2000). *Learning theories: An educational perspective* (3rd ed.). Upper Saddle River, NJ: Merrill/Prentice-Hall.

Schunk, D. H., & Cox, P. D. (1986). Strategy training and attributional feedback with learning disabled students. *Journal of Educational Psychology, 78,* 201–209.

Schunk, D. H., & Ertmer, P. A. (1999). Self-regulatory processes during computer skill acquisition: Goal and self-evaluative influences. *Journal of Educational Psychology, 91,* 251–260.

Schunk, D. H., & Hanson, A. R. (1985). Peer models: Influence on children's self-efficacy and achievement. *Journal of Educational Psychology, 77,* 313–322.

Schunk, D. H., & Hanson, A. R. (1989a). Influence of peer-model attributes on children's beliefs and learning. *Journal of Educational Psychology, 81,* 431–434.

Schunk, D. H., & Hanson, A. R. (1989b). Self-modeling and children's cognitive skill learning. *Journal of Educational Psychology, 81,* 155–163.

Schunk, D. H., Hanson, A. R., & Cox, P. D. (1987). Peer-model attributes and children's achievement behaviors. *Journal of Educational Psychology, 79,* 54–61.

Schunk, D. H., & Rice, J. M. (1986). Extended attributional feedback: Sequence effects during remedial reading instruction. *Journal of Early Adolescence, 6,* 55–66.

Schunk, D. H., & Rice, J. M. (1987). Enhancing comprehension skill and self-efficacy with strategy value information. *Journal of Reading Behavior, 19,* 285–302.

Schunk, D. H., & Swartz, C. W. (1993). Goals and progress feedback: Effects on self-efficacy and writing achievement. *Contemporary Educational Psychology, 18,* 337–354.

Schunk, D. H., & Zimmerman, B. J. (Eds.) (1994). *Self-regulation of learning and performance: Issues and educational applications.* Hillsdale, NJ: Erlbaum.

Schunk, D. H., & Zimmerman, B. J. (1996). Modeling and self-efficacy influences on children's development of self-regulation. In J. Juvonen & K. R. Wentzel (Eds.), *Social motivation: Understanding children's school adjustment* (pp. 154–180). Cambridge, England: Cambridge University Press.

Schunk, D. H., & Zimmerman, B. J. (1997). Social origins of self-regulatory competence. *Educational Psychologist, 32,* 195–208.

Schunk, D. H., & Zimmerman, B. J. (Eds.) (1998). *Self-regulated learning: From teaching to self-reflective practice.* New York: Guilford Press.

Schutz, P., & Davis, H. (2000). Emotions and self-regulation during test taking. *Educational Psychologist, 35,* 243–256.

Schwarz, N., & Clore, G. (1996). Feelings and phenomenal experiences. In E. T. Higgins & A. Kruglanski (Eds.), *Social psychology: Handbook of basic principles* (pp. 433–465). New York: Guilford.

Schwarzer, R., van der Ploeg, H., & Spielberger, C. D. (1989). *Advances in test anxiety research* (Vol. 6). Amsterdam: Swets & Zeitlinger.

Shah, J., & Kruglanski, A. (2000). Aspects of goal networks: Implications for self-regulation. In M. Boekaerts, P. R. Pintrich, & M. Zeidner (Eds.), *Handbook of self-regulation* (pp. 85–110). San Diego, CA: Academic Press.

Sharan, S. (1980). Cooperative learning in small groups: Recent methods and effects on achievement, attitudes, and ethnic relations. *Review of Educational Research, 50,* 241–271.

Shavelson, R., & Bolus, R. (1982). Self concept: The interplay of theory and methods. *Journal of Educational Psychology, 74,* 3–17.

Shedd, J., & Bacharach, S. B. (1991). *Tangled hierarchies: Teachers as professionals and the management of schools.* San Francisco: Jossey-Bass.

Shell, D., Murphy, C., & Bruning, R. (1989). Self-efficacy and outcome expectancy mechanisms in reading and writing achievement. *Journal of Educational Psychology, 81,* 91–100.

Shirey, L. (1992). Importance, interest, and selective attention. In K. A. Renninger, S. Hidi, & A. Krapp (Eds.), *The role of interest in learning and development* (pp. 281–296). Hillsdale, NJ: Erlbaum.

Shulman, L. S. (1986). Paradigms and research programs in the study of teaching: A contemporary perspective. In M. C. Wittrock (Ed.), *Handbook of research on teaching* (3rd ed., pp. 3–36). New York: Macmillan.

Shultz, T. R., & Lepper, M. R. (1996). Cognitive dissonance reduction as constraint satisfaction. *Psychological Review, 103,* 219–240.

Simmons, R., & Blyth, D. (1987). *Moving into adolescence: The impact of pubertal change and school context.* Hawthorn, NY: Aldine de Gruyter.

Singer, J., Marx, R., Krajcik, J. & Chambers, J. C. (2000). Constructing extended inquiry projects: Curriculum materials for science education reform. *Educational Psychologist, 35,* 165–178.

Sizer, T. (1984). *Horace's compromise: The dilemma of the American high school.* Boston: Houghton Mifflin.

Sizer, T. (1992). *Horace's compromise: Redesigning the American high school.* Boston: Houghton Mifflin.

Skaalvik, E. (1997). Self-enhancing and self-defeating ego orientation: Relations with task avoidance orientation, achievement, self-perceptions, and anxiety. *Journal of Educational Psychology, 89,* 71–81.

Skaalvik, E. M., & Hagtvet, K. (1990). Academic achievement and self-concept: An analysis of causal predominance in a developmental perspective. *Journal of Personality and Social Psychology, 58,* 292–307.

Skaalvik, E., Valas, H., & Sletta, O. (1994). Task involvement and ego involvement: Relations with academic achievement, academic self-concept and self-esteem. *Scandinavian Journal of Educational Research, 38,* 231–243.

Skinner, B. F. (1953). *Science and human behavior.* New York: Free Press.

Skinner, B. F. (1968). *The technology of teaching*. New York: Appleton-Century-Crofts.

Skinner, E. A. (1995). *Perceived control, motivation, and coping*. Thousand Oaks, CA: Sage Publications.

Skinner, E. A. (1996). A guide to constructs of control. *Journal of Personality and Social Psychology, 71*, 549–570.

Skinner, E. A., & Belmont, M. (1993). Motivation in the classroom: Reciprocal effects of teacher behavior and student engagement across the school year. *Journal of Educational Psychology, 85*, 571–581.

Skinner, E. A., Chapman, M., & Baltes, P. (1988a). Children's beliefs about control, means-ends, and agency: Developmental differences during middle childhood. *International Journal of Behavioral Development, 11*, 369–388.

Skinner, E. A., Chapman, M., & Baltes, P. (1988b). Control, means-ends, and agency beliefs: A new conceptualization and its measurement during childhood. *Journal of Personality and Social Psychology, 54*, 117–133.

Skinner, E. A., Wellborn, J. G., & Connell, J. P. (1990). What it takes to do well in school and whether I've got it: A process model of perceived control and children's engagement and achievement in school. *Journal of Educational Psychology, 82*, 22–32.

Slaughter-Defoe, D., Nakagawa, K., Takanishi, R., & Johnson, D. (1990). Toward cultural/ecological perspectives on schooling and achievement in African- and Asian-American Children. *Child Development, 61*, 363–383.

Slavin, R. (1983a). *Cooperative learning*. New York: Longman.

Slavin, R. (1983b). When does cooperative learning increase student achievement? *Psychological Bulletin, 94*, 429–445.

Slavin, R. (1995). *Cooperative learning*. Boston: Allyn & Bacon.

Smith, C. A., & Kirby, L. D. (2000). Consequences require antecedents: Towards a process model of emotion elicitation. In J. Forgas (Ed.), *Feeling and thinking: The role of affect in social cognition* (pp. 83–106). New York: Cambridge University Press.

Smith, C. P. (1992). *Motivation and personality: Handbook of thematic content analysis*. New York: Cambridge University Press.

Smith, E. R., & Miller, F. (1983). Mediation among attributional inferences and comprehension processes: Initial findings and a general method. *Journal of Personality and Social Psychology, 44*, 492–505.

Smith, M. L. (1980). Meta-analysis of research on teacher expectations. *Evaluation in Education, 4*, 53–55.

Smith, P. L., & Fouad, N. A. (1999). Subject-matter specificity of self-efficacy, outcome expectancies, interests, and goals: Implications for the social-cognitive model. *Journal of Counseling Psychology, 46*, 461–471.

Snow, R. (1989). Cognitive-conative aptitude interactions in learning. In R. Kanfer, P. L. Ackerman, & R. Cudeck (Eds.), *Abilities, motivation, and methodology* (pp. 435–473). Hillsdale, NJ: Erlbaum.

Sohn, D. (1982). Sex differences in achievement self-attributions: An effect size analysis. *Sex Roles, 8*, 345–357.

Sorensen, A. (1987). The organizational differentiation of students in schools as an opportunity structure. In M. Hallinan (Ed.), *The social organization of schools* (pp. 103–129). New York: Plenum Press.

Sorensen, A., & Hallinan, M. (1986). Effects of ability grouping on growth in academic achievement. *American Educational Research Journal, 23*, 519–542.

Spangler, W. D. (1992). Validity of questionnaire and TAT measures of need for achievement: Two meta-analyses. *Psychological Bulletin, 112*, 140–154.

Spear, P. S., & Armstrong, S. (1978). Effects of performance expectancies created by peer comparison as related to social reinforcement, task difficulty, and age of child. *Journal of Experimental Child Psychology, 25*, 254–266.

Spence, K. W. (1960). *Behavior theory and learning: Selected papers*. Englewood Cliffs, NJ: Prentice-Hall.

Spielberger, C. D. (1972). Anxiety as an emotional state. In C. D. Spielberger (Ed.), *Anxiety: Current trends in theory and research* (pp. 23–49). New York: Academic Press.

Steele, C. (1988). The psychology of self-affirmation: Sustaining the integrity of the self. In L. Berkowitz (Ed.), *Advances in experimental social psychology* (Vol. 21, pp. 261–302). New York: Academic Press.

Steele, C. (1997). A threat in the air: How stereotypes shape intellectual identity and performance. *American Psychologist, 52*, 613–629.

Steinberg, L., Brown, B. B., & Dornbusch, S. M. (1996). *Beyond the classroom: Why school reform has failed and what parents need to do*. New York: Simon & Schuster.

Sternberg, R. (1990). Prototypes of competence and incompetence. In R. Sternberg & J. Kolligian (Eds.), *Competence considered* (pp. 117–145). New Haven, CT: Yale University Press.

Stevenson, H., Chen, C., & Uttal, D. (1990). Beliefs and achievement: A study of black, white, and Hispanic children. *Child Development, 61,* 508–523.

Stevenson, H., & Stigler, J. (1992). *The learning gap.* New York: Summit Books.

Stipek, D. (1981). Children's perceptions of their own and their classmates' ability. *Journal of Educational Psychology, 73,* 404–410.

Stipek, D. (1984). Young children's performance expectations: Logical analysis or wishful thinking? In J. Nicholls (Ed.), *Advances in motivation and achievement: The development of achievement motivation* (Vol. 3, pp. 33–56). Greenwich, CT: JAI Press.

Stipek, D. J. (1996). Motivation and instruction. In D. C. Berliner & R. C. Calfee (Eds.), *Handbook of educational psychology* (pp. 85–113). New York: Macmillan.

Stipek, D. (1998). *Motivation to learn: From theory to practice.* Boston: Allyn & Bacon.

Stipek, D., & Kowalski, P. (1989). Learned helplessness in task-orienting versus performance-orienting testing conditions. *Journal of Educational Psychology, 81,* 384–391.

Stipek, D., & Mac Iver, D. (1989). Developmental change in children's assessment of intellectual competence. *Child Development, 60,* 521–538.

Stipek, D. J., & Ryan, R. H. (1997). Economically disadvantaged preschoolers: Ready to learn but further to go. *Developmental Psychology, 33,* 711–723.

Storms, M. D. (1973). Videotape and the attribution process: Reversing actors' and observers' points of view. *Journal of Personality and Social Psychology, 27,* 165–175.

Sue, S., & Okazaki, S. (1990). Asian-American educational achievement: A phenomenon in search of an explanation. *American Psychologist, 45,* 913–920.

Suls, J., & Sanders, G. S. (1982). Self-evaluation through social comparison: A developmental analysis. In L. Wheeler (Ed.), *Review of personality and social psychology* (Vol. 3, pp. 171–197). Beverly Hills, CA: Sage.

Suppes, P. (1974). The place of theory in educational research. *Educational Researcher, 3,* 3–10.

Swann, W. B., & Pittman, T. S. (1977). Initiating play activity of children: The moderating influence of verbal cues on intrinsic motivation. *Child Development, 48,* 1128–1132.

Tamis-LeMonda, C. S., & Cabrera, N. (1999). *Perspectives on father involvement: Research and policy* (Social Policy Report, Vol. 13, No. 2). Ann Arbor, MI: Society for Research in Child Development.

Tarde, G. (1903). *The laws of imitation* (2nd ed.). New York: Holt.

Taylor, R., Casten, R., Flickinger, S., & Roberts, D. (1994). Explaining the school performance of African-American adolescents. *Journal of Research on Adolescence, 4,* 21–44.

Thelen, M. H., Fry, R. A., Fehrenbach, P. A., & Frautschi, N. M. (1979). Therapeutic videotape and film modeling: A review. *Psychological Bulletin, 86,* 701–720.

Thorkildsen, T. A., & Nicholls, J. (1991). Students' critiques as motivation. *Educational Psychologist, 26,* 347–368.

Thorkildsen, T., & Nicholls, J. (1998). Fifth graders' achievement orientations and beliefs: Individual and classroom differences. *Journal of Educational Psychology, 90,* 179–201.

Thorndike, E. L. (1912). *Education: A first book.* New York: Macmillan.

Thorndike, E. L. (1913). *Educational psychology: Vol. 2. The psychology of learning.* New York: Teachers College Press.

Thorndike, E. L. (1932). *The fundamentals of learning.* New York: Teachers College Press.

Timberlake, W., & Farmer-Dougan, V. A. (1991). Reinforcement in applied settings: Figuring out ahead of time what will work. *Psychological Bulletin, 110,* 379–391.

Tobias, S. (1980). Anxiety and instruction. In I. G. Sarason (Ed.), *Test anxiety: Theory, research, and applications* (pp. 289–309). Hillsdale, NJ: Erlbaum.

Tobias, S. (1985). Test anxiety: Interference, defective skills, and cognitive capacity. *Educational Psychologist, 20,* 135–142.

Tobias, S. (1994). Interest, prior knowledge, and learning. *Review of Educational Research, 64,* 37–54.

Tolman, E. C. (1932). *Purposive behavior in animals and men.* New York: Appleton-Century-Crofts. (Reprinted 1949, 1951, University of California Press, Berkeley).

Tolman, E. C. (1949). There is more than one kind of learning. *Psychological Review, 56,* 144–155.

Tolman, E. C., & Honzik, C. H. (1930). Introduction and removal of reward, and maze performance in rats. *University of California Publications in Psychology, 4,* 257–275.

Tolman, E. C., Ritchie, B. F., & Kalish, D. (1946). Studies in spatial learning. I. Orientation and the short-cut. *Journal of Experimental Psychology, 36,* 13–24.

Triandis, H. C. (1972). *The analysis of subjective culture.* New York: Wiley-Interscience.

Tschannen-Moran, M., & Woolfolk Hoy, A. E., & Hoy, W. (1998). Teacher efficacy: Its meaning and measure. *Review of Educational Research, 68,* 202–248.

Trope, Y. (1975). Seeking information about one's ability as a determinant of choice among tasks. *Journal of Personality and Social Psychology, 32,* 1004–1013.

Tryon, G. S. (1980). The measurement and treatment of test anxiety. *Review of Educational Research, 50,* 343–371.

Turner, J., Thorpe, P., & Meyer, D. (1998). Students' reports of motivation and negative affect: A theoretical and empirical analysis. *Journal of Educational Psychology, 90,* 758–771.

Urdan, T. (1997). Achievement goal theory: Past results, future directions. In M. Maehr & P. R. Pintrich (Eds.), *Advances in motivation and achievement* (Vol. 10, pp. 99–141). Greenwich, CT: JAI Press.

Urdan, T., & Maehr, M. (1995). Beyond a two-goal theory of motivation: A case for social goals. *Review of Educational Research, 65,* 213–244.

Urdan, T., Midgley, C., & Wood, S. (1995). Special issues in reforming middle level schools. *Journal of Early Adolescence, 15,* 9–37.

VanderStoep, S., Pintrich, P. R., & Fagerlin, A. (1996). Disciplinary differences in self-regulated learning in college students. *Contemporary Educational Psychology, 21,* 345–362.

Veroff, J. (1969). Social comparison and the development of achievement motivation. In C. P. Smith (Ed.), *Achievement-related motives in children* (pp. 46–101). New York: Russell Sage Foundation.

Volling, B. L., & Elins, J. L. (1998). Family relationships and children's emotional adjustment as correlates of maternal and paternal differential treatment: A replication with toddler and preschool siblings. *Child Development, 69,* 1640–1656.

Vygotsky, L. S. (1962). *Thought and language.* Cambridge, MA: MIT Press.

Vygotsky, L. S. (1978). *Mind in society: The development of higher psychological processes.* Cambridge, MA: Harvard University Press.

Ware, J. E., & Williams, R. G. (1975). The Dr. Fox effect: A study of lecturer effectiveness and ratings of instruction. *Journal of Medical Education, 50,* 149–156.

Watson, D., & Tellegen, A. (1985). Toward a consensual structure of mood. *Psychological Bulletin, 98,* 219–235.

Watson, D., Wiese, D., Vaidya, J., & Tellegen, A. (1999). Two general activation systems of affect: Structural findings, evolutionary considerations, and psychobiological evidence. *Journal of Personality and Social Psychology, 76,* 820–838.

Watson, J. B. (1914). *Behavior: An introduction to comparative psychology.* New York: Henry Holt.

Watson, J. B. (1924). *Behaviorism.* New York: Norton.

Webb, N. M., & Palincsar, A. S. (1996). Group processes in the classroom. In D. C. Berliner & R. C. Calfee (Eds.), *Handbook of educational psychology* (pp. 841–873). New York: Macmillan.

Wegner, D. M., & Wheatley, T. (1999). Apparent mental causation: Sources of the experience of will. *American Psychologist, 54,* 480–492.

Weiner, B. (1979). A theory of motivation for some classroom experiences. *Journal of Educational Psychology, 71,* 3–25.

Weiner, B. (1980a). A cognitive (attributional)-emotion-action model of motivated behavior: An analysis of judgments of help-giving. *Journal of Personality and Social Psychology, 39,* 186–200.

Weiner, B. (1980b). May I borrow your class notes? An attributional analysis of judgments of help-giving in an achievement-related context. *Journal of Educational Psychology, 72,* 676–681.

Weiner, B. (1985a). An attributional theory of achievement motivation and emotion. *Psychological Review, 92,* 548–573.

Weiner, B. (1985b). *Human motivation.* New York: Springer-Verlag.

Weiner, B. (1986). *An attributional theory of motivation and emotion.* New York: Springer-Verlag.

Weiner, B. (1990). History of motivational research in education. *Journal of Educational Psychology, 82,* 616–622.

Weiner, B. (1991). Metaphors in motivation and attribution. *American Psychologist, 46,* 921–930.

Weiner, B. (1992). *Human motivation: Metaphors, theories, and research.* Newbury Park, CA: Sage.

Weiner, B. (1994). Integrating social and personal theories of achievement striving. *Review of Educational Research, 64,* 557–573.

Weiner, B. (1995). *Judgments of responsibility: A foundation for a theory of social conduct.* New York: Guilford Press.

Weiner, B., Frieze, I., Kukla, A., Reed, L., Rest, S., & Rosenbaum, R. (1971). *Perceiving the causes of success and failure.* Morristown, NJ: General Learning Press.

Weiner, B., Graham, S., & Chandler, C. (1982). Pity, anger, and guilt: An attributional analysis. *Personality and Social Psychology Bulletin, 8,* 226–232.

Weiner, B., Graham, S., Taylor, S., & Meyer, W. (1983). Social cognition in the classroom. *Educational Psychologist, 18,* 109–124.

Weiner, B., & Kukla, A. (1970). An attributional analysis of achievement motivation. *Journal of Personality and Social Psychology, 15,* 1–20.

Weiner, B., & Peter, N. (1973). A cognitive-developmental analysis of achievement and moral judgments. *Developmental Psychology, 9,* 290–309.

Weiner, B., Russell, D., & Lerman, D. (1978). Affective consequences of causal ascriptions. In J. Harvey, W. Ickes, & R. Kidd (Eds.), *New directions in attribution research* (Vol. 2, pp. 59–88). Hillsdale, NJ: Erlbaum.

Weinstein, C. E., & Mayer, R. (1986). The teaching of learning strategies. In M. C. Wittrock (Ed.), *Handbook of research on teaching* (3rd ed., pp. 315–327). New York: Macmillan.

Weinstein, R. (1985). Student mediation of classroom expectancy effects. In J. Dusek (Ed.), *Teacher expectancies* (pp. 329–350). Hillsdale, NJ: Erlbaum.

Weinstein, R. (1989). Perceptions of classroom processes and student motivation. Children's view of self-fulfilling prophecies. In C. Ames & R. Ames (Eds.), *Research on motivation in education. Vol. 3. Goals and cognitions* (pp. 187–221). New York: Academic Press.

Weinstein, R. (1993). Children's knowledge of differential treatment in school: Implications for motivation. In T. Tomlinson (Ed.), *Motivating students to learn: Overcoming barriers to achievement* (pp. 197–224). Berkeley, CA: McCutchan.

Weinstein, R., & Middlestadt, S. (1979). Student perceptions of teacher interactions with male high and low achievers. *Journal of Educational Psychology, 71,* 421–431.

Weisz, J. (1983). Can I control it? The pursuit of veridical answers across the life-span. In P. Baltes & O. Brim (Eds.), *Life-span development and behavior* (Vol. 5, pp. 233–300). New York: Academic Press.

Weisz, J. (1984). Contingency judgments and achievement behavior: Deciding what is controllable and when to try. In J. Nicholls (Ed.), *Advances in motivation and achievement: The development of achievement motivation* (Vol. 3, pp. 107–136). Greenwich, CT: JAI Press.

Weisz, J., Rothbaum, F., & Blackburn, T. (1984). Standing out and standing in: The psychology of control in America and Japan. *American Psychologist, 39,* 955–969.

Wentzel, K. (1989). Adolescent classroom goals, standards for performance, and academic achievement: An interactionist perspective. *Journal of Educational Psychology, 81,* 131–142.

Wentzel, K. (1991a). Relations between social competence and academic achievement in early adolescence. *Child Development, 62,* 1066–1078.

Wentzel, K. (1991b). Social and academic goals at school: Motivation and achievement in context. In M. L. Maehr & P. R. Pintrich (Eds.), *Advances in motivation and achievement: Goals and self-regulatory processes* (Vol. 7, pp. 185–212). Greenwich, CT: JAI Press.

Wentzel, K. (1991c). Social competence at school: Relation between social responsibility and academic achievement. *Review of Educational Research, 61,* 1–24.

Wentzel, K. (1992). Motivation and achievement in adolescence. A multiple goals perspective. In D. Schunk & J. Meece (Eds.), *Student perceptions in the classroom: Causes and consequences* (pp. 287–306). Hillsdale, NJ: Erlbaum.

Wentzel, K. (1993). Social and academic goals at school: Motivation and achievement in early adolescence. *Journal of Early Adolescence, 13,* 4–20.

Wentzel, K. (1994). Relations of social goal pursuit to social acceptance, classroom behavior, and perceived social support. *Journal of Educational Psychology, 86,* 73–182.

Wentzel, K. (1996). Social goals and social relationships as motivators of school adjustment. In J. Juvonen & K. R. Wentzel (Eds.), *Social motivation: Understanding children's school adjustment* (pp. 226–247). Cambridge, England: Cambridge University Press.

Wentzel, K. (1999). Social-motivational processes and interpersonal relationships: Implications for understanding students' academic success. *Journal of Educational Psychology, 91,* 76–97.

Wentzel, K. (2000). What is it that I'm trying to achieve? Classroom goals from a content perspective. *Contemporary Educational Psychology, 25,* 105–115.

Werner, H. (1957). *Comparative psychology of mental development.* New York: International Universities Press.

Wertsch, J., & Tulviste, P. (1992). L. S. Vygotsky and contemporary developmental psychology. *Developmental Psychology, 28,* 548–557.

Westen, D. (1998). The scientific legacy of Sigmund Freud: Towards a psychodynamically informed psychological science. *Psychological Bulletin, 124,* 333–371.

White, P. (1988). Causal processing: Origins and development. *Psychological Bulletin, 104,* 36–52.

White, P. H., Kjelgaard, M. M., & Harkins, S. G. (1995). Testing the contribution of self-evaluation to goal-setting effects. *Journal of Personality and Social Psychology, 69,* 69–79.

White, R. W. (1959). Motivation reconsidered: The concept of competence. *Psychological Review, 66,* 297–333.

Whitehead, G., Smith, S., & Eichorn, J. (1982). The effect of subject's race and other's race on judgments of causality for success and failure. *Journal of Personality, 50,* 193–202.

Wigfield, A. (1994). Expectancy-value theory of achievement motivation: A developmental perspective. *Educational Psychology Review, 6,* 49–78.

Wigfield, A., & Eccles, J. (1989). Test anxiety in elementary and secondary school students. *Educational Psychologist, 24,* 159–183.

Wigfield, A., & Eccles, J. (1992). The development of achievement task values: A theoretical analysis. *Developmental Review, 12,* 265–310.

Wigfield, A., & Eccles, J. (2000). Expectancy-value theory of achievement motivation. *Contemporary Educational Psychology, 25,* 68–81.

Wigfield, A., Eccles, J., Mac Iver, D., Reuman, D., & Midgley, C. (1991). Transitions during early adolescence: Changes in children's domain-specific self-perceptions and general self-esteem across the transition to junior high school. *Developmental Psychology, 27,* 552–565.

Wigfield, A., Eccles, J., & Pintrich, P. R. (1996). Development between the ages of 11 and 25. In D. Berliner & R. Calfee (Eds.), *Handbook of educational psychology* (pp. 148–185). New York: Wiley.

Wigfield, A., & Karpathian, M. (1991). Who am I and what can I do? Children's self-concepts and motivation in achievement situations. *Educational Psychologist, 26,* 233–262.

Wild, K.-P., Krapp, A., Schreyer, I., & Lewalter, D. (1998). The development of interest and motivational orientations: Gender differences in vocational education. In L. Hoffman, A. Krapp, A. Renninger, & J. Baumert (Eds.), *Interest and learning* (pp. 441–454). Kiel, Germany: IPN-The University of Kiel.

Wiley, M., & Eskilson, A. (1978). Why did you learn in school today? Teachers' perceptions of causality. *Sociology of Education, 51,* 261–269.

Wilson, T., & Linville, P. (1982). Improving the academic performance of college freshmen: Attribution therapy revisited. *Journal of Personality and Social Psychology, 42,* 367–376.

Wilson, T., & Linville, P. (1985). Improving the performance of college freshmen with attributional techniques. *Journal of Personality and Social Psychology, 49,* 287–293.

Wine, J. (1971). Test anxiety and direction of attention. *Psychological Bulletin, 76,* 92–104.

Winell, M. (1987). Personal goals: The key to self-direction in adulthood. In M. E. Ford & D. H. Ford (Eds.), *Humans as self-constructing living systems: Putting the framework to work* (pp. 261–287). Hillsdale, NJ: Erlbaum.

Winne, P. H., & Marx, R. W. (1982). Students' and teachers' views of thinking processes for classroom learning. *Elementary School Journal, 82,* 493–518.

Winter, D. G., John, O. P., Stewart, A. J., Klohnen, E. C., & Duncan, L. E. (1998). Traits and motives: Toward an integration of two traditions in personality research. *Psychological Review, 105,* 230–250.

Wittrock, M. C. (1986). Students' thought processes. In M. C. Wittrock (Ed.), *Handbook of research on teaching* (3rd ed., pp. 297–314). New York: Macmillan.

Wolters, C., Yu, S., & Pintrich, P. R. (1996). The relation between goal orientation and students' motivational beliefs and self-regulated learning. *Learning and Individual Differences, 8,* 211–238.

Wong, P., Derlaga, V., & Colson, W. (1988). The effects of race on expectancies and performance attributions. *Canadian Journal of Behavioral Science, 20,* 29–39.

Woodworth, R. S. (1918). *Dynamic psychology.* New York: Columbia University Press.

Woolfolk, A. E., & Hoy, W. K. (1990). Prospective teachers' sense of efficacy and beliefs about control. *Journal of Educational Psychology, 82,* 81–91.

Woolfolk Hoy, A. E., & Murphy, P. K. (2001). Teaching educational psychology to the implicit mind. In B. Torff & R. J. Sternberg (Eds.), *Understanding and teaching the intuitive mind: Student and teacher learning* (pp. 145–185). Mahwah, NJ: Erlbaum.

Wylie, R. C. (1974). *The self-concept* (Vol. 1). Lincoln, NE: University of Nebraska Press.

Wylie, R. C. (1979). *The self-concept* (Vol. 2). Lincoln, NE: University of Nebraska Press.

Wylie, R. C. (1989). *Measures of the self-concept.* Lincoln, NE: University of Nebraska Press.

Yerkes, R. M., & Dodson, J. D. (1908). The relation of strength of stimulus to rapidity of habit-formation. *Journal of Comparative Neurology and Psychology, 18,* 459–482.

Yogman, M. W., Kindlon, D., & Earls, F. (1995). Father involvement and cognitive/behavioral outcomes in preterm infants. *Journal of the American Academy of Child and Adolescent Psychiatry, 343,* 58–66.

Zahorik, J. A. (1975). Teachers' planning models. *Educational Leadership, 33,* 134–139.

Zajonc, R. B. (1980). Feeling and thinking: Preferences need no inferences. *American Psychologist, 35,* 151–175.

Zajonc, R. B. (1998). Emotions. In D. Gilbert, S. Fiske, & G. Lindzey (Eds.), *The handbook of social psychology* (Vol. 1., 4th ed., pp. 591–632). New York: McGraw-Hill.

Zajonc, R. B. (2000). Feeling and thinking: Closing the debate over the independence of affect. In J. Forgas (Ed.), *Feeling and thinking: The role of affect in social cognition* (pp. 31–58). New York: Cambridge University Press.

Zatz, S., & Chassin, L. (1985). Cognitions of test-anxious children under naturalistic test-taking conditions. *Journal of Consulting and Clinical Psychology, 53,* 393–401.

Zeidner, M. (1998). *Test anxiety: The state of the art.* New York: Plenum.

Zimmerman, B. J. (1989). A social cognitive view of self-regulated academic learning. *Journal of Educational Psychology, 81,* 329–339.

Zimmerman, B. J. (1990). Self-regulating academic learning and achievement: The emergence of a social cognitive perspective. *Educational Psychology Review, 2,* 173–201.

Zimmerman, B. J. (1994). Dimensions of academic self-regulation: A conceptual framework for education. In D. H. Schunk & B. J. Zimmerman (Eds.), *Self-regulation of learning and performance: Issues and educational applications* (pp. 3–21). Hillsdale, NJ: Erlbaum.

Zimmerman, B. J. (1998). Developing self-fulfilling cycles of academic regulation: An analysis of exemplary instructional models. In D. H. Schunk & B. J. Zimmerman (Eds.), *Self-regulated learning: From teaching to self-reflective practice* (pp. 1–19). New York: Guilford Press.

Zimmerman, B. J., Bandura, A., & Martinez-Pons, M. (1992). Self-motivation for academic attainment: The role of self-efficacy beliefs and personal goal setting. *American Educational Research Journal, 29,* 663–676.

Zimmerman, B. J., Greenberg, D., & Weinstein, C. E. (1994). Self-regulating academic study time: A strategy approach. In D. H. Schunk & B. Zimmerman (Eds.), *Self-regulation of learning and performance: Issues and educational applications* (pp. 181–199). Hillsdale, NJ: Erlbaum.

Zimmerman, B. J., & Martinez-Pons, M. (1990). Student differences in self-regulated learning: Relating grade, sex, and giftedness to self-efficacy and strategy use. *Journal of Educational Psychology, 82,* 51–59.

Zimmerman, B. J., & Martinez-Pons, M. (1992). Perceptions of efficacy and strategy use in the self-regulation of learning. In D. H. Schunk & J. L. Meece (Eds.), *Student perceptions in the classroom* (pp. 185–207). Hillsdale, NJ: Erlbaum.

Zimmerman, B. J., & Ringle, J. (1981). Effects of model persistence and statements of confidence on children's self-efficacy and problem solving. *Journal of Educational Psychology, 73,* 485–493.

Zimmerman, B. J., & Rosenthal, T. J. (1974). Observational learning of rule governed behavior by children. *Psychological Bulletin, 81,* 29–42.

Zuckerman, M., Porac, J., Lathin, D., Smith, R., & Deci, E. L. (1978). On the importance of self-determination for intrinsically motivated behavior. *Personality and Social Psychology Bulletin, 4,* 443–446.

Name Index

445

Subject Index